HOUGHTON MIFFLIN HARCOURT

JOURNEYS

Unit 4

Printed in China

ISBN   978-0-547-61007-8

3 4 5 6 7 8 9 10   1548   20 19 18 17 16 15 14 13 12

4500351499   A B C D E F G

HOUGHTON MIFFLIN HARCOURT

JOURNEYS

Grade 5

TEACHER'S EDITION

Program Authors

James F. Baumann · David J. Chard · Jamal Cooks
J. David Cooper · Russell Gersten · Marjorie Lipson
Lesley Mandel Morrow · John J. Pikulski · Héctor H. Rivera
Mabel Rivera · Shane Templeton · Sheila W. Valencia
Catherine Valentino · MaryEllen Vogt

Consulting Author

Irene Fountas

HOUGHTON MIFFLIN HARCOURT

Authors and Reviewers

Program Authors

James F. Baumann
Wyoming Excellence Chair of Literacy Education
University of Wyoming
Laramie, Wyoming

RESEARCH CONTRIBUTIONS:
Reading teacher effectiveness, national trends in elementary reading instruction

David J. Chard
Leon Simmons Endowed Chair
Southern Methodist University
Dallas, Texas

RESEARCH CONTRIBUTIONS:
Reading interventions, direct instruction of comprehension, alphabetic principle on the reading development of first graders

Jamal Cooks
Associate Professor
San Francisco State University
San Francisco, California

RESEARCH CONTRIBUTIONS:
Urban education; language, literacy, and culture; popular culture in the classroom

J. David Cooper
Professor of Education, Retired
Ball State University
Muncie, Indiana

RESEARCH CONTRIBUTIONS:
Classroom instruction, classroom management, development of programs for Response to Intervention

Russell Gersten
Professor Emeritus, College of Education
University of Oregon
Eugene, Oregon

RESEARCH CONTRIBUTIONS:
English language learners, studies of implementation, measurement of classroom instruction, reading comprehension

Marjorie Lipson
Professor Emerita
Principal Investigator, Vermont Reads Institute
University of Vermont
Burlington, Vermont

RESEARCH CONTRIBUTIONS:
Struggling readers and reading disabilities, reading comprehension, school change and literacy improvement

Lesley Mandel Morrow
Professor of Literacy, Graduate School of Education
Rutgers University, The State University of New Jersey
New Brunswick, New Jersey

RESEARCH CONTRIBUTIONS:
Early literacy development, organization and management of language arts programs

John J. Pikulski
Professor Emeritus, School of Education
University of Delaware
Newark, Delaware

RESEARCH CONTRIBUTIONS:
Early intervention to prevent reading difficulties, teaching and developing vocabulary

Héctor H. Rivera
Assistant Professor, School of Education and Human Development
Southern Methodist University
Dallas, Texas

RESEARCH CONTRIBUTIONS:
Professional development for educators who work with adolescent newcomers

Mabel Rivera
Research Assistant Professor at the Texas Institute for Measurement, Evaluation, and Statistics
University of Houston
Houston, Texas

RESEARCH CONTRIBUTIONS:
Education and prevention of reading difficulties in English learners

Shane Templeton
Foundation Professor of Literacy Studies
The University of Nevada, Reno
Reno, Nevada

RESEARCH CONTRIBUTIONS:
Morphological knowledge in vocabulary and spelling development; integrated word study in the development of phonics, spelling, and vocabulary

Sheila W. Valencia
Professor, Curriculum and Instruction
University of Washington
Seattle, Washington

RESEARCH CONTRIBUTIONS:
Literacy assessment, reading and writing instruction, teacher development

Catherine Valentino
Author-in-Residence
Houghton Mifflin Harcourt
West Kingston, Rhode Island

RESEARCH CONTRIBUTIONS:
Inquiry-based learning in reading and writing, motivating reluctant learners, literacy through early childhood problem-solving projects

MaryEllen Vogt
Distinguished Professor Emerita, College of Education
California State University, Long Beach
Long Beach, California

RESEARCH CONTRIBUTIONS:
English language learners, Sheltered Instruction Observation Protocol Model for teaching English-language arts to English language learners

Consulting Author

Irene Fountas
Professor of Education
Lesley University
Cambridge, Massachusetts

RESEARCH CONTRIBUTIONS:
Leveled texts, readers' and writers' workshop, assessment, classroom management and professional development

Reviewers

Jan Eckola
Lake Geneva Schools
Lake Geneva, WI

Sue Fleming
Gracemor Elementary School
Kansas City, MO

Laura Heyboer
Woodside Elementary School
Holland, MI

Nicole Lehr
Riverview Elementary
Wautoma, WI

Jessica Martin
Gracemor Elementary
Kansas City, MO

Valerie McCall
Elmwood Park Community Unit School District
Elmwood Park, IL

Edie Stearns
Bluff Creek Elementary
Chanhassen, MN

Connie Vang
Webster Elementary
Green Bay, WI

Steven Wernick
Washington County Public Schools
Hagerstown, MD

What's Your Story?

Contents

Lesson 16

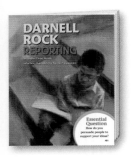

and Unit Wrap-Up T349

Intervention

ELL English Language Learners

Resources

JOURNEYS DIGITAL

Powered by DESTINATIONReading®

Implementing Interactive Instruction

http://www.hmhschool.com

 **LAUNCH >**

Whole Group & Small Group Instruction

Transforming teacher-led instruction

- Teach critical reading skills using interactive lessons and *Projectables*
- Project eBook selections and target skills
- Provide guided practice for target skills
- Teach vocabulary words

 **LAUNCH >**

Digital Centers

Application and Practice

- Interactive centers reinforce weekly skills
- *Leveled Readers*, *Student eBooks*, practice activities
- Full audio support for all *Leveled Readers*

 **LAUNCH >**

Family Support @ Home

Extend learning opportunities

- Interactive activities for homework
- Keep parents involved with school-home connections in English and Spanish

Additional Digital Support
Teacher Resources
Lesson Planning
Professional Development

- Teacher One-Stop Lesson Planning
- Comprehension Expedition CD-ROM
- WriteSmart CD-ROM
- Picture Card Bank for ELL Support
- Student Book Audiotext CD

Focus Wall

Easy Navigation for Teachers

to Suggested Weekly Plan

Student Book
- Student eBook
- Online Teacher's Edition

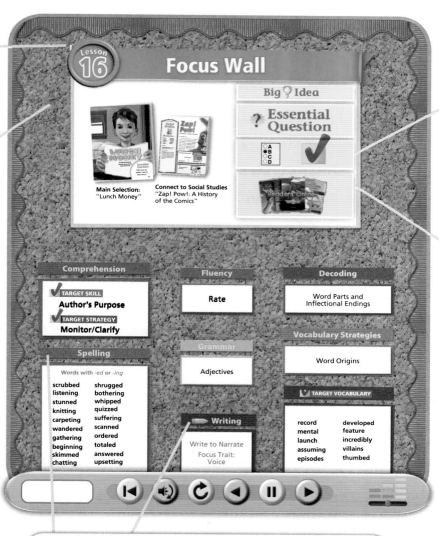

Online Assessment System
- Link to this lesson's Weekly Test
- Unit and Benchmark Tests available

Online Leveled Readers
- Link to this lesson's Readers
- Full audio support

Instruction and Resources on Demand
- Links to *Student Book* and *Teacher's Edition* pages for this lesson
- Game-like practice, powered by *Destination Reading*
- *Projectables, BLMs,* and other lesson resources
- Differentiated Instruction

Single Log In

Big Idea
Everyone has a story to tell.

? Essential Question

Whole Group

	Lesson 16 — *Why does an author want to tell a story?*	Lesson 17 — *What problem does the character face?*
Vocabulary Vocabulary Strategies	☑ Target Vocabulary ☑ Word Origins	☑ Target Vocabulary ☑ Using Reference Sources: Dictionary, Glossary, Thesaurus
Comprehension Reading	☑ **Target Skill** Author's Purpose **Target Strategy** Monitor/Clarify **Author's Craft** Repetition **Main Selection** "Lunch Money" **Paired Selection** "Zap! Pow!: A History of the Comics"	☑ **Target Skill** Story Structure **Target Strategy** Infer/Predict **Author's Craft** Onomatopoeia **Main Selection** "LAFFF" **Paired Selection** "From Dreams to Reality"
Fluency Decoding	☑ **Fluency** Rate ☑ **Decoding** Word Parts and Inflectional Endings	☑ **Fluency** Intonation ☑ **Decoding** Recognizing Common Word Parts
Research Skill/ Media Literacy Listening/Speaking	Record Data Analyze a Media Message	Identify Source Information Prepare an Oral Summary

Whole Group Language Arts

	Lesson 16	Lesson 17
Grammar Spelling Writing	☑ **Grammar** Adjectives ☑ **Spelling** Words with *-ed* or *-ing* ✏ **Writing** Friendly Letter Focus Trait: Voice	☑ **Grammar** Adverbs ☑ **Spelling** More Words with *-ed* or *-ing* ✏ **Writing** Character Description ☑ Focus Trait: Word Choice

SMALL GROUP Options

	Lesson 16	Lesson 17
Vocabulary Reader Leveled Readers	Differentiate *Job Sense* ● *Dog Walker, Inc.* ▲ *Incognito* ■ *The Three R's* ◆ *The Lost Comic Book*	Differentiate *That's a Wacky Idea* ● *Robot Rescue* ▲ *The Watch Girl* ■ *Pancakes* ◆ *Kendria's Watch*
Differentiate Instruction	Differentiate Comprehension and Vocabulary Strategies	Differentiate Comprehension and Vocabulary Strategies

Key ● Struggling Readers ▲ On-Level Readers ■ Advanced Readers ◆ English Language Learners

Unit Project

Oscar Time
Students create storyboards for a movie trailer of an unusual personal experience they have had, or of a favorite book that they would like to see made into a movie.

Checkpoints
- ☐ Brainstorm possible topics.
- ☐ Plan storyboards.
- ☐ Obtain and provide feedback on the storyboards of others, throughout.
- ☐ Write and illustrate the storyboards.
- ☐ Present the storyboards to the class.

Lesson 18 	Lesson 19 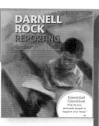	Lesson 20 
What part do facts and opinions play in a story?	*How do you persuade people to support your ideas?*	*How do the beliefs of a character affect a story?*
☑ Target Vocabulary ☑ Analogies	☑ Target Vocabulary ☑ Greek and Latin Suffixes: *-ism, -ist, -able, -ible*	☑ Target Vocabulary ☑ Idioms
☑ **Target Skill** Fact and Opinion **Target Strategy** Analyze/Evaluate **Author's Craft** Flashback **Main Selection** "The Dog Newspaper" **Paired Selection** "Poetry About Poetry"	☑ **Target Skill** Persuasion **Target Strategy** Summarize **Author's Craft** Dialogue **Main Selection** "Darnell Rock Reporting" **Paired Selection** "De Zavala: A Voice for Texas"	☑ **Target Skill** Understanding Characters **Target Strategy** Question **Author's Craft** Imagery **Main Selection** "Don Quixote and the Windmills" **Paired Selection** "LitBeat: Live from La Mancha"
☑ **Fluency** Phrasing: Punctuation ☑ **Decoding** Recognizing Suffixes	☑ **Fluency** Stress ☑ **Decoding** More Common Suffixes	☑ **Fluency** Accuracy ☑ **Decoding** Stress in Three-Syllable Words
Use Technology to Identify Relationships Deliver Oral Summaries	Analyze Graphic/Visual Sources Persuasive Techniques	Paraphrasing vs. Plagiarism View Symbols and Images
☑ **Grammar** Prepositions and Prepositional Phrases ☑ **Spelling** Changing Final *y* to *i* ▭▷ **Writing** Personal Narrative Paragraph Focus Trait: Voice	☑ **Grammar** More Kinds of Pronouns ☑ **Spelling** Suffixes: *-ful, -ly, -ness, -less, -ment* ▭▷ **Writing** Plan a Personal Narrative Focus Trait: Ideas	☑ **Grammar** Contractions ☑ **Spelling** Words from Other Languages ▭▷ **Writing** Write a Personal Narrative Focus Trait: Voice
Differentiate *Print It!*	Differentiate *From Parking Lot to Garden*	Differentiate *A Knight in Armor*
● *Maria Tallchief, American Ballerina* ▲ *B. B. King* ■ *Isabelle Allende* ◆ *The Life of B. B. King*	● *The Big Interview* ▲ *Saving the General* ■ *Another View* ◆ *The Old Tree*	● *Donald Quixote* ▲ *El Camino Real* ■ *A Night in the Kingdom* ◆ *The Royal Road*
Differentiate Comprehension and Vocabulary Strategies	Differentiate Comprehension and Vocabulary Strategies	Differentiate Comprehension and Vocabulary Strategies

Test Preparation and Assessment

5 Steps for Success

1

Where Do I Start?

Comprehensive Screening Assessment

- Group-administered tests
- Initial screening of previous year's skills: Language Arts, Decoding, and Writing, plus passages for Comprehension and Vocabulary
- Includes an optional group Spelling test

Diagnostic Assessment

- Individually administered tests
- Diagnosis of basic reading skills, plus passages for reading in context

2

In Your Teacher's Edition

Every Day

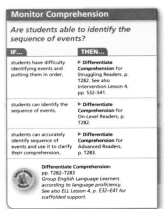

Monitor Progress features in the Teacher's Edition

- Monitor progress
- Differentiate instruction successfully

Corrective Feedback in the Teacher's Edition

- Provide immediate and helpful feedback

Online Assessment System

- Weekly Tests
- Benchmark and Unit Tests

 Common Core Assessment

- All Journeys assessments are correlated to the Common Core State Standards.

 3

Every Week

Group-administered assessment of

- Target Vocabulary
- Comprehension
- Decoding
- Vocabulary Strategies
- Language Arts

4

Every Unit

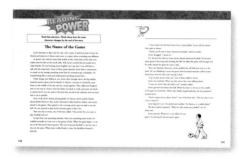

Reading Power in the Student Book

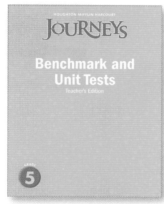

Benchmark and Unit Tests

- Group-administered, criterion-referenced
- Measure the unit's reading and writing skills

 5

Twice a Year

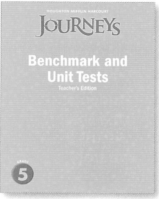

Units 3 and 5 Benchmark Tests

- Comprehensive, cumulative midyear and yearly assessments
- Group-administered, criterion-referenced

Diagnostic Assessment

- Can be re-administered to document progress of struggling readers

 # Unit 4 Launch the Unit

Discuss the Unit: What's Your Story?

- Have students turn to the Unit 4 Opener photograph. Have a volunteer read the unit title aloud.

- Guide students to describe how the photograph of the souvenirs and memorabilia connects to the unit title.

  1 Ask students to tell their favorite story. Is it a true story? Is it something that happened to you or someone you know?

  2 Have students summarize a story about something that happened to them personally.

  3 Encourage students to talk about a book they have read in which a character tells an interesting story. Have them discuss the character's conflict and its impact on the story's plot.

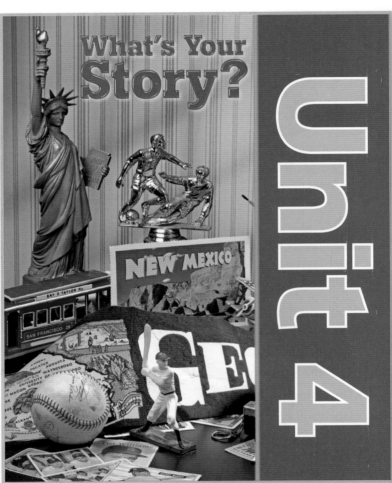

Student Book

Connect to the Big Idea

Everyone has a story to tell.

- Have students turn the page to the photograph of more memorabilia. Ask them to talk about how special things like those in this photograph can remind people of their own personal stories.

- Have a volunteer read the Big Idea aloud for the class. Lead students in a discussion about what kinds of stories people like to tell.

- Briefly discuss the Big Idea. What kinds of stories do you know? Have you ever told someone your own made-up story?

- Encourage students to make up their own fantastic stories and tell them aloud.

Student Book

Preview the Literature

- Ask students to scan the Table of Contents on **Student Book p. 401**, noting titles and topics of interest to them.

- Have students make predictions, based on selection titles and covers, about how the selections expand upon concepts related to the Big Idea. Prompt discussion by asking how the following are all examples of people who have stories to tell: a boy who writes and draws his own comics; a girl who desperately needs a story for her school's writing competition; a girl who writes her own newspaper stories about a special dog; a seventh-grader who writes an article for his school paper that sparks a community discussion about homeless people; and a tall, sad man who believes his own story that he is really a knight.

Oscar Time

Students will create a storyboard for a movie trailer based either on an unusual experience they have had or the plot of a favorite book that they would like to make into a movie. The storyboards will include a clear depiction of story elements such as conflict, resolution, and plot events.

SHARE OBJECTIVES

- Describe story incidents that give rise to future events.
- Explain characters' roles and functions in a plot.
- Give an organized and effective presentation.

DEVELOP BACKGROUND

- Tell students that one of the first steps in making a movie is the creation of a storyboard. The storyboard is a visual summary or map of the movie content.
- Explain that in this unit students will create and present a storyboard for a trailer, or preview, of a movie on an unusual experience they have had or a favorite book.

Materials

- storyboard paper or paper with open squares and writing lines next to them
- colored pencils or markers

Step 1

Plan and Gather Students plan the purpose of and criteria for the project. They gather their thoughts and materials.

- **a** Students brainstorm personal experiences they have had or favorite books that they might like to make into a movie.
- **b** Students will be working on their own but will share their ideas with a partner to obtain feedback and suggestions.
- **c** Students brainstorm and sketch initial ideas for their storyboards for the movie trailer.

Step 2

Organize Students brainstorm, design, create, and organize information that supports the project.

a Students review and revise notes and sketches of the sequence of events that will be depicted on their storyboards.

b Students conference with their partner to obtain and provide feedback on each other's storyboards.

c Students draft and draw their storyboards.

Step 3

Complete and Present Remind students that they will give a presentation. Allow time to rehearse.

a Students revise their storyboards to ensure that the characters and plot are clearly depicted and that events are in a clear and appropriate sequence.

b Students rehearse their presentations with their partners, who provide feedback.

c Students present their storyboards to the class.

Study Skills

For instruction in the following applicable study skills, see the lessons in the **Resources** section, pp. R2–R7.

ELL ENGLISH LANGUAGE LEARNERS

Scaffold

Beginning Explain to students the meanings of the following words *trailer, preview, scene*, and *storyboard* using gestures, objects, or simplified language.

Advanced Work with students to brainstorm and then connect words that relate to movies.

Intermediate Work with students to explain the meanings of the words *storyboard, movie trailer*, and *preview*.

Advanced High Lead a discussion on the purpose of a movie trailer and the elements needed to make it an effective one.

Developing English Learners' Language and Literacy

Sheltered Instruction Is Critical

Chan-sook is thrilled when she is named this month's outstanding student for her fifth grade class. She can hardly wait to tell her parents about this honor, and knows they will be very proud. Her teacher, Mr. Williamson, has worked hard to help her learn to read and write in English, a language that is still new and challenging. To help Chan-sook and other ELs understand, Mr. Williamson talks clearly and slowly when introducing new material, breaks concepts into parts, provides many examples, and carefully teaches new vocabulary words and ideas by using photos, realia, and gestures to clarify their meaning. Chan-sook thinks she should share this special award with her teacher because of all he has done to help her learn to read and write in English.

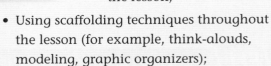

MaryEllen Vogt

Chan-sook is one of thousands of students in U.S. schools who are English learners (ELs). She emigrated with her family from Korea, but many other ELs are native-born children and youths whose home language (L1) is other than English (their L2). What can you do as a teacher to assist your ELs in becoming literate in English?

To assist your English learners in developing requisite academic language for reading and writing in various content areas, you can incorporate a variety of techniques and methods that will make your teaching more comprehensible. While effective instruction for ELs is more complex than just checking off a "to-do" list, careful attention to the following will provide the kind of teaching that promotes success (Echevarria, Vogt, & Short, 2008):

- Posting content and language objectives for each lesson and orally sharing them with students;

- Using supplemental materials to a high degree (for example, photos, illustrations, models);

- Explicitly linking content concepts to students' backgrounds and past learning experiences;

- Explicitly teaching, displaying, and later reviewing key vocabulary for the lesson;

- Using scaffolding techniques throughout the lesson (for example, think-alouds, modeling, graphic organizers);

- Incorporating hands-on materials and manipulatives as appropriate;

- Providing regular and frequent academic feedback throughout the lesson.

As you consider each of these features of an effective sheltered lesson for ELs, you will undoubtedly note that each of these can also be beneficial for native English speakers. You're right . . . but the thing to remember is that they are of critical importance for your English learners.

Writing Standards

The Common Core State Standards provide rigorous and increasingly complex student expectations in crucial areas of learning. In the Writing strand, emphasis is placed on real-world writing forms and applications. As students progress across grade levels, they are asked to write longer and more sophisticated pieces.

A main objective of the Common Core writing standards is to develop students' competencies in integrating and using digital tools and technology to produce and publish their writing as well to collaborate with others. Beyond their school years, students will continue to build on those competencies as they move toward success.

Research

One of the most challenging aspects of the Common Core writing standards is the emphasis they place on independent research. The goal is to empower students to be thoughtful, focused writers who gather and analyze evidence and produce logical, well-supported written arguments.

Textual Evidence

When working with students to incorporate textual evidence into their writing, it is important to provide students with models of writing that effectively incorporate paraphrases and direct quotations from source texts. As students take notes, remind them to paraphrase the information or quote exact words. As students write, they can use their notes to incorporate the paraphrases or direct quotations in their writing. Emphasize to students that they should always credit sources whether they paraphrase or use direct quotes.

Additional Support

It is important to establish a learning environment in which students feel comfortable collaborating with peers and exchanging constructive feedback about writing projects. Offer encouragement in the form of positive feedback at every opportunity. Use Routines to support struggling students and use Options for Reteaching to support students' mastery of skills. *HMH Journeys* provides teachers with the texts and comprehensive instruction they need to help students meet the Common Core State Standards and reach educational goals appropriate to each grade level.

Extending the Common Core State Standards: A Preview

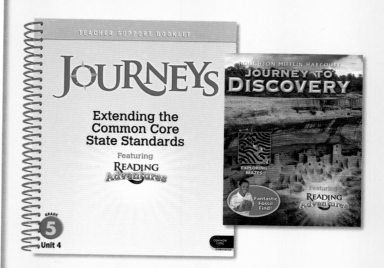

Unit 4: What's Your Story?
Extend the Common Core State Standards with these lessons.

- Introduce the Play: "A Royal Mystery"
- Comprehension: Theme
- Vocabulary Strategies: Adages and Proverbs
- Listening and Speaking: Use Formal English
- Grammar: Interjections
- Writing: Using Pacing in Narratives

Reading Standards for Literature K–5

Key Ideas and Details

RL.5.1 Quote accurately from a text when explaining what the text says explicitly and when drawing inferences from the text.

Craft and Structure

RL.5.4 Determine the meaning of words and phrases as they are used in a text, including figurative language such as metaphors and similes.

Integration of Knowledge and Ideas

RL.5.7 Analyze how visual and multimedia elements contribute to the meaning, tone, or beauty of a text (e.g., graphic novel, multimedia presentation of fiction, folktale, myth, poem).

Range of Reading and Level of Text Complexity

RL.5.10 By the end of the year, read and comprehend literature, including stories, dramas, and poetry, at the high end of the grades 4–5 text complexity band independently and proficiently.

Reading Standards for Informational Text K–5

Key Ideas and Details

RI.5.2 Determine two or more main ideas of a text and explain how they are supported by key details; summarize the text.

Integration of Knowledge and Ideas

RI.5.9 Integrate information from several texts on the same topic in order to write or speak about the subject knowledgeably.

Range of Reading and Level of Text Complexity

RI.5.10 By the end of the year, read and comprehend informational texts, including history/social studies, science, and technical texts, at the high end of the grades 4–5 text complexity band independently and proficiently.

Reading Standards: Foundational Skills K–5

Phonics and Word Recognition

RF.5.3a Use combined knowledge of all letter-sound correspondences, syllabication patterns, and morphology (e.g., roots and affixes) to read accurately unfamiliar multisyllabic words in context and out of context.

Fluency

RF.5.4a Read grade-level text with purpose and understanding.

RF.5.4b Read grade-level prose and poetry orally with accuracy, appropriate rate, and expression.

Writing Standards K–5

Production and Distribution of Writing

W.5.4 Produce clear and coherent writing in which the development and organization are appropriate to task, purpose, and audience. (Grade-specific expectations for writing types are defined in standards 1–3 above.)

W.5.5 With guidance and support from peers and adults, develop and strengthen writing as needed by planning, revising, editing, rewriting, or trying a new approach.

Research to Build and Present Knowledge

W.5.7 Conduct short research projects that use several sources to build knowledge through investigation of different aspects of a topic.

W.5.8 Recall relevant information from experiences or gather relevant information from print and digital sources; summarize or paraphrase information in notes and finished work, and provide a list of sources.

W.5.9a Apply *grade 5 Reading standards* to literature (e.g., "Compare and contrast two or more characters, settings, or events in a story or a drama, drawing on specific details in the text [e.g., how characters interact]").

Speaking & Listening Standards K–5

Comprehension and Collaboration

SL.5.1a Come to discussions prepared, having read or studied required material; explicitly draw on that preparation and other information known about the topic to explore ideas under discussion.

SL.5.1c Pose and respond to specific questions by making comments that contribute to the discussion and elaborate on the remarks of others.

Presentation of Knowledge and Ideas

SL.5.4 Report on a topic or text or present an opinion, sequencing ideas logically and using appropriate facts and relevant, descriptive details to support main ideas or themes; speak clearly at an understandable pace.

Language Standards K–5

Conventions of Standard English

L.5.2e Spell grade-appropriate words correctly, consulting references as needed.

Vocabulary Acquisition and Use

L.5.4a Use context (e.g., cause/effect relationships and comparisons in text) as a clue to the meaning of a word or phrase.

SUGGESTIONS FOR BALANCED LITERACY

Use *Journeys* materials to support a Readers' Workshop approach. See the Lesson 16 resources on pages 24, 70–71.

Focus Wall

Main Selection:
"Lunch Money"

Connect to Social Studies
"Zap! Pow!: A History
of the Comics"

Big 💡 Idea
Everyone has
a story to tell.

❓ Essential Question

Why does an author
want to tell a story?

Comprehension

✔ **TARGET SKILL**
Author's Purpose

✔ **TARGET STRATEGY**
Monitor/Clarify

Spelling

Words with -ed or -ing

scrubbed	shrugged
listening	bothering
stunned	whipped
knitting	quizzed
carpeting	suffering
wandered	scanned
gathering	ordered
beginning	totaled
skimmed	answered
chatting	upsetting

Fluency

Rate

Grammar

Adjectives

✏ Writing

Write to Narrate

Focus Trait:
Voice

Decoding

Word Parts and
Inflectional Endings

Vocabulary Strategies

Word Origins

✔ TARGET VOCABULARY

record	developed
mental	feature
launch	incredibly
assuming	villains
episodes	thumbed

Key Skills This Week

Target Skill:
Author's Purpose

Target Strategy:
Monitor/Clarify

Vocabulary Strategies:
Word Origins

Fluency:
Rate

Decoding:
Word Parts and Inflectional Endings

Research Skills:
Record Data

Grammar:
Adjectives

Spelling:
Words with *-ed* or *-ing*

 Writing:
Write to Narrate:
Friendly Letter

✓ Assess/Monitor

☑ **Vocabulary**
p. T54

☑ **Comprehension**
p. T54

☑ **Decoding**
p. T55

☑ **Language Arts**
p. T55

☑ **Fluency**
p. T55

Whole Group

READING

Paired Selections

Lunch Money
Realistic Fiction
Student Book pp. 406–416

Practice Quizzes for the Selection

Zap! Pow!: A History of the Comics
SOCIAL STUDIES/Informational Text

Student Book pp. 418–420

Vocabulary

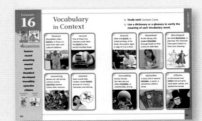

Student Book pp. 402–403

Background and Comprehension

Student Book pp. 404–405

LANGUAGE ARTS

Grammar
Student Book pp. 422–423

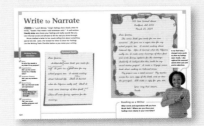

 Writing
Student Book pp. 424–425

Small Group

See page T58–T59 for Suggested Small Group Plan.

TEACHER-LED

Leveled Readers

● **Struggling Readers**

▲ **On Level**

■ **Advanced**

◆ **English Language Learners**

Vocabulary Reader

WHAT MY OTHER STUDENTS ARE DOING

Ready-Made Work Stations

Comprehension and Fluency

Word Study

Think and Write

Digital Center

● **Struggling Readers**

■ **Advanced**

◆ **English Language Learners**

▲ **On Level**

Grab-and-Go!

Lesson 16 Blackline Masters
- Target Vocabulary 16.1
- Selection Summary 16.2
- Graphic Organizer 16.3–16.6 ●▲■◆
- Critical Thinking 16.7–16.10 ●▲■◆
- Running Records 16.11–16.14 ●▲■◆
- Weekly Tests 16.1–16.10

Graphic Organizer Transparency 8

Additional Resources
- Genre: Fiction, p. 4
- Reading Log, p. 12
- Vocabulary Log, p. 13
- Listening Log, p. 14
- Proofreading Checklist, p. 15
- Proofreading Marks, p. 16
- Writing Conference Form, p. 17
- Writing Rubric, p. 18
- Instructional Routines, pp. 19–26
- Graphic Organizer 8: Inference Map, p. 34

JOURNEYS DIGITAL Powered by DESTINATION Reading

For Students
- Student eBook
- Comprehension Expedition CD-ROM
- Leveled Readers Online
- WriteSmart CD-ROM

For Teachers
- Online TE and Focus Wall
- Online Assessment System
- Teacher One-Stop
- Destination Reading Instruction

Intervention

STRATEGIC INTERVENTION: TIER II

Use these materials to provide additional targeted instruction for students who need Tier II strategic intervention.

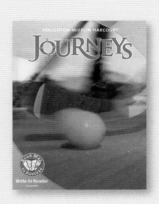

Supports the Student Book selections

Write-in Reader:

Making a Movie

- Engaging selection connects to main topic.
- Reinforces this week's target vocabulary and comprehension skill and strategy.
- Opportunities for student interaction on each page.

Assessment

Progress monitoring every two weeks.

For this week's Strategic Intervention lessons, see Teacher's Edition pages S2–S11.

INTENSIVE INTERVENTION: TIER III

- The materials in the Literacy Tool Kit help you provide a different approach for students who need Tier III intensive intervention.
- Interactive lessons provide focused instruction in key reading skills, targeted at students' specific needs.
- Lesson cards are convenient for small-group or individual instruction.
- Blackline masters provide additional practice.
- A leveled book accompanies each lesson to give students opportunities for additional reading and skill application.
- Assessments for each lesson help you evaluate the effectiveness of the intervention.

Lessons provide support for

- Phonics and Word Study Skills
- Vocabulary
- Comprehension Skills and Literary Genres
- Fluency

ELL English Language Learners

SCAFFOLDED SUPPORT

Use these materials to ensure that students acquire social and academic language proficiency.

Language Support Card

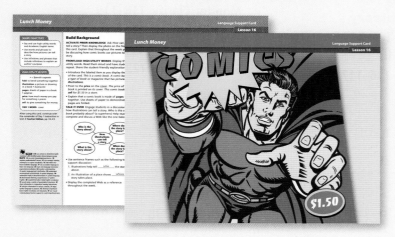

- Builds background for the main topic and promotes oral language.
- Develops high-utility vocabulary and academic language.

Leveled Reader

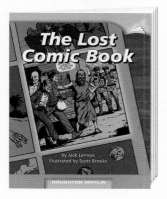

- Sheltered text connects to the main selection's topic, vocabulary, skill, and strategy.

Scaffolded Support

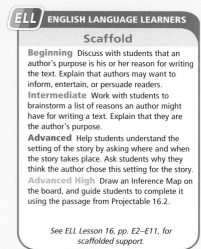

ELL ENGLISH LANGUAGE LEARNERS

Scaffold

Beginning Discuss with students that an author's purpose is his or her reason for writing the text. Explain that authors may want to inform, entertain, or persuade readers.

Intermediate Work with students to brainstorm a list of reasons an author might have for writing a text. Explain that they are the author's purpose.

Advanced Help students understand the setting of the story by asking where and when the story takes place. Ask students why they think the author chose this setting for the story.

Advanced High Draw an Inference Map on the board, and guide students to complete it using the passage from Projectable 16.2.

See ELL Lesson 16, pp. E2–E11, for scaffolded support.

- Notes throughout the Teacher's Edition scaffold instruction to each language proficiency level.

Vocabulary in Context Cards 151–160

- Provide visual support and additional practice for Target Vocabulary words.

For this week's English Language Learners lessons, see Teacher's Edition pages E2–E11.

Weekly Plan

		Day 1	Day 2
Whole Group	**Oral Language** Listening Comprehension	**Teacher Read Aloud** "Japanese Cartoons Are Manga-nificent," T12–T13 ☑ Target Vocabulary, T13	**Turn and Talk,** T19
	Vocabulary Comprehension Skills and Strategies **Reading**	☑ **Comprehension** Preview the Target Skill, T13 ☑ **Introduce Vocabulary** Vocabulary in Context, T14–T15 **Develop Background** ☑ Target Vocabulary, T16–T17	**Introduce Comprehension** ☑ Author's Purpose, T18–T19 Monitor/Clarify, T18–T19 **Read "Lunch Money,"** T20–T30 Focus on Genre, T20 Stop and Think, T23, T25, T29
	Cross-Curricular Connections Fluency Decoding	☑ **Fluency** Model Rate, T12	☑ **Fluency** Teach Rate, T38
Whole Group Language Arts	**Spelling Grammar Writing**	☑ **Spelling** Words with -ed or -ing: Pretest, T44 ☑ **Grammar** Daily Proofreading Practice, T46 Teach Adjectives, T46 ☑ **Write to Narrate: Friendly Letter** Analyze the Model, T50	☑ **Spelling** Words with -ed or -ing: Word Sort, T44 ☑ **Grammar** Daily Proofreading Practice, T47 Extend Adjectives, T47 ☑ **Write to Narrate: Friendly Letter** Focus Trait: Voice, T51
	Writing Prompt	*Describe your favorite movie that was based on a comic book.*	*Write descriptions of a hero and villain that would make a great Chunky Comic.*

COMMON CORE
Correlations

Introduce Vocabulary RL.5.4, L.5.4a **Develop Background** RL.5.4, L.5.4a **Fluency** RF.5.4a, RF.5.4b **Spelling** L.5.2e **Write to Narrate** W.5.4, W.5.5	**Turn and Talk** SL.5.1a **Read** RL.5.1, RL.5.4, RL.5.7, RL.5.10 **Fluency** RF.5.4a, RF.5.4b **Spelling** L.5.2e **Write to Narrate** W.5.4, W.5.5

Suggestions for Small Groups (See pp. T58–T59.)
Suggestions for Intervention (See pp. S2–S11.)
Suggestions for English Language Learners (See pp. E2–E11.)

JOURNEYS DIGITAL Powered by DESTINATIONReading®
Teacher One-Stop: Lesson Planning

Day 3

Turn and Talk, T31
Oral Language, T31

Read "Lunch Money," T20–T30
Develop Comprehension, T22, T24,
T26, T28, T30
☑ **Target Vocabulary**
"Lunch Money," T22, T24, T28, T30
Your Turn, T31
Deepen Comprehension
☑ Infer Author's Purpose, T36–T37

Cross-Curricular Connection
Social Studies, T27
☑ **Fluency** Practice Rate, T27
☑ **Decoding**
Word Parts and Inflectional
Endings, T39

☑ **Spelling**
Words with -ed or -ing: Analogies,
T45
☑ **Grammar**
Daily Proofreading Practice, T47
Teach Articles, T47
☑ **Write to Narrate: Friendly
Letter**
Prewrite, T5

*Create an outline for a story in
a new series of Chunky Comics.*

Oral Language SL.5.1a, SL.5.1c
Read RL.5.1, RL.5.4, RL.5.7, RL.5.10
Deepen Comprehension W.5.9a,
SL.5.1a, SL.5.1c
Fluency RF.5.4a, RF.5.4b
Spelling L.5.2e
Write to Narrate W.5.4, W.5.5

Day 4

Text to World, T35

**Read "Zap! Pow!: A History
of the Comics,"** T32–T34
Connect to Social Studies, T32
Target Vocabulary Review, T33
Develop Comprehension, T34
Weekly Internet Challenge, T34–T35
Making Connections, T35
☑ **Vocabulary Strategies**
Word Origins, T40–T41

☑ **Fluency**
Practice Rate, T33

☑ **Spelling**
Words with -ed or -ing: Connect to
Writing, T45
☑ **Grammar**
Daily Proofreading Practice, T48
Review Adjectives, T48
☑ **Write to Narrate: Friendly
Letter**
Draft, T52

*Explain why you feel a comics
code would be good or bad.*

Read RI.5.2, RI.5.10
Making Connections RI.5.9, W.5.7
Fluency RF.5.4a, RF.5.4b
Spelling L.5.2e
Write to Narrate W.5.4, W.5.5

Day 5

Listening and Speaking, T43

Connect and Extend
Read to Connect, T42
Independent Reading, T42
Extend Through Research, T43

☑ **Fluency**
Progress Monitoring, T55

☑ **Spelling**
Words with -ed or -ing: Assess, T45
☑ **Grammar**
Daily Proofreading Practice, T48
Connect Grammar to Writing,
T48–T49
☑ **Write to Narrate: Friendly
Letter**
Revise for Voice, T52

*Write a letter to Greg from
"Lunch Money" with ideas on
how to raise money.*

Listening and Speaking W.5.7, W.5.8,
SL.5.4
Connect and Extend RL.5.7, W.5.7,
W.5.8, SL.5.1a, SL.5.1c
Fluency RF.5.4a, RF.5.4b
Spelling L.5.2e
Write to Narrate W.5.4, W.5.5

Your Skills for the Week

☑ **Vocabulary**
Target Vocabulary
Strategies: Word
Origins

☑ **Comprehension**
Author's Purpose
Monitor/Clarify

☑ **Decoding**
Word Parts and
Inflectional
Endings

☑ **Fluency**
Rate

☑ **Language Arts**
Spelling
Grammar
Writing

Weekly Leveled Readers

Differentiated Support for This Week's Targets

 **TARGET SKILL**

Author's Purpose

✓ **TARGET STRATEGY**

Monitor/Clarify

✓ **TARGET VOCABULARY**

record	developed
mental	feature
launch	incredibly
assuming	villains
episodes	thumbed

Additional Tools

Vocabulary in Context Cards

Comprehension Tool: Graphic Organizer Transparency 8

❔ Essential Question

Why does an author want to tell a story?

Vocabulary Reader

Level P

Build Target Vocabulary

• Introduce the Target Vocabulary in context and build comprehension using the Target Strategy.

Job Sense

Blackline Master 16.1

Intervention

Scaffolded Support

• Provide extra support in applying the Target Vocabulary, Target Skill, and Target Strategy in context.

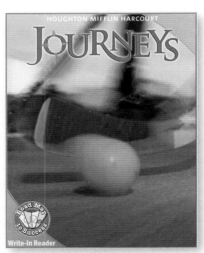

Write-In Reader

 For Vocabulary Reader Lesson Plans, see Small Group pages T60–T61.

Leveled Readers

Struggling Readers
Level P

Objective: Use Author's Purpose and the Monitor/Clarify strategy to read *Dog Walker, Inc.*

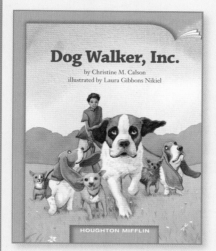

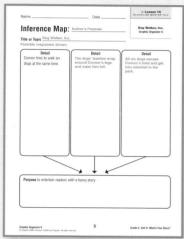

Blackline Master 16.3

On Level
Level S

Objective: Use Author's Purpose and the Monitor/Clarify strategy to read *Incognito.*

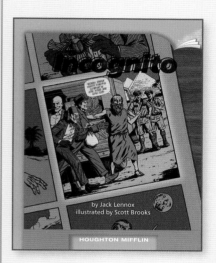

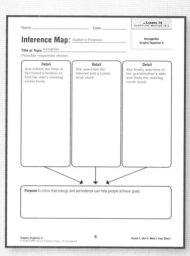

Blackline Master 16.4

Advanced
Level U

Objective: Use Author's Purpose and the Monitor/Clarify strategy to read *The Three R's.*

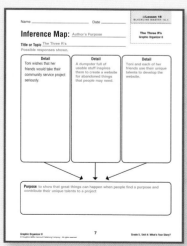

Blackline Master 16.5

English Language Learners
Level S

Objective: Use Author's Purpose and the Monitor/Clarify strategy to read *The Lost Comic Book.*

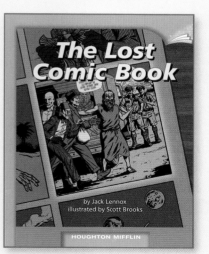

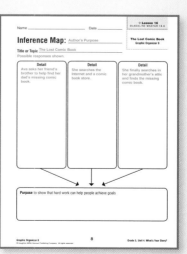

Blackline Master 16.6

 For Leveled Reader Lesson Plans, see Small Group pages T64–T67.

Ready-Made Work Stations

Managing Independent Activities

Use the Ready-Made Work Stations to establish a consistent routine for students working independently. Each station contains three activities. Students who experience success with the *Get Started!* activity move on to the *Reach Higher!* and *Challenge Yourself!* activities, as time permits.

Comprehension and Fluency

Materials
- Audiotext CD/ CD player/headphones
- dictionary
- Vocabulary and Reading Logs
- pencil or pen
- tape recorder
- **Student Book**

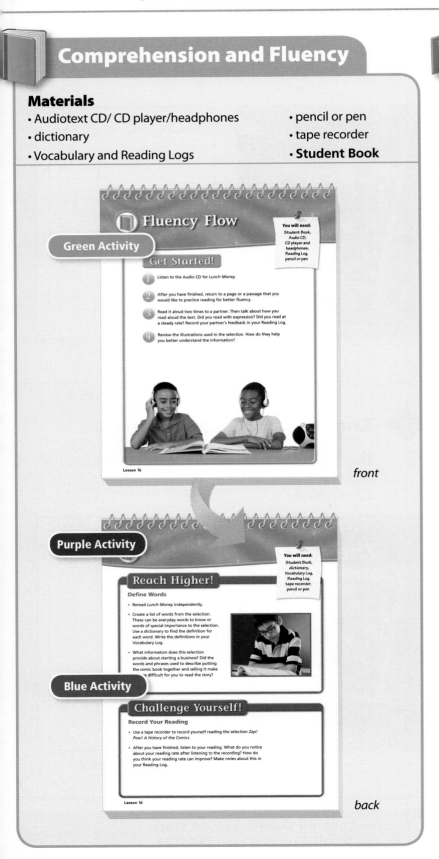

Fluency Flow

Green Activity

You will need: Student Book, Audio CD, CD player and headphones, Reading Log, pencil or pen

Get Started!

1. Listen to the Audio CD for *Lunch Money*.

2. After you have finished, return to a page or a passage that you would like to practice reading for better fluency.

3. Read it aloud two times to a partner. Then talk about how you read aloud the text. Did you read with expression? Did you read at a steady rate? Record your partner's feedback in your Reading Log.

4. Review the illustrations used in the selection. How do they help you better understand the information?

Lesson 16   *front*

Purple Activity

You will need: Student Book, dictionary, Vocabulary Log, Reading Log, tape recorder, pencil or pen

Reach Higher!

Define Words

- Reread *Lunch Money* independently.

- Create a list of words from the selection. These can be everyday words to know or words of special importance to the selection. Use a dictionary to find the definition for each word. Write the definitions in your Vocabulary Log.

- What information does this selection provide about starting a business? Did the words and phrases used to describe putting the comic book together and selling it make [it] difficult for you to read the story?

Blue Activity

Challenge Yourself!

Record Your Reading

- Use a tape recorder to record yourself reading the selection *Zap! Pow! A History of the Comics*.

- After you have finished, listen to your reading. What do you notice about your reading rate after listening to the recording? How do you think your reading rate can improve? Make notes about this in your Reading Log.

Lesson 16   *back*

Word Study

Materials
- dictionary
- paper
- pencil or pen
- **Vocabulary in Context Cards**

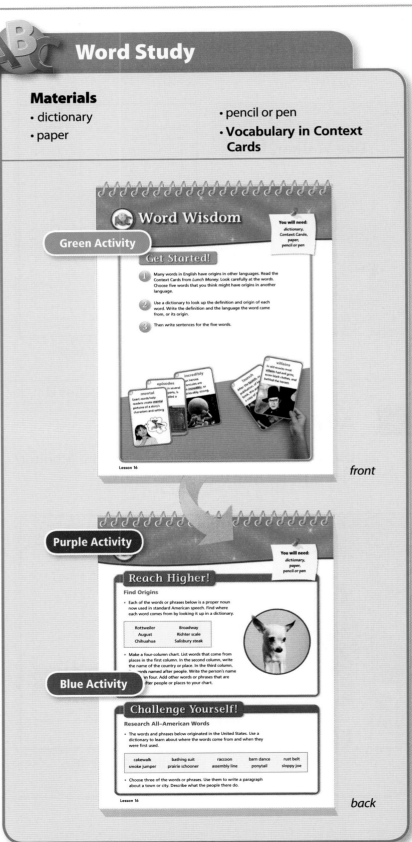

Word Wisdom

Green Activity

You will need: dictionary, Context Cards, paper, pencil or pen

Get Started!

1. Many words in English have origins in other languages. Read the Context Cards from *Lunch Money*. Look carefully at the words. Choose five words that you think might have origins in another language.

2. Use a dictionary to look up the definition and origin of each word. Write the definition and the language the word came from, or its origin.

3. Then write sentences for the five words.

Lesson 16   *front*

Purple Activity

You will need: dictionary, paper, pencil or pen

Reach Higher!

Find Origins

- Each of the words or phrases below is a proper noun now used in standard American speech. Find where each word comes from by looking it up in a dictionary.

Rottweiler	Broadway
August	Richter scale
Chihuahua	Salisbury steak

- Make a four-column chart. List words that come from places in the first column. In the second column, write the name of the country or place. In the third column, [wri]te words named after people. Write the person's name [in] four. Add other words or phrases that are [named] after people or places to your chart.

Blue Activity

Challenge Yourself!

Research All–American Words

- The words and phrases below originated in the United States. Use a dictionary to learn about where the words come from and when they were first used.

cakewalk	bathing suit	raccoon	barn dance	rust belt
smoke jumper	prairie schooner	assembly line	ponytail	sloppy joe

- Choose three of the words or phrases. Use them to write a paragraph about a town or city. Describe what the people there do.

Lesson 16   *back*

Think and Write

Materials
- computer with word processing program
- paper
- pencil or pen

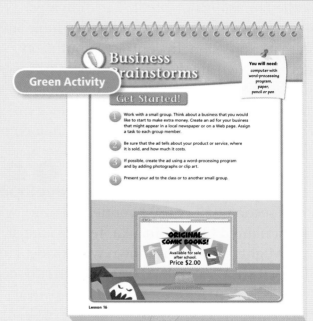

Green Activity

Business Brainstorms

You will need:
computer with word-processing program, paper, pencil or pen

Get Started!

1. Work with a small group. Think about a business that you would like to start to make extra money. Create an ad for your business that might appear in a local newspaper or on a Web page. Assign a task to each group member.

2. Be sure that the ad tells about your product or service, where it is sold, and how much it costs.

3. If possible, create the ad using a word-processing program and by adding photographs or clip art.

4. Present your ad to the class or to another small group.

ORIGINAL COMIC BOOKS!
Available for sale after school
Price $2.00

Lesson 16

front

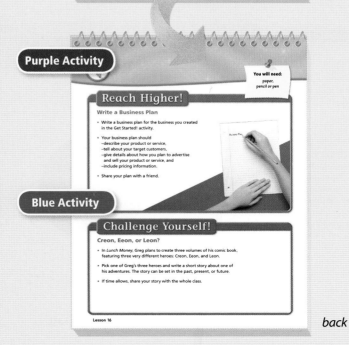

Purple Activity

You will need:
paper, pencil or pen

Reach Higher!

Write a Business Plan

- Write a business plan for the business you created in the Get Started! activity.

- Your business plan should
  –describe your product or service,
  –tell about your target customers,
  –give details about how you plan to advertise and sell your product or service, and
  –include pricing information.

- Share your plan with a friend.

Blue Activity

Challenge Yourself!

Creon, Eeon, or Leon?

- In *Lunch Money*, Greg plans to create three volumes of his comic book, featuring three very different heroes: Creon, Eeon, and Leon.

- Pick one of Greg's three heroes and write a short story about one of his adventures. The story can be set in the past, present, or future.

- If time allows, share your story with the whole class.

Lesson 16

back

Independent Activities

Have students complete these activities at a computer center or a center with an audio CD player.

 LAUNCH **Comprehension and Grammar Activities**

Practice and apply this week's skills.

 LAUNCH **Student eBook**

Read and listen to this week's selections and skill lessons.

 LAUNCH **WriteSmart CD-ROM**

Review student versions of this week's writing model.

 LAUNCH **Audiotext CD**

Listen to books or selections on CD.

Single Log In

Teacher Read Aloud

- Listen to fluent reading.
- Listen for the author's purpose.
- Listen to learn the Target Vocabulary words.

Model Fluency

Rate Explain to students that good readers can read quickly without errors, and that they read at a rate appropriate for understanding the text.

- Display **Projectable 16.1**. As you read the passage, vary your rate to allow students to hear the difference between slow and fast rates.

- Demonstrate how natural pauses and punctuation affect your reading rate.

- Reread the passage with students at a comfortable rate. Reread a second time at a faster rate. Tell students that they can improve their reading rate with practice.

Japanese Cartoons Are Manga-nificent

Imagine walking into a comic book store, or scanning your newspaper's funny pages. With one glance, you can see the variety: superheroes and **villains**, jokesters and fantasy daredevils—each one drawn in an artist's unique style. But, even with all this variety, one section stands out. You can tell by the look of its characters, created in one style by different cartoonists. This style is so unique, it is considered its own cartoon genre. It is called *manga*. **1**

In Japanese, manga means "humorous pictures." Some people have been introduced to manga at the movies, in its animated form called *animanga* or *anime*. The drawings **feature** the characters' eyes. Huge and oval, they look out at the reader with great expression. In contrast, mouths on manga characters are drawn small, in thin, black ink. Noses are tiny wedges. Hair is big, shown not as many single strands, but in thick tufts that fly out from the characters' heads as if blown by a strong wind. Often, manga hair comes in wild colors, like bright purple, electric pink, and fluorescent orange. That's quite a **mental** picture. **2** **3**

How did this amazing style emerge? Manga **developed** in Japan during the second half of the twentieth century with the work of an artist named Osamu Tezuka. Tezuka's most popular creation, "Mighty Atom," is known worldwide. Here in the United States, it showed up in animated form under

Projectable 16.1

Lunch Money | Fluency | Rate

Read Aloud: Model Oral Fluency

Japanese Cartoons Are Manga-nificent

Imagine walking into a comic book store, or scanning your newspaper's funny pages. With one glance, you can see the variety: superheroes and villains, jokesters and fantasy daredevils—each one drawn in an artist's unique style. But, even with all this variety, one section stands out. You can tell by the look of its characters, created in one style by different cartoonists. This style is so unique, it is considered its own cartoon genre. It is called *manga*.

Japan's Flag

the name "Astro Boy." However, one of Tezuka's first works was destined to **launch** manga as something that, in Japan, is not just a cartoon, but actual literature.

In 1947, Tezuka released his version of *Treasure Island*, Robert Louis Stevenson's classic novel. Two hundred pages long, it was the very first *tankoubon*. Here, we would call it a "graphic novel." With **record**-setting sales, this book shone a spotlight on its creator. Tezuka started using his signature style to produce new works with original characters. Other artists began using this style, **assuming** it would mean success for them, too. Then something **incredibly** unexpected occurred.

In Japan, at that time, reading comics was mostly a kids' pastime. As children left their teens behind, their literary interests moved on, but they never outgrew manga. Instead, they demanded new manga characters and story lines that appealed to their more grown-up tastes.

Now, there's a type of manga for just about everyone— and a name to go with it. Children's manga is called *kodomo*. Boys read *shonen*, and girls read *shojo*. For adults, manga contains **episodes** of action, adventure, romance, and fantasy. Of course, people can choose from any category they like. By the time the year 2000 rolled around, manga made up more than forty percent of all Japanese publications. **4**

If you have ever **thumbed** through the racks at a comic book store, you probably know what manga looks like. If not, you might just be curious to find out.

Listening Comprehension
Preview the Target Skill

Read aloud the passage, using appropriate rate. Then ask students the following questions.

1 **Main Idea and Details** *What is the first paragraph mainly about? Manga is a unique cartoon genre that stands out among the other varieties.*

2 **Author's Purpose** *Why do you think the author goes into such detail about what manga looks like? so readers can visualize what the drawings look like even if they have never seen them before*

3 **Compare and Contrast** *How would you describe the difference between manga characters and other cartoon characters? Manga characters have prominent eyes, big, colorful hair, and small noses and mouths.*

4 **Author's Purpose** *What is the author's purpose, or reason, for writing this article? Sample answer: The purpose is to inform readers that there is more than one way to tell a story and to give information about the manga style and its history.*

 **Target Vocabulary**

- Reread "Japanese Cartoons Are Manga-nificent" aloud.
- As you read, pause briefly to explain each highlighted vocabulary word.
- Discuss the meaning of each word as it is used in the Read Aloud.

villains characters that oppose heroes

feature to give something special importance

mental something in the mind

developed brought into being or made bigger and more complex

launch to officially start something

record the most remarkable achievement known

assuming accepting that something is true; supposing

incredibly especially hard to believe; amazing

episodes distinct parts of a longer series of events

thumbed turned pages quickly

☑ Introduce Vocabulary

SHARE OBJECTIVE

• Understand and use the Target Vocabulary words.

Teach

Display the **Vocabulary in Context Cards**, using the routine below. Direct students to **Student Book pp. 402–403.** See also **Instructional Routine 9.**

1 **Read and pronounce the word.** Read the word once alone, then together with students.

2 **Explain the word.** Read the explanation under *What Does It Mean?*

3 **Discuss vocabulary in context.** Together, read aloud the sentence on the front of the card. Help students explain and use the word in new sentences.

4 **Engage with the word.** Ask and discuss the *Think About It* question with students.

Apply

Give partners or small groups one or two **Vocabulary in Context Cards**.

• Help students start the *Talk It Over* activity on the back of their card.

• Have students complete activities for all the cards during the week.

Lesson 16

☑ **TARGET VOCABULARY**

feature

record

assuming

mental

launch

thumbed

developed

incredibly

episodes

villains

Vocabulary Reader   Context Cards

402

Vocabulary in Context

1 feature
Storytellers often feature, or focus on, tales from their own cultural tradition.

2 record
One of these tiny volumes could claim the record as the world's smallest book.

3 assuming
Mimes can tell stories without words, assuming viewers follow their motions.

4 mental
Exact words help readers create mental pictures of a story's characters and setting.

ELL ENGLISH LANGUAGE LEARNERS

Scaffold

Beginning Use actions to demonstrate the meaning of *thumbed*. Then have students perform the action as you say the word.

Advanced Ask students questions to confirm their understanding. For example, *Do you prefer watching movies or episodes of television shows? Why?*

Intermediate Guide students to complete sentence frames for each Vocabulary word. For example, *If you complete math exercises in your head, you're doing _____ math. (mental)*

Advanced High Have partners ask and answer questions about each Vocabulary word. For example, *Do you find heroes or villains more interesting? Why?*

See ELL Lesson 16, pp. E2–E11, for scaffolded support.

● Study each Context Card.

● Use a dictionary or a glossary to verify the meaning of each Vocabulary word.

5 launch

After the launch, or initial printing, of his book, this author signs a copy of it at a store.

6 thumbed

At the library, this student thumbed through books to find a story to read later.

7 developed

An artist developed, or planned, this character from pencil sketch to final color drawing.

8 incredibly

Roman heroes like Hercules are often incredibly, or unbelievably, strong.

9 episodes

A story told in several episodes, or parts, is sometimes called a series.

10 villains

In old movies most villains had evil grins, wore black clothes, and battled the heroes.

403

Monitor Vocabulary

Are students able to understand and use Target Vocabulary words?

IF...	THEN...
students have difficulty understanding and using most of the Target Vocabulary words,	▶ use **Vocabulary in Context Cards** and differentiate the **Vocabulary Reader**, *Job Sense*, for Struggling Readers, p. T60. *See also Intervention Lesson 16, pp. S2–S11.*
students can understand and use most of the Target Vocabulary words,	▶ use **Vocabulary in Context Cards** and differentiate the **Vocabulary Reader**, *Job Sense*, for On-Level Readers, p. T60.
students can understand and use all of the Target Vocabulary words,	▶ differentiate the **Vocabulary Reader**, *Job Sense*, for Advanced Readers, p. T61.

Vocabulary Reader, pp. T60–T61.

Group English Language Learners according to language proficiency.

SMALL GROUP Options

VOCABULARY IN CONTEXT CARDS 151–160

feature

Storytellers often feature, or focus on, tales from their own cultural tradition.

front

feature

What Does It Mean?
To feature something means to give it special importance.

Think About It.
If you owned a restaurant, what kind of food would you feature?

Talk It Over.
Create a chart like the one below. Write something that each place might feature. Compare your choices with a partner.

Place	What might it *feature*?
seafood restaurant	
aquarium	
movie theater	
zoo	

back

Develop Background

ENGLISH LANGUAGE LEARNERS

Scaffold

Beginning Discuss with students some features of comic books. Use visuals to illustrate each feature.

Intermediate Help students discuss familiar words related to comic books. Have students share what they know about comics.

Advanced Have partners list the difficulties a writer might face while trying to come up with ideas for new stories. Have students use the Target Vocabulary in their discussion.

Advanced High Have students discuss ideas for a new comic book in small groups, using the Target Vocabulary.

See ELL Lesson 16, pp. E2–E11, for scaffolded support.

 Target Vocabulary

1 Teach/Model

- Use the drawings on **Student Book p. 404** to discuss how a comic book is created. Tell students that "Lunch Money" is about a boy who wants to **launch** his own comic book.
- Use **Vocabulary in Context Cards** to review the student-friendly explanations of the Target Vocabulary words.
- Have students silently read **Student Book p. 404**. Then read the passage aloud.

2 Guided Practice

Ask students the first item below and discuss their responses. Continue in this way until students have answered a question about each Target Vocabulary word.

1. What magazines have you **thumbed** through while waiting for an appointment?
2. What are some steps that need to be taken before you **launch** a new project?
3. What **record** would you most like to break?
4. If you **developed** a comic book, what types of actions might the heroes take?
5. Describe two **episodes** of your favorite television show.
6. If you had a talk show, who would you most like to **feature**?
7. Who is your favorite movie **villain**?
8. Identify someone who is **incredibly** fast.
9. Explain the term "**mental** gymnastics."
10. **Assuming** that you had your own airplane, where would you fly?

Background

✓ **TARGET VOCABULARY** **Making a Comic Book** You have probably thumbed through a lot of comic books in your time. Before the launch of any comic book, writers and authors must do a lot of work.

The writers don't try to set a speed record when writing the story. The plot must be carefully developed to capture readers' interest. Writers decide where to split the story into episodes. They try to feature strong characters, both good guys and villains, who may be incredibly strong or fast.

Before the artist starts to draw, he or she must form a mental image of the characters. Assuming that everyone has done their job, a new superhero adventure is born.

Behind every successful comic book is a team of talented writers and artists.

04

3 | Apply

- Have partners take turns reading a paragraph on **Student Book p. 404** to one another.

- Tell partners to stop when they come to a highlighted word and have their partner explain it. Have partners switch roles and repeat the procedure.

Drawing is a skill that must be developed.

Introduce Comprehension

SHARE OBJECTIVES

- Identify the author's purpose.
- Monitor and clarify understanding of the text to determine the author's purpose.

SKILL TRACE

Author's Purpose

Introduce	T18–T19, T36–T37
Differentiate	T62–T63
Reteach	T70
Review	T310–T311, Unit 5
Test	Weekly Tests, Lesson 16

ELL ENGLISH LANGUAGE LEARNERS

Scaffold

Beginning Discuss with students that an author's purpose is his or her reason for writing the text. Explain that authors may want to inform, entertain, or persuade readers.

Intermediate Work with students to brainstorm a list of reasons an author might have for writing a text. Explain that those reasons are the author's purpose.

Advanced Help students understand the setting of the story by asking where and when the story takes place. Ask students why they think the author chose this setting for the story.

Advanced High Draw an Inference Map on the board, and guide students to complete it using the passage from Projectable 16.2.

See ELL Lesson 16, pp. E2–E11, for scaffolded support.

✔ Author's Purpose; Monitor/Clarify

1 Teach/Model

AL *Academic Language*

author's purpose the reason that the author wrote the selection

monitor to pay attention to how well you understand what you read

clarify to make clear and understandable

- Remind students that they can use text clues to **monitor** and **clarify** the **author's purpose** and viewpoint.
- Read and discuss **Student Book p. 405** with students. Have them use the Academic Language and related terms.
- Display **Projectable 16.2**. Have students read "The Lemonade Stand."

AUTHOR'S PURPOSE Tell students that they can determine an author's purpose for writing from story details. Explain that students will use an Inference Map to record details to determine the author's purpose.

> **Think Aloud** *The text explains how hard Tracy had to work to run a lemonade stand. I think that the author's purpose is to show that hard work pays off.*

MONITOR/CLARIFY Explain that monitoring the text and clarifying confusing details help readers better understand the author's purpose.

Projectable 16.2

Lunch Money | **Introduce Comprehension** Author's Purpose; Monitor/Clarify

Author's Purpose; Monitor/Clarify

The Lemonade Stand

Tracy had no idea just how much work a lemonade stand would be. She soon learned that she needed many supplies: lemons, sugar, water, ice, cups, change, a cooler, and napkins!

With everything in hand, she made her lemonade and put it in a cooler. She made a sign so people would know that it cost 25 cents per cup. She put a tablecloth on her table and set out her cups. She worked up quite a sweat. And then she waited.

Soon, her first customer appeared, and then four more in a row. In just an hour, she sold all her lemonade—40 cups in all. Her hard work had finally paid off. She made $10 from all her hard work.

Author's Purpose Use an Inference Map to record three details from the story. Then use those details to infer the author's purpose.

Detail	**Detail**	**Detail**
She learned the supplies she needed to have a lemonade stand.	She worked up quite a sweat setting up her lemonade stand.	She sold all of her lemonade in an hour and made $10 from it.

Author's Purpose
The author wanted to influence readers' thinking. The author chose specific details to provide an example that shows hard work can pay off. Tracy worked hard to set up her lemonade stand, but she was rewarded when she sold all of her lemonade in an hour and made $10.

Comprehension

✔ **TARGET SKILL** **Author's Purpose**

The author of "Lunch Money" provides details from which you can infer his viewpoint. As you read, think about how a character's thoughts and actions help you figure out the author's viewpoint, even when it is not directly stated. Use a graphic organizer like this one to help you understand the author's purpose.

✔ **TARGET STRATEGY** **Monitor/Clarify**

You can preview a selection to get an idea of the author's purpose or viewpoint. Before you begin reading, look at the illustrations in "Lunch Money." Then set a purpose for reading, based on what you think the author wants you to learn from the story. As you read, pay close attention to, or monitor, details. Monitoring what you read will help clarify the author's purpose and give you a better understanding of characters and events.

JOURNEYS DIGITAL Powered by DESTINATIONReading®
Comprehension Activities: Lesson 16

405

Monitor Vocabulary

Are students able to identify the author's purpose?

IF...	THEN...
students have difficulty identifying the author's purpose,	▶ **Differentiate Comprehension** for Struggling Readers, p. T62. *See also Intervention Lesson 16, pp. S2–S11.*
students can identify the author's purpose,	▶ **Differentiate Comprehension** for On Level Readers, p. T62.
students can monitor and clarify text details to identify the author's purpose,	▶ **Differentiate Comprehension** for Advanced Readers, p. T63.

 Differentiate Comprehension: pp. T62–T63.

Group English Language Learners according to language proficiency. See also ELL Lesson 16, pp. E2–E11, for scaffolded support.

2 Guided Practice

Guide students as they copy and complete their own Inference Maps for "The Lemonade Stand." Review their Inference Maps with them.

3 Apply

Turn and Talk Have students review their Inference Maps with the class and discuss the details that clarify and support their understanding of the author's purpose.

Ask students to identify the author's purpose in another text they have read recently. Have them record the author's purpose and text details in an Inference Map.

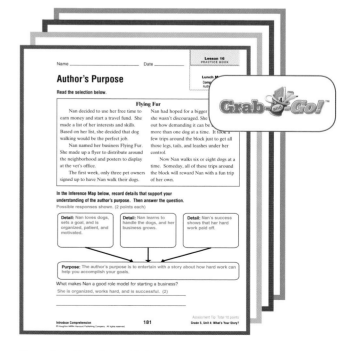

Practice Book p. 181
See Grab-and-Go™ Resources for additional leveled practice.

Introduce the
Main
Selection

✓ **TARGET SKILL**

AUTHOR'S PURPOSE Explain that as they read, students will use **Graphic Organizer 8: Inference Map** to record text clues that help them determine the author's viewpoint and purpose. Have students consider:

- which details the author stresses most
- the author's word choices

✓ **TARGET STRATEGY**

MONITOR/CLARIFY Students will use **Graphic Organizer 8** to **monitor** their understanding and to **clarify** the author's purpose.

GENRE: Realistic Fiction

- Read the genre information on **Student Book p. 406** with students.
- Share and discuss the **Genre Blackline Master: Fiction**.
- Preview the selection and model identifying the characteristics of the genre.

Think Aloud *The illustrations in this selection suggest that the story is fiction. However, on pp. 412–413, there are instructions on how to make something real.*

- As you preview, ask students to identify other features of realistic fiction.

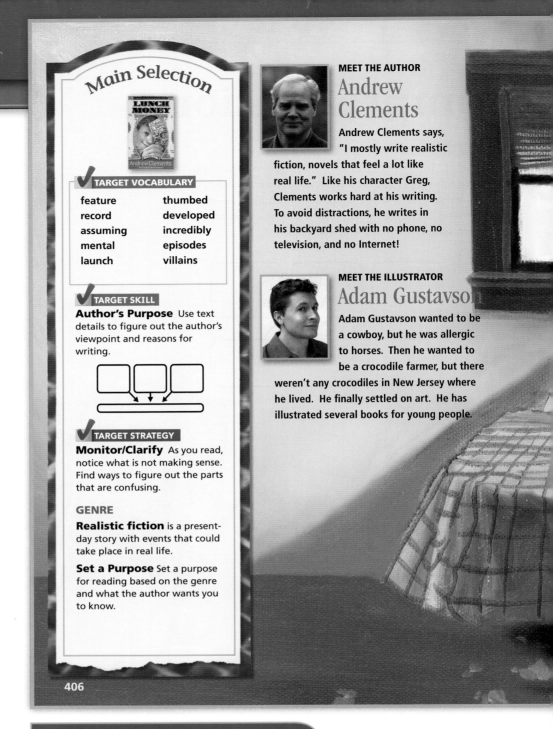

Main Selection

✓ **TARGET VOCABULARY**

feature	thumbed
record	developed
assuming	incredibly
mental	episodes
launch	villains

✓ **TARGET SKILL**

Author's Purpose Use text details to figure out the author's viewpoint and reasons for writing.

✓ **TARGET STRATEGY**

Monitor/Clarify As you read, notice what is not making sense. Find ways to figure out the parts that are confusing.

GENRE

Realistic fiction is a present-day story with events that could take place in real life.

Set a Purpose Set a purpose for reading based on the genre and what the author wants you to know.

406

MEET THE AUTHOR
Andrew Clements

Andrew Clements says, "I mostly write realistic fiction, novels that feel a lot like real life." Like his character Greg, Clements works hard at his writing. To avoid distractions, he writes in his backyard shed with no phone, no television, and no Internet!

MEET THE ILLUSTRATOR
Adam Gustavson

Adam Gustavson wanted to be a cowboy, but he was allergic to horses. Then he wanted to be a crocodile farmer, but there weren't any crocodiles in New Jersey where he lived. He finally settled on art. He has illustrated several books for young people.

Reading the Selection

	Pre-Reading	Reading
Supported	**SELECTION SUMMARY** Use **Blackline Master 16.2** to give students an overview before they read. **AUDIOTEXT CD** Have students listen to the selection as they follow along in their books.	**AUTHOR'S MESSAGE** After reading, have students discuss the author's message about careful planning and working hard.
Independent	**PREVIEW** Have students use the title and illustrations to discuss what they know about comic books. Some students may read the story independently.	**TEXT EVIDENCE** Have students read silently, listing questions for a class discussion in which students will answer the questions, citing text evidence.

by Andrew Clements

selection illustrated by
Adam Gustavson

**Essential
Question**

Why does an
author want to
tell a story?

407

Name _____ Date _____

Lunch Money

Lesson 16
BLACKLINE MASTER 16.2

Lunch Money
Selection Summary

Pages 408–409
Greg Kenton has been selling mini comic books to kids at
school. Greg made his books, which he calls Chunky Comics, on
his own. He stands in the lunch line adding up how much money
he has made. Greg can't think about anything besides his sales.
He doesn't even notice how his food tastes. Greg hopes to make
$25 in a week. His books are popular, but it seems like he might
not meet his goal.

Pages 410–411
Next, the story goes back in time and tells how Greg came
up with his business plan. Since everyone reads at school, he
thought it would be the perfect place to sell books. He learned
all about comics from his dad's huge collection. Greg has loved
drawing for years. He also likes to earn money. The summer
before sixth grade, he decided to find out how to make a comic
book that he could sell.

Pages 412–413
Making comic books is a ten-step process. The author uses
pictures and words to show how Greg made his Chunky Comics.

Pages 414–415
Greg developed story ideas for a whole series of books. He
thought out the details and even an ending. Superheroes from
the past, present, and future will all meet for some final stories.
Greg put a lot of work into the drawings for his first book, which
features Creon, his Stone Age hero.

Page 416
The last page tells how Greg printed his comic books using his
dad's copy machine. When he finished his first book, he felt
really proud.

Selection Summary   4   Grade 5, Unit 4: What's Your Story?
© Houghton Mifflin Harcourt Publishing Company. All rights reserved.

Blackline Master 16.2

? Essential Question

- Read aloud the **Essential Question** on **Student Book p. 407**. *Why does an author want to tell a story?*

- Tell students to think about this question as they read "Lunch Money."

Set Purpose

- Explain that good readers set a purpose for reading, based on their preview of the selection and what they know about the genre. Tell them they can also think about what the author wants them to know.

- Model setting a reading purpose based on the author's desired outcomes.

Think Aloud
In my preview, I see many illustrations about comic books and how to make them. I see a lot of money, and I know the title is "Lunch Money." I wonder how the author connects all of these things together. One purpose for writing the selection might have been to teach readers about the comic book business and how it relates to money.

- Have students share their reading purposes and record them in their journals.

JOURNEYS
DIGITAL **Powered by**
DESTINATIONReading®
Student eBook: Read and Listen

Develop Comprehension

Pause at the stopping points to ask students the following questions.

1 Character Traits

How many times does Greg count what is in his pencil case? What does this tell you about him? Sample answer: He counts whatever it is twice. It tells me that he is thorough and wants to be accurate.

2 ✔ **TARGET VOCABULARY**

*If Greg set another sales **record** before lunch tomorrow, how many units would he need to sell? He would have to sell eighteen units.*

3 Supporting Details

Based on the title of Greg's first comic book, what types of comics do you think Greg likes? Sample answer: The title is "Creon: Return of the Hunter," which sounds like the title of an action or superhero comic.

Standing in the cafeteria line, Greg opened his red plastic pencil case. He counted once, and then he counted again, just to be sure. Then he grinned. There were thirteen left. **1**

Sweet! That means I sold seventeen units.

That's what Greg called the comic books he'd been selling—units. And selling seventeen units before lunch was a new sales record.

Greg's comic books weren't the kind for sale at stores. Regular comic books were sort of tall. Also a little floppy. Not Greg's. **2**

Greg's comic books were about the size of a credit card, and they could stand up on one end all by themselves. They were only sixteen pages long, and he could fit about fifty of them into his pencil case. These comic books were short and sturdy. And that's why they were called Chunky Comics.

Greg loved that name. He had chosen it himself. He got to pick the name because he was the author of all the Chunky Comics stories. He had drawn all the pictures too. And he was also the designer, the printer, and the binder. Plus he was the marketing manager, the advertising director, and the entire sales force. Chunky Comics was a one-kid operation, and that one kid was Greg Kenton.

Greg snapped the pencil case shut and grabbed a tray. He took a grilled cheese sandwich, a cup of carrot sticks, and then looked over the fruit cocktail bowls until he found one with three chunks of cherry. He got a chocolate milk from the cooler, and as he walked toward his seat, Greg did some mental math.

Monday, the first day Chunky Comics had gone on sale, he had sold twelve units; Tuesday, fifteen units; Wednesday, eighteen units; and today, Thursday, he had already sold seventeen units—before lunch. So that was . . . sixty-two units since Monday morning, and each little book sold for $.25. So the up-to-the-minute sales total for September 12 was . . . $15.50.

408

ELL **ENGLISH LANGUAGE LEARNERS**

Scaffold

Beginning Use the illustrations to preview the selection with students. Help them name objects they recognize.	**Advanced** After reading pages 408–409, have partners briefly summarize the story up to this point.
Intermediate While reading the beginning of the story aloud, pause to ask what students have learned about Greg Kenton.	**Advanced High** After reading pp. 408–409, have students write one or two sentences summarizing what they have learned so far.

See ELL Lesson 16, pp. E2–E11, for scaffolded support.

Greg knew why sales were increasing: word of mouth. Kids had been telling other kids about his comic book. The cover illustration was powerful, the inside pictures were strong, and the story was loaded with action. The title was *Creon: Return of the Hunter*, and it was volume 1, number 1, the very first of the Chunky Comics. So that made it a collector's item.

Greg sat down at his regular lunch table, next to Ted Kendall. Ted nodded and said, "Hi," but Greg didn't hear him. Greg picked up his sandwich and took a big bite. He chewed the warm bread and the soft cheese, but he didn't taste a thing. Greg was still thinking about sales.

Fifteen fifty in three and a half days—not so hot.

Greg had set a sales goal for the first week: twenty-five dollars— which meant that he had to sell one hundred units. It looked like he was going to fall short.

 3

> **STOP AND THINK**
> **Monitor/Clarify** To clarify why Greg needs to sell one hundred units to make twenty-five dollars, reread the previous page. What happens when you multiply the price of one unit times one hundred?

409

STOP AND THINK

✓ **TARGET STRATEGY**
Monitor/Clarify

- Remind students that monitoring, or checking the text as they read, will help them better understand what they read. When they find an idea that seems confusing, they should stop to clarify what they have read.

- Have students answer the **Stop and Think** question on **Student Book p. 409.**

- If students have difficulty using the Monitor/Clarify strategy, see Comprehension Intervention for extra support.

- Display **Projectable 16.3a**. Tell students that an Inference Map can help them record details to determine the author's purpose. Model how to fill in the Inference Map, using the Monitor/Clarify strategy.

- Have students use **Graphic Organizer 8** to begin their own Inference Maps.

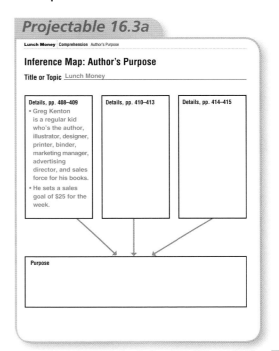

Projectable 16.3a

Lunch Money | Comprehension Author's Purpose

Inference Map: Author's Purpose
Title or Topic Lunch Money

Details, pp. 408–409	Details, pp. 410–413	Details, pp. 414–415
• Greg Kenton is a regular kid who's the author, illustrator, designer, printer, binder, marketing manager, advertising director, and sales force for his books. • He sets a sales goal of $25 for the week.		

Purpose

COMPREHENSION INTERVENTION

✓ **TARGET STRATEGY**   **Monitor/Clarify**

STRATEGY SUPPORT Remind students that *monitoring* means checking understanding while reading. When they come to text that doesn't make sense, they must clarify it by using strategies such as rereading or reading ahead. Model the Monitor/Clarify strategy by reviewing Greg's thoughts and actions at lunch.

When Greg's classmate says hello to him, Greg doesn't notice him. He also doesn't taste the sandwich he's eating. Clearly he's very distracted.

Read aloud p. 409. *How much money did Greg make in three and a half days?* fifteen dollars and fifty cents *What was his sales goal for the week?* twenty-five dollars *Why is Greg so distracted at lunch?* He's thinking about how short he is of his sales goal.

Guide students to begin working on their Inference Maps.

Develop Comprehension

4 **Identify Author's Purpose**
In the second line on page 410, the word KRAK is written as it would be in a comic book. Why does the author use this technique here? Sample answer: The style provides a connection to comic books and a visual for how Greg came up with his idea.

5 **Supporting Details**
On page 410, the author writes: "reading a comic book wasn't exactly the same as reading a regular book." Explain this statement. Sample answer: Comics have more pictures than regular books, and the words are sometimes in speech balloons. Comics are not typically used in school.

6 **Draw Conclusions**
Why do you think Greg had to show that he could take care of the comic books before he could read and look at them? Sample answer: The comics are worth money, but if they were damaged, they wouldn't be worth anything anymore.

7 ✓ **TARGET VOCABULARY**
How does Greg feel about the **launch** *of Chunky Comics? Sample answer: He is confident, but there are a lot of questions he needs to answer before it begins.*

The idea of making and selling comic books had hit Greg like a KRAK over the head from Superman himself. It made perfect sense. Candy and gum were against school rules, and tiny toys were boring—and also against the rules. But how could he go wrong selling little books? School was all about books and reading. True, reading a comic book wasn't exactly the same as reading a regular book, but still, there was a rack of comics right in the kids' section at the public library downtown, and some new graphic novels, too.

Comic books had been part of Greg's life forever, mostly because of his dad's collection. His dad's collection filled three shelves in the family room—and it was worth over ten thousand dollars. Once Greg had shown he knew how to take care of the comic books, he had been allowed to read and look at them all he wanted. Greg had even bought a few collectible comics of his own, mostly newer ones that weren't very expensive.

410

It was his love of comic books that had first gotten Greg interested in drawing. Comics had led Greg to books like *How to Draw Comic Book Villains*, *You Can Draw Superheroes*, *Make Your Own Comic-Book Art*, and *Draw the Monsters We Love to Hate*. Back in third grade Greg had used his own money to buy india ink, dip pens, brushes, and paper at the art supply store. And drawing new comic-book characters was one of his favorite things to do—when he wasn't earning money.

That whole summer before sixth grade Greg had worked toward the launch of Chunky Comics. From the start he had felt pretty sure he could come up with a story idea, and he knew he would be able to do the drawings.

But first he'd had to deal with a lot of *hows*: How does a whole comic book get put together? How big should each be? How was he going to print them? How much would it cost him to make each one? And finally, how much money should he charge for his finished comic books—assuming he could actually make some?

But one by one, Greg had found the answers. An encyclopedia article about printing books had helped a lot. It showed how pages of a book start as one large sheet of paper that gets folded in half several times. Each time the sheet is folded, the number of pages is doubled. So Greg took a piece of regular letter-size paper, and folded it in half three times the way it showed in the encyclopedia. That one piece of paper turned into a chunky little sixteen-page book—Chunky Comics. It was so simple.

7

> **STOP AND THINK**
> **Author's Craft** Authors often use **repetition**, repeating a word or phrase, to bring extra attention to something. Why do you think the author repeats the word *how* so many times in the third paragraph on this page?

411

STOP AND THINK
Author's Craft: Repetition

- Explain to students that **repetition** is a device authors use in which they repeat a word or phrase several times.

- Point out that authors use repetitive language for emphasis. A word or phrase may be repeated to bring extra attention to something and to help readers connect to what's most important.

> **Think Aloud** *In the third paragraph on page 411, we learn that Greg is dealing with a lot of "how" questions. There are five* how *questions listed. I think the author does this for a reason.*

- Have students answer the **Stop and Think** question on **Student Book p. 411**.

- Display **Projectable 16.3b** and work with students to fill in the Inference Map with details about the author's use of repetition.

- Have them continue filling out text details that allow them to infer the author's purpose while looking at the process on the following pages.

Projectable 16.3b

Lunch Money | Comprehension | Author's Purpose

Inference Map: Author's Purpose

Title or Topic Lunch Money

Details, pp. 408–409	Details, pp. 410–413	Details, pp. 414–415
• Greg Kenton is a regular kid who's the author, illustrator, designer, printer, binder, marketing manager, advertising director, and sales force for his books. • He sets a sales goal of $25 for the week.	• The author tells about all the "hows" Greg has to answer before he can get started. • The author uses pictures and written instructions to clarify the ten-step process Greg follows to make his book.	

Purpose

Develop Comprehension

8 **Identify Author's Purpose**
Why does the author include pictures with the written instructions? Sample answer: It might be hard to know how to paste the minipages on the master copy without a picture.

9 **Supporting Details**
What is a press sheet? a paper that is used for printing

10 **Sequence of Events**
What should you do after you have carefully folded the minipages? The pages should be stapled and trimmed.

But not really. Greg figured out that making little comic books was a ten-step process.

1. Write a story that can be told on twelve to fourteen mini-comic book pages.

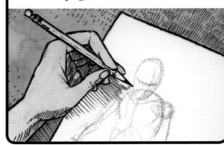

2. Sketch, draw, ink, and then letter all sixteen minipages—which include the front and back covers.

8 3. Paste eight of the minipage drawings into their correct positions on a piece of paper to make "master copy one"—a sheet that can be copied again and again.

4. Paste up the other eight minipages to make "master copy two."

412

ELL **ENGLISH LANGUAGE LEARNERS**

Scaffold

Beginning Use gestures and the instructions on pp. 412–413 to explain the steps Greg takes to complete a comic book.

Advanced Have partners orally summarize the instructions for making the comic books on pp. 412–413 and look for clues to define the word *develop*.

Intermediate Work with students to describe the steps Greg takes to complete one of his Chunky Comics.

Advanced High Have partners write two or three sentences about how Greg developed his book-making process.

See ELL Lesson 16, pp. E2–E11, for scaffolded support.

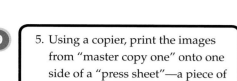

9

5. Using a copier, print the images from "master copy one" onto one side of a "press sheet"—a piece of regular letter-size paper.

6. Print "master copy two" onto the flip side of the press sheet—making eight page images on the front, and eight on the back.

7. Carefully fold the press sheet with the sixteen copied minipages on it.

8. Put in two staples along the crease at the very center of the little book—between pages 8 and 9.

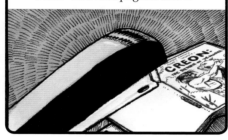

10

9. Trim the three unstapled edges— and that makes one finished mini-comic book.

10. Repeat.

And each of the ten steps had to be done perfectly, or no one would ever want to spend money on his little comics.

413

Practice Fluency

Rate Read aloud the first paragraph on **Student Book p. 414** as students follow along. As you read the paragraph, model reading at a conversational rate appropriate to the text.

Ask students to explain why reading at a slower rate might be more appropriate for this paragraph.

• Tell students that good readers don't rush, but keep a steady reading rate.

• Explain that when readers come to a difficult phrase, they should sound out the words. Remind students that they can look up or ask about a difficult word like *marauders*, which means "thieves."

• Have students do guided repeated readings with a partner. Tell partners to keep a steady reading rate.

See **p. T38** for a complete fluency lesson on reading at an appropriate rate.

CROSS-CURRICULAR CONNECTION

Social Studies

Explain to students that in the United States we have a free enterprise system, in which people can own and operate their own businesses privately with minimal government intervention. People have the freedom to develop an idea, create a product, and earn money for that product. Their product can compete against similar products, and people have the freedom to choose which product they would prefer.

Ask: *If someone at Greg's school already sold comic books, would Greg still be able to sell his Chunky Comics? Why or why not? Sample answer: Yes; the free enterprise system would allow Greg's comics to compete against the other students' comics. It would be the students' choice as to whose comic books they bought.*

Develop Comprehension

11 **Understanding Characters**
How does Greg's publishing plan help readers understand him? Sample answer: He's organized, creative, and determined, which shows that if a person works hard enough, he or she can accomplish anything.

12 ✔ **TARGET VOCABULARY**
*Why do you think Greg decides to **feature** three different characters in his comic books? Sample answer: He uses three different characters so people with different interests will enjoy his comics.*

13 **Draw Conclusions**
Explain why some illustrations are in black and white, while others are in color. Sample answer: The color illustrations are from the story "Lunch Money," while the black and white drawings are Greg's comics.

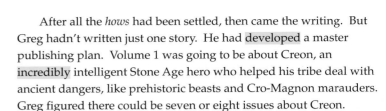

After all the *hows* had been settled, then came the writing. But Greg hadn't written just one story. He had developed a master publishing plan. Volume 1 was going to be about Creon, an incredibly intelligent Stone Age hero who helped his tribe deal with ancient dangers, like prehistoric beasts and Cro-Magnon marauders. Greg figured there could be seven or eight issues about Creon.

Chunky Comics volume 2 would feature the future, where a superhero named Eeon tried to protect a small colony of humans living in a world of melting ice caps and mutant life-forms that were part human, part toxic sludge, and part recycled trucks and airplanes. Again, there would be seven or eight issues featuring Eeon.

STOP AND THINK
Author's Purpose Why do you think the author explains how Greg makes comic books in such detail?

414

Then Chunky Comics volume 3 would feature Leon, a fairly normal modern-age technodude who suddenly finds himself energized when his digital atomic watch overheats and burns its circuits into the nerves on his wrist. Leon learns that the watch can be set for the future or the past. The six or seven time-travel adventures of volume 3 would follow Leon to the past, where he would team up with Creon, and then to the future, where he would offer his services to the amazing Eeon. And eventually, all three characters would have some final episodes together: Creon, Leon, and Eeon—past, present, and future. **(11)** **(12)**

Once the master plan was set, writing the first Creon story, *Return of the Hunter*, had been pretty easy for Greg. But the drawing was more difficult than he'd thought it would be. It had taken a long time to get each small page looking just the way he wanted. It wasn't like doodling or sketching. These pictures had to be good—good enough to sell.

415

STOP AND THINK

✓ TARGET SKILL
Author's Purpose

- Remind students that an author's purpose is his or her reason for writing. Tell students that thinking about the author's purpose can help them understand the text.

- Have students answer the **Stop and Think** question on **Student Book p. 414.**

- If students have difficulty identifying the author's purpose, see Comprehension Intervention for extra support.

- Display **Projectable 16.3c.** Work with students to complete the Inference Map.

Turn and Talk

? Essential Question

Discuss why the author chose to tell the story of Greg and his comic books.

COMPREHENSION INTERVENTION

✓ TARGET SKILL Author's Purpose

SKILL SUPPORT Remind students that the author's purpose is what the author wants a reader to learn from a text. Sometimes it is directly stated, and other times you must use text details to infer the author's purpose.

Model using details from the text to determine the author's purpose.
The author provides step-by-step instructions on how to make a book, which shows that anyone could do it. The author wants people to know that with organization and planning, they could also do something great.

Read aloud the top paragraph on page 415. Ask: *What does the author want us to learn from this paragraph? Sample answer: Greg is thinking far ahead and has an ending planned out. In order to get something done, you must have a plan.*

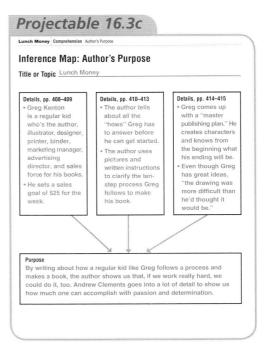

Projectable 16.3c

Lunch Money | Comprehension | Author's Purpose

Inference Map: Author's Purpose
Title or Topic Lunch Money

Details, pp. 408–409	Details, pp. 410–413	Details, pp. 414–415
• Greg Kenton is a regular kid who's the author, illustrator, designer, printer, binder, marketing manager, advertising director, and sales force for his books. • He sets a sales goal of $25 for the week.	• The author tells about all the "hows" Greg has to answer before he can get started. • The author uses pictures and written instructions to clarify the ten-step process Greg follows to make his book.	• Greg comes up with a "master publishing plan." He creates characters and knows from the beginning what his ending will be. • Even though Greg has great ideas, "the drawing was more difficult than he'd thought it would be."

Purpose
By writing about how a regular kid like Greg follows a process and makes a book, the author shows us that, if we work really hard, we could do it, too. Andrew Clements goes into a lot of detail to show us how much one can accomplish with passion and determination.

Develop Comprehension

14 ✔ **TARGET VOCABULARY** *How do you think Greg felt when he **thumbed** through his book for the first time?*
Sample answers: excited, proud, tired

When both covers and the fourteen inside pages had been drawn and inked and pasted in place to make the two master copies, Greg tackled his first printing.

The copier he used was his dad's, and it was actually part of the printer that was hooked up to the computer in the family room. It was an ink-jet printer, plus a scanner, plus a copier—one of those "all-in-one" machines. It made copies in either black and white or color.

Greg had stuffed about forty ruined sheets of paper into the recycling bin before he had figured out how to get all sixteen page images copied correctly onto the front and back of one sheet of paper.

But finally, he had folded his first perfectly printed sheet, stapled it twice, and trimmed the top, front, and bottom edges. And then, one hot night in the middle of July, Greg stood there in his
14 family room and thumbed through the very first volume of Chunky Comics. It had been a proud moment.

416

ELL **ENGLISH LANGUAGE LEARNERS**

Scaffold

Beginning Point to the picture of Greg holding the completed comic. Have students repeat these summary sentences. *Greg developed and made a comic book. Greg likes the comic book. He feels proud.*

Advanced Guide students to summarize the last paragraph. Ask: *Can you clarify the events of the last paragraph?* Allow students to answer in their own words.

Intermediate Read aloud the last paragraph of the selection. Have volunteers look for context clues to define a *proud moment.*

Advanced High Have students describe the reasons why Greg is proud. *Can you clarify why Greg is proud?*

See ELL Lesson 16, pp. E2–E11, for scaffolded support.

Your Turn

A Proud Moment

Short Response One hot night in July, Greg thumbed through the first volume of his comic book series. It was a proud moment for him. Have you, or has someone you know, worked so hard to create something that the resulting feelings of pride and accomplishment were as strong as Greg's? Write a paragraph explaining what happened. Be sure to include vivid details. PERSONAL RESPONSE

Buy Chunky Comics!

Create a Poster Work with a partner to design and create a promotional poster for a bookstore or library that can help Greg advertise his comic books. Use details from the selection to make the comic books come alive. PARTNERS

Past, Present, Future

Turn and Talk Do you think Creon, Leon, and Eeon will be good characters for a series of comic books? Do you think Greg will be successful? Discuss with a partner what makes comic books popular and fun to read. Then discuss why the author might have included Greg's detailed plans for his Chunky Comics series. AUTHOR'S PURPOSE

417

Retelling Rubric

4	Excellent	Students **clearly describe all important story events** in order and explain how each event leads to the next.
3	Good	Students **describe most important story events** in order and explain how some events lead to others.
2	Fair	Students **describe a few story events** and **demonstrate a limited understanding** of how events are related.
1	Unsatisfactory	Students **cannot identify important story events**.

Your Turn

Have students complete the activities on **Student Book page 417.**

A Proud Moment Have partners brainstorm an accomplishment to write about. Encourage them to think of school projects and/or gifts they have made. Then suggest that students use a Flow Chart to plan their paragraph. They can first use the Flow Chart to organize the sequence of events and then add vivid details to the graphic organizer before writing. (PERSONAL RESPONSE)

Buy Chunky Comics! Before students begin work on their posters, discuss and list the elements of an effective advertisement. Then have partners review the selection to find details about the comic books that they can advertise in their poster. When students are finished, have them share their posters with the class and identify the effective elements of others' posters. (PARTNERS)

Past, Present, Future Ask questions to help partners consider whether or not Greg's project will succeed, such as: *Do you find the characters Creon, Eeon, and Leon interesting? Would you buy one of Greg's comic books? Why or why not? What did you learn from reading the details about Greg's plans?* (AUTHOR'S PURPOSE)

Oral Language Have students use the illustrations in the story to review details about Greg and his comic book business. Then have students retell "Lunch Money." Use the Retelling Rubric at left to evaluate their responses.

Connect to Social Studies

PREVIEW THE INFORMATIONAL TEXT

- Tell students that this selection includes facts, details, and a timeline about the history of comics. Ask students to preview the illustrations and headings. Then have students read the informational text independently.

DISCUSS TIMELINES

- Explain that informational texts often include graphic features such as an illustrated timeline.

- Remind students that timelines show when important events took place. The left side shows the earliest events, while the right side shows the most recent events. Discuss the use of the evenly spaced dates marked in purple on the timeline on **Student Book pp. 418–419.**

- Tell students to look for the following features of a timeline that will help them read and understand it.

date	the day, month, or year when an event took place
event	an important happening that relates to the timeline's subject
illustration	a picture that gives more information about an event on the timeline

- Have students read and answer the bulleted question on the bookmark of **Student Book p. 418.**

Connect to Social Studies

TARGET VOCABULARY

feature	thumbed
record	developed
assuming	incredibly
mental	episodes
launch	villains

GENRE
Informational text gives facts and examples about a topic.

TEXT FOCUS
A **timeline** marks the sequence of important events in a period of history or other span of time.
- Preview the timeline on pages 418–419. How do the facts and dates relate to the title of the selection?

Zap! Pow!
A History of the Comics
by Linda Cave

Do you read the funnies in the paper? They have been popular for more than one hundred years. They tell stories with words and pictures, and new episodes appear each day. Assuming you read comics, you know they can be funny. Sometimes they feature adventures or political issues. Some comics are in books, too.

Development of Comics

1896: *Yellow Kid*

1907: Daily comics

1934: *Flash Gordon*

1900

1920

1933: First comic books

1897: Speech balloons; story panels

418

ELL ENGLISH LANGUAGE LEARNERS

Scaffold

Beginning Point out to students the timeline and its important features on pp. 418–419. Then explain what a timeline is and how to read its parts.

Advanced Have students use text details to answer this question: *When did comics first become popular?*

Intermediate Pose questions about comics and how they developed, based on the timeline. Discuss students' responses and clarify their understanding.

Advanced High Have students orally summarize the first two pages of the informational text.

See ELL Lesson 16, pp. E2–E11, for scaffolded support.

Early Days

In 1896 the comic *Yellow Kid* appeared in a Sunday paper. The kid wore a wide yellow suit. The words he "spoke" were written on the suit. People thumbed through the papers just to read the comic. Soon comics were in many Sunday papers. When one artist used a speech balloon to show a character speaking, other artists began to use the balloons. At about the same time, artists developed panels, or boxes, to show a series of events. Later, publishers put comics in their papers every day.

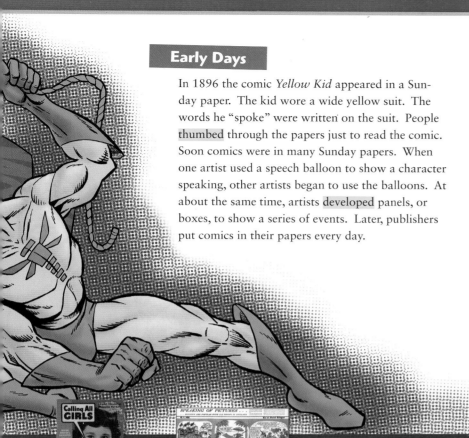

1941: *Calling All Girls,* first comic for girls

1939–1945: Comic books popular with WWII soldiers

1970s: Comic book collecting

1940   1960   1980

1938: First Superman

1954: Standards for comic books set by Comics Code Authority

1950s: First comics for grownups

Present: Motion pictures based on comic books

419

Practice Fluency

Rate Have students listen as you read aloud the paragraph on **Student Book p. 419.**

- Remind students that good readers establish a steady reading rate that is fast enough to keep a listener's attention, but slow enough to ensure comprehension. Good readers change their rate slightly to emphasize certain words or phrases.

- Have students do repeated readings with partners. Have them look up any challenging vocabulary so that their reading rate and comprehension can be maintained.

JOURNEYS DIGITAL **Powered by** DESTINATIONReading
Student eBook: Read and Listen

TARGET VOCABULARY REVIEW

✓ **TARGET VOCABULARY** Vocabulary in Context Cards — Word Pairs

Use the **Vocabulary in Context Cards** to reinforce Target Vocabulary as students get ready to read the selection. Have students work with partners to create word pairs. Tell students to mix the cards and then pick two at random. They should write a sentence that uses both words and then read the sentence aloud to other partners.

CONTEXT CARDS

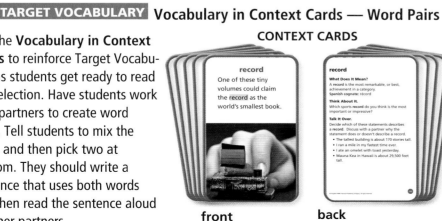

front   back

Develop Comprehension

Reread the selection with students. Pause at stopping points to ask students the following questions.

1 ✔️ **TARGET VOCABULARY**

*Why do you think comics were **incredibly** popular with soldiers during WWII? Sample answer: Comics were light to carry, quick to read, and provided the soldiers with entertainment.*

2 Main Idea and Details

What are some characteristics of superheroes in comic books? Sample answers: They fight villians, use amazing tools, and have super physical and mental powers.

3 Analyze Text Features

Under which heading will you find information about when comic books were very popular? Why? Sample answer: That information will be under the heading "The Golden Age of Comic Books" because golden age refers to something at its peak.

INTERPRET A TIMELINE

- Review the features of an illustrated timeline, and model interpreting information on **p. 420** by using the timeline on **pp. 418–419**.

- Model the thinking.

Think Aloud

On page 420, I learn that the first comic books were given away to people who bought a certain product. To find out when that happened, I can use the timeline. The first comic books were made in 1933.

Comic Strips to Comic Books

In the early 1930s, someone collected newspaper comics into books to give away to people who bought certain products. These were the first comic books. Writers and artists saw that people wanted the books and would buy them. Soon original stories began to appear in comic book form.

The Golden Age of Comic Books

1 Many historians say the golden age of comic books began with the launch of Superman in 1938. He was the first character to have super powers. His comic books were incredibly popular. They set a new sales record, with over one million copies sold per issue. Noticing the new superhero's popularity, other comic book artists created Batman, The Flash, the Green Lantern, Captain America, and Wonder Woman. They all fought villains. Some used amazing tools **2** or had super physical and mental powers.

The Comics Code and After

Some adults worried that comic books were bad for children. A comics code was established in 1954 to make sure comics were safe for kids to read. For many, this marked the end of a golden age. Today comic books are still popular, with new superheroes and villains appearing each year. Classic superheroes like Superman and Batman find new audiences through new comic book adventures and in movies. Using words and artwork together to tell a story is still a winning combination. **3**

420

Weekly Internet Challenge

Using Keywords

- Review the Internet Strategy, Step 1: Plan a Search.
- Review that the purpose of a search engine is to perform research on the Internet.
- Explain that good researchers can choose keywords effectively to achieve satisfactory results.

INTERNET STRATEGY

1. **Plan a Search** by identifying what you are looking for and how to find it.

2. **Search and Predict** which sites will be worth exploring.

3. **Navigate** a site to see how to get around it and what it contains.

4. **Analyze and Evaluate** the quality and reliability of the information.

5. **Synthesize** the information from multiple sites.

Making Connections

 Text to Self

Write a Letter to a Hero You do not have to be a superhero to do incredible things. Write a letter to someone you know who has done something special or out of the ordinary. In your letter, explain why you think what that person did is special.

 Text to Text

Create a Comic In "Lunch Money," Greg creates three comic book characters—Creon, Eeon, and Leon. Create a comic about an adventure one of these characters has. Use one of the comic book formats described in "Zap! Pow! A History of the Comics" to write your comic.

 Text to World

Expand a Timeline Work with a partner to add to the timeline in "Zap! Pow! A History of the Comics." Begin by studying the captions and illustrations on the timeline on pages 418–419. Use print sources or the Internet to find additional information to include on the timeline. Then add to the timeline three other important events in the history of comics. Review the new timeline. How has the audience for comics changed over the years?

421

"Zap! Pow!: A History of the Comics" Challenge

- Have students work in a group to choose a specific topic about comic books, such as "The Golden Age of Comic Books." Tell them to browse the selection if they need ideas for a topic.

- Then ask students to brainstorm a list of keywords for an Internet search about their chosen topic.

- Have students start with the first term on their list. Tell them to evaluate the results from the search. Discuss students' searches and whether they are yielding results that are too general or too narrow. Have them adjust their keywords accordingly and search again.

Making Connections

 Text to Self

Students may need help determining events that are special or extraordinary. Prompt them to brainstorm events that they remember well and then ask who was involved in that event.

 Text to Text

If students have difficulty coming up with an adventure, help them brainstorm ideas. Ask: *What happened on the way to school? Is there a funny story your family always tells?* Provide examples of comics and subjects.

 Text to World

Have students closely examine how the timeline on pp. 418–419 was constructed and use it as a base for their new timeline. Guide them to Internet sites that focus on the history of comics.

Deepen Comprehension

SHARE OBJECTIVES

- Determine the author's viewpoint.
- Describe how the author's viewpoint affects the theme of the text.

SKILL TRACE

Author's Purpose

Introduce	T18–T19, T36–T37
Differentiate	T62–T63
Reteach	T70
Review	T310–T311, Unit 5
Test	Weekly Tests, Lesson 16

ELL ENGLISH LANGUAGE LEARNERS

Scaffold

Beginning Discuss with students some of the text clues in "Lunch Money" that might point to the author's viewpoint. Help students complete this sentence frame: *Greg creates the first volume of Chunky Comics by _____ .*

Intermediate Provide the sentence frame above, and have students complete it orally using text clues from the selection.

Advanced Have students discuss how the following text from p. 416 shows the author's viewpoint: *. . . Greg stood there in the family room and thumbed through the very first volume of Chunky Comics. It was a proud moment.*

Advanced High Have partners infer the author's viewpoint about Greg on p. 409. Tell them to write sentences about how the author views Greg.

See ELL Lesson 16, pp. E2–E11, for scaffolded support.

☑ Author's Viewpoint and Purpose

1 Teach/Model

AL *Academic Language*

author's viewpoint the way the author thinks or feels about something

inference a conclusion a reader makes using clues in the text

---

- Explain that an **author's viewpoint** reflects how the author feels toward what he or she is writing about. It affects the author's purpose and the way in which the author writes the selection.

- Tell students that they can help determine an author's viewpoint by examining the author's purpose and theme of the selection, and the way the characters, setting, and events are presented.

- Have students reread **Student Book pp. 408–411** of "Lunch Money."

- Display **Projectable 16.4.** Discuss **Deepen Comprehension Question 1.**

- Remind students that an Inference Map helps organize details so readers can infer the author's viewpoint.

- Model adding details to the Inference Map to answer the first question and make an **inference** about the author's viewpoint.

Projectable 16.4

Lunch Money | Deepen Comprehension | Author's Purpose

Inference Map: Author's Viewpoint

Deepen Comprehension Question 1
How does the author describe Greg Kenton? What inference can you make about how the author thinks and feels about Greg? p. 411

Details	Details	Details
a regular kid with a lot to think about	does everything for his comic book	kept track of sales and profits

Author's Viewpoint
Greg is hard working. That is a good characteristic.

Deepen Comprehension Question 2
What details does the author provide to show how Greg makes his comic books? How do the details support how the author feels about Greg? pp. 412–413

Details	Details	Details
Greg read how in an encyclopedia	instructions describing each of the ten steps	each step has to be done perfectly

Author's Viewpoint
These details show how the author is impressed with Greg for being able to do all of this work.

Deepen Comprehension Question 3
What are some other ways that the author's feelings about Greg support the theme?

Think Aloud *What details can I find in the text that help me understand how the author thinks and feels about Greg? I see that Greg spends a lot of time thinking about how to design and write his comic books and how to sell them. I'll add those details to my Inference Map. The author wants to show me that Greg is hard-working and that this characteristic is admirable.*

2 Guided Practice

• Reread with students on **Student Book p. 412–413** of "Lunch Money." Discuss **Deepen Comprehension Question 2** on **Projectable 16.4**. Use these prompts to guide students.

• What process is explained on these pages? *how to create little comic books*

• Why does each step have to be done perfectly? *If the comics are not made well, no one will spend money on them.*

• Guide students to complete the Inference Map for **Question 2**.

GUIDED DISCUSSION Have students reread **pp. 412–413** and work with them to infer other details that reveal the author's viewpoint. Prompt students with questions such as the one below:

• How does the author view the way that Greg spends most of his time? *Since the author includes many details about the lengthy process Greg uses to create comics, he must admire his passion and hard work.*

3 Apply

 TURN AND TALK Have students reread **Student Book pp. 414–416** of "Lunch Money." Then have small groups make an Inference Map and work together to complete **Deepen Comprehension Question 3** on **Projectable 16.4**.

WRITE ABOUT READING Have students write their responses to **Deepen Comprehension Question 3**. Ask students to share their responses.

Monitor Comprehension

Are students able to infer the author's viewpoint and purpose in a selection?

IF...	THEN...
students have difficulty inferring the author's viewpoint and purpose,	▶ use the Leveled Reader for **Struggling Readers**, *Dog Walker, Inc.*, p. T64.
students understand and are able to infer the author's viewpoint and purpose,	▶ use the Leveled Reader for **On-Level Readers**, *Incognito*, p. T65.
students can connect the author's viewpoint and purpose to the story's theme,	▶ use the Leveled Reader for **Advanced Readers**, *The Three R's*, p. T66

Use the Leveled Reader for **English Language Learners**, *The Lost Comic Book*, p. T67. *Group English Language Learners according to language proficiency.*

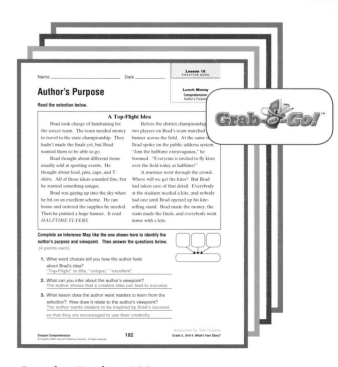

Practice Book p. 182
See Grab-and-Go™ Resources for additional leveled practice.

Fluency

SHARE OBJECTIVES

- Read aloud with grade-appropriate fluency.
- Read fluently by changing rate as needed for comprehension.

 Rate

1 Teach/Model

- Tell students that good readers can read a passage quickly and without errors. However, even when they read quickly, they must understand what they read. Their reading rate, or how fast or slow they read, must be appropriate for the text.

- Have students follow along as you read aloud **Student Book p. 414**. Show students how you slow your reading rate to be able to correctly read and comprehend the text.

- Explain that students might need to read at a slower rate to understand a difficult text. If they are reading for enjoyment, they can read faster.

2 Guided Practice

- Read aloud **Student Book p. 411** with students.

- Work with students to adjust their reading rate as needed to understand the passage.

- If students are struggling to read at an appropriate rate, practice choral-reading **pp. 411–413** with students. Guide them to change their reading rate when the difficulty of the text changes.

- See also **Instructional Routine 7**.

3 Apply

- Tell students that with practice, they can improve comprehension by learning to adjust their reading rate as necessary.

- Have partners take turns reading **Student Book pp. 411–413** aloud to each other at a rate appropriate for understanding.

- Allow students to read the pages three or four times.

Decoding

 Word Parts and Inflectional Endings

SHARE OBJECTIVES

- Recognize word parts and words with inflectional endings.
- Use word parts and inflectional endings to decode longer words.

1 Teach/Model

ANALYZE WORD PARTS AND INFLECTIONAL ENDINGS Model how to recognize word parts and inflectional endings by breaking apart the word *struggled*. Point out the base word *struggle* and the inflectional ending *-ed*. Read the word aloud and have students repeat after you: *strug | gled*.

Tell students that:

- If a base word ends in a *d* or a *t*, the inflection *-ed* will form the last syllable; otherwise *-ed* will be part of the preceding syllable.
- For base words that end in a vowel-plus consonant, double the consonant and add the inflection.
- For base words that end in *e*, drop the *e* before adding the ending.

Use Projectable S1 to guide instruction with the decoding strategy.

2 Practice/Apply

DECODE WORDS WITH *–ED* OR *–ING* Write the following words on the board: *supposed, disturbing, complained, forgetting, muttered, featured, publishing, computing*.

- Guide students to break the first two words into parts and then divide them into syllables.

  suppos | ed; sup | posed   disturb | ing; dis | turb | ing

- Have partners work to decode the remaining words.
- Call on students to identify each base word and inflectional ending.
- Use **Corrective Feedback** if students need additional help.

Corrective Feedback

If students have trouble decodir words with inflectional endings use the model below.

Correct the error. Divide the word into its parts. *The word is* computing. *The parts are* comput *and* ing.

Model the correct way to decode the word. *Look for word parts that you know. Identify the base word. Look for an inflectional ending.*

Guide students to identify the base word and the inflectional ending. *What is the base word?* (compute) *What is the inflectional ending?* (-ing)

Check students' understanding. *What is the word?* (computing)

Reinforce Have students repeat the process with the word *muttered*.

Vocabulary Strategies

SHARE OBJECTIVE

- Learn and use word origins to see how words change over time.

SKILL TRACE

Word Origins	
Introduce	T40–T41
Differentiate	T68–T69
Reteach	T70
Review	T212–T213, Unit 6
Test	Weekly Tests, Lesson 16

ELL ENGLISH LANGUAGE LEARNERS

Scaffold

Beginning Show students a world map. Point to Mexico and say that the word *cafeteria* was first used in Mexico. Move your finger up to the United States and say that we still use the word *cafeteria* today. Work with students to use prior knowledge to define the word.

Intermediate Write *riso* on the board. Pronounce the word and ask what English word sounds similar to this Italian word. Explain that *rice* came from the word *riso*.

Advanced Discuss with students why the Spanish word *rosa* and the English word *rose* sound alike. Then have them use a dictionary to identify the relationship between the words.

Advanced High Ask students to look up *lariat* in a dictionary to find where the word came from. Then have students discuss how the origins of *lariat* can help them understand the word's history and meaning.

See ELL Lesson 16, pp. E2–E11, for scaffolded support.

✔ Word Origins

1 Teach/Model

AL *Academic Language*

word origin the language or region in which a word originated

- Explain that **word origins** tell where a word comes from, or where it originated. Word origins can give us an idea of what a word means, why and where it was created, and by whom.

- Point out that many English words came from words in other languages, such as Greek, Latin, and French.

- Write the following sentence on the board: *Greg learned how to draw pictures of villains for his comic book series.* Read the sentence aloud for students.

- Model using word origins to better understand the meaning of *villains*.

Think Aloud *I know that in comic books, heroes usually take action against villains. I am not sure about the word origin of* villains. *Maybe finding out the origin will help me understand the word's meaning. When I look in the dictionary, I see that* villain *has a Latin origin, but it also has a more recent French origin. In French, it was spelled* vilain *and it meant "a serf—a peasant or unskilled worker—who caused trouble." I know villains in comic books usually do bad things. Villains must be people who cause problems.*

2 Guided Practice

- Display the top half of **Projectable 16.5** and read "The Purse" aloud.

- Display the T-Map at the bottom of **Projectable 16.5**.

- Have students identify the bold-faced words in the passage. Circle or highlight the words.

- Point out the columns of the T-Map labeled *Word* and *Origin*. List the words from the word list under *Word*. Then work with students to use a dictionary to find the words' origins. Write them in the *Origin* column. Explain that in dictionaries, the letter *L* indicates Latin origin, the letter *F* indicates French origin, and the abbreviation *Gk* indicates Greek origin.

- Point out that English has changed a lot over time, and that some words and word roots were created during the Old or Middle English periods. English also uses words that are originally from other languages, such as Spanish and German.

Projectable 16.5

Lunch Money **Vocabulary Strategies** Word Origins

Word Origins

The Purse

Eliza ate a **banana** at her lunch table while reading an **encyclopedia**. She gazed around the **cafeteria**. Her glance fell proudly on her new purse. Eliza brought the purse to school so her friends could admire it. Eliza and her grandmother had spent a large amount of time sewing the pieces together by hand. But it had been worth the effort.

After school, Eliza went to her weekly **guitar** lesson with John. He told Eliza she would be an excellent **solo** performer, because she had such a great voice. John said she could perform as soon as she wrote some original songs.

Eliza sat down on the **patio** table to write. As soon as she picked up her pencil, she knew she would write a song about sewing the purse with her grandmother. She would title her new song: *The Purse!*

Vocabulary
- banana
  - *banano
- encyclopedia
  - *enciclopedia
- cafeteria
  - *cafeteria
- guitar
  - *guitarra
- solo
  - *solo
- patio
  - *patio

* Spanish cognates

Word	Origin
cafeteria	French
guitar	French from Greek
solo	Italian from Latin
banana	Spanish
patio	Spanish
encyclopedia	Greek

Monitor Vocabulary Strategies

Are students able to identify and use word origins?

IF...	THEN...
students have difficulty identifying and using word origins,	▶ **Differentiate Vocabulary Strategies** for Struggling Readers, p. T68. *See also Intervention Lesson 16, pp. S2–S11.*
students can identify and use word origins most of the time,	▶ **Differentiate Vocabulary Strategies** for On-Level Readers, p. T68.
students can consistently identify and use word origins,	▶ **Differentiate Vocabulary Strategies** for Advanced Readers, p. T69.

Differentiate Vocabulary Strategies: pp. T68–T69.
Group English Language Learners according to language proficiency.

3 Apply

- Have partners determine the meanings of the following words: *adobe, klutz, al fresco, protegé,* and *á la carte*. Then have them use a dictionary to determine the origins of the words. Ask volunteers to share their findings with the class.

- Have students write each word in a sentence to demonstrate understanding of the word's meaning.

Practice Book p. 183
See Grab-and-Go™ Resources for additional leveled practice.

Connect and Extend

- Make connections across texts.
- Read independently for a sustained period of time.
- Effectively record data.
- Analyze and communicate a media message.

"Lunch Money"   **"Zap! Pow!: A History of the Comics"**

Vocabulary Reader

Struggling Readers   *On-Level Readers*

Advanced Readers   *English Language Learners*

Read to Connect

SHARE AND COMPARE TEXTS Have students compare and contrast this week's reading selections. Use the following prompts to guide the discussion:

- Compare the ways pictures in these selections help you to follow a sequence of events.

- Using evidence from the selections you have read this week, explain how authors and artists decide what pictures or other graphics to include in a story.

CONNECT TEXT TO WORLD Have students write several questions related to the overall meanings of this week's texts. Have them trade papers with a partner and answer each other's questions. Use the following prompt to deepen their thinking and discussion.

- How do pictures help you find information both in books and in places in your community?

Independent Reading

BOOK TALK Have partners discuss their independent reading for the week. Tell them to refer to their Reading Log or journal and summarize the main ideas. Have them paraphrase a favorite section, maintaining its meaning and logical order, to give their partner a better idea of what they read. Then have students discuss the following:

- how the cultural or historical contexts of the texts support their understanding

- the selections' themes

- the authors' purposes

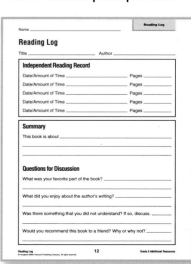

Reading Log

Extend Through Research

RECORD DATA Explain to students that while they are doing research for a report or other project, they should take notes and record data so they can analyze it and find relationships between ideas. Tell students that recording data as they research will help them give stronger presentations and write better-organized essays.

- Tell students they will work in groups to research the history of comic books.

- Discuss how to create a research plan. Ask students to brainstorm a list of open-ended questions that will guide their research. Have students use the Internet, encyclopedias, or other reliable sources to gather relevant information and visual data such as charts and timelines.

- Have students use a word processing program to record data as they research. Remind students that they can use the spell-check function in the program as they go to be sure they are spelling information correctly. Point out that they will still need to proofread carefully for misspelled names and improper word choice.

- Tell students they should convert any visual data into written notes so that they can easily explain it to others. Have them share their findings with another group.

Listening and Speaking

ANALYZE A MEDIA MESSAGE Tell students they will give an oral presentation that analyzes a media message. Explain that they will build on the comic book topic they researched in the above activity.

- Have students use the Internet to find several media sources related to the public's response to comic books. Suggest topics such as: comic book popularity, comic book sales in recent years, the audience for comics, comic books that have been made into animated cartoons or films.

- Tell students to take notes on their media and compile the information into a short presentation. Have them include an analysis of the messages in their media and whether the media sources are reliable.

- Have students give their oral presentations. Before they begin, remind presenters to employ good eye contact, an appropriate speaking rate and volume, and natural gestures to communicate their ideas.

While students give their presentations, have audience members use the Listening Log to record what they learn and which points they agree or disagree with. Discuss the presentations with the class, including points of agreement and disagreement.

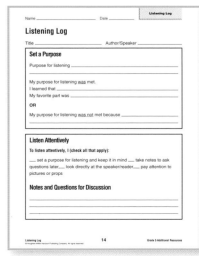

Listening Log

Spelling ☑ Words with -ed or -ing

SHARE OBJECTIVE

- Spell words that have the -ed or -ing ending.

Spelling Words

Basic

scrubbed	beginning	suffering
listening	skimmed	✪ scanned
stunned	chatting	ordered
knitting	shrugged	✪ totaled
carpeting	bothering	✪ answered
wandered	whipped	upsetting
gathering	quizzed	

Review

wandering, dimmed, stripped, ✪ ordered, ✪ snapping

Challenge

compelling, deposited, occurred, threatening, canceled

✪ Forms of these words appear in "Lunch Money."

 ENGLISH LANGUAGE LEARNERS

Preteach

Spanish Cognates

Write and discuss these Spanish cognates for Spanish-speaking students.

suffering • *sufrimiento*

ordered • *ordenado*

totaled • *totalizaron*

Day 1

❶ TEACH THE PRINCIPLE

- Administer the **Pretest**. Use the Day 5 Sentences.

- Write *scrub* and *listen* on the board. Use the chart below to help students spell the word when adding -ed or -ing.

If a base word ending with VC...	...then before adding -ed or -ing
has one syllable	double the final consonant, as in *scrubbed* and *knitting*
has two or more syllables	maintain a single final consonant, as in *totaled* or *listening*

❷ PRACTICE/APPLY

- Guide students to identify syllables and endings in the remaining Spelling Words.

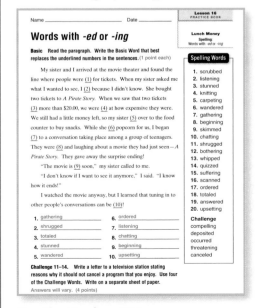

Practice Book p. 184

Day 2

❶ TEACH WORD SORT

- Set up two columns as shown. Model adding a Spelling Word to each column.

- Have students copy the chart. Guide students to write each Spelling Word where it belongs.

No change	Double final consonant
bothering	skimmed

❷ PRACTICE/APPLY

- Have students add words from "Lunch Money" to the chart.

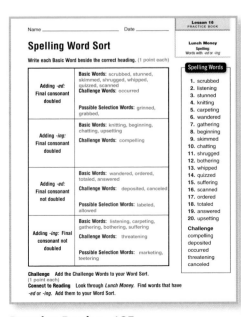

Practice Book p. 185

Day 3

① TEACH ANALOGIES

- **WRITE** this analogy: *Create is to make as strolled is to _____.* Explain that an *analogy* is an equation in which the first pair of words has the same relationship as the second pair of words.

- **ASK** *How are create and make related? same meaning; synonyms*

- **ASK** *Which Spelling Word has almost the same meaning as strolled? wandered*

- Follow the steps above with this analogy: *Start is to stop as ending is to _____.* Guide students to determine that the word pairs are opposites (antonyms). Ask them to find the missing Spelling Word. *beginning*

② PRACTICE/APPLY

- **WRITE** these analogies: *Find is to discover as talking is to _____; Smiled is to frowned as questioned is to _____; Threw is to tossed as tested is to _____.*

- **ASK** *Which Spelling Word belongs on each blank?*

➤ Have students write their answers.

Day 4

① CONNECT TO WRITING

- Read and discuss the prompt below.

> ✏ **Write to Narrate**
>
> Write a friendly letter about the story you would tell if you created a comic book. Use details from your reading this week.

② PRACTICE/APPLY

- Guide students as they plan and write their friendly letters. See p. T52.

- Remind them to proofread their writing for errors in spelling words with -*ed* or -*ing*.

Proofreading for Spelling — Practice Book p. 186

Day 5

ASSESS SPELLING

- Say each boldfaced word, read the sentence, and then repeat the word.

- Have students write only the boldfaced word.

Basic

1. The cleaners **scrubbed** the floors.
2. Are you **listening** to me?
3. He was **stunned** by the news.
4. Grandma is **knitting** a sweater.
5. The room has **carpeting**.
6. Ana **wandered** into the room.
7. He is **gathering** facts for his report.
8. It is **beginning** to rain.
9. I **skimmed** some pages.
10. Layla is **chatting** with me.
11. Bob **shrugged** his shoulders.
12. Please stop **bothering** me.
13. The chef **whipped** the eggs.
14. The teacher **quizzed** the class.
15. Jim is **suffering** from a headache.
16. I **scanned** the list of names.
17. Lois **ordered** them to leave.
18. The bill **totaled** thirty dollars.
19. Have I **answered** your question?
20. The story is **upsetting** her.

Grammar ✓ Adjectives

SHARE OBJECTIVES

- Identify adjectives and descriptive adjectives.
- Use adjectives and articles in writing and speaking.

ELL ENGLISH LANGUAGE LEARNERS

Scaffold

Beginning Explain to students that an adjective describes a noun. Work with them to complete the following sentence frames using adjectives.

The comic book had _____ pages. sixteen

Greg carried _____ boxes. big

Intermediate Work with students to complete the sentence frames above using adjectives that tell *what kind. tiny; cardboard*

Advanced Ask students to use adjectives to orally describe objects in the room, telling *how many* and *what kind.* Example:

There are *(ten)* books on the shelf.

There are *(ten, red)* books on the shelf.

Advanced High Have student pairs take turns orally describing objects in the room and in the selection, using adjectives that tell *how many* and *what kind.*

See ELL Lesson 16, pp. E2–E11, for scaffolded support.

JOURNEYS DIGITAL **Powered by DESTINATIONReading®**
Grammar Activities: Lesson 16
Grammar Songs CD: Track 7

Day 1 TEACH

DAILY PROOFREADING PRACTICE
where did Greg buy his comic books. *Where; books?*

❶ TEACH ADJECTIVES

- Display **Projectable 16.6.** Explain that an **adjective** gives information about a noun, such as *how many* and *what kind.* One special kind of **descriptive adjective** tells the origin of the person, place, or thing it describes.

Projectable **16.6**

- Model identifying the adjectives used in the example sentences: *I ate **twelve** egg rolls. I ate **delicious** Chinese food. I ate **Chinese** food.*

Think Aloud *To identify adjectives, I ask these Thinking Questions:* **Which word gives information about a noun?** *twelve; delicious; Chinese* **Does it describe the noun or tell the origin of the noun?** *Twelve tells how many; delicious tells what kind; Chinese is a descriptive noun that tells the origin of the food.*

❷ PRACTICE/APPLY

- Complete the items on the bottom of **Projectable 16.6** with students.

- Write the following nouns on the board.

pencil	book
food	cars
paper	rules

- Work with students to brainstorm adjectives that might describe each one. *Sample answers: wooden pencil; French book; Thai food; compact cars; yellow paper; school rules*

Practice Book p. 187

Day 2 TEACH

DAILY PROOFREADING PRACTICE

The desert I ate was sweet, good. *dessert; sweet and*

1 EXTEND ADJECTIVES

Projectable 16.7

• Display **Projectable 16.7**. Explain that a linking verb may connect the subject in a sentence to an adjective describing it. Some linking verbs are forms of the verb "to be," such as *is, are, am,* and *was.*

• Model identifying the linking verbs used in the example sentences: *The food in the cafeteria smells good. Greg is happy to write comic books.*

Think Aloud *To identify a subject, linking verb, and adjective describing the subject, I ask these Thinking Questions:* **What is the subject? What is the adjective? What word connects the subject to the adjective?** *The subjects are* food *and* Greg*. The adjectives are* good *and* happy*. Smells* and *is connect the subjects and adjectives.*

2 PRACTICE/APPLY

• Complete 1–6 on **Projectable 16.7** with students.

• Write the following sentence frames on the board. Have students identify the linking verb and add an adjective that describes the noun.

The apple seems _____. *seems; fresh*

Bob looks_____. *looks; tall*

The children feel _____. *feel; happy*

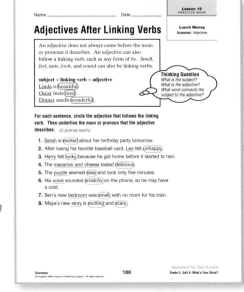

Practice Book p. 188

Day 3 TEACH

DAILY PROOFREADING PRACTICE

The workers seem are happy? *delete* seem *or* are; *happy.*

1 TEACH ARTICLES

Projectable 16.8

• Display **Projectable 16.8**. Explain that the words *a, an,* and *the* are **articles**. Point out that articles are kinds of adjectives that refer to and give information about a noun.

• Use the first example on the projectable to explain when to use the articles *a* and *an*. Use the second example to explain when to use the article *the*.

2 PRACTICE/APPLY

• Complete items 1–8 on **Projectable 16.8** with students.

• Display several short phrases from the selection containing an adjective and a noun. Have students respond orally using the articles *a, an,* or *the,* as appropriate, to describe the noun.

standing in _____ cafeteria line *the*

_____ marketing director of his company *the*

took _____ big bite of his sandwich *a*

_____ ink-jet printer *an*

developed _____ master plan *a*

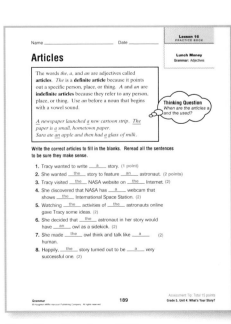

Practice Book p. 189

Adjectives • **T47**

Day 4 REVIEW

DAILY PROOFREADING PRACTICE

Creon were a interesting hero in the story. *was; an*

1 REVIEW ADJECTIVES

• Remind students that an **adjective** is a word that describes a noun. A **linking verb** connects the subject in a sentence to an adjective that tells about it. Point out that an **article** is a type of adjective that refers to a specific noun or a general noun. Review with students the different kinds of adjectives.

2 SPIRAL REVIEW

Kinds of Pronouns Review with students that personal pronouns are nouns that take the place of a specific person, place, or thing. Two categories of personal pronouns include **subject pronouns** (*I, you, she, he, they, we, it*) and **object pronouns** (*me, you, him, her, them, us, it, whom*).

Write the following sentences on the board. Work with students to identify the correct subject or object pronouns.

(He, Him) writes a comic called *Chunky Comics*. *He*

(They, them) hope that she will present it to (they, them). *They; them*

Write the following words on the board: *I, she, them, us, it, you, he, him, whom, we.* Have students identify the subject pronouns. *I, she, it, you, he, we*

Practice Book p. 190

Day 5 CONNECT TO WRITING

DAILY PROOFREADING PRACTICE

Mr. Brown helped he right the comic book. *him; write*

1 CONNECT TO WRITING

• Tell students that using precise descriptive adjectives helps create clear images for the reader.

• Point out that an important part of revising is using descriptive adjectives correctly.

2 PRACTICE/APPLY

• Display the following sentences. Have partners work together to provide adjectives to describe the nouns. Tell students to choose the correct article, when necessary.

Greg wrote a/an _____ comic book.

It was about a/an _____ man and his _____ friends.

The _____ man and his _____ friends saved some _____ people from a/an _____ monster.

• Have students turn to **Student Book p. 422.** Review with them the different ways to make their writing more interesting by using adjectives.

• Then have students form pairs and complete the **Turn and Talk** activity.

Practice Book p. 191

Grammar

What Is an Adjective? An **adjective** is a word that gives information about a noun, such as *how many* and *what kind*. An adjective that tells *what kind* is called a **descriptive adjective**. One special type of descriptive adjective tells the origin of the person, place, or thing being described. These adjectives are formed from names of places, so they are capitalized.

Academic Language
adjective
descriptive adjective

descriptive adjective	Suzette likes comics with dynamic artwork.
descriptive adjective giving origin	She especially likes the Japanese comics called manga.

Turn and Talk **Work with a partner. Find the descriptive adjectives in these sentences. Tell which identify the origin of a person, place, or thing.**

1. Her favorite adventures take place in Asian cities.
2. Modern buildings make a great background for intense action.
3. Korean costumes from ancient times add appeal.
4. Phil has a comic with Chinese warriors in it!
5. A capable superhero knows karate, jiujitsu, and kickboxing.

Word Choice When you write, use precise descriptive adjectives to create clear images for your readers. Using precise descriptive adjectives will help make your writing more interesting.

Vague Adjective	Precise Adjectives
I photographed a big pyramid.	I photographed a massive Mexican pyramid.

Connect Grammar to Writing

As you revise your friendly letter, look for opportunities to replace vague adjectives with precise descriptive adjectives. Using descriptive adjectives will help readers visualize what you are writing about.

422

423

Turn and Talk

- descriptive adjectives: *favorite, Asian, Modern, great, intense, Korean, ancient, Chinese, capable*
- descriptive adjectives that identify origin: *Asian, Korean, Chinese*

CONNECT GRAMMAR TO WRITING

- Have students turn to **Student Book p. 423**. Read the Word Choice paragraph with students.

- Read the sentences on the chart. Tell students that the word *big* is a good adjective, but precise adjectives can make the sentence even more interesting.

- Tell students that as they revise their friendly letters, they should use interesting descriptive adjectives to create clear images.

- Review the Common Errors at right with students.

COMMON ERRORS

Error: Greg wrote a **book comic**.

Correct: Greg wrote a **comic book**.

Error: He is **a** excellent writer.

Correct: He is **an** excellent writer.

Error: An only hero in the story is named Creon.

Correct: The only hero in the story is named Creon.

Write to Narrate

Focus Trait: Voice

SHARE OBJECTIVES

- Understand the structure of a friendly letter.
- Write a friendly letter that conveys ideas, information, and closure.

Academic Language

friendly informal and showing kind interest

heading includes the writer's address and the date

salutation a word of greeting to begin a letter

closing the ending part of a letter, just before the signature

ELL ENGLISH LANGUAGE LEARNERS

Scaffold

Beginning Work with students to understand words used as friendly greetings in conversations and letters.

Intermediate Place the categories *Formal* and *Informal* on the board. Write the greetings *Good morning* and *Hello*. Have students change them to informal greetings. *Samples: Hey!, What's up/happening?)*

Advanced Have students think of formal substitutes for the following: Let's grab a bite. *Let's get something to eat.* It makes me jump and clap! *It makes me happy.*

Advanced High Write a short, formal paragraph on the board. Challenge partners to work together to rewrite the formal paragraph into one that is informal and friendly.

See Lesson 16, pp. E2–E11, for scaffolded support.

Powered by
DESTINATIONReading®
WriteSmart CD-ROM

Day 1 ANALYZE THE MODEL

1 INTRODUCE THE MODEL

- Tell students that they will be writing a friendly, letter in this lesson.

- Display **Projectable 16.9** and read aloud Writing Model 1. Discuss the following:

> #### What Is a Friendly Letter?
>
> - It includes **friendly**, informal words that express the writer's real feelings and personality.
>
> - The **heading** is the writer's address and the date.
>
> - The **salutation** usually starts with the word *Dear* followed by the person's name.
>
> - A **closing**, such as *Your friend*, followed by a comma, completes the letter.

- Use Writing Model 1 on **Projectable 16.9** to point out the words and phrases showing the writer's thoughts and feelings. Explain where the closing and signature should be at the end of the letter.

2 PRACTICE/ APPLY

Work with students, using Writing Model 2 on **Projectable 16.9,** to identify and label the heading, the body, and the words and phrases that show the writer's thoughts and feelings.

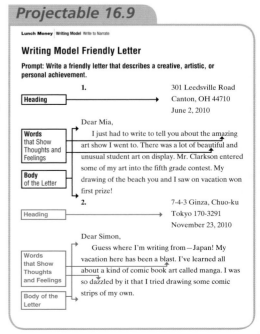

Projectable 16.9

Lunch Money Writing Model Write to Narrate

Writing Model Friendly Letter

Prompt: Write a friendly letter that describes a creative, artistic, or personal achievement.

1.   301 Leedsville Road
Canton, OH 44710
June 2, 2010

[Heading]

Dear Mia,
    I just had to write to tell you about the amazing art show I went to. There was a lot of beautiful and unusual student art on display. Mr. Clarkson entered some of my art into the fifth grade contest. My drawing of the beach you and I saw on vacation won first prize!

[Words that Show Thoughts and Feelings]

[Body of the Letter]

2.   7-4-3 Ginza, Chuo-ku
Tokyo 170-3291
November 23, 2010

[Heading]

Dear Simon,
    Guess where I'm writing from—Japan! My vacation here has been a blast. I've learned all about a kind of comic book art called manga. I was so dazzled by it that I tried drawing some comic strips of my own.

[Words that Show Thoughts and Feelings]

[Body of the Letter]

LESSON	FORM	TRAIT
16	**Friendly Letter**	**Voice**
17	Character Description	Word Choice
18	Personal Narrative Paragraph	Voice
19	Prewrite: Personal Narrative	Ideas
20	Draft, Revise, Edit, Publish: Personal Narrative	Voice

Language Arts

Writing

Day 2 TEACH THE FOCUS TRAIT

① INTRODUCE THE FOCUS TRAIT: VOICE

- Tell students that their writing *voice* is the feelings and personality that come through in the words and phrases they use.

- Explain that informal language can help express a writer's voice. Informal language is friendly and casual, like natural conversation.

Connect to "Lunch Money"	
Instead of this...	**...the author wrote this.**
I was glad I sold seventeen units.	"Sweet! That means I sold seventeen units." (p. 408)

- Point out that the author's use of informal words and phrases allow Greg's thoughts and feelings to come through and helps readers understand him.

② PRACTICE/APPLY

- Write: *Greg had a good idea.* Work with students to write a sentence that describes what is happening, using a more informal voice. *Sample answer: Greg's idea was so cool!*

- Write: *I bought a comic book.* Have students add descriptive, friendly words to this sentence to reveal feelings and personality. *Sample answer: There are some really out-of-this-world drawings in the comic book I bought.*

Name _____ Date _____

Lesson 16
PRACTICE BOOK

Lunch Money
Writing: Write to Narrate

Focus Trait: Voice
Using Informal Language

Formal Language	Informal Language
Children had been talking about his comic book.	Kids had been going on like crazy about his comic book.

A. Read each formal sentence. Replace the formal words or phrases with informal words. Write your new sentence in the box. Possible responses shown.
(1 point each)

Formal Language	Informal Language
1. My father is an attorney.	My dad's a lawyer.
2. Kindly respond to my request in a timely fashion.	Please call me as soon as you can!

B. Read each formal sentence. Rewrite each sentence using informal language that shows feelings and personality.

Pair/Share Work with a partner to rewrite each sentence with informal words and phrases that show feelings and personality. Possible responses shown.
(1 point each)

Formal Language	Informal Language
3. I am greatly looking forward to attending the art show.	I'm totally psyched to go to the show!
4. My mother will not allow me to draw until my homework is done.	I can't believe Mom won't let me draw until I'm done with my homework.

Practice Book p. 192

Day 3 PREWRITE

① TEACH PLANNING A FRIENDLY LETTER

- Display **Projectable 16.10** and read aloud the prompt. Guide students to think about a creative, artistic, or personal achievement that they might describe in a friendly letter.

- Explain that an Idea-Support Map can help them plan their writing.

② PRACTICE/APPLY

- Point out the topic at the top of **Projectable 16.10**. Tell students that the topic should be mentioned in the first sentence of their letter.

- Explain that the main idea tells more about the topic. Point out that each supporting detail relates to the main idea. Tell students that these details will make up the body of the letter.

- Work with students to complete the Idea-Support Map.

- Have students choose a topic for their friendly letters. Distribute **Graphic Organizer 7**. Guide students to complete the Idea-Support Map.

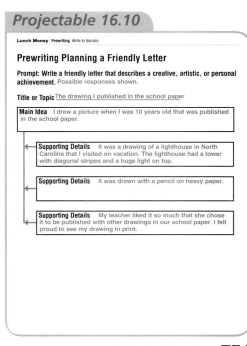

Projectable 16.10

Lunch Money | Prewriting Write to Narrate

Prewriting Planning a Friendly Letter

Prompt: Write a friendly letter that describes a creative, artistic, or personal achievement. Possible responses shown.

Title or Topic The drawing I published in the school paper

Main Idea I drew a picture when I was 10 years old that was published in the school paper.

Supporting Details It was a drawing of a lighthouse in North Carolina that I visited on vacation. The lighthouse had a tower with diagonal stripes and a huge light on top.

Supporting Details It was drawn with a pencil on heavy paper.

Supporting Details My teacher liked it so much that she chose it to be published with other drawings in our school paper. I felt proud to see my drawing in print.

Day 4 DRAFT

1 BEGIN A DRAFT

• Have the students begin their drafts using their Idea-Support Maps. Discuss with them the following:

> **1. Introduce** the letter format by using a heading and a salutation, such as "Dear _____,".

> **2. Organize** the main idea and supporting details so they make sense to the reader.

> **3. Include** informal words and expressions that really sound like you, helping your feelings and personality come through.

> **4. Conclude** with an informal closing, ending in a comma. Place your signature below.

2 PRACTICE/APPLY

• Have students draft their own friendly letters with correct formatting. Remind them to use the Idea-Support Maps that they completed for prewriting.

Day 5 REVISE FOR VOICE

1 INTRODUCE THE STUDENT MODEL

• Remind students that good writers use voice in their friendly letters by choosing informal words and phrases that show their feelings and personality.

• Read the top of **Student Book p. 424** with students. Discuss the revisions made by the student writer, Nicole. Point out the revision in the first two sentences. Explain that using informal, friendly words helps readers understand the writer's feelings and personality.

2 PRACTICE/APPLY

• Display **Projectable 16.11**. Work with students to revise the rest of Nicole's letter. Point out places where a friendly voice could show more of Nicole's warm personality.

• Work with students to answer the *Reading as a Writer* questions on **Student Book p. 425**. Discuss students' responses.

• **Revising** Have students revise their letters using the Writing Traits Checklist on **Student Book p. 424**.

• **Proofreading** For proofreading support, have students use the **Proofreading Checklist Blackline Master**.

Projectable 16.11

Lunch Money : Revising Write to Narrate

Revising Nicole's Narrative Paragraph

Proofread Nicole's draft. Use proofreading marks to correct any errors or make any improvements.

Dear Jerome,
   The comic book you made for me was awesome!
It gave me a supper idea for my school project, too. I
started reading about colonial life. After I learned what
the Pilgrims really ate, I made some drawings of there
food and wrote funny captions for the drawings.
   Suddenly I realized that this could be my social
studies project. I made a 12-page comic book. It was
about cooking in Colonial times. My teacher wants her
own copy of the book. The principal wants a copy, too.
   Your very best cousin,
   Goodbye,

   Nicole

Write to Narrate

☑ **Voice** In "Lunch Money," Greg's feelings show clearly when he thinks, "Sweet! That means I sold seventeen units." A well-written **friendly letter** also shows your feelings and really sounds like you. Use informal words and phrases to let the real you shine through.

Nicole drafted a letter to her cousin telling him about something special she did. Later, she revised her letter to show her feelings. Use the Writing Traits Checklist below as you revise your writing.

Writing Traits Checklist

☑ **Ideas**
Do all of the details in my letter fit my purpose?

☑ **Organization**
Did I use the correct format for a friendly letter?

☑ **Sentence Fluency**
Did I vary my sentence types?

☑ **Word Choice**
Did I use informal words and expressions?

☑ **Voice**
Do my feelings and personality come through?

☑ **Conventions**
Did I use correct spelling, grammar, and punctuation?

Revised Draft

Dear Jerome,
              The
I liked the comic book you made for
                    super
me. It gave me a ~~good~~ idea for my
school project, too. I started reading
              After
about Colonial life. ~~Then~~ I learned
what the Pilgrims really ate. ~~Then~~ I
                              and
made some drawings of their food.
~~Then~~ I wrote funny captions for the
drawings.

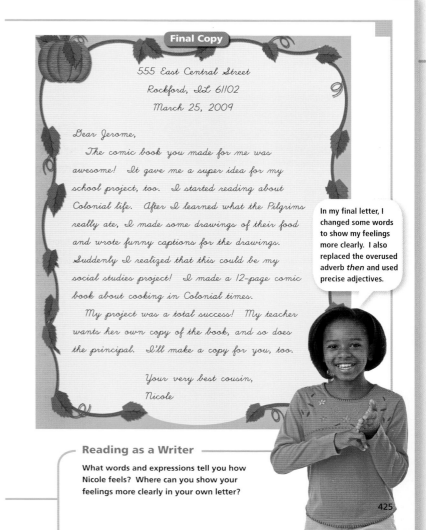

Final Copy

555 East Central Street
Rockford, IL 61102
March 25, 2009

Dear Jerome,
    The comic book you made for me was awesome! It gave me a super idea for my school project, too. I started reading about Colonial life. After I learned what the Pilgrims really ate, I made some drawings of their food and wrote funny captions for the drawings. Suddenly I realized that this could be my social studies project! I made a 12-page comic book about cooking in Colonial times.
    My project was a total success! My teacher wants her own copy of the book, and so does the principal. I'll make a copy for you, too.

              Your very best cousin,
              Nicole

In my final letter, I changed some words to show my feelings more clearly. I also replaced the overused adverb *then* and used precise adjectives.

Reading as a Writer

What words and expressions tell you how Nicole feels? Where can you show your feelings more clearly in your own letter?

424

425

Writing Traits Scoring Rubric

	Focus/Ideas	☑ **Organization**	**Voice**	☑ **Word Choice**	☑ **Sentence Fluency**	**Conventions**
4	Adheres to the topic, is interesting, has a sense of completeness. Ideas are well developed.	Ideas and details are clearly presented and well organized.	Connects with reader in a unique, personal way.	Includes vivid verbs, strong adjectives, specific nouns.	Includes a variety of complete sentences that flow smoothly, naturally.	Shows a strong command of grammar, spelling, capitalization, punctuation.
3	Mostly adheres to the topic, is somewhat interesting, has a sense of completeness. Ideas are adequately developed.	Ideas and details are mostly clear and generally organized.	Generally connects with reader in a way that is personal and sometimes unique.	Includes some vivid verbs, strong adjectives, specific nouns.	Includes some variety of mostly complete sentences. Some parts flow smoothly, naturally.	Shows a good command of grammar, spelling, capitalization, punctuation.
2	Does not always adhere to the topic, has some sense of completeness. Ideas are superficially developed.	Ideas and details are not always clear or organized. There is some wordiness or repetition.	Connects somewhat with reader. Sounds somewhat personal, but not unique.	Includes mostly simple nouns and verbs, and may have a few adjectives.	Includes mostly simple sentences, some of which are incomplete.	Some errors in grammar, spelling, capitalization, punctuation.
1	Does not adhere to the topic, has no sense of completeness. Ideas are vague.	Ideas and details are not organized. Wordiness or repetition hinders meaning.	Does not connect with reader. Does not sound personal or unique.	Includes only simple nouns and verbs, some inaccurate. Writing is not descriptive.	Sentences do not vary. Incomplete sentences hinder meaning.	Frequent errors in grammar, spelling, capitalization, punctuation.

See also Writing Rubric Blackline Master and Teacher's Edition pp. R18–R21.

 # Progress Monitoring

Assess

 Grab & Go!

- Weekly Tests
- Fluency Tests
- Periodic Assessments

Vocabulary
Target Vocabulary
Strategies: Word Origins

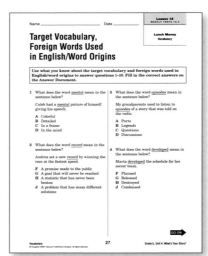

Weekly Tests 16.2–16.4

Comprehension
Author's Purpose

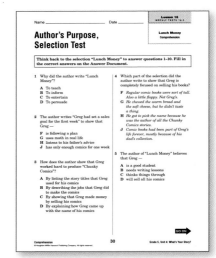

Weekly Tests 16.5–16.6

Respond to Assessment

IF	a Student Scores...	THEN...
7–10 of 10		▶ Continue Core Instructional Program.
4–6 of 10		▶ **Reteaching Lesson,** p. T70
1–3 of 10		▶ **Intervention** Lesson 16, pp. S2–S11

IF	a Student Scores...	THEN...
7–10 of 10		▶ Continue Core Instructional Program.
4–6 of 10		▶ **Reteaching Lesson,** p. T70
1–3 of 10		▶ **Intervention** Lesson 16, pp. S2–S11

Powered by DESTINATIONReading®
- Online Assessment System
- Weekly Tests

✓ Decoding
Word Parts and Inflectional Endings

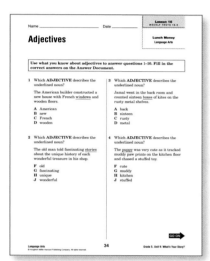

Weekly Tests 16.7–16.8

IF a Student Scores...	THEN...
7–10 of 10	▶ Continue Core Instructional Program.
4–6 of 10	▶ **Reteaching Lesson,** p. T71
1–3 of 10	▶ **Intervention** Lesson 16, pp. S2–S11

✓ Language Arts
Grammar: Adjectives

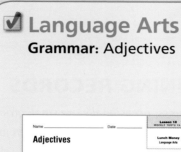 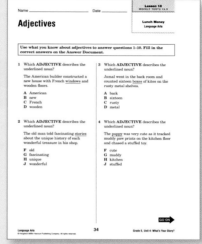

Weekly Test 16.9–16.10

Writing Traits Rubrics
See TE pp. R18–R21.

IF a Student Scores...	THEN...
7–10 of 10	▶ Continue Core Instructional Program.
4–6 of 10	▶ **Reteaching Lesson,** p. T71
1–3 of 10	▶ **Intervention** Lesson 16, pp. S2–S11

✓ Fluency

Fluency Plan
Assess one group per week.
Use this suggested plan below.

🔵 **Struggling Readers**	**Weeks 1, 3, 5**
▲ **On Level**	**Week 2**
⬛ **Advanced**	**Week 4**

Oral Reading Practice
Use the Student Book, the Leveled Readers, or other reading materials in this unit to help students improve fluency in preparation for assessment in the next unit.

Fluency Scoring Rubric
See *Grab-and-Go™ Resources Assessment* for help in measuring progress.

Progress Monitoring

Small Group

RUNNING RECORDS

To assess individual progress, occasionally use small group time to take a reading record for each student. Use the results to plan instruction.

 **Struggling Readers**

 On Level

 Advanced

 **English Language Learners**

For running records, see
Grab and Go™ Resources: Lesson 16,
pp. 13–16.

Behaviors and Understandings to Notice

- Self-corrects errors that detract from meaning.

- Self-corrects intonation when it does not reflect the meaning.

- Rereads to solve words and resumes normal rate of reading.

- Demonstrates phrased and fluent oral reading.

- Reads dialogue with expression.

- Demonstrates awareness of punctuation.

- Automatically solves most words in the text to read fluently.

- Demonstrates appropriate stress on words, pausing and phrasing, intonation, and use of punctuation.

- Reads orally at an appropriate rate.

Weekly
Small Group Instruction

 Day 1

Vocabulary Reader
• *Job Sense,* T60–T61

 Day 2

Differentiate Comprehension
• Target Skill: Author's Purpose, T62–T63
• Target Strategy: Monitory/Clarify, T62–T63

 Day 3

Leveled Readers
● *Dog Walker, Inc.,* T64
▲ *Incognito,* T65
■ *The Three R's,* T66
◆ *The Lost Comic Book,* T67

 Day 4

Differentiate Vocabulary Strategies
• Word Origins, T68–T69

 Day 5

Options for Reteaching
• Vocabulary Strategies: Word Origins, T70
• Comprehension Skill: Author's Viewpoint and Purpose, T70
• Language Arts: Adjectives/Write to Narrate, T71
• Decoding: Word Parts and Inflectional Endings, T71

Ready-Made Work Stations

Ready-Made Practice
• Comprehension and Fluency, T10
• Word Study, T10
• Think and Write, T11
• Digital Center, T11

Comprehension and Fluency

Word Study

Think and Write

Digital Center

Suggested Small Group Plan

	Day 1	**Day 2**	**Day 3**
Teacher-Led			
Struggling Readers	**Vocabulary Reader** *Job Sense*, Differentiated Instruction, p. T60	**Differentiate Comprehension** Author's Purpose; Monitor/Clarify, p. T62	**Leveled Reader** *Dog Walker, Inc.*, p. T64
On Level	**Vocabulary Reader** *Job Sense*, Differentiated Instruction, p. T60	**Differentiate Comprehension** Author's Purpose; Monitor/Clarify, p. T62	**Leveled Reader** *Incognito*, p. T65
Advanced	**Vocabulary Reader** *Job Sense*, Differentiated Instruction, p. T61	**Differentiate Comprehension** Author's Purpose; Monitor/Clarify, p. T63	**Leveled Reader** *The Three R's*, p. T66
English Language Learners	**Vocabulary Reader** *Job Sense*, Differentiated Instruction, p. T61	**Differentiate Comprehension** Author's Purpose; Monitor/Clarify, p. T63	**Leveled Reader** *The Lost Comic Book*, p. T67

	Day 1	**Day 2**	**Day 3**
What are my other students doing?			
Struggling Readers	**Reread** *Job Sense*	**Vocabulary in Context Cards** 151–160 *Talk It Over* Activities **Complete** Leveled Practice SR16.1	**Listen** to Audiotext CD of "Lunch Money;" Retell and discuss **Complete** Leveled Practice SR16.2
On Level	**Reread** *Job Sense*	**Reread** "Lunch Money" with a partner **Complete** Practice Book p. 181	**Reread** for Fluency: *Incognito* **Complete** Practice Book p. 182
Advanced	**Vocabulary in Context Cards** 151–160 *Talk It Over* Activities	**Reread and Retell** "Lunch Money" **Complete** Leveled Practice A16.1	**Reread** for Fluency: *The Three R's* **Complete** Leveled Practice A16.2
English Language Learners	**Reread** *Job Sense*	**Listen** to Audiotext CD of "Lunch Money" Retell and discuss **Complete** Leveled Practice ELL16.1	**Vocabulary in Context Cards** 151–160 *Talk It Over* Activities **Complete** Leveled Practice ELL16.2

Ready-Made Work Stations
Assign these activities across the week to reinforce and extend learning.

Comprehension and Fluency
Fluency Flow

Word Study
Word Wisdom

Day 4

Differentiate Vocabulary Strategies
Word Origins, p. T68

Differentiate Vocabulary Strategies
Word Origins, p. T68

Differentiate Vocabulary Strategies
Word Origins, p. T69

Differentiate Vocabulary Strategies
Word Origins, p. T69

Partners: Reread for Fluency
Dog Walker, Inc
Complete Leveled
Practice SR16.3

Vocabulary in Context Cards
151–160
Talk It Over Activities
Complete Practice Book p. 183

Reread for Fluency: "Lunch Money"
Complete Leveled Practice A16.3

Partners: Reread for Fluency: *The Lost Comic Book*
Complete Leveled
Practice ELL16.3

 **Think and Write**
Business Brainstorm

Day 5

Options for Reteaching,
pp. T70–T71

Options for Reteaching,
pp. T70–T71

Options for Reteaching,
pp. T70–T71

Options for Reteaching,
pp. T70–T71

Reread for Fluency: "Lunch Money"
Complete Work Station activities
Independent Reading

Complete Work Station activities
Independent Reading

Complete Work Station activities
Independent Reading

Reread *Job Sense* or "Lunch Money"
Complete Work Station activities

 JOURNEYS DIGITAL Powered by DESTINATION Reading **Digital Center**

Weekly To-Do List

This Weekly To-Do List helps students see their own progress and move on to additional activities independently.

Reading Log

Summary

This book explores how students can earn money and helps them identify any special interests and skills they may have. Students learn what types of jobs they could do and how to get customers.

✔ TARGET VOCABULARY

record	developed
mental	feature
launch	incredibly
assuming	villains
episodes	thumbed

Vocabulary Reader

Job Sense

Struggling Readers

- Explain to students that they each have skills they can use to earn money.

- Guide students to preview the **Vocabulary Reader.** Read aloud the headings. Ask students to describe the images, using Target Vocabulary words whenever possible. Model doing this for them.

- Have students alternate reading the text aloud. Guide them to use context clues to determine the meanings of unfamiliar words. As necessary, use the **Vocabulary in Context Cards** to review the meanings of Target Vocabulary words.

- Assign the **Responding Page** and **Blackline Master 16.1.** Have partners work together to complete the pages.

On Level

- Explain to students that many people want to own and run their own business. A person must possess certain skills to become a successful entrepreneur. Guide students to preview the **Vocabulary Reader.**

- Remind students that context clues can help them determine the meaning of an unknown word. Tell students to use context clues to confirm their understanding of Target Vocabulary words and to learn the meanings of new words that are unfamiliar.

- Have partners alternate reading pages of the **Vocabulary Reader** aloud. Tell them to use context clues to determine the meanings of unknown words.

- Assign the **Responding Page** and **Blackline Master 16.1.** Have students discuss their responses with a partner.

Advanced

- Have students preview the **Vocabulary Reader** and make predictions about what they will read, using information from their preview and their own prior knowledge.

- Remind students to use context clues to help them determine the meanings of unknown words.

- Tell students to read the text with a partner. Ask them to stop and discuss the meanings of unknown words as necessary.

- Assign the **Responding Page** and **Blackline Master 16.1**. For the Write About It activity, remind students to use facts and details to support their ideas. Tell them to include information on how an entrepreneur could finance and market a new business.

(ELL) English Language Learners

Group English Language Learners according to language proficiency.

Beginning

Conduct a picture walk with students. Then read *Job Sense* aloud with them, pausing to explain the Target Vocabulary words as necessary. Have students repeat each word with you.

Intermediate

Use visuals, simplified language, and gestures to preteach the following selection vocabulary: *launch, assuming, feature,* and *villains.* Have partners use the words in oral sentences.

Advanced

Read *Job Sense* aloud with students. Check student's understanding of the Target Vocabulary words by having them write sentences using *record, mental, incredibly,* and *thumbed.*

Advanced High

Have students reread *Job Sense* and discuss why they think the author wrote the text. Tell them to think about the character's thoughts and actions. Have them use the Target Vocabulary words.

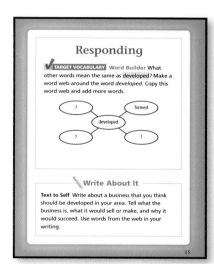

Job Sense, p. 15

Blackline Master 16.1

Differentiate Comprehension

✓ Author's Purpose; Monitor/Clarify

Struggling Readers

I DO IT

- Review *author's purpose* with students. Explain how monitoring key text details can help them clarify the author's purpose.

- Read aloud p. 408 of "Lunch Money." Model identifying details that support the author's purpose.

 Think Aloud *The detail "Greg loved that name" shows he is proud of the comics business he runs.*

WE DO IT

- Read aloud with students p. 411 of "Lunch Money."

- Help them find a key detail that tells what Greg does and how he feels about it.

- Guide students to enter the detail in the "Detail" box of an Inference Map.

- Explain that they can connect key details about the character's thoughts and actions to help understand the author's purpose.

YOU DO IT

- Have students find two more key details about Greg's thoughts and actions, and enter them into their Inference Maps.

- Have them work with a partner to identify the author's purpose by connecting these details.

- Have students write their inferences in the bottom box of their Inference Maps.

On Level

I DO IT

- Read aloud p. 408 of "Lunch Money."

- Review with students *author's purpose*. Explain how monitoring key details helps clarify the author's purpose.

- Model identifying details that support author's purpose.

Think Aloud *The phrase "one-kid operation" shows Greg's hard work and dedication to his business.*

WE DO IT

- Have students read pp. 414–415 of "Lunch Money."

- Guide them as they point out some of the key details the author uses when he describes Greg's actions and thoughts.

- Encourage students to use the Monitor/Clarify strategy to figure out details that are confusing.

- Help students as they add these details to an Inference Map.

YOU DO IT

- Have partners create their own Inference Maps using key text details.

- Then have them work together to identify the author's purpose and write it in the bottom box of the Inference Map. *The author wants to show readers that hard work and determination can produce rewarding results.*

Advanced

I DO IT

- Explain that a reader can often gain an understanding of the author's purpose(s) for writing by monitoring and clarifying text details.
- Read aloud p. 416 of "Lunch Money."
- Identify how the author has provided more details about the hard work Greg has put into making his comic book business succeed.

WE DO IT

- Have students review p. 416 and monitor the author's word choices that can help them understand the author's purpose.
- Point out the phrase "But finally." Explain that by adding this word choice, the author is emphasizing just how long Greg had to work to finish the comic.
- Support students as they write details in an Inference Map.

YOU DO IT

- Have partners add more details to their Inference Maps and then identify how the details support the author's purpose.
- Have small groups discuss the author's purpose. Remind students that an author can have more than one purpose for writing.
- Invite students to model how they used the Monitor/Clarify strategy to complete their Inference Maps.

ELL English Language Learners

Group English Language Learners according to language proficiency. Write the following sentence frames on the board: *The author gives the detail _____ to show that Greg _____. I think the author wants me to learn a lesson about _____.* Complete an Inference Map on the board. Then choose one of the following activities, as needed.

Beginning

Read aloud p. 408 of "Lunch Money." Model filling in the first part of the first sentence frame with *"Greg loved the name."* Guide students to fill in the second part of the frame. *is proud; loves his work*

Intermediate

Read aloud pp. 412–413 of "Lunch Money." Have students read aloud the first two sentences on p. 412. Have them complete the first sentence frame.

Advanced

Have students work in pairs to provide several examples that will complete the first sentence frame. Have them think about why the author wrote the selection.

Advanced High

Have students work in pairs to complete the frames on the board with examples from the selection. Have them write a few sentences about the author's purpose.

Targets for Lesson 16

TARGET SKILL

Author's Purpose

TARGET STRATEGY

Monitor/Clarify

TARGET VOCABULARY

record	developed
mental	feature
launch	incredibly
assuming	villains
episodes	thumbed

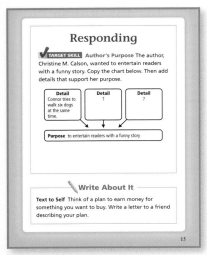

Dog Walker, Inc., p. 15

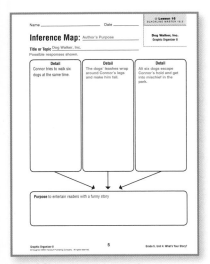

Blackline Master 16.3

Leveled Readers

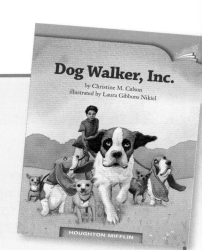

Struggling Readers

 Dog Walker, Inc.

GENRE: REALISTIC FICTION

Summary Connor decides to become a dog walker to earn money to buy his own dog. He is so eager to show his mom how responsible he is that he ends up walking too many dogs. He soon learns that controlling six dogs is not easy money.

Before Reading

• Explain that adopting a pet costs money. If Connor can show that he is responsible and can earn the money, his mother will consider getting a pet.

• Remind students that using an Inference Map can help them understand the author's purpose for writing the story.

Supporting the Reading

• As you listen to students read, pause to discuss these questions.

AUTHOR'S PURPOSE p. 4 *Why does the author describe Connor imagining his life with a pet? The author wants us to know how much Connor wants a dog. He even has a name picked out.*

MONITOR/CLARIFY p. 13 *How does the woman at the park use the cheese crackers to help Connor? She uses them to coax the dogs to come back to Connor after they run away.*

Discussing and Revisiting the Text

CRITICAL THINKING After they discuss *Dog Walker, Inc.,* have students read the instructions on **Responding p. 15**. Use these points to revisit the text.

• Have students list details from the story that support the author's purpose in the top boxes of **Blackline Master 16.3**.

• Distribute **Blackline Master 16.7** to further develop students' critical thinking skills.

FLUENCY: RATE Have partners practice reading a paragraph while using a timer. First, they should concentrate on accuracy. Then have them reread the selection again focusing on reading at a slightly quicker, but still comfortable, pace.

Small Group

JOURNEYS
DIGITAL Powered by
DESTINATIONReading®
Leveled Readers Online

Day 3

On Level

▲ *Incognito*

GENRE: REALISTIC FICTION

Summary When Ava Madera's father cannot find his prized comic book, Ava decides she will do whatever it takes to find him a new one. After an exhaustive search, she finally realizes that his comic book may have been misplaced during her family's move.

Introducing the Text

• Explain that interest in comic books increased in the 1940s because of the popularity of superheroes. By the 1960s, collecting and trading comic books had become commonplace.

• Remind students that authors write with a purpose. Good readers can detect an author's bias, or viewpoint.

Supporting the Reading

• As you listen to students read, pause to discuss these questions.

AUTHOR'S PURPOSE pp. 13–14 *Why does the author write the scene in which the clerk tries to trick Ava? to show that Ava is smart and a good researcher*

MONITOR/CLARIFY pp. 15–16 *What does Ava do when her mother mentions they may have left some summer clothes at Grandma's house? She wonders if they might have left something besides clothes there. She finds the missing comic book when she searches inside a box.*

Discussing and Revisiting the Text

CRITICAL THINKING After they discuss *Incognito,* have students read the instructions on **Responding p. 19**. Use these points to revisit the text.

• Have students list details from the story that support the author's purpose on **Blackline Master 16.4**.

• Distribute **Blackline Master 16.8** to further develop students' critical thinking skills.

FLUENCY: RATE Have students read a paragraph aloud using a timer. Have them first concentrate on accuracy. Then have them practice reading at a faster pace.

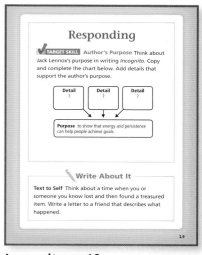

Incognito, p. 19

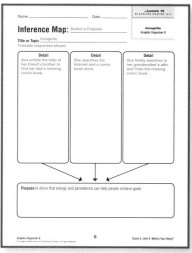

Blackline Master 16.4

SMALL GROUP Options

Targets for Lesson 16

✔ **TARGET SKILL**

Author's Purpose

✔ **TARGET STRATEGY**

Monitor/Clarify

✔ **TARGET VOCABULARY**

record	developed
mental	feature
launch	incredibly
assuming	villains
episodes	thumbed

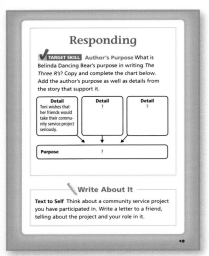

The Three R's, p. 19

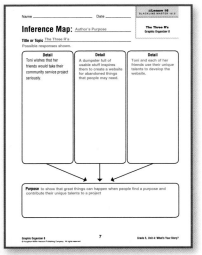

Blackline Master 16.5

Leveled Readers

Advanced

 The Three R's

GENRE: REALISTIC FICTION

Summary Toni and her team have a hard time developing an idea for a community service project. By accident, they come up with a creative way to do the Three R's: Reclaim! Repair! Reuse!

Introducing the Text

• Tell students that recycling protects Earth's resources and reduces the amount of waste people throw away as garbage.

• Remind students that authors write with a purpose in mind. Good readers are able to infer the author's viewpoint.

Supporting the Reading

• As you listen to students read, pause to discuss these questions.

AUTHOR'S PURPOSE pp. 8–9 *Carmen and her friends discover a rusty tricycle and an old barbecue that people have thrown away. What is the author's viewpoint? The author thinks fixing up old stuff is worthwhile.*

MONITOR/CLARIFY pp. 16–17 *How is the group able to pool their talents when presenting their community service project? Carmen does the illustration; Lee comes up with the mascot; Marcus takes care of the computer work; and Toni organizes the group and sums up their idea.*

Discussing and Revisiting the Text

CRITICAL THINKING After they discuss *The Three R's,* have students read the instructions on **Responding p. 19**. Use these points as they revisit the text.

• Have students list details from the story that support the author's purpose on **Blackline Master 16.5**. Have them list the author's purpose in the bottom box.

• Distribute **Blackline Master 16.9** to further develop students' critical thinking skills.

FLUENCY: RATE Have partners practice reading a paragraph aloud while using a timer. Have them compare their times and decide on the best rate.

JOURNEYS DIGITAL Powered by **DESTINATION**Reading®
Leveled Readers Online

ELL **English Language Learners**

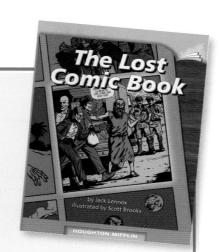

◆ *The Lost Comic Book*

GENRE: REALISTIC FICTION

Summary When Ava Madera's father cannot find his prized comic book, Ava decides she will do whatever it takes to find him a new one. After a long search, she realizes that the comic book may have been misplaced during her family's recent move.

Introducing the Text

• Explain that collecting comic books became commonplace in the 1960s and that some first editions are extremely valuable.

• Remind students that using an Inference Map can help them identify the author's purpose for writing the story.

Supporting the Reading

• As you listen to students read, pause to discuss these questions.

AUTHOR'S PURPOSE pp. 2–3 *Ava's father enjoys showing his daughter his comic book collection. Why does the author give this information? The author wants us to understand how important the comic is to Ava's dad and how sad he is to lose it.*

MONITOR/CLARIFY p. 13 *Why doesn't Ava buy the comic book the clerk tries to sell her? She notices a break in the story, and the cover isn't the original.*

Discussing and Revisiting the Text

CRITICAL THINKING After discussing *The Lost Comic Book*, have students read the instructions on **Responding p. 19**. Use these points to revisit the text.

• Have students list three details from the story that support the author's purpose on **Blackline Master 16.6**.

• Distribute **Blackline Master 16.10** to further develop students' critical thinking skills.

FLUENCY: RATE Have partners practice reading a paragraph aloud while using a timer. For the first reading, they should concentrate on accuracy. For the next reading, they should try to read slightly faster.

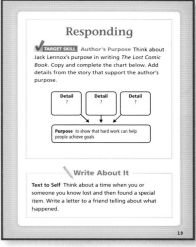

The Lost Comic Book, p. 19

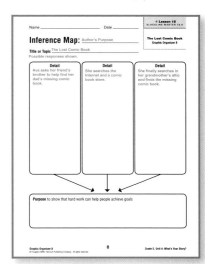

Blackline Master 16.6

Differentiate Vocabulary Strategies ☑ Word Origins

Struggling Readers

I DO IT

- Remind students that many words have a long history and were first used by people in other countries.

- Explain that students can use a dictionary to learn a word's origin, or history.

- Display the **Vocabulary in Context Card** for *feature*.

WE DO IT

- Help students use a dictionary to read about the origin of the word *feature*. *Middle English, from Old French, from Latin: a working or making, to make or do*

- Discuss with students how the word origin relates to the meaning of the word today.

YOU DO IT

- Have students use the **Vocabulary in Context Card** for *feature* to restate the context sentence for *feature* and to tell its meaning.

- Then have them write a short sentence to demonstrate their understanding of the meaning of *feature*.

- Ask students how the meaning of the word has changed over time.

On Level

I DO IT

- Explain that language, including English, is always changing.

- Point out that one way languages evolve is to borrow words from other languages. Many English words come from Greek, Latin, and French.

- Tell students that over time, English speakers used these words in different ways, creating new words.

- Explain that a word's origin, or history, can be found in a dictionary.

WE DO IT

- Display the **Vocabulary in Context Card** for *incredibly*.

- Have a volunteer look up the base word, *incredible*, in a dictionary.

- Have them read the origins of the word. *Middle English, Latin: not believable*

- Ask students how the word origin relates to the meaning today.

- Guide students to recognize the familiar Latin prefix *in-*, meaning "not."

YOU DO IT

- Have partners use the same process to figure out the origins of five of the Target Vocabulary words of this lesson.

- Have students write each word and its origins on a separate index card.

Advanced

I DO IT

- Point out that language is always changing, including English. One way that language evolves, or slowly changes over time, is through the borrowing of words from other languages.

- Explain that many English words came from Greek, Latin, French, Old or Middle English, or German.

- Similarly, some English words have been borrowed by other languages, as well.

WE DO IT

- Explain to students that to learn a word's origin, or history, they can look it up in a dictionary.

- Have a volunteer look up *villain* and share its history with the class.

- Have students look up unfamiliar words in the information they found about *villain*. Guide them to see that over time, *villain's* meaning changed from "peasant" to "evil person."

YOU DO IT

- Have students look up the remaining Target Vocabulary words in a dictionary and write their word origins on separate index cards.

- Have small groups discuss what the words' origins have in common, as well as how their meanings have changed over time.

ELL English Language Learners

Group English Language Learners according to language proficiency. Write *record, mental, launch, episodes, developed, feature, incredibly, villains, assuming,* and *thumbed* on the board. Have students repeat after you as you pronounce each word.

Beginning

Display the **Vocabulary in Context Card** for *villains*. Have students repeat the word. Point to France on a map and explain that the word came from there. Then point to the United States and say we use the word here. Help students define the word.

Intermediate

Model looking up the definition and word origin of one of the words on the board. Explain the origin and the meaning of the word. Help partners look up the origins of one or more of the other words and read their findings aloud.

Advanced

Display all of the **Vocabulary in Context Cards** from Lesson 16. Have students choose a card, and look up the vocabulary word in a dictionary. Have them write each word's origin, along with its definition.

Advanced High

Have pairs of students choose a Target Vocabulary word. Have them find the word in a dictionary, noting the word's origin. Then have them search the dictionary for three more words with the same origin.

Options for Reteaching

Vocabulary Strategies

Word Origins

I DO IT

- Remind students that a word's origin explains its history and the language in which the word was first used.
- Explain that language is constantly changing and new words are developed to reflect the latest trends.
- Remind students that many English words began as words in other languages, such as French and Spanish.

WE DO IT

- Write the word *lariat* on the board.
- Help students look up *lariat* in a dictionary.
- Model how to find the word origin in the entry and use it to understand the word *lariat*.

Think Aloud *I'll look up* lariat *in a dictionary to find out its meaning and word origin. Cowboys use a* lariat *to tie up animals that get loose. The dictionary entry tells me that the word* lariat *has a Spanish origin. It comes from the Spanish words meaning "to tie again." That helps me understand the word better.*

YOU DO IT

- Have partners work together to identify the origins of *cafeteria, encyclopedia,* and *patio.*
- Have them use a dictionary or the Internet to help them find the origins to verify their answers.
- Have students compare the original meanings of these words with their meanings today.

Comprehension Skill

Author's Viewpoint and Purpose

I DO IT

- Remind students that an author's purpose can be to inform, entertain, describe, or persuade.
- Point out that the author's viewpoint is the way that the author thinks and feels about a subject. This affects the author's reasons for writing.
- Remind students to use the words, details, facts, and examples the author chooses, as well as the way the text is organized, to figure out the author's purpose.

WE DO IT

- Have students read the third paragraph of **Student Book p. 411** aloud and infer the author's viewpoint.
- Model how to identify words, facts, and examples to help infer the author's viewpoint.

Think Aloud *The author lists the many "how" questions Greg had to answer before he could begin making his comic books. The author seems to think that making comic books is a big job that requires a lot of planning.*

- Help volunteers identify other clues that support this inference.

YOU DO IT

- Distribute **Graphic Organizer 7.**
- Have students list details from the story that will help them infer the author's viewpoint and lead to discovering the author's purpose. *Sample details: Greg worked on comic books all summer; he did research and solved problems.*
- Have partners work together to complete the graphic organizer.
- Review their completed graphic organizers.

Language Arts

 # Adjectives/Write to Narrate

I DO IT

- Review that an adjective describes a noun or a pronoun and that adjectives answer the questions *what kind* or *how many*.
- Write: *flag, flowers*. Model assigning adjectives to nouns.

> **Think Aloud**
> *To describe a flag, I ask "What kind of flag hangs in our classroom?" I can answer: an American flag. To describe flowers, I ask "How many flowers are in the bouquet?" I can answer: twelve flowers.*

WE DO IT

- Work together to write sentences using adjectives to describe nouns. Include one proper adjective that describes the origin of a person, place, or thing. *Sample answer: American car* Point out that proper adjectives are formed from names of places, so they are capitalized.
- Guide students to identify which question (*what kind, how many*) is answered by the adjective used in each sentence.
- Have partners work together to write a sentence that describes. Have them explain which question is answered by the adjectives they have used.
- Have volunteers share their sentences with the class.

YOU DO IT

- Have students write a short narrative paragraph describing a place that is special to them. Have them use adjectives to enliven their descriptions. Ask them to underline the adjectives they used.
- Invite students to share their paragraphs with the class. Have students listen and note which adjectives are used and which question each one answers.

Decoding

 # Word Parts and Inflectional Endings

I DO IT

- Remind students that some long words have a base word and an inflectional ending.
- Recall that there may be spelling changes to words when inflectional endings are added.

WE DO IT

- Write *featuring, publishing, figured,* and *recycled* on the board.
- Have students open to **Student Book p. 414**.
- Help students find the sentences containing these words.
- Help students identify the base words and inflectional endings.
- Model how to decode *featuring* step by step.

> **Think Aloud**
> *I know that some words are made up of a base word followed by a suffix or inflectional ending. This word has the ending, -ing. The base word must be feature. The spelling changes when the ending is added. The silent e is dropped.*

YOU DO IT

- Have partners decode the other words.
- Ask them to note the spelling changes in the base words.
- Use the **Corrective Feedback** on p. T39 if students need additional help.

Teacher Notes

Preteaching for Success!

Comprehension:

Story Structure

Remind students that every story has a structure.

- Review with students that story structure is the sum of the parts that make up a story, such as the characters, the plot, and the setting.
- To illustrate the concept, refer students to the story map on Student Book p. 430. Have them fill in the story map with setting and characters as well as conflicts, events, and the resolution as they read "LAFFF."

Challenge Yourself!

Research Time Machines

After reading the selection "LAFFF," have students research stories about time machines.

- Tell students that myths and folk tales about time machines have been around for thousands of years. More recent examples include H.G. Wells' "The Time Machine" and Mary Pope Osborne's "The Magic Treehouse" books.
- Have available books about time travel and time machines.
- Have pairs of students write adventure stories about a time machines. Hold a contest for the most exciting adventure.

Short Response

W.5.1b Provide logically ordered reasons that are supported by facts and details.

Write a new ending to "LAFFF." Describe what Angela might have done if someone else had written the winning story.

Scoring Guidelines	
Excellent	Student has written a new ending with a satisfying conclusion.
Good	Student has written a new ending with a plausible conclusion.
Fair	Student has written a new ending that has little to do with the story.
Unsatisfactory	Student has not written a paragraph or has written one that is not an ending to the story.

Writing Minilesson

Skill: Write to Narrate—Character Description

Teach: Explain to students that clear character descriptions help in writing good narrations.

Thinking Beyond the Text

Writing Prompt: Write a character description of Angela.

1. Tell students to write one-paragraph character descriptions of Angela. Have them include Angela's thoughts, actions, and words.
2. Remind students to check that they have used adverbs correctly.
3. Tell students to choose the right words to make their descriptions clear and focused.

Group Share: Invite students to read and discuss their descriptions with partners.

Cross-Curricular Activity: Science

The Future of My State

In the selection, students read about how the LAFFF machine only travels to the future. Ask students to think about how their state has changed in the last hundred years. Then ask them to pretend they could travel 100 years into their state's future. What do they see? Have each student write a paragraph about his or her ideas. Tell students that they must support their explanations by including examples of how their state has changed in the past.

Reading Standards for Literature K–5

Key Ideas and Details

RL.5.1 Quote accurately from a text when explaining what the text says explicitly and when drawing inferences from the text.

Craft and Structure

RL.5.4 Determine the meaning of words and phrases as they are used in a text, including figurative language such as metaphors and similes.

Range of Reading and Level of Text Complexity

RL.5.10 By the end of the year, read and comprehend literature, including stories, dramas, and poetry, at the high end of the grades 4–5 text complexity band independently and proficiently.

Reading Standards for Informational Text K–5

Integration of Knowledge and Ideas

RI.5.9 Integrate information from several texts on the same topic in order to write or speak about the subject knowledgeably.

Range of Reading and Level of Text Complexity

RI.5.10 By the end of the year, read and comprehend informational texts, including history/social studies, science, and technical texts, at the high end of the grades 4–5 text complexity band independently and proficiently.

Reading Standards: Foundational Skills K–5

Phonics and Word Recognition

RF.5.3a Use combined knowledge of all letter-sound correspondences, syllabication patterns, and morphology (e.g., roots and affixes) to read accurately unfamiliar multisyllabic words in context and out of context.

Fluency

RF.5.4b Read grade-level prose and poetry orally with accuracy, appropriate rate, and expression.

Writing Standards K–5

Text Types and Purposes

W.5.3a Orient the reader by establishing a situation and introducing a narrator and/or characters; organize an event sequence that unfolds naturally.

W.5.3b Use narrative techniques, such as dialogue, description, and pacing, to develop experiences and events or show the responses of characters to situations.

W.5.3d Use concrete words and phrases and sensory details to convey experiences and events precisely.

W.5.3e Provide a conclusion that follows from the narrated experiences or events.

Production and Distribution of Writing

W.5.4 Produce clear and coherent writing in which the development and organization are appropriate to task, purpose, and audience. (Grade-specific expectations for writing types are defined in standards 1–3 above.)

W.5.5 With guidance and support from peers and adults, develop and strengthen writing as needed by planning, revising, editing, rewriting, or trying a new approach.

Research to Build and Present Knowledge

W.5.7 Conduct short research projects that use several sources to build knowledge through investigation of different aspects of a topic.

W.5.8 Recall relevant information from experiences or gather relevant information from print and digital sources; summarize or paraphrase information in notes and finished work, and provide a list of sources.

Speaking & Listening Standards K–5

Comprehension and Collaboration

SL.5.1a Come to discussions prepared, having read or studied required material; explicitly draw on that preparation and other information known about the topic to explore ideas under discussion.

SL.5.1b Follow agreed-upon rules for discussions and carry out assigned roles.

SL.5.1c Pose and respond to specific questions by making comments that contribute to the discussion and elaborate on the remarks of others.

SL.5.2 Summarize a written text read aloud or information presented in diverse media and formats, including visually, quantitatively, and orally.

Presentation of Knowledge and Ideas

SL.5.4 Report on a topic or text or present an opinion, sequencing ideas logically and using appropriate facts and relevant, descriptive details to support main ideas or themes; speak clearly at an understandable pace.

Language Standards K–5

Conventions of Standard English

L.5.1c Use verb tense to convey various times, sequences, states, and conditions.

L.5.2e Spell grade-appropriate words correctly, consulting references as needed.

Vocabulary Acquisition and Use

L.5.4a Use context (e.g., cause/effect relationships and comparisons in text) as a clue to the meaning of a word or phrase.

L.5.4c Consult reference materials (e.g., dictionaries, glossaries, thesauruses), both print and digital, to find the pronunciation and determine or clarify the precise meaning of key words and phrases.

L.5.5a Interpret figurative language, including similes and metaphors, in context.

SUGGESTIONS FOR BALANCED LITERACY

Use *Journeys* materials to support a Readers' Workshop approach.
See the Lesson 17 resources on pages 25, 72–73.

Focus Wall

Main Selection:
"LAFFF"

Connect to Science:
"From Dreams to Reality"

Big 💡 Idea
Everyone has a
story to tell.

❓ Essential
Question

What problem does
the character face?

Comprehension

✔ **TARGET SKILL**
Story Structure

✔ **TARGET STRATEGY**
Infer/Predict

Spelling

More Words with -ed or -ing

tiring	related
amazing	expected
practicing	whispered
borrowed	attending
performing	amusing
supported	losing
freezing	damaged
resulting	repeated
united	decided
delivered	remarked

Fluency

Intonation

Grammar

Adverbs

Writing

Write to Narrate

Focus Trait:
Word Choice

Decoding

Recognizing Common
Word Parts

Vocabulary Strategies

Using Reference Sources

✔ TARGET VOCABULARY

impressed	concentrate
admitted	collected
produced	rumor
destination	suspense
original	compliment

Week at a Glance

Key Skills This Week

Target Skill:
Story Structure

Target Strategy:
Infer/Predict

Vocabulary Strategies:
Using Reference Sources

Fluency:
Intonation

Decoding:
Recognizing Common Word Parts

Research Skill:
Identify Source Information

Grammar:
Adverbs

Spelling:
More Words with -ed or -ing

 Writing:
Write to Narrate:
Character Description

✔ Assess/Monitor

☑ **Vocabulary,**
   p. T130

☑ **Comprehension,**
   p. T130

☑ **Decoding,**
   p. T131

☑ **Language Arts,**
   p. T131

☑ **Fluency,**
   p. T131

Whole Group

READING

Paired Selections

LAFFF from *Best Shorts*
Science Fiction
Student Book, pp. 430–444

From Dreams to Reality
Science/Informational Text
Student Book, pp. 446–448

 Accelerated Reader
Practice Quizzes for the Selection

Vocabulary

Student Book, pp. 426–427

Background and Comprehension

Student Book, pp. 428–429

LANGUAGE ARTS

Grammar
Student Book, pp. 450–451

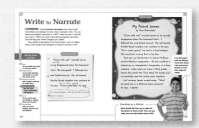

Writing
Student Book, pp. 452–453

Small Group

See page T134–T135 for Suggested Small Group Plan.

TEACHER-LED

Leveled Readers

● **Struggling Readers**

▲ **On Level**

■ **Advanced**

◆ **English Language Learners**

Vocabulary Reader

That's a Wacky Idea by Sarah Glasscock

WHAT MY OTHER STUDENTS ARE DOING

Ready-Made Work Stations

Comprehension and Fluency

Word Study

Think and Write

Digital Center

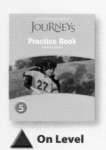

JOURNEYS Practice Book

● **Struggling Readers**

■ **Advanced**

◆ **English Language Learners**

▲ **On Level**

Lesson 17 Blackline Masters
- Target Vocabulary 17.1
- Selection Summary 17.2
- Graphic Organizer 17.3–17.6 ●▲■◆
- Critical Thinking 17.7–17.10 ●▲■◆
- Running Records 17.11–17.14 ●▲■◆
- Weekly Tests 17.1–17.10

Graphic Organizer Transparency 11

Additional Resources
- Genre: Fiction, p. 4
- Reading Log, p. 12
- Vocabulary Log, p. 13
- Listening Log, p. 14
- Proofreading Checklist, p. 15
- Proofreading Marks, p. 16
- Writing Conference Form, p. 17
- Writing Rubric, p. 18
- Instructional Routines, pp. 19–26
- Graphic Organizer 11: Story Map, p. 37

JOURNEYS DIGITAL Powered by DESTINATION Reading

For Students
- Student eBook
- Comprehension Expedition CD-ROM
- Leveled Readers Online
- WriteSmart CD-ROM

For Teachers
- Online TE and Focus Wall
- Online Assessment System
- Teacher One-Stop
- Destination Reading Instruction

Week at a Glance

Intervention

STRATEGIC INTERVENTION: TIER II

Use these materials to provide additional targeted instruction for students who need Tier II strategic intervention.

Supports the Student Book selections

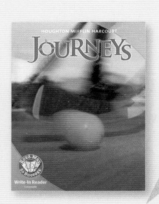

Interactive Work-text for Skills Support

Write-In Reader:

In the Year 2525
- Engaging selection connects to main topic.
- Reinforces this week's target vocabulary and comprehension skill and strategy.
- Opportunities for student interaction on each page.

Assessment

Progress monitoring every two weeks.

For this week's Strategic Intervention lessons, see Teacher's Edition pages S12–S21.

INTENSIVE INTERVENTION: TIER III

- The materials in the Literacy Tool Kit help you provide a different approach for students who need Tier III intensive intervention.
- Interactive lessons provide focused instruction in key reading skills, targeted at students' specific needs.
- Lesson cards are convenient for small-group or individual instruction.
- Blackline masters provide additional practice.
- A leveled book accompanies each lesson to give students opportunities for additional reading and skill application.
- Assessments for each lesson help you evaluate the effectiveness of the intervention.

Lessons provide support for

- Phonics and Word Study Skills
- Vocabulary
- Comprehension Skills and Literary Genres
- Fluency

ELL English Language Learners

SCAFFOLDED SUPPORT

Use these materials to ensure that students acquire social and academic language proficiency.

Language Support Card

- Builds background for the main topic and promotes oral language.
- Develops high-utility vocabulary and academic language.

Leveled Reader

- Sheltered text connects to the main selection's topic, vocabulary, skill, and strategy.

Scaffolded Support

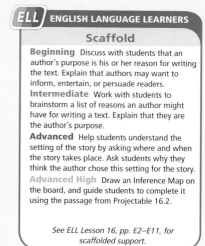

ELL ENGLISH LANGUAGE LEARNERS

Scaffold

Beginning Discuss with students that an author's purpose is his or her reason for writing the text. Explain that authors may want to inform, entertain, or persuade readers.

Intermediate Work with students to brainstorm a list of reasons an author might have for writing a text. Explain that they are the author's purpose.

Advanced Help students understand the setting of the story by asking where and when the story takes place. Ask students why they think the author chose this setting for the story.

Advanced High Draw an Inference Map on the board, and guide students to complete it using the passage from Projectable 16.2.

See ELL Lesson 16, pp. E2–E11, for scaffolded support.

- Notes throughout the Teacher's Edition scaffold instruction to each language proficiency level.

Vocabulary in Context Cards 161–170

- Provide visual support and additional practice for Target Vocabulary words.

For this week's English Language Learners lessons, see Teacher's Edition pages E12–E21.

Weekly Plan

	Day 1	**Day 2**
Whole Group		
Oral Language Listening Comprehension	**Teacher Read Aloud** "The Visitor," T84–T85 ☑ Target Vocabulary, T85	**Turn and Talk,** T91
Vocabulary Comprehension Skills and Strategies **Reading**	☑ **Comprehension** Preview the Target Skill, T85 ☑ **Introduce Vocabulary** Vocabulary in Context, T86–T87 **Develop Background** ☑ Target Vocabulary, T88–T89	**Introduce Comprehension** ☑ Story Structure, T90–T91 Infer/Predict, T90–T91 **Read "LAFFF,"** T92–T106 Focus on Genre, T92 Stop and Think, T95, T99, T103
Cross-Curricular Connections Fluency Decoding	☑ **Fluency** Model Intonation, T84	☑ **Fluency** Teach Intonation, T114
Whole Group Language Arts		
Spelling Grammar Writing	☑ **Spelling** More Words with -ed or -ing: Pretest, T120 ☑ **Grammar** Daily Proofreading Practice, T122 Teach Adverbs, T122 ☑ **Write to Narrate: Character Description** Analyze the Model, T126	☑ **Spelling** More Words with -ed or -ing: Word Sort, T120 ☑ **Grammar** Daily Proofreading Practice, T123 Extend Adverbs, T123 ☑ **Write to Narrate: Character Description** Focus Trait: Word Choice, T127
Writing Prompt	*Write about a time period you would travel to and why you would like to go there.*	*Describe a moment when time seemed to move very quickly or slowly.*

COMMON CORE Correlations

Day 1
Teacher Read Aloud RL.5.4
Introduce Vocabulary RL.5.4, L.5.4a
Develop Background RL.5.4, L.5.4a
Fluency RF.5.4b
Spelling L.5.2e
Write to Narrate W.5.3a, W.5.3b, W.5.3d, W.5.4, W.5.5

Day 2
Read RL.5.1, RL.5.4, RL.5.10, L.5.5a
Fluency RF.5.4b
Spelling L.5.2e
Write to Narrate W.5.3a, W.5.3b, W.5.3d, W.5.4, W.5.5

Suggestions for Small Groups (See pp. T134–T135.)
Suggestions for Intervention (See pp. S12–S21.)
Suggestions for English Language Learners (See pp. E12–E21.)

JOURNEYS DIGITAL Powered by
DESTINATIONReading
Teacher One-Stop: Lesson Planning

Day 3

Turn and Talk, T107
Oral Language, T107

Read "LAFFF," T92–T106
Develop Comprehension, T94, T96, T98, T100, T102, T104, T106
☑ **Target Vocabulary**
"LAFFF," T94, T96, T100, T102, T104
YourTurn , T107
Deepen Comprehension
☑ Analyze Story Structure, T112–T113

Cross-Curricular Connection
Social Studies, T99
☑ **Fluency**
Practice Intonation, T101
☑ **Decoding**
Recognizing Common Word Parts, T115

☑ **Spelling**
More Words with *-ed* or *-ing*: Teach Synonyms, T121
☑ **Grammar**
Daily Proofreading Practice, T123
Teach Using Adverbs, T123
☑ **Write to Narrate:**
Character Description
Prewrite, T127

Explain why you think Angela was right or wrong to copy the story.

Oral Language SL.5.1a, SL.5.1c
Read RL.5.1, RL.5.4, RL.5.10, L.5.5a
Your Turn SL.5.1a, SL.5.1b, SL.5.1c, SL.5.2
Deepen Comprehension SL.5.1a, SL.5.1c
Fluency RF.5.4b
Decoding RF.5.3a
Spelling L.5.2e
Write to Narrate W.5.3a, W.5.3b, W.5.3d, W.5.4, W.5.5

Day 4

Weekly Internet Challenge, T111

Read "From Dreams to Reality," T108–T110
Connect to Science, T108
Target Vocabulary Review, T109
Develop Comprehension, T110
Weekly Internet Challenge, T110–T111
Making Connections, T111
☑ **Vocabulary Strategies**
Using Reference Sources, T116–T117

☑ **Fluency**
Practice Intonation, T109

☑ **Spelling**
More Words with *-ed* or *-ing*: Connect to Writing, T121
☑ **Grammar**
Daily Proofreading Practice, T124
Review Adverbs, T124
☑ **Write to Narrate:**
Character Description
Draft, T128

Think of a problem you have and write about an invention that solves it.

Read RI.5.10
Making Connections RI.5.9, W.5.7
Vocabulary Strategies L.5.4c
Fluency RF.5.4b
Spelling L.5.2e
Grammar L.5.1c
Write to Narrate W.5.3a, W.5.3b, W.5.3d, W.5.3e, W.5.4, W.5.5

Day 5

Listening and Speaking, T119

Connect and Extend
Read to Connect, T118
Independent Reading, T118
Extend Through Research, T119

☑ **Fluency**
Progress Monitoring, T131

☑ **Spelling**
More Words with *-ed* or *-ing*: Assess, T121
☑ **Grammar**
Daily Proofreading Practice, T124
Connect Grammar to Writing, T124–T125
☑ **Write to Narrate:**
Character Description
Revise for Word Choice, T128

Compare and contrast Greg from "Lunch Money" with Peter from "LAFFF."

Listening and Speaking W.5.8, SL.5.2
Connect and Extend W.5.7, W.5.8, SL.5.1a, SL.5.1c, SL.5.4
Fluency RF.5.4b
Spelling L.5.2e
Write to Narrate W.5.3a, W.5.3b, W.5.3d, W.5.3e, W.5.4, W.5.5

Your Skills for the Week

☑ **Vocabulary**
Target Vocabulary Strategies: Using Reference Sources

☑ **Comprehension**
Story Structure
Infer/Predict

☑ **Decoding**
Recognizing Common Word Parts

☑ **Fluency**
Intonation

☑ **Language Arts**
Spelling
Grammar
Writing

Weekly Leveled Readers

Additional Tools

Vocabulary in Context Cards

Comprehension Tool: Graphic Organizer Transparency 11

Differentiated Support for This Week's Targets

 **TARGET SKILL**

Story Structure

 **TARGET STRATEGY**

Infer/Predict

✔ **TARGET VOCABULARY**

impressed	concentrate
admitted	collected
produced	rumor
destination	suspense
original	compliment

❓ Essential Question

What problem does the character face?

Vocabulary Reader

Build Target Vocabulary **Level R**

• Introduce the Target Vocabulary in context and build comprehension using the Target Strategy.

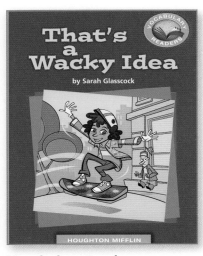

Vocabulary Reader

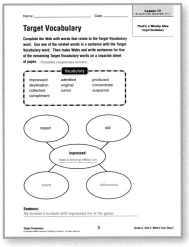

Blackline Master 17.1

Intervention

Scaffolded Support

• Provide extra support in applying the Target Vocabulary, Target Skill, and Target Strategy in context.

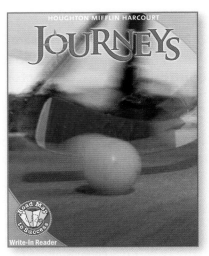

Write-In Reader

 For Vocabulary Reader Lesson Plans, see Small Group pages T136–T137.

Leveled Readers

Level R

Struggling Readers

Objective: Use Story Structure and the Infer/Predict strategy to read *Robot Rescue*.

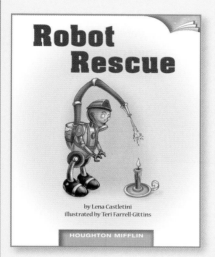

Robot Rescue
by Lena Castletini
illustrated by Teri Farrell-Gittins
HOUGHTON MIFFLIN

Blackline Master 17.3

Level S

On Level

Objective: Use Story Structure and the Infer/Predict strategy to read *The Watch Girl*.

The Watch Girl
by John Vogt
illustrated by Carol Heyer
HOUGHTON MIFFLIN

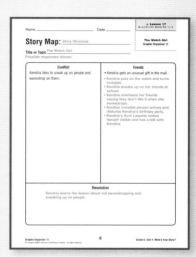

Blackline Master 17.4

Level W

Advanced

Objective: Use Story Structure and the Infer/Predict strategy to read *Pancakes*.

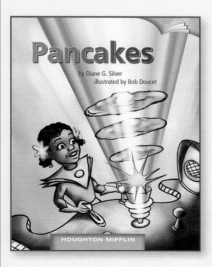

Pancakes
by Diane G. Silver
illustrated by Bob Doucet
HOUGHTON MIFFLIN

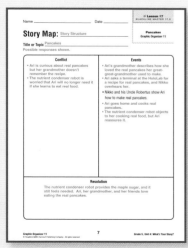

Blackline Master 17.5

Level S

English Language Learners

Objective: Use Story Structure and the Infer/Predict strategy to read *Kendria's Watch*.

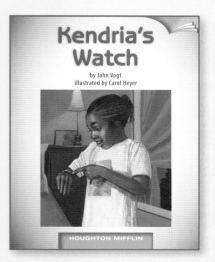

Kendria's Watch
by John Vogt
illustrated by Carol Heyer
HOUGHTON MIFFLIN

Blackline Master 17.6

 SMALL GROUP Options

For Leveled Reader Lesson Plans, see Small Group pages T140–T143.

Ready-Made Work Stations

Managing Independent Activities

Use the Ready-Made Work Stations to establish a consistent routine for students working independently. Each station contains three activities. Students who experience success with the *Get Started!* activity move on to the *Reach Higher!* and *Challenge Yourself!* activities, as time permits.

Comprehension and Fluency

Materials
- **Student Book**
- tape recorder
- Reading Log
- pencil or pen

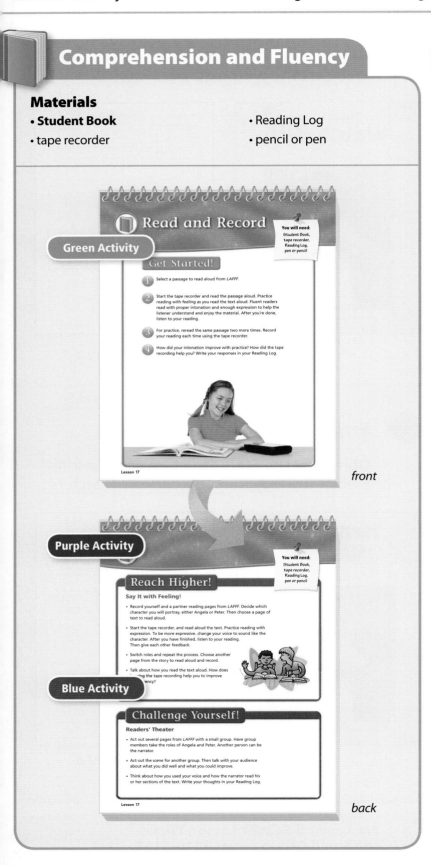

Green Activity

Read and Record

You will need:
Student Book, tape recorder, Reading Log, pen or pencil

Get Started!

1. Select a passage to read aloud from *LAFFF*.

2. Start the tape recorder and read the passage aloud. Practice reading with feeling as you read the text aloud. Fluent readers read with proper intonation and enough expression to help the listener understand and enjoy the material. After you're done, listen to your reading.

3. For practice, reread the same passage two more times. Record your reading each time using the tape recorder.

4. How did your intonation improve with practice? How did the tape recording help you? Write your responses in your Reading Log.

Lesson 17   *front*

Purple Activity

You will need:
Student Book, tape recorder, Reading Log, pen or pencil

Reach Higher!

Say It with Feeling!

- Record yourself and a partner reading pages from *LAFFF*. Decide which character you will portray, either Angela or Peter. Then choose a page of text to read aloud.

- Start the tape recorder, and read aloud the text. Practice reading with expression. To be more expressive, change your voice to sound like the character. After you have finished, listen to your reading. Then give each other feedback.

- Switch roles and repeat the process. Choose another page from the story to read aloud and record.

- Talk about how you read the text aloud. How does ___ing the tape recording help you to improve ___ency?

Blue Activity

Challenge Yourself!

Readers' Theater

- Act out several pages from *LAFFF* with a small group. Have group members take the roles of Angela and Peter. Another person can be the narrator.

- Act out the scene for another group. Then talk with your audience about what you did well and what you could improve.

- Think about how you used your voice and how the narrator read his or her sections of the text. Write your thoughts in your Reading Log.

Lesson 17   *back*

Word Study

Materials
- pencil or pen, paper
- **Vocabulary in Context Cards**
- graph paper
- dictionary
- **Student Book**
- thesaurus

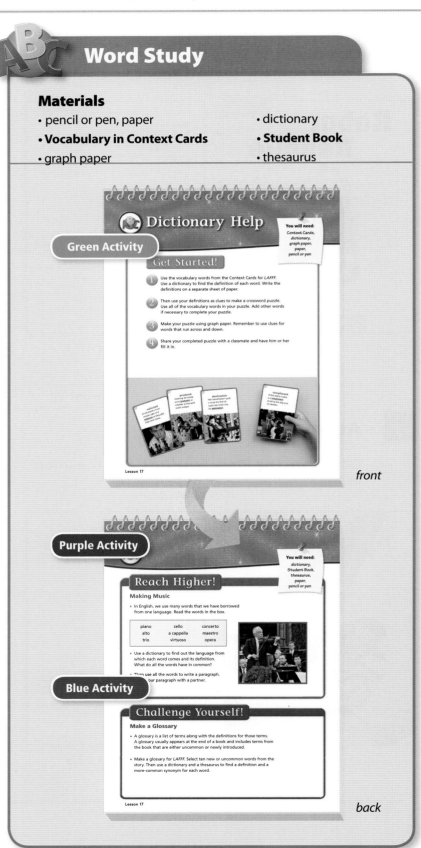

Green Activity

Dictionary Help

You will need:
Context Cards, dictionary, graph paper, paper, pencil or pen

Get Started!

1. Use the vocabulary words from the Context Cards for *LAFFF*. Use a dictionary to find the definition of each word. Write the definitions on a separate sheet of paper.

2. Then use your definitions as clues to make a crossword puzzle. Use all of the vocabulary words in your puzzle. Add other words if necessary to complete your puzzle.

3. Make your puzzle using graph paper. Remember to use clues for words that run across and down.

4. Share your completed puzzle with a classmate and have him or her fill it in.

Lesson 17   *front*

Purple Activity

You will need:
dictionary, Student Book, thesaurus, paper, pencil or pen

Reach Higher!

Making Music

- In English, we use many words that we have borrowed from one language. Read the words in the box.

piano	cello	concerto
alto	a cappella	maestro
trio	virtuoso	opera

- Use a dictionary to find out the language from which each word comes and its definition. What do all the words have in common?

- Then use all the words to write a paragraph. ___ your paragraph with a partner.

Blue Activity

Challenge Yourself!

Make a Glossary

- A glossary is a list of terms along with the definitions for those terms. A glossary usually appears at the end of a book and includes terms from the book that are either uncommon or newly introduced.

- Make a glossary for *LAFFF*. Select ten new or uncommon words from the story. Then use a dictionary and a thesaurus to find a definition and a more-common synonym for each word.

Lesson 17   *back*

Think and Write

Materials
- library books
- paper
- pencil or pen

- **Student Book**
- short stories
- magazines and journals

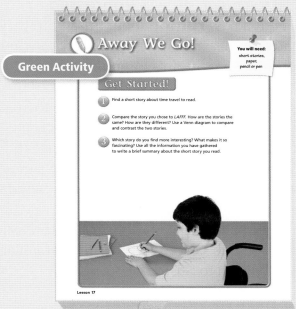

Away We Go!

Green Activity

You will need:
short stories,
paper,
pencil or pen

Get Started!

1. Find a short story about time travel to read.

2. Compare the story you chose to *LAFFF*. How are the stories the same? How are they different? Use a Venn diagram to compare and contrast the two stories.

3. Which story do you find more interesting? What makes it so fascinating? Use all the information you have gathered to write a brief summary about the short story you read.

Lesson 17

front

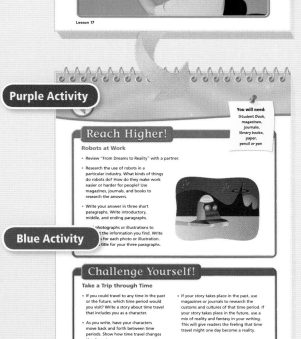

Purple Activity

You will need:
Student Book,
magazines,
journals,
library books,
paper,
pencil or pen

Reach Higher!

Robots at Work

- Review "From Dreams to Reality" with a partner.

- Research the use of robots in a particular industry. What kinds of things do robots do? How do they make work easier or harder for people? Use magazines, journals, and books to research the answers.

- Write your answer in three short paragraphs. Write introductory, middle, and ending paragraphs.

- photographs or illustrations to the information you find. Write for each photo or illustration. title for your three paragraphs.

Blue Activity

Challenge Yourself!

Take a Trip through Time

- If you could travel to any time in the past or the future, which time period would you visit? Write a story about time travel that includes you as a character.

- As you write, have your characters move back and forth between time periods. Show how time travel changes the characters.

- If your story takes place in the past, use magazines or journals to research the customs and cultures of that time period. If your story takes place in the future, use a mix of reality and fantasy in your writing. This will give readers the feeling that time travel might one day become a reality.

Lesson 17

back

JOURNEYS DIGITAL · Powered by DESTINATIONReading®

Independent Activities

Have students complete these activities at a computer center or a center with an audio CD player.

LAUNCH ❯ **Comprehension and Grammar Activities**

Practice and apply this week's skills.

LAUNCH ❯ **Student eBook**

Read and listen to this week's selections and skill lessons.

LAUNCH ❯ **WriteSmart CD-ROM**

Review student versions of this week's writing model.

LAUNCH ❯ **Audiotext CD**

Listen to books or selections on CD.

Single Log In

Teacher Read Aloud

- Listen to fluent reading.
- Identify story structure.
- Listen to learn the Target Vocabulary words.

Model Fluency

Intonation Explain that good readers vary the pitch of their voice to emphasize meaning.

- Display **Projectable 17.1**. Read two or three sentences with no intonation. Then reread the same sentences with proper intonation to demonstrate the difference.

- Explain that the events occuring in the story play a large part in how vocal pitch should be varied.

- Reread the sentences together with students, modeling good intonation based on what is happening in the passage.

The Visitor

No matter how much the new girl tried to blend in, thought Hillary, she stood out like a polar bear in the desert. On the first day of school, Susan had arrived in clothes that even the most **original** student wouldn't dare risk: metallic silver leggings and a knee-length tunic that actually changed colors. Her flat ankle boots grew heels—two inches one minute, three inches the next—depending on what she was doing. One word described her style: Futuristic.

1

Her behavior **produced** a **compliment** or two. Sure, she was quiet. But Susan was an absolute whiz at history. Most of the time, she knew more than their teacher. Yes, Hillary **admitted** to herself, she was **impressed**.

Each day brought a new **rumor** about Susan Smith. One girl swore she had seen her in two places at once. A whole classroom was positive that Susan's forgotten science homework had suddenly materialized out of nowhere.

Today after school, Hillary was supposed to go to Susan's house to work on their English project. After school, however, Susan insisted on working at Hillary's instead.

"Can't," said Hillary. "Mom's having her writer's group today." She stayed cool and **collected** as they gathered stuff from their lockers and walked outside.

"So, why don't we just go to your house?" Hillary asked, but Susan couldn't seem to **concentrate** on what Hillary was saying. "Susan? Earth to Susan."

Projectable 17.1

LAFF | Fluency Intonation

Read Aloud: Model Oral Fluency

The Visitor

No matter how much the new girl tried to blend in, thought Hillary, she stood out like a polar bear in the desert. On the first day of school, Susan had arrived in clothes that even the most original student wouldn't dare risk: metallic silver leggings and a knee-length tunic that actually changed colors. Her flat ankle boots grew heels-two inches one minute, three inches the next-depending on what she was doing. One word described her style: Futuristic.

Her behavior produced a compliment or two. Sure, she was quiet. But, Susan was an absolute whiz at history. Most of the time, she knew more than their teacher. Yes, Hillary admitted to herself, she was impressed.

"Sorry," Susan replied. "Okay. But, it's not a good day for you to be on my street. I'm just warning you." Hillary rolled her eyes. Susan was always making predictions.

They turned onto Susan's street. They were almost to their **destination** when Hillary noticed Susan scanning her surroundings, as if she were expecting something. Hillary wondered why Susan acted so oddly sometimes. "Come on Susan. Let's hurry up so we can get to our studying." Hillary said as she stepped into the street.

It all happened in a few seconds, but Hillary remembered it later in slow motion **suspense**. The sudden rattle of the truck, the blare of the horn, the screech of wheels . . . and the pain in her ribs as Susan grabbed her and flung her safely down on the sidewalk.

Hillary sat there. How did Susan know the truck was coming? It came out of nowhere. There is no way she could have seen it speeding around the corner. She just knew it was there. The whole thing was impossible.

Susan helped Hillary up and gave her a hug. "This is good-bye," Susan explained. "Now that you're safe, I must go forward, but, from now on, you must take care. You are destined to do great things." With that, Susan disappeared—just popped into nothing.

How did she do that? Hillary wondered later. One thing was certain: When Susan had snatched her from the path of the oncoming truck, she had altered the course of history. Just what sort of role, Hillary wondered, was she herself going to play?

Listening Comprehension
Preview the Target Skill

Read aloud the passage, using appropriate intonation. Then ask students the following questions.

1 **Understanding Characters** *Why is the description of how Susan dresses important to the story? It lets the reader know that Susan is different, and it makes the reader curious to find out why she is so different.*

2 **Make Inferences** *Why could Susan not concentrate on what Hillary was saying? Susan knew that Hillary was about to get hit by the truck, so she was trying to think of what the best way to avoid that would be.*

3 **Story Structure** *What problem arises for Hillary? How is it taken care of? Hillary is about to step out in front of a truck, but Susan grabs her and flings her out of harm's way.*

4 **Draw Conclusions** *What might have been the purpose for Susan meeting Hillary? Susan was sent from the future to save Hillary because Hillary is destined to do great things.*

Target Vocabulary

- Reread "The Visitor" aloud.
- As you read, pause briefly to explain each highlighted vocabulary word.
- Discuss the meaning of each word as it is used in the Read Aloud.

original first or fresh

produced created, made

compliment a positive, admiring, or respectful remark

admitted agreed that something is true

impressed left with a positive feeling

rumor a piece of information people talk about that may not be true

collected calm and sensible; together

concentrate focus one's attention

destination a place to which people travel

suspense tension felt when waiting for something to happen

☑️ Introduce Vocabulary

SHARE OBJECTIVE

- Understand and use the Target Vocabulary words.

Teach

Display the **Vocabulary in Context Cards**, using the routine below. Direct students to **Student Book pp. 426–427**. See also **Instructional Routine 9**.

1 **Read and pronounce the word.** Read the word once alone, then together with students.

2 **Explain the word.** Read the explanation under *What Does It Mean?*

3 **Discuss vocabulary in context.** Together, read aloud the sentence on the front of the card. Help students explain and use the word in new sentences.

4 **Engage with the word.** Ask and discuss the *Think About It* question with students.

Apply

Give partners or small groups one or two **Vocabulary in Context Cards**.

- Help students start the *Talk It Over* activity on the back of their card.

- Have students complete activities for all of the cards during the week.

Lesson 17

Vocabulary in Context

☑️ TARGET VOCABULARY

impressed

collected

produced

destination

original

concentrate

suspense

admitted

compliment

rumor

Vocabulary Reader

Context Cards

1 impressed
This judge was impressed and awed by a young writer's remarkable talent.

2 collected
Chess players must remain calm and collected as they plot their next move.

3 produced
Amazing structures were produced, or created, at this sand castle contest.

4 destination
This marathoner's goal is to be the first to reach the finish line, his destination.

426

ELL ENGLISH LANGUAGE LEARNERS

Scaffold

Beginning Use actions and facial expressions to demonstrate the meanings of *impressed, concentrate,* and *suspense*. Then have students perform the actions as you say each word.

Advanced Ask students questions to confirm their understanding. For example, *Would you start a rumor about your best friend? Why not?*

Intermediate Have students complete sentence frames for each Vocabulary word. For example, *When you are at the end of your journey, you have reached your____. destination*

Advanced High Have partners ask and answer questions about each Vocabulary word. For example, *Why is it important to stay collected in an emergency?*

See ELL Lesson 17, pp. E12–E21, for scaffolded support.

- **Study each** Context Card.
- **Use a glossary to determine the pronunciation of each Vocabulary word.**

original

Olympia, Greece, is the original, or first, place where Olympic Games were held.

concentrate

This tennis player has to concentrate on the ball in order to hit it back to her opponent.

suspense

These fans are in suspense, wondering who will win the big game.

admitted

This spelling bee contestant admitted, or confessed, how nervous he was.

compliment

A first-place trophy is a compliment praising the dog and its handler.

rumor

Sometimes a rumor, or unproved news, can spread about who won a contest.

427

VOCABULARY IN CONTEXT CARDS 161–170

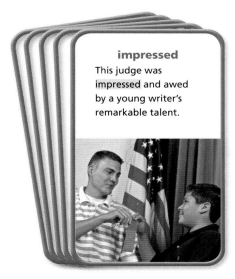

front   **back**

Monitor Vocabulary

Are students able to understand and use Target Vocabulary words?

IF...	THEN...
students have difficulty understanding and using most of the Target Vocabulary Words,	▶ use **Vocabulary in Context Cards** and differentiate the **Vocabulary Reader,** *That's a Wacky Idea,* for Struggling Readers, p. T136. *See also Intervention Lesson 17, pp. S12–S21.*
students can understand and use most of the Target Vocabulary words,	▶ use **Vocabulary in Context Cards** and differentiate the **Vocabulary Reader,** *That's a Wacky Idea,* for On-Level Readers, p. T136.
students can understand and use all of the Target Vocabulary words,	▶ differentiate the **Vocabulary Reader,** *That's a Wacky Idea,* for Advanced Readers, p. T137.

Vocabulary Reader, pp. T137–T136.
Group English Language Learners according to language proficiency.

Develop Background

SHARE OBJECTIVES

- Learn about important ideas in "LAFFF."
- Build background using the Target Vocabulary words.

 ENGLISH LANGUAGE LEARNERS

Scaffold

Beginning Review the Target Vocabulary words in "Imagining the Future" using gestures, visuals, and simplified language. Then have students mimic your gestures as they repeat the words.

Intermediate Review the Target Vocabulary words in "Imagining the Future" using gestures, visuals, and simplified language. Have students act out a vocabulary word such as *concentrate* for the class.

Advanced Discuss what it might be like to travel to a different time period. Use the Target Vocabulary to guide conversation.

Advanced High Tell students that the machine in the pictures on page 428 is a time machine. Have students draw a picture of their own invention and write a short paragraph about it using the Target Vocabulary.

See ELL Lesson 17, pp. E12–E21, for scaffolded support.

Target Vocabulary

1 Teach/Model

- Use the picture on **Student Book p. 428** to discuss time machines. Tell students that "LAFFF" is a story about a boy who **produced** a time machine called LAFFF.
- Use **Vocabulary in Context Cards** to review the student-friendly explanations of the Target Vocabulary words.
- Have students silently read **Student Book p. 428.** Then read the passage aloud.

2 Guided Practice

Ask students the first item below and discuss their responses. Continue in this way until students have answered a question about each Target Vocabulary word.

1. What usually happens when someone has **admitted** to making a mistake?
2. Tell about a time when you were kept in **suspense**.
3. Why might it be more exciting to see an **original** painting in a museum than a copy in a book?
4. Would you be surprised if someone **produced** a rabbit from a hat? Why or why not?
5. What do you do to help yourself **concentrate** when you do your homework?
6. Why might a time traveler from the past be **impressed** by modern technology?
7. Describe how someone who is calm and **collected** looks and acts.
8. What is your favorite vacation **destination**? Why?
9. How might a **rumor** hurt someone?
10. Would you expect someone to be angry at a **compliment**? Explain.

Background

✓ **TARGET VOCABULARY** **Imagining the Future** At one time or another, we have all admitted that we are curious about the future. If the suspense of waiting to see what's in store is too much, you can always read science fiction. Even the earliest, or original, science fiction authors, such as H.G. Wells, produced stories about time travel. The stories often concentrate on new inventions and changes in society that impressed the fictional time travelers. There are often cool and collected scientists and brave adventurers who select another time for their destination. However, time travel is only a rumor. It could never really happen. It is a compliment to the skill of science fiction writers that they can make us believe in their imaginary futures.

Some science fiction stories feature mechanical devices that send characters forward or backward in time.

8

Readers are often impressed by the imagination of authors.

3 Apply

- Have partners take turns reading a paragraph on **Student Book p. 428** to one another.

- Tell partners to pause and explain each highlighted word as they read aloud. When they have finished, have students use the Target Vocabulary to begin a class conversation about what the future will be like.

Introduce Comprehension

SHARE OBJECTIVES

- Identify story elements, such as conflict, plot, and resolution.
- Use story details to make inferences and predictions.

SKILL TRACE

Story Structure

Introduce	T90–T91
Differentiate	T138–T139
Reteach	T146
Review	T112–T113
Test	Weekly Tests, Lesson 17

ELL ENGLISH LANGUAGE LEARNERS

Scaffold

Beginning Display and discuss the term *predict*. Use the illustration on **p. 431** to help students make simple predictions about the selection.

Intermediate Display this sentence frame: *If a character is smart, I predict that _____.* Have students complete the sentence and share their responses.

Advanced Have students use the following sentence frame to make oral predictions about simple occurrences, such as the weather or which team will win an upcoming game: *I predict that _____ because _____.*

Advanced High Have partners write prediction sentences about simple occurrences, such as the weather or which team will win an upcoming game.

See ELL Lesson 17, pp. E12–E21, for scaffolded support.

1 | Teach/Model

AL *Academic Language*

story structure how the author organizes important parts of the story, called story elements, including characters, setting, and plot

plot the story events, including a conflict and its resolution

resolution how the conflict or problem in a story is solved

- Tell students that the main elements of a **story's structure** are the characters; setting (where and when it takes place); and **plot**, including the conflict, or problem, and **resolution**, or solution to the problem.
- Read and discuss with students **Student Book p. 429**. Have them use the Academic Language in the discussion.
- Display **Projectable 17.2**. Have students read "Tate's New Ride."

STORY STRUCTURE Explain that understanding each element of a story helps readers understand the story as a whole.

- Explain that you will use the Story Map to record the elements of the story's structure.

Think Aloud I'll begin my Story Map by filling in the Conflict section with the problem that the main character is facing.

INFER/PREDICT Explain that inferring and predicting can help readers better understand the story as they read.

Think Aloud Tate pays extra attention in science class when they learn about space and time. From that, I can infer that Tate's machine must have something to do with space and time. I also predict that his space-time machine would solve his problem.

Projectable 17.2

LAFFF | Introduce Comprehension Story Structure; Infer/Predict

Story Structure; Infer/Predict

Tate's New Ride

Tate hated the long bus ride to school. "I wish somehow I could just be there," he complained. Suddenly, he had an idea. That day, Tate invented the Incredible No-Bus-Needed Machine.

Tate worked on his machine for a year. He worked on weekends and after school. He paid extra attention in science class when they studied time and space.

One morning it was done. He left the house wearing his backpack. He didn't walk to the bus; he walked into his machine. He closed the door and pressed "On."

Tate felt funny all over. When the machine stopped, he was standing outside school. Success!

Then it hit him. He still had to take the bus home.

STORY STRUCTURE Use a Story Map to organize information about the plot in a science fiction story.

Conflict:	Events:
Tate hates riding the bus to school.	• Tate has an idea for the Incredible No-Bus-Needed Machine.
	• Tate works on the machine for a year.
	• Tate tries out the machine.
Resolution: Tate's machine instantly transports him to school.	

INFER/PREDICT You can use the information in your Story Map to predict what might happen next in the story.

Comprehension

✔ TARGET SKILL **Story Structure**

As you read "LAFFF," identify a character's problem or conflict and the events in the story that resolve the conflict, or lead to a solution. Think about the character's role in what happens, when it happens, and why. Use a story map like the one below to help you understand how a story unfolds. Remember to list story events in sequential order.

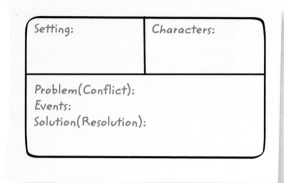

```
Setting:              Characters:

Problem(Conflict):
Events:
Solution(Resolution):
```

✔ TARGET STRATEGY **Infer/Predict**

When a character has a conflict or a problem, think about the way the story unfolds to bring about a resolution. Look to the events in a story to predict what will happen next. Making predictions and finding out if they come true can make reading fun.

JOURNEYS DIGITAL — Powered by DESTINATIONReading
Comprehension Activities: Lesson 17

429

Monitor Comprehension

Are students able to identify elements of story structure?

IF...	THEN...
students have difficulty identifying elements of story structure,	▶ **Differentiate Comprehension** for Struggling Readers, p. T138. *See also Intervention Lesson 17, pp. S12–S21.*
students can identify elements of story structure,	▶ **Differentiate Comprehension** for On-Level Readers, p. T138.
students can infer and predict elements of story structure,	▶ **Differentiate Comprehension** for Advanced Readers, p. T139.

Differentiate Comprehension: pp. T138–T139

Group English Language Learners according to language proficiency. See also ELL Lesson 17, pp. E12–E21, for scaffolded support.

---

2 Guided Practice

Help students complete their own Story Maps for "Tate's New Ride." Use **Projectable S2** to guide inferring and predicting story elements. Then review students' Story Maps with them.

3 Apply

Turn and Talk   Have partners use their Story Maps to discuss what they can infer about Tate's personality and to make predictions about what Tate might do next.

Have student pairs choose a story they have read recently and identify story elements, such as characters' roles, the conflict, and the resolution. Have them record the information in a Story Map.

Practice Book p. 193
See Grab-and-Go™ Resources for additional leveled practice.

Introduce the
Main Selection

TARGET SKILL

STORY STRUCTURE Explain that as they read, students will use **Graphic Organizer 11: Story Map** to identify the following elements of story structure:

- the main problem or conflict

- events that lead to the resolution

TARGET STRATEGY

INFER/PREDICT Students will use **Graphic Organizer 11** to help them infer and predict events in the story.

GENRE: Science Fiction

- Read the genre information on **Student Book p. 430** with students.

- Share and discuss the **Genre Blackline Master: Fiction**.

- Preview the selection and model identifying the characteristics of the genre.

Think Aloud *The strange title and the futuristic cover illustration make me think that this selection is about something unusual based on science. The text is full of dialogue, like a story.*

- As you preview, ask students to identify other features of science fiction.

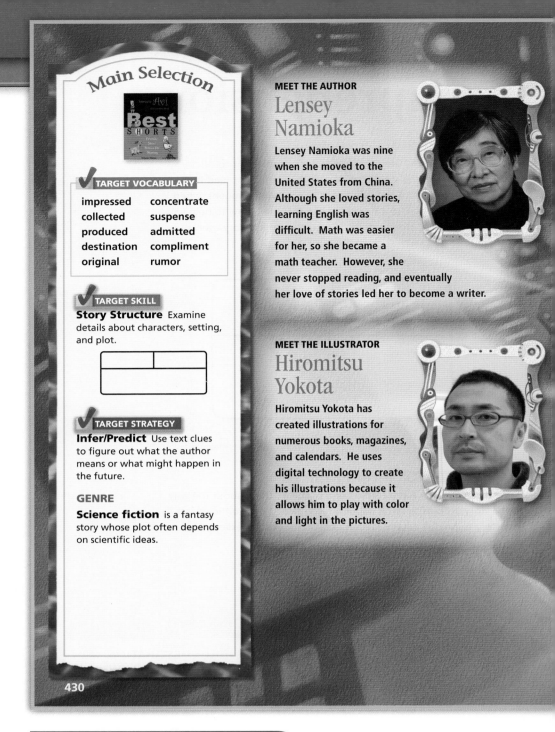

Main Selection

✓ TARGET VOCABULARY

impressed	concentrate
collected	suspense
produced	admitted
destination	compliment
original	rumor

✓ TARGET SKILL

Story Structure Examine details about characters, setting, and plot.

✓ TARGET STRATEGY

Infer/Predict Use text clues to figure out what the author means or what might happen in the future.

GENRE

Science fiction is a fantasy story whose plot often depends on scientific ideas.

MEET THE AUTHOR
Lensey Namioka

Lensey Namioka was nine when she moved to the United States from China. Although she loved stories, learning English was difficult. Math was easier for her, so she became a math teacher. However, she never stopped reading, and eventually her love of stories led her to become a writer.

MEET THE ILLUSTRATOR
Hiromitsu Yokota

Hiromitsu Yokota has created illustrations for numerous books, magazines, and calendars. He uses digital technology to create his illustrations because it allows him to play with color and light in the pictures.

430

Reading the Selection

	Pre-Reading	Reading
Supported	**SELECTION SUMMARY** Use **Blackline Master 17.2** to give students an overview. **AUDIOTEXT CD** Have students listen to the selection as they follow along in their books.	**AUTHOR'S MESSAGE** After reading the selection, discuss with students the author's message about honesty and competition.
Independent	**PREVIEW** Have students use the title, genre information, and illustrations to discuss predictions and clues. Some students may read the story independently.	**TEXT EVIDENCE** Pause after reading pp. 433, 437, 441, and 444. Have students write questions and answers and note where evidence for the answer is found. Discuss student questions and answers.

LAFFF
from *Best Shorts*

by Lensey Namioka
selection illustrated by Hiromitsu Yokota

Essential Question

What problem
does the
character face?

431

? Essential Question

- Read aloud the **Essential Question** on **Student Book p. 431.** *What problem does the character face?*

- Tell students to think about this question as they read "LAFFF."

Set Purpose

- Explain that good readers set a purpose for reading based on their preview of the selection and what they know about the genre, as well as what they want to learn by reading.

- Model setting a reading purpose.

Think Aloud *Science fiction has imagined details about science and technology. One purpose for reading the story might be to see what science and technology have to do with the title and the characters.*

- Have students share their personal reading purposes and record them in their journals.

JOURNEYS DIGITAL — Powered by DESTINATIONReading
Student eBook: Read and Listen

Name _____ Date _____

Lesson 17
BLACKLINE MASTER 17.2

LAFFF

LAFFF
Selection Summary

Pages 432–435
Angela, the narrator of the story, thinks Peter, a member of her class, is a genius. Peter is great at school, but he keeps to himself around other people. He spends all his time alone working on an amazing machine in his garage. Angela wants to know what it is. One night she peeks through the window. Peter sees her. He explains that it is a time machine that can send people into the future, but only for a few minutes.

Pages 436–437
Peter and Angela become friends. Peter tries to make his machine work so that people can stay longer in the future. Unfortunately anything taken from the future will soon return to its own time. The machine is not very useful, until Angela has an idea.

Pages 438–439
Angela tells Peter her idea. She wants to win a writing contest at school. She will go into the future, read the winning story, and then copy it. She thinks she is sure to win. Peter sends Angela into the future through his machine.

Pages 440–441
Angela arrives three weeks in the future. She rushes to her house to get the story. She almost runs into her future self, and she confuses her mother. She finds the story, but does not get to read the whole thing or the name of the author before it disappears.

Pages 442–444
Angela is anxiously waiting to learn who wins the writing contest. Angela feels guilty because she used the time machine to write her winning story. Then Peter teases her and she realizes that she had thought of the story all along. Angela's story was about using the time machine.

Selection Summary   4   Grade 5, Unit 4: What's Your Story?

Blackline Master 17.2

Develop Comprehension

Pause at the stopping points to ask students the following questions.

1 Drawing Conclusions
Use text details to draw a conclusion about Peter's traits and relationships with other students. Sample answer: Peter looks and acts like a normal kid, even though he is very smart, quiet, and always thinking and reading. He does not fit in well with other kids his age.

2 ✔ TARGET VOCABULARY
*Why were the other kids **impressed** when they saw Peter? Sample answer: The other kids thought Peter's mad scientist costume was cool.*

3 Identify Story Structure
What element of story structure begins here? How do you know? Sample answer: Rising action; the story has changed from giving background information to plot events that happen in the present time.

In movies, geniuses have frizzy white hair, right? They wear thick glasses and have names like Dr. Zweistein.

Peter Lu didn't have frizzy white hair. He had straight hair, as black as licorice. He didn't wear thick glasses, either, since his vision was normal.

Peter's family, like ours, had immigrated from China, but they had settled here first. When we moved into a house just two doors down from the Lus, they gave us some good advice on how to get along in America.

I went to the same school as Peter, and we walked to the school bus together every morning. Like many Chinese parents, mine made sure that I worked very hard in school.

In spite of all I could do, my grades were nothing compared to Peter's. He was at the top in all his classes. We walked to the school bus without talking because I was a little scared of him. Besides, he was always deep in thought.

Peter didn't have any friends. Most of the kids thought he was a nerd because they saw his head always buried in books. I didn't think he even tried to join the rest of us or cared what the others thought of him.

432

ELL ENGLISH LANGUAGE LEARNERS

Scaffold

Beginning Using the illustrations, preview the selection with students. Help them name objects they recognize and describe the setting.

Intermediate Read aloud the first three paragraphs on p. 432. Discuss with students these words using gestures, visuals, and simplified language: *geniuses, immigrated.*

Advanced After reading pp. 432–433, have students restate the ideas and ask clarifying questions.

Advanced High After reading pp. 432–433, have students write one or two sentences summarizing what they have learned to this point.

See ELL Lesson 17, pp. E12–E21, for scaffolded support.

Then he surprised us all. As I went down the block trick-or-treating, dressed as a zucchini in my green sweats, I heard a strange, deep voice behind me say, "How do you do."

I yelped and turned around. Peter was wearing a long, black Chinese gown with slits in the sides. On his head he had a little round cap, and down each side of his mouth drooped a thin, long mustache.

"I am Dr. Lu Manchu, the mad scientist," he announced, putting his hands in his sleeves and bowing.

He smiled when he saw me staring at his costume. It was a scary smile, somehow.

2 Some of the other kids came up, and when they saw Peter, they were impressed. "Hey, neat!" said one boy.

I hadn't expected Peter to put on a costume and go trick-or-treating like a normal kid. So maybe he did want to join the others after all—at least some of the time. After that night he wasn't a nerd anymore. He was Dr. Lu Manchu. Even some of the teachers began to call him that.

When we became too old for trick-or-treating, Peter was still Dr. Lu Manchu. The rumor was that he was working on a fantastic machine in his parents' garage. But nobody had any idea what it was.

3 One evening, as I was coming home from a baby-sitting job, I cut across the Lus' backyard. Passing their garage, I saw through a little window that the light was on. My curiosity got the better of me, and I peeked in.

> **STOP AND THINK**
>
> **Infer/Predict** Think about what you know about Peter and the narrator. What might Peter's "fantastic machine" be, and how might it affect the plot? As you read, think about your prediction and adjust it as you learn new details.

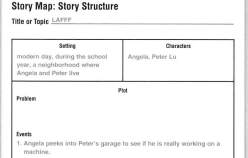

433

STOP AND THINK

 **TARGET STRATEGY**

Infer/Predict

- Tell students that authors do not always state every detail. Remind students that inferring unstated details and using them to predict what might happen next in the text will help them understand the story.

- Have students complete the **Stop and Think** activity on **Student Book p. 433**.

- If students have difficulty using the Infer/Predict strategy, see **Comprehension Intervention** for extra support.

- Display **Projectable 17.3a**. Tell students that a Story Map can help them organize story structure. Model how to fill out the Story Map.

- Have students use **Graphic Organizer 11** to begin their own Story Maps.

COMPREHENSION INTERVENTION

 **TARGET STRATEGY**   **Infer/Predict**

STRATEGY SUPPORT Remind students that inferring details in the text means understanding what the author does not state. Point out that they should predict what might happen based on their inferences. Model the Infer/Predict strategy by reviewing the other kids' reaction to Peter's costume.

Peter dresses up as a mad scientist and from that point, he is known as "Dr. Lu Manchu" to his classmates. Read aloud p. 433. *Ask: How does the narrator feel about Peter's costume? She is surprised he dressed up at all. What can you infer about the narrator's attitude toward Peter? She sees him as not normal but also as impressive and surprising. Predict how this may affect the relationship between Peter and the narrator. They will learn more about each other as the story continues.*

Projectable 17.3a

LAFFF Comprehension Story Structure

Story Map: Story Structure

Title or Topic LAFFF

Setting	Characters
modern day, during the school year, a neighborhood where Angela and Peter live	Angela, Peter Lu

Plot

Problem

Events
1. Angela peeks into Peter's garage to see if he is really working on a machine.

Solution

Develop Comprehension

④ Identify Author's Purpose
Why does the author include details about Peter's strange voice? Sample answer: The author wants to build suspense by having Peter act mysteriously.

⑤ ✓ **TARGET VOCABULARY**
*Why had Peter used his normal voice when he **admitted** the machine's faults? Sample answer: Peter was being truthful, so he used his real voice.*

⑥ Analyze Story Structure
How might this "problem" with the machine be important to the story structure? Sample answer: The problem with the machine only being able to send things forward for a short time might end up becoming a bigger issue once we learn what the main conflict of the story is.

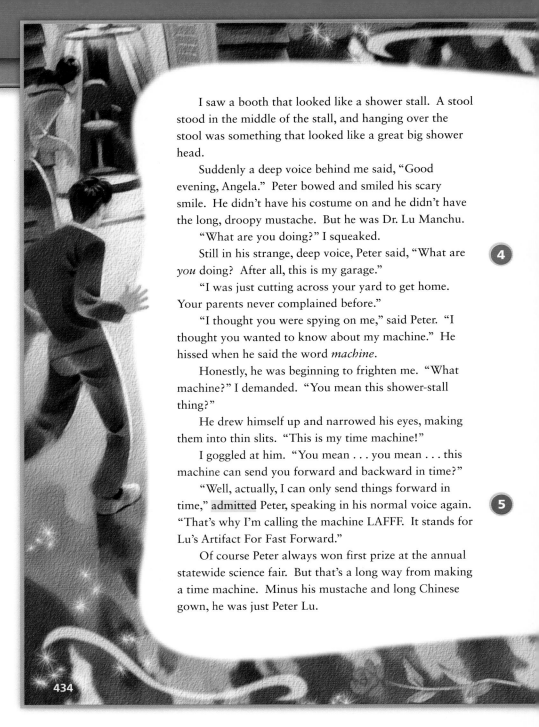

I saw a booth that looked like a shower stall. A stool stood in the middle of the stall, and hanging over the stool was something that looked like a great big shower head.

Suddenly a deep voice behind me said, "Good evening, Angela." Peter bowed and smiled his scary smile. He didn't have his costume on and he didn't have the long, droopy mustache. But he was Dr. Lu Manchu.

"What are you doing?" I squeaked.

Still in his strange, deep voice, Peter said, "What are *you* doing? After all, this is my garage." ④

"I was just cutting across your yard to get home. Your parents never complained before."

"I thought you were spying on me," said Peter. "I thought you wanted to know about my machine." He hissed when he said the word *machine*.

Honestly, he was beginning to frighten me. "What machine?" I demanded. "You mean this shower-stall thing?"

He drew himself up and narrowed his eyes, making them into thin slits. "This is my time machine!"

I goggled at him. "You mean . . . you mean . . . this machine can send you forward and backward in time?"

"Well, actually, I can only send things forward in time," admitted Peter, speaking in his normal voice again. "That's why I'm calling the machine LAFFF. It stands for Lu's Artifact For Fast Forward." ⑤

Of course Peter always won first prize at the annual statewide science fair. But that's a long way from making a time machine. Minus his mustache and long Chinese gown, he was just Peter Lu.

434

ELL ENGLISH LANGUAGE LEARNERS

Scaffold

Beginning For each question, accept one-word responses and expand student responses into sentences. Have students repeat the expanded sentences.

Advanced Have students respond to the questions in complete sentences. Provide corrective feedback as needed.

Intermediate Provide part of a response for each question and have students say the complete response and confirm their understanding.

Advanced High Have students tell how they know the answer to each question based on details from the story.

See ELL Lesson 17, pp. E12–E21, for scaffolded support.

"I don't believe it!" I said. "I bet LAFFF is only good for a laugh."

"Okay, Angela. I'll show you!" hissed Peter.

He sat down on the stool and twisted a dial. I heard some *bleeps*, *cheeps*, and *gurgles*. Peter disappeared.

He must have done it with mirrors. I looked around the garage. I peeked under the tool bench. There was no sign of him.

"Okay, I give up," I told him. "It's a good trick, Peter. You can come out now."

Bleep, *cheep*, and *gurgle* went the machine, and there was Peter sitting on the stool. He held a red rose in his hand. "What do you think of that?"

I blinked. "So you produced a flower. Maybe you had it under the stool."

"Roses bloom in June, right?" he demanded.

That was true. And this was December.

"I sent myself forward in time to June when the flowers were blooming," said Peter. "And I picked the rose from our yard. Convinced, Angela?"

It was too hard to swallow. "You said you couldn't send things back in time," I objected. "So how did you bring the rose back?"

But even as I spoke I saw that his hands were empty. The rose was gone.

6

"That's one of the problems with the machine," said Peter. "When I send myself forward, I can't seem to stay there for long. I snap back to my own time after only a minute. Anything I bring with me snaps back to its own time, too. So my rose has gone back to this June."

435

✔ **TARGET STRATEGY**

Infer/Predict

- Remind students that as they read a selection, they should look for text clues that will help them infer the author's meaning or predict what will happen in the future. Details and dialogue, for example, can offer text clues about what might happen next.

- Display **Projectable 17.3a** again and work with students to add to the Story Map. Remind them that a Story Map organizes text clues that will help them make inferences and predictions to better understand the story structure.

- Model inferring details that can be added to the Story Map.

Think Aloud *At first Angela finds it hard to believe that Peter can send himself forward in time. She watches and is not sure, but when she sees that the rose disappears, I can infer that she must be impressed. I predict that Angela will want to use the time machine.*

- Have students continue to add details to the Story Map.

Develop Comprehension

7 ## Infer Character Motives
Why does Peter not want anyone to know about LAFFF until he has gotten it just right? Sample answer: Peter seems like a person who takes pride in getting things right. He probably only wants to show his work if he has it right.

8 ## Character Traits
How does Angela feel about the usefulness of LAFFF? Sample answer: She doesn't think it's very useful even though it can go into the future. She wants to determine how she can put it to use for herself.

9 ## Draw Conclusions
What do you think is the importance of the writing contest? Sample answer: Angela wants to impress her parents, but she doesn't think she can win the contest.

I was finally convinced, and I began to see possibilities. "Wow, just think: If I don't want to do the dishes, I can send myself forward to the time when the dishes are already done."

"That won't do you much good," said Peter. "You'd soon pop back to the time when the dishes were still dirty."

Too bad. "There must be something your machine is good for," I said. Then I had another idea. "Hey, you can bring me back a piece of fudge from the future, and I can eat it twice: once now, and again in the future."

"Yes, but the fudge wouldn't stay in your stomach," said Peter. "It would go back to the future."

"That's even better!" I said. "I can enjoy eating the fudge over and over again without getting fat!"

It was late, and I had to go home before my parents started to worry. Before I left, Peter said, "Look, Angela, there's still a lot of work to do on LAFFF. Please don't tell anybody about the machine until I've got it right."

A few days later I asked him how he was doing.

"I can stay in the future time a bit longer now," he said. "Once I got it up to four minutes."

"Is that enough time to bring me back some fudge from the future?" I asked.

"We don't keep many sweets around the house," he said. "But I'll see what I can do."

A few minutes later, he came back with a spring roll for me. "My mother was frying these in the kitchen, and I snatched one while she wasn't looking."

7

436

I bit into the hot, crunchy spring roll, but before I finished chewing, it disappeared. The taste of soy sauce, green onions, and bean sprouts stayed a little longer in my mouth, though.

8 It was fun to play around with LAFFF, but it wasn't really useful. I didn't know what a great help it would turn out to be.

Every year our school held a writing contest, and the winning story for each grade got printed in our school magazine. I wanted desperately to win. I worked awfully hard in school, but my parents still thought I could do better.

9 Winning the writing contest would show my parents that I was really good in something. I love writing stories, and I have lots of ideas. But when I actually write them down, my stories never turn out as good as I thought. I just can't seem to find the right words, because English isn't my first language.

I got an honorable mention last year, but it wasn't the same as winning and showing my parents my name, Angela Tang, printed in the school magazine.

The deadline for the contest was getting close, and I had a pile of stories written, but none of them looked like a winner.

Then, the day before the deadline, *boing*, a brilliant idea hit me.

I thought of Peter and his LAFFF machine.

I rushed over to the Lus' garage and, just as I had hoped, Peter was there, tinkering with his machine.

STOP AND THINK

Author's Craft When authors use words, such as *buzz* or *clang*, that sound like the noises they describe, it is called **onomatopoeia**. Where has the author used onomatopoeia on this page and how does it help the story?

437

STOP AND THINK
Author's Craft: Onomatopoeia

- Explain to students that onomatopoeia is a literary device that authors use to mimic noises. Authors purposely choose words that sound like the noises they describe.

- Point out that authors may use onomatopoeia to help readers visualize something in a story.

- Have students brainstorm words that sound like the noise they describe.

- Model the **Stop and Think** activity on **Student Book p. 437**.

Think Aloud *Examples of onomatopoeia might include the words "buzz" and "clang." Both of these words sound like the noises they describe. An author might use "buzz" to describe bees rushing by, which makes the reader hear the noise in his or her mind.*

- Have students answer the **Stop and Think** question.

- Remind students to continue working on their Story Maps.

CROSS-CURRICULAR CONNECTION

Social Studies

Tell students that there are many references to culture in this story. Remind students that the United States has many people who have come from other countries that still observe their culture's traditions.

What references to Chinese culture do you find in the story? Peter's mother makes spring rolls, a Chinese food.

How can you tell that Peter and Angela observe American traditions? Sample answer: Angela and Peter dress up for Halloween, which is a tradition observed by many young Americans.

Have students use the Internet to research other Chinese traditions that are observed in the United States. Tell them to write a summary of their findings.

Develop Comprehension

10 ## Draw Conclusions

Explain whether you think Angela's decision to go forward in time to find the winning story is a good idea. Sample answer: It's a bad idea because she might get stuck in the future.

11 ✔ **TARGET VOCABULARY**

At what point in the future is Angela's **destination***? Sample answer: Angela wants to go three weeks into the future, when the winning essay is already chosen.*

12 ## Understanding Characters

Explain what you think is most likely to happen if Angela meets her future self in her room. Why? Sample answer: The future Angela would not be surprised because she would remember that she went forward in time. Maybe she would help herself by telling her earlier self who wrote the winning story.

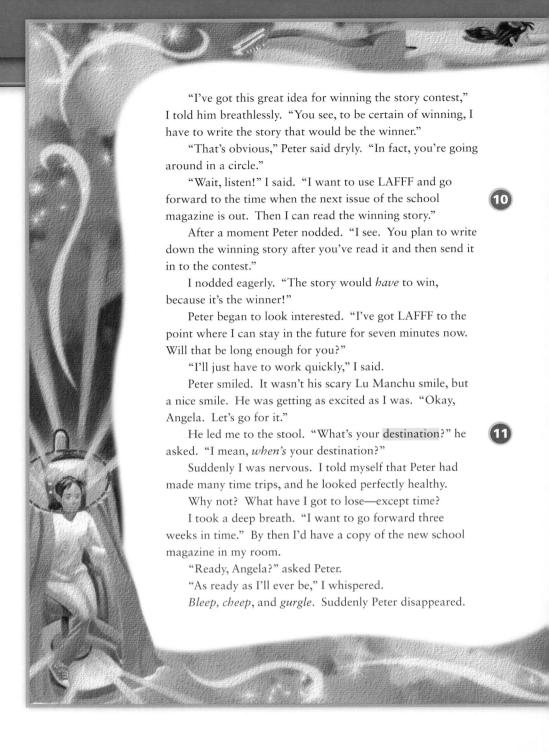

"I've got this great idea for winning the story contest," I told him breathlessly. "You see, to be certain of winning, I have to write the story that would be the winner."

"That's obvious," Peter said dryly. "In fact, you're going around in a circle."

"Wait, listen!" I said. "I want to use LAFFF and go forward to the time when the next issue of the school magazine is out. Then I can read the winning story." **10**

After a moment Peter nodded. "I see. You plan to write down the winning story after you've read it and then send it in to the contest."

I nodded eagerly. "The story would *have* to win, because it's the winner!"

Peter began to look interested. "I've got LAFFF to the point where I can stay in the future for seven minutes now. Will that be long enough for you?"

"I'll just have to work quickly," I said.

Peter smiled. It wasn't his scary Lu Manchu smile, but a nice smile. He was getting as excited as I was. "Okay, Angela. Let's go for it."

He led me to the stool. "What's your destination?" he asked. "I mean, *when's* your destination?" **11**

Suddenly I was nervous. I told myself that Peter had made many time trips, and he looked perfectly healthy.

Why not? What have I got to lose—except time?

I took a deep breath. "I want to go forward three weeks in time." By then I'd have a copy of the new school magazine in my room.

"Ready, Angela?" asked Peter.

"As ready as I'll ever be," I whispered.

Bleep, cheep, and *gurgle*. Suddenly Peter disappeared.

Whole Group

During Reading

What went wrong? Did Peter get sent by mistake, instead of me?

Then I realized what had happened. Three weeks later in time Peter might be somewhere else. No wonder I couldn't see him.

There was no time to be lost. Rushing out of Peter's garage, I ran over to our house and entered through the back door.

Mother was in the kitchen. When she saw me, she stared.

"Angela! I thought you were upstairs taking a shower!"

"Sorry!" I panted. "No time to talk!"

12 I dashed up to my room. Then I suddenly had a strange idea. What if I met *myself* in my room? Argh! It was a spooky thought.

There was nobody in my room. Where was I? I mean, where was the I of three weeks later?

Wait. Mother had just said she thought I was taking a shower. Down the hall, I could hear the water running in the bathroom. Okay. That meant I wouldn't run into me for a while.

I went to the shelf above my desk and frantically pawed through the junk piled there. I found it! I found the latest issue of the school magazine, the one with the winning stories printed in it.

How much time had passed? Better hurry.

439

Practice Fluency

Intonation Read aloud the first two paragraphs on **Student Book p. 439** as students follow along.

- Tell students that when sudden things happen in stories, good readers change their intonation, or the tone of their voice, to let listeners know something has changed.

- Point out to students that words and punctuation marks in text can signal places to change their tone as they read.

- Have students echo-read each sentence of the first two paragraphs after you read them. Tell them to mimic your intonation as they read.

See **p. T114** for a complete fluency lesson on reading with intonation.

Main Selection (SB p. 439) • **T101**

Develop Comprehension

13 ✔ **TARGET VOCABULARY**

*Why might Peter not be acting like his usual **collected** self? Sample answer: He's excited that someone else has used his machine.*

14 **Character Traits**

Based on the story so far, how do you think Angela feels about herself as a writer? Sample answer: She doesn't think she is good enough to win the contest on her own.

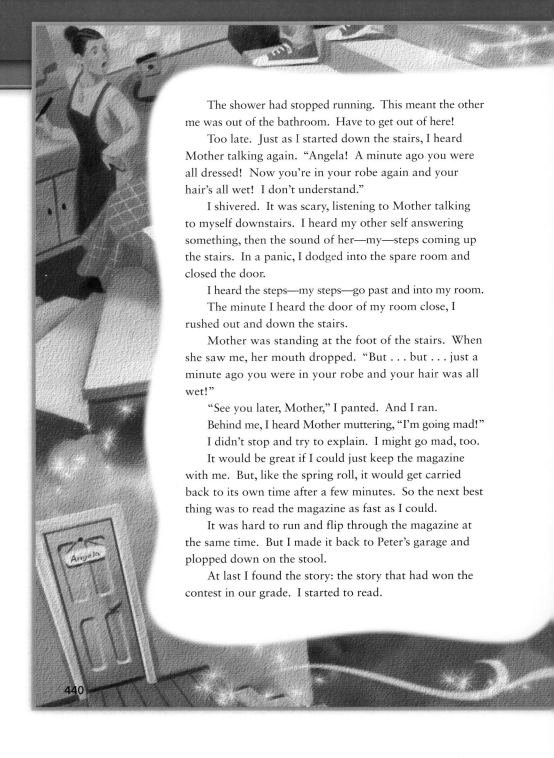

The shower had stopped running. This meant the other me was out of the bathroom. Have to get out of here!

Too late. Just as I started down the stairs, I heard Mother talking again. "Angela! A minute ago you were all dressed! Now you're in your robe again and your hair's all wet! I don't understand."

I shivered. It was scary, listening to Mother talking to myself downstairs. I heard my other self answering something, then the sound of her—my—steps coming up the stairs. In a panic, I dodged into the spare room and closed the door.

I heard the steps—my steps—go past and into my room.

The minute I heard the door of my room close, I rushed out and down the stairs.

Mother was standing at the foot of the stairs. When she saw me, her mouth dropped. "But . . . but . . . just a minute ago you were in your robe and your hair was all wet!"

"See you later, Mother," I panted. And I ran.

Behind me, I heard Mother muttering, "I'm going mad!"

I didn't stop and try to explain. I might go mad, too.

It would be great if I could just keep the magazine with me. But, like the spring roll, it would get carried back to its own time after a few minutes. So the next best thing was to read the magazine as fast as I could.

It was hard to run and flip through the magazine at the same time. But I made it back to Peter's garage and plopped down on the stool.

At last I found the story: the story that had won the contest in our grade. I started to read.

440

Suddenly I heard *bleep*, *cheep*, and *gurgle*, and Peter loomed up in front of me. I was back in my original time again.

But I still had the magazine! Now I had to read the story before the magazine popped back to the future. It was hard to concentrate with Peter jumping up and down impatiently, so different from his usual calm, collected self. **13**

I read a few paragraphs, and I was beginning to see how the story would shape up. But before I got any further, the magazine disappeared from my hand.

So I didn't finish reading the story. I didn't reach the end, where the name of the winning writer was printed.

That night I stayed up very late to write down what I remembered of the story. It had a neat plot, and I could see why it was the winner.

I hadn't read the entire story, so I had to make up the ending myself. But that was okay, since I knew how it should come out. **14**

> ✔ **STOP AND THINK**
> **Story Structure** Setting, where the story happens, is often an important part of a story's structure. How does the setting make Angela's trip to the future exciting and funny?

441

STOP AND THINK

✔ **TARGET SKILL**

Story Structure

- Remind students that paying close attention to the setting, or the time and place, will help them understand the sequence of events in a story. Point out that they should also pay attention to the conflict of the story and how the characters solve it.

- Have students answer the **Stop and Think** question on **Student Book p. 441**.

- If students have difficulty identifying elements of the story's structure, see **Comprehension Intervention** for extra support.

- Have students continue filling in their graphic organizers. Display **Projectable 17.3b** and work with students to add to the Story Map.

COMPREHENSION INTERVENTION

✔ **TARGET SKILL**   **Story Structure**

SKILL SUPPORT Remind students that the main elements of a story are characters, setting, and plot, which includes the conflict and the way it is solved. Model using story structure to understand the story.

One conflict in the story is that the narrator wants to win the story contest, and her plan to solve this problem is to use LAFFF to travel to the future to read the winning story. In real life, time travel is not possible, so her solution is exciting and funny as she deals with other challenges presented by traveling to the future.

Read aloud **p. 440.** Ask students to pay close attention as they listen to understand what happens. Ask how time travel affects the story structure. *The narrator's solution to her problem—traveling to the future—causes further problems that she must solve.*

Projectable 17.3b

LAFFF Comprehension Story Structure

Story Map: Story Structure
Title or Topic LAFFF

Setting	Characters
modern day, during the school year, a neighborhood where Angela and Peter live	Angela, Peter Lu

Plot	

Problem
1. Angela wants to win her school's writing contest.

Events
1. Angela peeks into Peter's garage to see if he's really working on a machine.
2. Angela discovers the time machine, and Peter proves that it works.

Solution

Comprehension
© Houghton Mifflin Harcourt Publishing Company. All rights reserved.

Grade 5, Unit 4: What's Your Story?

Develop Comprehension

15 ✔ **TARGET VOCABULARY**

Why might Angela feel **suspense** *as she waits? Sample answer: She is anxious to know who won because she used the time machine to help her win.*

16 **Character's Motives**

Why doesn't Angela feel good about winning? Sample answer: She feels like she has cheated to win.

17 ✔ **TARGET VOCABULARY**

What **compliment** *does Peter give to Angela? Sample answer: He says that he likes Angela's original stories.*

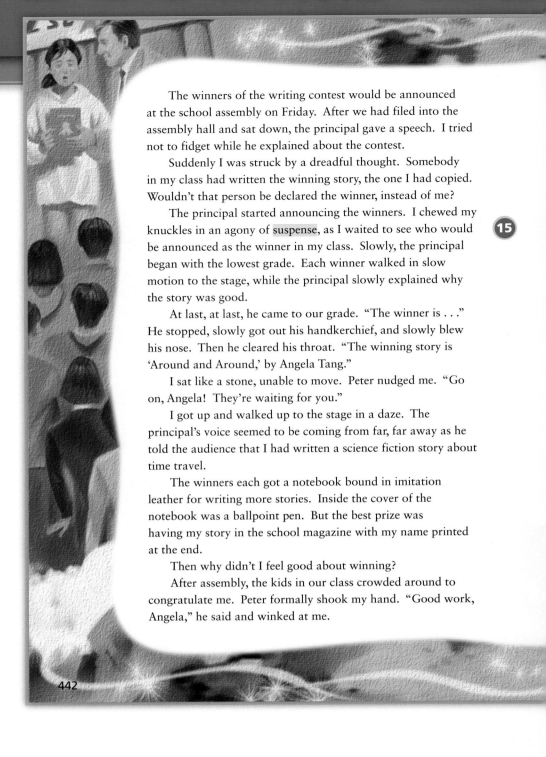

The winners of the writing contest would be announced at the school assembly on Friday. After we had filed into the assembly hall and sat down, the principal gave a speech. I tried not to fidget while he explained about the contest.

Suddenly I was struck by a dreadful thought. Somebody in my class had written the winning story, the one I had copied. Wouldn't that person be declared the winner, instead of me?

The principal started announcing the winners. I chewed my knuckles in an agony of suspense, as I waited to see who would be announced as the winner in my class. Slowly, the principal began with the lowest grade. Each winner walked in slow motion to the stage, while the principal slowly explained why the story was good. **15**

At last, at last, he came to our grade. "The winner is . . ." He stopped, slowly got out his handkerchief, and slowly blew his nose. Then he cleared his throat. "The winning story is 'Around and Around,' by Angela Tang."

I sat like a stone, unable to move. Peter nudged me. "Go on, Angela! They're waiting for you."

I got up and walked up to the stage in a daze. The principal's voice seemed to be coming from far, far away as he told the audience that I had written a science fiction story about time travel.

The winners each got a notebook bound in imitation leather for writing more stories. Inside the cover of the notebook was a ballpoint pen. But the best prize was having my story in the school magazine with my name printed at the end.

Then why didn't I feel good about winning?

After assembly, the kids in our class crowded around to congratulate me. Peter formally shook my hand. "Good work, Angela," he said and winked at me.

442

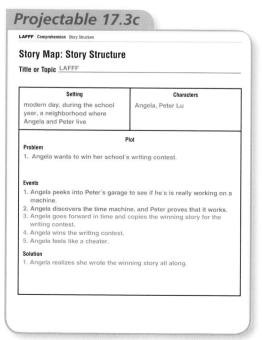

16 That didn't make me feel any better. I hadn't won the contest fairly. Instead of writing the story myself, I had copied it from the school magazine.

That meant someone in our class—one of the kids here—had actually written the story. Who was it?

My heart was knocking against my ribs as I stood there and waited for someone to complain that I had stolen his story.

Nobody did.

As we were riding the school bus home, Peter looked at me. "You don't seem very happy about winning the contest, Angela."

"No, I'm not," I mumbled. "I feel just awful."

"Tell you what," suggested Peter. "Come over to my house and we'll discuss it."

"What is there to discuss?" I asked glumly. "I won the contest because I cheated."

"Come on over, anyway. My mother bought a fresh package of humbow in Chinatown."

I couldn't turn down that invitation. Humbow, a roll stuffed with barbecued pork, is my favorite snack.

Peter's mother came into the kitchen while we were munching, and he told her about the contest.

Mrs. Lu looked pleased. "I'm very glad, Angela. You have a terrific imagination, and you deserve to win."

"I like Angela's stories," said Peter. "They're original."

17 It was the first compliment he had ever paid me, and I felt my face turning red.

After Mrs. Lu left us, Peter and I each had another humbow. But I was still miserable. "I wish I had never started this. I feel like such a jerk."

Peter looked at me, and I swear he was enjoying himself. "If you stole another student's story, why didn't that person complain?"

"I don't know!" I wailed.

443

Story Structure

- Display **Projectable 17.3c** and work with students to add events that lead to the conflict's resolution to the Story Map. Then have students add the solution to the graphic organizer.

? Essential Question

Display the following: *When the contest winner is announced, Angela doesn't feel good about winning. She knows she didn't win fairly.* Discuss the new problem and compare it to the main conflict Angela faces in the story.

Projectable 17.3c

LAFFF | Comprehension Story Structure

Story Map: Story Structure

Title or Topic LAFFF

Setting	Characters
modern day, during the school year, a neighborhood where Angela and Peter live	Angela, Peter Lu

Plot

Problem

1. Angela wants to win her school's writing contest.

Events

1. Angela peeks into Peter's garage to see if he's is really working on a machine.
2. Angela discovers the time machine, and Peter proves that it works.
3. Angela goes forward in time and copies the winning story for the writing contest.
4. Angela wins the writing contest.
5. Angela feels like a cheater.

Solution

1. Angela realizes she wrote the winning story all along.

Develop Comprehension

18 **Understanding Characters**

How is Angela's definition of smart different from Peter's? Which definition do you think is most accurate? Sample answer: Angela thinks being smart means getting good grades and winning contests. Peter thinks that a good imagination can make someone smart. I think they are both right.

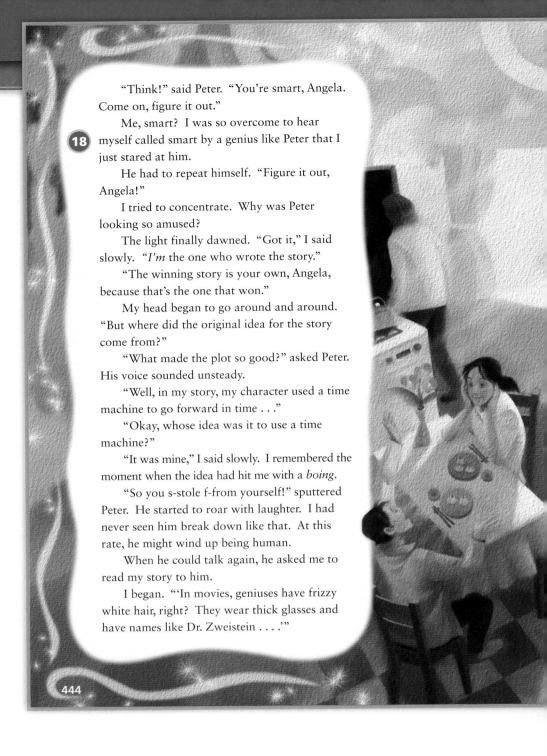

"Think!" said Peter. "You're smart, Angela. Come on, figure it out."

18 Me, smart? I was so overcome to hear myself called smart by a genius like Peter that I just stared at him.

He had to repeat himself. "Figure it out, Angela!"

I tried to concentrate. Why was Peter looking so amused?

The light finally dawned. "Got it," I said slowly. "*I'm* the one who wrote the story."

"The winning story is your own, Angela, because that's the one that won."

My head began to go around and around. "But where did the original idea for the story come from?"

"What made the plot so good?" asked Peter. His voice sounded unsteady.

"Well, in my story, my character used a time machine to go forward in time . . ."

"Okay, whose idea was it to use a time machine?"

"It was mine," I said slowly. I remembered the moment when the idea had hit me with a *boing*.

"So you s-stole f-from yourself!" sputtered Peter. He started to roar with laughter. I had never seen him break down like that. At this rate, he might wind up being human.

When he could talk again, he asked me to read my story to him.

I began. "'In movies, geniuses have frizzy white hair, right? They wear thick glasses and have names like Dr. Zweistein . . . .'"

444

Your Turn

Future Plans

Short Response Angela uses Peter's time machine to read the story that won the writing contest. What if you were able to travel into the future? Think about your goal and purpose. Write a paragraph that describes how far forward in time you would choose to go and what you would do when you got there. PERSONAL RESPONSE

Imagine the Future

Drawing Tomorrow Imagine what your classroom might look like in 100 years. How do you think important subjects such as reading, math, science, and social studies might be taught? With a partner, illustrate and label the classroom setting, showing changes in technology and other features that would make learning fun and exciting. PARTNERS

Time Travel

 Turn and Talk Think about how the plot of the story unfolds after Angela uses Peter's time machine to travel three weeks into the future. Discuss with a partner how the time machine affects Peter's and Angela's lives. STORY STRUCTURE

445

Retelling Rubric

4	Excellent	Students **clearly describe all important story events** in order and explain how each event leads to the next.
3	Good	Students **describe most important story events** in order and explain how some events lead to others.
2	Fair	Students **describe a few story events** and **demonstrate a limited understanding** of how events are related.
1	Unsatisfactory	Students **cannot identify important story events.**

Your Turn

Have students complete the activities on **Student Book page 445**.

Future Plans Have students brainstorm ideas before they write. Ask: *What specific times in the future do you wish you could know about? What could you learn about the future that would help you now? Is there something that you could help someone else with by traveling into the future and back?*

PERSONAL RESPONSE

Imagine the Future Tell students to think about their activities during a typical school day. Have them consider what parts of the classroom are used for these activities and how those objects and elements of a classroom might change over 100 years. PARTNERS

Time Travel Have partners review the selection to find details about how Peter and Angela use the time machine. If students have trouble describing the ways the machine affects the characters' lives, encourage them to fill out an Inference Map with events from that part of the story. STORY STRUCTURE

Oral Language Have partners retell "LAFFF." Have them use the illustrations to identify important details and the sequence of events. Also have students discuss how each story event leads to the next. Tell them to think about the experiences Angela and Peter share. Then have small groups discuss how Angela and Peter's relationship changes as they work to help Angela win the writing contest. Tell groups to allow each person to speak and then take turns asking questions about what others said. Use the Retelling Rubric at the left to evaluate students' responses.

Connect to Science

PREVIEW THE INFORMATIONAL TEXT

- Tell students that this selection is a magazine article that gives facts and examples about the imagination of science fiction authors and the genre's relationship to the future. Ask students to read the title, headings, and captions, and to preview the photographs and illustrations on pages 446–448. Then have students read the informational text independently.

DISCUSS PHOTOGRAPHS AND ILLUSTRATIONS

- Tell students that photographs and illustrations work with the text to present the information.

- Point out that most photographs and illustrations have captions that briefly explain the image being presented.

- Photographs and illustrations can help clarify facts and examples presented in articles and may also provide additional information not found in the text.

photographs	present accurate images that relate to the topic of a magazine article
illustrations	show an artist's rendering of ideas and concepts

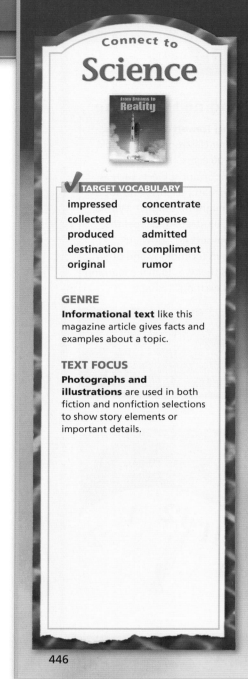

Connect to Science

✓ **TARGET VOCABULARY**

impressed	concentrate
collected	suspense
produced	admitted
destination	compliment
original	rumor

GENRE

Informational text like this magazine article gives facts and examples about a topic.

TEXT FOCUS

Photographs and illustrations are used in both fiction and nonfiction selections to show story elements or important details.

446

from Dreams to Reality

Sci Fi Authors Predict the Future

Long ago, computers, fax machines, and satellites seemed impossible. There was not a hint or a rumor that they could ever be a part of our lives. Yet now we use them every day. ①
They were first dreamed up not by engineers, but by science fiction writers. Jules Verne was a writer who could concentrate on amazing ideas. In 1863, he published an early science fiction book, *Five Weeks in a Balloon*. Since then, people have been impressed by how the genre can predict the future. Many predictions, like time travel, are not possible in the real world. But sometimes machines first dreamed up by writers *do* become real.

In this drawing from Verne's *From the Earth to the Moon*, a crowd watches in suspense as the space capsule is prepared to take off.

ELL ENGLISH LANGUAGE LEARNERS

Scaffold

Beginning Discuss with students the meaning of *science fiction* and the illustration on page 446. Explain that the term *sci fi* is an abbreviation, or shortened form, of *science fiction*.

Intermediate Work with students to brainstorm a list of words, concepts, and phrases associated with science fiction and fantasy. Demonstrate how to use each in a sentence.

Advanced Ask students simple questions about the genre of science fiction and its relationship to the future. Discuss with students their responses, and clarify understanding.

Advanced High Have partners use evidence from the text to answer this question: *How do Jules Verne's ideas about space travel in 1864 compare with space travel today?*

See ELL Lesson 17, pp. E12–E21, for scaffolded support.

Manned Flight to the Moon

Verne was a master at predicting what lay ahead. In 1864, he wrote *From the Earth to the Moon.* The book tells about a flight to the moon. This was 105 years before the first manned mission to the moon reached its destination.

Verne's mission has a three-man team. That's the same number used in real moon landings. His space travelers are sent from Florida. NASA sends astronauts into space from there, too. The size of Verne's space capsule is also very close to that of the real Apollo spacecraft. ②

Not all the ideas that Verne produced are true. His space capsule is shot from a cannon. Today, rocket engines propel modern spacecraft.

A *Saturn V* rocket blasts off for the moon. On July 20, 1969, the world watched *Apollo 11* astronaut Neil Armstrong step onto the moon's surface. They heard him say in a collected voice, "That's one small step for a man, one giant leap for mankind."

447

Practice Fluency

Intonation Have students listen as you read aloud the first paragraph on **Student Book p. 446.**

- Remind students that good readers read aloud with an intonation that matches the tone of the selection, and vary their intonation to keep the interest of their listeners.

- Have students partner read each sentence aloud. Remind them to use appropriate intonation and to vary their intonation to match what's happening in each sentence.

JOURNEYS DIGITAL | **Powered by** DESTINATIONReading®
Student eBook: Read and Listen

TARGET VOCABULARY REVIEW

 **TARGET VOCABULARY** Vocabulary in Context Cards – Pantomime

Ask pairs of students to take turns using gestures and movements to pantomime each Target Vocabulary word. Have students guess the correct word. Ask them to use the word in a sentence, such as *I am impressed.* As the game progresses, ask students to use longer sentences, such as *I am impressed by the skill you showed in chess today.*

CONTEXT CARDS

front   back

Develop Comprehension

Reread the selection with students. Pause at the stopping points to ask students the following questions.

1 ✔ **TARGET VOCABULARY**

What clue does the author give in the following sentence that helps you understand the meaning of **rumor***? "There was not a hint or a* **rumor** *that they could ever be a part of our lives." The word hint helps us understand the meaning of rumor.*

2 Author's Purpose

Why do you think the author included information about NASA's space mission? Sample answer: The author uses the information to compare Verne's sci-fi story about space travel with NASA's actual mission 105 years later.

3 Make Inferences

Why do you think science fiction authors sometimes create stories that become reality? Sample answer: Science fiction authors use their imaginations to figure out what things might be like in the future.

INTERPRET PHOTOGRAPHS AND ILLUSTRATIONS

- Tell students that the illustrations and photographs in this selection clarify the ideas introduced by the author.

- Model the thinking.

Think Aloud *By looking at the illustration and photograph on pp. 446–447, I can see that Verne's space capsule looks similar to NASA's.*

These robots working in a car plant don't look much like the original fictional ones.

Robots

The word *robot* first entered our language through a play, not a laboratory. Czech writer Karel Čapek used the word in his 1921 play, *R.U.R.: Rossum's Universal Robots.* In the play, robots look like humans and are used for cheap labor. Fifty years later real labor-saving robots would be putting together manufactured goods in factories.

Not everyone is a fan of science fiction. But most people have admitted that these writers seem to see the future. It is a compliment to the power of imagination that so many sci-fi dreams do become true. The next time you read science fiction, remember, you *may* be reading about your future.

3

Karel Čapek's imaginary robots looked like humans.

448

Weekly Internet Challenge

Using Links

- Review Internet Strategy, Step 2: Search and Predict.
- Review the different URL endings, such as *.org, .edu,* and *.com.* Point out that reliable sites will most likely end with *.org, .edu,* or *.gov.*
- Explain that good researchers search and predict which sites will be worth exploring in order to save time and to ensure accurate information.

INTERNET STRATEGY

1. **Plan a Search** by identifying what you are looking for and how to find it.

2. **Search and Predict** which sites will be worth exploring.

3. **Navigate** a site to see how to get around it and what it contains.

4. **Analyze and Evaluate** the quality and reliability of the information.

5. **Synthesize** the information from multiple sites.

Making Connections

Making Connections

Text to Self

Describe a Talent In "LAFFF," Angela has a talent for writing. Think of something you are good at. Write a paragraph describing a time when you got to show off that talent to others. Describe how you felt as you displayed your talent.

Text to Text

Compare and Contrast Science Fiction In "Lunch Money," Greg plans to write a comic book set in the future. Compare Greg's science fiction ideas to those in Lensey Namioka's story "LAFFF." How are they alike? How are they different? Use examples from both texts to support your response.

Text to World

Research Technology With a partner, review the photographs, illustrations, and captions in "From Dreams to Reality." Use print sources or the Internet to find three additional facts about the United States space program or the car-making industry discussed in the captions. Create a timeline using all your information.

449

Text to Self

Students may need help thinking of ways in which they are talented. Remind them that there are different talents that people can have. They may be talented academically, physically, or artistically. Remind students that leadership is another type of talent.

Text to Text

To help students identify similarities and differences between Greg's science fiction ideas and Lensey Namioka's story, have them create a Venn diagram to compare and contrast the ideas.

Text to World

Have students use information in photographs, illustrations, and captions to get ideas about facts to research. For example, the photograph and caption on **p. 448** are about robots in a car plant. The students might research which auto manufacturer first used robots.

"From Dreams to Reality" Challenge

- Ask students to search for sites that would give additional information about science fiction authors. Have them predict what information could be found at each site.

- Have students make a list of questions about each author that they would like to find answers to.

- Have students review and compare the information located on the various sites. Discuss what can be found on an encyclopedia site compared to a website created by the author or the author's fans.

Deepen Comprehension

SHARE OBJECTIVES

- Explore events from the story to analyze plot development.
- Make inferences about story elements.

SKILL TRACE

Story Structure

Introduce	T90–T91
Differentiate	T138–T139
Reteach	T146
Review	**T112–T113**
Test	Weekly Tests, Lesson 17

ELL ENGLISH LANGUAGE LEARNERS

Scaffold

Beginning Review with students that the conflict of a story is the main problem the character faces. Work with them to answer simple questions about the conflict, such as: *What does Angela want to win? Does she think she can win?*

Intermediate Review *conflict* with students. Provide the questions above and have students complete them orally as you discuss with them the conflict in the story.

Advanced Read aloud pp. 436–437. Have partners identify the conflict and the important events that follow. Then have them predict how the conflict will be resolved.

Advanced High Have partners identify the characters' problems and the events that lead to their resolutions.

See ELL Lesson 17, pp. E12–E21, for scaffolded support.

 Analyze Story Structure

1 Teach/Model

 Academic Language

plot, resolution, story structure

- Remind students that the **plot** is the story's events, including the conflict, or problem, and its **resolution**, or solution. The **story's structure** includes the plot, characters, and setting.

- Point out to students that some conflicts in a story are not as obvious as others. Making inferences and predictions can help readers analyze story elements and understand how they interact.

- Display **Projectable 17.4** and discuss **Deepen Comprehension Question 1.**

- Remind students that a Story Map can help students analyze story structure.

- Model completing the Story Map to answer the question.

> **Think Aloud** *The narrator writes that she works hard in school. She compares her grades to Peter's, who does very well in school. I think that this will be a problem for her since she seems to worry about her grades. I'll write this detail in the Problem section of the Story Map.*

Projectable 17.4

LAFFF | Deepen Comprehension | Analyze Story Structure

Story Map: Analyze Story Structure

Deepen Comprehension Question 1
What is the conflict that Angela has with herself at the beginning of the story? What makes it worse? Support your answer with details from *LAFFF.* p. 432

Setting	
Angela's neighborhood; Peter's garage	

Problem: Angela doesn't feel she does well enough in school. She feels she can never be as smart as Peter.
Events:

Solution: Her parents push her to do well.

Deepen Comprehension Question 2
What problem does Angela face with the writing contest? How does she solve it? Support your answer with details from the story. p. 438

Setting	
Angela's neighborhood; Peter's garage	

Problem: Angela doesn't feel she does well enough in school. She feels she can never be as smart as Peter.
Events: Angela wants to win the writing contest.
Angela goes ahead in time in Peter's time machine to read the winning story.
She does not get to finish the story to see how it ends or who wrote it.
Solution: Her parents push her to do well.

Deepen Comprehension Question 3
What conflict does Angela struggle with at the end of the story? What should you infer about the ending in order to know that this conflict has been resolved? Support your answer with details from *LAFFF.* p. 444

2 Guided Practice

- Reread with students **Student Book p. 438** of "LAFFF." Discuss with them what Angela means when she says, "The story would *have* to win because it's the winner."

- Read and discuss **Deepen Comprehension Question 2** on **Projectable 17.4**. Use these prompts to guide students:

- *Why is the writing contest important to Angela?* She wants to win so she can show her parents that she does well in school.

- *What idea does Angela have to help her win the contest?* She wants to use Peter's machine to go into the future to see the winning story.

- *How does her idea solve her problem?* She can see the winning story so she'll know what she has to write to win.

- Guide students to complete the Story Map for Question 2.

3 Apply

Turn and Talk Have students reread **Student Book pp. 443–444** of "LAFFF." Then have partners make a Story Map and work together to discuss and complete **Deepen Comprehension Question 3** on **Projectable 17.4**.

EXTEND DISCUSSION Remind students that an important part of a story's structure is the conclusion. Explain to students that the author of "LAFFF" uses a circular ending to show that Angela would have written the winning story anyway. Have students form groups to discuss this question: *How does the ending change your perspective of what came before?* Tell students to give each person in their group a chance to speak and ask any questions they may have about each person's ideas.

Monitor Comprehension

Are students able to analyze the problem and solution in a story?

IF...	THEN...
students have difficulty analyzing story structure,	▶ use the Leveled Reader for **Struggling** Readers, *Robot Rescue*, p. T140.
students can analyze story structure,	▶ use the Leveled Reader for **On-Level** Readers, *The Watch Girl*, p. T141.
students can analyze and make inferences about story structure,	▶ use the Leveled Reader for **Advanced** Readers, *Pancakes*, p. T142.

 Use the Leveled Reader for **English Language Learners,** *Kendria's Watch*, p. T143. *Group English Language Learners according to language proficiency.*

Practice Book p. 194
See Grab-and-Go™ Resources for additional leveled practice.

Fluency

SHARE OBJECTIVES

- Read aloud with grade-appropriate fluency.
- Adjust intonation to increase fluency and comprehension.

 Intonation

1 Teach/Model

- Tell students that good readers read with the correct intonation. Explain that intonation is the rise and fall of the pitch of your voice. Your intonation should reflect the meaning of what's being read.

- Have students follow along as you read aloud the last seven paragraphs on **Student Book p. 438**. First, read in a flat voice, with no intonation. Then read with expressive intonation. Discuss with students why your second reading is an example of good intonation.

2 Guided Practice

- Read aloud with students the first two paragraphs on **Student Book p. 440**. Read each paragraph sentence by sentence, using the correct intonation.

- Work with students to help them adjust their pitch to read the passage aloud with proper intonation.

- If students are struggling to read with intonation, have them echo-read **Student Book p. 440** with you. Tell them to pay special attention to the rise and fall of their pitch.

- See also **Instructional Routine 5**.

3 Practice/Apply

- Tell students that with practice, they can improve their intonation.

- Have partners take turns reading aloud **Student Book p. 441,** using correct intonation. Listen in to monitor fluency.

- Allow students to read the page three or four times.

Decoding

 Recognizing Common Word Parts

1 Teach/Model

ANALYZE COMMON WORD PARTS Write the word *unrelated* on the board and read it aloud. Have students repeat the word. Point out the prefix *un-* and the inflectional ending *-ed*. Then break the word into syllables, using the word parts as a guide. Then read the word aloud to students: un | re | lat | ed

- Tell students that they should look for familiar word parts in unfamiliar words when trying to decode a word.

- Model how to recognize common word parts in the word *underperforming*. Break the word into word parts: under | perform | ing

- Point out the familiar base word *perform* along with the prefix *under-* and the inflectional ending *-ing*.

- Remind students that after they have identified the word parts, they may have to divide them into syllables to decode the entire word. For example, the prefix *under* and the base word *perform* have a VCCV pattern and should be divided between the consonants.

2 Practice/Apply

DECODE WORDS WITH COMMON WORD PARTS Write the following words on the board: *unrelated, informing, disappearing, immigrated, reposted, mistreated, subfreezing, transplanted.*

- Have students read the words aloud. Review how to identify the prefix, base word, and inflectional ending in the first word step by step. Words parts may need to be divided into syllables.

un | re | lat | ed	in | form | ing
dis | ap | pear | ing	im | mi | grat | ed
re | post | ed	mis | treat | ed
sub | freez | ing	trans | plant | ed

- Have partners work to decode the remaining words.

- Call on students to read the words and identify each prefix, base word, and inflectional ending. Then ask them if any of the word parts should be divided into syllables.

- Use **Corrective Feedback** if students need additional help.

SHARE OBJECTIVES

- Recognize words with common word parts.
- Use common word parts to decode longer words.

Corrective Feedback

If students have difficulty decoding words with common word parts, use the model below.

Correct the error. Divide the word into its parts. *The word is un | relat | ed.*

Model the correct way to decode the word. *This word has a prefix, un-. Its base word is relate. There is also an inflectional ending, -ed. I'll put the sounds of the word parts together, then adjust the sounds.*

Guide students to identify the common word parts. *What is the prefix?* un- *What is the base word?* relate *What is the inflectional ending?* -ed

Check students' understanding. *What is the word?* unrelated

Reinforce Have students repeat the process with the word *misbehaving*.

Vocabulary Strategies

SKILL TRACE

Using Reference Sources	
Introduce	T42–T43, Unit 3
Differentiate	T144–T145
Reteach	T146
▶ Review	**T116–T117; T116–T117, Unit 5**
Test	Weekly Tests, Lesson 17

ELL **ENGLISH LANGUAGE LEARNERS**

Scaffold

Beginning Explain that a dictionary provides information about a word, including its part of speech and meaning. Write *rumor* on the board. Show students the entry for the word in a dictionary. Point out the part of speech and definition.

Intermediate Display the dictionary entry for the word *original*. Point to the part of speech, the date of origin, and the first meaning. Explain that a dictionary can give more than one meaning.

Advanced Explain that a dictionary lists words alphabetically. Ask which word—*hamster* or *hill*—would be listed first in a dictionary.

Advanced High Have students look *concentrate* up in a dictionary and then say how that defintion compares to the one in their textbook's glossary.

See ELL Lesson 17, pp. E12–E21, for scaffolded support.

✓ Using Reference Sources: Dictionary, Glossary, Thesaurus

1 Teach/Model

AL *Academic Language*

dictionary entry the definition, part of speech, origin, pronunciation, and spelling of the entry word

glossary entry information on the words in a specific text, such as a school book, including the definition and pronunciation

thesaurus entry a listing of synonyms and antonyms for a word

---

• Point out that when an entry appears in a dictionary, the part of speech is identified before the word's definition. Parts of speech include nouns, adjectives, verbs, pronouns, and adverbs. The part of speech may be abbreviated; for example, *verb = v*.

• Explain that glossaries function much like dictionaries, but they are specific to a text, such as a textbook. Glossaries contain the meaning of the entry word as it is used in the text, the pronunciation, and sometimes, where it is used in the text.

• Point out that a thesaurus is a resource of synonyms and antonyms. Students can use a thesaurus to add more descriptive words to their writing and to identify words related to the entry word. They can also use a thesaurus to find antonyms for the entry word.

• Write the following on the board: "I concentrate while I play chess." Read the sentence aloud to students.

• Model using reference sources to understand the word *concentrate*.

Think Aloud *I can look up the meaning of* concentrate *in a dictionary. I know that a dictionary also tells me the word's part of speech: a noun, pronoun, verb, adjective, or adverb. The dictionary entry for* concentrate *has a "v." before the definition, so it must be a verb.*

2 | Guided Practice

- Display the top half of **Projectable 17.5** and read "The Famous Dancer" aloud.

- Display the Column Chart at the bottom of **Projectable 17.5**.

- Tell students to imagine that this is a text from their **Student Book**. Where might they find the meanings of words in the text? *(the glossary)* Guide students to fill in the first column.

- Explain that a dictionary or glossary can be used to find the meanings, syllabication, pronunciation, and parts of speech of words. A thesaurus is used to find alternate word choices.

- Complete the Column Chart with students. Work with them to determine when to use a dictionary, glossary, or thesaurus to find information about another unknown word.

Projectable 17.5

LAFFF Vocabulary Strategies Using Reference Sources

Use Reference Sources

The Famous Dancer

I have always wanted to become a famous dancer. My friends often laugh at how seriously I take my dancing. They talk about movies, shopping, and other things I don't care much about. When the subject of dancing comes up, I have a lot to say!

My teacher is helping me get ready for the annual dance competition. I did not take first place last year, but she encouraged me to move forward and try again.

This year's first place prize is a trip to Los Angeles. I have to dress in my favorite costume for the contest. I hope it brings me luck.

Later today I will go the studio to check the dance schedule. I will search the fine print for my name and dance time. I'm already thinking ahead to when I will dance for the judges. I hope the writing on the first place ribbon reads my name. Then off to Los Angeles I'll travel!

Word List
laugh
subject
forward
dress
print
writing
travel

Use a Glossary	Use a Thesaurus	Use a Dictionary
to find the specific meaning of a word within a text	to find synonyms for words; to find a more exact term when writing	to find the meaning, syllabication, pronunciation, and part of speech for a word

3 | Apply

- Have partners create a 4-Column Chart with the following headings: Word, Meaning, Syllabication, Part of Speech. Have them list the words on **Projectable 17.5** in the Word column and use a dictionary to identify the items for each word. Have partners record their answers in the chart. Then have them use the pronunciation feature in a dictionary to say each word aloud. Have students write the words in a sentence using the meaning and part of speech they located in the reference source.

- Have students use a thesaurus to list any possible alternate word choices for each word. Tell them to use an alternate word choice in a sentence.

Monitor Vocabulary Strategies

Are students able to identify and use reference sources?

IF...	THEN...
students have difficulty identifying and using reference sources,	▶ **Differentiate Vocabulary Strategies** for Struggling Readers, p. T144. *See also Intervention Lesson 17, pp. S12–S21.*
students can identify and use reference sources most of the time,	▶ **Differentiate Vocabulary Strategies** for On-Level Readers, p. T144.
students can consistently identify and use reference sources,	▶ **Differentiate Vocabulary Strategies** for Advanced Readers, p. T145.

Differentiate Vocabulary Strategies: pp. T144–T145
Group English Language Learners according to language proficiency.

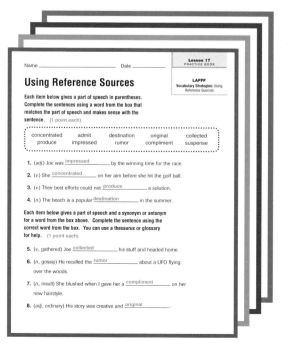

Name _____ Date _____

Lesson 17
PRACTICE BOOK

Using Reference Sources

LAFFF
Vocabulary Strategies: Using Reference Sources

Each item below gives a part of speech in parentheses. Complete the sentences using a word from the box that matches the part of speech and makes sense with the sentence. (1 point each)

concentrated	admit	destination	original	collected
produce	impressed	rumor	compliment	suspense

1. (adj.) Joe was <u>impressed</u> by the winning time for the race.

2. (v.) She <u>concentrated</u> on her aim before she hit the golf ball.

3. (v.) Their best efforts could not <u>produce</u> a solution.

4. (n.) The beach is a popular <u>destination</u> in the summer.

Each item below gives a part of speech and a synonym or antonym for a word from the box above. Complete the sentence using the correct word from the box. You can use a thesaurus or glossary for help. (1 point each)

5. (v., gathered) Joe <u>collected</u> his stuff and headed home.

6. (n., gossip) He recalled the <u>rumor</u> about a UFO flying over the woods.

7. (n., insult) She blushed when I gave her a <u>compliment</u> on her new hairstyle.

8. (adj., ordinary) His story was creative and <u>original</u>.

Practice Book p. 195
See Grab-and-Go™ Resources for additional leveled practice.

Connect and Extend

SHARE OBJECTIVES

- Make connections across texts.
- Read independently for a sustained period of time.
- Identify source information.
- Prepare an oral summary.

"LAFFF"   **"From Dreams to Reality"**

Vocabulary Reader

Struggling Readers   **On-Level Readers**

Advanced Readers   **English Language Learners**

Read to Connect

SHARE AND COMPARE TEXTS Have students compare and contrast this week's reading selections. Use the following prompts to guide the discussion:

- What role does the future play in both selections?
- Using evidence from the selections you have read this week, support or challenge the idea that it is possible to predict the future.

CONNECT TEXT TO WORLD Use these prompts to help deepen student thinking and discussion. Accept students' opinions, but encourage them to support their ideas with text details and other information from their reading.

- Why do you think so many writers like to write about what might happen?
- Consider what all of the inventors from the selections have in common. Use examples to come up with a list of basic qualities that an inventor must have.

Independent Reading

BOOK TALK Have partners discuss their independent reading for the week. Tell them to refer to their Reading Log or journal and summarize the main ideas, maintaining the meaning and logical order. Have them paraphrase a favorite section. Then have students discuss the following:

- how the cultural or historical contexts of the texts support their understanding
- the selections' messages
- the authors' styles

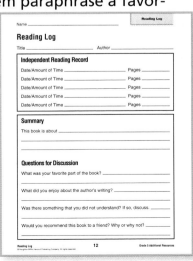

Reading Log

Extend Through Research

IDENTIFY SOURCE INFORMATION Tell students that when they conduct research for a report or other project, it is important to identify the sources they use. Explain that in order to write a strong research report, they should use information from at least three sources. Explain that as they research, they should write down information from each source in their own words.

If they want to include some information word for word in their report, they should frame it in direct quotes and include information as to where the quote came from. Remind students to write down the title, author, date, and page number of the source. Discuss these guidelines for identifying sources.

- Ask students to conduct research on a science fiction author. Have them work with a partner to generate a research question based on what they would like to know about the author. Then have them locate three sources of information that can be used to answer the question.

- Review with students primary and secondary sources. Tell them that they should include information from both types of sources. Have them document their sources on note cards. Then have them share their information and their sources with the class. Have students determine the relevance, validity, and reliability of each other's sources.

Listening and Speaking

PREPARE AN ORAL SUMMARY Tell students they will give a brief oral summary of a text they have read recently. Explain that readers who want to share a shortened version of a text often prepare an oral summary. Remind students that to prepare an oral summary, a speaker must:

- **Take Notes** The speaker should begin by noting the main ideas and important details in a selection.

- **Organize** The speaker should organize notes so that the most important information is presented in the same order that events and information are presented in the text.

- **Create Structure** The speaker creates an introduction, a body that is organized logically, and a conclusion.

- **Practice** The speaker practices presenting the summary, adjusting eye contact, voice, and gestures as necessary.

While students give their presentations, have audience members use the Listening Log to record what they learned.

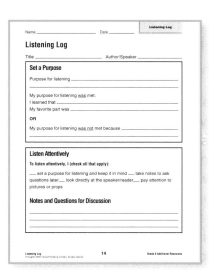

Listening Log

Spelling ☑ More Words with *-ed* or *-ing*

SHARE OBJECTIVE

- Spell words with the *-ed* or *-ing* ending.

Spelling Words

Basic

tiring	amazing	practicing
borrowed	performing	supported
freezing	resulting	united
delivered	related	✪ expected
✪ whispered	attending	✪ amusing
losing	damaged	repeated
decided	remarked	

Review ✪ pleasing, dared, traveled, checking, landed

Challenge
assigned, entertaining, operated, rehearsing, donated

✪ Forms of these words appear in "LAFFF."

ELL ENGLISH LANGUAGE LEARNERS

Preteach

Spanish Cognates

- Write and discuss these Spanish cognates for Spanish-speaking students.

decided • decidió

united • unida

repeated • repetida

Day 1

❶ TEACH THE PRINCIPLE

- Administer the **Pretest**. Use the Day 5 sentences.
- Write *freeze* and *perform* on the board. Use the chart below to help students spell the word endings correctly.

If a base word...	Then...
ends in e	drop final e before adding *-ed* or *-ing*, as in *united* and *freezing*
does not end in e	make no spelling change, as in *supported* and *performing*

❷ PRACTICE/APPLY

- Guide students to identify the spellings/endings in the remaining Spelling Words.

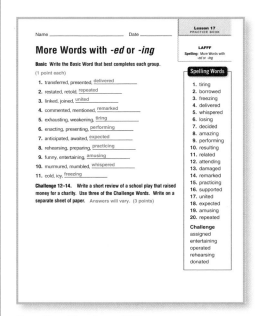

Practice Book p. 196

Day 2

❶ TEACH WORD SORT

- Set up two columns as shown. Model adding a Spelling Word to each column.
- Have students copy the chart. Have them complete it by writing each Spelling Word in its proper column.

No change	Drop final *e*
borrow + *-ed* = borrowed	amaze + *-ing* = amazing relate + *-ed* = related

❷ PRACTICE/APPLY

- Have students add words from "LAFFF."

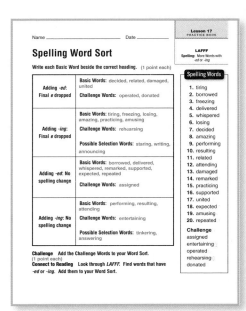

Practice Book p. 197

Day 3

① TEACH SYNONYMS

- **WRITE** *tiring* and *exhausting*.

- **ASK** *How are these two words related?* *(same meaning)* Point out that words with the same meaning are called *synonyms*.

- **WRITE** *remarked*. With students, list and discuss words that have almost the same meaning. *(Samples: commented, stated, observed, mentioned)*

② PRACTICE/APPLY

- **WRITE** the following words in a column: *delivered, amazing, related, damaged, supported, amusing*.

- Have students copy the words.

- Then have students look up each word in a thesaurus or an electronic resource to find a synonym. Ask them to write the synonym next to that Spelling Word. *(Samples: delivered/brought, amazing/remarkable, related/connected, damaged/injured, supported/encouraged, amusing/entertaining)*

- Have students use their synonyms in sentences.

Day 4

① CONNECT TO WRITING

- Read and discuss the prompt below.

> **WRITE TO NARRATE**
> Imagine that you are writing a story about time travel. Think about one character you would have in your story and write a description of that character. Use details from your readings this week.

② PRACTICE/APPLY

- Guide students as they plan and write their character descriptions. See p. T128.

- Remind students to proofread their writing for errors in words ending with -*ed* or -*ing*.

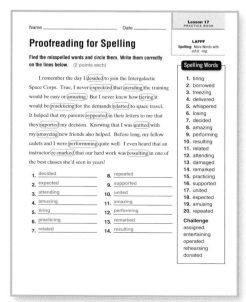

Practice Book p. 198

Day 5

ASSESS SPELLING

- Say each boldfaced word, read the sentence, and then repeat the word.

- Have students write only the boldfaced word.

Basic

1. A long hike can be very **tiring**.
2. I **borrowed** my sister's sweater.
3. The pond is **freezing** over.
4. Who **delivered** this package?
5. Kim **whispered** the secret.
6. Bill is **losing** weight on a diet.
7. I **decided** to carry an umbrella.
8. Her athletic ability is **amazing**.
9. Who is **performing** first?
10. Floods are **resulting** from the heavy rains.
11. The two events are **related**.
12. My son is **attending** college.
13. Raul's car was badly **damaged**.
14. He **remarked** about the weather.
15. Mia is **practicing** for the concert.
16. My friends **supported** me during a difficult time.
17. The two **united** in marriage.
18. She **expected** a better grade.
19. The movie was **amusing**.
20. I **repeated** my question.

Grammar ✓ Adverbs

SHARE OBJECTIVES

- Identify adverbs and the verbs they describe.
- Use adverbs in writing and speaking.

ELL ENGLISH LANGUAGE LEARNERS

Scaffold

Beginning Work with students to identify the adverbs in the following short sentences:

Stella spoke slowly. *(slowly)*
Jim played today. *(today)*

Use gestures, pantomime, and simplified language to demonstrate how the adverb adds meaning to the sentence.

Intermediate Provide the sentence frame below, and have students complete it with an adverb. Then have them demonstrate the adverb.

I speak _____. *(slowly, quickly, loudly)*

Advanced Tell students that most adverbs are formed by adding *-ly* to adjectives. Write the following adjectives on the board. Work with students to form adverbs and to use them in sentences.

quick   silent   slow   loud   correct

Advanced High Have partners use the list of adjectives above to form adverbs. Then have them write sentences using the adverbs.

See ELL Lesson 17, pp. E12–E21, for scaffolded support.

JOURNEYS DIGITAL **Powered by DESTINATIONReading**
Grammar Activities: Lesson 17

Day 1 TEACH

PROJECTABLE
17.6

DAILY PROOFREADING PRACTICE

The time machene was fast, fun. *machine; fast and*

❶ TEACH ADVERBS

- Display **Projectable 17.6**. Explain that an **adverb** is a word that tells something about a verb. Some adverbs tell *how, when,* or *where*. Many adverbs end in *-ly*.

- Model identifying what verb the adverb describes in the example sentence: *I will wait patiently for the time machine to be built.*

Think Aloud *To identify the adverb in the sentence, I'll ask the Thinking Questions. Patiently ends in -ly and tells how the subject of the sentence,* I, *will wait. So,* patiently *must be the adverb that describes the verb* will wait.

❷ PRACTICE/APPLY

- Complete the other examples on **Projectable 17.6** with students.

- List the following verbs on the board. Work with students to identify adverbs that might describe each one.

walk *(briskly)*
wandered *(slowly)*
thought *(quickly)*
stood *(silently)*
jumped *(suddenly)*

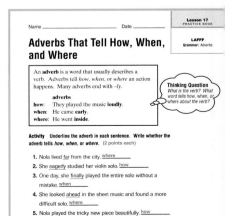

Practice Book p. 199

AL *Academic Language*

adverb describes a verb
adverb of frequency tells how often an action happens
adverb of intensity tells how much or to what degree an action happens

Day 2 TEACH

DAILY PROOFREADING PRACTICE

Angela smiled happy at the childen?
happily; children.

① **EXTEND ADVERBS**

PROJECTABLE
17.7

- Display **Projectable 17.7**. Tell students that some adverbs tell *how often* an action happens. They are called *adverbs of frequency*. Adverbs that tell *how much* or to what degree an action happens are called *adverbs of intensity*.

- Model identifying adverbs of frequency and adverbs of intensity in the example sentences: *I usually like stories about the future. I read a lot of science fiction.*

  Think Aloud   *In the first sentence, I see the verb* like *and the word* usually. *It ends in -ly and tells* how often. *It must be the adverb that describes the verb* like. *I'll try using the Thinking Questions with the second sentence.*

② **PRACTICE/APPLY**

- Complete the other examples on **Projectable 17.7** with students.

- Write these sentences on the board. Have students orally add adverbs of frequency or intensity.

  Peter _____ rides his bike. *(always)*

  Angela _____ listened to the boy talk. *(hardly)*

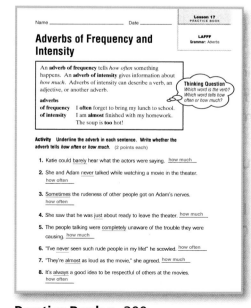

Practice Book p. 200

Day 3 TEACH

DAILY PROOFREADING PRACTICE

Greg oftin travells in time. *often; travels*

① **TEACH USING ADVERBS**

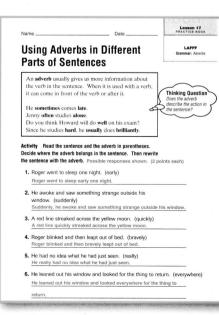

- Display **Projectable 17.8**. Explain that an adverb needs to make sense when it describes a verb.

- Model recognizing when an adverb makes sense in these example sentences: *He happily buys comic books. He perfectly buys comic books.*

  Think Aloud   *When I ask the Thinking Question, I see that the adverb* happily, *in the first sentence, describes the action. The adverb* perfectly *does not describe the action.*

- Tell students that when they write a sentence, they can place the adverb before or after the verb.

② **PRACTICE/APPLY**

- Complete the other examples on **Projectable 17.8** with students.

- Display the following sentence pairs that use adverbs correctly and incorrectly. Have students determine when the adverb makes sense describing the verb.

  Greg quickly sold seventeen units before lunch.
  (correct)

  Greg softly sold seventeen units before lunch.
  (incorrect)

Practice Book p. 201

Day 4 REVIEW

DAILY PROOFREADING PRACTICE

He usual talks animated about travel. *usually; animatedly*

1 REVIEW ADVERBS

- Remind students that an **adverb** is a word that describes a verb. Adverbs tell *how, when,* or *where* an action happens. Many adverbs end with *-ly*. **Adverbs of frequency** tell *how often*. **Adverbs of intensity** tell *how much*.

2 SPIRAL REVIEW

Simple Verb Tenses Review with students that present, past, and future verb tenses are all **simple verb tenses**. Present tense tells what is happening now or what is happening over and over. Past tense tells what happened in the past, and future tense tells what will happen in the future.

Write the following sentences on the board. Have students identify the verb and its tense in each sentence.

Brenda dropped the dog off at home. *(dropped; past)*

Alex waits for her presents. *(waits; present)*

We will stay with Paolo. *(will stay; future)*

Practice Book p. 202

Day 5 CONNECT TO WRITING

DAILY PROOFREADING PRACTICE

Greg mom quick fried the spring rolls. *Greg's; quickly*

1 CONNECT TO WRITING

- Tell students that using precise adverbs to make descriptions more vivid helps readers visualize images clearly.

- Point out that an important part of revising is using precise adverbs.

2 PRACTICE/APPLY

- Have students turn to **Student Book p. 450.** Review with them the different ways to make writing more interesting by using adverbs to describe verbs. Then have students complete the *Turn and Talk* activity.

- Display the following sentences. Guide students to provide adverbs to describe the verbs.

Angela was _____ convinced to try the time machine. *(easily)*

Angela departed _____ on a trip to the future. *(immediately)*

Angela _____ traveled in the time machine. *(frequently)*

Practice Book p. 203

Grammar

What Is an Adverb? A word that describes a verb is an **adverb**. Adverbs tell *how, when,* or *where* an action happens. Many adverbs end with *–ly*.

Academic Language

adverb
adverb of frequency
adverb of intensity

How	The time machine buzzed loudly.
When	Soon its door opened.
Where	I took a deep breath and stepped inside.

An **adverb of frequency** tells *how often* something happens. **Adverbs of intensity** often tell *how much* about a verb.

Adverb of Frequency: I sometimes feel cramped in small spaces.

Adverb of Intensity: When the time machine door closed, I almost screamed!

Turn and Talk **Identify the adverb that describes each underlined verb. Explain to a partner whether the adverb tells *how, when, where, how often,* or *how much.***

1. Karl <u>stared</u> intently at the blank screen.

2. He usually <u>found</u> himself with no inspiration.

3. He <u>closed</u> his eyes again and thought of story ideas.

4. Karl imagined a future world in which time machines <u>worked</u> everywhere.

5. He typed the story at top speed and almost <u>sprained</u> his fingers.

450

Word Choice To make your descriptions more vivid, try using precise adverbs. By doing this, you can make your writing more lively and create details that help readers visualize images clearly.

Less Precise Adverb	More Precise Adverb
The time traveler walked **slowly** down the corridor.	The time traveler walked **stealthily** down the corridor.

Connect Grammar to Writing

As you revise your character description, look for opportunities to use precise adverbs. These adverbs will help readers visualize your descriptions, and they will make your writing interesting.

451

Try This!

1. *intently; how*
2. *usually; how often*
3. *again; how often*
4. *everywhere; where*
5. *almost; how much*

CONNECT GRAMMAR TO WRITING

- Have students turn to **Student Book p. 451**. Read the Word Choice paragraph with students.

- Read the sentences in the chart. Point out to students that using a precise adverb, like *stealthily*, creates details that help readers visualize images clearly.

- Tell students that as they revise their character descriptions, they should look for opportunities to use adverbs to make their writing more interesting.

- Review the Common Errors at right with students.

COMMON ERRORS

Error: Angela walked **quick** to school.

Correct: Angela walked **quickly** to school.

Error: Greg used the machine happy.

Correct: Greg used the machine **happily**.

Write to Narrate ✓ Focus Trait: Word Choice

- Use proper punctuation and spacing for quotations.
- Write a character description using dialogue.

Academic Language

character the qualities that form the personality or nature of a person

vivid detail a detail that helps readers clearly picture what is being described

dialogue the words spoken between two or more people

ELL ENGLISH LANGUAGE LEARNERS

Scaffold

Beginning Write the words *Person* and *Appearance* on the board. Invite students to name a person and tell one thing they remember about that person's appearance. *(Sample answer: happy, red shirt)*

Intermediate Write *Actions* and *Dialogue* on the board. Have students say actions that people might do and dialogue that people might say.

Advanced Have students act out a simple action, like putting away a book. Have them describe the appearance/action of the person.

Advanced High Have students write dialogue to match the appearances/actions above. Check for the correct placement of quotation marks.

See also ELL Lesson 17, pp. E12–E21, for scaffolded support.

JOURNEYS DIGITAL **Powered by** **DESTINATION**Reading®
WriteSmart CD-ROM

Day 1 ANALYZE THE MODEL

❶ INTRODUCE THE MODEL

- Tell students that they will be writing a character description in this lesson.
- Display **Projectable 17.9** and read aloud the Writing Model prompt. Discuss the following:

What Is a Character Description?

- It shows different aspects of a person's **character**.
- It includes **vivid details** to describe the person's appearance, thoughts, and actions.
- Describing the person's actions in detail tells the reader how that person acts.
- **Dialogue** helps the reader understand how the person thinks, talks, and feels.

- Point out that the character description includes dialogue, vivid details, and actions.

❷ PRACTICE/APPLY

- Work with students to complete the second section of the Projectable by labeling vivid details, actions, and dialogue.

- Have them identify a place to insert the following dialogue: *"My clothing is unique," my friend Jack likes to say.* (Insert the dialogue before the first sentence.)

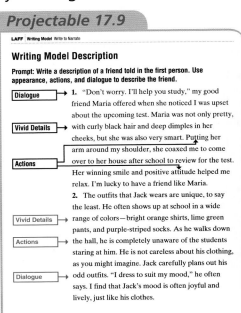

Projectable 17.9

LAFF Writing Model Write to Narrate

Writing Model Description

Prompt: Write a description of a friend told in the first person. Use appearance, actions, and dialogue to describe the friend.

Dialogue → 1. "Don't worry. I'll help you study," my good friend Maria offered when she noticed I was upset about the upcoming test. Maria was not only pretty,

Vivid Details → with curly black hair and deep dimples in her cheeks, but she was also very smart. Putting her

Actions → arm around my shoulder, she coaxed me to come over to her house after school to review for the test. Her winning smile and positive attitude helped me relax. I'm lucky to have a friend like Maria.
2. The outfits that Jack wears are unique, to say the least. He often shows up at school in a wide

Vivid Details → range of colors—bright orange shirts, lime green pants, and purple-striped socks. As he walks down

Actions → the hall, he is completely unaware of the students staring at him. He is not careless about his clothing, as you might imagine. Jack carefully plans out his

Dialogue → odd outfits. "I dress to suit my mood," he often says. I find that Jack's mood is often joyful and lively, just like his clothes.

LESSON	FORM	TRAIT
16	Friendly Letter	Voice
17	**Character Description**	**Word Choice**
18	Personal Narrative Paragraph	Voice
19	Prewrite a Personal Narrative	Ideas
20	Draft, Revise, Edit, Publish a Personal Narrative	Voice

Day 2 TEACH THE FOCUS TRAIT

1 INTRODUCE THE FOCUS TRAIT: WORD CHOICE

• Remind students that good word choice means carefully selecting the best words to express your ideas.

• Exact words can bring a character description to life. They can make the reader feel like he or she is actually seeing and hearing the person.

Connect to "LAFFF"	
Instead of this...	**...the author wrote this.**
He wore a small cap on his head and had a mustache.	"On his head he had a little round cap, and down each side of his mouth drooped a thin, long mustache." (p. 433)

• Point out that this vivid description helps the reader imagine how the person appears.

2 PRACTICE/APPLY

• Write: *His voice scared me.* Have students suggest more descriptive words, such as adjectives and precise verbs, to make this sentence more colorful and interesting. *(Sample answer: His mysterious, deep voice terrified me.)*

• Write: *Peter opened a door to show the device.* Have students improve the sentence using exact and vivid words. *(Sample: Peter proudly opened the garage door to show his time machine.)*

Name _____ Date _____

Lesson 17
PRACTICE BOOK

Focus Trait: Word Choice
Using Exact Words

LAFFF
Writing: Write to Narrate

Basic Description	Description with Exact Words
Tara had blonde hair.	Tara's long, straight hair was the color of sunlit wheat.

Think about the characters Angela and Peter from *LAFFF*. Read each sentence. Make it more vivid by adding exact words.

Basic Description	Description with Exact Words
1. Angela felt odd when she looked into the room.	Angela felt nervous _____ when she peeked into the garage. (1 point)
2. Peter waited to hear about what Angela did.	Peter anxiously waited _____ to hear about Angela's voyage. (1)

Pair/Share Work with a partner to brainstorm exact words to add to each sentence. Possible responses shown.

Basic Description	Description with Exact Words
3. Angela saw something in the kitchen.	Angela saw the magazine in the small kitchen. (1)
4. Peter laughed at the funny thing.	Peter roared with laughter at the joke. (1)
5. Angela ran away.	Angela bolted from the garage. (1)

Practice Book p.204

Day 3 PREWRITE

1 TEACH PLANNING A CHARACTER DESCRIPTION

• Display **Projectable 17.10** and read aloud the prompt. Ask students to think about a friend they would like to write about.

• Explain that a Column Chart can help them plan their writing.

2 PRACTICE/ APPLY

• Point out the three headers—*Appearance, Actions,* and *Dialogue*—in the Column Chart on **Projectable 17.10**. Explain to students that good writers reveal character traits by showing their characters' appearance, actions, and dialogue.

• Tell students that they should give examples of what characters say and do, rather than just listing their qualities.

• Work with students to complete the Column Chart.

• Have students choose a person for their character descriptions. Distribute **Graphic Organizer 1**. Guide students to complete their own Column Charts.

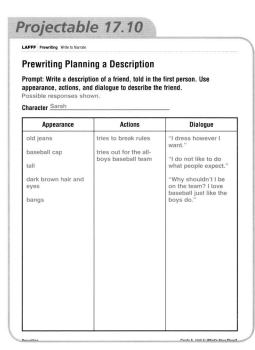

Projectable 17.10

LAFFF Prewriting Write to Narrate

Prewriting Planning a Description

Prompt: Write a description of a friend, told in the first person. Use appearance, actions, and dialogue to describe the friend.
Possible responses shown.

Character Sarah

Appearance	Actions	Dialogue
old jeans	tries to break rules	"I dress however I want."
baseball cap	tries out for the all-boys baseball team	
tall		"I do not like to do what people expect."
dark brown hair and eyes		"Why shouldn't I be on the team? I love baseball just like the boys do."
bangs		

Day 4 DRAFT

1 BEGIN A DRAFT

- Have students begin their drafts using their Column Charts. Discuss with them the following:

> **1. Introduce** using a vivid dialogue or a colorful description to show what your person is like.

> **2. Organize** your writing to include the person's appearance, actions, and speech.

> **3. Include** natural sounding dialogue that brings the person to life. Use colorful details when describing the person's actions and appearance. Clearly describe actions that reveal the person's character.

> **4. Conclude** with action or dialogue that reinforces the character of your person.

2 PRACTICE/APPLY

- Have students draft their character descriptions. Remind them to use the Column Charts they completed for prewriting on Day 3.

Day 5 REVISE FOR WORD CHOICE

1 INTRODUCE THE STUDENT MODEL

- Remind students that good writers choose interesting, exact words to show their character's appearance, actions, and speech.

- Read the top of **Student Book p. 452** with the class. Discuss the revisions made by the student writer, Theo. Point out that Theo added exact describing words to make his writing more vivid.

2 PRACTICE/ APPLY

- Display **Projectable 17.11**. Work with students to revise the rest of the character description. Point out where more exact words in dialogue, actions, and appearance could create clearer images for the reader.

- Discuss Theo's Final Copy on **Student Book p. 453**. Work with students to answer the *Reading As a Writer* questions. Discuss students' responses.

- **Revising** Have students revise their descriptions using the Writing Traits Checklist on **Student Book p. 452**.

- **Proofreading** For proofreading support, have students use the **Proofreading Checklist Blackline Master**.

Projectable 17.11

LAFF Revising Write to Narrate

Revising Theo's Narrative Paragraph

Proofread Theo's draft. Use proofreading marks to correct any errors or make any improvements.

"Come with me!" shouted James as he quickly disappeared down the basement stairs. I followed him and looked around. My red-haired, freckle-faced neighbor was nowhere to be seen. "I am in the box," he said in a loud whisper. The sound was coming from a big box.

That was my introduction to James McGinnis and his fabulous imagination. His box could be a submarine, an intergalactic transporter, or a time machine. Later, when we were in third grade, James discovered the Time Warp Trio books, and we excitedly read the whole series together.

Last summer, James moved away. "What we need now is a distance-warp machine," he says. I agree!

Write to Narrate

☑ **Word Choice** A good **character description** uses exact words, vivid details, and dialogue to show what a character is like. You can almost see Angela's expression in "LAFFF" when she says, "I feel like such a jerk." When you write a descriptive paragraph, use words that will help your readers imagine your subject.

Theo drafted a description of his friend James. Later, he added details and changed some dialogue to bring his character to life.

Writing Traits Checklist

☑ **Ideas**
Do my details show what my character is like?

☑ **Organization**
Are my topic sentences and details in an order that makes sense?

☑ **Sentence Fluency**
Did I combine sentences for better flow?

☑ **Word Choice**
Did I use exact words, vivid details, and dialogue?

☑ **Voice**
Do my words reveal my feelings or attitude about my character?

☑ **Conventions**
Did I use correct spelling, grammar, and punctuation?

Revised Draft

"Come with me!" shouted James
                    quickly
as he disappeared down the basement
stairs. ~~He was quick.~~ I followed him
and looked around. My red-haired,
freckle-faced neighbor was nowhere to
                        I'm in outer space!
be seen. "~~I am in the box,~~" he said.
in a loud whisper. The sound was coming
from a big box

452

Final Copy

My Friend James
by Theo Pothoulakis

"Come with me!" shouted James as he quickly disappeared down the basement stairs. I followed him and looked around. My red-haired, freckle-faced neighbor was nowhere to be seen. "I'm in outer space!" he said in a loud whisper. The sound was coming from a big box.

That was my introduction to James McGinnis and his fabulous imagination. His box could be a submarine, an intergalactic transporter, or a time machine. Later, when we were in third grade, James discovered the Time Warp Trio books, and we excitedly read the whole series together.

Last summer, James moved away. "What we need now is a distance-warp machine," he says. I agree!

In my final paper, I made the dialogue sound more natural. I also used precise adverbs to create clear images for readers.

Reading as a Writer

What details did Theo use to make his description of James vivid? How can you make your own description more vivid?

453

Writing Traits Scoring Rubric

	Focus/Ideas	☑ Organization	Voice	☑ Word Choice	☑ Sentence Fluency	Conventions
4	Adheres to the topic, is interesting, has a sense of completeness. Ideas are well developed.	Ideas and details are clearly presented and well organized.	Connects with reader in a unique, personal way.	Includes vivid verbs, strong adjectives, specific nouns.	Includes a variety of complete sentences that flow smoothly, naturally.	Shows a strong command of grammar, spelling, capitalization, punctuation.
3	Mostly adheres to the topic, is somewhat interesting, has a sense of completeness. Ideas are adequately developed.	Ideas and details are mostly clear and generally organized.	Generally connects with reader in a way that is personal and sometimes unique.	Includes some vivid verbs, strong adjectives, specific nouns.	Includes some variety of mostly complete sentences. Some parts flow smoothly, naturally.	Shows a good command of grammar, spelling, capitalization, punctuation.
2	Does not always adhere to the topic, has some sense of completeness. Ideas are superficially developed.	Ideas and details are not always clear or organized. There is some wordiness or repetition.	Connects somewhat with reader. Sounds somewhat personal, but not unique.	Includes mostly simple nouns and verbs, and may have a few adjectives.	Includes mostly simple sentences, some of which are incomplete.	Some errors in grammar, spelling, capitalization, punctuation.
1	Does not adhere to the topic, has no sense of completeness. Ideas are vague.	Ideas and details are not organized. Wordiness or repetition hinders meaning.	Does not connect with reader. Does not sound personal or unique.	Includes only simple nouns and verbs, some inaccurate. Writing is not descriptive.	Sentences do not vary. Incomplete sentences hinder meaning.	Frequent errors in grammar, spelling, capitalization, punctuation.

See also **Writing Rubric Blackline Master** and Teacher's Edition pp. R18–R21.

Progress Monitoring

Assess

- **Weekly Tests**
- **Fluency Tests**
- **Periodic Assessments**

Vocabulary
Target Vocabulary
Strategies: Using Reference Sources

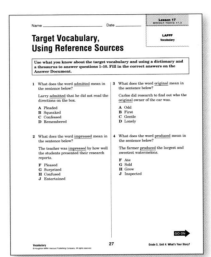

Weekly Tests 17.2–17.4

Comprehension
Story Structure

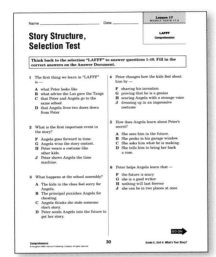

Weekly Tests 17.5–17.6

Respond to Assessment

IF a Student Scores...	THEN...
7–10 of 10	▶ Continue Core Instructional Program.
4–6 of 10	▶ **Reteaching Lesson,** p. T146
1–3 of 10	▶ **Intervention** Lesson 17, pp. S12–S21

IF a Student Scores...	THEN...
7–10 of 10	▶ Continue Core Instructional Program.
4–6 of 10	▶ **Reteaching Lesson,** p. T146
1–3 of 10	▶ **Intervention** Lesson 17, pp. S12–S21

Powered by DESTINATIONReading®
- Weekly Tests
- Online Assessment System

☑ Decoding
Recognizing Common Word Parts

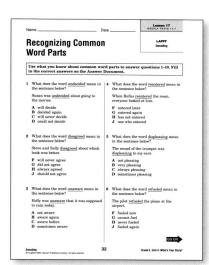

Weekly Tests 17.7–17.8

IF a Student Scores...	THEN...
7–10 of 10	▶ Continue Core Instructional Program.
4–6 of 10	▶ **Reteaching Lesson,** p. T147
1–3 of 10	▶ **Intervention** Lesson 17, pp. S12–S21

☑ Language Arts
Grammar: Adverbs

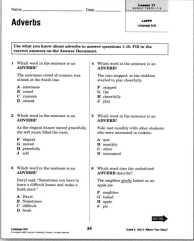

Weekly Tests 17.9–17.10

Writing Traits Rubric
See TE pp. R18–R21.

IF a Student Scores...	THEN...
7–10 of 10	▶ Continue Core Instructional Program.
4–6 of 10	▶ **Reteaching Lesson,** p. T147
1–3 of 10	▶ **Intervention** Lesson 17, pp. S12–S21

☑ Fluency

Fluency Plan
Assess one group per week.
Use this suggested plan below.

	Struggling Readers	Weeks 1, 3, 5
▲	On Level	Week 2
■	Advanced	Week 4

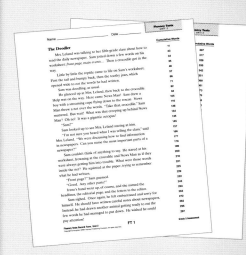

Fluency Record Form

Fluency Scoring Rubric
See *Grab-and-Go™ Resources Assessment* for help in measuring progress.

Progress Monitoring

Small Group

RUNNING RECORDS

To assess individual progress, occasionally use small group time to take a reading record for each student. Use the results to plan instruction.

 **Struggling Readers**

 On Level

 Advanced

English Language Learners

For running records, see
Grab-and-Go™ Resources: Lesson 17, pp. 13–16.

Behaviors and Understandings to Notice

- Self-corrects errors that detract from meaning.
- Self-corrects intonation when it does not reflect the meaning.
- Rereads to solve words and resumes normal rate of reading.
- Demonstrates phrased and fluent oral reading.
- Reads dialogue with expression.

- Demonstrates awareness of punctuation.
- Automatically solves most words in the text to read fluently.
- Demonstrates appropriate stress on words, pausing and phrasing, intonation, and use of punctuation.
- Reads orally at an appropriate rate.

Weekly
Small Group Instruction

Day 1
Vocabulary Reader
- *That's A Wacky Idea*, T136–T137

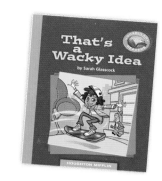

Day 2
Differentiate Comprehension
- Target Skill: Story Structure, T138–T139
- Target Strategy: Infer/Predict, T138–T139

Day 3
Leveled Readers
- ● *Robot Rescue*, T140
- ▲ *The Watch Girl*, T141
- ■ *Pancakes*, T142
- ◆ *Kendria's Watch*, T143

Day 4
Differentiate Vocabulary Strategies
- Using Reference Sources, T144–T145

Day 5
Options for Reteaching
- Vocabulary Strategies: Using Reference Sources, T146
- Comprehension Skill: Analyze Story Structure, T146
- Language Arts: Adverbs/Write to Narrate, T147
- Decoding: Recognizing Common Word Parts, T147

Ready-Made Work Stations

Ready-Made Practice
- Comprehension and Fluency, T82
- Word Study, T82
- Think and Write, T83
- Digital Center, T83

Comprehension and Fluency

Word Study

Think and Write

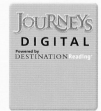
Digital Center

		Day 1	**Day 2**	**Day 3**
Teacher-Led	**Struggling Readers**	**Vocabulary Reader** *That's a Wacky Idea*, Differentiated Instruction, p. T136	**Differentiate Comprehension** Story Structure; Infer/Predict, p. T138	Leveled Reader *Robot Rescue*, p. T140
	On Level	**Vocabulary Reader** *That's a Wacky Idea*, Differentiated Instruction, p. T136	**Differentiate Comprehension** Story Structure; Infer/Predict, p. T138	Leveled Reader *The Watch Girl*, p. T141
	Advanced	**Vocabulary Reader** *That's a Wacky Idea*, Differentiated Instruction, p. T137	**Differentiate Comprehension** Story Structure; Infer/Predict, p. T139	Leveled Reader *Pancakes*, p. T142
	English Language Learners	**Vocabulary Reader** *That's a Wacky Idea*, Differentiated Instruction, p. T137	**Differentiate Comprehension** Story Structure; Infer/Predict, p. T139	Leveled Reader *Kendria's Watch*, p. T143
What are my other students doing?	**Struggling Readers**	**Reread** *That's a Wacky Idea*	**Vocabulary in Context Cards** 161–170 *Talk It Over* Activities **Complete** Leveled Practice SR17.1	**Listen** to Audiotext CD of "LAFFF"; Retell and discuss **Complete** Leveled Practice SR17.2
	On Level	**Reread** *That's a Wacky Idea*	**Reread** "LAFFF" with a partner **Complete** Practice Book p. 193	**Reread** for Fluency: *The Watch Girl* **Complete** Practice Book p. 194
	Advanced	**Vocabulary in Context Cards** 161–170 *Talk It Over* Activities	**Reread and Retell** "LAFFF" **Complete** Leveled Practice A17.1	**Reread** for Fluency: *Pancakes* **Complete** Leveled Practice A17.2
	English Language Learners	**Reread** *That's a Wacky Idea*	**Listen** to Audiotext CD of "LAFFF"; Retell and discuss **Complete** Leveled Practice ELL17.1	**Vocabulary in Context Cards** 161–170 *Talk It Over* Activities **Complete** Leveled Practice ELL17.2

Ready-Made Work Stations

Assign these activities across the week to reinforce and extend learning.

Comprehension and Fluency Read and Record

Word Study Dictionary Help

Day 4

Differentiate Vocabulary Strategies
Using Reference Sources, p. T144

Differentiate Vocabulary Strategies
Using Reference Sources, p. T144

Differentiate Vocabulary Strategies
Using Reference Sources, p. T145

Differentiate Vocabulary Strategies
Using Reference Sources, p. T145

Day 5

Options for Reteaching,
pp. T146–T147

Options for Reteaching,
pp. T146–T147

Options for Reteaching,
pp. T146–T147

Options for Reteaching,
pp. T146–T147

Partners: Reread for Fluency:
Robot Rescue
Complete Leveled
Practice SR17.3

Vocabulary in Context Cards
161–170
Talk It Over Activities
Complete Practice Book p. 195

Reread for Fluency: "LAFFF"
Complete Leveled Practice A17.3

Partners: Reread for Fluency:
Kendria's Watch
Complete Leveled
Practice ELL17.3

Reread for Fluency: *That's a Wacky Idea*
Complete Work Station activities
Independent Reading

Complete Work Station activities
Independent Reading

Complete Work Station activities
Independent Reading

Reread *That's a Wacky Idea* or "LAFFF"
Complete Work Station activities

Think and Write
Away We Go

Digital Center

Weekly To-Do List

This Weekly To-Do List helps students see their own progress and move on to additional activities independently.

Reading Log

Vocabulary Reader

That's a Wacky Idea

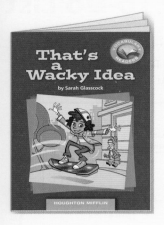

Summary

People invent things for different reasons. Some want to solve problems or make life easier. Others want to make people happy. Students will learn about all kinds of wacky inventions.

✓ TARGET VOCABULARY

impressed	concentrate
admitted	collected
produced	rumor
destination	suspense
original	compliment

Struggling Readers

- Explain that every invention starts out as an idea in someone's mind. However, only a very few inventions actually get made and widely used.

- Guide students to preview the **Vocabulary Reader**. Read aloud the headings. Ask students to describe the images, using Target Vocabulary when possible. Ask students if every invention is *original*. Ask them what invention has *impressed* them the most.

- Have students alternate reading pages of the text aloud. Guide them to use context clues to determine the meanings of unfamiliar words. As necessary, use the **Vocabulary in Context Cards** to review the meanings of vocabulary words.

- Assign the **Responding Page** and **Blackline Master 17.1**. Have partners work together to complete the pages.

On Level

- Explain that many inventions, such as the windshield wiper, were created to solve a problem. Guide students to preview the **Vocabulary Reader**.

- Remind students that context clues can help them determine the meaning of an unknown word. Tell students to use context clues to confirm their understanding of Target Vocabulary and to learn the meanings of new words.

- Have partners alternate reading pages of the text aloud. Tell them to use context clues to determine the meanings of unknown words.

- Assign the **Responding Page** and **Blackline Master 17.1**. Have students discuss their responses with a partner.

Advanced

- Have students preview the **Vocabulary Reader** and make predictions about what they will read, using information from their preview and prior knowledge.

- Remind students to use context clues to help them determine the meanings of unknown words.

- Tell students to read the **Vocabulary Reader** with a partner. Ask them to stop and discuss the meanings of unknown words as necessary.

- Assign the **Responding Page** and **Blackline Master 17.1**. For the Write About It activity, remind students to use facts and details to support their ideas. Ask students to choose an invention from the selection and to describe how this invention changed the way people live.

ELL English Language Learners

Group English Language Learners according to language proficiency.

Beginning	Advanced
Read the Vocabulary Reader aloud. For each Target Vocabulary word, show the corresponding Vocabulary in Context Card picture. Ask students to repeat the sentences after you and to describe the pictures.	Have students reread the Vocabulary Reader. Have them choose one part of the selection and work in pairs to summarize it using at least three Target Vocabulary words.

Intermediate	Advanced High
Ask questions using five vocabulary words, relating them to students' lives. For example, ask *Is it nice to get a compliment about how you look?* Next, have partners generate simple oral sentences using each word.	Have students reread the Vocabulary Reader. Have partners describe an invention they would like to create. Have them use at least four of the Target Vocabulary words.

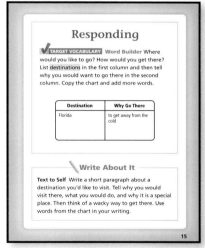

Responding

✓ **TARGET VOCABULARY** Word Builder Where would you like to go? How would you get there? List **destinations** in the first column and then tell why you would want to go there in the second column. Copy the chart and add more words.

Destination	Why Go There
Florida	to get away from the cold

Write About It

Text to Self Write a short paragraph about a destination you'd like to visit. Tell why you would visit there, what you would do, and why it is a special place. Then think of a wacky way to get there. Use words from the chart in your writing.

15

That's a Wacky Idea, p. 15

Blackline Master 17.1

Differentiate Comprehension

☑ Story Structure; Infer/Predict

Struggling Readers

I DO IT

- Review the elements of story structure: setting, characters, plot (conflict, resolution).

- Explain that readers can make predictions about story events.

- Read aloud p. 436 of "LAFFF" and model making a prediction about what Angela will do.

> **Think Aloud** *Angela is trying to find a use for Peter's machine. I predict she will come up with a plan, which may affect the plot.*

WE DO IT

- Have students read p. 432 of "LAFFF."

- Have them identify the setting and two main characters.

- Guide students to identify one of the problems and predict how it might affect the plot.

- Write students' predictions on the board; have them confirm or revise their predictions as they read more of the text.

YOU DO IT

- Have students fill in a Story Map for the first few pages of "LAFFF" up to p. 437.

- Have them use the events they have already written into the Story Map to predict what might happen later in the story.

- Point out that inferring and making predictions can help them connect story elements and understand story structure.

On Level

I DO IT

- Review the elements of story structure: setting, characters, plot (conflict, resolution).

- Read aloud p. 433 of "LAFFF." Explain that one aspect of story structure that readers should pay attention to is plot development, or how a plot becomes more complicated.

- Model how to complete a Story Map. Explain how one plot event can be used to predict later plot developments, or changes.

WE DO IT

- Have students read p. 434.

- Have them describe how Angela's feelings toward Peter change when Peter speaks in the strange voice. Then have students predict how their relationship will change.

- Help students add details to the Story Map that will help them predict later story events.

YOU DO IT

- As they read, have pairs work together to make predictions based on plot events. Have pairs complete their own Story Maps, identifying setting, characters, plot events, the problem, and the resolution.

- Then have students go back through the story and identify events from "LAFFF" that helped them make predictions as they read.

- Have them discuss their completed Story Maps and predictions.

Advanced

I DO IT

- Read aloud p. 441 of "LAFFF."
- Explain that students should use text details and personal experience to make inferences and predictions about story elements such as plot events.

Experience	I've wanted to win before.
Text detail	She read part of the winning story.
Prediction	Angela will win.

WE DO IT

- Have students contrast how Angela feels before the contest with how she feels after.
- Help students infer why Angela's attitude has changed. Have them look at details in the beginning and refer to personal experience for support.
- Model using a Story Map to help students use their inferences and predictions to identify and understand elements of the story structure.

YOU DO IT

- Have students complete their Story Maps and use them to write a short paragraph about the circular plot of the story. (You may want to point out that the first and last lines are the same.)
- Invite students to model how they used their Story Maps to make predictions.

ELL English Language Learners

Group English Language Learners according to language proficiency.

Review story structure with students. Write the following sentence frames on the board:
The story takes place ____; Important events in the story include ____; The characters in the story are____; The main problem of a story is____; The solution to the problem is____. Guide students to complete the sentence frames. Say each completed sentence aloud. Have students repeat.

Beginning

Review with students that *characters* are the *people* in the story. Have students name the main characters. Repeat for *setting*.

Intermediate

Review with students that the *plot* includes *the events* in the story. Guide students to explain what happens in the story.

Advanced

Explain that the *problem* and the *solution* of the story are parts of the plot. Discuss with students the main problem of the story and how it was solved.

Advanced High

Have pairs work together to write a paragraph summarizing the plot of "LAFFF." Have them include the problem and its solution, as well as the other elements of the story structure.

Targets for Lesson 17

✓ TARGET SKILL

Story Structure

✓ TARGET STRATEGY

Infer/Predict

✓ TARGET VOCABULARY

impressed	concentrate
admitted	collected
produced	rumor
destination	suspense
original	compliment

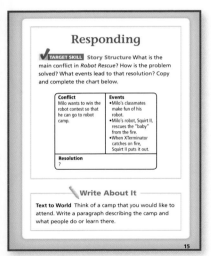

Robot Rescue, p. 15

Blackline Master 17.3

Struggling Readers

● *Robot Rescue*

GENRE: SCIENCE FICTION

SUMMARY In the year 2040, Camilla starts rumors that Milo does not have a robot for the robot contest. Milo is the laughing stock of the school. The day of the big contest, though, everyone is impressed with Squirt II, Milo's fire-fighting robot.

Introducing the Text

• Explain that sometimes science fiction stories take place in the future. This selection takes place in 2040, when robots are everywhere.

• Remind students that using a Story Map can help them keep track of the conflict, or problem, and resolution of a story.

Supporting the Reading

• As you listen to students read, pause to discuss these questions.

STORY STRUCTURE pp. 5–6 *Why does Milo want to win the contest so much? His mom can't afford robot camp, and the contest winner gets two free weeks there.*

INFER/PREDICT p. 14 *What do you predict will happen when XTerminator's head goes up in flames? Squirt II will help put out the fire, and Milo will win the competition.*

Discussing and Revisiting the Text

CRITICAL THINKING After discussing *Robot Rescue*, have students read the instructions on **Responding p. 15**. Use these teaching points to revisit the text.

• Have partners identify the main conflict and write it on **Blackline Master 17.3**.

• Have them write the main events that lead to the resolution in the events box. Then have them write the problem's solution in the resolution box.

• Distribute **Blackline Master 17.7** to develop students' critical thinking skills.

FLUENCY: INTONATION Have pairs practice reading paragraphs two through five on p. 6 to each other. Have students focus on intonation.

JOURNEYS DIGITAL | **Powered by** **DESTINATIONReading**
Leveled Readers Online

On Level

▲ *The Watch Girl*

GENRE: SCIENCE FICTION

SUMMARY Kendria receives a birthday watch in the mail from her long-lost Aunt Laqueta. She learns that this special gift can make her invisible. Although she finds it amusing to sneak up on people, Kendria soon learns a valuable lesson about eavesdropping.

Introducing the Text

• Explain to students that Kendria has a reputation for being sneaky and an eavesdropper.

• Remind students that all stories have a structure, including a conflict, important plot events, and a resolution.

Supporting the Reading

• As you listen to students read, pause to discuss these questions.

STORY STRUCTURE pp. 8–9 *What does Kendria do that causes conflict at school? She sneaks up on little kids on the playground, goes through the cafeteria line a second time, and overhears her friends talking about her.*

INFER/PREDICT p. 18 *What might the blue and yellow buttons on Kendria's watch do? The blue button will allow her to travel in time, and the yellow button will probably bring her back to the present.*

Discussing and Revisiting the Text

CRITICAL THINKING After discussing *The Watch Girl*, have students read the instructions on **Responding p. 19**. Use these teaching points to revisit the text.

• Have students identify the main conflict in *The Watch Girl*. Have them record the conflict on **Blackline Master 17.4**. Then ask them to add the main events that lead to the resolution and how the problem is solved.

• Distribute **Blackline Master 17.8** to develop students' critical thinking skills.

FLUENCY: INTONATION Have students practice reading paragraphs two through the end of the page on p. 9. They should focus on intonation, especially when reading dialogue.

The Watch Girl, p. 19

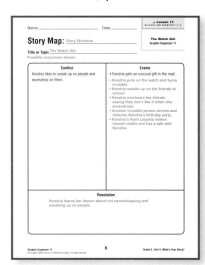

Blackline Master 17.4

Leveled Readers

Targets for Lesson 17

TARGET SKILL

Story Structure

TARGET STRATEGY

Infer/Predict

TARGET VOCABULARY

impressed	concentrate
admitted	collected
produced	rumor
destination	suspense
original	compliment

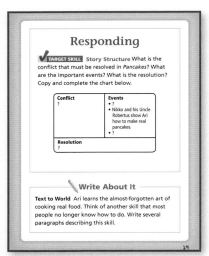

Pancakes, p. 19

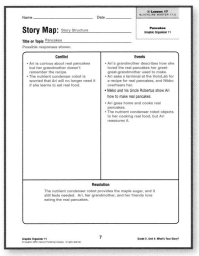

Blackline Master 17.5

Advanced

 Pancakes

GENRE: SCIENCE FICTION

SUMMARY In this story set in the future, Ari is curious after she learns about pancakes, a delicious food people used to cook before nutrient pellets were invented. A new student introduces Ari to cooking, and Ari decides to surprise her grandma with a pancake breakfast.

Introducing the Text

- Explain that science fiction is often set in the future. In this story, people eat nutrient pellets because they consider food preparation time-consuming.

- Remind students that recognizing a story's structure, including its conflict, main events, and resolution, will help them to understand the text.

Supporting the Reading

- As you listen to students read, pause to discuss these questions.

STORY STRUCTURE pp. 4–5 *What does Ari learn about Nikko, the new boy at school? He's from the Hinterlands, a "backward" area where people still cook.*

INFER/PREDICT pp. 17–18 *Although everyone enjoys the pancakes, Ari realizes a lot of preparation goes into a meal. What can we infer Ari will do? She will still take the pellets, since life in the future is so fast-paced.*

Discussing and Revisiting the Text

CRITICAL THINKING After discussing *Pancakes*, have students read the instructions on **Responding p. 19**. Use these teaching points to revisit the text.

- Have students work individually or in pairs to identify the story's structure.

- Have them identify the conflict and write it on **Blackline Master 17.5**. Then have them add the main events that lead to the resolution and how the problem is solved.

- Distribute **Blackline Master 17.9** to develop students' critical thinking skills.

FLUENCY: INTONATION Have students practice reading p. 4 aloud, focusing on using intonation to show what's happening in the text.

JOURNEYS DIGITAL Powered by **DESTINATION Reading®**
Leveled Readers Online

◆ English Language Learners

◆ *Kendria's Watch*

GENRE: SCIENCE FICTION

SUMMARY Kendria receives a birthday watch in the mail from her long-lost Aunt Laqueta. She learns that this special gift can make her invisible. Kendria soon discovers that using the watch to eavesdrop is a bad idea.

Introducing the Text

- Explain that eavesdropping means to listen in on other people's conversations without them knowing. Most people consider this behavior rude.

- Remind students that a Story Map helps readers keep track of a story's conflict, major events, and resolution.

Supporting the Reading

- As you listen to students read, pause to discuss these questions.

STORY STRUCTURE p. 9 *According to Kendria's friends, what does she do that bothers them? She eavesdrops, or listens, to private conversations.*

INFER/PREDICT p. 11 *Kendria thinks that someone is eavesdropping on her. How do you think this will make her feel? She'll be irritated, just like everyone is when she eavesdrops.*

Discussing and Revisiting the Text

CRITICAL THINKING After discussing *Kendria's Watch*, have students read the instructions on **Responding p. 19**. Use these teaching points to revisit the text.

- Have partners identify the story's main conflict, events, and resolution. Have them enter the information on **Blackline Master 17.6**. Help them to locate and list the events that happen to Kendria that lead her to realize that eavesdropping is wrong.

- Distribute **Blackline Master 17.10** to develop students' critical thinking skills.

FLUENCY: INTONATION Have partners practice reading p. 6 to each other. Have them focus on their intonation as they read.

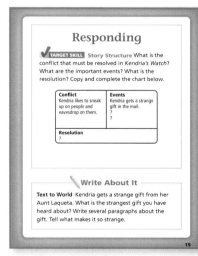

Kendria's Watch p. 19

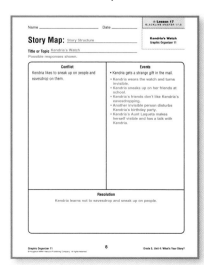

Blackline Master 17.6

Differentiate Vocabulary Strategies ☑ Using Reference Sources

Struggling Readers

I DO IT

- Remind students that a dictionary is a reference book, or a book that gives information or facts. Looking in a dictionary is a way to find a word's meaning and its part of speech.

- Explain that a thesaurus is a reference used to look up synonyms and antonyms, and a glossary is a reference for terms found inside a book.

WE DO IT

- Display the **Vocabulary in Context Card** for *concentrate*.

- Read aloud the context sentence on the front of the card.

- Model using a dictionary to verify the part of speech of *concentrate*.

- Have a volunteer read aloud the dictionary definition of *concentrate* that matches its use in the sample sentence.

YOU DO IT

- Have pairs use a dictionary to look up the parts of speech of the following Target Vocabulary words: *impressed, collected, original, suspense, produced, destination, admitted, compliment, rumor*.

- Have them group words into three parts of speech: noun, verb, and adjective.

On Level

I DO IT

- Remind students that dictionary entries include a word's part of speech: noun, pronoun, verb, adjective, or adverb.

- Remind students that a thesaurus is a book that gives synonyms and antonyms for a word.

- Explain that a glossary is a type of condensed dictionary that lists only certain terms and words contained inside a book.

WE DO IT

- Have students use a dictionary to look up the Target Vocabulary word *concentrate*.

- Have them read aloud the definition and identify how many different parts of speech there are for the word *concentrate*. *two: verb and noun*

- Have them read the sample sentence on the **Vocabulary in Context Card** and tell which definition entry matches it most closely.

YOU DO IT

- Have students use a thesaurus to find a synonym for each of the following Target Vocabulary words: *impressed, original, suspense, admitted, compliment*.

- Have students then use a dictionary to record the matching definition and part of speech of for each word.

Advanced

I DO IT

- Remind students that context can help them figure out an unfamiliar word's meaning, and they can use a reference source to confirm.

- Remind them that dictionary entries identify parts of speech as well as word meaning.

- Remind students that informational textbooks often have a glossary, or a section of the book where words or terms are defined.

WE DO IT

- Display the **Vocabulary in Context Card** for *compliment*.

- Ask students to tell you the part of speech of *compliment* in the sample sentence. *verb*

- Have students use a dictionary to identify the parts of speech for each definition of *compliment*.

- Guide students to understand that *compliment* can be used as a noun or a verb.

YOU DO IT

- Tell students to use a dictionary to determine which other Target Vocabulary words for Lesson 17 have different parts of speech. *original, (adj., noun); concentrate (verb, noun)*

- Have them write sentences using the words in each form. Then ask them to identify multiple-meaning words from the Target Vocabulary list. *concentrate, impressed, admitted, compliment*

ELL English Language Learners

Group English Language Learners according to language proficiency.

Write *impressed, collected, produced, destination, original, concentrate, suspense, admitted, compliment,* and *rumor.* Have students repeat after you as you pronounce each word.

Beginning	**Intermediate**	**Advanced**	**Advanced High**
Display **Vocabulary in Context Card** for *impressed.* Show students the picture. Read the card with the students. Model how to look up the word in a dictionary using guidewords. Point out the definition and the part of speech. Ask: *What makes you* impressed*?*	Read each **Vocabulary in Context Card** with students. Have them look up two of the words in a thesaurus. Have them pronounce each Target Vocabulary word and list the synonyms they find.	Have students find the Lesson 17 Target Vocabulary words in a thesaurus. Have partners use a synonym for each word in a sentence.	Have students find each Target Vocabulary word from Lesson 17 in a dictionary. Have them write their own context sentences for each word using the matching dictionary definition as a guide.

Options for Reteaching

Vocabulary Strategies

 ## Using Reference Sources

I DO IT

- Review using a glossary, dictionary, and thesaurus.

- Remind students a dictionary can be used to find meanings, spelling, pronunciation, origin, and the part of speech of a word. A thesaurus can be used to find synonyms and antonyms.

- Explain that a glossary contains many features of a dictionary, but lists only certain words from the book the glossary is in.

WE DO IT

- Write the following sentence on the board: *What was the subject of the movie you saw?*

- Model using a dictionary to find the meaning of the word *subject*.

> **Think Aloud** *I usually think of* subject *as something we study in school, but that doesn't really make sense here. I'll check the dictionary, using guidewords to locate the word. I see* subject *can also mean "something discussed; a topic." I think that makes sense here.*

- Have a volunteer look up *subject* in a dictionary and read the definitions and parts of speech aloud.

YOU DO IT

- Have students work together to review the Target Vocabulary words.

- Then have partners use a dictionary to look up five of the words and write the meaning that matches the context of the word as it is used in the main selection.

Comprehension Skill

 ## Story Structure

I DO IT

- Remind students that the main elements of a story are the characters, the setting, and the plot. The plot is made up of the sequence of story events, and usually involves a central problem, or conflict, and its resolution.

- Remind students that analyzing the problem and solution can help them understand the story and how the elements fit together.

WE DO IT

- Have students read **Student Book p. 432** aloud. Ask them to identify any possible problems in the story.

- Model analyzing how this problem might affect the rest of the story.

> **Think Aloud** *I read that Angela works very hard in school, but she doesn't think her grades will ever be as good as Peter's. I can tell that part of Angela's conflict is with herself. She wants to do better but is afraid she can't. I predict that the plot of the story will have to do with Angela's attempts to improve at school.*

- Help volunteers analyze how Angela feels about her own abilities. Then have them predict how her feelings might affect the story.

YOU DO IT

- Distribute **Graphic Organizer 11**.

- Have students read **Student Book p. 438**.

- Have students describe the problem Angela has. *Angela has to make sure she doesn't meet herself in the future.*

- Have students work with a partner to complete the graphic organizer. Review students' graphic organizers with them.

Language Arts

 Adverbs/Write to Narrate

I DO IT

- Remind students that adverbs tell how, when, or where an action takes place.

- List the following verbs: *read, walk, run*. Model asking and answering questions to add an adverb.

Think Aloud *How do you read? I read* carefully. *When do you walk? I walk* daily. *Where do you run? I run* outside.

WE DO IT

- Work together to list verbs for actions that take place in school, such as *study, write, work, talk*.

- Guide students to use precise, vivid adverbs to describe the action. Write: *He studied _____ in his room*. Ask students to suggest a word for the blank that tells how someone might study, such as *alone, quietly, diligently*.

- Have students work with a partner to write a similar sentence for the other verbs listed, adding an adverb that tells how, when, or where.

- Have students explain which question is answered by the adverbs they have used.

- Remind students that adverbs often, but don't always, end with the suffix *–ly*.

YOU DO IT

- Have students write 3–4 interesting sentences that include precise adverbs. Tell students to help a reader visualize the action.

- Have pairs exchange papers and underline the adverbs and tell what question is answered by each adverb their partner used.

Decoding

 Recognizing Common Word Parts

I DO IT

- Remind students that recognizing common word parts, such as prefixes and suffixes, can help them decode words.

- Point out that separating a base word or word root from its affixes can help students determine its pronunciation.

WE DO IT

- Ask students to brainstorm a list of common prefixes and suffixes. Write them on the board.

- Then write *replaced, underperforming, prerequested, overvalued, mispronouncing*, and *explorer* on the board.

- Model how to decode *replaced* step by step. Break the word into syllables. Point out the prefix *re-*, the base word *place*, and the inflectional ending *-ed*.

- Call on students to help you repeat the process for *underperforming*. Have volunteers come to the board to draw lines to syllabicate the word and to circle the affixes and underline the base word.

YOU DO IT

- Have partners decode the remaining words.

- Ask them to identify the prefix, base word, and suffix in each word.

- Use the **Corrective Feedback** on p. T115 if students need additional help.

Teacher Notes

Preteaching for Success!

Comprehension:

Fact and Opinion

Remind students that understanding the difference between fact and opinion will clarify their reading.

- Review with students that facts are ideas that can be proven true. Opinions are ideas that express a thought or feeling and cannot be proven true.
- Form two groups of volunteers – the Opinions and the Facts. Have a member of the Opinions make a statement that is clearly false, such as "I believe the sun revolves around the Earth." Have a member of the Facts refute that opinion. Continue for several rounds until all the volunteers have had a chance.

Challenge Yourself!

Research Dogs in the Military

After reading the selection "The Dog Newspaper," have students research the history of dogs in the military.

- Discuss with students that dogs have worked in the military since ancient times. Dogs have been used to pull carts, carry messages, guard and track, or simply as mascots.
- Brainstorm the traits and characteristics dogs have that help them perform well in military situations.
- Have each student write a newspaper article about a dog he or she knows and describe the dog's imagined exploits in the military.

Short Response

W.5.3d Use concrete words and phrases and sensory details to convey experiences and events precisely.

Find the words *canteen*, *company mascot*, and *foxholes* on Student Book p. 461. Write a statement for each, explaining how the words add to your understanding of the story.

Scoring Guidelines	
Excellent	Student has written a statement for each word explaining how it contributes to understanding the story.
Good	Student has written a statement for two of the words explaining how they contribute to understanding the story.
Fair	Student has written a statement for one word explaining how it contributes to understanding the story.
Unsatisfactory	Student has not written a statement.

Writing Minilesson

Skill: Write to Narrate—Personal Narrative Paragraph

Teach: Explain to students that when they write to narrate, they tell about experiences they have had.

Thinking Beyond the Text

Writing Prompt: Write a paragraph about an encounter you have had with an animal.

1. Tell each student to think about an experience he or she has had with an animal. The animal can be a pet or a wild animal.
2. Remind students to correctly use prepositions and prepositional phrases.
3. Tell students to use a voice that sounds like their own.

Group Share: Have students read their paragraphs aloud to each other.

Cross-Curricular Activity: Science

Helpful Features

In the selection, students read that B.J. adapted to life among the soldiers. Discuss some of the reasons dogs are suited to make rescues or find people and objects. Have students brainstorm lists of rescues that are more suitable for dogs to make than for people, and why.

Reading Standards for Literature K–5

Craft and Structure

RL.5.5 Explain how a series of chapters, scenes, or stanzas fits together to provide the overall structure of a particular story, drama, or poem.

Integration of Knowledge and Ideas

RL.5.7 Analyze how visual and multimedia elements contribute to the meaning, tone, or beauty of a text (e.g., graphic novel, multimedia presentation of fiction, folktale, myth, poem).

Range of Reading and Level of Text Complexity

RL.5.10 By the end of the year, read and comprehend literature, including stories, dramas, and poetry, at the high end of the grades 4–5 text complexity band independently and proficiently.

Reading Standards for Informational Text K–5

Key Ideas and Details

RI.5.1 Quote accurately from a text when explaining what the text says explicitly and when drawing inferences from the text.

RI.5.2 Determine two or more main ideas of a text and explain how they are supported by key details; summarize the text.

Range of Reading and Level of Text Complexity

RI.5.10 By the end of the year, read and comprehend informational texts, including history/social studies, science, and technical texts, at the high end of the grades 4–5 text complexity band independently and proficiently.

Reading Standards: Foundational Skills K–5

Phonics and Word Recognition

RF.5.3a Use combined knowledge of all letter-sound correspondences, syllabication patterns, and morphology (e.g., roots and affixes) to read accurately unfamiliar multisyllabic words in context and out of context.

Fluency

RF.5.4a Read grade-level text with purpose and understanding.

Writing Standards K–5

Text Types and Purposes

W.5.3a Orient the reader by establishing a situation and introducing a narrator and/or characters; organize an event sequence that unfolds naturally.

W.5.3b Use narrative techniques, such as dialogue, description, and pacing, to develop experiences and events or show the responses of characters to situations.

W.5.3d Use concrete words and phrases and sensory details to convey experiences and events precisely.

W.5.3e Provide a conclusion that follows from the narrated experiences or events.

Production and Distribution of Writing

W.5.4 Produce clear and coherent writing in which the development and organization are appropriate to task, purpose, and audience. (Grade-specific expectations for writing types are defined in standards 1–3 above.)

W.5.5 With guidance and support from peers and adults, develop and strengthen writing as needed by planning, revising, editing, rewriting, or trying a new approach.

Research to Build and Present Knowledge

W.5.7 Conduct short research projects that use several sources to build knowledge through investigation of different aspects of a topic.

W.5.8 Recall relevant information from experiences or gather relevant information from print and digital sources; summarize or paraphrase information in notes and finished work, and provide a list of sources.

W.5.9b Apply *grade 5 Reading standards* to informational texts (e.g., "Explain how an author uses reasons and evidence to support particular points in a text, identifying which reasons and evidence support which point[s]").

Speaking & Listening Standards K–5

Comprehension and Collaboration

SL.5.1a Come to discussions prepared, having read or studied required material; explicitly draw on that preparation and other information known about the topic to explore ideas under discussion.

SL.5.1c Pose and respond to specific questions by making comments that contribute to the discussion and elaborate on the remarks of others.

SL.5.2 Summarize a written text read aloud or information presented in diverse media and formats, including visually, quantitatively, and orally.

Presentation of Knowledge and Ideas

SL.5.4 Report on a topic or text or present an opinion, sequencing ideas logically and using appropriate facts and relevant, descriptive details to support main ideas or themes; speak clearly at an understandable pace.

Language Standards K–5

Conventions of Standard English

L.5.1a Explain the function of conjunctions, prepositions, and interjections in general and their function in particular sentences.

L.5.1c Use verb tense to convey various times, sequences, states, and conditions.

L.5.2e Spell grade-appropriate words correctly, consulting references as needed.

Knowledge of Language

L.5.3a Expand, combine, and reduce sentences for meaning, reader/listener interest, and style.

Vocabulary Acquisition and Use

L.5.4a Use context (e.g., cause/effect relationships and comparisons in text) as a clue to the meaning of a word or phrase.

L.5.4c Consult reference materials (e.g., dictionaries, glossaries, thesauruses), both print and digital, to find the pronunciation and determine or clarify the precise meaning of key words and phrases.

L.5.5c Use the relationship between particular words (e.g., synonyms, antonyms, homographs) to better understand each of the words.

SUGGESTIONS FOR BALANCED LITERACY

Use *Journeys* materials to support a Readers' Workshop approach. See the Lesson 18 resources on pages 26, 74–75.

Lesson 18

Focus Wall

Main Selection:
The Dog Newspaper

Connect to Poetry:
Poetry about Poetry

Big Idea
Everyone has a story to tell.

? Essential Question
What part do facts and opinions play in a story?

Comprehension

✔ **TARGET SKILL**
Fact and Opinion

✔ **TARGET STRATEGY**
Analyze/Evaluate

Spelling

Changing Final *y* to *i*

duties	trophies
earlier	cozier
loveliest	enemies
denied	iciest
ferries	greediest
sunnier	drowsier
terrified	victories
abilities	horrified
dirtier	memories
scariest	strategies

Fluency

Phrasing:
Punctuation

Grammar

Prepositions and
Prepositional
Phrases

Writing

Write to Narrate

Focus Trait:
Voice

Decoding

Recognizing Suffixes

Vocabulary Strategies

Analogies

▼ TARGET VOCABULARY

career	formula
publication	background
household	insights
edition	uneventful
required	destruction

Key Skills This Week

Target Skill:
Fact and Opinion

Target Strategy:
Analyze/Evaluate

Vocabulary Strategies:
Analogies

Fluency:
Phrasing: Punctuation

Decoding:
Recognizing Suffixes

Research Skill:
Use Technology to Identify Relationships

Grammar:
Prepositions and Prepositional Phrases

Spelling:
Changing Final *y* to *i*

Writing:
Write to Narrate: Personal Narrative Paragraph

✓ Assess/Monitor

☑ **Vocabulary,**
p. T200

☑ **Comprehension,**
p. T200

☑ **Decoding,**
p. T201

☑ **Language Arts,**
p. T201

☑ **Fluency,**
p. T201

Whole Group

READING

Paired Selections

The Dog Newspaper
Autobiography
Student Book, pp. 458–466

Poetry About Poetry
Poetry
Student Book, pp. 468–471

Accelerated Reader
Practice Quizzes for the Selection

Vocabulary

Student Book, pp. 454–455

Background and Comprehension

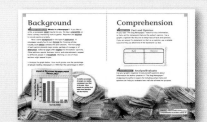

Student Book, pp. 456–457

LANGUAGE ARTS

Grammar
Student Book, pp. 472–473

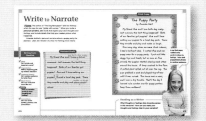

Writing
Student Book, pp. 474–475

Small Group

See pages T204–T205 for Suggested Small Group Plan.

TEACHER-LED

Leveled Readers

● Struggling Readers

▲ On Level

■ Advanced

◆ English Language Learners

Vocabulary Reader

WHAT MY OTHER STUDENTS ARE DOING

Ready-Made Work Stations

Comprehension and Fluency

Word Study

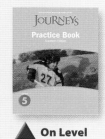

Think and Write

Digital Center

● Struggling Readers

■ Advanced

◆ English Language Learners

▲ On Level

Grab-and-Go!

Lesson 18 Blackline Masters
- Target Vocabulary 18.1
- Selection Summary 18.2
- Graphic Organizer 18.3–18.6 ●▲■◆
- Critical Thinking 18.7–18.10 ●▲■◆
- Running Records 18.11–18.14 ●▲■◆
- Weekly Tests 18.1–18.14

Graphic Organizer Transparency 12

Additional Resources
- Genre: Autobiography, p. 8
- Reading Log, p. 12
- Vocabulary Log, p. 13
- Listening Log, p.14
- Proofreading Checklist, p.15
- Proofreading Marks, p.16
- Writing Conference Form, p. 17
- Writing Rubric, p.18
- Instructional Routines, pp.19–26
- Graphic Organizer 12: T-Map, p. 38

JOURNEYS DIGITAL Powered by DESTINATION Reading

For Students
- Student eBook
- Comprehension Expedition CD-ROM
- Leveled Readers Online
- WriteSmart CD-ROM

For Teachers
- Online TE and Focus Wall
- Online Assessment System
- Teacher One-Stop
- Destination Reading Instruction

Week at a Glance

Intervention

STRATEGIC INTERVENTION: TIER II

Use these materials to provide additional targeted instruction for students who need Tier II strategic intervention.

Supports the Student Book selections

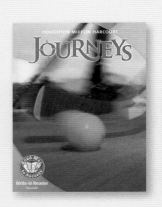  

Interactive Work-text for Skills Support

Write-In Reader:

Making a Magazine

- Engaging selection connects to main topic.
- Reinforces this week's target vocabulary and comprehension skill and strategy.
- Opportunities for student interaction on each page.

Assessment

Progress monitoring every two weeks.

For this week's Strategic Intervention lessons, see Teacher's Edition pages S22–S31.

INTENSIVE INTERVENTION: TIER III

- The materials in the Literacy Tool Kit help you provide a different approach for students who need Tier III intensive intervention.
- Interactive lessons provide focused instruction in key reading skills, targeted at students' specific needs.
- Lesson cards are convenient for small-group or individual instruction.
- Blackline masters provide additional practice.
- A leveled book accompanies each lesson to give students opportunities for additional reading and skill application.
- Assessments for each lesson help you evaluate the effectiveness of the intervention.

Lessons provide support for

- Phonics and Word Study Skills
- Vocabulary
- Comprehension Skills and Literary Genres
- Fluency

ELL English Language Learners

JOURNEYS DIGITAL Powered by DESTINATIONReading®
- Leveled Readers Online
- Picture Card Bank Online

SCAFFOLDED SUPPORT

Use these materials to ensure that students acquire social and academic language proficiency.

Language Support Card

- Builds background for the main topic and promotes oral language.
- Develops high-utility vocabulary and academic language.

Leveled Reader

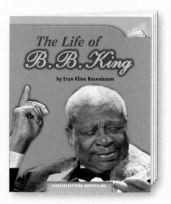

- Sheltered text connects to the main selection's topic, vocabulary, skill, and strategy.

Scaffolded Support

ELL ENGLISH LANGUAGE LEARNERS

Scaffold

Beginning Show children two classroom objects. Have them repeat *same* if the objects are the same and *different* if the objects are different. Repeat with more objects.

Intermediate Have children draw two objects that are the same. Then have them draw two objects that are different.

Advanced Name an object. First, ask children to name another object that is similar. Then, have them name an object that is different from the object you named.

Advanced High Show children two objects. Ask them to use complete sentences to describe multiple similarities and differences between the two.

- Notes throughout the Teacher's Edition scaffold instruction to each language proficiency level.

Vocabulary in Context Cards 171–180

specialty A schoolroom may be set up for one skill, or **specialty**. In this room, students use computers.

disturbing Loud noises are **disturbing** students working in the library. Please be courteous.

collapsed After a hard practice, you might find a tired team **collapsed** onto benches in the gym.

- Provide visual support and additional practice for Target Vocabulary words.

For this week's English Language Learners lessons, see Teacher's Edition, pages E22–E31.

Weekly Plan

	Day 1	Day 2
Whole Group		
Oral Language Listening Comprehension	**Teacher Read Aloud** "Hundreds Rally at Fullerton High," T160–T161 ☑ Target Vocabulary, T161	**Turn and Talk,** T167
Vocabulary Comprehension Skills and Strategies **Reading**	☑ **Comprehension** Preview the Target Skill, T161 ☑ **Introduce Vocabulary** Vocabulary in Context, T162–T163 **Develop Background** ☑ Target Vocabulary, T164–T165	**Introduce Comprehension** ☑ Fact and Opinion, T166–T167 Analyze/Evaluate, T166–T167 **Read "The Dog Newspaper,"** T168–T176 Focus on Genre, T168 Stop and Think, T173, T175, T176
Cross-Curricular Connections Fluency Decoding	☑ **Fluency** Model Phrasing: Punctuation, T160	☑ **Fluency** Teach Phrasing: Punctuation, T184
Whole Group Language Arts		
Spelling Grammar Writing	☑ **Spelling** Changing Final *y* to *i*: Pretest, T190 ☑ **Grammar** Daily Proofreading Practice, T192 Teach Prepositions, T192 ☑ **Write to Narrate: Personal Narrative Paragraph** Analyze the Model, T196	☑ **Spelling** Changing Final *y* to *i*: Word Sort, T190 ☑ **Grammar** Daily Proofreading Practice, T193 Teach Prepositional Phrases, T193 ☑ **Write to Narrate: Personal Narrative Paragraph** Focus Trait: Voice, T197
Writing Prompt	*Explain which section of a newspaper you would like to write.*	*Write a blog entry for a pet-owners' website with two facts and two opinions.*
COMMON CORE Correlations	Introduce Vocabulary L.5.4a Develop Background L.5.4a Fluency RF.5.4a Spelling L.5.2e Grammar L.5.1a Write to Narrate W.5.3a, W.5.3b, W.5.3d, W.5.4, W.5.5	Turn and Talk SL.5.1a Read RI.5.2, RI.5.10 Fluency RF.5.4a Spelling L.5.2e Grammar L.5.1a Write to Narrate W.5.3a, W.5.3b, W.5.3d, W.5.4, W.5.5

Suggestions for Small Groups (See pp. T204–T205.)
Suggestions for Intervention (See pp. S22–S31.)
Suggestions for English Language Learners (See pp. E22–E31.)

JOURNEYS DIGITAL · Powered by DESTINATIONReading®
Teacher One-Stop: Lesson Planning

Day 3

Turn and Talk, T177
Oral Language, T177

Read "The Dog Newspaper," T168–T176
Develop Comprehension, T170, T172, T174
☑ **Target Vocabulary**
"The Dog Newspaper," T170, T172
Your Turn, T177
Deepen Comprehension
☑ Fact and Opinion, T182–T183

Cross-Curricular Connection
Social Studies, T173
☑ **Fluency:** Practice Phrasing: Punctuation, T171
☑ **Decoding**
Recognizing Suffixes, T185

☑ **Spelling**
Changing Final *y* to *i*: Antonyms, T191
☑ **Grammar**
Daily Proofreading Practice, T193
Teach Object Pronouns, T193
☑ **Write to Narrate: Personal Narrative Paragraph**
Prewrite, T197

Write a diary entry for a day in the life of a dog.

Oral Language SL.5.1a
Read RI.5.2, RI.5.10
Your Turn SL.5.1c
Deepen Comprehension RI.5.1, W.5.9b, SL.5.1a, SL.5.1c
Fluency RF.5.4a
Decoding RF.5.3a
Spelling L.5.2e
Grammar L.5.1a
Write to Narrate W.5.3a, W.5.3b, W.5.3d, W.5.4, W.5.5

Day 4

Text to World, T181

Read "Poetry about Poetry," T178–T180
Connect to Poetry, T178
Target Vocabulary Review, T179
Develop Comprehension, T180
Weekly Internet Challenge, T180–T181
Making Connections, T181
☑ **Vocabulary Strategies**
Analogies, T186–T187

Fluency
Practice Phrasing: Punctuation, T179

☑ **Spelling**
Changing Final *y* to *i*: Connect to Writing, T191
☑ **Grammar**
Daily Proofreading Practice, T194
Review Prepositions and Prepositional Phrases, T194
☑ **Write to Narrate: Personal Narrative Paragraph**
Draft, T198

Describe how you can touch, taste, and smell words.

Read RL.5.5, RL.5.7, RL.5.10
Making Connections W.5.7
Vocabulary Strategies L.5.4c, L.5.5c
Fluency RF.5.4a
Spelling L.5.2e
Grammar L.5.1c
Write to Narrate W.5.3a, W.5.3b, W.5.3d, W.5.3e, W.5.4, W.5.5

Day 5

Listening and Speaking, T189

Connect and Extend
Read to Connect, T188
Independent Reading, T188
Extend Through Research, T189

Fluency
Progress Monitoring, T201

☑ **Spelling**
Changing Final *y* to *i*: Assess, T191
☑ **Grammar**
Daily Proofreading Practice, T194
Connect Grammar to Writing, T194–T195
☑ **Write to Narrate: Personal Narrative Paragraph**
Revise for Voice, T198

Create a concrete poem for Peter Lu's time machine.

Listening and Speaking SL.5.2, SL.5.4
Connect and Extend W.5.7, W.5.8, SL.5.1a, SL.5.1c
Fluency RF.5.4a
Spelling L.5.2e
Grammar L.5.1a, L.5.3a
Write to Narrate W.5.3a, W.5.3b, W.5.3d, W.5.3e, W.5.4, W.5.5

Your Skills for the Week

☑ **Vocabulary**
Target Vocabulary
Strategies: Analogies

☑ **Comprehension**
Fact and Opinion
Analyze/Evaluate

☑ **Decoding**
Recognizing Suffixes

☑ **Fluency**
Phrasing:
Punctuation

☑ **Language Arts**
Spelling
Grammar
Writing

Weekly Leveled Readers

Differentiated Support for This Week's Targets

 **TARGET SKILL**

Fact and Opinion

 **TARGET STRATEGY**

Analyze/Evaluate

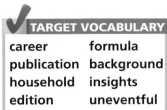 **TARGET VOCABULARY**

career	formula
publication	background
household	insights
edition	uneventful
required	destruction

Additional Tools

Vocabulary in Context Cards

Comprehension Tool: Graphic Organizer Transparency 12

? Essential Question

What part do facts and opinions play in a story?

Vocabulary Reader

Level R

Build Target Vocabulary

- Introduce the Target Vocabulary in context and build comprehension using the Target Strategy.

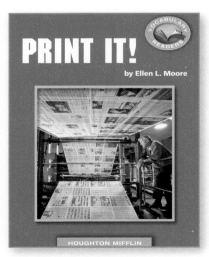

Vocabulary Reader

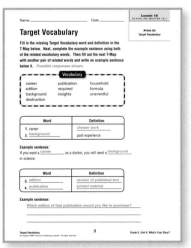

Blackline Master 18.1

Intervention

Scaffolded Support

- Provide extra support in applying the Target Vocabulary, Target Skill, and Target Strategy in context.

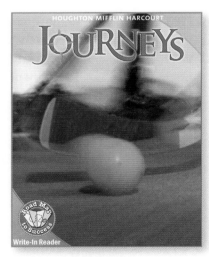

Write-In Reader

 SMALL GROUP Options

For Vocabulary Reader Lesson Plans, see pp. T206–T207.

Leveled Readers

Struggling Readers
Level P

Objective: Use Fact and Opinion and the Analyze/Evaluate strategy to read *Maria Tallchief, American Ballerina*.

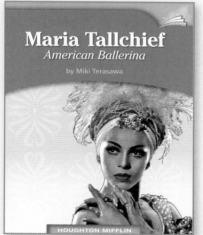

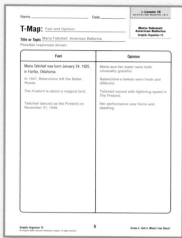

Blackline Master 18.3

On Level
Level U

Objective: Use Fact and Opinion and the Analyze/Evaluate strategy to read *B.B. King*.

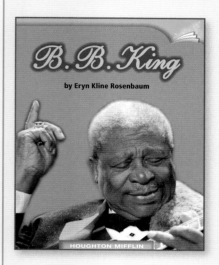

Blackline Master 18.4

Advanced
Level X

Objective: Use Fact and Opinion and the Analyze/Evaluate strategy to read *Isabel Allende*.

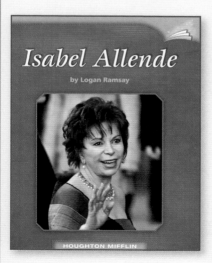

Blackline Master 18.5

English Language Learners
Level U

Objective: Use Fact and Opinion and the Analyze/Evaluate strategy to read *The Life of B.B. King*.

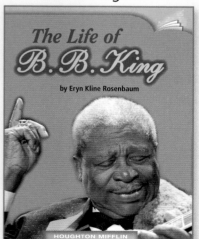

Blackline Master 18.6

For Leveled Reader Lesson Plans, see pp. T210–T213.

Ready-Made Work Stations

Managing Independent Activities

Use the Ready-Made Work Stations to establish a consistent routine for students working independently. Each station contains three activities. Students who experience success with the *Get Started!* activity move on to the *Reach Higher!* and *Challenge Yourself!* activities, as time permits.

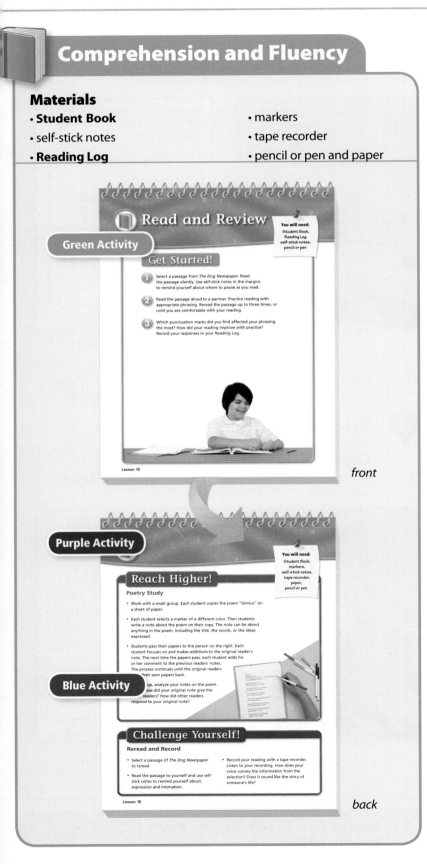

Comprehension and Fluency

Materials
- **Student Book**
- self-stick notes
- **Reading Log**
- markers
- tape recorder
- pencil or pen and paper

Read and Review

Green Activity

You will need: Student Book, Reading Log, self-stick notes, pencil or pen

Get Started!

1. Select a passage from *The Dog Newspaper*. Read the passage silently. Use self-stick notes in the margins to remind yourself about where to pause as you read.

2. Read the passage aloud to a partner. Practice reading with appropriate phrasing. Reread the passage up to three times, or until you are comfortable with your reading.

3. Which punctuation marks did you find affected your phrasing the most? How did your reading improve with practice? Record your responses in your Reading Log.

Lesson 18   *front*

Purple Activity

You will need: Student Book, markers, self-stick notes, tape recorder, paper, pencil or pen

Reach Higher!

Poetry Study

- Work with a small group. Each student copies the poem "Genius" on a sheet of paper.

- Each student selects a marker of a different color. Then students write a note about the poem on their copy. The note can be about anything in the poem, including the title, the words, or the ideas expressed.

- Students pass their papers to the person on the right. Each student focuses on and makes additions to the original reader's note. The next time the papers pass, each student adds his or her comment to the previous readers' notes. The process continues until the original readers [get] their own papers back.

Blue Activity

[...] up, analyze your notes on the poem. [...] did your original note give the [...] readers? How did other readers respond to your original note?

Challenge Yourself!

Reread and Record

- Select a passage of *The Dog Newspaper* to reread.

- Read the passage to yourself and use self-stick notes to remind yourself about expression and intonation.

- Record your reading with a tape recorder. Listen to your recording. How does your voice convey the information from the selection? Does it sound like the story of someone's life?

Lesson 18   *back*

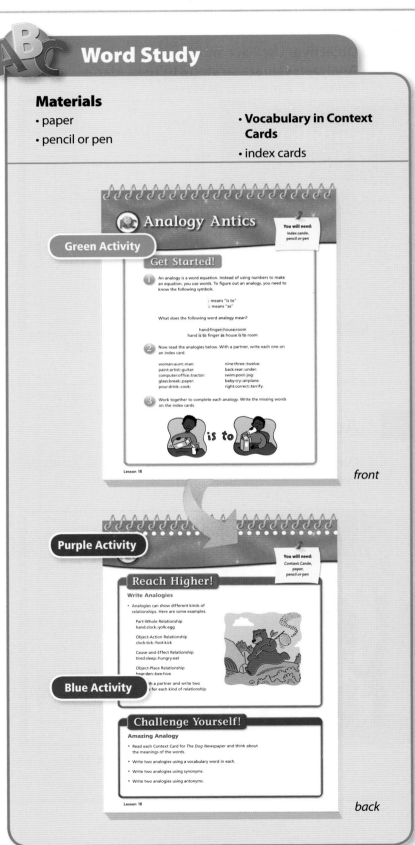

Word Study

Materials
- paper
- pencil or pen
- **Vocabulary in Context Cards**
- index cards

Analogy Antics

Green Activity

You will need: index cards, pencil or pen

Get Started!

1. An analogy is a word equation. Instead of using numbers to make an equation, you use words. To figure out an analogy, you need to know the following symbols.

   : means "is to"
   :: means "as"

   What does the following word analogy mean?

   hand:finger::house:room
   hand is to finger as house is to room

2. Now read the analogies below. With a partner, write each one on an index card.

   woman:aunt::man: nine:three::twelve:
   paint:artist::guitar: back:rear::under:
   computer:office::tractor: swim:pool::jog:
   glass:break::paper: baby:cry::airplane:
   pour:drink::cook: right:correct::terrify:

3. Work together to complete each analogy. Write the missing words on the index cards.

   is to

Lesson 18   *front*

Purple Activity

You will need: Context Cards, paper, pencil or pen

Reach Higher!

Write Analogies

- Analogies can show different kinds of relationships. Here are some examples.

   Part-Whole Relationship
   hand:clock::yolk:egg

   Object-Action Relationship
   clock:tick::foot:kick

   Cause-and-Effect Relationship
   tired:sleep::hungry:eat

   Object-Place Relationship
   heard en::bee:hive

Blue Activity

[...] h a partner and write two [...] s for each kind of relationship.

Challenge Yourself!

Amazing Analogy

- Read each Context Card for *The Dog Newspaper* and think about the meanings of the words.

- Write two analogies using a vocabulary word in each.

- Write two analogies using synonyms.

- Write two analogies using antonyms.

Lesson 18   *back*

Think and Write

Materials
- computer with Internet access
- art supplies
- pencil or pen and paper
- library books
- clip art or photographs
- poster board

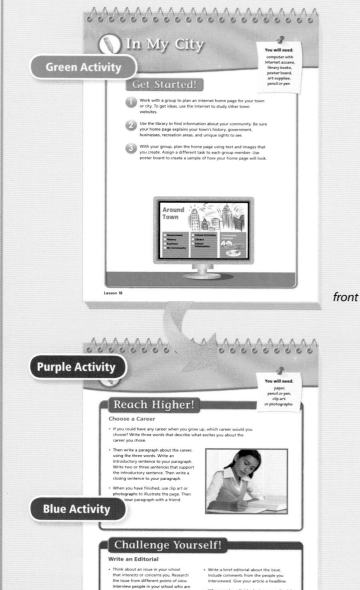

In My City

Green Activity

You will need:
computer with Internet access, library books, poster board, art supplies, pencil or pen

Get Started!

1. Work with a group to plan an Internet home page for your town or city. To get ideas, use the Internet to study other town websites.

2. Use the library to find information about your community. Be sure your home page explains your town's history, government, businesses, recreation areas, and unique sights to see.

3. With your group, plan the home page using text and images that you create. Assign a different task to each group member. Use poster board to create a sample of how your home page will look.

Around Town

Lesson 18

front

Purple Activity

You will need:
paper, pencil or pen, clip art or photographs

Reach Higher!

Choose a Career

- If you could have any career when you grow up, which career would you choose? Write three words that describe what excites you about the career you chose.

- Then write a paragraph about the career, using the three words. Write an introductory sentence to your paragraph. Write two or three sentences that support the introductory sentence. Then write a closing sentence to your paragraph.

- When you have finished, use clip art or photographs to illustrate the page. Then share your paragraph with a friend.

Blue Activity

Challenge Yourself!

Write an Editorial

- Think about an issue in your school that interests or concerns you. Research the issue from different points of view. Interview people in your school who are involved with the issue. To prepare for the interviews, write questions to ask each person.

- Write a brief editorial about the issue. Include comments from the people you interviewed. Give your article a headline.

- When you have finished, give your editorial to the students and teachers you interviewed. Did they agree, or disagree, with what you wrote?

Lesson 18

back

Independent Activities

Have students complete these activities at a computer center or a center with an audio CD player.

LAUNCH **Comprehension and Grammar Activities**

- Practice and apply this week's skills.

LAUNCH **Student eBook**

- Read and listen to this week's selections and skill lessons.

LAUNCH **WriteSmart CD-ROM**

- Review student versions of this week's writing model.

LAUNCH **Audiotext CD**

- Listen to books or selections on CD.

Single Log In

Teacher Read Aloud

Model Fluency

Phrasing: Punctuation Explain that good readers use punctuation to group words into phrases.

- Display **Projectable 18.1**. As you read each sentence, model how to group words into phrases, using the punctuation as a guide.

- Point out that commas and end punctuation help show where some, but not all, pauses should occur when reading aloud.

- Reread the sentences together with students, grouping the words together into natural phrases. Make sure students pay attention to punctuation.

Hundreds Rally at Fullerton High

Yesterday, students at Fullerton High School gathered to protest the firing of their school newspaper's editor. The rally was followed by a meeting with the principal, where students presented petitions asking him to reinstate the editor. When Principal Ross Miller refused, students decided to discuss their case with the school board.

The unrest stems from Miller's decision last Thursday, which **required** Senior Blake Wilson to give up his position as editor-in-chief of the *Fullerton Crier*. The principal acted after Wilson wrote an editorial in last week's **edition**, **(1)** defending students whose behavior caused disruption at school.

The editorial criticized Miller for taking privileges away from students who had worn T-shirts that had a political message and a peace sign in the **background**.

Some expressed surprise that the T-shirts generated controversy. "Who doesn't want peace?" asked Senior Jenna O'Brien.

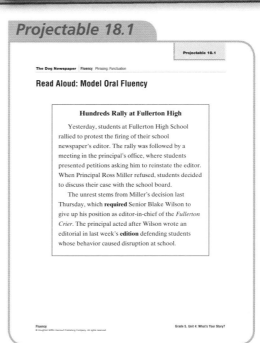

Projectable 18.1

Projectable 18.1

The Dog Newspaper | Fluency Phrasing: Punctuation

Read Aloud: Model Oral Fluency

Hundreds Rally at Fullerton High

Yesterday, students at Fullerton High School rallied to protest the firing of their school newspaper's editor. The rally was followed by a meeting in the principal's office, where students presented petitions asking him to reinstate the editor. When Principal Ross Miller refused, students decided to discuss their case with the school board.

The unrest stems from Miller's decision last Thursday, which **required** Senior Blake Wilson to give up his position as editor-in-chief of the *Fullerton Crier*. The principal acted after Wilson wrote an editorial in last week's **edition** defending students whose behavior caused disruption at school.

Fluency
© Houghton Mifflin Harcourt Publishing Company. All rights reserved.

Grade 5, Unit 4: What's Your Story?

The U.S. Constitution

According to Junior Sienna Deval, her graphic arts class made a few T-shirts as a team project. As they became controversial, demand for the shirts grew. "A few of us stayed after school making more," said Deval, whose **career** goals include art. She believes that wearing the T-shirt means something different to each student. "Some feel strongly that we should promote world peace. To others, it is the in thing."

Principal Miller decided to ban the T-shirts because "they were a **formula** for disruption." Miller said, "Discussions about the shirt's message carried over into class time. There were debates. It seemed like every **household** was talking about this topic." After a parent called to complain, Miller issued the ban. The next day, nine students wore the shirts and were sent to the principal's office.

Miller admits there is no prohibition against other T-shirt slogans, and he insists that this ban has nothing to do with the shirt's message. The key, he says, is the disruption. "Wearing a T-shirt to school should be **uneventful**."

Wilson, the former newspaper editor, believes it was important for the student **publication** to stand up for free speech. "We have the right to state our opinions," he said. Wilson believes that neither the T-shirt nor the editorial violated school rules. He offered these **insights**: "The shirt doesn't whip up hatred or **destruction**. Provoking discussion is a good thing."

Listening Comprehension
Preview the Target Skill

Read aloud the passage using correct phrasing. Then ask the following questions.

1 **MAKE INFERENCES** *What can you learn about Blake Wilson's beliefs from his newspaper editorial? He values students' rights and thinks that they are worth fighting for.*

2 **FACT AND OPINION** *Is it a fact or an opinion that T-shirts were a "formula for disruption"? It is Principal Miller's opinion that they are a disruption, but he uses facts to support his opinion.*

3 **FACT AND OPINION** *What facts led Principal Miller to issue the T-shirt ban? disrupted classes, debates, and a parent complaint*

4 **MAIN IDEA AND DETAILS** *Why does Blake Wilson think it is important for the newspaper to support the students? He believes that people have a right to express their opinions in a sensible way.*

✓ Target Vocabulary

- Reread "Hundreds Rally at Fullerton High" aloud.
- As you read, pause briefly to explain each highlighted vocabulary word.
- Discuss the meaning of each word as it is used in the Read Aloud.

required necessary, called for

edition version; specific issue

background the details of a person's or thing's past

career profession; the work a person does to earn a living

formula set of rules or steps

household the people who live in a house

uneventful unimportant, insignificant

publication any print product, such as a magazine, book, or newspaper

insights understanding on an issue; point of view

destruction vast damage or devastation; ruin

☑ Introduce Vocabulary

SHARE OBJECTIVE

- Understand and use the Target Vocabulary words.

Teach

Display the **Vocabulary in Context Cards,** using the routine below. Direct students to **Student Book pp. 454–455.** See also **Instructional Routine 9.**

1 Read and pronounce the word. Read the word once alone, then together with students.

2 **Explain the word.** Read the explanation under *What Does It Mean?*

3 **Discuss vocabulary in context.** Together, read aloud the sentence on the front of the card. Help students explain and use the word in new sentences.

4 **Engage with the word.** Ask and discuss the *Think About It* question with students.

Apply

Give partners or small groups one or two **Vocabulary in Context Cards.**

- Help students start the *Talk It Over* activity on the back of their card.

- Have students complete activities for all the cards during the week.

Lesson 18

Vocabulary in Context

☑ **TARGET VOCABULARY**

career
publication
background
household
insights
required
uneventful
edition
formula
destruction

Vocabulary Reader   Context Cards

1 career
The career, or chosen work, of a journalist involves carefully gathering the facts.

2 publication
A news publication might take the form of a newspaper, news magazine, or website.

3 background
Years of experience as reporters often give TV newscasters their needed background.

4 household
This boy delivers newspapers to nearly every household in his neighborhood.

454

ELL ENGLISH LANGUAGE LEARNERS

Scaffold

Beginning Use actions to show the meanings of *background*, *publication*, and *destruction.* Then have students perform the action as you say each word.

Advanced Ask students questions to confirm their understanding. For example, *What is required for you to do well on an exam?*

Intermediate Have students complete sentence frames for each Vocabulary word. For example, *Nothing happened yesterday. Overall it was very _____.* (*uneventful*)

Advanced High Have partners ask and answer questions about each Vocabulary word. For example, *What kind of career would you like to have?*

See ELL Lesson 18, pp. E22–E31, for scaffolded support.

- Study each Context Card.

- Break each Vocabulary word into syllables. Use a dictionary to verify your answers.

5 insights

During interviews, reporters hear the insights and opinions of other people.

6 required

TV cameras are often required, or needed, to record all the action at a sports event.

7 uneventful

This meteorologist predicts an uneventful week. The weather won't change much.

8 edition

A special edition, or version, of a newspaper might be published after a huge news event.

9 formula

Use this formula, or rule, in all news articles: tell *who*, *what*, *when*, *where*, *why*, and *how*.

10 destruction

Papers reported that the destruction caused by the hurricane left some people homeless.

455

Monitor Vocabulary

Are students able to understand and use Target Vocabulary words?

IF...	THEN...
students have difficulty understanding and using most of the Target Vocabulary Words,	▶ use **Vocabulary in Context Cards** and differentiate the **Vocabulary Reader**, *Print It!*, for Struggling Readers, p. T206. *See also Intervention Lesson 18, pp. S22–S31.*
students can understand and use most of the Target Vocabulary words,	▶ use **Vocabulary in Context Cards** and differentiate the **Vocabulary Reader**, *Print It!*, for On-Level Readers, p. T206.
students can understand and use all of the Target Vocabulary words,	▶ differentiate the **Vocabulary Reader** *Print It!*, for Advanced Readers, p. T207.

SMALL GROUP Options

Vocabulary Reader, pp. T206–T207. *Group English Language Learners according to language proficiency.*

VOCABULARY IN CONTEXT CARDS 171–180

career

The career, or chosen work, of a journalist involves carefully gathering the facts.

front

career

What Does It Mean?
A career is a job that becomes a person's life's work.
Spanish cognate: carrera

Think About It.
What do you think your **career** will be? Why?

Talk It Over.
Think about the kinds of things people do to prepare for a **career**. Point to match each activity with a possible future **career**.

If you like to:	your *career* might be:
take care of cats and dogs	singer
help a friend learn about fractions	chef
make delicious sandwiches	veterinarian
illustrate your stories	teacher
sing in a talent show	artist

back

Develop Background

SHARE OBJECTIVES

- Learn about important ideas in "The Dog Newspaper."
- Build background using the Target Vocabulary words.

 ENGLISH LANGUAGE LEARNERS

Scaffold

Beginning Help students list familiar publications including newspapers, books, magazines, and the Internet by demonstrating and showing examples of each.

Intermediate Pre-teach unfamiliar words in "The Dog Newspaper" using gestures, visuals, or simplified language. Have volunteers generate sentences with these words.

Advanced Have students discuss what it would be like to work at a newspaper for a day. Use Target Vocabulary to guide students' conversation.

Advanced High Point out that most Americans have relatives who moved here within the past 200 years. Have students use the Target Vocabulary to write a short fictional newspaper story about a person's first days in America.

See ELL Lesson 18, p. E22–E31, for scaffolded support.

 Target Vocabulary

1 Teach/Model

- Use the graph on **Student Book p. 456** to discuss the newspaper business. Tell students that "The Dog Newspaper" is about a girl who is trying to create her own newspaper **publication**.

- Use **Vocabulary in Context Cards** to review the student-friendly explanations of the Target Vocabulary words.

- Have students silently read **Student Book p. 456**. Then read the passage aloud.

2 Guided Practice

Ask students the first item below and discuss their responses. Continue in this way until students have answered a question about each Target Vocabulary word.

1. What part of a **career** in the newspaper business do you find most interesting?

2. What type of **publication** do you most enjoy reading?

3. How many people would make up a full **household**?

4. How might a special **edition** of a newspaper differ from a daily edition?

5. What is **required** in order to be a successful student?

6. How would you describe the **formula** for a great news article?

7. Tell what kind of career you would like to have. What **background** would be helpful in that career?

8. If a person has good **insights,** is that person considered to be smart? Why?

9. Describe what an **uneventful** day of school would be like.

10. Name some ways people can help fix the **destruction** caused by a hurricane.

Background

✓ **TARGET VOCABULARY** **What's in a Newspaper?** If you like to write, a newspaper **career** may be for you. No day is **uneventful**, so there is always interesting news to gather. Reporters are **required** to record events accurately.

Here is some **background** on this type of **publication**. A newspaper usually has its own **formula** for choosing articles. Usually, each **edition** contains the same sections. The front page of each section presents major stories, perhaps of courage or of **destruction**. Editorial pages offer **insights** into the editors' opinions. Other sections—sports, business, comics, and entertainment—appeal to different people in a **household**. Working on one of these sections might appeal to you.

• Analyze the graph below. How much greater was the percentage of people reading newspapers in 1994 than the percentage in 2002?

PEOPLE READING NEWSPAPERS REGULARLY

A smaller percentage of people are reading newspapers now than in the past. More people are getting their news from television and the Internet.

Most city newspapers have a daily **edition**.

3 | Apply

• Have partners take turns reading a paragraph on **Student Book p. 456** to one another.

• Tell partners to pause at and explain each highlighted word as they read. Have students continue their discussion by using the Target Vocabulary to tell about a neighborhood activity they enjoy doing.

• Review the graph with students. Discuss the steps required to correctly read a graph. Have students use the graph to answer the bulleted question. *(7% fewer people read newspapers in 2002 than in 1994)*

Introduce Comprehension

SHARE OBJECTIVES

- Analyze how an author uses facts and opinions.
- Evaluate how well an author uses facts to support opinions.

SKILL TRACE

Fact and Opinion

Introduce	T166–T167, T182–T183
Differentiate	T208–T209
Reteach	T216
Review	T104–T105, Unit 6
Test	Weekly Tests, Lesson 18

ELL ENGLISH LANGUAGE LEARNERS

Scaffold

Beginning Say the words *fact* and *opinion* aloud and have students repeat. Then demonstrate how to use the words in sentence frames such as these: *One fact about newspapers is _____. One opinion is _____.*

Intermediate Give students practice in expressing opinions. Have students complete these sentence frames: *I think that_____. I believe that _____. In my opinion, _____.*

Advanced Discuss the difference between the fact that a book weighs two pounds and a students' opinion on whether the book is heavy or light.

Advanced High Have students write opinion sentences using the signal phrases *I think* or *I believe that.*

See ELL Lesson 18, pp. E22–E31, for scaffolded support.

✔ Fact and Opinion; Analyze/Evaluate

1 Teach/Model

AL *Academic Language*

evaluate to form an opinion or judgment about something

opinion a statement that tells a thought, feeling, or belief

- Remind students that facts can be proven true or false, but **opinions** cannot. Tell students they will analyze text to **evaluate** the author's use of facts and opinions.

- Read and discuss **Student Book p. 457** with students. Have them use the Academic Language in the discussion.

- Display **Projectable 18.2**. Have students read "Mice Weekly Squeaks to a Close."

FACT AND OPINION Point out that phrases like "I think" and "it seems" indicate an opinion. Facts can easily be proven true or false.

- Explain that you will use the T-Map to record facts and opinions from the passage.

Think Aloud
The author writes that "Mice Weekly" was not a success. This can't be proven, so it's an opinion. I'll see if there are any facts to support this opinion.

ANALYZE/EVALUATE Explain that analyzing a text to evaluate the author's use of facts and opinions and asking questions about why certain information is included will help students better understand a selection.

Think Aloud
The author states that "Lee couldn't understand the newspaper's failure" because the first edition sold well. The author thinks that the newspaper sold because people bought it out of fear of mice.

Projectable 18.2

The Dog Newspaper | Introduce Comprehension | Fact and Opinion; Analyze/Evaluate

Fact and Opinion; Analyze/Evaluate

Mice Weekly Squeaks to a Close

Lee Norris likes mice. One day he decided to combine his favorite things—mice and writing—into a weekly newspaper, "Mice Weekly." It was not a success. Lee published only two editions. He sold just one copy of the second edition. Lee's brother bought it because he owed Lee a dollar.

Lee couldn't understand the newspaper's failure. He thought it was great. His first edition sold twenty copies! Most people were drawn by the front-page headline of that edition, "Mice Escaping All Over Town!" The story was about an experiment that timed mice to see how quickly they could escape a maze. It wasn't that mice were loose in the city, as people who bought the paper had feared.

Fact and Opinion Use a T-Map to show opinions and supporting facts.

Supporting Facts	Opinion
Lee published only two editions. Lee sold just one copy of the second edition. Lee's brother bought a copy only because he owed Lee a dollar.	He thought it was great.
The first edition sold 20 copies. The first edition had a headline about mice escaping all over the city.	People bought the first edition only out of fear.

Analyze/Evaluate Evaluate how well the author's opinion is supported by facts.

Comprehension

✓ **TARGET SKILL** **Fact and Opinion**

As you read "The Dog Newspaper," watch for true information, or facts, and for statements that are the author's opinion. Use a graphic organizer like this one to keep track of facts and opinions. If you are unsure if a statement is a fact or an opinion, use a reliable source to help you determine if the statement is a fact.

Facts	Opinions
•	•
•	•
•	•

✓ **TARGET STRATEGY** **Analyze/Evaluate**

Use your graphic organizer to ask yourself questions about information the author presents in "The Dog Newspaper." Analyzing the author's reasons for including certain facts and opinions can help you evaluate how well she achieves her purpose.

JOURNEYS DIGITAL **Powered by** DESTINATION Reading®
Comprehension Activities: Lesson 18

457

2 Guided Practice

Use **Projectable S7** to further explain the analyze/evaluate strategy. Then have students copy and complete their own T-Maps for "Mice Weekly Squeaks to a Close." Review their T-Maps with them and guide students to ask themselves questions about information in the passage.

3 Apply

Turn and Talk Have partners analyze the facts presented in the passage and discuss other opinions that could be supported with those facts.

Ask students to locate facts and opinions in another text they have read recently. Have them record the facts and opinions in a T-Map and use an encyclopedia or other source to verify the facts.

Monitor Comprehension

Are students able to analyze text to evaluate an author's use of fact and opinion?

IF...	THEN...
students are having difficulty distinguishing fact from opinion,	▶ **Differentiate Comprehension** for Struggling Readers, p. T208. *See also Intervention Lesson 18, p. S22–S31.*
students can distinguish fact from opinion,	▶ **Differentiate Comprehension** for On-Level Readers, p. T208.
students can analyze text to evaluate fact and opinion,	▶ **Differentiate Comprehension** for Advanced Readers, p. T209.

 SMALL GROUP Options

Differentiate Comprehension: pp. T208–T209.

Group English Language Learners according to language proficiency. See also ELL Lesson 18, pp. E22–E31 for scaffolded support.

Practice Book p. 205

See Grab-and-Go™ Resources for additional leveled practice.

Introduce the
Main Selection

TARGET SKILL

FACT AND OPINION Explain that as they read, students will use **Graphic Organizer 12: T-Map** to distinguish between two types of statements:

• facts—ideas that can be proven true

• opinions—ideas that cannot be proven true

TARGET STRATEGY

ANALYZE/EVALUATE Students will use **Graphic Organizer 12** to analyze and evaluate the author's use of facts and opinions.

GENRE: Autobiography

• Read the genre information on **Student Book p. 458** with students.

• Share and discuss **Genre Blackline Master: Biography, Autobiography**.

• Preview the selection and model identifying characteristics of the genre.

Think Aloud *I see from the first sentence that the author is writing from her own point of view. The title tells me the selection is about a newspaper.*

• As you preview, ask students to identify other features of autobiographies.

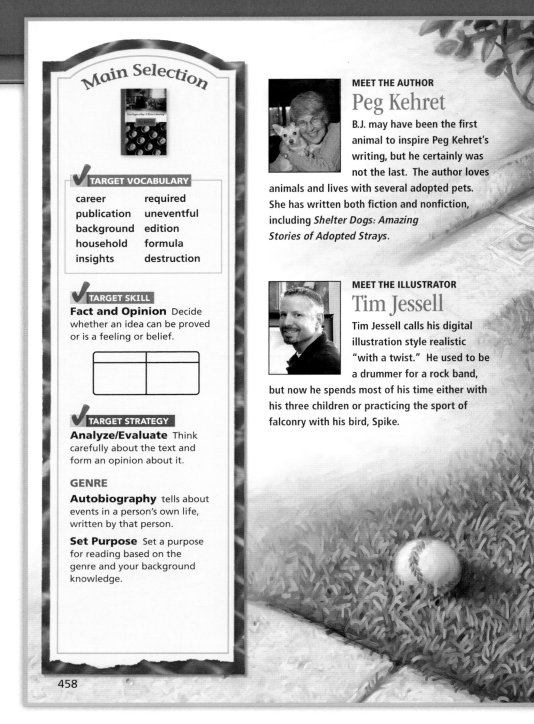

Main Selection

TARGET VOCABULARY

career	required
publication	uneventful
background	edition
household	formula
insights	destruction

TARGET SKILL

Fact and Opinion Decide whether an idea can be proved or is a feeling or belief.

TARGET STRATEGY

Analyze/Evaluate Think carefully about the text and form an opinion about it.

GENRE

Autobiography tells about events in a person's own life, written by that person.

Set Purpose Set a purpose for reading based on the genre and your background knowledge.

458

MEET THE AUTHOR
Peg Kehret

B.J. may have been the first animal to inspire Peg Kehret's writing, but he certainly was not the last. The author loves animals and lives with several adopted pets. She has written both fiction and nonfiction, including *Shelter Dogs: Amazing Stories of Adopted Strays.*

MEET THE ILLUSTRATOR
Tim Jessell

Tim Jessell calls his digital illustration style realistic "with a twist." He used to be a drummer for a rock band, but now he spends most of his time either with his three children or practicing the sport of falconry with his bird, Spike.

Reading the Selection

	Pre-Reading	Reading
Supported	**SELECTION SUMMARY** Use **Blackline Master 18.2** to give students an overview before they read. **AUDIOTEXT CD** Have students listen to the selection as they follow along in their books.	**AUTHOR'S PURPOSE** After reading, reread each page and have students retell the key life events the author describes. As a whole group discuss the author's purpose for focusing on these events.
Independent	**PREVIEW** Have students use the title, genre information, and illustrations to discuss predictions and clues. Some students may read the story independently.	**TEXT EVIDENCE** Pause after reading pp. 461, 463, 465, 466. Have students write questions that can be answered using text evidence in the story. Discuss students' questions and answers.

The Dog Newspaper

from Five Pages a Day

by Peg Kehret • selection illustrated by Tim Jessell

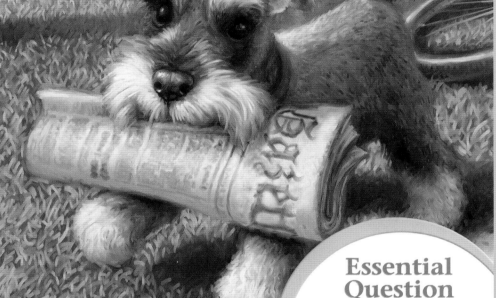

Essential Question

What part do facts and opinions play in a story?

459

Blackline Master 18.2

? Essential Question

- Read aloud the **Essential Question** on **Student Book p. 459.** *What part do facts and opinions play in a story?*

- Tell students to think about this question as they read "The Dog Newspaper."

Set Purpose

- Explain that good readers set a purpose for reading based on their preview of the selection, what they know about the genre, as well as what they want to learn by reading. Tell them they can also think about what the author wants them to know.

- Model setting a reading purpose based on the author's desired outcomes.

> **Think Aloud**
> *An autobiography tells about major events in a person's life and is written by that person. One purpose for reading is to find out how the author is involved with this newspaper and why this event is important in her life.*

- Have students share their purposes for reading and record them in their journals.

JOURNEYS DIGITAL **Powered by** **DESTINATIONReading**
Student eBook: Read and Listen

Develop Comprehension

Pause at the stopping points to ask students the following questions.

1 Character Traits

Based on the details in the first four paragraphs on p. 460, what character traits does the author possess? How does her use of dialogue reinforce these traits? Sample answers: outgoing, curious, persistent, and creative; The dialogue gives readers an idea of how she conducted interviews and research for her newspaper.

2 Draw Conclusions

Why does the author conclude that the local dogs' lives are boring? Sample answer: They follow the same routines day after day.

3 ✔ **TARGET VOCABULARY**

Why would it be surprising to find a puppy alive amid all the **destruction***? Sample answer: Almost everything else in the area was damaged or killed.*

4 Understanding Characters

How is B.J.'s life different from that of Fluffy, Max, and the other local dogs? Sample answer: B.J. was rescued during a war. His life has been filled with adventure.

I began my writing career at the age of ten when I wrote and sold the *Dog Newspaper*. This weekly publication, which cost five cents a copy, reported on the local dogs.

I interviewed every neighbor who had a dog. "What exciting thing has your dog done?" I asked.

People responded, "All Fluffy does is eat, sleep, and bark at the mailman." Or, "Max's only excitement is his daily walk on the leash." Such answers did not lead to important news stories.

I didn't give up. "If your dog could talk," I asked, "what do you think he would say?"

1

"Feed me," was the most common answer, followed by, "Let's play."

What could a writer do with such boring material? The solution sat at my feet, wagging his tail.

2

The first issue of the *Dog Newspaper* featured my dog, B.J., on the entire front page. Although his life at that time was as uneventful as the lives of the other neighborhood dogs, B.J. had a unique background.

460

ELL **ENGLISH LANGUAGE LEARNERS**

Scaffold

Beginning Review with students the ways in which the soldiers take care of B.J. As you read, use gestures to show *tucked*, *fed*, and *shared water*.

Advanced Have students look at the selection. *What does B.J. offer the soldiers? He helps them feel less sad; he gives them love.*

Intermediate Help students evaluate the soldiers' decision to take care of B.J. *What did the soldiers see too much of? death and destruction*

Advanced High After reading pages 460–461, have students write a few sentences summarizing why the soldiers decided to keep B.J.

See ELL Lesson 18, pp. E22–E31, for scaffolded support.

Uncle Bill, my mother's younger brother, was a soldier in the U.S. Army during World War II. While in Germany, his unit went into a town that had recently been bombed. As they searched for survivors in a destroyed building, they came across a mother dog and her litter of puppies. The mother dog was dead. So were all the puppies except one.

3 The soldiers, who had seen far too much of death and destruction, carefully lifted that little brown dog from his littermates. One soldier tucked the puppy inside his jacket to keep him warm. The men fed him from their own food supplies, shared water from their canteens, and decided to keep him as the company mascot.

From then on, wherever Uncle Bill and his comrades went, the dog went, too. They named him B.J. because he was a Big Job to take care of, especially when they were fighting a war.

B.J. grew bigger and stronger as he traveled with the soldiers, tagging along on every mission and somehow surviving even when the men were too busy to pay attention to him.

4 As the soldiers fought to protect the free world, B.J. did his duty, too. He slept with them in foxholes; he trudged long miles across burned and barren land; he helped search rubble for signs of life. Most of all, he offered love and laughter to a group of lonely, weary men who were far from home.

461

Projectable 18.3a

The Dog Newspaper | Comprehension Fact and Opinion

T-Map: Fact and Opinion

Title or Topic The Dog Newspaper

Facts	Opinions
Sample answers: pp. 460–461 • Author began writing career at the age of ten. • Made up a newspaper that reported on local dogs. • Uncle Bill was a soldier in the U.S. Army during World War II. • He brought home B. J., a dog that became the family pet, from Germany.	Sample answers: pp. 460–461 • The dogs' lives were boring.

Practice Fluency

Phrasing Read aloud the fifth paragraph on **Student Book p. 461** as students follow along. As you read, model using consistent phrasing appropriate to the text.

Discuss with students how punctuation marks give clues to the reader on when to pause.

- *What punctuation marks in the paragraph signal places to pause?* commas, periods, and semicolons

- Have students choral-read the paragraph, pausing after phrases.

See **p. T184** for a complete fluency lesson on using punctuation to guide phrasing.

Analyze/Evaluate

- Display **Projectable 18.3a**. Remind students that a T-Map can help them list facts and opinions from the selection.

- Model how to fill out the T-Map using the Analyze/Evaluate strategy for **Student Book pp. 460–461** to analyze and evaluate the author's use of facts and opinions.

Think Aloud *The author says the dog went with the soldiers. This is a fact which gives the reader background. When she says the dog was a "Big Job" to take care of, she is giving an opinion.*

- Have students use **Graphic Organizer 12** to begin their own T-Map as they read, using the Analyze/Evaluate strategy to help them organize facts and opinions.

Develop Comprehension

5 Draw Conclusions

Explain whether you think the soldiers' decision to send B.J. to the United States was a good idea.
Sample answer: Yes, because the people of Germany already had a lot of responsibilities.

6 ✔ **TARGET VOCABULARY**

*How might your **household** be affected by the arrival of a dog like B.J.? Sample answer: A dog could bring great fun to my family, but he might also create a big mess around our house.*

7 Author's Craft

How does the author's word choice help readers understand her reaction to having B.J. join her family? Sample answers: "delighted by the addition"; "showered him with loving attention"

When the war ended, the soldiers rejoiced. Soon they would be going home to their loved ones. But what about B.J.? They knew they could not leave him in Germany. The German people were faced with the task of rebuilding their cities and their lives; no one wanted to bother with a dog, especially a dog who belonged to the Americans.

5 The men decided to chip in enough money to fly B.J. back to the United States. Then they had a drawing to see who got to keep him. Each soldier wrote his name on a slip of paper and put the paper in a helmet. The winning name was drawn: Bill Showers! My uncle.

Uncle Bill lived with my family, so B.J. was flown from Germany to Minneapolis, where my parents picked him up at the airport and drove him to our home in Austin, Minnesota.

6 I was nine years old and delighted by the addition of this wire-haired schnauzer (at least, we thought he might be a schnauzer) to our household.

According to Uncle Bill, B.J. understood many commands in both English and German. Since none of us spoke German, we had no way to prove this claim.

B.J. quickly became my dog. Although B.J. was overjoyed when my uncle arrived home after his discharge, Uncle Bill did not stay in Austin long. He got married and headed to the University of Minnesota, where dogs were not allowed in student housing. B.J. stayed with my family.

7 I showered him with loving attention. I brushed him, tied ribbons on his collar, took him for walks, and read aloud to him. B.J. seemed especially fond of the Raggedy Ann and Andy stories, which were favorites of mine as well.

> **STOP AND THINK**
> **Author's Craft** The author uses a **flashback**, a scene that shows earlier events, to tell about B.J.'s life before he came to live with her. Why is this information important to the story? Why is a flashback a good way to present information?

462

ELL **ENGLISH LANGUAGE LEARNERS**

Scaffold

Beginning For each question, accept one-word responses and expand student responses into sentences.	**Advanced** Have students respond to the questions in complete sentences. Provide corrective feedback as needed.
Intermediate Provide part of a response for each question and have students complete it. Then have students repeat the complete response and confirm their understanding.	**Advanced High** Have students tell how they know the answer to each question based on details from the story.

See ELL Lesson 18, pp. E22–E31, for scaffolded support.

B.J. had lived with us for a year when I launched the *Dog Newspaper*. He was a fascinating front-page subject, and the first edition of the *Dog Newspaper* sold twelve copies.

Even though my lead story required little research, this sixty cents was not easy money. All those interviews about the neighbor dogs took time. Also, I grew up before there were copy machines, so I couldn't just go to the local copy center and run off twelve copies of the paper. Using a pencil, I wrote every word twelve times. Then I delivered my newspapers and collected my pay.

B.J. and I became famous on our block. Neighbors were enthralled by the story, and I gobbled up congratulations on my writing the way B.J. ate his dinner. All of my customers agreed to purchase the next issue of the *Dog Newspaper*.

Giddy with success, I immediately began writing the second issue. The neighborhood dogs were still every bit as boring as they had been a week earlier, so I decided to repeat my winning formula and use B.J. as the main article again. Since I had already told the only unusual thing about my dog, this time I wrote a story called "B.J.'s Gingerbread House."

463

STOP AND THINK
Author's Craft: Flashback

- Explain to students that a flashback is a reference to events that happened earlier than the current scene in a story.

- Point out that authors use flashbacks to provide background about the setting or characters or to provide additional information in an interesting way.

- Have students answer the **Stop and Think** questions on **Student Book p. 462**.

CROSS-CURRICULAR CONNECTION

Social Studies

Tell students that World War II, the war in which Uncle Bill was a soldier for the U.S. Army, lasted from 1939–1945. It was the largest war in history, and it involved almost every part of the world. The United States was on the side of the Allies, along with France, Great Britain, and the Soviet Union. The other side, the Axis, included Germany, Japan, and Italy. Many millions of people died in the war. Eventually, the Allies won.

Where was Uncle Bill when he found B.J.? Germany

Was he in friendly territory or hostile territory? How do you know? He was probably in hostile territory because the U.S. and Germany fought on opposite sides of the war.

Develop Comprehension

8 **Infer/Predict**

Why do you think the neighbors enjoy the second issue of The Dog Newspaper *so much less than the first? Sample answer: The stories focus on ordinary events. They are not as exciting as the story in the first issue.*

9 **Supporting Details** *What happened during issues three and four?* Issue three was a publishing disaster and the author's grandfather was the only person to purchase issue four.

10 **Infer Character Motives**

Why does the author stop writing The Dog Newspaper? *Do you think this is a good decision? Why or why not? Sample answer: The author stops writing because people quit buying her newspaper. It was a good decision because she was not able to find worthwhile stories to write about.*

Our new washing machine had arrived in a large cardboard box. I kept the box to create a special house for B.J., who slept in the basement every night.

I spent hours decorating the box, copying a picture of a gingerbread house that was in one of my books. I colored curlicues; I blistered my hands cutting designs in the cardboard; I painted flowers on the sides. The gingerbread house was absolutely breathtaking.

At bedtime that night, I took B.J. down to the basement and put his blanket in the beautiful gingerbread house. I petted him and kissed him and told him I knew he would sleep well.

The next morning, I couldn't believe my eyes. B.J. had licked the glue from the cardboard, creating a sticky mess in his beard, and had chewed the house into dozens of pieces. He pranced toward me through the wreckage that littered the floor.

8 This story was quite a bit shorter than the story of B.J.'s rescue from a bombed-out house in Germany—and far less interesting. I filled the rest of issue number two of the *Dog Newspaper* with stirring reports such as "Rusty Knocks over Garbage Can" and "Cleo Chases Cat." After I delivered my papers, I eagerly waited for more compliments on my exciting journalism. None came. The next issue was even worse. Since B.J. still had done nothing newsworthy, I used the front page to describe what a beautiful and great dog he was. The other dogs, as always, got brief mention on the back page. Desperate to fill the space, I even wrote a story titled "Skippy Gets a Bath."

9 Issue number three was a publishing disaster. Few people read it, and the only person who purchased issue number four was my grandpa. Less than one month after its launch, the *Dog Newspaper* **10** went out of business.

✓ STOP AND THINK

Fact and Opinion Why is the author's statement above, "Less than one month after its launch, the *Dog Newspaper* went out of business," a fact? What are some other facts on this page?

464

465

STOP AND THINK

 TARGET SKILL

Fact and Opinion

- Remind students that facts can be proven true or false, while opinions cannot. Thinking about an author's use of facts and opinions can help readers judge what they read.

- Have students answer the **Stop and Think** question on **Student Book p. 464**.

- If students have difficulty finding facts and opinions, see Comprehension Intervention below for extra support.

- Have students continue working on their graphic organizers. Display **Projectable 18.3b** and work with students to add facts and opinions to the T-Map.

Turn and Talk

❓ Essential Question

Discuss the role that facts and opinions play in this selection.

COMPREHENSION INTERVENTION

 **TARGET SKILL**   Fact and Opinion

SKILL SUPPORT Remind students that a fact can be proven true, but an opinion cannot. Discuss some facts and opinions in the story so far:

- *Fact: The neighbors told stories about their dogs' daily lives.*

- *Opinion: These stories were dull.*

Read aloud the first three paragraphs of p. 464. Guide students in identifying the facts and opinions in the passage. Facts: The washing machine came in a large cardboard box; the author used the box to make a house for B.J.; and B.J. slept in the basement every night. Opinion: The house was special.

Guide students to continue working on their graphic organizers.

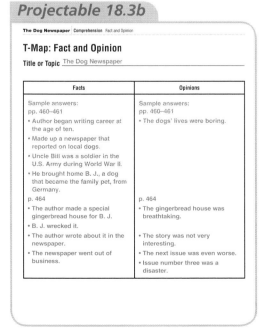

Projectable 18.3b

The Dog Newspaper | Comprehension | Fact and Opinion

T-Map: Fact and Opinion

Title or Topic The Dog Newspaper

Facts	Opinions
Sample answers: pp. 460–461	Sample answers: pp. 460–461
• Author began writing career at the age of ten.	• The dogs' lives were boring.
• Made up a newspaper that reported on local dogs.	
• Uncle Bill was a soldier in the U.S. Army during World War II.	
• He brought home B. J., a dog that became the family pet, from Germany.	
p. 464	p. 464
• The author made a special gingerbread house for B. J.	• The gingerbread house was breathtaking.
• B. J. wrecked it.	
• The author wrote about it in the newspaper.	• The story was not very interesting.
• The newspaper went out of business.	• The next issue was even worse.
	• Issue number three was a disaster.

STOP AND THINK

 **TARGET STRATEGY**

Analyze/Evaluate

- Explain to students that readers analyze text to evaluate its content. Readers may compare text content to what they know, and then evaluate whether what they are reading is fact or opinion.

- Have students use their completed graphic organizers to discuss how the author used facts and opinions to achieve her purpose.

- Have students answer the **Stop and Think** question on **Student Book p. 466.**

- Tell students that they should analyze the examples and evaluate how effectively the author presents her ideas to teach a lesson.

- If students have difficulty using the Analyze/Evaluate strategy, see **Comprehension Intervention** below for extra support.

I believed my writing career was over. My mistake, I thought then, was always putting my own dog on the front page. Now I realize that having dull material was an even bigger error. Would the *Dog Newspaper* have succeeded if I had featured Rusty or Fluffy or Cleo? Probably not, because Rusty, Fluffy, Cleo, and all the other neighborhood dogs hadn't done anything special.

If Fluffy had gotten lost and been returned home in a police car, or if Cleo had won a prize in a dog show, or if Rusty had given birth to puppies, then perhaps the neighbors would have wanted to read my articles.

Now I know that if I want people to read what I write, I must write something that they find interesting. I need exciting plots, unique information, and fresh insights.

When I wrote the *Dog Newspaper*, I was so caught up in the fun of creating a newspaper and getting paid for my work that I lost sight of my audience. What was in it for them? Except for the first issue, not much.

B.J. took one more plane ride, from Minneapolis to Fresno, California, where my parents moved shortly after I got married. He loved the California sunshine and spent his old age sleeping on the patio. He lived to be sixteen, a good long life for an orphaned puppy who entered the world during a wartime bombing.

No one bothered to save any issues of the *Dog Newspaper*. I can't imagine why.

STOP AND THINK
Analyze/Evaluate What lesson does the author try to teach? How does this story help to teach that lesson?

466

COMPREHENSION INTERVENTION

 **TARGET STRATEGY**   Analyze/Evaluate

STRATEGY SUPPORT Remind students that analyzing a text to evaluate facts and opinions can help them better understand what they are reading.

Point out that at first, the author believes that putting her own dog on the front page was her mistake. Tell students that analyzing the facts in the story does not support this opinion.

Read aloud the first paragraph on p. 466. *What does the author realize was her error?* having dull material

Tell students that they can use the information they record about facts to evaluate whether or not an opinion is valid.

Your Turn

True Tales

Short Response The most popular issue of the *Dog Newspaper* included the true story of how the soldiers found B.J. in Germany. Have you, or has someone you know, had an unusual adventure with a pet that you think others might find interesting? Write a paragraph describing that adventure.
PERSONAL RESPONSE

Publish It!

Plan a Newspaper The failure of her first newspaper teaches the author a lot about how to be a successful writer. If you were to start a newspaper of your own, what would you do to make it successful? Work with a small group to plan an edition of a school or community newspaper. Decide what kinds of articles, photographs, editorial features, and advertisements or comics you would include. Then share your ideas with the class.
SMALL GROUP

In Your Opinion

Turn and Talk Think about the facts and opinions the author includes in the story. With a partner, analyze the author's reasons for including various facts and her own opinions about her newspaper. Discuss what the information reveals about the author's outlook and how it has changed since the time in which the story's events took place. FACT AND OPINION

467

Retelling Rubric

4	Excellent	The retelling clearly and thoroughly explains how the author's reflections reveal what she learned.
3	Good	The retelling accurately explains how the author's reflections reveal what she learned.
2	Fair	The retelling gives a limited explanation of how the author's reflections reveal what she learned.
1	Unsatisfactory	The retelling does not explain how the author's reflections reveal what she learned.

Your Turn

Have students complete the activities on page 467.

True Tales Before students write, ask them to make a list of pets they know. If none of these pets have ever been involved in an adventure, students can search for newspaper articles about amazing pets. Once students have chosen a pet and an adventure, encourage them to use a Flow Chart to plan their paragraph. PERSONAL RESPONSE

Publish It! With the class, before students begin their plan, list and discuss the common features of a newspaper. Then remind students of the author's realization that to be successful, writing needs to interest an audience. Ask: *Who is your audience? What kinds of topics would they like to read about?* Allow time for students to share their plans. SMALL GROUP

In Your Opinion Have partners review the selection and list facts and opinions that the author includes. Then tell them to consider how the opinions change over time and how the author uses facts both to support her opinions and to interest the reader. FACT AND OPINION

Oral Language Have partners discuss how the author's reflections on page 466 help readers understand what she learned from working on the *Dog Newspaper*. If necessary, review that reflections are careful thoughts about past activities. Use the Retelling Rubric at the left to evaluate students' responses.

Connect to Poetry

PREVIEW THE POEM

- Tell students that this selection includes three poems, and information about poets and writing poetry. Ask students to read the titles of the poems and preview the pictures and subtitles in the text. Have students set a purpose for reading the poems based on the genre and their background knowledge. Then have students read the poetry independently.

DISCUSS POETIC FORM

- Tell students that poems are arranged in lines and stanzas. A stanza is a group of lines that form a unit. Stanzas are like the paragraphs of a poem.

- Tell students that rhythm is the repetition of stressed and unstressed syllables that gives a musical quality to poetry. Every poem has a rhythm. Some rhythms follow a specific pattern, while others do not.

- Explain that a pattern of rhyming words is a poem's rhyme scheme. Poets use rhyme scheme to appeal to readers' emotions.

- Tell students to look for the following elements of poetry as they read the poems that follow:

rhythm	a pattern of stressed and unstressed syllables in the words of a poem
rhyme scheme	a pattern of rhyming words or lines in a poem

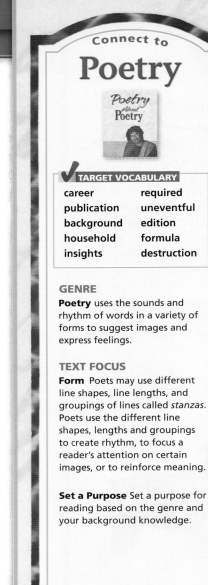

Connect to Poetry

✔ **TARGET VOCABULARY**

career	required
publication	uneventful
background	edition
household	formula
insights	destruction

GENRE

Poetry uses the sounds and rhythm of words in a variety of forms to suggest images and express feelings.

TEXT FOCUS

Form Poets may use different line shapes, line lengths, and groupings of lines called *stanzas*. Poets use the different line shapes, lengths and groupings to create rhythm, to focus a reader's attention on certain images, or to reinforce meaning.

Set a Purpose Set a purpose for reading based on the genre and your background knowledge.

468

Poetry About Poetry

Poetry lovers agree that a really great poem can turn an uneventful afternoon into an exciting one for the reader. The poets on these pages write about their love of poetry or about poetry itself. Think about what you like most about poetry. Is it the rhythm of the language, the images it creates, or the way it makes you feel?

To Write Poetry/ Para escribir poesía

by Francisco X. Alarcón

To Write Poetry
we must
first touch
smell and taste
every word

Para escribir poesía
debemos
primero tocar
oler y saborear
cada palabra

ELL ENGLISH LANGUAGE LEARNERS

Scaffold

Beginning Read aloud the poem titles and have students repeat. Define *genius* and help them use it in simple descriptive sentences.

Advanced Have partners discuss the connections between the poems they read on pp. 468–469.

Intermediate Prompt students to answer simple questions about poetic form. Discuss particularly difficult figurative language that poets may use.

Advanced High Have students use support from the poems to write a response to this question: *How does a poet convey her thoughts?*

See ELL Lesson 18, pp. E22–E31, for scaffolded support.

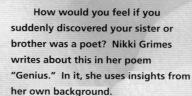

Genius
by Nikki Grimes

"Sis! Wake up!" I whisper
in the middle of the night.

Urgently, I shake her
till she switches on the light.

The spiral notebook in my hand
provides her quick relief.

It tells her there's no danger
of a break-in by a thief.

"Okay," she says, then props herself
up vertically in bed.

She nods for me to read my work.
I cough, then forge ahead.

The last verse of my poem leaves
her silent as a mouse.

I worry till she says, "We have
a genius in the house."

How would you feel if you suddenly discovered your sister or brother was a poet? Nikki Grimes writes about this in her poem "Genius." In it, she uses insights from her own background.

Grimes had always wanted a career as a poet and writer. Her first poem was accepted for publication while she was in high school and was printed in an edition of a poetry journal. She was always close to members of her household, especially her sister. As you read "Genius," think about how Grimes shows the sisters' feelings for each other.

469

Practice Fluency

Phrasing: Punctuation Have students listen as you read aloud the first stanza of "Genius" on **Student Book p. 469**.

- Remind students that to read poetry, good readers pause at commas and periods. They do not stop at the ends of lines unless punctuation indicates to do so.

- Have students choral-read the stanzas in "Genius." Remind them to group the phrases based on punctuation and meaning, not line by line.

JOURNEYS DIGITAL Powered by **DESTINATION Reading**
Student eBook: Read and Listen

TARGET VOCABULARY REVIEW

TARGET VOCABULARY Vocabulary in Context Cards – Word Webs

Have partners write each Target Vocabulary word in the center of a word web. Have one student pick a card at random from the pile, and then have partners work together to create the web. In the outer circles of the web, they should place words or phrases that relate to the vocabulary word. Discuss students' completed webs.

CONTEXT CARDS 171–180

front   back

Develop Comprehension

Reread the selection with students. Pause at the stopping points to ask students the following questions.

1 **Identify Details** *Why does the speaker of "Genius" wake up her sister?* She wakes her sister up to read her the poem.

2 **Author's Purpose** *Why has the author of "A Seeing Poem" decided to write his poem in the shape of a lightbulb?* Sample answer: It further emphasizes turning "on a light in someone's mind."

3 ✓ **TARGET VOCABULARY**

*What **formula** is **required** to write a concrete poem?* Sample answer: The words should create the shape of what is described in the poem.

Interpret Poetry

• Review the definitions of *rhythm*, *rhyme scheme*, and *form*. Remind students that poets use different forms to emphasize their meaning. Explain how form is used in each of the poems.

• Model the thinking.

> **Think Aloud** *"To Write Poetry" has varied line lengths. "Genius" has a regular rhythm formed by the stanzas, and "A Seeing Poem" uses the shape of the poem to reinforce meaning.*

A Seeing Poem
by Robert Froman

A SEEING POEM HAPPENS WHEN WORDS TAKE A SHAPE THAT HELPS THEM TO TURN ON A LIGHT IN SOMEONE'S MIND

2

Write a Concrete Poem

3 Write your own concrete, or seeing, poem. There is no exact formula for writing one. The only element required is that the words you use create the shape of the object or action your poem describes. For instance, how could you create a concrete poem to show the destruction B.J. caused to Peg's gingerbread house in "The Dog Newspaper?"

470

Weekly Internet Challenge

Navigating a Site

• Review the Internet Strategy, Step 3: Navigate.

• Review common features that can be found on websites, such as menus, search engines, and hyperlinks.

• Tell students that each feature can help them find more information about a topic.

INTERNET STRATEGY

1. **Plan a Search** by identifying what you are looking for and how to find it.

2. **Search and Predict** which sites will be worth exploring.

3. **Navigate** a site to see how to get around it and what it contains.

4. **Analyze and Evaluate** the quality and reliability of the information.

5. **Synthesize** the information from multiple sites.

Making Connections

Making Connections

 Text to Self

Write About Yourself Think about how the author of "The Dog Newspaper" tells the story of her creation of the first issue of her neighborhood paper. What language and devices does she use to help readers relate to her experience? Write a short paragraph about an interesting project you have worked on. Present your information in ways that will help readers relate to you and your experience.

 Text to Text

Analyze Poetry Reread Nikki Grimes's poem "Genius," and Jane Yolen's poem "Karate Kid" from Lesson 4. Look for examples of imagery in each selection. Pay special attention to sound effects, such as rhyme and repetition, used by the poets. Then compare the two pieces of poetry and tell how they are alike and different. How does each poet convey a certain feeling about the activity featured in her poem?

 Text to World

Research Rescue Dogs Revisit Peg Kehret's flashback about B.J. on page 461. Think about how B.J.'s rescue and experiences with the soldiers helped him survive his time in Germany. Then work with a group to find information, either in print or online, about rescue dogs. Discuss with your group whether you think B.J. would have made a good rescue dog. Take time to consider each person's point of view.

471

"Poetry About Poetry" Challenge

- Have partners select keywords and search for sites about concrete poems.

- When partners have found a relevant website, ask them to evaluate what makes it helpful and what makes it difficult to locate information on the site.

- Have students discuss the followings questions: *Are the menu options clear? Is there a built-in site map or search tool? If not, is one needed? Why or why not? Is it easy to find where to click for links? Is there distracting commercial information? What would make the site better, and why?*

Making Connections

Making Connections

 Text to Self

Guide students to places where they can find information about literary devices. They may need help thinking of an interesting project.

 Text to Text

To help students identify similarities and differences between Nikki Grimes's "Genius" and Jane Yolen's "Karate Kid," have them create a Venn diagram to compare and contrast the sound effects used by each poet.

 Text to World

Help students identify sources of information about rescue dogs. Tell them that finding good information will make the task of evaluting B.J. easier.

Deepen Comprehension

SHARE OBJECTIVE

• Analyze facts and opinions to evaluate an author's messages.

SKILL TRACE

Fact and Opinion	
Introduce	T166–T167, T182–T183
Differentiate	T208–T209
Reteach	T216
Review	T104–T105, Unit 6
Test	Weekly Tests, Lesson 18

ELL ENGLISH LANGUAGE LEARNERS

Scaffold

Beginning Discuss with students some of the statements made on pp. 462–463 of "The Dog Newspaper." Work with them to say words that describe the picture on p. 463.

Intermediate Provide these sentence frames: *It's true that_____. The author believes that_____.* Help students complete them orally using statements from pp. 462–463.

Advanced Have students point out the details of the scene on p. 462. Ask them to analyze/evaluate these actions.

Advanced High Have partners analyze and evaluate the events on p. 462 by writing statements of fact and opinion.

See ELL Lesson 18, pp. E22–E31, for scaffolded support.

✔ Analyze Fact and Opinion

1 Teach/Model

AL *Academic Language*

fact a statement that can be proven to be true

opinion a statement that tells a thought, feeling, or belief

• Explain that many authors include facts to support their opinions. Point out that they often use facts and opinions to help readers think about their message.

• Good readers **analyze,** or study carefully, an author's statements. They decide when an author is giving opinions and whether the opinions are based on facts that can be proven. This analysis helps readers evaluate an author's message.

• Have students reread the first paragraph of **Student Book p. 463** of "The Dog Newspaper."

• Display **Projectable 18.4.** Discuss **Deepen Comprehension Question 1.**

• Remind students that a T-Map helps readers organize facts and opinions so they can evaluate the author's message.

• Model using a T-Map to analyze how an author presents facts and opinions.

Think Aloud *The author's opinion tells what she believes. She supports it with a fact that can be proven. I realize that she used fact and opinion this way to show why the first edition sold well.*

Projectable 18.4

The Dog Newspaper | Deepen Comprehension Analyze Fact and Opinion

T-Map: Analyze Fact and Opinion

Deepen Comprehension Question 1

Analyze the first paragraph of p. 463 of *The Dog Newspaper*. How does the author support her opinion? Use the T-Map organize facts and opinions. p. 463

Opinion	Fact
B.J. was a fascinating front-page subject.	The first edition sold twelve copies.

Deepen Comprehension Question 2

Reread the last paragraph of p. 464 of *The Dog Newspaper*. Organize facts and opinions on the T-Map. Analyze why the author uses facts and opinions this way. p. 464

Opinion	Fact
Issue number three was a publishing disaster.	Few people read it. Her grandpa was the only person to purchase issue number four. The paper went out of business.

Deepen Comprehension Question 3

Do you agree with the author that it is important for a newspaper to publish interesting articles? Does the author present enough evidence to support her opinion? Use examples from the text to support your answer. p. 466

2 | Guided Practice

- Reread p. 464 with students. Read and discuss **Deepen Comprehension Question 2** on **Projectable 18.4**. Use these prompts to guide students:

- *What does the author think of issue number three of "The Dog Newspaper"?* She thinks it was a publishing disaster.

- *How does the author support this opinion?* She gives us facts that tell us why she considers it a publishing disaster.

- *How do these facts help support the author's message?* The facts help support the author's opinion that it was a publishing disaster. These facts help readers believe the author's message.

- *Can the facts be proven?* Yes, they all can be proven true.

- Complete the T-Map for Question 2 with students.

GUIDED DISCUSSION Have students reread p. 464, and work with them to analyze other facts and opinions. Prompt students with questions like the one below:

- *What does the narrator think about the lead story for issue number two?* It's far less interesting than the story of B.J.'s rescue.

Monitor Comprehension

Are students able to analyze how authors use facts to support their opinions?

IF...	THEN...
students have difficulty analyzing how facts can support opinions,	▶ use the Leveled Reader for **Struggling Readers**, *Maria Tallchief, American Ballerina*, p. T210.
students can analyze how facts can support opinions,	▶ use the Leveled Reader for **On Level Readers**, *B.B King*, p. T211.
students can clearly analyze how and why authors present facts to support their own opinions,	▶ use the Leveled Reader for **Advanced Readers**, *Isabelle Allende*, p. T212.

 SMALL GROUP Options Use the Leveled Reader for **English Language Learners**, *The Life of B.B. King*, p. T213.

3 | Apply

Turn and Talk Have students discuss **Deepen Comprehension Question 3** on **Projectable 18.4**. Discuss students' responses. *Sample answer: I agree with the author. Without interesting articles, no one would want to read the newspaper. The author presents a lot of strong evidence to support her opinion. For example, she uses B.J. as the main article twice and gets no compliments from readers.*

WRITE ABOUT READING Have students write their opinions about the role facts and opinions play in this selection. Tell them to present their opinions and the facts that support their opinions. Then have partners evaluate each other's opinions.

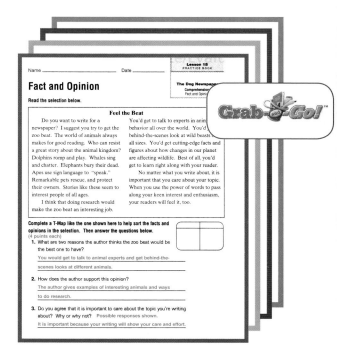

Practice Book p. 206
See Grab-and-Go™ Resources for additional leveled practice.

Fluency

Phrasing: Punctuation

1 | Teach/Model

- Tell students that good readers pay attention to punctuation because it can help them group words into meaningful phrases.

- Review with students the punctuation marks that help guide phrasing, including quotes, dashes, and parentheses.

- Have students follow along as you read aloud the first two paragraphs of **Student Book p. 462.** First, read them without using punctuation to help guide your phrasing. Then, reread, paying attention to punctuation.

- Discuss the differences in the two readings. Tell students that grouping words into appropriate phrases makes their reading sound more natural and can impact their understanding of the text.

2 | Guided Practice

- Together, read aloud paragraphs 3 and 4 on **Student Book p. 462.**

- Work with students to use punctuation to group words into meaningful phrases.

- If students are struggling with phrasing, have them echo-read **Student Book p. 463,** using punctuation to guide their phrasing.

- Allow each student to read the section three or four times.

- See also **Instructional Routine 6.**

3 | Apply

- Tell students that with practice, they can improve their phrasing.

- Then have students read the paragraphs independently several times or as needed to read fluently and with appropriate phrasing.

Decoding

 Recognizing Suffixes

RECOGNIZE SUFFIXES Write the word *greedy* on the board and read it aloud. Have students repeat the word.

- Break the word into syllables and read each one aloud with students: greed | y.

- Point out that a suffix adds a syllable to the end of a word. Tell students that identifying the suffix first can help them decode the whole word.

- Model how to recognize suffixes by identifying the base word *greed* and the suffix *-y* in *greedy*.

- Note that when a word ends in a consonant and *y*, the final *y* is changed to *i* when *-er* or *-est* is added. For example:

ear | ly	ear | li | er
hap | py	hap | pi | est

2 Practice/Apply

DECODE WORDS WITH SUFFIXES Write on the board the following words with suffixes: *sunnier, dirtier, iciest, greediest, drowsier*.

- Have students break the words into syllables, identify the suffix and the base word, and read the words aloud.

sunnier	sun | ni | er	sunny
dirtier	dirt | i | er	dirty
iciest	ic | i | est	icy
greediest	greed | i | est	greedy
drowsier	drows | i | er	drowsy

- Use **Corrective Feedback** if students need additional help.

SHARE OBJECTIVES

- Recognize words with suffixes.
- Use knowledge of suffixes to decode longer words.

Corrective Feedback

If students have trouble decoding words with suffixes, use the model below.

Correct the error. Say the word aloud. *What is the last syllable in the word iciest?* (-est) *The suffix is -est.*

Model the correct way to decode the word. *When I separate the suffix from the word, I'm left with i-c-i. I don't recognize that word, but when I try blending the sounds together, I recognize the adjective icy. I remember that words that end in a consonant and y change the y to i before -er or -est is added. I'll put all the parts together: ic | i | est.*

Guide students to identify the base word and the suffix. *What is the base word?* (icy) *What is the suffix?* (est)

Check students' understanding. *What is the word?* (iciest)

Reinforce Have students repeat the process with the word *sunnier*.

Vocabulary Strategies

SHARE OBJECTIVE

• Complete analogies using synonyms and antonyms to make comparisons.

SKILL TRACE

Analogies	
Introduce	T332–T333, Unit 2
Differentiate	T214–T215
Reteach	T216
▶ Review	**T186–T187; T332–T333, Unit 5**
Test	Weekly Tests, Lesson 18

ELL ENGLISH LANGUAGE LEARNERS

Scaffold

Beginning Draw a child next to a man on one side of the board and a house next to a tall building on the other. Then state this analogy: *Child is to man as house is to skyscraper.* Discuss the relationships.

Intermediate Explain that an analogy shows the relationship between word pairs. For example, *a cat is like a lion the way a dog is like a wolf.* This analogy compares a tame animal to a wild animal.

Advanced Have students say this analogy as a sentence. *blue : sky :: orange : carrot.* (Blue is to sky as orange is to carrot.)

Advanced High Have students complete this analogy and explain the relationship it represents: *tired : awake :: tense : ____*

See ELL Lesson 18, pp. E22–E31, for scaffolded support.

✔ Analogies

1 Teach/Model

AL *Academic Language*

analogies comparisons of two pairs of words that are related in the same way
antonyms words that have opposite or very different meanings
synonyms words that have the same, or almost the same, meaning

---

• Explain that analogies compare one pair of words to another pair of words that are related in the same way. To understand an analogy, look at the first pair of words and identify how they are related. Then apply that relationship to the second pair of words to confirm that they are related in the same way.

• Point out that antonyms and synonyms are commonly used to create analogies. Tell students that when an analogy uses synonyms, it compares one pair of words that have similar meanings with another pair that have similar meanings. When an analogy uses antonyms, the words in each pair have opposite meanings.

• Write the following on the board. Then model completing the analogy:

> *destruction : ruin :: solution : answer*
> *famous : unknown :: short : _____ (long)*

Think Aloud *I can say the first analogy as a sentence: "Destruction is to ruin as solution is to answer." I know that destruction and ruin both mean "the act of damaging something." They are synonyms. Solution and answer are synonyms, too. I am comparing one pair of synonyms to another. I can also make an analogy by comparing antonyms. Famous and unknown are antonyms. To make an analogy, I need an antonym for short. Long would work. Famous is to unknown as short is to long.*

• Tell students that a thesaurus can help them find synonyms and antonyms.

2 Guided Practice

- Display the top half of **Projectable 18.5** and read "A Lost Memory" aloud.

- Have students identify the words from the list in the passage. Circle or highlight the words.

- Display the graphic organizer on the bottom of **Projectable 18.5**.

- Have students use the graphic organizer to complete analogies using some of the vocabulary words.

- For each analogy, have students identify the relationship between words. Discuss the meanings of any unknown words.

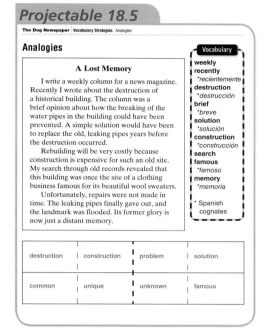

Projectable 18.5

The Dog Newspaper Vocabulary Strategies Analogies

Analogies

A Lost Memory

I write a weekly column for a news magazine. Recently I wrote about the destruction of a historical building. The column was a brief opinion about how the breaking of the water pipes in the building could have been prevented. A simple solution would have been to replace the old, leaking pipes years before the destruction occurred.

Rebuilding will be very costly because construction is expensive for such an old site. My search through old records revealed that this building was once the site of a clothing business famous for its beautiful wool sweaters.

Unfortunately, repairs were not made in time. The leaking pipes finally gave out, and the landmark was flooded. Its former glory is now just a distant memory.

Vocabulary
weekly
recently
*recientemente
destruction
*destrucción
brief
*breve
solution
*solución
construction
*construcción
search
famous
*famoso
memory
*memoria

* Spanish cognates

destruction	construction	problem	solution
common	unique	unknown	famous

3 Apply

- In the following word analogies, have students identify the comparison (synonyms or antonyms), say the analogy as a sentence, and complete it. Remind students to use a thesaurus to find synonyms or antonyms.

  serious : cheerful :: timid : _____ *(antonyms; sample answer: bold)*

  talkative : chatty :: clever : _____ *(synonyms; sample answer: smart)*

Then have students work with a partner to create two new synonym and two new antonym word analogies and write each as a sentence.

Practice Book p. 207
See Grab-and-Go™ Resources for additional leveled practice.

Connect and Extend

"The Dog Newspaper" "Poetry about Poetry"

Vocabulary Reader

Struggling Readers   ***On-Level Readers***

Advanced Readers   ***English Language Learners***

Read to Connect

SHARE AND COMPARE TEXTS Have students compare and contrast this week's reading selections. Use the following questions to guide the discussion:

- Why might these selections be considered good stories? What makes a story good to you?
- Using evidence from the selections you have read this week, explain how writers think of and develop their ideas for stories.

CONNECT TEXT TO WORLD Use these prompts to help deepen student thinking and discussion. Accept students' opinions, but encourage them to support their ideas with text details and other information from their reading.

- Why do people have different opinions about what makes a good story or poem?
- Should an author write a story even if others might not think it is a good idea? Why or why not?

Independent Reading

BOOK TALK Have partners discuss their independent reading for the week. Tell them to refer to their Reading Log or journal and summarize the main ideas. Have them paraphrase a favorite section, maintaining its meaning and logical order. Then have students discuss the following:

- how the cultural or historical context of the text supports their understanding
- the selections' sequence of events or plot events

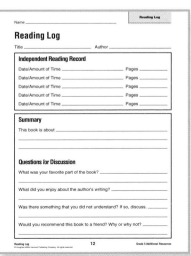

Reading Log

Extend Through Research

USE TECHNOLOGY TO IDENTIFY RELATIONSHIPS Tell students that as they conduct research, they should use technology to help them see relationships between ideas.

- Tell students they will work in small groups to research another person who has written an autobiography.

- Review how to create a research plan. Ask students to list questions that will guide their research. Have them use the Internet or other electronic sources to gather information about the person they have selected.

- Have students use internet links or key words in online articles to direct them to additional information. Have students use note cards or a word processing program to record data as they research. Students should note the relationships among the ideas they found.

- Discuss with students the importance of using technology to connect ideas for research. Have students identify the kinds of relationships they found among the sources they examined.

Listening and Speaking

DELIVER ORAL SUMMARIES Tell students that they will give a brief oral summary of the research they did in the activity above. Explain that they should organize their thoughts by stating a main idea and then including details to support it. Have students talk about why the relationships they found between ideas are important to understanding the person who wrote the autobiography.

Allow time for students to rehearse. Tell them to focus on:
- making eye contact with people in the audience.
- speaking at an appropriate rate, or speed.
- pronouncing each word clearly.
- using an appropriate volume.

While students give their summaries, have audience members use the Listening Log to record notes about the speaker's message. Allow time for students to ask questions to clarify the speaker's purpose or perspective.

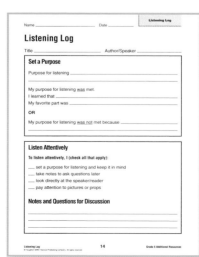

Listening Log

Spelling ☑ Changing Final *y* to *i*

SHARE OBJECTIVE

- Spell words in which final *y* is changed to *i*.

Spelling Words

Basic

✪ duties	abilities	greediest
✪ earlier	✪ dirtier	drowsier
loveliest	✪ scariest	victories
denied	trophies	horrified
ferries	cozier	memories
sunnier	enemies	strategies
terrified	iciest	

Review ✪ easier, ✪ families, studied, countries, happiest

Challenge

unified, dictionaries, boundaries, satisfied, tragedies

✪ Forms of these words appear in "The Dog Newspaper."

ELL ENGLISH LANGUAGE LEARNERS

Preteach

Spanish Cognates

Write and discuss these Spanish cognates for Spanish-speaking students.

trophies • *trofeos*
enemies • *enemigos*
victories • *victorias*

Day 1

1 TEACH THE PRINCIPLE

- Administer the **Pretest**. Use the Day 5 sentences.
- Write *ferry*, *deny*, *early*, and *icy* on the board. Use the chart below to help students understand when to change *y* to *i* before adding *–es*, *–ed*, *–er*, *–est*.

Words ending in a consonant and *y* plus the ending...	Change *y* to *i*
ferry + es *deny + ed* *early + er* *icy + est*	ferries denied earlier iciest

2 PRACTICE/APPLY

Guide students to identify the *y* to *i* spelling change in the remaining Spelling Words.

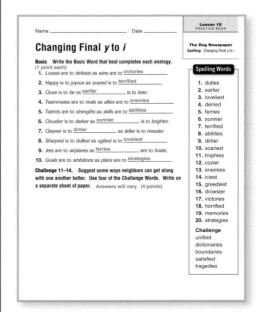

Practice Book p. 208

Day 2

1 TEACH WORD SORT

- Set up two columns as shown. Have students copy the chart. Guide them to add each Spelling word to the chart.

Words ending in *-es* or *-ed*	Words ending in *-er* or *-est*
abilities horrified	sunnier greediest

2 PRACTICE/APPLY

- Have students add to the chart words from "The Dog Newspaper."

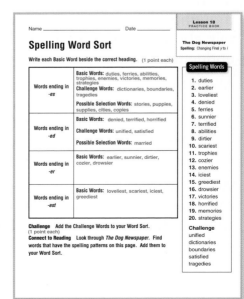

Practice Book p. 209

Day 3

1 TEACH ANTONYMS

- **WRITE** *earlier* and *later*.

- **ASK** *What is the connection between these words? (opposite meanings)* Point out that words with opposite meanings are called *antonyms*.

- **WRITE** *enemies*. With students, list and discuss words that have the opposite meaning. *(Samples: friends, allies, pals, buddies)*

2 PRACTICE/APPLY

- **WRITE** the following words in a column: *loveliest, denied, sunnier, terrified, dirtier, victories.*

- Have students copy the words.

- Then have students look up each word in a dictionary or an electronic resource to find the meaning. Have them decide on an antonym and write it next to that Spelling Word. *(Samples: loveliest/ugliest, denied/permitted, sunnier/gloomier, terrified/calmed, dirtier/cleaner, victories/defeats)*

➤ Have students write their answers.

Day 4

1 CONNECT TO WRITING

- Read and discuss the prompt below.

> ➤ **Write to Narrate**
> Think of an interesting incident involving your pet or the pet of someone you know. Write a story about it as you would want it to appear in a local newspaper. Use details from your readings this week.

2 PRACTICE/APPLY

- Guide students as they plan and write their stories. See p. T198.

- Remind them to proofread their writing for errors in spelling.

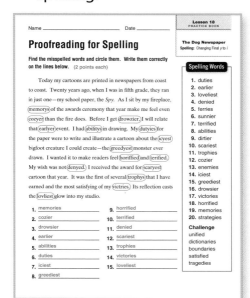

Practice Book p. 210

Day 5

ASSESS SPELLING

- Say each boldfaced word, read the sentence, and then repeat the word.

- Have students write the boldfaced word.

> **Basic**
>
> 1. What are the **duties** of a senator?
> 2. That flight arrives one hour **earlier**.
> 3. The rose is the **loveliest** flower.
> 4. My request was **denied**.
> 5. **Ferries** are passenger boats.
> 6. Today is **sunnier** than yesterday.
> 7. The big dog **terrified** the child.
> 8. I admire your many **abilities**.
> 9. Your hands are **dirtier** than mine.
> 10. What is the **scariest** movie ever made?
> 11. The athlete won many **trophies**.
> 12. This sofa is **cozier** than that one.
> 13. Good people have few **enemies**.
> 14. This is the **iciest** winter on record.
> 15. He is the **greediest** person I know.
> 16. The pill made me **drowsier** than I thought.
> 17. Our team has had many **victories**.
> 18. I was **horrified** by his rudeness.
> 19. Lynn has many fond **memories**.
> 20. Let's discuss different **strategies**.

Grammar ☑ Prepositions and Prepositional Phrases

- Identify prepositions and prepositional phrases.
- Use prepositional phrases in writing and speaking.

ELL **ENGLISH LANGUAGE LEARNERS**

Scaffold

Beginning Use the following sentence frames to demonstrate the use of prepositions.

She stopped ___ the store. (at)

He played basketball ___ an hour. (for)

Intermediate Work with students to use the sentence frames above to identify the prepositional phrases and explain their use.

Advanced Have students describe the relationship of objects in the classroom by creating sentences using prepositional phrases. Example: The teacher's desk is located in the corner.

Advanced High Have student pairs write sentences that use prepositions, showing relationships of location, time, or direction, or prepositional phrases that add details.

See ELL Lesson 18, pp. E22–E31, for scaffolded support.

JOURNEYS DIGITAL **Powered by DESTINATIONReading**
Grammar Activities: Lesson 18
Grammar Songs CD, Track 8

Day 1 TEACH

DAILY PROOFREADING PRACTICE
The police dog moved quick thrugh the burning building. *quickly; through*

PROJECTABLE
18.6

❶ TEACH PREPOSITIONS

- Display **Projectable 18.6.** Explain that prepositions are words that show relationships between other words in a sentence. Point out that prepositions convey relationships of location, time, or direction. Tell students that some common prepositions are *above, after, at, during, for, through, in, on, of, to,* and *with.*

- Model identifying the preposition in the following sentence: *The dog walker traveled after school.*

Think Aloud *To identify the preposition, I ask this Thinking Question:* **What words give information about time, direction, or location?** *I see the words* **after school.** *They tell me when, or what time, the dog walker traveled. I know that* **after** *is a common preposition. I'll try using the Thinking Question and my knowledge of common prepositions with the other sentences.*

❷ PRACTICE/APPLY

- Complete items 1–8 on **Projectable 18.6** with students.

- List prepositions on the board. Have students provide a phrase using each one. Ask them to tell under which heading their phrases should be categorized: *direction, location, time.*

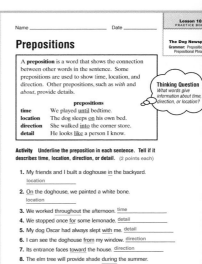

Practice Book p. 211

preposition a word that gives information about location, time, or direction

prepositional phrase a phrase that includes a preposition and a noun or pronoun

---

Day 2 TEACH

DAILY PROOFREADING PRACTICE

The reporter didn't need no interviews for his artical. *any; article*

PROJECTABLE 18.7

1 TEACH PREPOSITIONAL PHRASES

- Display **Projectable 18.7**. Explain that a prepositional phrase begins with a preposition and ends with a noun or pronoun. Point out that the noun or pronoun is the object of the preposition. Tell students that prepositional phrases add meaning and details to sentences.

- Model identifying the prepositional phrase in this example sentence: *Animal shelters provide refuge for homeless dogs.*

Think Aloud *When I ask the Thinking Questions, I can identify the preposition, for. I see that the phrase ends with the noun dogs. The prepositional phrase is for homeless dogs, and dogs is the object of the preposition. This prepositional phrase helps explain why animal shelters are needed.*

2 PRACTICE/APPLY

- Complete items 1–8 on **Projectable 18.7** with students.

- Write this sentence frame on the board. Have students provide a prepositional phrase to complete it.

The students found the dog _____. *(under the table)*

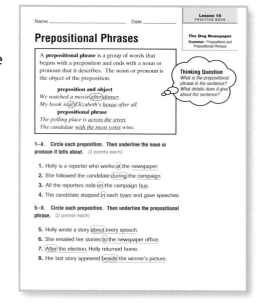

Practice Book p. 212

Day 3 TEACH

DAILY PROOFREADING PRACTICE

All the peaple moved safe from the burning building. *people; safely*

PROJECTABLE 18.8

1 TEACH OBJECT PRONOUNS

- Display **Projectable 18.8**. Use the examples to explain how to combine short sentences using a prepositional phrase. Point out that if two sentences tell about one subject, the prepositional phrase can be moved from one sentence to the other. Complete items 1–6 on the projectable with students.

- Explain that sometimes the object of a preposition is the noun or pronoun that follows the preposition. Tell students that some common object pronouns are *it, me, you, us,* and *them.*

- Display the following sentence: **Our dog Bailey runs beside us when we ride our bikes.**

- Then work with students to identify the prepositional phrase and the object pronoun. *(beside us; us)*

2 PRACTICE/APPLY

- Display these sentences:
  My cat watches birds. There are birds in the yard.
  Work with students to combine the sentences using a prepositional phrase.

- Display the following sentence. Then have students identify the object pronoun and the prepositional phrase.
  Bret read the camera's instructions to them. *(them; to them)*

Practice Book p. 213

Day 4 REVIEW

DAILY PROOFREADING PRACTICE

The firefighters finaly rescued there hero dog. *finally; their*

❶ REVIEW PREPOSITIONAL PHRASES

- Remind students how to find the prepositional phrases and object pronouns in a sentence. Review with students that prepostions begin a preposional phrase. The object pronoun follows the preposition. Review some common prepositions and object pronouns.

❷ SPIRAL REVIEW

Verbs in the Present Review with students that a verb showing action that is happening right now is in the present tense. Point out that the form of the verb changes to show the present tense when a singular noun is the subject.

- Display the following sentence pairs. Guide students to identify the subject and verb in each one. Then ask them which subject is a singular noun. *(paper)*

The paper costs five cents a copy. *(paper/ costs)*

The dogs live in my neighborhood. *(dogs/ live)*

- Display the following sentences. Have students identify the verb in the present tense in each sentence.

Birds flap their wings rapidly. *(flap)*

This bird always eats at the feeder. *(eats)*

The bird house rarely has birds in it. *(has)*

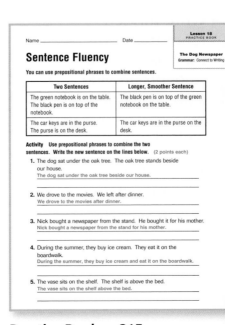

Practice Book p. 214

Day 5 CONNECT TO WRITING

DAILY PROOFREADING PRACTICE

The dog wag his tale back and forth. *wags; tail*

❶ CONNECT TO WRITING

- Remind students that combining two short sentences by moving a prepositional phrase makes their writing interesting to read. Discuss these two examples.

Short Sentences
I feed my dog.
He eats in the morning.

Longer Sentence
I feed my dog in the morning.

- Point out that an important part of revising is combining sentences using a prepositional phrase.

❷ PRACTICE/APPLY

- Have students turn to **Student Book p. 472**. Review with them prepositions and prepositional phrases. Then have students complete the *Try This!* activity.

Practice Book p. 215

Grammar

What Is a Preposition? Prepositions are words that show relationships between other words in a sentence. Prepositions convey location, time, or direction. **Prepositional phrases** begin with a preposition and end with a noun or pronoun. They add meaning and details to sentences. Some common prepositions are *above, after, at, during, for, through, in, of, to,* and *with*.

Academic Language

preposition
prepositional phrase

Prepositions and Prepositional Phrases	
Direction	A dog walker was moving toward the east.
Time	She had been walking three dogs for an hour.
Location	She stopped at the smallest dog's home.
Additional Details	A woman with red hair happily patted her dog.

Try This! **Copy these sentences onto a sheet of paper. Circle each preposition. Then underline each prepositional phrase and tell whether it conveys location, time, or direction, or provides details.**

❶ I am the dog walker for our family's dog.

❷ We always walk to the south.

❸ We visit the park on Seventh Street.

❹ We play fetch the stick until five o'clock.

❺ I write entries in my dog walker's diary.

472

Sentence Fluency In your writing, you can combine two short sentences by moving a prepositional phrase. If two sentences tell about one subject, you can combine them by moving a prepositional phrase from one sentence to the other.

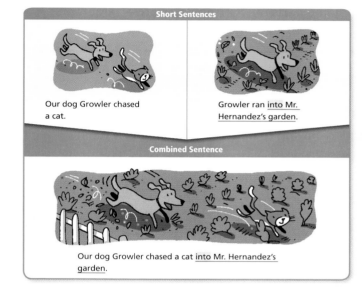

Short Sentences

Our dog Growler chased a cat.

Growler ran into Mr. Hernandez's garden.

Combined Sentence

Our dog Growler chased a cat into Mr. Hernandez's garden.

Connect Grammar to Writing

As you revise your personal narrative paragraph, look for short sentences that you can combine by moving a prepositional phrase from one sentence to the other. Using a variety of sentence lengths will make your writing more interesting to read.

473

Try This!

1. (for) our family's dog (details)
2. (to) the south (direction)
3. (on) Seventh Street (location)
4. (until) five o'clock (time)
5. (in) my dog walker's diary (location)

 CONNECT GRAMMAR TO WRITING

- Have students turn to **Student Book p. 473**. Read the Sentence Fluency paragraph with students.

- Read aloud the sentences in the chart. Note that using a variety of sentence lengths will make students' writing more interesting to read.

- Tell students that as they revise their personal narrative paragraphs, they should look for opportunities to combine sentences.

- Review the Common Errors at right with students.

COMMON ERRORS

Error: My friend brings me **at** school.

Correct: My friend brings me **to** school.

Error: We went to the store **at** Main Street.

Correct: We went to the store **on** Main Street.

Write to Narrate   Focus Trait: Voice

SHARE OBJECTIVES

- Identify the parts of a personal narrative paragraph.
- Write a personal narrative paragraph.

Academic Language

narrative a story told in detail

personal having to do with someone's private life

vivid detail a detail that helps readers clearly picture what is being described

ELL   ENGLISH LANGUAGE LEARNERS

Scaffold

Beginning Write a simple subject, such as "dog" on the board. Invite volunteers to describe a dog in vivid detail. *(Sample: black, furry, barks, wags tail)*

Intermediate Ask students to use vivid details to tell what they feel or think about the simple subject. *(Sample: dogs are fun/scare me/play with balls)*

Advanced Have students say sentences in the first person about about the simple subject. *(Sample: I love big dogs. My dog's name is Duke.)*

Advanced High Have partners take turns writing thoughts or feelings, in the first person, about simple subjects like dogs, pizza, movies, or games.

JOURNEYS DIGITAL **Powered by** DESTINATIONReading®
WriteSmart CD-ROM

① INTRODUCE THE MODEL

- Tell students that they will be writing a personal narrative paragraph in this lesson.

- Display **Projectable 18.9** and read aloud the Writing Model prompt. Discuss the following:

What is a Personal Narrative?

- It is the writing of an event or experience in the writer's own life.

- The **narrative** focuses on one **personal** experience and is written in the first person, using *I*.

- Includes **personal** thoughts and feelings to help the reader imagine the experience.

- **Vivid details** keep readers interested by helping them form a picture in their minds.

- Use the Projectable to identify the lead, supporting, and concluding sentences.

② PRACTICE/APPLY

With students, label the lead, supporting, and concluding sentences in section 2 on the Projectable.

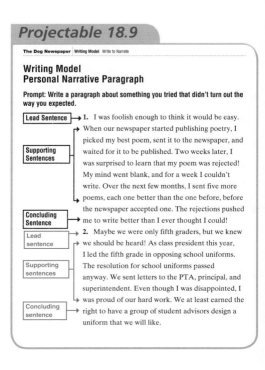

Projectable 18.9

The Dog Newspaper : Writing Model : Write to Narrate

Writing Model
Personal Narrative Paragraph

Prompt: Write a paragraph about something you tried that didn't turn out the way you expected.

Lead Sentence → 1. I was foolish enough to think it would be easy. When our newspaper started publishing poetry, I picked my best poem, sent it to the newspaper, and waited for it to be published. Two weeks later, I was surprised to learn that my poem was rejected! My mind went blank, and for a week I couldn't write. Over the next few months, I sent five more poems, each one better than the one before, before the newspaper accepted one. The rejections pushed me to write better than I ever thought I could!

Supporting Sentences

Concluding Sentence

Lead sentence → 2. Maybe we were only fifth graders, but we knew we should be heard! As class president this year, I led the fifth grade in opposing school uniforms. The resolution for school uniforms passed anyway. We sent letters to the PTA, principal, and superintendent. Even though I was disappointed, I was proud of our hard work. We at least earned the right to have a group of student advisors design a uniform that we will like.

Supporting sentences

Concluding sentence

LESSON	FORM	TRAIT
16	Friendly Letter	Voice
17	Character Description	Word Choice
18	**Personal Narrative Paragraph**	**Voice**
19	Prewrite: Personal Narrative	Ideas
20	Draft, Revise, Edit, Publish: Personal Narrative	Voice

Day 2 TEACH THE FOCUS TRAIT

1 INTRODUCE THE FOCUS TRAIT: VOICE

- Tell students that in good personal narratives, writers create a voice that shows their personality.

- One way writers can sound like themselves is by sharing their inner thoughts and feelings.

Connect to "The Dog Newspaper"	
Instead of this...	**...the author wrote this.**
"I liked the dog. I cared about him."	"I showered him with loving attention. I brushed him, tied ribbons on his collar, . . . " (p. 462)

- Point out that the author chose vivid words in her description to better show her personality.

2 PRACTICE/APPLY

- Write: *B.J. made a mess.* Have students look at the picture on **Student Book p. 465**. Ask them to be the narrator and tell what happened, using words and details that convey their feelings. *Sample: I couldn't believe my eyes! B.J. had shredded the gingerbread house.*

- Write: *I liked B.J.* Have students think about the story and write a sentence using words and details that better show how the narrator felt about B.J. *Sample: I was sure that B.J. was the most brilliant of all dogs.*

Name _____ Date _____

Lesson 18
PRACTICE BOOK

The Dog Newspaper
Writing: Write to Narrate

Focus Trait: Voice
Adding Vivid Words and Details

Weak Voice	Strong Voice
I gave Spot lots of attention.	I brushed Spot's coat, gave him a red collar, and played catch with him.

A. Read each weak sentence. Fill in the missing words and details that add voice and show the narrator's thoughts and feelings. Possible responses shown.

Weak Voice	Description with Exact Words
1. Spot was in the newspaper.	I beamed with pride when I saw that Spot was in a big picture on the front page of the local newspaper. (2 points)
2. Neighbors enjoyed the story, and I liked receiving their compliments on how great Spot looked in the photo.	Neighbors laughed out loud at the story, and I will never forget their compliments on how adorable Spot looked in the photo, saluting the camera with his paw. (2)

B. Read each weak sentence. Then rewrite it to add voice. Use words and details that show your feelings.

Pair/Share Work with a partner to brainstorm new words and details.
Possible responses shown. (2 points each)

Weak Voice	Strong Voice
3. Dogs are good pets.	Loyal and cuddly, dogs are the best pets because they make such good friends.
4. I liked to talk about my pet.	I could talk about my cat Nico all day long and still have more to say.
5. I enjoyed taking my puppy to the beach.	I loved how my puppy barked with excitement and rolled in the sand at the beach.

Practice Book, p. 216

Day 3 PREWRITE

1 TEACH PLANNING A PARAGRAPH

- Display **Projectable 18.10** and read aloud the prompt. Ask students to think about a personal experience they would like to share.

- Explain that a flow chart can help them plan their writing.

2 PRACTICE/APPLY

- Point out the topic at the top of **Projectable 18.10**. Explain to students that their topic should be addressed in the first few sentences of their paragraph, either by a vivid quote or a sentence.

- Tell students that each event listed in the flow chart should relate to the topic. Tell them that the events and their details will make up the body of the narrative.

- Work with students to complete the flow chart.

- Have students choose a topic for their personal narratives. Distribute **Graphic Organizer 4**. Guide students to fill in their own flow charts.

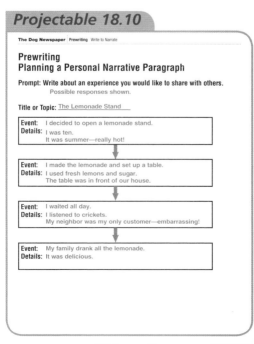

Projectable 18.10

The Dog Newspaper | Prewriting | Write to Narrate

Prewriting
Planning a Personal Narrative Paragraph

Prompt: Write about an experience you would like to share with others.
Possible responses shown.

Title or Topic: The Lemonade Stand

| **Event:** I decided to open a lemonade stand. |
| **Details:** I was ten. |
| It was summer—really hot! |

| **Event:** I made the lemonade and set up a table. |
| **Details:** I used fresh lemons and sugar. |
| The table was in front of our house. |

| **Event:** I waited all day. |
| **Details:** I listened to crickets. |
| My neighbor was my only customer—embarrassing! |

| **Event:** My family drank all the lemonade. |
| **Details:** It was delicious. |

Day 4 DRAFT

1 BEGIN A DRAFT

- Have students begin their drafts using their prewriting flow charts from Day 3. Discuss with them the following:

> **1. Introduce** by writing something interesting, funny, or surprising to grab readers' attention.

> **2. Organize** by focusing on one experience or event, and writing in the first person, using *I*.

> **3. Include** vivid details, as well as personal thoughts, feelings, and reactions. The reader should feel like he or she is really there.

> **4. Conclude** with an ending that explains what the writer learned from the experience.

2 PRACTICE/APPLY

- Have students draft their own personal narrative paragraphs. Remind them to refer to their completed flow charts.

Day 5 REVISE FOR VOICE

1 INTRODUCE THE STUDENT MODEL

- Remind students that one way writers give voice to a personal narrative is by using words and details that convey their thoughts and feelings about the events.

- Read the top of **Student Book p. 474** with the class. Discuss the revisions made by the student writer, Amanda. Point out how Amanda's revisions in the first and last sentences show how she really feels about dogs.

2 PRACTICE/APPLY

- Display **Projectable 18.11.** Work with students to revise the second paragraph. Point out where vivid details can improve Amanda's voice.

- Work with students to answer the *Reading as a Writer* questions on **Student Book p. 475.**

- **Revising** Have students revise their paragraphs using the Writing Traits Checklist on **Student Book p. 474.**

- **Proofreading** For proofreading support, have students use the **Proofreading Checklist Blackline Master.**

Projectable 18.11

The Dog Newspaper | Revising | Write to Narrate

Revising Amanda's Narrative Paragraph

Proofread Amanda's draft. Use proofreading marks to correct any errors or make any improvements.

Write to Narrate

☑ **Voice** The author of "The Dog Newspaper" tells her feelings when she says she was "giddy with success." When you revise a **personal narrative**, add words that express your own thoughts and feelings, and include details that help your readers picture what happened.

Amanda drafted a personal narrative about a puppy party she planned. Later, she revised it to show her feelings more clearly.

Writing Traits Checklist

☑ **Ideas**
Did I include only important events?

☑ **Organization**
Will my beginning grab my readers' attention?

☑ **Sentence Fluency**
Did I combine sentences for better flow?

☑ **Word Choice**
Did I use words that sound like me?

☑ **Voice**
Does my narrative reveal my inner thoughts and feelings?

☑ **Conventions**
Did I use correct spelling, grammar, and punctuation?

474

Revised Draft

My friend Ana and I ~~have a lot in~~ ^are both dog crazy.^

~~common.~~ Last summer, the best thing

happened! Both of our families got

puppies! Ana and I love walking our

puppies! ~~There's~~ ^to^ a local dog park. There

they wrestle and play and ~~chase each~~ ^make us laugh^

~~other.~~

Final Copy

The Puppy Party
by Amanda West

My friend Ana and I are both dog crazy. Last summer, the best thing happened! Both of our families got puppies! Ana and I love walking our puppies to a local dog park. There they wrestle and play and make us laugh.

One rainy day, when we were stuck indoors, I had a brilliant idea. I invited Ana and her puppy over for a puppy party. I put out little doggy toys and treats, but as soon as Ana arrived, the puppies started chasing each other around the house. A lamp crashed to the floor. A potted plant spilled out all over the rug. The pups grabbed a sock and played tug-of-war until it was ruined. The house was a mess, and I was in big trouble. That's the day I learned rule number one for puppy parties: Keep them outdoors!

In my final paper, I added some words to show my feelings. I also used prepositional phrases to combine sentences.

Reading as a Writer

What thoughts or feelings does Amanda express in this narrative? How can you make your thoughts and feelings clear in your narrative?

475

Writing Traits Scoring Rubric

	Focus/Ideas	☑ Organization	Voice	☑ Word Choice	☑ Sentence Fluency	Conventions
4	Adheres to the topic, is interesting, has a sense of completeness. Ideas are well developed.	Ideas and details are clearly presented and well organized.	Connects with reader in a unique, personal way.	Includes vivid verbs, strong adjectives, specific nouns.	Includes a variety of complete sentences that flow smoothly, naturally.	Shows a strong command of grammar, spelling, capitalization, punctuation.
3	Mostly adheres to the topic, is somewhat interesting, has a sense of completeness. Ideas are adequately developed.	Ideas and details are mostly clear and generally organized.	Generally connects with reader in a way that is personal and sometimes unique.	Includes some vivid verbs, strong adjectives, specific nouns.	Includes some variety of mostly complete sentences. Some parts flow smoothly, naturally.	Shows a good command of grammar, spelling, capitalization, punctuation.
2	Does not always adhere to the topic, has some sense of completeness. Ideas are superficially developed.	Ideas and details are not always clear or organized. There is some wordiness or repetition.	Connects somewhat with reader. Sounds somewhat personal, but not unique.	Includes mostly simple nouns and verbs, and may have a few adjectives.	Includes mostly simple sentences, some of which are incomplete.	Some errors in grammar, spelling, capitalization, punctuation.
1	Does not adhere to the topic, has no sense of completeness. Ideas are vague.	Ideas and details are not organized. Wordiness or repetition hinders meaning.	Does not connect with reader. Does not sound personal or unique.	Includes only simple nouns and verbs, some inaccurate. Writing is not descriptive.	Sentences do not vary. Incomplete sentences hinder meaning.	Frequent errors in grammar, spelling, capitalization, punctuation.

See also ***Writing Rubric Blackline Master*** and Teacher's Edition pp. R18–R21.

Progress Monitoring

Assess

- Weekly Tests
- Fluency Tests
- Periodic Assessments

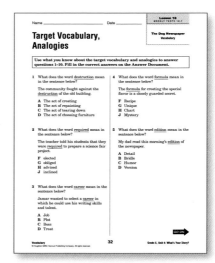

Weekly Tests 18.7–18.8

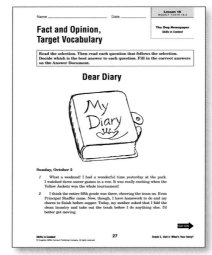

Weekly Tests 18.2–18.6

✓ Vocabulary
Target Vocabulary
Strategies: Analogies

✓ Skills in Context
Fact and Opinion
Target Vocabulary

Respond to Assessment

IF	a Student Scores...	THEN...
7–10 of 10		▶ Continue Core Instructional Program.
4–6 of 10		▶ **Reteaching Lesson,** page T216
1–3 of 10		▶ **Intervention** Lesson 18, pp. S22–S31

IF	a Student Scores...	THEN...
7–10 of 10		▶ Continue Core Instructional Program.
4–6 of 10		▶ **Reteaching Lesson,** page T216
1–3 of 10		▶ **Intervention** Lesson 18, pp. S22–S31

Powered by DESTINATIONReading®

- Online Assessment System
- Weekly Tests

☑ Decoding
Recognizing Suffixes

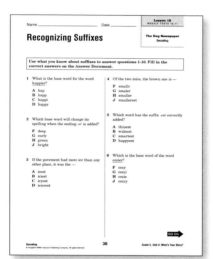

Weekly Tests 18.11–18.12

IF	a Student Scores...	THEN...
7–10 of 10	▶ Continue Core Instructional Program.	
4–6 of 10	▶ Reteaching Lesson, page T217	
1–3 of 10	▶ Intervention Lesson 18, pp. S22–S31	

☑ Language Arts
Grammar: Prepositions and Prepositional Phrases

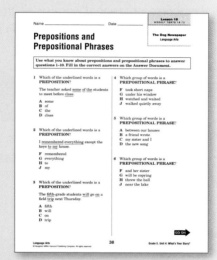

Weekly Tests 18.13–18.14

Writing Traits Rubrics
See TE pp. R18–R21.

IF	a Student Scores...	THEN...
7–10 of 10	▶ Continue Core Instructional Program.	
4–6 of 10	▶ Reteaching Lesson, page T217	
1–3 of 10	▶ Intervention Lesson 18, pp. S22–S31	

☑ Fluency

Fluency Plan
Assess one group per week.
Use this suggested plan below.

● Struggling Readers	Weeks 1, 3, 5
▲ On Level	Week 2
■ Advanced	Week 4

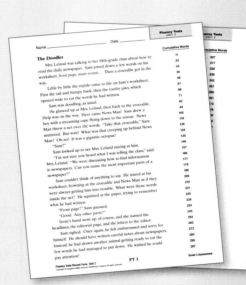

Fluency Record Form

Fluency Scoring Rubrics
See Grade 5 *Assessment* in *Grab-and-Go™ Resources* for help measuring progress.

Progress Monitoring

 ## Small Group

RUNNING RECORDS

To assess individual progress, occasionally use small group time to take a reading record for each student. Use the results to plan instruction.

● **Struggling Readers**

▲ **On Level**

■ **Advanced**

◆ **English Language Learners**

For running records, see **Grab-and-Go™ Resources: Lesson 18, pp. 13–16.**

Behaviors and Understandings to Notice

- Self-corrects errors that detract from meaning.

- Self-corrects intonation when it does not reflect the meaning.

- Rereads to solve words and resumes normal rate of reading.

- Demonstrates phrased and fluent oral reading.

- Reads dialogue with expression.

- Demonstrates awareness of punctuation.

- Automatically solves most words in the text to read fluently.

- Demonstrates appropriate stress on words, pausing and phrasing, intonation, and use of punctuation.

- Reads orally at an appropriate rate.

Vocabulary Reader
- *Print It!*, T206–T207

Differentiate Comprehension
- Target Skill: Fact and Opinion, T208–T209
- Target Strategy: Analyze/Evaluate, T208–T209

Leveled Readers
- ● *Maria Tallchief, American Ballerina*, T210
- ▲ *B.B. King*, T211
- ■ *Isabelle Allende*, T212
- ◆ *The Life of B.B. King*, T213

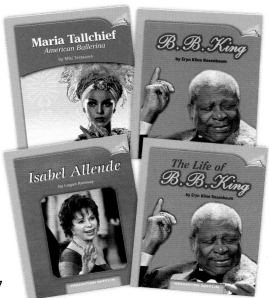

Differentiate Vocabulary Strategies
- Analogies, T214–T215

Options for Reteaching
- Vocabulary Strategies: Analogies, T216
- Comprehension Skill: Analyze Fact and Opinion, T216
- Language Arts: Prepositions and Prepositional Phrases/Write to Narrate, T217
- Decoding: Recognizing Suffixes, T217

Ready-Made Work Stations

Independent Practice
- Comprehension and Fluency, T158
- Word Study, T158
- Think and Write, T159
- Digital Center, T159

Comprehension and Fluency

Word Study

Think and Write

Digital Center

Suggested Small Group Plan

PRINT IT!

		Day 1	Day 2	Day 3
Teacher-Led	**Struggling Readers**	**Vocabulary Reader** *Print It!*, Differentiated Instruction, p. T206	**Differentiate Comprehension** Fact and Opinion; Analyze/Evaluate, p. T208	**Leveled Reader** *Maria Tallchief, American Ballerina*, p. T210
	On Level	**Vocabulary Reader** *Print It!*, Differentiated Instruction, p. T206	**Differentiate Comprehension** Fact and Opinion; Analyze/Evaluate, p. T208	**Leveled Reader** *B.B. King*, p. T211
	Advanced	**Vocabulary Reader** *Print It!*, Differentiated Instruction, p. T207	**Differentiate Comprehension** Fact and Opinion; Analyze/Evaluate, p. T209	**Leveled Reader** *Isabelle Allende*, p. T212
	English Language Learners	**Vocabulary Reader** *Print It!*, Differentiated Instruction, p. T207	**Differentiate Comprehension** Fact and Opinion; Analyze/Evaluate, p. T209	**Leveled Reader** *The Life of B.B. King*, p. T213

		Day 1	Day 2	Day 3
What are my other students doing?	**Struggling Readers**	**Reread** *Print It!*	**Vocabulary in Context Cards** 171–180 *Talk It Over* Activities **Complete** Leveled Practice SR18.1	**Listen** to Audiotext CD of "The Dog Newspaper"; Retell and discuss **Complete** Leveled Practice, SR18.2
	On Level	**Reread** *Print It!*	**Reread** "The Dog Newspaper" with a partner **Complete** Practice Book p. 205	**Reread** for Fluency: *B.B. King* **Complete** Practice Book p. 206
	Advanced	**Vocabulary in Context Cards** 171–180 *Talk It Over* Activities	**Reread and Retell** "The Dog Newspaper" **Complete** Leveled Practice A18.1	**Reread** for Fluency: *Isabelle Allende* **Complete** Leveled Practice A18.2
	English Language Learners	**Reread** *Print It!*	**Listen** to Audiotext CD of "The Dog Newspaper"; Retell and discuss **Complete** Leveled Practice ELL18.1	**Vocabulary in Context Cards** 171–180 *Talk It Over* Activities **Complete** Leveled Practice ELL18.2

Ready-Made Work Stations

Assign these activities across the week to reinforce and extend learning.

Comprehension and Fluency
Read and Review

Word Study
Analogy Antics

Day 4

Differentiate Vocabulary Strategies
Analogies, p. T214

Differentiate Vocabulary Strategies
Analogies, p. T214

Differentiate Vocabulary Strategies
Analogies, p. T215

Differentiate Vocabulary Strategies
Analogies, p. T215

Day 5

Options for Reteaching,
pp. T216–T217

Options for Reteaching,
pp. T216–T217

Options for Reteaching,
pp. T216–T217

Options for Reteaching,
pp. T216–T217

Partners: Reread *Maria Tallchief, American Ballerina*
Complete Leveled
Practice SR18.3

Vocabulary in Context Cards
171–180 *Talk It Over* Activities
Complete Practice Book p. 207

Reread for Fluency: "The Dog Newspaper"
Complete Leveled Practice A18.3

Partners: Reread for Fluency:
The Life of B.B. King
Complete Leveled
Practice ELL18.3

Reread for Fluency: "The Dog Newspaper"
Complete Work Station activities
Independent Reading

Complete Work Station activities
Independent Reading

Complete Work Station activities
Independent Reading

Reread *Print It!*
or "The Dog Newspaper"
Complete Work Station activities

Think and Write
In My City

JOURNEYS DIGITAL **Powered by** DESTINATIONReading®
Digital Center

Weekly To-Do List

This Weekly To-Do List helps students see their own progress and move on to additional activities independently.

Reading Log

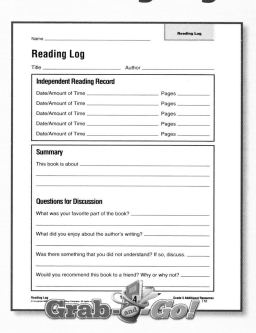

Vocabulary Reader

Print It!

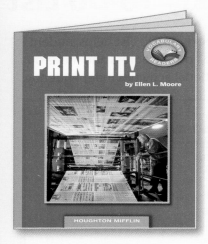

PRINT IT!
by Ellen L. Moore

HOUGHTON MIFFLIN

Summary

This selection explains how a newspaper is made. Reporters, photographers, editors, and designers all have unique responsibilities in the production of a newspaper.

✔ **TARGET VOCABULARY**

career	formula
publication	background
household	insights
edition	uneventful
required	destruction

Struggling Readers

- Explain to students that many people with different skills and talents are needed to publish a newspaper.

- Guide students to preview the **Vocabulary Reader**. Read aloud the headings. Ask students to describe the images, using Target Vocabulary when possible. Ask if they know of anyone who has or has had a *career* at a newspaper.

- Have partners alternate reading pages of the text aloud. Guide them to use context clues to determine the meanings of unfamiliar words. As necessary, use the **Vocabulary in Context Cards** to review the meanings of vocabulary words.

- Assign the **Responding Page** and **Blackline Master 18.1**. Have partners work together to complete the pages.

On Level

- Explain to students that technology has shaped how news is reported, published, and distributed, or shared, with readers. Guide students to preview the selection.

- Remind students that context clues can help them determine the meaning of an unknown word. Tell students to use context clues to confirm their understanding of Target Vocabulary and to learn the meanings of new words.

- Have partners alternate reading pages of the **Vocabulary Reader** aloud. Tell them to use context clues to determine the meanings of unknown words.

- Assign the **Responding Page** and **Blackline Master 18.1**. Have students discuss their responses with a partner.

Advanced

- Have students preview the **Vocabulary Reader** and make predictions about what they will read, using information from their preview and prior knowledge.

- Remind students to use context clues to help them determine the meanings of unknown words.

- Tell students to read the selection with a partner. Ask them to stop and discuss the meanings of unknown words as necessary.

- Assign the **Responding Page** and **Blackline Master 18.1.** For the Write About It activity, remind students to use facts and details to support their ideas. Ask students to describe how a reporter gets information to write a story.

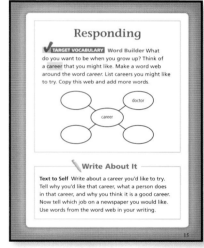

Print It!, p. 15

ELL English Language Learners

Group English Language Learners according to language proficiency.

Beginning

Conduct a picture walk of *Print It!* with students, stopping to write each Target Vocabulary word on the board. Have students repeat each word. Ask them to describe the Vocabulary in Context Card photos for each word.

Advanced

Have students write sentences about a possible career they might like to have when they are older. Have them include in their sentences one vocabulary word and a requirement for that career.

Intermediate

Have partners read *Print It!*, pausing at Target Vocabulary they have difficulty understanding. Encourage pairs to figure out the meaning through context or by using a dictionary or glossary. Have them read the meaning of the word aloud.

Advanced High

Have students reread *Print It!* Have partners discuss a job at a newspaper, using vocabulary words to describe that job's tasks and responsibilities.

Blackline Master 18.1

Differentiate Comprehension

✔ Fact and Opinion; Analyze/Evaluate

Struggling Readers

I DO IT

- Explain that analyzing statements will help readers determine whether they are fact or opinion.

- Remind students that facts can be proven true, but opinions can't.

- Read aloud p. 460 of "The Dog Newspaper" and model analyzing to identify fact or opinion.

Think Aloud The Dog Newspaper *cost five cents. This statement can be proven. It is a fact.*

WE DO IT

- Have students read the first paragraph on p. 463 of "The Dog Newspaper."

- Help students identify one fact that can be proven and one opinion that states a belief, thought, or feeling. *Opinon: "fascinating" front-page subject; Fact: first edition sold 12 copies*

- Help students begin to fill in a T-Map with facts and opinions from the first paragraph.

YOU DO IT

- Have students fill in T-Maps with examples of facts and opinions from the rest of "The Dog Newspaper."

- Have them take turns reading the facts and opinions from their T-Maps.

- Ask them to explain how they used the Analyze/Evaluate strategy to determine whether statements were facts or opinions.

On Level

I DO IT

- Read aloud p. 464 of "The Dog Newspaper."

- Explain that identifying facts and opinions requires a close analysis of the words in each statement.

- Model analyzing the following statement, pointing out that the words *absolutely breathtaking* express an opinion that cannot be proven true or false. Explain that adjectives sometimes signal opinions.

The gingerbread house was absolutely breathtaking.

WE DO IT

- Have students read p. 466 of "The Dog Newspaper."

- Have them suggest statements that were hard to identify as facts or opinions. For example, have them explain why the following statement is an opinion. *"My mistake, I thought then, was always putting my own dog on the front page."*

- Help students understand how this opinion of the author's relates to her message. Then have students enter this opinion in a T-Map.

YOU DO IT

- Have students reread pp. 460–461, recording facts and opinions in their T-Maps.

- Have partners analyze the opinions from their T-Maps and explain how the facts support them. Then discuss how they relate to the author's message that interesting stories are needed to sell newspapers.

- Have volunteers share their work with the class.

Advanced

I DO IT

- Remind students that adjectives sometimes can signal an opinion, as in: *This article is very entertaining and funny.*

- Explain that analyzing sentence parts will reveal whether facts are given along with opinions.

- Read aloud p. 462 of "The Dog Newspaper." Model analyzing the last sentence by breaking it into parts. *The first part is an opinion; the second part is a fact.*

WE DO IT

- Have students read p. 463 of "The Dog Newspaper."

- Have a volunteer suggest a long sentence that has two or more parts. *He was a fascinating front-page subject, and the first edition of* The Dog Newspaper *sold twelve copies.*

- Work together to break the sentence into parts and evaluate whether it has both facts and opinions. Decide whether the opinions are supported by other facts in the story.

YOU DO IT

- Have partners find two complex sentences in the story.

- Have them break the sentences into parts and decide whether each part is fact or opinion. Have them discuss whether the opinions are supported by facts. Then have them record their findings on a T-Map.

- Invite students to model how they used the Analyze/Evaluate strategy to complete their T-Maps.

ELL English Language Learners

Group English Language Learners according to language proficiency.

Write the following sentence frames on the board. *A _____ can be proven true. An _____ can NOT be proven true.* Have students help you to fill in the blanks and to enter examples of facts and opinions onto a T-Map on the board. Then choose one of the following activities for additional support, as appropriate.

Beginning

Describe objects around the room, using both facts and opinions. After each statement, ask the following questions: *Is this true? Is this a fact or an opinion? How do you know?*

Intermediate

Write the following opinion on the board: *Dogs are better than cats.* Record how many agree and disagree. Ask why students have different responses. *It's an opinion.* Repeat the exercise for other opinions offered by students.

Advanced

Have student pairs fill out a T-Map as they read "The Dog Newspaper." Have them enter the most important facts and opinions. Have pairs share their T-Maps with the class. Ask them to explain how they could tell the facts from the opinions.

Advanced High

After reading "The Dog Newspaper," have students discuss the most important facts and opinions of the story. Have them explain why they think the author included certain key facts and opinions.

Targets for Lesson 18

TARGET SKILL

Fact and Opinion

TARGET STRATEGY

Analyze/Evaluate

TARGET VOCABULARY

career	formula
publication	background
household	insights
edition	uneventful
required	destruction

Responding

✔ **TARGET SKILL** Fact and Opinion Think about the facts and opinions the author gives about Maria Tallchief. Then copy the chart below. Add an opinion from the story to complete the chart.

Fact	Opinion
Maria Tallchief was born on January 24, 1925, in Fairfax, Oklahoma.	?

✎ **Write About It**

Text to Self Maria Tallchief was proud of her Native American background. Think of something about yourself that you are proud of. Write a paragraph that tells what makes you proud of that part of yourself.

Maria Tallchief, p. 15

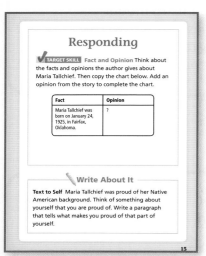

Blackline Master 18.3

Leveled Readers

Struggling Readers

 Maria Tallchief, American Ballerina

GENRE: BIOGRAPHY

SUMMARY Maria Tallchief became a famous ballerina despite the prejudice that Americans would never become great ballet dancers. This biography describes how she took pride in her Native American heritage and excelled as a dancer.

Introducing the Text

- Explain that ballet began in Europe in the 1500s. It came to the United States in 1900, which meant Americans were new to ballet.

- Remind students that a **T-Map** can help them keep track of facts and opinions when they are reading.

Supporting the Reading

- As you listen to students read, pause to discuss these questions.

FACT AND OPINION p. 8 *What is the director's opinion of Betty Marie's name? She needs to change it to a Russian-sounding name to be successful.*

ANALYZE/EVALUATE p. 12 *Evaluate Maria's accomplishments. Did she deserve awards? Yes, her dancing brought attention to the Osage tribe and helped develop the art of ballet.*

Discussing and Revisiting the Text

CRITICAL THINKING After discussing *Maria Tallchief*, have students read the instructions on **Responding p. 15**. Use these points as they revisit the text.

- Have students identify facts and opinions about George Balanchine on p. 10. Tell them to list facts and opinions on **Blackline Master 18.3**.

- Distribute **Blackline Master 18.7** to develop students' critical thinking skills.

FLUENCY: PHRASING: PUNCTUATION Model phrasing. Then have partners practice reading the first paragraph on p. 4 to each other, listening for phrasing based on punctuation.

JOURNEYS DIGITAL | **Powered by** DESTINATIONReading®
Leveled Readers Online

On Level

 ### B. B. King

GENRE: BIOGRAPHY

Summary B. B. King grew up in hard times, losing family members and living on his own by the time he was nine. This biography describes how he eventually became the world-famous musician known as "The King of the Blues."

Introducing the Text

- Explain that working in the cotton fields was hard, and that B. B. King would have been eager to find different work.

- Remind students that they can use facts in a text and their own experiences to decide whether they agree or disagree with an author's opinion.

Supporting the Reading

- As you listen to students read, pause to discuss these questions.

FACT AND OPINION p. 7 *What was one fact that made it difficult for African-Americans to become well-known musicians? Radio stations didn't play their music.*

ANALYZE/EVALUATE p. 12 *Evaluate King's rise to fame. Do you agree with the author? Yes, B. B. King worked hard to overcome many obstacles; he has a unique style that influenced other musicians; he has a likable personality.*

Discussing and Revisiting the Text

CRITICAL THINKING After discussing *B. B. King*, have students read the instructions on **Responding p. 19**. Use these points as they revisit the text.

- Have students identify facts and opinions about B. B. King on pp. 8–9. Have them enter them on **Blackline Master 18.4** and evaluate the author's opinions of King.

- Distribute **Blackline Master 18.8** to develop students' critical thinking skills.

FLUENCY: PHRASING: PUNCTUATION Have partners practice reading the first paragraph on p. 14 to each other. Remind them to use the punctuation to help guide phrasing and expression.

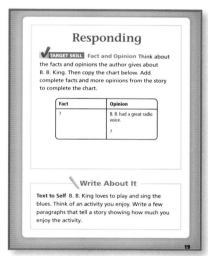

B. B. King, p. 19

Blackline Master 18.4

Targets for Lesson 18

✔ **TARGET SKILL**

Fact and Opinion

✔ **TARGET STRATEGY**

Analyze/Evaluate

✔ **TARGET VOCABULARY**

career	formula
publication	background
household	insights
edition	uneventful
required	destruction

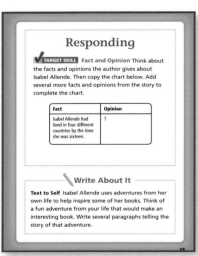

Isabel Allende, p. 19

Blackline Master 18.5

Leveled Readers

Advanced

■ *Isabel Allende*

GENRE: BIOGRAPHY

Summary Isabel Allende lived in many countries growing up and was always the "new girl," who sought comfort in books and writing. Eventually she became an award-winning author, but not without experiencing difficult times along the way.

Introducing the Text

- Explain that Chile, a country in South America, has had a history of changing and overturning governments.

- Remind students that authors often place their own opinions into their writing. A reader's opinion may be the same or different from the author's.

Supporting the Reading

- As you listen to students read, pause to discuss these questions.

FACT AND OPINION p. 11 *What was Neruda's opinion of Isabel Allende? Why?* *She was a terrible journalist, because she inserted her own views into her writing. She was better at writing fiction because her characters could offer their opinions.*

ANALYZE/EVALUATE p. 4 *Evaluate the effect of Isabel's upbringing on her writing. Do you think it helped or hindered her?* *It helped because the members of her family and her reading provided her with ideas.*

Discussing and Revisiting the Text

CRITICAL THINKING After discussing *Isabel Allende*, have students read the instructions on **Responding p. 19**. Use these points as they revisit the text.

- Have students identify facts and opinions about Isabel Allende from pp. 3–4.

- Tell them to list them on **Blackline Master 18.5**. Have them review the facts to see whether they support the stated opinions.

- Distribute **Blackline Master 18.9** to develop students' critical thinking skills.

FLUENCY: PHRASING: PUNCTUATION Have students practice reading paragraph two on p. 13 aloud. They should concentrate on phrasing and expression when reading quotations.

JOURNEYS DIGITAL **Powered by** DESTINATIONReading®
Leveled Readers Online

ELL **English Language Learners**

◆ **The Life of B. B. King**

GENRE: BIOGRAPHY

Summary As a young boy, Riley B. King worked on a cotton plantation. By age nine, his mother and grandmother had died, and he was left alone to make a living for himself. Music was always a part of his life, but it was not until many years later that he experienced success.

Introducing the Text

- Explain that B. B. King's love for music and life helped him get noticed and become a successful musician.

- Remind students that biographies often contain both facts and opinions. Good readers learn to identify both types of statements.

Supporting the Reading

- As you listen to students read, pause to discuss these questions.

FACT AND OPINION p. 7 *What fact shows that King felt guilty for going off and leaving his boss with the broken tractor? He returned to Indianola and gave his boss money for repairs.*

ANALYZE/EVALUATE pp. 13–14 *Evaluate B. B. King's rise to fame. What do you think made him successful? Sample Answer: B. B. King worked hard, learned from others, had great talent, and a likable personality.*

Discussing and Revisiting the Text

CRITICAL THINKING After discussing *The Life of B. B. King,* have students read the instructions on **Responding p. 19**. Use these points as they revisit the text.

- Have students identify facts and opinions about B. B. King from pp. 8–9. Have them list these facts and opinions on **Blackline Master 18.6**. Then have partners discuss whether the facts support the opinions.

- Distribute **Blackline Master 18.10** to further develop critical thinking skills.

FLUENCY: PHRASING: PUNCTUATION Have students practice reading paragraph one on p. 14. Remind them to use the punctuation to help with phrasing. Then have students read to partners.

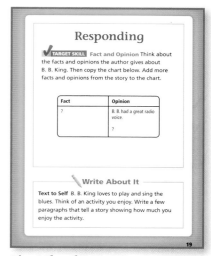

The Life of B. B. King, p. 19

Blackline Master 18.6

Differentiate Vocabulary Strategies ☑ Analogies

Struggling Readers

I DO IT

- Tell students that an analogy is a comparison in which one pair of words has the same type of relationship as the second pair.

- Point out that pairs of words are often compared using synonyms and antonyms:

  worried : concerned :: calm : peaceful synonym

  high : low :: straight : crooked antonym

WE DO IT

- Display the **Vocabulary in Context Card** for *destruction*. Write the following on the board:

  destruction : ruin :: construction : build

- Point out that both word pairs share the same relationship. Have students explain the relationship. *synonym*

- Work with students to complete this analogy: *uneventful : boring :: eventful : exciting*

YOU DO IT

- On the board, write the following analogy: *career : occupation :: education : ___*

- Have students offer words that complete the analogy. *learning*

- Ask volunteers to explain the relationship the analogy uses. *synonyms*

- Repeat for this problem: *destruction : construction :: ruin : ___*

  build, create; antonyms

On Level

I DO IT

- Explain that an analogy is a kind of comparison in which one pair of words is compared to another. The second two words have the same relationship to each other as the first two words have.

- Explain that among the types of relationships two word pairs can share are synonyms, antonyms, and degrees, or general-to-specific categories.

- Give an example of each type.

WE DO IT

- On the board, write the following analogy: *career : teacher :: publication : _____*

- Ask students how *career* and *teacher* are related. *"Teacher" is a specific example, or degree, of the general category "career." Teacher is a type of career.* Have them determine choices for the blank. *newspaper, magazine, book are specific examples of the general category of publication.*

YOU DO IT

- Have students write their own analogies using five Target Vocabulary words.

- Have them write analogies using as many relationship types as they can.

- Have them copy their analogies, leaving one word blank. Have pairs exchange analogy problems and solve them. Review selected analogies with the class.

Advanced

I DO IT

- Explain to students that an analogy is a kind of comparison in which one pair of words is compared to another. Each pair has the same relationship.

- Explain that among the types of relationships two word pairs can share are synonyms, antonyms, parts of a whole, degrees, or general-to-specific categories.

- Give an example of each type.

WE DO IT

- Help students describe the relationship between the words in the following analogies:
  career : teacher :: tree : oak
  chain : link :: book : page

- Guide students to see that the first analogy uses degrees, or categories that are general to specific. Ask students to tell you the relationship of the second analogy. *parts of a whole*

- Help students create an analogy using this analogy starter *writer : novel :: artist : _____ painting*

YOU DO IT

- Have students create analogies using as many of the Target Vocabulary words listed below as they can:

  career, publication, household, edition, required, formula, background, insights, uneventful

- Tell students to vary the types of relationships their analogies use.

- Have pairs exchange their analogies to determine the types of relationships used or to offer feedback if the analogies are unsound.

ELL English Language Learners

Group English Language Learners according to language proficiency. Write *career, publication, background, household, insights, required, uneventful, edition, formula,* and *destruction.* Have students repeat after you as you pronounce each word. Have students list synonyms, antonyms, or examples that come to mind for each word.

Beginning

Copy this analogy on the board: *up : down :: left : right.* Ask students what *up* and *down* have in common. *antonyms* Repeat for *left* and *right.* Guide them to see that the word pairs share the same antonym relationship.

Intermediate

Copy this analogy on the board: *up : climb :: left : _____.* Ask students what *up* and *climb* have in common. *You climb to go up.* Ask them to name the word that shows the same relationship to *left. turn*

Advanced

Display the Context Cards for the lesson. Have students choose a card and create the first part of an analogy using a synonym or antonym. Have them trade it with a partner who will complete the analogy.

Advanced High

Display the Context Cards. Have students write an analogy using one of the words. Have them trade analogies with a partner and then write a sentence explaining the relationship between the words.

☑ Options for Reteaching

Vocabulary Strategies

☑ Analogies

I DO IT

- Remind students that an analogy is a kind of comparison in which one pair of words is compared to another.
- Explain that the first pair of words has the same relationship to each other as the second pair of words.
- Remind students that antonyms and synonyms are commonly used to make analogies.

WE DO IT

- Write the following analogy on the board and model how to complete it:
  destruction : construction :: problem : _____

  Think Aloud *Destruction is to construction as problem is to what? Destruction and construction are antonyms. So, to complete the analogy, I need to find an antonym for* problem. Solution *is an antonym for* problem. *I'll use* solution *to complete the analogy. Destruction is to construction as problem is to solution.*

- Guide students to complete the following analogy:
  fire : hot :: snow : _____

YOU DO IT

- Have partners work together to complete the following analogies:
  common : unique :: short : _____ long
  common : popular :: short : _____ short
- Have students use a thesaurus or dictionary to find synonyms and antonyms.

Comprehension Skill

☑ Fact and Opinion

I DO IT

- Remind students that authors use both fact and opinion statements in their writing. They often use facts to support their opinions. Remind students that they can often identify opinions by signal words, such as *think* or *believe*.
- Remind students that good readers *analyze,* or study closely, how authors use fact and opinion in order to *evaluate,* or make a judgment about, the author's work.

WE DO IT

- Have students reread **Student Book p. 460** and identify an opinion statement supported by fact.
- Model how to identify an opinion and analyze the use of facts to support it.

  Think Aloud *The author says she began her writing career at age ten. This is a fact; it can be proven. Then a little further on, she calls the news boring. This is an opinion. But it's a fact that her neighbors shared her opinion that their dogs were not exciting. That fact supports her opinion.*

- Help volunteers identify another fact-supported opinion in the last paragraph of the passage.

YOU DO IT

- Distribute **Graphic Organizer 12.**
- Have students list facts and opinions on p. 462. *Fact: German people were faced with rebuilding. Opinion: No one wanted to bother with a dog.*
- Have students work in pairs to complete the graphic organizer.
- Have students discuss how some of the facts support opinions.

Language Arts

 # Prepositions and Prepositional Phrases/ Write to Narrate

I DO IT

- Explain that prepositions act as links between ideas in sentences. They often tell a time, direction, or location. Prepositional phrases start with a preposition and end with a noun or pronoun.

- Write *after, on,* and *in* on the board. Then write *We go to art after lunch.*

> **Think Aloud** *I know* after *is a preposition.* After lunch *is the prepositional phrase. This phrase tells me a time.*

WE DO IT

- Work together to write on the board a sentence using a preposition that tells a place, such as, *We had lunch in the park.*
- Guide students to identify the preposition and the prepositional phrase in the sentence.
- Have partners work together to write sentences with prepositional phrases. Help them to explain whether the preposition tells a time, direction, or location.

YOU DO IT

- Have pairs of students write a short narrative with at least 3 sentences using prepositional phrases. Have them underline the prepositional phrase, and identify whether the preposition they used tells a time, direction, or location.

Decoding

 # Recognizing Suffixes

I DO IT

- Remind students that a suffix is added to the ending of a word. It changes the word's meaning.
- Sometimes the spelling of the base word changes when adding a suffix.
- Some words have more than one suffix.

WE DO IT

- Write *loveliest, earlier, helpful,* and *iciest* on the board.
- Help students identify the base words and suffixes.
- Model how to decode *loveliest.*

> **Think Aloud** *I know that some words are made up of a base word followed by one or more suffixes. The base word here is* love. *This word has both the suffix -ly and the suffix -est added. But when the suffix -est is added, the spelling changes.*

YOU DO IT

- Have partners decode the other words.
- Ask them to note the spelling changes in *loveliest* and *earlier.*
- Use the **Corrective Feedback** on p. T185 if students need additional help.

Teacher Notes

Preteaching for Success!

Comprehension:

Persuasion

Tell students that recognizing persuasion helps the reader make up his or her own mind.

- Review with students that persuasion is how the author convinces the reader to think a certain way, or to agree with something.
- To illustrate the concept, help students fill in the graphic organizer on Student Book p. 480. Write in the top box "new playground." Brainstorm with students how to persuade the city council to vote for a new playground in your town.

Challenge Yourself!

Research Community Gardens

After reading the selection "Darnell Rock Reporting," have students research real community gardens.

- Review with students that community gardens are not a new idea. During wartime, citizens often maintain vegetable gardens for extra food.
- Have students research community gardens in their town or city. If there are none, ask students for suggestions for spaces for one.
- Have pairs of students design community gardens. Tell them to research what kinds of plants grow in their climate. Have them draw pictures or diagrams of their gardens.

Short Response

W.5.1b Provide logically ordered reasons that are supported by facts and details.

Write a paragraph about how Sweeby Jones's comments affected or changed your thinking about homeless people.

Scoring Guidelines	
Excellent	Student has written a paragraph about his or her reaction to Sweeby Jones's comments.
Good	Student has written a paragraph about Sweeby Jones but has not included his or her reaction.
Fair	Student has written a paragraph about the story but not about Sweeby Jones's comments.
Unsatisfactory	Student has not written a paragraph.

Writing Minilesson

Skill: Write to Narrate—Personal Narrative

Teach: Explain to students that one of the best ways to narrate is to retell personal experiences.

Thinking Beyond the Text

Writing Prompt: Write a short personal narrative about a good deed you once did.

1. Tell students to think about things they did that were helpful to others. Students should retell these events in one or two paragraphs.
2. Remind students to check that they have used pronouns correctly.
3. Tell students to make sure their ideas are expressed clearly.

Group Share: Invite students to share their personal narratives with the class.

Cross-Curricular Activity: Science

Nutrients in Fruits and Vegetables

The selection tells of Darnell's plan to build a community garden. Discuss some of the vitamins and minerals people get by eating different fruits and vegetables. Encourage students to research which fruits and vegetables people should eat each day to get plenty of protein, vitamins, and minerals. Have them make charts to show their findings.

Reading Standards for Literature K–5

Key Ideas and Details
RL.5.1 Quote accurately from a text when explaining what the text says explicitly and when drawing inferences from the text.

Craft and Structure
RL.5.4 Determine the meaning of words and phrases as they are used in a text, including figurative language such as metaphors and similes.

Range of Reading and Level of Text Complexity
RL.5.10 By the end of the year, read and comprehend literature, including stories, dramas, and poetry, at the high end of the grades 4–5 text complexity band independently and proficiently.

Reading Standards for Informational Text K–5

Integration of Knowledge and Ideas
RI.5.8 Explain how an author uses reasons and evidence to support particular points in a text, identifying which reasons and evidence support which point(s).

Reading Standards: Foundational Skills K–5

Phonics and Word Recognition
RF.5.3a Use combined knowledge of all letter-sound correspondences, syllabication patterns, and morphology (e.g., roots and affixes) to read accurately unfamiliar multisyllabic words in context and out of context.

Fluency
RF.5.4b Read grade-level prose and poetry orally with accuracy, appropriate rate, and expression.

Writing Standards K–5

Text Types and Purposes
W.5.3a Orient the reader by establishing a situation and introducing a narrator and/or characters; organize an event sequence that unfolds naturally.

W.5.3b Use narrative techniques, such as dialogue, description, and pacing, to develop experiences and events or show the responses of characters to situations.

W.5.3d Use concrete words and phrases and sensory details to convey experiences and events precisely.

W.5.3e Provide a conclusion that follows from the narrated experiences or events.

Production and Distribution of Writing
W.5.4 Produce clear and coherent writing in which the development and organization are appropriate to task, purpose, and audience. (Grade-specific expectations for writing types are defined in standards 1–3 above.)

W.5.5 With guidance and support from peers and adults, develop and strengthen writing as needed by planning, revising, editing, rewriting, or trying a new approach.

Research to Build and Present Knowledge
W.5.7 Conduct short research projects that use several sources to build knowledge through investigation of different aspects of a topic.

Speaking & Listening Standards K–5

Comprehension and Collaboration
SL.5.1a Come to discussions prepared, having read or studied required material; explicitly draw on that preparation and other information known about the topic to explore ideas under discussion.

SL.5.1c Pose and respond to specific questions by making comments that contribute to the discussion and elaborate on the remarks of others.

SL.5.1d Review the key ideas expressed and draw conclusions in light of information and knowledge gained from the discussions.

SL.5.2 Summarize a written text read aloud or information presented in diverse media and formats, including visually, quantitatively, and orally.

Presentation of Knowledge and Ideas
SL.5.4 Report on a topic or text or present an opinion, sequencing ideas logically and using appropriate facts and relevant, descriptive details to support main ideas or themes; speak clearly at an understandable pace.

SL.5.6 Adapt speech to a variety of contexts and tasks, using formal English when appropriate to task and situation.

Language Standards K–5

Conventions of Standard English
L.5.1c Use verb tense to convey various times, sequences, states, and conditions.

L.5.2e Spell grade-appropriate words correctly, consulting references as needed.

Knowledge of Language
L.5.3b Compare and contrast the varieties of English (e.g., dialects, registers) used in stories, dramas, or poems.

Vocabulary Acquisition and Use
L.5.4a Use context (e.g., cause/effect relationships and comparisons in text) as a clue to the meaning of a word or phrase.

L.5.4b Use common, grade-appropriate Greek and Latin affixes and roots as clues to the meaning of a word (e.g., *photograph, photosynthesis*).

SUGGESTIONS FOR BALANCED LITERACY

Use *Journeys* materials to support a Readers' Workshop approach. See the Lesson 19 resources on pages 27, 76–77.

Focus Wall

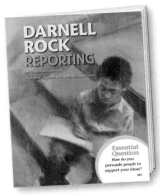

Main Selection:
"Darnell Rock
Reporting"

Connect to Social Studies:
"De Zavala: A Voice
for Texas"

Big Idea
Everyone has a
story to tell.

? Essential Question
How do you persuade
people to support
your ideas?

Comprehension

✔ **TARGET SKILL**

Persuasion

✔ **TARGET STRATEGY**

Summarize

Fluency

Stress

Decoding

More Common Suffixes

Vocabulary Strategies

Greek and Latin Suffixes
-ism, -ist, -able, -ible

Grammar

More Kinds of
Pronouns

Spelling

Suffixes: *-ful, -ly, -ness, -less, -ment*

lately	delightful
government	appointment
forgiveness	steadily
settlement	noisily
agreement	effortless
harmless	closeness
watchful	tardiness
cloudiness	plentiful
enjoyment	calmly
countless	forgetful

✐ Writing

Write to Narrate
Focus Trait: Ideas

✔ TARGET VOCABULARY

issue	effective
deteriorating	urge
dependent	violations
exception	ordinance
granted	minimum

Week at a Glance

Key Skills This Week

Target Skill:
Persuasion

Target Strategy:
Summarize

Vocabulary Strategies:
Greek and Latin Suffixes -ism, -ist, -able, -ible

Fluency:
Stress

Decoding:
More Common Suffixes

Research Skill:
Create Graphic/Visual Data

Grammar:
More Kinds of Pronouns

Spelling:
Suffixes: -ful, -ly, -ness, -less, -ment

 Writing:
Write to Narrate: Personal Narrative

✔ Assess/Monitor

☑ **Vocabulary,**
p. *T274*

☑ **Comprehension,**
p. *T274*

☑ **Decoding,**
p. *T275*

☑ **Language Arts,**
p. *T275*

☑ **Fluency,**
p. *T275*

Whole Group

READING

Paired Selections

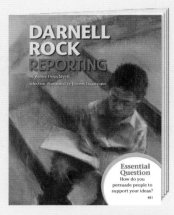

Darnell Rock Reporting
Realistic Fiction
Student Book pp. 480–492

De Zavala: A Voice for Texas
SOCIAL STUDIES/Persuasive Text
Student Book pp. 494–496

Practice Quizzes for the Selection

Vocabulary

Student Book pp. 476–477

Background and Comprehension

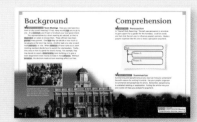

Student Book pp. 478–479

LANGUAGE ARTS

Grammar
Student Book pp. 498–499

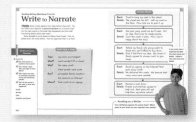

Writing
Student Book pp. 500–501

Whole Group — **Small Group** — Intervention — **ELL**

Small Group

See page T278–T279 for Suggested Small Group Plan.

TEACHER-LED

Leveled Readers

 Struggling Readers ▲ **On Level**

■ **Advanced** ◆ **English Language Learners**

Vocabulary Reader

WHAT MY OTHER STUDENTS ARE DOING

Ready-Made Work Stations

Word Study **Think and Write**

Comprehension and Fluency **Digital Center**

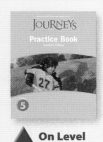 

 ● **Struggling Readers**

 ■ **Advanced**

◆ **English Language Learners**

 ▲ **On Level**

Grab-and-Go!

Lesson 19 Blackline Masters
- Target Vocabulary 19.1
- Selection Summary 19.2
- Graphic Organizer 19.3-19.6 ●▲■◆
- Critical Thinking 19.7-19.10 ●▲■◆
- Running Records 19.11-19.14 ●▲■◆
- Weekly Tests 19.1–19.9

Graphic Organizer Transparency 7

Additional Resources
- Genre: Fiction, p. 4
- Reading Log, p. 12
- Vocabulary Log, p. 13
- Listening Log, p. 14
- Proofreading Checklist, p. 15
- Proofreading Marks, p. 16
- Writing Conference Form, p. 17
- Writing Rubric, p. 18
- Instructional Routines, pp. 19–26
- Graphic Organizer 7: Idea-Support Map, p. 33

JOURNEYS DIGITAL Powered by DESTINATION Reading

For Students
- Student eBook
- Comprehension Expedition CD-ROM
- Leveled Readers Online
- WriteSmart CD-ROM

For Teachers
- Online TE and Focus Wall
- Online Assessment System
- Teacher One-Stop
- Destination Reading Instruction

Week at a Glance

STRATEGIC INTERVENTION: TIER II

Use these materials to provide additional targeted instruction for students who need Tier II strategic intervention.

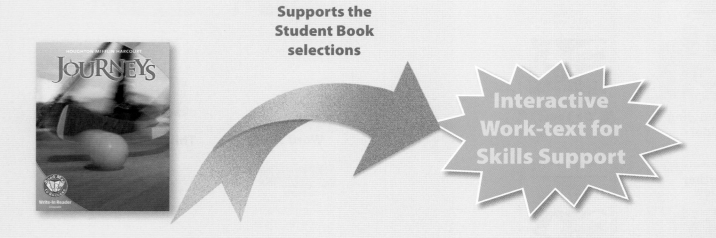

Supports the Student Book selections

Interactive Work-text for Skills Support

Write-in Reader:

Sojourner Truth, Speaker for Equal Rights

- Engaging selection connects to main topic.
- Reinforces this week's target vocabulary and comprehension skill and strategy.
- Opportunities for student interaction on each page.

Assessment

Progress monitoring every two weeks.

For this week's Strategic Intervention lessons, see Teacher's Edition pages S32–S41.

INTENSIVE INTERVENTION: TIER III

- The materials in the Literacy Tool Kit help you provide a different approach for students who need Tier III intensive intervention.
- Interactive lessons provide focused instruction in key reading skills, targeted at students' specific needs.
- Lesson cards are convenient for small-group or individual instruction.
- Blackline masters provide additional practice.
- A leveled book accompanies each lesson to give students opportunities for additional reading and skill application.
- Assessments for each lesson help you evaluate the effectiveness of the intervention.

Lessons provide support for:

- Phonics and Word Study Skills
- Vocabulary
- Comprehension Skills and Literary Genres
- Fluency

ELL English Language Learners

SCAFFOLDED SUPPORT

Use these materials to ensure that students acquire social and academic language proficiency.

JOURNEYS DIGITAL Powered by **DESTINATION Reading**
• Leveled Readers Online
• Picture Card Bank Online

Language Support Card

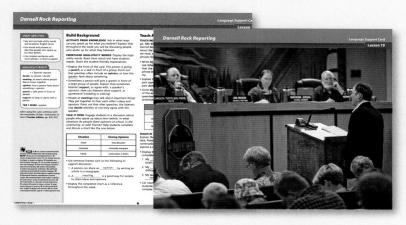

• Builds background for the main topic and promotes oral language.
• Develops high-utility vocabulary and academic language.

Leveled Reader

• Sheltered text connects to the main selection's topic, vocabulary, skill, and strategy.

Scaffolded Support

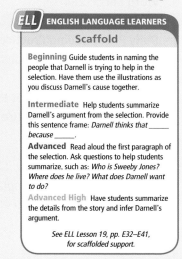

ELL ENGLISH LANGUAGE LEARNERS

Scaffold

Beginning Guide students in naming the people that Darnell is trying to help in the selection. Have them use the illustrations as you discuss Darnell's cause together.

Intermediate Help students summarize Darnell's argument from the selection. Provide this sentence frame: *Darnell thinks that _____ because _____.*

Advanced Read aloud the first paragraph of the selection. Ask questions to help students summarize, such as: *Who is Sweeby Jones? Where does he live? What does Darnell want to do?*

Advanced High Have students summarize the details from the story and infer Darnell's argument.

See ELL Lesson 19, pp. E32–E41, for scaffolded support.

• Notes throughout the Teacher's Edition scaffold instruction to each language proficiency level.

Vocabulary in Context Cards 181–190

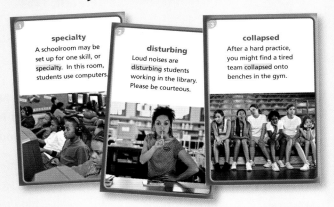

specialty A schoolroom may be set up for one skill, or specialty. In this room, students use computers.

disturbing Loud noises are disturbing students working in the library. Please be courteous.

collapsed After a hard practice, you might find a tired team collapsed onto benches in the gym.

• Provide visual support and additional practice for Target Vocabulary words.

For this week's English Language Learners lessons, see Teacher's Edition pages E32–E41.

Lesson 19
Weekly Plan

? Essential Question How do you persuade people to support your ideas?

	Day 1	Day 2
Whole Group		
Oral Language Listening Comprehension	**Teacher Read Aloud** "The Power of Spirit Lake," T230–T231 ☑ Target Vocabulary, T231	**Turn and Talk**, T237
Vocabulary **Comprehension** Skills and Strategies **Reading**	☑ **Introduce Comprehension** Preview the Target Skill, T231 ☑ **Introduce Vocabulary** Vocabulary in Context, T232–T233 **Develop Background** ☑ Target Vocabulary, T234–T235	**Introduce Comprehension** ☑ Persuasion, T236–T237 Summarize, T236–T237 **Read "Darnell Rock Reporting,"** T238–T250 Focus on Genre, T238 Stop and Think, T243, T247, T249
Cross-Curricular **Connections** **Fluency** **Decoding**	☑ **Fluency** Model Stress, T230	☑ **Fluency** Teach Stress, T258
Whole Group Language Arts		

Spelling
Grammar
Writing
	☑ **Spelling**
	Suffixes: -ful, -ly, -ness, -less, -ment:
	Pretest, T264
	☑ **Grammar**
	Daily Proofreading Practice, T266
	Teach Indefinite Pronouns, T266
	
	☑ **Write to Narrate: Plan a**
	    Personal Narrative
	Analyze the Model, T270
		☑ **Spelling**
		Suffixes: -ful, -ly, -ness, -less, -ment:
		Word Sort, T264
		☑ **Grammar**
		Daily Proofreading Practice, T267
		Teach Possessive Pronouns, T267
		
		☑ **Write to Narrate: Plan a**
		    Personal Narrative
		Focus Trait: Ideas, T271

Writing Prompt	*Describe an issue you feel your city council should address.*	*Write a persuasive paragraph asking for a no-homework weekend once a month.*

COMMON CORE Correlations

Day 1
Introduce Vocabulary RL.5.4, L.5.4a
Develop Background RL.5.4, L.5.4a
Fluency RF.5.4b
Spelling L.5.2e
Write to Narrate W.5.3a, W.5.3e, W.5.4, W.5.5

Day 2
Turn and Talk SL.5.3
Introduce Comprehension SL.5.2
Read RL.5.1, RL.5.4, RL.5.10, SL.5.2, L.5.3b
Fluency RF.5.4b
Spelling L.5.2e
Write to Narrate W.5.3a, W.5.3b, W.5.3d,
    W.5.4, W.5.5

Suggestions for Small Groups (See pp. T278–T279.)
Suggestions for Intervention (See pp. S32–S41.)
Suggestions for English Language Learners (See pp. E32–E41.)

JOURNEYS DIGITAL Powered by DESTINATIONReading
Teacher One-Stop: Lesson Planning

Day 3

Turn and Talk, T251
Oral Language, T251

Read "Darnell Rock Reporting," T238–T250
Develop Comprehension, T240, T242, T244, T246, T248, T250
☑ **Discuss Vocabulary**
"Darnell Rock Reporting," T240, T242, T248
Your Turn, T251
Deepen Comprehension
☑ Analyze and Evaluate Persuasion, T256–T257

Cross-Curricular Connection
Social Studies, T243
☑ **Fluency** Practice Stress, T245
☑ **Decoding**
More Common Suffixes, T259

☑ **Spelling**
Suffixes: *-ful, -ly, -ness, -less, -ment*: Related Words, T265
☑ **Grammar**
Daily Proofreading Practice, T267
Teach Interrogative Pronouns, T267

☑ **Write to Narrate: Plan a Personal Narrative**
Prewrite, T272

Describe how the author made you feel about Darnell and Linda.

Oral Language SL.5.3
Read RL.5.1, RL.5.4, RL.5.10, SL.5.2, L.5.3b
Your Turn SL.5.1a, SL.5.1c
Deepen Comprehension SL.5.1a, SL.5.1c, SL.5.1d
Fluency RF.5.4b
Decoding RF.5.3a
Spelling L.5.2e
Write to Narrate W.5.3a, W.5.3b, W.5.3d, W.5.4, W.5.5

Day 4

Text to World, T255

Read "De Zavala: A Voice for Texas," T252–T254
Connect to Social Studies, T252
Target Vocabulary Review, T253
Develop Comprehension, T254
Weekly Internet Challenge, T254–T255
Making Connections, T255
☑ **Vocabulary Strategies**
Greek and Latin Suffixes *-ism, -ist, -able, -ible,* T260–T261

☑ **Fluency**
Practice Stress, T253

☑ **Spelling**
Suffixes: *-ful, -ly, -ness, -less, -ment*: Connect to Writing, T265
☑ **Grammar**
Daily Proofreading Practice, T268
Review More Kinds of Pronouns, T268

☑ **Write to Narrate: Plan a Personal Narrative**
Prewrite, T272

Write a speech about an issue you would present to the school's student council.

Read RI.5.8, RF.5.4b
Vocabulary Strategies RF.5.3a, L.5.4b
Fluency RF.5.4b
Spelling L.5.2e
Grammar L.5.1c
Write to Narrate W.5.3a, W.5.3b, W.5.3d, W.5.4, W.5.5

Day 5

Listening and Speaking, T263

Connect and Extend
Read to Connect, T262
Independent Reading, T262
Extend Through Research, T263

☑ **Fluency**
Progress Monitoring, T275

☑ **Spelling**
Suffixes: *-ful, -ly, -ness, -less, -ment*: Assess, T265
☑ **Grammar**
Daily Proofreading Practice, T268
Connect Grammar to Writing, T268–T269

☑ **Write to Narrate: Plan a Personal Narrative**
Prewrite, T272

Explain which is more persuasive: a speech or an online newspaper article.

Listening and Speaking SL.5.6
Connect and Extend W.5.7, SL.5.1a, SL.5.1c, SL.5.4
Fluency RF.5.4b
Spelling L.5.2e
Write to Narrate W.5.3a, W.5.3b, W.5.3d, W.5.4, W.5.5

Your Skills for the Week

☑ **Vocabulary**
Target Vocabulary
Strategies: Greek and Latin Suffixes *-ism, -ist, -able, -ible*

☑ **Comprehension**
Persuasion
Summarize

☑ **Decoding**
More Common Suffixes

☑ **Fluency**
Stress

☑ **Language Arts**
Spelling
Grammar
Writing

Weekly Leveled Readers

Additional Tools

Vocabulary in Context Cards

Comprehension Tool: Graphic Organizer Transparency 7

Differentiated Support for This Week's Targets

✓ **TARGET SKILL**
Persuasion

✓ **TARGET STRATEGY**
Summarize

✓ **TARGET VOCABULARY**

issue	effective
deteriorating	urge
dependent	violations
exception	ordinance
granted	minimum

? Essential Question

How do you persuade people to support your ideas?

Vocabulary Reader

Build Target Vocabulary · **Level R**

- Introduce the Target Vocabulary in context and build comprehension using the Target Strategy.

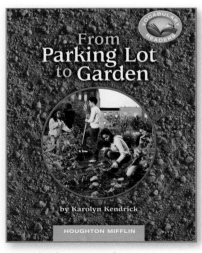

Vocabulary Reader

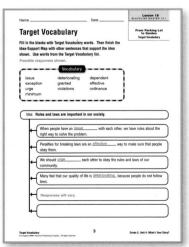

Blackline Master 19.1

Intervention

Scaffolded Support

- Provide extra support in applying the Target Vocabulary, Target Skill, and Target Strategy in context.

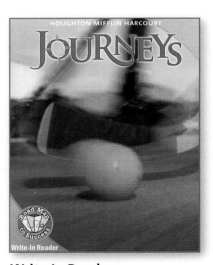

Write-In Reader

SMALL GROUP Options
For Vocabulary Reader Lesson Plans, see Small Group pages T280–T281.

Leveled Readers

 Struggling Readers   **Level R**

Objective: Use Persuasion and the Summarize strategy to read *The Big Interview.*

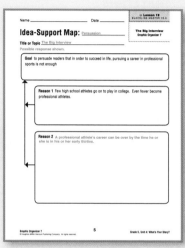

Blackline Master 19.3

 On Level   **Level T**

Objective: Use Persuasion and the Summarize strategy to read *Saving the General.*

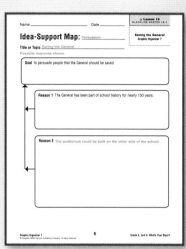

Blackline Master 19.4

Advanced   **Level X**

Objective: Use Persuasion and the Summarize strategy to read *Another View.*

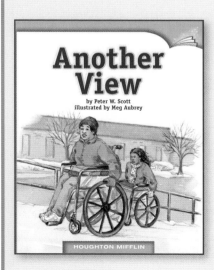

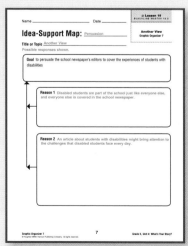

Blackline Master 19.5

English Language Learners   **Level T**

Objective: Use Persuasion and the Summarize strategy to read *The Old Tree.*

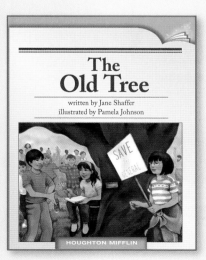

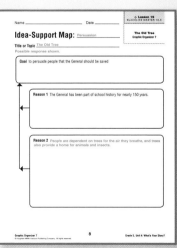

Blackline Master 19.6

 For Leveled Reader Lesson Plans, see Small Group pages T284–T287.

Ready-Made Work Stations

Managing Independent Activities

Use the Ready-Made Work Stations to establish a consistent routine for students working independently. Each station contains three activities. Students who experience success with the *Get Started!* activity move on to the *Reach Higher!* and *Challenge Yourself!* activities, as time permits.

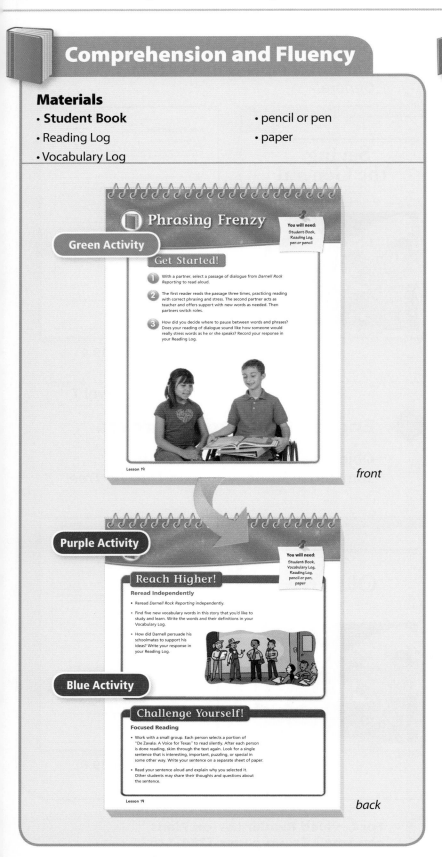

Comprehension and Fluency

Materials
- **Student Book**
- Reading Log
- Vocabulary Log
- pencil or pen
- paper

Phrasing Frenzy

You will need: Student Book, Reading Log, pen or pencil

Green Activity

Get Started!

1. With a partner, select a passage of dialogue from *Darnell Rock Reporting* to read aloud.

2. The first reader reads the passage three times, practicing reading with correct phrasing and stress. The second partner acts as teacher and offers support with new words as needed. Then partners switch roles.

3. How did you decide where to pause between words and phrases? Does your reading of dialogue sound like how someone would really stress words as he or she speaks? Record your response in your Reading Log.

Lesson 19   *front*

Purple Activity

You will need: Student Book, Vocabulary Log, Reading Log, pencil or pen, paper

Reach Higher!

Reread Independently

- Reread *Darnell Rock Reporting* independently.
- Find five new vocabulary words in this story that you'd like to study and learn. Write the words and their definitions in your Vocabulary Log.
- How did Darnell persuade his schoolmates to support his ideas? Write your response in your Reading Log.

Blue Activity

Challenge Yourself!

Focused Reading

- Work with a small group. Each person selects a portion of "De Zavala: A Voice for Texas" to read silently. After each person is done reading, skim through the text again. Look for a single sentence that is interesting, important, puzzling, or special in some other way. Write your sentence on a separate sheet of paper.
- Read your sentence aloud and explain why you selected it. Other students may share their thoughts and questions about the sentence.

Lesson 19   *back*

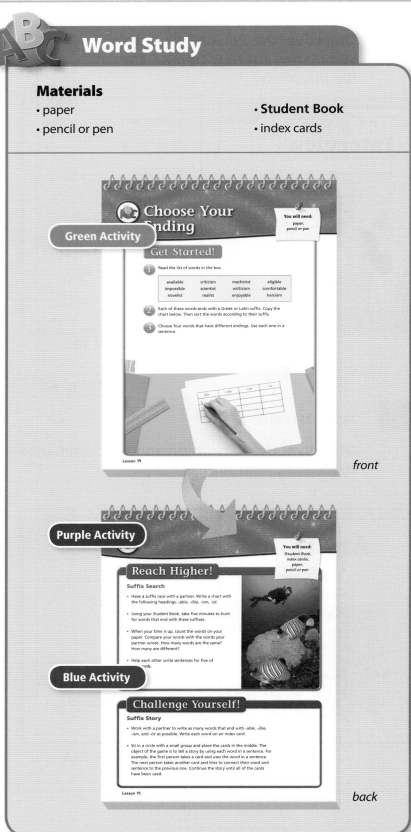

Word Study

Materials
- paper
- pencil or pen
- **Student Book**
- index cards

Choose Your Ending

You will need: paper, pencil or pen

Green Activity

Get Started!

1. Read the list of words in the box.

available	criticism	machinist	eligible
impossible	scientist	witticism	comfortable
novelist	realist	enjoyable	heroism

2. Each of these words ends with a Greek or Latin suffix. Copy the chart below. Then sort the words according to their suffix.

3. Choose four words that have different endings. Use each one in a sentence.

Lesson 19   *front*

Purple Activity

You will need: Student Book, index cards, paper, pencil or pen

Reach Higher!

Suffix Search

- Have a suffix race with a partner. Write a chart with the following headings: -able, -ible, -ism, -ist.
- Using your Student Book, take five minutes to hunt for words that end with these suffixes.
- When your time is up, count the words on your paper. Compare your words with the words your partner wrote. How many words are the same? How many are different?
- Help each other write sentences for five of words.

Blue Activity

Challenge Yourself!

Suffix Story

- Work with a partner to write as many words that end with -able, -ible, -ism, and -ist as possible. Write each word on an index card.
- Sit in a circle with a small group and place the cards in the middle. The object of the game is to tell a story by using each word in a sentence. For example, the first person takes a card and uses the word in a sentence. The next person takes another card and tries to connect their word and sentence to the previous one. Continue the story until all of the cards have been used.

Lesson 19   *back*

Think and Write

Materials
- paper
- pencil or pen
- construction paper
- colored markers
- stapler

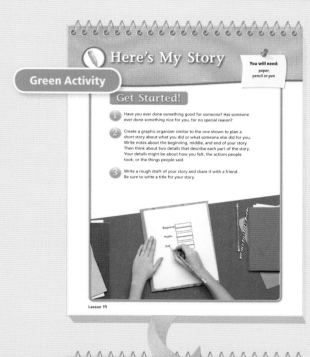

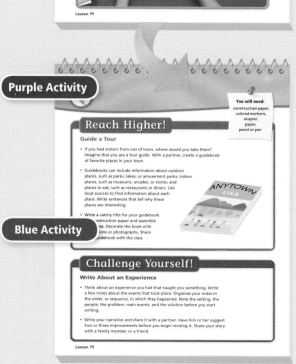

front

back

Powered by
DESTINATIONReading®

Independent Activities

Have students complete these activities at a computer center or a center with an audio CD player.

LAUNCH **Comprehension and Grammar Activities**

Practice and apply this week's skills.

LAUNCH **Student eBook**

Read and listen to this week's selections and skill lessons.

LAUNCH **WriteSmart CD-ROM**

Review student versions of this week's writing model.

LAUNCH **Audiotext CD**

Listen to books or selections on CD.

Ready-Made Work Stations • **T229**

Teacher Read Aloud

SHARE OBJECTIVES

- Listen to fluent reading.
- Listen for persuasion.
- Listen to learn the Target Vocabulary words.

Model Fluency

Stress Explain that good readers emphasize particular words or syllables through volume and pitch.

- Display **Projectable 19.1**. Read each sentence and explain how stressing, or emphasizing, particular words or syllables affects the meaning of what is read.

- Demonstrate how stressing certain words or syllables correctly adds emphasis to the point that the author makes to the reader.

- Reread the passage together. Tell students to stress certain words and syllables to enhance meaning.

The Power of Spirit Lake

The town of Spirit Lake, population 4,048, sits in a lonely corner of northern Iowa. Yet this tiny community has put itself on the map. This is their story.

1 Fifteen years ago, with about 1300 students in the system, Spirit Lake schools faced a **deteriorating** budget. The cause was a common national problem: huge energy costs.

On Earth Day 1991, Superintendent Harold Overmann visited a biology class. As Overmann recalls it, students took **exception** to the idea that officials really cared about any environmental **issue**. "The students challenged me as I had never been challenged before," he reports. "'If the school is so interested in preserving our environment,' they asked, 'why do we use Styrofoam cups in our lunch program? Why do we rely so much on fossil fuels?' They really grilled me."

The students would **urge** Overmann to think: Maybe cleaner energy could solve the school's budget woes. The question was—how?

One afternoon, Overmann and a parent were watching their kids play flag football on the school field. It was a windy day—pretty ordinary for Spirit Lake. This town sits on Buffalo Ridge, about 200 feet above the Iowa grasslands. "Wouldn't it be nice if we could do something with this?" the parent shouted above the wind. And with that, a project began to take shape.

Projectable 19.1

Darnell Rock Reoprting | Fluency Stress

Read Aloud: Model Oral Fluency

The Power of Spirit Lake

The town of Spirit Lake, population 4,048, sits in a lonely corner of northern Iowa. Yet this tiny community has put itself on the map. This is their story.

Fifteen years ago, with about 1300 students in the system, Spirit Lake schools faced a deteriorating budget. The cause was a common national problem: huge energy costs.

On Earth Day 1991, Superintendent Harold Overmann visited a biology class. As Overmann recalls it, students took exception to the idea that officials really cared about any environmental issue. "The students challenged me as I had never been challenged before," he reports. "'If the school is so interested in preserving our environment,' they asked, 'why do we use Styrofoam cups in our lunch program? Why do we rely so much on fossil fuels?' They really grilled me."

A windmill used to create electricity

Overmann and other officials did some homework. They read up on wind turbines and researched the local building **ordinance** list. They discovered that a wind turbine works in a way opposite to that of a fan. You plug in a fan, using electricity to make wind. But a wind turbine uses wind to make electricity. When the wind blows, it turns three tall blades that spin a shaft. This connects to a generator, which makes electricity. The electricity is transmitted underground to a substation, which routes it to users.

Spirit Lake submitted their proposal to the Federal Department of Energy, which **granted** them a loan to build its first wind turbine. How did the experiment turn out? Within four years, the wind turbine had produced enough electricity to pay off the building costs. Now, it actually *makes* money by selling about $20,000 of excess electricity back to the utility each year. **②**

The project was so **effective** that they built a second, larger wind turbine. Now, the schools in Spirit Lake produce all their own energy. This amounts to a savings of $120,000 per year—money that goes right back into improving the schools. And that's not all. Instead of racking up **violations**, Spirit Lake has reduced carbon dioxide emissions by a **minimum** of two tons per year. After being **dependent** on fossil fuels, the town has eliminated their use. This amounts to a savings of 4,000 barrels of oil or about 1,000 tons of coal per year. **③**

That is how one Iowa town became the first in the nation to run its schools completely on the power of its own winds—and the strength of its community spirit. **④**

Listening Comprehension
Preview the Target Skill

Read aloud the passage at a natural rate. Pause to ask the following questions.

❶ Details *How does the author portray the town of Spirit Lake? It's a tiny town that is looking for ways to save money.*

❷ Summarize *Briefly tell the important details about the outcome of the Spirit Lake wind turbine experiment. Within four years, the wind turbine paid off the building costs and began to sell excess electricity back to the utility.*

❸ Persuasion *Identify reasons supporting the argument that a second wind turbine increases savings. The town saved $120,000 in energy costs annually; it used savings for school improvement; it reduced carbon emissions; it eliminated dependence on fossil fuels.*

❹ Persuasion *How does the author of this selection try to convince readers? The author explains how a small town made a difference.*

✔ Target Vocabulary

- Reread "The Power of Spirit Lake" aloud.
- As you read, pause briefly to explain each highlighted vocabulary word.
- Discuss the meaning of each word as it is used in the Read Aloud.

deteriorating becoming worse; falling apart

exception something that does not fit into a general rule

issue a subject or problem that people think and talk about

urge to try to persuade strongly

ordinance a law or rule made by authorities

granted given in an official way

effective successful and achieves desired results

violations acts that show disrespect or break the rules

minimum the very least

dependent relying on others

✓ Introduce Vocabulary

Teach

Display the **Vocabulary in Context Cards**, using the routine below. Direct students to **Student Book pp. 476–477**. See also **Instructional Routine 9**.

1 **Read and pronounce the word.** Read the word once alone, then together with students.

2 **Explain the word.** Read the explanation under *What Does It Mean?*

3 **Discuss vocabulary in context.** Together, read aloud the sentence on the front of the card. Help students explain and use the word in new sentences.

4 **Engage with the word.** Ask and discuss the *Think About It* question with students.

Apply

Give partners or small groups one or two **Vocabulary in Context Cards**.

• Help students start the *Talk It Over* activity on the back of their card.

• Have students complete activities for all the cards during the week.

Lesson 19

✓ **TARGET VOCABULARY**

urge

minimum

effective

deteriorating

dependent

violations

granted

issue

ordinance

exception

Vocabulary Reader

Context Cards

476

Vocabulary in Context

1 urge
Teachers can urge, or coax, students to get involved in helping their community.

2 minimum
The food collected by students exceeded the minimum, or least, amount needed.

3 effective
Picking up litter can be effective in keeping parks and beaches clean. It gets results.

4 deteriorating
Many deteriorating buildings will only get worse if volunteers don't help repair them.

ELL ENGLISH LANGUAGE LEARNERS

Scaffold

Beginning Use simplified language to help students understand the Vocabulary words. Ask yes/no questions to confirm students' understanding.

Advanced Ask students questions to confirm their understanding. For example, *Is smiling and being helpful an effective way to make new friends?*

Intermediate Have students complete sentence frames for each Vocabulary word. For example, *UNESCO tries to save works of art that are _____ or falling apart.* (deteriorating)

Advanced High Have partners ask and answer questions about each Vocabulary word. For example, *Why are pets dependent on their owners?*

See ELL Lesson 19, pp. E32–E41, for scaffolded support.

- **Study each Context Card.**
- **Use a thesaurus to find an alternate word for each Vocabulary word.**

5 dependent

A literacy group may be dependent on volunteers. It needs them as reading tutors.

6 violations

If they pollute too much, companies can be fined for violations of clean air laws.

7 granted

The principal granted, or gave, these students and teacher permission to hold a car wash.

8 issue

Providing better care for senior citizens is an issue, or concern. You can help in many ways.

9 ordinance

An ordinance, or city law, can create volunteer community service groups.

10 exception

With the exception of rainy days, this class works in the school garden every day.

477

Monitor Vocabulary

Are students able to understand and use Target Vocabulary words?

IF...	THEN...
students have difficulty understanding and using most of the Target Vocabulary words,	▶ use **Vocabulary in Context Cards** and differentiate the **Vocabulary Reader,** *From Parking Lot to Garden,* for Struggling Readers, p. T280. *See also Intervention Lesson 19, pp. S32–S41.*
students can understand and use most of the Target Vocabulary words,	▶ use **Vocabulary in Context Cards** and differentiate the **Vocabulary Reader,** *From Parking Lot to Garden,* for On-Level Readers, p. T280.
students can understand and use all of the Target Vocabulary words,	▶ differentiate the **Vocabulary Reader,** *From Parking Lot to Garden,* for Advanced Readers, p. T281.

SMALL GROUP Options

Vocabulary Reader, pp. T280–T281. *Group English Language Learners according to language proficiency.*

VOCABULARY IN CONTEXT CARDS 181–190

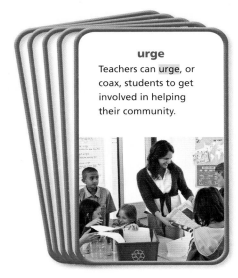

urge

Teachers can urge, or coax, students to get involved in helping their community.

front

urge

What Does It Mean?
To **urge** is to recommend or argue for strongly.

Think About It.
What kinds of things do your parents or relatives **urge** you to do?

Talk It Over.
Working with a partner, think of five things you could do or say to **urge** other students to help clean up a public park.

181

back

Develop Background

 ENGLISH LANGUAGE LEARNERS

Scaffold

Beginning Work with students to name some common community buildings. Use photographs or other images to point out libraries, town halls, sports arenas, and schools as you name each building aloud with students.

Intermediate Guide students to use the Target Vocabulary words in simple sentences. For example, *I urge you to vote.*

Advanced Have students work in small groups to discuss something they would like to add to their community, such as a new park or library. Have them use the Target Vocabulary in their discussion.

Advanced High Ask students to imagine that they are mayor of their city or town. Have them write a plan describing what they will do for the community in the coming year. Have them use the Target Vocabulary in their writing.

See ELL Lesson 19, pp. E32–E41, for scaffolded support.

 Target Vocabulary

1 Teach/Model

- Use the photos on **Student Book p. 478** to discuss what occurs at town meetings. Tell students that "Darnell Rock Reporting" is about a boy who presents an **effective** idea at a town council meeting.

- Use **Vocabulary in Context Cards** to review the student-friendly explanations of the Target Vocabulary words.

- Have students silently read **Student Book p. 478.** Then read the passage aloud.

2 Guided Practice

Ask students the first item below and discuss their responses. Continue in this way until students have answered a question about each Target Vocabulary word.

1. Why do people **urge** students to stay in school?
2. How do you feel about the **minimum** ages to drive a car and vote?
3. How are you personally **dependent** on your local government?
4. If you were **granted** one wish, what would it be?
5. Identify an important **issue** at your school.
6. Why is it necessary to have an **ordinance** about noise at night?
7. What do you believe are fair consequences for littering **violations**?
8. How might a **deteriorating** sidewalk make it difficult for some people to walk safely?
9. Describe an **effective** homework assignment that helped you learn about a topic
10. Name an **exception** to a spelling or grammar rule.

Background

✓ **TARGET VOCABULARY** **Town Meetings** Have you ever been to a town or city council meeting? If not, many would <mark>urge</mark> you to go to one. At a <mark>minimum</mark>, you'll learn a lot about your local government.

The representatives to a town meeting are elected, so they're <mark>dependent</mark> on voters to choose them. These officials have been <mark>granted</mark> many powers. One <mark>issue</mark> they can decide is how much to tax people so the town has money. Another task is to vote on each local <mark>ordinance</mark>, or rule. When <mark>violations</mark> of town rules occur, town meeting members decide how to punish the rule breakers. Finally, they vote on how to spend the town's money. For example, they may decide to repair a <mark>deteriorating</mark> town building or to give a town department more money to make it more <mark>effective</mark>. Without <mark>exception</mark>, the decisions made at town meetings affect our lives.

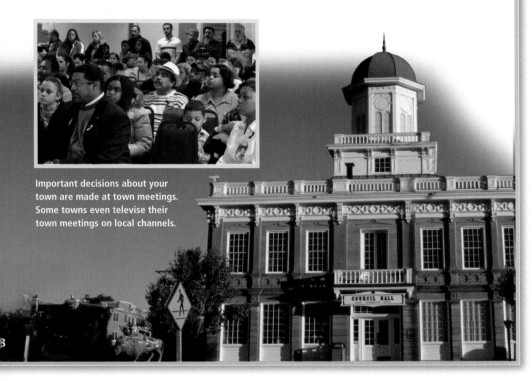

Important decisions about your town are made at town meetings. Some towns even televise their town meetings on local channels.

3 | Apply

- Have partners take turns reading a paragraph on **Student Book p. 478** to one another.
- Tell partners to stop when they come to a highlighted vocabulary word and have their partner explain it. Have partners take turns explaining each word.

This **ordinance** protects against pollution.

Introduce Comprehension

- Analyze and evaluate the author's attempts to persuade.
- Summarize the author's arguments.

SKILL TRACE

Persuasion	
Introduce	T236–T237
Differentiate	T282–T283
Reteach	T290
Review	T256–T257
Test	Weekly Tests, Lesson 19

ELL ENGLISH LANGUAGE LEARNERS

Scaffold

Beginning Role-play both characters in this conversation: *Boy: Let's go play basketball. Girl: I want to ride bikes. Boy: It will be fun. I'll let you have the ball first.* Explain why this is an example of persuasion. Then have students talk about experiences they have had with persuasion.

Intermediate Help students state a persuasive goal. Provide this sentence frame: *I think you should_____.* Point out the signal word *should.* Guide students to complete the sentence with something they want someone else to think or do.

Advanced Draw an Idea-Support Map on the board and discuss with students how a persuasive goal relates to the reasons that support it.

Advanced High Have partners use the information from Projectable 19.2 to write persuasive sentences.

See ELL Lesson 19, pp. E32–E41, for scaffolded support.

✔ Persuasion; Summarize

1 Teach/Model

 Academic Language

author's goal what an author wants readers to think or do

persuade to convince someone to think or act a certain way

summarize to briefly tell the important parts of a text in your own words

---

- Remind students that the author of a persuasive text might state a goal and give reasons why the goal is important.
- Read and discuss **Student Book p. 479** with students. Have them use the Academic Language.
- Display **Projectable 19.2**. Have students read "A Case for Chewing Gum."

PERSUASION Explain that the author of a persuasive text might give facts and examples to support each reason.

- Explain that you will use an Idea-Support Map to record the goal and supporting reasons of a persuasive text.

Think Aloud *The author agrees with Mr. Palmer. The author gives reasons why it's good to chew gum during tests. The author wants to persuade readers that students should be allowed to chew gum during tests.*

SUMMARIZE Explain that summarizing an argument helps readers understand how the author's reasons support the goal.

Think Aloud *I will write down the supporting reasons the author gives. Then I can use these reasons to summarize the argument.*

Projectable 19.2

Darnell Rock Reporting | Introduce Comprehension | Persuasion; Summarize

Persuasion; Summarize

A Case for Chewing Gum

Oakdale Middle School is holding a debate later this week. The topic of the debate is: Should students be allowed to chew gum during tests?

Usually chewing gum is against school rules, but Mr. Palmer, the new sixth grade teacher, has asked Principal Leroy for an exception. I agree with Mr. P. At his old school, students who chewed gum during exams seemed to do better on tests. Mr. P claims that chewing gum keeps students alert during long exams. He also cites several newspaper articles that report how chewing gum is a relaxing activity that calms nervous test-takers.

Persuasion Use an Idea-Support Map to show how the author tries to persuade the reader with statements in the passage.

Goal: Allow students to chew gum during tests.

Reason: Students who chewed gum during tests at Mr. P's old school got better results.

Reason: Chewing gum keeps students alert during exams.

Reason: Chewing gum calms nervous test-takers.

Summarize Use the Idea-Support Map to summarize, or briefly restate, the argument.

Comprehension

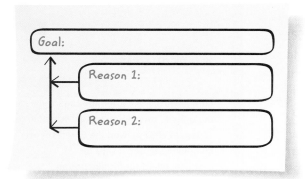

✔ TARGET SKILL Persuasion

In "Darnell Rock Reporting," Darnell uses persuasion in an article to gain support for a garden for the homeless. Look for words and facts that Darnell uses to influence people's opinions. Make a graphic organizer like this one to show a persuasive argument.

Goal:

→ Reason 1:

→ Reason 2:

✔ TARGET STRATEGY Summarize

Summarizing and paraphrasing as you read can help you understand Darnell's reasons for writing his article. Use your graphic organizer to summarize and paraphrase his article. Remember, paraphrasing is a detailed retelling or explanation. Putting the article into your own words will help you analyze his argument.

JOURNEYS DIGITAL
Powered by DESTINATIONReading®
Comprehension Activities: Lesson 19

479

Monitor Comprehension

Are students able to analyze persuasive arguments?

IF...	THEN...
students are having trouble analyzing persuasive arguments,	▶ **Differentiate Comprehension** for Struggling Readers, p. T282. *See also Intervention Lesson 19, pp. S32–S41.*
students can analyze persuasive arguments,	▶ **Differentiate Comprehension** for On-Level Readers, p. T282.
students can analyze and summarize persuasive arguments,	▶ **Differentiate Comprehension** for Advanced Readers, p. T283.

 Differentiate Comprehension: pp. T282–T283.
Group English Language Learners according to language proficiency. See also ELL Lesson 19, pp. E32–E41, for scaffolded support.

2 Guided Practice

Guide students to copy and complete their own Idea-Support Maps for "A Case for Chewing Gum." Then guide students to summarize the argument by using **Projectable S6**.

3 Apply

Turn and Talk Have students share their completed Idea-Support Maps and summaries of the author's argument.

Then ask students to summarize the author's argument in another text they have read recently.

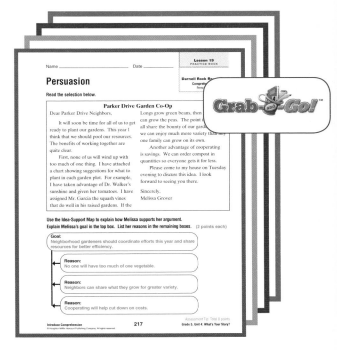

Practice Book p. 217
See Grab-and-Go™ Resources for additional leveled practice.

Introduce the Main Selection

TARGET SKILL

PERSUASION Explain that as they read, students will use **Graphic Organizer 7: Idea-Support Map** to identify

- Darnell's goal.
- reasons that support making an old basketball court a community garden.

TARGET STRATEGY

SUMMARIZE Students will use **Graphic Organizer 7** to summarize reasons that support the idea.

GENRE: Realistic Fiction

- Read the genre information on **Student Book p. 480** with students.
- Share and discuss the **Genre Blackline Master: Fiction**.
- Preview the selection and model identifying characteristics of the genre.

Think Aloud *This story tells how Darnell Rock speaks up about turning a basketball court near the school into a garden. This is a situation that could happen in real life, but I don't think Darnell Rock is a real person.*

- As you preview, ask students to identify other features of realistic fiction.

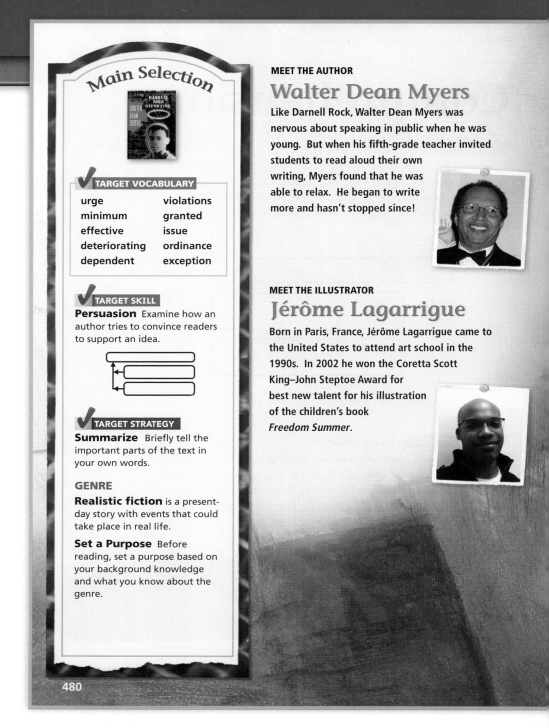

Main Selection

TARGET VOCABULARY

urge	violations
minimum	granted
effective	issue
deteriorating	ordinance
dependent	exception

TARGET SKILL

Persuasion Examine how an author tries to convince readers to support an idea.

TARGET STRATEGY

Summarize Briefly tell the important parts of the text in your own words.

GENRE

Realistic fiction is a present-day story with events that could take place in real life.

Set a Purpose Before reading, set a purpose based on your background knowledge and what you know about the genre.

480

MEET THE AUTHOR

Walter Dean Myers

Like Darnell Rock, Walter Dean Myers was nervous about speaking in public when he was young. But when his fifth-grade teacher invited students to read aloud their own writing, Myers found that he was able to relax. He began to write more and hasn't stopped since!

MEET THE ILLUSTRATOR

Jérôme Lagarrigue

Born in Paris, France, Jérôme Lagarrigue came to the United States to attend art school in the 1990s. In 2002 he won the Coretta Scott King–John Steptoe Award for best new talent for his illustration of the children's book *Freedom Summer*.

Reading the Selection

	Pre-Reading	Reading
Supported	**SELECTION SUMMARY** Use **Blackline Master 19.2** to give students an overview before they read. **AUDIOTEXT CD** Have students listen to the selection as they follow along in their books.	**AUTHOR'S PURPOSE** After reading, have students write about the author's message about the power of persuasion.
Independent	**PREVIEW** Have students use the title and illustrations to discuss predictions and clues. Some students may read the story independently.	**TEXT EVIDENCE** Pause periodically while reading the selection. Have students write questions that can be answered using text evidence. After reading, discuss students' questions and answers.

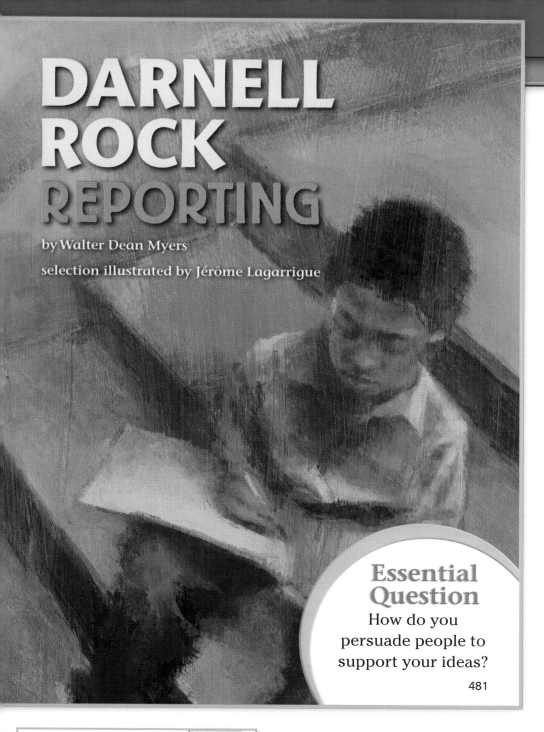

DARNELL ROCK REPORTING

by Walter Dean Myers

selection illustrated by Jérôme Lagarrigue

Essential Question

How do you persuade people to support your ideas?

481

? Essential Question

- Read aloud the **Essential Question** on **Student Book p. 481.** *How do you persuade people to support your ideas?*

- Tell students to think about this question as they read "Darnell Rock Reporting."

Set Purpose

- Explain that good readers set a purpose for reading based on their preview of the selection, what they know about the genre, as well as what they want to learn by reading.

- Model setting a reading purpose.

Think Aloud
Sometimes it can be hard to speak up in front of other people. I wonder if the main character has to overcome nervousness in order to persuade people that a garden is the best use for the old basketball court. One purpose might be to learn from how he handles the situation.

- Have students share their personal reading purposes and record them in their journals.

JOURNEYS DIGITAL **Powered by**
DESTINATIONReading®
Student eBook: Read and Listen

Name _____ Date _____

Lesson 19
BLACKLINE MASTER 19.2

Darnell Rock Reporting

Darnell Rock Reporting
Selection Summary

Pages 482–483
Darnell writes an article for the school newspaper that suggests turning old basketball courts into a garden to feed the homeless. Another student named Linda Gold also writes an article that says the basketball courts should become a teacher's parking lot. Both articles appear in the town newspaper as well. The issue is to be talked about at a City Council meeting.

Pages 484–485
Darnell and his sister Tamika arrive at the City Council meeting. The city clerk says that the basketball courts will be the last item the Council will talk about that night. Then the Council discusses a building that was built too close to the street.

Pages 486–487
Many people boo when the Council decides there is no money to give to the library. Darnell is nervous because it's almost his turn to speak about the garden. Linda speaks first.

Pages 488–489
Darnell explains how a garden would help both the homeless people and kids in the school. Kids would see that they can also make their lives better. Darnell tells the Council how his life changed for the better after his article was printed in the *Journal*.

Pages 490–491
One councilman doesn't think that a garden for the homeless near the school is a good idea. Then Sweeby Jones speaks. He tells the Council to listen to Darnell. But the Council votes against the garden.

Page 492
Darnell is disappointed, but after the meeting he learns that someone who heard him speak wants to donate some other land for a garden.

Selection Summary
© Houghton Mifflin Harcourt Publishing Company. All rights reserved.

4

Grade 5, Unit 4: What's Your Story?

Blackline Master 19.2

Develop Comprehension

Pause at the stopping points to ask students the following questions.

1 ✔ **TARGET VOCABULARY**
Why might **deteriorating** *basketball courts near the school pose a problem for Oakdale? Sample answers: They are unsafe; it costs money to fix them.*

2 Author's Purpose
Why does the author begin Darnell's article with words spoken by a man who is homeless? Sample answer: Reading Sweeby Jones's words adds a personal side to the persuasion.

3 Supporting Details
According to Linda, how does a parking lot benefit students? Sample answer: It supports teachers, who are important to students.

1 Darnell Rock feels that his teachers only notice him, his friends, and his sister Tamika, when they get into trouble. Then a homeless man, Sweeby Jones, inspires Darnell to write an article in his school newspaper about turning a deteriorating basketball court into a garden to feed the homeless. Soon editor Peter Miller publishes Darnell's article in the town newspaper. Not everyone agrees with him, though, including student Linda Gold and teacher Miss Joyner. A city council meeting will decide what to do with the basketball court. Darnell is nervous about presenting his opinion, but his parents, and teachers like Mr. Baker and Miss Seldes, all support him. Before the meeting, everyone at school has read Darnell's article (pictured below) and an opposing article written by Linda that ran in the school newspaper (shown on page 483).

2 "Nobody wants to be homeless," Sweeby Jones said. He is a homeless man who lives in our city of Oakdale. It is for him and people like him that I think we should build a garden where the basketball courts were, near the school. That way the homeless people can help themselves by raising food.

"You see a man or woman that's hungry and you don't feed them, or help them feed themselves, then you got to say you don't mind people being hungry," Mr. Jones said. "And if you don't mind people being hungry, then there is something wrong with you."

This is what Mr. Sweeby Jones said when I spoke to him. I don't want to be the kind of person who says it's all right for some people to be hungry. I want to do something about it. But I think there is another reason to have the garden.

Things can happen to people that they don't plan. You can get sick, and not know why, or even homeless. But sometimes there are things you can do to change your life or make it good. If you don't do anything to make your life good, it will probably not be good.

"I was born poor and will probably be poor all my life," Mr. Sweeby Jones said.

I think maybe it is not how you were born that makes the most difference, but what you do with your life. The garden is a chance for some people to help their own lives.

Darnell Rock is a seventh-grader at South Oakdale Middle School. The school board has proposed that the site that Mr. Rock wants to make into a garden be used as a parking lot for teachers. The City Council will decide the issue tomorrow evening.

482

ELL ENGLISH LANGUAGE LEARNERS

Scaffold

Beginning Point out that when things grow old, they deteriorate. Have students locate *deteriorating* on the page and ask them to name objects that deteriorate.

Advanced After reading page 482, have students restate what it is Darnell wants to do with the deteriorating basketball court.

Intermediate Have students describe what they think the deteriorating basketball court looks like. Provide descriptive words, such as *old, broken, falling down, empty.*

Advanced High After reading p. 482, have students write one or two sentences, summarizing what they have learned about Darnell's plan.

See ELL Lesson 19, pp. E32–E41, for scaffolded support.

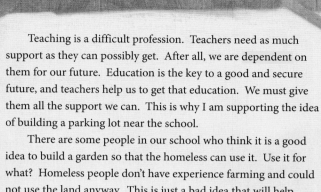

Teaching is a difficult profession. Teachers need as much support as they can possibly get. After all, we are dependent on them for our future. Education is the key to a good and secure future, and teachers help us to get that education. We must give them all the support we can. This is why I am supporting the idea of building a parking lot near the school.

There are some people in our school who think it is a good idea to build a garden so that the homeless can use it. Use it for what? Homeless people don't have experience farming and could not use the land anyway. This is just a bad idea that will help nobody and will hurt the teachers. The teachers give us good examples of how we should live and how we should conduct ourselves. The homeless people, even though it is no fault of theirs, don't give us good examples.

On Friday evening at 7:00 p.m., the City Council will meet to make a final decision. I urge them to support the teachers, support education, and support the students at South Oakdale.

3

483

✓ TARGET STRATEGY

Summarize

- Remind students that summarizing sections of text as they read can help them better understand what they are reading. Review summarizing with students.

- Display **Projectable 19.3a**. Tell students that using an Idea-Support Map is a good way to summarize an argument.

- Model how to fill out the title and first box of the Idea-Support Map for **Student Book pp. 482–483,** using the Summarize strategy.

> **Think Aloud** *I wonder what Darnell Rock thinks the city should do with the basketball court. By summarizing, I will make sure I understand his plan. His article on page 482 tells me that he thinks it should be a garden. He believes that a garden would help the homeless people in his neighborhood.*

- Have students use **Graphic Organizer 7** to begin their own Idea-Support Maps as they read, using the Summarizing strategy to clarify their understanding.

Projectable 19.3a

Darnell Rock Reporting Comprehension Persuasion

Idea-Support Map: Persuasion

Title or Topic Darnell Rock Reporting

Goal: Make the basketball courts into a community garden.

Develop Comprehension

4 **TARGET VOCABULARY**

Why is it important to have rules about the **minimum** *distance from the street for large buildings?*
Sample answer: Without the rule, the distance could be unsafe for pedestrians.

5 Persuasion

How does the author portray the builder? Sample answer: The author says the builder "sounded like a kid" in trouble. He wants to make the builder appear childish.

6 Cause and Effect

Why does the builder say, "This is going to ruin me"? Sample answers: It will be very expensive to change the building; the project and his business might go bankrupt.

"You see anybody from the school?" Larry looked over the large crowd at the Oakdale Court building.

"There goes Mr. Derby *and* Mr. Baker." Tamika pointed toward the front of the building.

Darnell felt a lump in the pit of his stomach. There were at least a hundred people at the City Council meeting.

Tamika led them through the crowd to where she had spotted Mr. Derby and South Oakdale's principal. The large, high-ceilinged room had rows of benches that faced the low platform for the City Council. Linda Gold was already sitting in the front row. Darnell saw that her parents were with her.

He had brought a copy of the *Journal* with him and saw that a few other people, grown-ups, also had copies of the paper.

The nine members of the City Council arrived, and the meeting was called to order. The city clerk said that there were five items on the agenda, and read them off. The first three items were about Building Code violations. Then came something about funding the city's library.

"The last item will be the use of the basketball courts as a parking lot at South Oakdale Middle School," the clerk said. "We have three speakers scheduled."

Linda turned and smiled at Darnell.

484

ELL ENGLISH LANGUAGE LEARNERS

Scaffold

Beginning For each question, accept one-word responses and expand student responses into sentences, having students repeat.	**Advanced** Have students respond to the questions in complete sentences. Provide corrective feedback as needed.
Intermediate Provide part of a response for each question and have students complete it. Then have students repeat the complete response and confirm their understanding.	**Advanced High** Have students tell how they know the answer to each question based on details from the story.

See ELL Lesson 19, pp. E32–E41, for scaffolded support.

Darnell didn't know what Building Code violations were but watched as building owners showed diagrams explaining why there were violations. The first two weren't that interesting, but the third one was. A company had built a five-story building that was supposed to be a minimum of twenty feet from the curb, but it was only fifteen feet.

4

"You mean to tell me that your engineers only had fifteen-foot rulers?" one councilman asked.

"Well, er, we measured it right the first time"—the builder shifted from one foot to the other—"but then we made some changes in the design and somehow we sort of forgot about the er . . . you know . . . the other five feet."

To Darnell the builder sounded like a kid in his homeroom trying to make an excuse for not having his homework.

5

"Can you just slide the building back five or six feet?" the Councilman asked.

Everybody laughed and the builder actually smiled, but Darnell could tell he didn't think it was funny.

Somebody touched Darnell on his shoulder, and he turned and saw his parents.

"We have this ordinance for a reason," a woman on the Council was saying. "I don't think we should lightly dismiss this violation. An exception granted here is just going to encourage others to break the law."

"This is going to ruin me," the builder said. "I've been in Oakdale all of my life and I think I've made a contribution."

6

"Let's have a vote." The head of the Council spoke sharply.

> **STOP AND THINK**
> **Author's Craft** Authors try to make **dialogue,** or conversation, reflect the way people speak. What does the author do in the third paragraph on this page that makes the builder's speech seem realistic?

485

STOP AND THINK
Author's Craft: Dialogue

- Explain to students that dialogue is conversation between characters in a story. Authors use dialogue to move the plot of a story along and to tell readers about the characters.

- Point out to students that dialogue is written to sound like spoken words. It may include incomplete sentences, interjections, and slang.

- Have students answer the **Stop and Think** question on **Student Book p. 485**.

- Have them continue adding to their Idea-Support Maps with information from **Student Book pp. 484–485**.

CROSS-CURRICULAR CONNECTION

Social Studies

Ask students to think about people who have made a difference by speaking up. Point out that Darnell Rock is a fictional character, but that many real people speak up about important issues. Suggest that students read about someone who speaks up about important issues. Guide the discussion with the following questions.

Who has spoken up about an important issue? Sample answer: Dr. Martin Luther King What did this person do? He spoke out for equal rights.

What are some ways that we can speak up about an important issue? Sample answer: write a letter to a newspaper

Develop Comprehension

7 **Understanding Characters**
What do the words, "if he didn't have to speak, he would have enjoyed the meeting," tell us about Darnell? Sample answers: He is nervous; he does not like to speak in public.

8 **Understanding Characters**
Why does the author tell us that Linda read her speech in "the snootiest voice that Darnell had ever heard"? Sample answers: He wants readers to know more about Linda's personality and to know that she does not seem nervous.

9 **Supporting Details**
What other evidence provides a clue as to how Darnell feels? Sample answer: His hands are shaking.

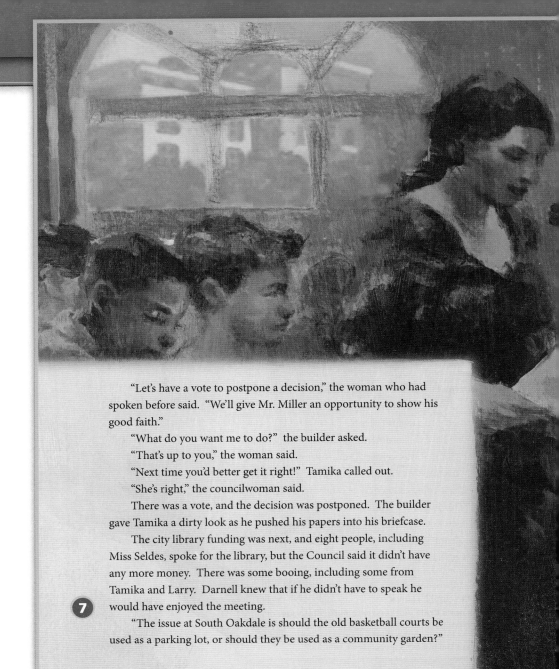

"Let's have a vote to postpone a decision," the woman who had spoken before said. "We'll give Mr. Miller an opportunity to show his good faith."

"What do you want me to do?" the builder asked.

"That's up to you," the woman said.

"Next time you'd better get it right!" Tamika called out.

"She's right," the councilwoman said.

There was a vote, and the decision was postponed. The builder gave Tamika a dirty look as he pushed his papers into his briefcase.

The city library funding was next, and eight people, including Miss Seldes, spoke for the library, but the Council said it didn't have any more money. There was some booing, including some from Tamika and Larry. Darnell knew that if he didn't have to speak he **7** would have enjoyed the meeting.

"The issue at South Oakdale is should the old basketball courts be used as a parking lot, or should they be used as a community garden?"

486

"Who's going to pay for paving the lot?" a councilman asked. "Does it have to be paved?"

"It's my understanding that it doesn't have to be paved," the head of the Council answered. "Am I right on that?"

"Yes, you are," Miss Joyner spoke up from the audience.

"We have two young people from the school to speak," the councilwoman said. "The first is a Miss Gold."

Linda went into the middle aisle, where there was a microphone. She began reading her article in the snootiest voice that Darnell had ever heard. He felt a knot in his stomach. He turned to look at his mother, and she was smiling. On the stage some of the councilmen were looking at some papers. **8**

"I hope I don't mess up," he whispered to Tamika.

"You won't," Tamika said.

Linda finished reading her article and then turned toward Darnell.

"Although everybody would like to help the homeless," she said, "schools are supposed to be for kids, and for those who teach kids! Thank you."

There was applause for Linda, and Miss Joyner stood up and nodded toward her. Darnell felt his hands shaking. **9**

487

Practice Fluency

Stress Read aloud the last sentence of Linda's speech on **Student Book p. 487** as students follow along.

Ask students to explain what words at the end of Linda's speech might be stressed to make her point.

- Explain that when people try to persuade someone, putting stress on certain words gives clues to their feelings.

- Tell students that when someone has strong feelings, they stress certain words by slowing their speech and changing their pitch and volume.

- Have students echo-read each sentence after you, taking care to slow down and stress key words.

See **p. T258** for a complete fluency lesson on reading with appropriate stress.

Develop Comprehension

10 **Make Comparisons**
What is the connection the author draws between schoolchildren and the world of adults outside school?
Sample answer: At times, everyone can have problems.

11 **Analyze Characters**
What changed for Darnell after his article appeared in the Journal?
Sample answers: People started treating him differently; people who wouldn't have listened to him before are listening to him now.

12 **Draw Conclusions**
According to Darnell's speech, what problems do some homeless people and some kids have in common?
Sample answers: People get mad at them; they might stop trying because people expect them to fail.

Darnell's name was called, and he made the long trip to the microphone.

"When I first thought about having a garden instead of a parking lot, I thought it was just a good idea," Darnell said. "Then, when the *Journal* asked me to send them a copy of my interview with Mr. Jones, I was thinking that it was mainly a good idea to have a garden to help out the homeless people. But now I think it might be a good idea to have the garden to help out the kids—some of the kids—in the school.

"Sometimes, when people go through their life they don't do the things that can make them a good life. I don't know why they don't do the right thing, or maybe even if they know what the right thing is sometimes.

"But I see the same thing in my school, South Oakdale. Some of the kids always do okay, but some of us don't. Maybe their parents are telling them something, or maybe they know something special. But if you're a kid who isn't doing so good, people start off telling you what you should be doing, and you know it, but sometimes you still don't get it done and mess up some more. Then people start expecting you to mess up, and then *you* start expecting to mess up. Teachers get mad at you, or the principal, or your parents, and they act like you're messing up on purpose. Like you want to get bad marks and stuff like that. Then you don't want people getting on your case all the time so you don't do much because the less you do the less they're going to be on your case. Only that doesn't help anything, and everybody knows it, but that's the way it goes."

10

"You seem to be doing all right, young man," the head of the City Council said.

"I wasn't doing too hot before," Darnell said, taking a quick look over to where Mr. Baker sat. "But when I got on the paper and the *Journal* printed my article, then everybody started treating me different. People came up to me and started explaining their points of view instead of just telling me what to do. And you people are listening to me. The kids I hung out with, they called us the Corner Crew, are mostly good kids, but you wouldn't listen to them unless they got into trouble.

11

488

ELL ENGLISH LANGUAGE LEARNERS

Scaffold

Beginning Ask students simple yes/no questions to help them understand the main ideas in Darnell's speech.

Advanced After students read pp. 488–489, ask them clarifying questions to demonstrate understanding.

Intermediate While reading pages 488–489, pause after each paragraph and have students say a sentence that summarizes Darnell's point.

Advanced High After reading pp. 488–489, have students summarize Darnell's argument in a few sentences.

See ELL Lesson 19, pp. E32–E41, for scaffolded support.

"In South Oakdale some kids have bad things happen to them—like they get sick—and I don't know why that happens, but all they can do is to go to the hospital. And some kids just get left out of the good things and can't find a way of getting back into them. People get mad at them the same way they get mad at the homeless people or people who beg on the street. Maybe the garden will be a way for the homeless people to get back into some good things, and maybe seeing the homeless people getting back into a better life will be a way for some of the kids to think about what's happening to them. Thank you."

12

STOP AND THINK
Persuasion What is Darnell's argument in favor of the community garden?

489

STOP AND THINK

 **TARGET SKILL** Persuasion

- Explain to students that writers and speakers use persuasion when they want to convince someone to think or act a certain way. To identify persuasive text, look for words and facts that might influence people's opinions.

- Have students answer the **Stop and Think** question on **Student Book p. 489**.

- If students have difficulty identifying persuasive information, see Comprehension Intervention below for extra support.

- Have students continue their graphic organizers. Display **Projectable 19.3b** and work with students to add to the Idea-Support Map.

COMPREHENSION INTERVENTION

 **TARGET SKILL** Persuasion

SKILL SUPPORT Remind students that Darnell wants to persuade the City Council to vote for the garden. Discuss the main reason for the garden given so far:

- *Darnell thinks the garden would help homeless people.*

Remind students that Darnell's ideas developed over time. Read the last paragraph on p. 489. Ask: *Why does Darnell think a garden for homeless people might be good for kids who are having problems? Kids would see that they could make their lives better, too.*

Guide students to continue working on their Idea-Support Maps.

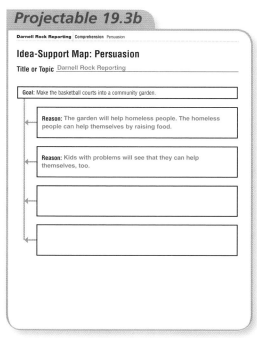

Projectable 19.3b

Darnell Rock Reporting Comprehension Persuasion

Idea-Support Map: Persuasion

Title or Topic Darnell Rock Reporting

Goal: Make the basketball courts into a community garden.

Reason: The garden will help homeless people. The homeless people can help themselves by raising food.

Reason: Kids with problems will see that they can help themselves, too.

Main Selection (SB p. 489) • **T247**

Develop Comprehension

✔ TARGET VOCABULARY

13 *What would an **effective** plan do for the homeless? Sample answer: It would give them shelter and food.*

14 **Understanding Characters**
How do we know that some people at the meeting, and the councilman, view Sweeby Jones differently than Darnell does? Sample answer: Darnell listens to Sweeby Jones and respects his opinion; other people whisper about Jones and do not want to hear his opinion.

15 **Cause and Effect**
Explain why the Council voted against the garden. Sample answers: The right decision was not clear; both sides had good arguments.

There was some applause as Darnell turned to go back to his seat.

"Just a minute, young man," one of the councilmen called to him. "The girl said that these people don't know anything about raising a garden. Is that true?"

"It doesn't matter," someone said from the audience. "I'm from the college, and we can help with technical advice."

"I didn't ask you," the councilman said.

"I'm telling you anyway," the man said.

13 "I don't know how effective a community garden would be," the councilman said. "You can't feed people from a garden."

"You could sell what you grow," Darnell heard himself saying.

"I think bringing people who are . . . nonschool people into that close a contact with children might not be that good an idea," the councilman said. "Who's the last speaker?"

"A Mr. Jones," the clerk said. Sweeby came into the middle aisle, and a lot of people began to talk among themselves. There were a lot of things they were interested in, and most of them were **14** not interested in the school parking lot.

490

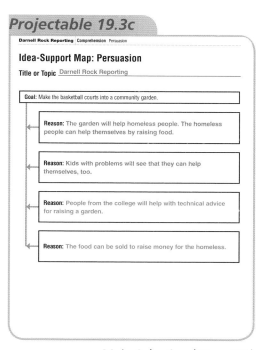

"I just wanted to ask you why you don't want to listen to this boy," Sweeby asked.

"You have four minutes to speak," the councilman said. He seemed angry. "We don't have to answer your questions."

"You don't have to answer my questions," Sweeby said. "And you don't have to have the garden. You don't have to think about us—what did you call us?—nonschool people?

"But it's a shame you don't want to listen to this boy. I wish he had been my friend when I was his age. Maybe I would be sitting in one of your seats instead of being over here."

"Is there anything more?" the councilman asked.

"No, you can just forget about the whole thing now," Sweeby said. "Go on back to your papers."

"I think we can vote on this issue now," the councilman said. "I think Mr."—the councilman looked at the agenda to find Darnell's name—"Mr. Darnell Rock had some good points, but it's still a tough issue. Let's get on with the vote."

The vote went quickly. Three councilpeople decided not to vote, five voted against the garden, and only one voted for it. **15**

Darnell took a deep breath and let it out slowly. Tamika patted him on his hand. When he looked at her she had tears in her eyes.

Darnell felt he had let Sweeby down. His father patted him on his back, and Miss Seldes came over.

"You did a good job," she said. "Really good."

"I lost," Darnell said.

"Sometimes you lose," Miss Seldes said. "But you still did a good job."

> **STOP AND THINK**
> **Summarize** Summarize the main events that happen on pages 490–491. Remember to include only the most important details.

491

STOP AND THINK

 **TARGET STRATEGY**

Summarize

- Remind students that summarizing will help them better understand what they read. At various points in a text, they should stop to summarize what they have read to confirm their understanding.

- Have students answer the **Stop and Think** question on **Student Book p. 491**.

- Have students complete their graphic organizers. Display **Projectable 19.3c** and discuss the persuasive arguments.

Turn and Talk

? Essential Question

Discuss how Darnell persuaded people to support his ideas.

COMPREHENSION INTERVENTION

 **TARGET STRATEGY** Summarize

STRATEGY SUPPORT Remind students that summarizing can help them understand a speaker's message. Remind them that summarizing is a brief recap including only the story's main ideas and most important details and events.

Read aloud **Student Book pp. 490–491.** Guide students in summarizing the events.

The councilman questions Darnell's argument, and Sweeby Jones speaks in favor of Darnell. But in the end, the council votes down the garden.

Discuss with students why certain events or ideas belong in a summary and others do not.

Projectable 19.3c

Darnell Rock Reporting Comprehension Persuasion

Idea-Support Map: Persuasion

Title or Topic Darnell Rock Reporting

Goal: Make the basketball courts into a community garden.

Reason: The garden will help homeless people. The homeless people can help themselves by raising food.

Reason: Kids with problems will see that they can help themselves, too.

Reason: People from the college will help with technical advice for raising a garden.

Reason: The food can be sold to raise money for the homeless.

Develop Comprehension

16 **Make Judgments**
Explain whether you think the Council's decision was fair. Sample answers: They had to consider many opinions; they did the best they could with the information presented; supporting teachers is important, too.

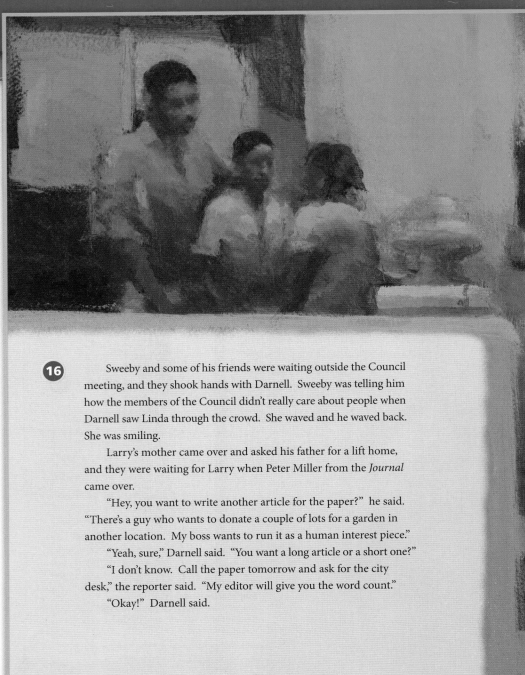

16 Sweeby and some of his friends were waiting outside the Council meeting, and they shook hands with Darnell. Sweeby was telling him how the members of the Council didn't really care about people when Darnell saw Linda through the crowd. She waved and he waved back. She was smiling.

Larry's mother came over and asked his father for a lift home, and they were waiting for Larry when Peter Miller from the *Journal* came over.

"Hey, you want to write another article for the paper?" he said. "There's a guy who wants to donate a couple of lots for a garden in another location. My boss wants to run it as a human interest piece."

"Yeah, sure," Darnell said. "You want a long article or a short one?"

"I don't know. Call the paper tomorrow and ask for the city desk," the reporter said. "My editor will give you the word count."

"Okay!" Darnell said.

492

Speak Your Mind

Short Response Darnell Rock spoke his mind even though others disagreed with him. Write a paragraph describing a time when you spoke up even though you knew others might disagree with you. Explain what you learned from the experience. PERSONAL RESPONSE

Use and Reuse

Make a Proposal Imagine that your school has an unused space like the one at South Oakdale Middle School. With a partner, think of three ways the space might be used. Choose your favorite one, and write a speech you might present to the community in order to convince them to support your idea. Then rehearse your speech, and deliver it to the class. PARTNERS

Powers of Persuasion

Turn and Talk Think about the speeches that Linda and Darnell give at the City Council meeting. With a partner, discuss how the two students use persuasion to gain support for their ideas. Then evaluate which student is more convincing and why. PERSUASION

493

Your Turn

Have students complete the activities on **Student Book page 493**.

Speak Your Mind Have students think about the questions Who? What? Where? When? How? and Why? to plan their writing. Ask: *Who disagreed with you? What did each side believe? Where, when, and how did you speak out? Why did you speak out?*
(PERSONAL RESPONSE)

Use and Reuse Before students begin writing, work as a class to identify the elements of an effective persuasive speech. Tell students to include these elements in their writing. Allow time for students to rehearse before they read their speeches to the class, and then have the class discuss what made the speeches persuasive. (PARTNERS)

Powers of Persuasion Have partners review the selection to find the facts and opinions that Linda and Darnell use to persuade their audiences, how Linda delivers her speech, and how Darnell feels about his speech. Suggest that students use a Venn diagram to compare and contrast the speeches.
(PERSUASION)

Oral Language Have students in small groups choose roles and reenact what happens at the City Council meeting. Use the Retelling Rubric at left to evaluate students' responses.

Retelling Rubric

4	Excellent	The students' reenactment **includes many details** that clearly and thoroughly represent what happened at the City Council meeting.
3	Good	The students' reenactment **includes some details** that accurately represent what happened at the City Council meeting.
2	Fair	The students' reenactment **gives a limited representation** of what happened at the City Council meeting.
1	Unsatisfactory	Students **cannot represent** what happened at the City Council meeting.

Connect to Social Studies

PREVIEW THE PERSUASIVE TEXT

- Tell students this selection is a speech that Lorenzo de Zavala may have given to persuade Texans to support the decision to declare independence from Mexico. Ask students to read the title and introduction on page 494. Ask them to set a purpose for reading the speech. Then have students read de Zavala's speech independently.

DISCUSS PERSUASIVE TECHNIQUES

- Tell students that persuasive techniques are used to persuade or convince a person to think or act a certain way.

- Explain that political speeches often contain persuasive techniques, such as emotional appeals, promises, and power words. Discuss the techniques identified in the chart below. Then tell students that as they read, they should look for these techniques.

emotional appeal	a statement that makes someone feel a certain emotion or feeling, such as excitement or patriotism
campaign promise	a statement of what the candidate will do if elected
power words	words that evoke strong feelings

Connect to Social Studies

DE ZAVALA: A VOICE FOR TEXAS

✓ **TARGET VOCABULARY**

urge	violations
minimum	granted
effective	issue
deteriorating	ordinance
dependent	exception

GENRE

Persuasive text, like this speech, seeks to persuade the reader to think or act a certain way.

TEXT FOCUS

Persuasive techniques may be used in a speech to persuade the reader to think or act a certain way.

494

DE ZAVALA: A VOICE FOR TEXAS

In February 1836, people living in the part of Mexico called Texas faced a big decision. The Mexican leader, General Santa Anna, was a cruel dictator who would not share power. Many Texans wanted to separate from Mexico. A year before, at a meeting, or "Consultation," they had voted to stay in Mexico but form their own government. One of the delegates to the Consultation was a respected Mexican statesman named Lorenzo de Zavala. He and others would meet again in March to vote on independence. We can imagine de Zavala giving a speech like this one to a crowd in Harrisburg, Texas, the town he represented.

ELL ENGLISH LANGUAGE LEARNERS

Scaffold

Beginning Use the Vocabulary words in simple questions that help develop students' understanding of the text.

Advanced Have students give oral sentences summarizing the persuasive speech they read on pages 495–496.

Intermediate Have students answer simple questions about the purpose of De Zavala's speech. Discuss with students their responses and clarify understanding.

Advanced High Have partners use evidence from the text to answer this question: *What does the speaker mean by the statement, "Today it is Texas that needs to be healed"?*

See ELL Lesson 19, pp. E32–E41 for scaffolded support.

My good friends, independence is an issue that affects all of us. I know that many of you were unhappy with the Consultation of 1835. I beg you to be patient. Our fight continues, and the solution is nearer than ever before.

I have fought for democracy since I was a young man. I went to prison for my beliefs. While I was there, I resolved to help people the best way I could. I thought I would become a doctor. Instead I became a politician. Today it is Texas that needs to be healed.

I know you work hard and love this land. You do not deserve to have your rights reduced to a minimum. You do not need another ordinance from leaders you did not elect. I tell you that we will have no justice as long as we are under Santa Anna's rule. Just as Mexico once declared its independence from Spain, today Texas has no choice but to declare its independence from Mexico!

495

Practice Fluency
Stress

Have students listen as you read aloud the third paragraph on **Student Book p. 495.**

- Remind students that good readers use their voices to stress words and phrases that they think are important and deserve extra attention.

- Have students partner-read each sentence of the paragraph aloud. Remind them to use their voices to stress words and phrases that they want to emphasize.

JOURNEYS DIGITAL — **Powered by** DESTINATIONReading®
Student eBook: Read and Listen

TARGET VOCABULARY REVIEW

✓ **TARGET VOCABULARY** Vocabulary in Context Cards – Persuasive Vocabulary

Ask pairs of students to write the Target Vocabulary words on index cards or slips of paper. Have students take turns choosing a vocabulary word and using it in a persuasive sentence. For example, the word *urge* could be used in the following persuasive sentence:
I would like to urge my fellow class-mates to sign this petition asking for a longer recess.

CONTEXT CARDS

front   back

Develop Comprehension

① Fact and Opinion

Explain whether the statement "Our fight continues, and the solution is nearer than ever before" is a fact or opinion? Sample answer: It is an opinion because it cannot be proven, and it is what the speaker believes.

② Persuasion

What persuasive technique does the author use by having the speaker say, "I know you work hard and love this land"? Sample answer: The author appeals to feelings of pride that listeners have for Texas.

③ ✔ **TARGET VOCABULARY**

What does the author mean when he says that freedom is **deteriorating***? Sample answer: He means Texans are losing their freedom.*

Persuasive Techniques

- Tell students that this speech is meant to persuade citizens that Texas needs to declare independence from Mexico. Tell them that one of the persuasive techniques used is a campaign promise.

- Model the thinking.

Think Aloud *De Zavala uses the last line of his speech to make a promise to the citizens. He says that if the citizens support the leaders, then the leaders will give the people the most effective government possible.*

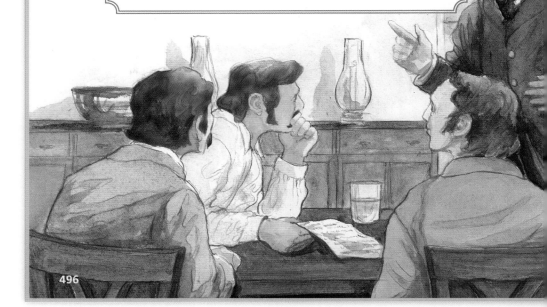

For a time, I believed in our leaders. But times have changed, and I have changed, too. Our freedom is deteriorating. **③** There have been violations of the law that I cannot ignore. Our leaders do not respect the Mexican constitution, and I can no longer work for them. There are others who feel the same way. We plan to write a new constitution for an independent Texas.

When we do, we will remember the rights of all Texans. We will never make an exception for the rich over the poor. The leaders of Texas are dependent on the trust of the people. They must be elected fairly and democratically.

My friends, we are being granted a chance to make an example of our republic. I urge you to give us your support, and in return we will give you the most effective government possible.

From March to October of 1836, Lorenzo de Zavala served as the first vice-president of the Republic of Texas. He died of pneumonia in November 1836. Nine years later, Texas joined the United States as the twenty-eighth state.

496

Weekly Internet Challenge

Skim and Scan

- Review Internet Strategy, Step 4: Analyze and Evaluate.
- Review with students the importance of analyzing and evaluating websites before using information found there.
- Explain that good researchers learn to skim and scan websites to determine the quality of the site and the reliability of the information.

INTERNET STRATEGY

1. **Plan a Search** by identifying what you are looking for and how to find it.

2. **Search and Predict** which sites will be worth exploring.

3. **Navigate** a site to see how to get around it and what it contains.

4. **Analyze and Evaluate** the quality and reliability of the information.

5. **Synthesize** the information from multiple sites.

Making Connections

 Text to Self

Evaluate a Speech Imagine you are a reporter in the crowd in Harrisburg, Texas, listening to De Zavala's speech. Write a short paragraph in which you summarize De Zavala's viewpoint and main ideas for your newspaper readers. Note any parts of the speech that you think are exaggerated. Then evaluate which parts of the speech are most effective. Describe the atmosphere and the mood of the crowd so readers will feel as if they are there, too.

 Text to Text

Compare Character Perspectives Lorenzo de Zavala was a respected Mexican statesman and a talented public speaker. If De Zavala could speak to Darnell Rock about his speech at the City Council meeting, what do you think he would say? What kinds of tips might he be able to give Darnell? What kinds of questions might Darnell ask De Zavala?

 Text to World

Discuss Media Techniques Darnell Rock writes a newspaper article to present to the public his thoughts on a community issue. Work with a small group to think of a community or national issue that has been covered in various media. Make a list of where you have seen information about the issue, such as in newspaper articles, magazine advertisements, television commercials, and documentaries. Then discuss how the different kinds of media present the issue. Consider how written text, sound effects, images, video, narration, and other techniques contribute to an overall message.

497

"De Zavala: A Voice for Texas" Challenge

- Ask students to locate several websites that have information about the events leading up to the independence of Texas and its joining the United States as the twenty-eighth state. Have students skim and scan the websites quickly and make an evaluation about each site's reliability.

- Then have students find other websites with persuasive speeches. Have them select a speech, identify the author's viewpoint and explain the relationships among the ideas in the argument. Then have them identify exaggerated, contradictory, and misleading statement from the texts.

Making Connections

 **Text to Self**

To help students identify De Zavala's viewpoint, have them use an Inference Map to keep track of important details that tell how he feels. Discuss with students whether they feel that any of his claims are exaggerated.

 Text to Text

To identify tips De Zavala might give Darnell, have students compare speeches and take notes on what is effective and what could be improved. Then write down questions that Darnell might ask De Zavala that could help Darnell improve his speech.

 Text to World

Remind students to consider the purpose of different media techniques when evaluating the effectiveness of the overall message. Guide students to create a rating system to evaluate the overall effectiveness of the various media techniques used.

Deepen Comprehension

SKILL TRACE

Persuasion	
Introduce	T236–T237
Differentiate	T282–T283
Reteach	T290
▶ Review	**T256–T257**
Test	Weekly Tests, Lesson 19

ELL ENGLISH LANGUAGE LEARNERS

Scaffold

Beginning Guide students in naming the people that Darnell is trying to help in the selection. Have them use the illustrations as you discuss Darnell's cause together.

Intermediate Help students summarize Darnell's argument from the selection. Provide this sentence frame: *Darnell thinks that _____ because _____.*

Advanced Read aloud the first paragraph of the selection. Ask questions to help students summarize, such as: *Who is Sweeby Jones? Where does he live? What does Darnell want to do?*

Advanced High Have students summarize the details from the story and infer Darnell's argument.

See ELL Lesson 19, pp. E32–E41, for scaffolded support.

✔ Analyze and Evaluate Persuasion

1 Teach/Model

AL *Academic Language*

assumption a statement that is accepted as true without proof

bias a strong feeling for or against without good reason

persuade to convince someone to think or act in a certain way

---

- Explain that authors and story characters may or may not support their arguments with reliable facts, examples, and details. Sometimes authors and characters make **assumptions** or use **bias** to get an audience to agree with them.

- Good readers can recognize the different ways authors try to persuade them and can make up their own minds based on the supporting evidence.

- Have students reread Darnell's article on p. 482.

- Display **Projectable 19.4.** Discuss **Deepen Comprehension Question 1.**

- Remind students that an Idea-Support Map helps organize the reasons given to support an argument.

- Model analyzing and evaluating Darnell's argument to complete the Idea-Support Map and answer the question.

Projectable 19.4

Darnell Rock Reporting | Deepen Comprehension | Persuasion

Idea-Support Map: Persuasion

Deepen Comprehension Question 1
What is the main argument of Darnell's article? List two of the persuasive details he used to support his argument. p. 482

> We should turn the old courts into a garden to help the homeless.
>> The quote from Mr. Jones: "...if you don't mind people being hungry, then there is something wrong with you."
>> "There are things you can do to change your life or make it good."

Deepen Comprehension Question 2
How does Darnell try to question the assumptions of his audience? Support your answer with details from the story. pp. 488–490

> Darnell tries to present the point of view of the people who usually get ignored.
>> He shows that homeless people want to do good and start a garden.
>> He explains that the Corner Crew are mostly good kids, but no one listens to them unless they're in trouble.
>> He explains how kids who get off track could use the example of the homeless people to help them find what's good.

Deepen Comprehension Question 3
What evidence of bias do you notice in Linda's argument? Why do you think the council votes for her idea rather than Darnell's? Support your answer with details from the story. pp. 483, 487

Think Aloud *Darnell includes a quote from Mr. Jones that supports his argument. The quote says there's something wrong with you if you don't mind people being hungry. The quote is emotionally charged and powerful. I'll put it in my Idea-Support Map.*

2 Guided Practice

- Reread pp. 488–490 of "Darnell Rock Reporting" with students. Clarify any confusion about how Darnell's argument develops from a simple emotional response to a supported argument.

- Read and discuss **Deepen Comprehension Question 2** on **Projectable 19.4**. Use these prompts to guide students:

- *Why does Darnell talk about how the garden could help students?* *He assumes that the council wants to help the school, not the homeless.*

- *Why does Darnell think the garden would provide a good example to young people who need help?* *He assumes the garden would help the homeless people improve their lives, and students would see that as a good example.*

- Guide students to complete the Idea-Support Map for Question 2.

GUIDED DISCUSSION Have students reread p. 488 and work with them to evaluate the key points of Darnell's argument. Prompt students with questions like the one below:

- *What group of students does Darnell focus on to make his point?* *The kids who are usually in trouble; the Corner Crew*

3 Apply

 Have students reread Linda's article on p. 483. Then have partners complete a new Idea-Support Map and work together to answer **Deepen Comprehension Question 3** on **Projectable 19.4**. Have volunteers share their responses.

EXTEND DISCUSSION Evaluate with students the persuasive techniques used by Darnell, Linda, and Sweeby Jones. Have students tell what they think makes each argument effective or what the character could have included to better support his or her argument. Then have them summarize the selection and discuss how the arguments help them understand the selection as a whole.

Monitor Comprehension

Are students able to analyze persuasion?

IF...	THEN...
students have difficulty analyzing persuasion,	▶ use the Leveled Reader for **Struggling Readers**, *The Big Interview*, p. T284.
students are able to analyze persuasion,	▶ use the Leveled Reader for **On-Level Readers**, *Saving the General*, p. T285.
students are able to analyze and evaluate persuasion,	▶ use the Leveled Reader for **Advanced Readers**, *Another View*, p. T286.

Leveled Readers, pp. T284–T287.

Use the Leveled Reader for **English Language Learners,** *The Old Tree,* p. T287. *Group English Language Learners according to language proficiency.*

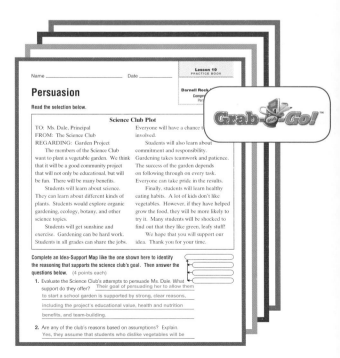

Practice Book p. 218
See Grab-and-Go™ Resources for additional leveled practice.

Fluency

- Read aloud with grade-appropriate fluency.
- Read fluently with comprehension by placing the correct stress on words.

☑ Stress

1 Teach/Model

- Tell students that good readers make text meaningful by stressing, or emphasizing, certain words.

- Have students follow along as you read aloud the first three paragraphs on **Student Book p. 485,** using appropriate emphasis. Read aloud individual sentences with the correct stress and then without stress so that students can hear the difference.

- Explain that knowing which words to stress in a sentence helps readers understand the overall meaning of a text.

2 Guided Practice

- Together, read aloud **Student Book p. 486.**

- Work with students to adjust their stress, or emphasis, as needed to reflect the importance of certain words or phrases.

- If students are struggling to read with proper stress, read each sentence aloud and have students repeat it after you, mimicking your pitch, tone, and volume. Then have them choral-read the passage with you, using appropriate emphasis.

- See also **Instructional Routine 6.**

3 Apply

- Tell students that with practice, they will improve their reading fluency and comprehension of a selection by learning to stress the correct words.

- Have small groups take turns reading a paragraph of the selection aloud to each other, focusing on stress.

- Allow students to read the paragraph three or four times.

Decoding

 More Common Suffixes

1 | Teach/Model

ANALYZE COMMON SUFFIXES Write the word *argument* on the board and read it aloud. Have students repeat the word. Break the word into syllables and read each syllable aloud with students.

- Point out the familiar base word *argue* along with the common suffix *-ment*. Have a student underline the suffix on the board.

- Explain that there are often spelling changes to a word when a suffix is added. In the word *argument,* the final *e* of a base word is dropped. Other spelling changes include changing the final *y* to *i*, or doubling the final consonant.

- Point out that adding a suffix often adds a syllable to a word. Common suffixes include *-ly, -ment, -less, -ness, -ion,* and *-er.*

2 | Practice/Apply

DECODE WORDS WITH COMMON SUFFIXES Write the following words on the board: *composition, effortless, entirely, challenger, friendliness, suspension.* Model how to decode the first two words step by step.

- Have partners work together to decode the remaining words. Ask students to read the words and identify each suffix. Have them note any spelling changes made to the base word when the suffix is added.

- Use **Corrective Feedback** if students need additional help.

Corrective Feedback

If students have difficulty decoding words with suffixes, use the model below.

Correct the error. Divide the word into its parts. *The word is* happiness. *The syllables are* happi- *and* -ness.

Model the correct way to decode the word. *Check for a suffix and see if you recognize it as a common suffix, such as -er, -ly, -ness, -ion, -less, or -ment. Then look for a familiar base word. Watch for a spelling change in the base before the suffix.*

Guide students to identify the word parts. *What is the suffix? (-ness) What is the base word? (happy)*

Check students' understanding. *What is the word? (happiness)*

Reinforce Have students repeat the process with the word *judgment.*

Vocabulary Strategies

 Greek and Latin Suffixes
-ism, -ist, -able, -ible

1 Teach/Model

AL *Academic Language*

suffix an affix attached to the end of a base word or root that changes the meaning of the word

---

• Explain that a suffix is an affix attached to the end of a base word or root that changes the meaning of the word. Two common Greek suffixes are *-ism* (belief in something) and *-ist* (one who is or does). Common Latin suffixes include *-able* and *-ible* (capable or worthy of an action).

• Point out that the word *biologist* contains the suffix *-ist*.

• Write "The marine biologist leaned over the tank to see the electric eels." on the board and read it aloud for students.

• Display **Projectable S8.** Model applying Steps 1 and 2 of the strategy to understand the meaning of the suffix *-ist* in the word *biologist*.

Think Aloud *When I look at this word, I see the suffix -ist. I know that biology is the study of life science. The suffix -ist means "one who does." So, biologist must mean "someone who does or studies biology." This definition makes sense in this sentence.*

• *What else can we do to figure out the meaning of a word with a suffix if using the suffix's meaning does not help? (Use context clues or look in a dictionary.)*

2 Guided Practice

- Display the passage on **Projectable 19.5** and read "Making a Difference" aloud.

- Display the Four-Square Map at the bottom of **Projectable 19.5**.

- Guide students to read the list of vocabulary words from the passage. Tell students that they will use these words to complete the Four-Square Map.

- Have students choose words from the list that end either in the Greek suffixes *-ism* and *-ist* or the Latin suffixes *-ible* and *-able*. Write them in the appropriate squares. Discuss the changes in meaning after each suffix is added to the base word or root.

Projectable 19.5

Darnell Rock Reporting Vocabulary Strategies Greek and Latin Suffixes -ism, -ist, -able, -ible

Greek Suffixes *-ism, -ist*
Latin Suffixes *-able, -ible*

Vocabulary
biologist
biólogo
heroism
heroísmo
terrible
terrible
horrible
horrible
activism
activismo
considerable
considerable
vulnerable
vulnerable

* Spanish cognates

Making a Difference

Reading was essential for Tim, and he spent a **considerable** amount of his time face down in a book. Books allowed Tim to be any person he chose, to go anywhere in the world, and to see anything he wanted to see. One day he was a **biologist** studying with a team off the coast of Australia, and the next a **terrible** dragon chasing peasants in medieval times. A day without reading was a **horrible** day, indeed.

As Tim grew older a funny thing happened: He began to live like some of the characters in the books he read. Many people praised Tim for his **heroism** and courage at times when most of his peers felt cowardly or **vulnerable**. When asked about his abilities Tim said, "**My activism** is nothing compared to wonderful characters in books like *Tom Sawyer*. Reading has allowed me to meet some of the best people on the planet."

heroism activism		biologist
	-ism, -ist *-ible, -able*	
terrible horrible		considerable vulnerable

3 Apply

- Have students read "Making a Difference" on **Projectable 19.5**. For each word, have students use the suffix and its meaning, as well as the context of a sentence, to identify the meaning of the word. Discuss the meanings of the words to confirm students' understanding.

- Have students use other texts to look for words that end in *-ism, -ist, -ible,* and *-able.* Have students use each suffix to determine the meaning of each word. Tell students to use a dictionary to confirm the meanings of the words. Remind students that adding a suffix may result in a spelling change in the base word. Tell students to be sure they spell words with Greek and Latin suffixes correctly.

Monitor Vocabulary Strategies

Are students able to identify and use Greek suffixes -ism and -ist and Latin suffixes -ible and -able?

IF...	THEN...
students have difficulty identifying and using Greek suffixes *-ism, -ist* and Latin suffixes *-ible, -able,*	▶ **Differentiate Vocabulary Strategies** for Struggling Readers, p. T288. *See also Intervention Lesson 19, pp. S31–S42.*
students can identify and use Greek suffixes *-ism, -ist* and Latin suffixes *-ible, -able* most of the time,	▶ **Differentiate Vocabulary Strategies** for On-Level Readers, p. T288.
students can consistently identify and use Greek suffixes *-ism, -ist* and Latin suffixes *-ible, -able,*	▶ **Differentiate Vocabulary Strategies** for Advanced Readers, p. T289.

Differentiate Vocabulary Strategies: pp. T288–T289. *Group English Language Learners according to language proficiency.*

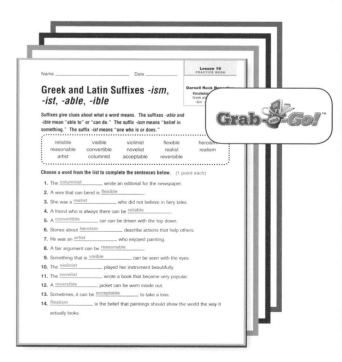

Name _____ Date _____

Lesson 19
PRACTICE BOOK

Greek and Latin Suffixes *-ism,*
-ist, -able, -ible

Darnell Rock Reporting
Vocabulary
Greek and Latin Suffixes
-ism, -ist...

Suffixes give clues about what a word means. The suffixes *-able* and *-ible* mean "able to" or "can do." The suffix *-ism* means "belief in something." The suffix *-ist* means "one who is or does."

reliable	visible	violinist	flexible	heroism
reasonable	convertible	novelist	realist	realism
artist	columnist	acceptable	reversible	

Choose a word from the list to complete the sentences below. (1 point each)

1. The <u>columnist</u> wrote an editorial for the newspaper.
2. A wire that can bend is <u>flexible</u>.
3. She was a <u>realist</u> who did not believe in fairy tales.
4. A friend who is always there can be <u>reliable</u>.
5. A <u>convertible</u> car can be driven with the top down.
6. Stories about <u>heroism</u> describe actions that help others.
7. He was an <u>artist</u> who enjoyed painting.
8. A fair argument can be <u>reasonable</u>.
9. Something that is <u>visible</u> can be seen with the eyes.
10. The <u>violinist</u> played her instrument beautifully.
11. The <u>novelist</u> wrote a book that became very popular.
12. A <u>reversible</u> jacket can be worn inside out.
13. Sometimes, it can be <u>acceptable</u> to take a loss.
14. <u>Realism</u> is the belief that paintings should show the world the way it actually looks.

Practice Book p. 219
See Grab-and-Go™ Resources for additional leveled practice.

Connect and Extend

"Darnell Rock Reporting"   **"De Zavala: A Voice for Texas"**

Vocabulary Reader

Struggling Readers   ***On-Level Readers***

Advanced Readers   ***English Language Learners***

Read to Connect

SHARE AND COMPARE TEXTS Have students compare and contrast this week's reading selections. Use the following prompts to guide the discussion.

- How do the characters try to get others to see their point of view? Are they effective? Why or why not?

- Summarize this week's selections. Explain in a sentence or two what the texts reveal about trying to persuade others.

CONNECT TEXT TO WORLD Use these prompts to help guide student discussion. Accept students' opinions, but encourage them to support their ideas with text details from their reading. Allow time for them to consider suggestions from others and identify points of agreement or disagreement.

- Why is it often so difficult to change peoples' minds about an issue?

- Think of a community issue in your area. What can you do to convince others of your point of view about the issue?

Independent Reading

BOOK TALK Have student pairs discuss their independent reading for the week. Tell them to refer to their Reading Logs or journals and summarize the main ideas, maintaining meaning and order. Have students retell a favorite section to give their partner a better idea of what they read. Then have students discuss the following:

- how the cultural or historical context of each text supports their understanding

- the selections' organizational patterns or plot events

- the authors' purposes

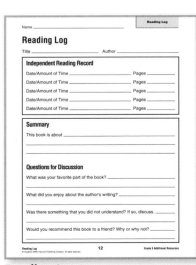

Reading Log

Extend Through Research

CREATE GRAPHIC/VISUAL DATA Remind students that information can be gathered not only from print or electronic text, but also from graphic/visual sources, such as charts, graphs, diagrams, and illustrations. Sometimes information is easier to understand when it is presented visually. Discuss with students a situation in which they used graphic/visual data to understand information.

- Tell students that they will be converting information from text into a graphic source or other visual data.

- Have students research the boom of immigration to America that took place during the early 1900s. Have them look for text information that could be presented visually in graphic sources such as timelines, charts, tables, and diagrams.

- Have students brainstorm ways to convert the text information they find into graphic information.

- Then have students discuss the kinds of graphic sources they used and how converting text into graphic information helped them better understand their research topic.

Listening and Speaking

PERSUASIVE TECHNIQUES Tell students they will give a brief persuasive speech explaining why graphic/visual sources they used in their research in the above activity were more useful than the same information in text form.

Allow students to prepare their presentations. Tell them to focus on:
- making eye contact with the audience.
- pronouncing each word clearly with appropriate rate, volume, and stress.
- speaking persuasively using natural gestures.

While students give their presentations, have audience members use the Listening Log to record notes about the speaker's main and supporting ideas and whether they agree with each speaker's perspective. Allow time for students to ask clarifying questions if needed.

Listening Log

Spelling ☑ Suffixes: *-ful, -ly, -ness, -less, -ment*

SHARE OBJECTIVE

- Spell words that have the suffixes *-ful, -ly, -ness, -less,* and *-ment.*

Spelling Words

Basic

lately	government	forgiveness
settlement	✪ agreement	harmless
✪ watchful	cloudiness	✪ enjoyment
✪ countless	✪ delightful	appointment
steadily	noisily	effortless
✪ closeness	tardiness	plentiful
calmly	✪ forgetful	

Review

clumsiness, movement, ✪ pavement, lonely, penniless

Challenge

suspenseful, merciless, seriousness, contentment, suspiciously

✪ Forms of these words appear in "Darnell Rock Reporting".

ELL ENGLISH LANGUAGE LEARNERS

Preteach

Spanish Cognates

Write and discuss these Spanish cognates for Spanish-speaking students.

calmly • *con calma*

tardiness • *tardanza*

Day 1

❶ TEACH THE PRINCIPLE

- Administer the **Pretest.** Use the Day 5 sentences.
- Write *steady* on the board. Use the chart to help students understand when to change *y* to *i* before adding a suffix.

If the base word…	Before adding the suffix *-ful, -ly, -ness, -less,* or *-ment*…
ends with a consonant and *y*	change *y* to *i,* as in *steadily, cloudiness*
does not end in a consonant and *y*	the spelling does not change, as in *lately*

❷ PRACTICE/APPLY

Guide students to identify the suffixes and spelling changes in the remaining Spelling Words.

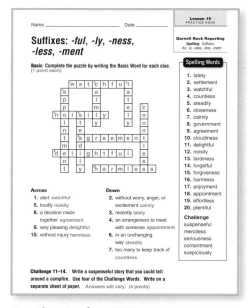

Practice Book p. 220

Day 2

❶ TEACH WORD SORT

- Set up five rows as shown. Label each row with a suffix. Model adding a Spelling Word to each row.
- Have students copy the chart. Guide students to write each Spelling Word where it belongs.

-ful	forgetful
-ly	noisily
-ness	cloudiness
-less	effortless
-ment	appointment

❷ PRACTICE/APPLY

Have students add words from "Darnell Rock Reporting" to the chart.

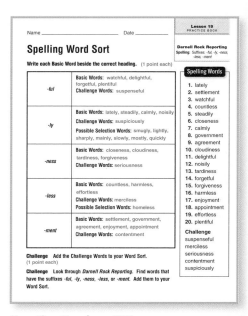

Practice Book p. 221

Day 3

1 TEACH RELATED WORDS

- **WRITE** *community, village, colony, _____.*

- **ASK** *What do these three words have in common? (They refer to a place where a group of people live.)*

- **ASK** *Which Spelling Word also refers to a place where people live? (settlement)*

- **WRITE** *settlement* on the line.

- With students, follow the steps above to complete the following word group with the correct Spelling Word: *meeting, engagement, date, _____.* (appointment)

2 PRACTICE/APPLY

- **WRITE** these word groups: *friendship, familiarity, relationship, _____; regime, administration, rule, _____; mercy, pity, pardon, _____.*

- Have students look these words up in a dictionary or an electronic resource to find their meanings.

- **ASK** *Which Spelling Word belongs on each blank? (closeness; government; forgiveness)*

✏️ Have students explain their answers in writing.

Day 4

1 CONNECT TO WRITING

- Read and discuss the prompt below.

✏️ **WRITE TO NARRATE**

Write a personal narrative that includes your thoughts and feelings about an experience you had. Use ideas about persuasion that you learned this week.

2 PRACTICE/APPLY

- Guide students as they plan and write their narratives. See page T272.

- Remind students to proofread their writing to make sure they have spelled words with suffixes correctly.

Name _____ Date _____

Proofreading for Spelling

Find the misspelled words and circle them. Write them correctly on the lines below. (2 points each)

> Katie's neighborhood had the feeling of closeness that might exist in a small setlement. It seemed almost to have its own goverment, with a homeowners' association group and a neighborhood crime watch. Katie decided to join the neighborhood community and start a babysitting club. She found it to be a nearly efortless job to sign up babysitters who wanted to be in the club. Everybody understood that there would be no forgivness for tardyness on the job—and that nobody could be forgettful. One rainy morning, Katie made flyers to advertise the babysitting club. As soon as she had finished, the rain stopped, and the sun erased all traces of cloudines. She then took enjoiment in distributing the flyers to the plentifull supply of prospective neighborhood clients!

1. closeness   6. tardiness
2. settlement   7. forgetful
3. government   8. cloudiness
4. effortless   9. enjoyment
5. forgiveness   10. plentiful

Lesson 19 PRACTICE BOOK

Darnell Rock Reporting
Spelling: Suffixes: -ful, -ly, -ness, -less, -ment

Spelling Words
1. lately
2. settlement
3. watchful
4. countless
5. steadily
6. closeness
7. calmly
8. government
9. agreement
10. cloudiness
11. delightful
12. noisily
13. tardiness
14. forgetful
15. forgiveness
16. harmless
17. enjoyment
18. appointment
19. effortless
20. plentiful

Challenge
suspenseful
merciless
seriousness
contentment
suspiciously

Practice Book p. 222

Day 5

ASSESS SPELLING

- Say each boldfaced word, read the sentence, and then repeat the word.

- Have students write the bold-faced word.

Basic

1. The weather has been cold **lately**.
2. The Pilgrims founded a **settlement**.
3. Be **watchful** when walking alone.
4. The sky has **countless** stars.
5. I ran **steadily** toward the finish line.
6. My sister and I share a special **closeness**.
7. He **calmly** explained his position.
8. We have a democratic **government**.
9. They could not reach an **agreement**.
10. **Cloudiness** will not ruin the picnic.
11. That funny show was **delightful**!
12. The children played **noisily**.
13. Teachers do not like **tardiness**.
14. Being tired makes me **forgetful**.
15. The prisoner sought **forgiveness** for his crime.
16. I have no fear of **harmless** spiders.
17. Dad plays golf for **enjoyment**.
18. Cora has a doctor's **appointment**.
19. You made that dive look **effortless**.
20. We have a **plentiful** supply of food.

Grammar ☑ More Kinds of Pronouns

- Identify indefinite, possessive, and interrogative pronouns.
- Use pronouns in writing and speaking.

ELL ENGLISH LANGUAGE LEARNERS

Scaffold

Beginning Use the following sentences to demonstrate that an indefinite pronoun replaces a person or thing that is not identified.

Someone came to the class.

Does anyone want to help?

Intermediate Use the sentence frames below to guide students to use indefinite pronouns.

_____ came to the class. *(Some, Few, All)*

Does _____ want to help? *(somebody, everybody, someone)*

Advanced Have students describe objects in the room using the following pronouns: *his, anyone, who, everything, their, both.*

Advanced High Have one partner name a pronoun. Have the other partner make up a sentence using that pronoun. Then have partners tell what kind of pronoun they used.

See ELL Lesson 19, pp. E32–E41, for scaffolded support.

JOURNEYS **Powered by**
DIGITAL **DESTINATIONReading**
Grammar Activities: Lesson 19

Day 1 TEACH

DAILY PROOFREADING PRACTICE
the people went too the garden. *The; to*

❶ TEACH INDEFINITE PRONOUNS

PROJECTABLE
19.6

- Display **Projectable 19.6.** Remind students that a pronoun is a word that takes the place of a noun. An **indefinite pronoun** refers to a person or thing that is not identified. Tell students that words such as *someone, something, anyone, everything, both, all, either, each, nothing, anything,* and *neither* are indefinite pronouns.

- Model identifying indefinite pronouns in this example sentence: *Someone volunteered to take over our community garden.*

Think Aloud *To identify the indefinite pronoun, I ask this Thinking Question:* **What pronoun refers to a person or thing that is not identified?** *The word* Someone *does not identify the person who volunteered.*

❷ PRACTICE/APPLY

- Complete items 1–10 on **Projectable 19.6** with students.

- Write the words *anyone, either, few, both* and *all* on the board. Ask students to provide sentences using each indefinite pronoun.

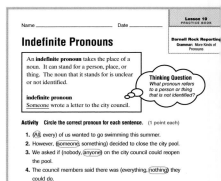

Practice Book p. 223

AL *Academic Language*

indefinite pronoun refers to a person or thing that is not identified
possessive pronoun shows ownership
interrogative pronoun begins questions

Language Arts

Grammar

Day 2 TEACH

DAILY PROOFREADING PRACTICE

is everyone ready to vote. *Is; vote?*

1 EXTEND POSSESSIVE PRONOUNS

PROJECTABLE
19.7

- Display **Projectable 19.7.** Remind students that a possessive noun shows ownership. Explain that a **possessive pronoun** replaces a possessive noun and shows ownership. Tell students that words such as *my, your, his, her, its our, their, mine, yours,* and *theirs* are possessive pronouns.

- Model identifying possessive pronouns in this example sentence: *Our town has a park with a community garden.*

Think Aloud *To identify the possessive pronoun, I ask the Thinking Question:* **What is the pronoun in the sentence that shows ownership?** *I see that the word* Our *appears before the word* town. Our *shows ownership by telling whose town it is. I think* Our *is the possessive pronoun.*

2 PRACTICE/APPLY

- Complete items 1–6 on **Projectable 19.7** with students.

- Write the following sentences on the board. Have students name a possessive pronoun to complete each one.

Peter and Carla read ___ report about Japan. *(their)*

We will make covers for ___ reports. *(our)*

Karen reviewed ___ favorite movies. *(her)*

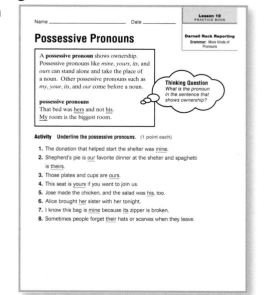

Practice Book p. 224

Day 3 TEACH

DAILY PROOFREADING PRACTICE

Darnell talking to Darnell's mom. *talks/talked; his*

1 TEACH INTERROGATIVE PRONOUNS

PROJECTABLE
19.8

- Display **Projectable 19.8.** Tell students that interrogative pronouns are words used to begin questions. Point out that the words *who, what,* and *which* are interrogative pronouns.

- Model identifying interrogative pronouns in this example sentence: *Who will ask the mayor if we can build a community park?*

Think Aloud *To identify an interrogative pronoun, I look to see if a pronoun begins a sentence. Then I ask this question:* **What pronoun begins the question in this sentence?** Who *is the interrogative pronoun.*

2 PRACTICE/APPLY

- Complete items 1–6 on **Projectable 19.8** with students.

- Have student pairs work together. Tell one partner to point to an object in the classroom and say one of the three interrogative pronouns: *who, what,* or *which.* Have the other partner make up a question about the object, using the interrogative pronoun.

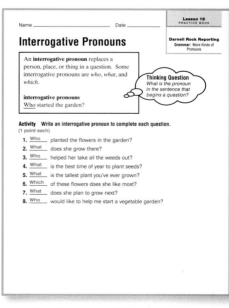

Practice Book p. 225
More Kinds of Pronouns • **T267**

Day 4 REVIEW

DAILY PROOFREADING PRACTICE

What wants to make the garden. *Who; garden?*

1 REVIEW MORE KINDS OF PRONOUNS

• Remind students that a **pronoun** is a word that replaces a noun. An **indefinite pronoun** refers to a person or thing that is not identified, such as *someone, anyone,* or *each.* A **possessive pronoun,** such as *yours, his,* or *mine,* is used to show ownership or possession. An **interrogative pronoun,** such as *who, what,* and *which,* begins a question.

2 SPIRAL REVIEW

Present and Past Tense Verbs Review with students that a **present tense** verb tells what is happening now. A **past tense** verb tells what happened before now. Remind students that many past tense verbs end with *–ed.*

Write the following sentences on the board. Have students change the verbs in the present tense to the past tense, and verbs in past tense to present.

Darnell is in the seventh grade. *(was)*

He wrote great articles. *(writes)*

Darnell talked to Sweeby Jones. *(talks)*

The City Council meets with Darnell. *(met)*

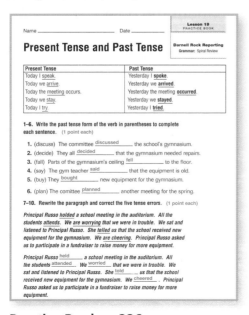

Practice Book p. 226

Day 5 CONNECT TO WRITING

DAILY PROOFREADING PRACTICE

Last weak he walks to the City Council. *week; walked*

1 CONNECT TO WRITING

• Tell students that an important part of revising is using pronouns correctly.

• Point out that using the correct pronouns in writing will make the ideas clear to readers.

2 PRACTICE/APPLY

• Display the following sentences. Have students identify the underlined pronouns as indefinite, possessive, or interrogative.

<u>Who</u> is <u>his</u> teacher? *(interrogative; possessive)*

<u>Neither</u> wanted to go to the meeting. *(indefinite)*

<u>What</u> does <u>everyone</u> want for lunch? *(interrogative; indefinite)*

<u>All</u> are welcome to <u>our</u> meeting. *(indefinite; possessive)*

• Have students turn to **Student Book p. 498**. Review with them different ways to use pronouns in their writing.

• Then have students complete the *Try This!* activity.

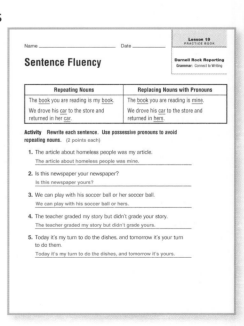

Practice Book p. 227

Grammar

More Kinds of Pronouns A **pronoun** is a word that takes the place of a noun. There are several kinds of pronouns. Words like *someone* and *something* refer to a person or thing that is not identified. These pronouns are called **indefinite pronouns**. Pronouns that replace possessive nouns are called **possessive pronouns**. Words such as *who*, *what*, and *which* can be used to begin questions. These pronouns are called **interrogative pronouns**.

Academic Language

indefinite pronouns
possessive pronouns
interrogative pronouns

Pronouns	Examples
indefinite pronoun	Anyone can become a gardener here.
possessive pronoun	Mr. Mogannum never had his own yard.
interrogative pronoun	What is that orange vegetable in the garden?

Try This! **Copy each sentence below onto a sheet of paper. Underline each indefinite pronoun. Circle each possessive pronoun. Draw a box around each interrogative pronoun.**

1. Who is the woman in the purple bonnet?
2. Everyone in the garden asks that woman for advice!
3. Her tomatoes are the biggest and reddest!
4. Which is Mr. Jackson's garden plot?
5. The plot with the sunflowers is his plot.

498

Sentence Fluency Possessive pronouns can help you avoid repeating proper nouns in your writing. When you use possessive pronouns, be sure that your readers will be able to understand to whom each possessive pronoun refers.

Poor Use of Possessive Pronouns

Carla will present Carla's proposal at the council meeting tonight. Carla's mother and aunt will attend the meeting, along with Carla's cousin. Carla has used their ideas in Carla's proposal.

Better Use of Possessive Pronouns

Carla will present her proposal at the council meeting tonight. Her mother and aunt will attend the meeting, and Carla's cousin will be there, too. Carla has used her mother's and aunt's ideas in her proposal.

Connect Grammar to Writing

As you revise your personal narrative next week, make sure you have used possessive pronouns effectively. Check to see that readers will understand to whom each possessive pronoun refers.

499

Try This!

1. *Who, interrogative*
2. *Everyone, indefinite*
3. *Her, Possessive*
4. *which, interrogative*
5. *his, possessive*

CONNECT GRAMMAR TO WRITING

- Have students turn to **Student Book p. 499**. Read the Sentence Fluency paragraph with them.

- Read the Poor Use of Possessive Pronouns paragraph. Point out that these sentences sound awkward because the name *Carla* is used often. Then read the Better Use of Possessive Pronouns paragraph. Tell students that using possessive pronouns helps them avoid the unnecessary repetition of proper nouns.

- Tell students that as they revise their personal narratives, they should use possessive, indefinite, and interrogative pronouns.

- Review the Common Errors at right with students.

COMMON ERRORS

Error: Darnell walked back to **Darnell's** seat.

Correct: Darnell walked back to **his** seat.

Error: I do not like **neither** the blue one or the white one.

Correct: I do not like **either** the blue one or the white one.

Write to Narrate ☑ Plan a Personal Narrative

- Study and evaluate personal narratives.
- Use the writing process to plan a personal narrative.
- Plan a first draft.

Academic Language

personal narrative a story in which the writer expresses his or her own experiences, thoughts, or feelings

body the part of an extended piece of writing that contains most of the details and content; it falls between the beginning and the ending

main idea what a story is mainly about

ELL ENGLISH LANGUAGE LEARNERS

Scaffold

Beginning Ask simple questions to help students generate topics for their personal narratives.

Intermediate Guide students to understand and use the pronouns *I, me, my, and mine* in their personal narratives.

Advanced Have partners take turns describing their ideas for their personal narratives. Then have them work together to brainstorm words, phrases, and other ideas appropriate to their topics.

Advanced High Have partners brainstorm main events and ideas and then list feelings that might be associated with the personal events they chose. Encourage them to use these words in their draft.

JOURNEYS DIGITAL Powered by DESTINATIONReading®
WriteSmart CD-ROM

Day 1 ANALYZE THE MODEL

❶ INTRODUCE THE MODEL

- Tell students that they will be planning a personal narrative in this lesson.
- Display **Projectable 19.9** and point out the prompt.

What Is a Personal Narrative?

- It is a story about someone's own experiences.
- It uses the pronoun *I*.
- The **beginning** introduces the topic and grabs readers' attention.
- The **body** presents details that describe the most important events. The events are arranged in time order.
- The **ending** wraps up the narrative, telling how events worked out, how the writer felt, or what the writer learned.

❷ PRACTICE/APPLY

- Using the Projectable, work with students to label the author's descriptive details, thoughts, and feelings in the Writing Model.

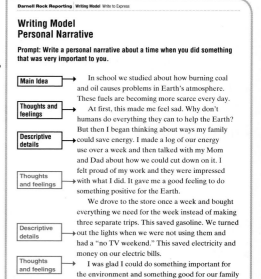

Projectable 19.9

Darnell Rock Reporting | Writing Model Write to Express

**Writing Model
Personal Narrative**

Prompt: Write a personal narrative about a time when you did something that was very important to you.

| Main Idea → | In school we studied about how burning coal and oil causes problems in Earth's atmosphere. These fuels are becoming more scarce every day. |

Thoughts and feelings → At first, this made me feel sad. Why don't humans do everything they can to help the Earth? But then I began thinking about ways my family

Descriptive details → could save energy. I made a log of our energy use over a week and then talked with my Mom and Dad about how we could cut down on it. I

Thoughts and feelings → felt proud of my work and they were impressed with what I did. It gave me a good feeling to do something positive for the Earth.

We drove to the store once a week and bought everything we need for the week instead of making three separate trips. This saved gasoline. We turned

Descriptive details → out the lights when we were not using them and had a "no TV weekend." This saved electricity and money on our electric bills.

Thoughts and feelings → I was glad I could do something important for the environment and something good for our family at the same time. I think the little things we do can make a difference.

LESSON	FORM	TRAIT
16	Friendly Letter	Voice
17	Character Description	Word Choice
18	Personal Narrative Paragraph	Voice
19	**Prewrite: Personal Narrative**	**Ideas**
20	Draft, Revise, Edit, Publish: Personal Narrative	Voice

Day 2 TEACH THE FOCUS TRAIT

1 INTRODUCE THE FOCUS TRAIT: IDEAS

- Tell students that writers present ideas in a way that helps readers understand why the writer feels a certain way.
- Explain that an idea presented in a personal narrative may be a main idea or it may be part of a descriptive detail in the narrative. Ideas in both of these places help the reader better understand the author's thoughts and feelings.

Connect to *Darnell Rock Reporting*	
Instead of this...	**...the author wrote this.**
Darnell was nervous to speak in front of the City Council.	Darnell felt a lump in the pit of his stomach. There were at least a hundred people at the City Council meeting. (p. 484)

- Discuss the idea of speaking in front of a large group of people and point out Darnell's thoughts and feelings about it.

2 PRACTICE/APPLY

- Tell students that the ideas in a personal narrative are related to each other. Explain that, although Darnell is nervous to talk in front of a group, he will do it because he wants to help the homeless.
- Suggest a topic such as *getting good grades*, and work with students to brainstorm a list of main ideas and descriptive details.

Practice Book p. 228

Day 3 PREWRITE

1 TEACH EXPLORING A TOPIC

- Explain that one way to explore ideas for a personal narrative is by creating an events chart.
- Tell students that you will list ideas for events that would be topics for a personal narrative.

Think Aloud *First, I'll think of possible events that will help me tell my story. I will use the heading "event" and then write the main events of my narrative. Then I will use the heading "details" and write more ideas, details, thoughts, and feelings related to each event.*

Event   *I could not find room in closet for my coat, so I decided to start a coat drive to help people in need.*

Details   *I had to leave my coat on the floor because there was no room. I told Mom my idea, and she liked it. People helped me start the coat drive.*

2 PRACTICE/APPLY

- Write the following prompt on the board: *Write a personal narrative about a time when you did something that was very important to you.*
- Work with students to begin planning their own personal narratives by brainstorming a list of ideas, events, and details. Have them save their lists for use on Day 4.

Day 4 PREWRITE

❶ TEACH PLANNING A PERSONAL NARRATIVE

- Point out that descriptive details of a story should help to support the main idea.

- Remind students of the following events from "Darnell Rock Reporting."

  - Building violations were discussed at the meeting.

  - Teachers wanted to build a parking lot where Darnell thought the community garden should be.

- Ask: *Which detail helps support the main idea? Why? Teachers want to build a parking lot; it gives a reason why people opposed Darnell's plan and why it was a challenge.*

- Tell students that discussing building violations at the meeting set a mood in the story, but it does not support the main idea. Explain that descriptive details in a story should help support the main idea.

❷ PRACTICE/APPLY

- Review the brainstorming ideas that you developed with the class on Day 3. Display **Projectable 19.10.**

- Together, choose important events in the story. Model how to use the Flow Chart.

- Distribute **Graphic Organizer 4.** Have students complete Flow Charts for their personal narratives.

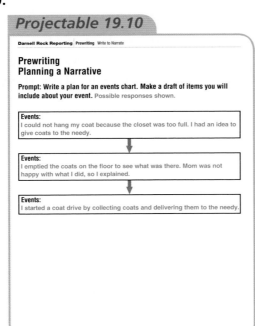

Projectable 19.10

Darnell Rock Reporting | Prewriting Write to Narrate

Prewriting
Planning a Narrative

Prompt: Write a plan for an events chart. Make a draft of items you will include about your event. Possible responses shown.

Events:
I could not hang my coat because the closet was too full. I had an idea to give coats to the needy.

⬇

Events:
I emptied the coats on the floor to see what was there. Mom was not happy with what I did, so I explained.

⬇

Events:
I started a coat drive by collecting coats and delivering them to the needy.

Day 5 PREWRITE

❶ TEACH PLANNING A PERSONAL NARRATIVE

- Tell students they will read how one writer explored a topic and planned his personal narrative.

- Read aloud **Student Book p. 500,** including the brainstorming ideas written by a student, Rama.

- Then read Rama's event chart on **p. 501.**

- Ask: *How did Rama organize his event chart so that it made sense to him? He answered questions to support his topic.*

❷ PRACTICE/APPLY

- Discuss students' responses to the *Reading as a Writer* questions on **Student Book p. 501.**

- Have students check their Flow Charts to be sure they have included details that support the main idea and thoughts and feelings about the event. Tell them to make any improvements needed.

Write to Narrate

☑ **Ideas** Good writers explore their ideas before they draft. You can collect your ideas for a **personal narrative** on an events chart. List the main events in the order they happened, and then add interesting details about each event.

Rama decided to write about his Warm Coat Project. First, he jotted down the notes below. Then he organized them in a chart.

Writing Process Checklist

▶ **Prewrite**
☑ Did I think about my audience and purpose?
☑ Did I choose a topic that I am eager to write about?
☑ Did I explore my topic to remember important events and interesting details?
☑ Did I list the events in the order in which they happened?

Draft

Revise

Edit

Publish and Share

500

Exploring a Topic

Topic:	my warm coat project
What?	coat wouldn't fit in closet
Why?	too many coats
	other people need coats
How?	persuaded family members
	did research on Internet
Where?	took coats to an agency

Events Chart

Event: Tried to hang my coat in the closet.
Details: The closet was too full. Left my coat on the floor. Mom told me to pick it up.

Event: Saw how many coats we don't wear. Got an idea. Give some to needy people.
Details: I put the coats in piles. Mom wasn't happy about the mess.

Event: Talked my family into giving coats to those who can't afford to buy them.
Details: First, I told Mom my idea. She loved it! Family agreed to choose coats to give away.

In my events chart, I organized my ideas into main events and details. I added a new event and some details.

Event: Found an agency on the Internet that gives away coats.
Details: We delivered the coats. We learned that many more were needed.

Event: Started a coat drive.
Details: Friends and relatives agreed to help out. Next year, will get help from my whole school.

Reading as a Writer

How did Rama organize his events chart? Which parts of your chart can you organize more clearly?

501

Writing Traits Scoring Rubric

	Focus/Ideas	☑ Organization	Voice	☑ Word Choice	☑ Sentence Fluency	Conventions
4	Adheres to the topic, is interesting, has a sense of completeness. Ideas are well developed.	Ideas and details are clearly presented and well organized.	Connects with reader in a unique, personal way.	Includes vivid verbs, strong adjectives, specific nouns.	Includes a variety of complete sentences that flow smoothly, naturally.	Shows a strong command of grammar, spelling, capitalization, punctuation.
3	Mostly adheres to the topic, is somewhat interesting, has a sense of completeness. Ideas are adequately developed.	Ideas and details are mostly clear and generally organized.	Generally connects with reader in a way that is personal and sometimes unique.	Includes some vivid verbs, strong adjectives, specific nouns.	Includes some variety of mostly complete sentences. Some parts flow smoothly, naturally.	Shows a good command of grammar, spelling, capitalization, punctuation.
2	Does not always adhere to the topic, has some sense of completeness. Ideas are superficially developed.	Ideas and details are not always clear or organized. There is some wordiness or repetition.	Connects somewhat with reader. Sounds somewhat personal, but not unique.	Includes mostly simple nouns and verbs, and may have a few adjectives.	Includes mostly simple sentences, some of which are incomplete.	Some errors in grammar, spelling, capitalization, punctuation.
1	Does not adhere to the topic, has no sense of completeness. Ideas are vague.	Ideas and details are not organized. Wordiness or repetition hinders meaning.	Does not connect with reader. Does not sound personal or unique.	Includes only simple nouns and verbs, some inaccurate. Writing is not descriptive.	Sentences do not vary. Incomplete sentences hinder meaning.	Frequent errors in grammar, spelling, capitalization, punctuation.

See also *Writing Rubric Blackline Master* and Teacher's Edition pp. R18–R21.

Progress Monitoring

Assess

- Weekly Tests
- Fluency Tests
- Periodic Assessments

☑ Vocabulary

Target Vocabulary
Strategies: Greek and Latin Suffixes *-ism, -ist, -able, -ible*

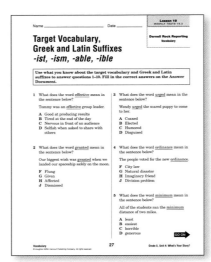

Weekly Tests 19.2–19.3

☑ Comprehension

Persuasion

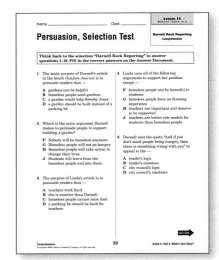

Weekly Tests 19.4–19.5

Respond to Assessment

IF	a Student Scores...	THEN...
	7–10 of 10	▶ Continue Core Instructional Program.
	4–6 of 10	▶ **Reteaching Lesson,** page T290
	1–3 of 10	▶ **Intervention** Lesson 19, pp. S32–S41

IF	a Student Scores...	THEN...
	7–10 of 10	▶ Continue Core Instructional Program.
	4–6 of 10	▶ **Reteaching Lesson,** page T290
	1–3 of 10	▶ **Intervention** Lesson 19, pp. S32–S41

Powered by DESTINATIONReading®
- Online Assessment System
- Weekly Tests

☑ Decoding
More Common Suffixes

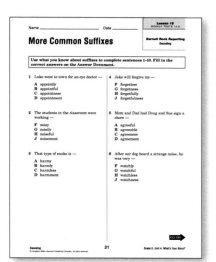

Weekly Tests 19.6–19.7

IF	a Student Scores...	THEN...
7–10 of 10	▶ Continue Core Instructional Program.
4–6 of 10	▶ **Reteaching Lesson,** page T291
1–3 of 10	▶ **Intervention** Lesson 19, pp. S32–S41

☑ Language Arts
Grammar: More Kinds of Pronouns

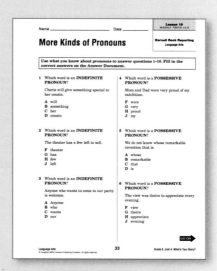

Weekly Tests 19.8–19.9

Writing Traits Rubrics
See TE pp. R18–R21.

IF	a Student Scores...	THEN...
7–10 of 10	▶ Continue Core Instructional Program.
4–6 of 10	▶ **Reteaching Lesson,** page T291
1–3 of 10	▶ **Intervention** Lesson 19, pp. S32–S41

☑ Fluency

Fluency Plan
Assess one group per week.
Use this suggested plan below.

●	Struggling Readers	Weeks 1, 3, 5
▲	On Level	Week 2
■	Advanced	Week 4

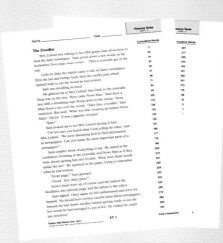

Fluency Record Form

Fluency Scoring Rubric
See *Grab-and-Go™ Resources Assessment* for help in measuring progress

✔ Progress Monitoring

Small Group

RUNNING RECORDS

To assess individual progress, occasionally use small group time to take a reading record for each student. Use the results to plan instruction.

● **Struggling Readers**

▲ **On Level**

■ **Advanced**

◆ **English Language Learners**

For running records, see
Grab and Go™ Resources: Lesson 19, pp. 13–16.

Behaviors and Understandings to Notice

- Self-corrects errors that detract from meaning.

- Self-corrects intonation when it does not reflect the meaning.

- Rereads to solve words and resumes normal rate of reading.

- Demonstrates phrased and fluent oral reading.

- Reads dialogue with expression.

- Demonstrates awareness of punctuation.

- Automatically solves most words in the text to read fluently.

- Demonstrates appropriate stress on words, pausing and phrasing, intonation, and use of punctuation.

- Reads orally at an appropriate rate.

Weekly
Small Group Instruction

 Day 1

Vocabulary Reader
- *From Parking Lot to Garden*, T280–T281

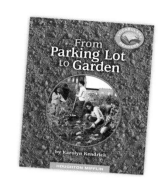

 Day 2

Differentiate Comprehension
- Target Skill: Persuasion, T282–T283
- Target Strategy: Summarize, T282–T283

 Day 3

Leveled Readers
- ● *The Big Interview*, T284
- ▲ *Saving the General*, T285
- ■ *Another View*, T286
- ◆ *The Old Tree*, T287

 Day 4

Differentiate Vocabulary Strategies
- Greek and Latin Suffixes *-ism, -ist, -able, -ible*, T288–T289

 Day 5

Options for Reteaching
- Vocabulary Strategies: Greek and Latin Suffixes *-ism, -ist, -able, -ible*, T290
- Comprehension Skill: Analyze and Evaluate Persuasion, T290
- Language Arts: More Kinds of Pronouns/ Write to Narrate, T291
- Decoding: More Common Suffixes, T291

Ready-Made Work Stations

Ready-Made Practice
- Comprehension and Fluency, T228
- Word Study, T228
- Think and Write, T229
- Digital Center, T229

Comprehension and Fluency

Word Study

Think and Write

Digital Center

Suggested Small Group Plan

		Day 1	Day 2	Day 3
Teacher-Led	**Struggling Readers**	**Vocabulary Reader** *From Parking Lot to Garden*, Differentiated Instruction, p. T280	**Differentiate Comprehension** Persuasion; Summarize, p. T282	**Leveled Reader** *The Big Interview*, p. T284
	On Level	**Vocabulary Reader** *From Parking Lot to Garden*, Differentiated Instruction, p. T280	**Differentiate Comprehension** Persuasion; Summarize, p. T282	**Leveled Reader** *Saving the General*, p. T285
	Advanced	**Vocabulary Reader** *From Parking Lot to Garden*, Differentiated Instruction, p. T281	**Differentiate Comprehension** Persuasion; Summarize, p. T283	**Leveled Reader** *Another View*, p. T286
	English Language Learners	**Vocabulary Reader** *From Parking Lot to Garden*, Differentiated Instruction, p. T281	**Differentiate Comprehension** Persuasion; Summarize, p. T283	**Leveled Reader** *The Old Tree*, p. T287
What are my other students doing?	**Struggling Readers**	**Reread** *From Parking Lot to Garden*	**Vocabulary in Context Cards** 181–190 *Talk It Over* Activities **Complete** Leveled Practice, SR19.1	**Listen** to Audiotext CD of "Darnell Rock Reporting"; Retell and discuss **Complete** Leveled Practice SR19.2
	On Level	**Reread** *From Parking Lot to Garden*	**Reread** "Darnell Rock Reporting" with a partner **Complete** Practice Book p. 217	**Reread** for Fluency: *Saving the General* **Complete** Practice Book p. 218
	Advanced	**Vocabulary in Context Cards** 181–190 *Talk It Over* Activities	**Reread and Retell** "Darnell Rock Reporting" **Complete** Leveled Practice A19.1	**Reread** for Fluency: *Another View* **Complete** Leveled Practice A19.2
	English Language Learners	**Reread** *From Parking Lot to Garden*	**Listen** to Audiotext CD of "Darnell Rock Reporting"; Retell and discuss **Complete** Leveled Practice ELL19.1	**Vocabulary in Context Cards** 181–190 *Talk It Over* Activities **Complete** Leveled Practice ELL19.2

Ready-Made Work Stations

Assign these activities across the week to reinforce and extend learning.

Comprehension and Fluency
Phrasing Frenzy

Word Study
Choose Your Ending

Day 4

Differentiate Vocabulary Strategies
Greek and Latin Suffixes *-ism, -ist, -able, -ible*, p. T288

Differentiate Vocabulary Strategies
Greek and Latin Suffixes *-ism, -ist, -able, -ible*, p. T288

Differentiate Vocabulary Strategies
Greek and Latin Suffixes *-ism, -ist, -able, -ible*, p. T289

Differentiate Vocabulary Strategies
Greek and Latin Suffixes *-ism, -ist, -able, -ible*, p. T289

Partners: Reread for Fluency: *The Big Interview*
Complete Leveled Practice SR19.3

Vocabulary in Context Cards
181–190
Talk It Over Activities
Complete Practice Book p. 219

Reread for Fluency: "Darnell Rock Reporting"
Complete Leveled Practice A19.3

Partners: Reread for Fluency: *The Old Tree*
Complete Leveled Practice ELL19.3

Think and Write
Here's My Story

Day 5

Options for Reteaching,
pp. T290–T291

Options for Reteaching,
pp. T290–T291

Options for Reteaching,
pp. T290–T291

Options for Reteaching,
pp. T290–T291

Reread for Fluency: "Darnell Rock Reporting"
Complete Work Station activities
Independent Reading

Complete Work Station activities
Independent Reading

Complete Work Station activities
Independent Reading

Complete Work Station activities

Reread *From Parking Lot to Garden* or "Darnell Rock Reporting"
Complete Work Station activities

JOURNEYS DIGITAL Powered by **DESTINATION**Reading
Digital Center

Weekly To-Do List

This Weekly To-Do List helps students see their own progress and move on to additional activities independently.

Reading Log

Vocabulary Reader

From Parking Lot to Garden

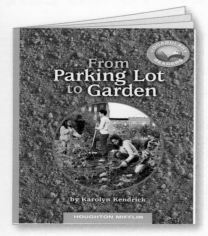

Summary

Community gardens allow people to garden, care for the Earth, and help feed the homeless. Students will learn how community gardens are created and who takes care of them.

✔ **TARGET VOCABULARY**

issue	effective
deteriorating	urge
dependent	violations
exception	ordinance
granted	minimum

Struggling Readers

- Explain to students that community gardens are often created on empty city lots. They allow people who may not have a backyard the chance to garden.

- Guide students to preview the **Vocabulary Reader**. Read aloud the headings. Ask students to describe the images, using Target Vocabulary when possible.

- Have students alternate reading pages of the text aloud. Guide them to use context clues to determine the meanings of unfamiliar words. As necessary, use the **Vocabulary in Context Card**s to review the meanings of vocabulary words.

- Assign the **Responding Page** and **Blackline Master 19.1**. Have partners work together to complete the pages.

On Level

- Explain to students that community gardens often help the environment by bringing plants and wildlife to urban areas. Guide students to preview the **Vocabulary Reader**.

- Remind students that context clues can help them determine the meaning of an unknown word. Tell students to use context clues to confirm their understanding of Target Vocabulary and to learn the meanings of new words.

- Have partners alternate reading pages of the text aloud. Tell them to use context clues to determine the meanings of unknown words.

- Assign the **Responding Page** and **Blackline Master 19.1**. Have students discuss their responses with a partner.

Advanced

- Have students preview the **Vocabulary Reader** and make predictions about what they will read, using information from their preview and prior knowledge.

- Remind students to use context clues to help them determine the meanings of unknown words.

- Tell students to read the text with a partner. Ask them to stop and discuss the meanings of unknown words as necessary.

- Assign the **Responding Page** and **Blackline Master 19.1**. For the Write About It activity, remind students to use facts and details to support their ideas. Ask students to describe the type of crops that could be planted in a community garden to benefit the homeless.

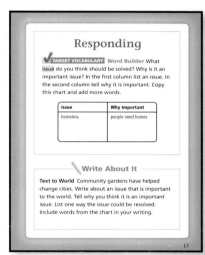

From Parking Lot to Garden,
p. 15

ELL English Language Learners

Group English Language Learners according to language proficiency.

Beginning

Go through the book with students, naming things in the illustrations and using the Target Vocabulary when possible. Then read the book together.

Advanced

Have students choose two events that occur in *From Parking Lot to Garden*. Have students restate each event using one of the Vocabulary words.

Intermediate

Give sentence frames using the Target Vocabulary, and have students complete them orally. Read the selection together. Ask simple questions about the story. Expand students' one-word answers and have them repeat the complete sentences.

Advanced High

Have students reread *From Parking Lot to Garden*. Have them find sentences that use the Target Vocabulary. Have them then write a synonym for as many Target Vocabulary words as they can.

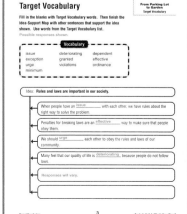

Blackline Master 19.1

Differentiate Comprehension

 Persuasion; Summarize

Struggling Readers

I DO IT

- The goal of a persuasive text is to get readers to think or act in a certain way. Authors (or their characters) use words and facts as reasons to support their ideas.

- Read aloud **p. 482** and model summarizing Darnell's argument. Point out clue words such as *should* and *because*.

> **Think Aloud** *Darnell thinks the basketball court should become a garden because it will help the homeless.*

WE DO IT

- Have students read **p. 483** of the selection.

- Have them identify what the main argument is on this page and who is making it.

- Have students identify the reasons given to support the main argument.

- Write students' reasons on the board. Help them use the list to summarize the passage.

YOU DO IT

- Have students fill in an Idea-Support Map for either Darnell's or Linda's argument.

- Have them take turns summarizing the two positions.

- Point out that listing the main point and reasons forms an effective summary of the argument.

On Level

I DO IT

- Explain that an author's (or character's) presentation may use assumptions to persuade.

- Read aloud **p. 482** of the selection.

- Model determining Darnell's argument by creating an Idea-Support Map.

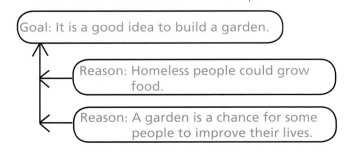

WE DO IT

- Have students read **p. 483** of the selection.

- Have a volunteer identify one of Linda's assumptions.

- Work with the class to complete an Idea-Support Map based on Linda's position.

YOU DO IT

- Have student pairs add boxes to the map to list more assumptions and supporting details Linda makes in her argument.

- Encourage pairs to decide how Linda's assumptions affect her argument.

- Have volunteer pairs use their completed Idea-Support Maps to summarize Linda's argument for the class.

Advanced

I DO IT	**WE DO IT**	**YOU DO IT**
• Read the first half of **p. 490** aloud.	• Have students read **pp. 490–491** independently. Ask:	• Have student pairs analyze how Darnell develops his argument and how effective it is by completing an Idea-Support Map. Point out that he does not need to win to present an effective argument.
• Point out that support can be strong or weak, emotional or logical. Explain that telling fact from opinion will help readers determine if an author's (or character's) support is strong.	• *What is Darnell's main argument? Seeing homeless people doing good might be a good example to kids.*	• Have pairs note Darnell's emotional reasoning and explain its effect.
• Point out that Darnell summarizes his own life experiences to persuade his audience.	• *Why is this an emotional argument? because people have different opinions about the kids Darnell wants to help*	• Invite students to model how they used the Summarize strategy to complete their Idea-Support Maps.

ELL English Language Learners

Group English Language Learners according to language proficiency. Review Persuasion with students. Draw an Idea-Support Map on the board. Then reread with students "Darnell Rock Reporting" and work together to complete the map with the goals and reasons cited in the selection. Choose one of the following activities for additional support, as appropriate.

Beginning	**Intermediate**	**Advanced**	**Advanced High**
Review the meaning of *persuade* and read the passage on **p. 490** aloud. Ask: *Does Darnell want to persuade the council to vote for the garden? yes How can he persuade them? by giving good reasons*	Read aloud **p. 490** and have students follow along. Ask: *Does Darnell want to persuade the council that a garden will be good or bad? good Why does Darnell believe this? He thinks it will help the homeless and the kids at school.*	Have students read **p. 490** and identify what Darnell wants to persuade people to do. Then have partners take turns identifying and writing down the information that Darnell provides to support his argument.	Have students work in pairs to summarize what Darnell wants to persuade the council to do in this selection. They should state Darnell's reasons and whether or not they effectively support his position.

TARGET SKILL

Persuasion

TARGET STRATEGY

Summarize

TARGET VOCABULARY

issue	effective
deteriorating	urge
dependent	violations
exception	ordinance
granted	minimum

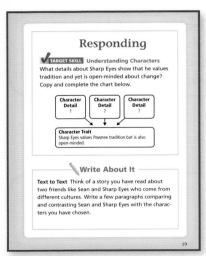

The Big Interview, p. 19

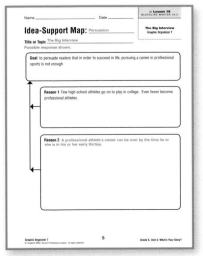

Blackline Master 19.3

Leveled Readers

Struggling Readers

 ### *The Big Interview*

GENRE: REALISTIC FICTION

SUMMARY Brenda Taylor cannot wait for her interview with Rashad Fuller, the star linebacker for the Blue Bay Pelicans. Brenda is surprised to learn that Rashad's role model isn't an athlete, but someone Brenda knows well.

Introducing the Text

- Explain that athletes often have short careers and must train for another career once they can no longer compete.

- Remind students that using a graphic organizer will help them organize the reasons the author gives to support her attempts to persuade.

Supporting the Reading

- As you listen to students read, pause to discuss these questions.

PERSUASION pp. 4–5 *Why does Brenda's father encourage her to find other role models besides athletes? He wants his children to develop their minds, not just their bodies.*

SUMMARIZE p. 6 *Why did the athlete, Arthur Ashe, encourage students to have doctors, engineers, and teachers as role models? Few people can be professional athletes. If students study hard and set high goals, these careers could be possibilities for them.*

Discussing and Revisiting the Text

CRITICAL THINKING After discussing *The Big Interview*, have students read the instructions on **Responding p. 19**. Use these points as students revisit the text.

- Have partners identify the author's goal.

- Have them list reasons for the author's opinion and enter them on **Blackline Master 19.3**. Have them explain how the reasons support the larger goal.

- Distribute **Blackline Master 19.7** to develop students' critical thinking skills.

FLUENCY: STRESS Have partners practice reading paragraph three on p. 5 to each other. They should listen for appropriate stress of syllables.

On Level

▲ *Saving the General*

GENRE: REALISTIC FICTION

SUMMARY Gardener Academy is in desperate need of a new auditorium. When students learn that the "General," an oak tree that dates back to the Civil War, will have to be cut down to build it, the school becomes divided over building the auditorium or saving the old tree.

Introducing the Text

- Explain that a writer might sign articles with a pen name, or fake name, to keep his or her identity private. In the story, P. Pod is a pen name.

- A good persuasive writer can show how both sides will benefit from the suggested solution.

Supporting the Reading

- As you listen to students read, pause to discuss these questions.

PERSUASION p. 6 *What are the benefits of building a new auditorium according to P. Pod? The existing auditorium will soon violate building rules. The curtains and spotlights don't work, the floorboards are squeaky, and the acoustics are poor.*

SUMMARIZE pp. 14–15 *Summarize Elena's suggestions for how to build the new auditorium. The auditorium could be built on the opposite side of the building away from the tree, making it more convenient for parking, causing fewer disruptions to classes during construction and adding more conveniences for students.*

Discussing and Revisiting the Text

CRITICAL THINKING After discussing *Saving the General*, have students read **Responding p. 19**. Use these points as students revisit the text.

- Have students identify the author's goal and write it on **Blackline Master 19.4**. Have them list the reasons for the author's opinion and explain why the supporting reasons may benefit everyone.

- Distribute **Blackline Master 19.8** to develop students' critical thinking skills.

FLUENCY: STRESS Have students practice reading aloud their favorite part of *Saving the General* with appropriate stress.

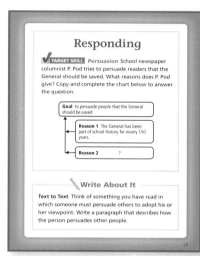

Savng the General, p. 19

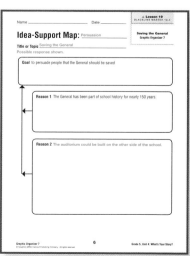

Blackline Master 19.4

Targets for Lesson 19

✓ **TARGET SKILL**

Persuasion

✓ **TARGET STRATEGY**

Summarize

✓ **TARGET VOCABULARY**

issue	effective
deteriorating	urge
dependent	violations
exception	ordinance
granted	minimum

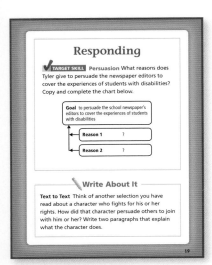

Responding

✓ **TARGET SKILL** Persuasion What reasons does Tyler give to persuade the newspaper editors to cover the experiences of students with disabilities? Copy and complete the chart below.

> **Goal** to persuade the school newspaper's editors to cover the experiences of students with disabilities
>
> Reason 1   ?
> Reason 2   ?

Write About It

Text to Text Think of another selection you have read about a character who fights for his or her rights. How did that character persuade others to join with him or her? Write two paragraphs that explain what the character does.

Another View, p. 19

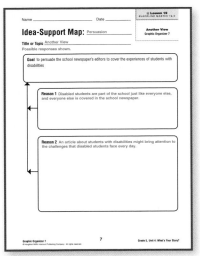

Blackline Master 19.5

Leveled Readers

Advanced

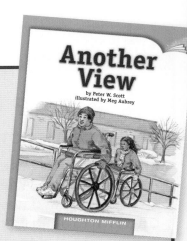

■ *Another View*

GENRE: REALISTIC FICTION

Summary When Tyler Chen notices that the school newspaper doesn't have any articles about students with disabilities, like himself, he decides to write a letter to the editor. The school takes notice when Chantel, a reporter, decides to experience life in a wheelchair.

Introducing the Text

- Explain that although buildings have to be handicapped accessible, some places meet only the minimum requirements, making it difficult for someone in a wheelchair to get around.

- Remind students that a good persuasive writer will show why his or her ideas are the best choice by including valid reasons.

Supporting the Reading

- As you listen to students read, pause to discuss these questions.

PERSUASION pp. 4–5 *What reasons does Tyler give for why the newspaper should include articles about disabled students? Disabled students are active in many school activities that would interest others.*

SUMMARIZE pp. 14–15 *Briefly summarize the hardships Chantel encounters using a wheelchair. She finds it challenging keeping up with Tyler and having to take longer routes to classes. Her mittens were wet from touching the wheels since there were puddles and slush to go through.*

Discussing and Revisiting the Text

CRITICAL THINKING After discussing *Another View*, have students read the instructions on **Responding p. 19**. Use these points as students revisit the text.

- Have students identify the author's goal and write it on **Blackline Master 19.5**. Have them list reasons that support the author's opinions.

- Distribute **Blackline Master 19.9 t**o develop students' critical thinking skills.

FLUENCY: STRESS Have students practice reading their favorite parts aloud with correct syllable stress.

JOURNEYS DIGITAL | Powered by DESTINATION Reading®
Leveled Readers Online

The Old Tree

written by Jane Shaffer
illustrated by Pamela Johnson

HOUGHTON MIFFLIN

ELL English Language Learners

◆ The Old Tree

GENRE: REALISTIC FICTION

Summary Gardener Academy needs a new auditorium. Then students learn that the "General," a favorite oak tree that dates back to the Civil War, will have to be cut down to build it. The school becomes divided over what to do.

Introducing the Text

- Explain that a newspaper opinion columnist with a hidden identity allows the students at Gardener Academy to see both sides of an important issue.

- Remind students that using a graphic organizer will help them record reasons the author gives for supporting his or her opinion.

Supporting the Reading

- As you listen to students read, pause to discuss these questions.

PERSUASION p. 8 *What is one reason why Beth believes the* "General" *should be saved? Trees help keep the air clean.*

SUMMARIZE p. 16 *After Elena describes how the new auditorium can be built without destroying the* "General," *what do we learn about her? She is the anonymous writer, P. Pod.*

Discussing and Revisiting the Text

CRITICAL THINKING After discussing *The Old Tree*, have students read the instructions on **Responding p. 19**. Use these points as students revisit the text.

- Have students work individually or in pairs to identify P. Pod's goal.

- Have students write P. Pod's goal on **Blackline Master 19.6**. Then have them list two reasons for P. Pod's opinion in the boxes below.

- Distribute **Blackline Master 19.10** to develop students' critical thinking skills.

FLUENCY: STRESS Have partners practice reading the article on p. 9 of *The Old Tree* to each other. They should listen for correct enunciation and stress of syllables.

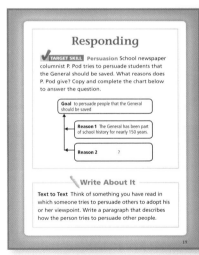

Responding

✔ **TARGET SKILL** Persuasion School newspaper columnist P. Pod tries to persuade students that the General should be saved. What reasons does P. Pod give? Copy and complete the chart below to answer the question.

Goal to persuade people that the General should be saved

Reason 1 The General has been part of school history for nearly 150 years.

Reason 2 ?

Write About It

Text to Text Think of something you have read in which someone tries to persuade others to adopt his or her viewpoint. Write a paragraph that describes how the person tries to persuade other people.

The Old Tree, p. 19

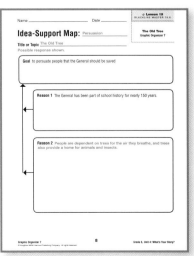

Name _____ Date _____

Lesson 19
BLACKLINE MASTER 19.6

Idea-Support Map: Persuasion

The Old Tree
Graphic Organizer 7

Title or Topic The Old Tree
Possible response shown.

Goal to persuade people that the General should be saved

Reason 1 The General has been part of school history for nearly 150 years.

Reason 2 People are dependent on trees for the air they breathe, and trees also provide a home for animals and insects.

Blackline Master 19.6

Differentiate Vocabulary Strategies ☑ Greek and Latin Suffixes

Struggling Readers

I DO IT

- Remind students that a suffix is a word part added to the end of a base word. The suffix changes the base word's meaning.

- Tell students that Greek suffixes include *–ism* and *–ist*, and Latin suffixes include *–able* and *–ible*.

- Write on the board that *–ism* means "a belief in," or "state of," *–ist* means "one who does or is," and *–able* and *–ible* mean "capable or worthy of an action."

WE DO IT

- Write the following word pairs on the board: *art/artist; agree/agreeable; value/valuable; sense/sensible*.

- Have students read the words aloud. Guide them to note how word meaning changes after each suffix is added.

- Work with students to use each of the words in a sentence.

  > We went to a museum to see **art**.
  >
  > Which **artist** do you like best?

YOU DO IT

- Have students write the words *violinist, agreeable, valuable, flexible, tourism,* and *tourist*.

- Have partners write a sentence for each word above.

- Have partners circle the suffix and identify it as Greek or Latin.

- Make sure students check their spelling.

On Level

I DO IT

- Remind students that a suffix is a word part added to the end of a base word. The suffix changes the base word's meaning and sometimes its spelling.

- Tell students that Greek suffixes include *–ism* and *–ist*, and Latin suffixes include *–able* and *–ible*.

- Write on the board that *–ism* means "a belief in," or "state of," *–ist* means "one who does or is," and *–able* and *–ible* mean "capable or worthy of an action."

WE DO IT

- Write the following word pairs on the board: *art/artist; patriot/patriotism; agree/agreeable; sense/sensible*.

- Have volunteers read a word pair aloud, and note how the suffix changes one word's meaning. *An artist is a person who makes art; patriotism is a belief in love for one's country; something agreeable is capable of agreeing; something sensible is capable of having sense.*

- Ask for more examples of words using these suffixes.

YOU DO IT

- Have students work in pairs to find more words with the suffixes *–ism, –ist, –able,* and *–ible*. *Sample answers: pianist, tourism, inseparable, visible*

- Have pairs write definitions for each of the new words.

- Have them label the suffixes as Greek or Latin.

- Make sure students check their spelling.

Advanced

I DO IT

- Remind students that a suffix is a word part added to the end of a base word. The suffix changes the base word's meaning and sometimes its spelling.

- Tell students that Greek suffixes include –ism and –ist, and Latin suffixes include –able and –ible.

- Write on the board that –ism means "a belief in," or "state of," –ist means "one who does or is," and –able and –ible mean "capable or worthy of an action."

WE DO IT

- Write on the board the following words and have a volunteer read them aloud: *active, activist, activism, tour, tourist, tourism, enjoy, enjoyable, tolerate, tolerable, sense, sensible.*

- Have students identify the suffixes and then tell you the definitions of each word. *Sample: an activist is a person who is active for a cause; activism is belief in a cause.*

YOU DO IT

- Have students work to write sentences using words with the Greek and Latin suffixes.

- They should brainstorm words that were not discussed in class. Have students share their sentences with the class.

- Students should identify whether the suffixes used are Latin or Greek.

- Make sure students check their spelling.

ELL English Language Learners

Group English Learners according to language proficiency. Write –ism = "belief in" or "state of"; –ist = "one who does or is"; –able and –ible = "capable or worthy of an action."

Beginning

Display a picture of a violin. Ask: *What is this? violin* Display a picture of a person playing a violin. Ask: *Who is this? a violinist* Tell students that *violinist* means *someone who plays the violin.* Repeat the exercise using other examples.

Intermediate

Ask students: *What or who is a patriot? someone who loves their country* Ask: *What is patriotism? the state of loving one's country* Write: *Our trip to the art museum was enjoyable. I loved the paintings by the artists there.* Have students define *enjoyable* and *artist.*

Advanced

Have students write a sentence using a word with each of the following Greek and Latin suffixes: *– ism, –ist, –able, –ible.* Have students identify whether each suffix is Greek or Latin and tell how the suffix changes the meanings of the base words.

Advanced High

Have students use the **Vocabulary in Context Cards** to identify which words could be modified to add the suffix –able. *dependable, exceptionable* Have them write sentences using the new words. Then have them write a short paragraph using each of the suffixes taught.

 # Options for Reteaching

Vocabulary Strategies

✔ Greek and Latin Suffixes

I DO IT

- Remind students that suffixes are word parts added to the end of a word, that change the meaning of the word.
- List the following suffixes on the board: *-ism, -ist, -able, -ible*.
- Tell students that the suffixes *–ism* and *–ist* are Greek, and the suffixes *–able and -ible* are Latin.

WE DO IT

- Work together to list words with Greek and Latin suffixes.
- Have volunteers come to the board and circle the base words.
- Model how to look up each word in the dictionary and note the etymology of the word.

> **Think Aloud** *I'll look up the word* accessible *and see what its etymology, or origin, is. I see that after the dictionary entry shows me the pronunciation and the part of speech, it puts in brackets* Late Latin - accessibilis. *This tells me* accessible *came from the Latin language.*

YOU DO IT

- Have partners work together to create a list of words using the suffixes *-ism, -ist, -able,* and *-ible*.
- Have them apply what they have learned about suffixes to determine the meanings of the words.
- Have students use dictionaries to verify their answers.

Comprehension Skill

✔ Analyze and Evaluate Persuasion

I DO IT

- Remind students that persuasive texts are written by authors who want to convince readers to think or act in a certain way.
- Remind students that authors have stated goals. Authors may support their goals, or arguments, with reliable facts, examples, and details. Readers must identify when and how authors try to persuade them.

WE DO IT

- Have students reread the first paragraph of Linda's article on **Student Book p. 483** aloud and identify Linda's goal and persuasive technique.
- Model how to identify Linda's reasoning and the persuasive technique she uses.

> **Think Aloud** *Linda gives only one reason for building a parking lot, and that's to support teachers. I think it is her persuasive technique to get readers to think that they must support teachers as they are the key to a good education. Her technique is to shift the focus to what teachers need.*

YOU DO IT

- Distribute **Graphic Organizer 7.**
- Have students list reasons for Linda's argument. *A parking lot would support teachers; teachers deserve support; homeless people can't farm anyway and don't help the school.*
- Have student pairs complete the graphic organizer.
- Review completed graphic organizers.

Language Arts

 # More Kinds of Pronouns/Write to Narrate

I DO IT

- Remind students a pronoun takes the place of a noun.
- List the following pronouns on the board: *my, somebody, which.* Model using the pronouns in sentences.

Think Aloud *My is a possessive pronoun. It shows ownership. Example:* My dog likes to go for a walk. *An indefinite pronoun takes the place of a noun, but doesn't show specifically which noun. Example:* Somebody donated money to the school. *An interrogative pronoun is used to ask a question. Example:* Which sweater do you like best?

WE DO IT

- Work together to write sentences with pronouns.
- Guide students to identify the pronoun in each sentence. Have them tell you if the pronoun is indefinite, possessive, or interrogative.
- Have partners work together to write sentences using pronouns. Have them identify the kind of pronoun in each sentence.

YOU DO IT

- Have pairs of students write three sentences using one type of pronoun in each sentence.
- Invite students to read their sentences aloud and explain to other students why they used each pronoun.

Decoding

 # More Common Suffixes

I DO IT

- Remind students that there is sometimes a spelling change to a base word when a suffix is added.
- Some common suffixes are *-ful, -ly, -ness, -less, -ment.* Write on the board: *They built a settlement near the river.*

Think Aloud *In the word* settlement, *I recognize the common suffix* -ment *and the base word* settle.

WE DO IT

- Write *watchful, countless, steadily,* and *closeness* on the board.
- Help students decode each word.
- Have volunteers circle the base word in each word on the board. Discuss whether the spelling of the base word changes when a suffix is added.

YOU DO IT

- Ask partners to find and decode other words using suffixes in "Darnell Rock Reporting."
- Use the **Corrective Feedback** on p. T259 if students need additional help.

Teacher Notes

Preteaching for Success!

Comprehension:

Understanding Characters

Tell students that understanding the characters helps them understand the whole story.

- Review with students that understanding characters requires paying attention to what they say, think, and do.
- To illustrate the concept, help students fill in the graphic organizer on Student Book p. 506. Think of a character from a familiar book. Brainstorm the character's thoughts and actions and put them in the corresponding columns in the chart. Add the character's words, from memory or paraphrased, to the Words column.

Challenge Yourself!

Research Knights in Armor

After reading the selection "Don Quixote and the Windmills," have students research knights of medieval times.

- Review with students that knights were warriors in the Middle Ages. They are associated with chivalry which means "they were courageous, honorable, and loyal."
- Have students read more about the Middle Ages and the role knights played.
- Have students draw pictures or diagrams of knights' suits of armor. Tell them to label the parts and write paragraphs about why the knights needed armor.

Short Response

W.5.4 Produce clear and coherent writing in which the development and organization are appropriate to task, purpose, and audience.

Write a story about a time you imagined that something could happen, and then it did. Your story should include characters and dialogue.

Scoring Guidelines

Excellent	Student has written a story on the topic with characters and dialogue.
Good	Student has written a story on the topic with either characters or dialogue but not both.
Fair	Student has written a story on the topic but has not included characters or dialogue.
Unsatisfactory	Student has not written a story.

Writing Minilesson

Skill: Write to Narrate—Personal Narrative

Teach: Explain to students that a personal narrative can be long or short.

Thinking Beyond the Text

Writing Prompt: Write a two-paragraph narrative about an adventure you once had.

1. Brainstorm about the adventures students have experienced. Ask each student to choose one adventure.
2. Remind students to use contractions correctly.
3. Tell students to write their narratives in their own voice and in the first person.

Group Share: Have students put their adventure stories in a binder for the class to read.

Cross-Curricular Activity: Science

Identify Types of Machines

The selection tells of Don Quixote's fight with the windmill. Have students research how a windmill works. How are the blades used? How is energy harnessed? Ask students to think of other ways that the wind is used to power things.

Reading Standards for Literature K–5

Key Ideas and Details

RL.5.1 Quote accurately from a text when explaining what the text says explicitly and when drawing inferences from the text.

RL.5.2 Determine a theme of a story, drama, or poem from details in the text, including how characters in a story or drama respond to challenges or how the speaker in a poem reflects upon a topic; summarize the text.*

RL.5.3 Compare and contrast two or more characters, settings, or events in a story or drama, drawing on specific details in the text (e.g., how characters interact).*

Craft and Structure

RL.5.4 Determine the meaning of words and phrases as they are used in a text, including figurative language such as metaphors and similes.

RL.5.5 Explain how a series of chapters, scenes, or stanzas fits together to provide the overall structure of a particular story, drama, or poem.*

Integration of Knowledge and Ideas

RL.5.9 Compare and contrast stories in the same genre (e.g., mysteries and adventure stories) on their approaches to similar themes and topics.

Reading Standards: Foundational Skills K–5

Phonics and Word Recognition

RF.5.3a Use combined knowledge of all letter-sound correspondences, syllabication patterns, and morphology (e.g., roots and affixes) to read accurately unfamiliar multisyllabic words in context and out of context.

Fluency

RF.5.4b Read grade-level prose and poetry orally with accuracy, appropriate rate, and expression.

Writing Standards K–5

Text Types and Purposes

W.5.3a Orient the reader by establishing a situation and introducing a narrator and/or characters; organize an event sequence that unfolds naturally.

W.5.3b Use narrative techniques, such as dialogue, description, and pacing, to develop experiences and events or show the responses of characters to situations.

W.5.3c Use a variety of transitional words, phrases, and clauses to manage the sequence of events.*

W.5.3d Use concrete words and phrases and sensory details to convey experiences and events precisely.

W.5.3e Provide a conclusion that follows from the narrated experiences or events.

Production and Distribution of Writing

W.5.4 Produce clear and coherent writing in which the development and organization are appropriate to task, purpose, and audience. (Grade-specific expectations for writing types are defined in standards 1–3 above.)

W.5.5 With guidance and support from peers and adults, develop and strengthen writing as needed by planning, revising, editing, rewriting, or trying a new approach.

W.5.6 With some guidance and support from adults, use technology, including the Internet, to produce and publish writing as well as to interact and collaborate with others; demonstrate sufficient command of keyboarding skills to type a minimum of two pages in a single sitting.

Research to Build and Present Knowledge

W.5.7 Conduct short research projects that use several sources to build knowledge through investigation of different aspects of a topic.

W.5.8 Recall relevant information from experiences or gather relevant information from print and digital sources; summarize or paraphrase information in notes and finished work, and provide a list of sources.

W.5.9a Apply *grade 5 Reading standards* to literature (e.g., "Compare and contrast two or more characters, settings, or events in a story or a drama, drawing on specific details in the text [e.g., how characters interact]").

Speaking & Listening Standards K–5

Comprehension and Collaboration

SL.5.1c Pose and respond to specific questions by making comments that contribute to the discussion and elaborate on the remarks of others.

Presentation of Knowledge and Ideas

SL.5.4 Report on a topic or text or present an opinion, sequencing ideas logically and using appropriate facts and relevant, descriptive details to support main ideas or themes; speak clearly at an understandable pace.

SL.5.5 Include multimedia components (e.g., graphics, sound) and visual displays in presentations when appropriate to enhance the development of main ideas or themes.

SL.5.6 Adapt speech to a variety of contexts and tasks, using formal English when appropriate to task and situation. (See grade 5 Language standards 1 and 3 on pages 28 and 29 for specific expectations.)*

Language Standards K–5

Conventions of Standard English

L.5.1a Explain the function of conjunctions, prepositions, and interjections in general and their function in particular sentences.*

Knowledge of Language

L.5.3b Compare and contrast the varieties of English (e.g., dialects, registers) used in stories, dramas, or poems.

Vocabulary Acquisition and Use

L.5.5b Recognize and explain the meaning of common idioms, adages, and proverbs.

L.5.6 Acquire and use accurately grade-appropriate general academic and domain-specific words and phrases, including those that signal contrast, addition, and other logical relationships (e.g., *however, although, nevertheless, similarly, moreover, in addition*).*

* Extending the Common Core State Standards

SUGGESTIONS FOR BALANCED LITERACY

Use *Journeys* materials to support a Readers' Workshop approach. See the Lesson 20 resources on pages 28, 78–79.

Lesson 20

Focus Wall

Main Selection:
"Don Quixote and the Windmills"

Connect to Social Studies:
"LitBeat: Live from La Mancha"

Big 💡 Idea
Everyone has a story to tell.

❓ Essential Question
How do the beliefs of a character affect a story?

Comprehension

 **TARGET SKILL**

Understanding Characters

 **TARGET STRATEGY**

Question

Spelling

Words from Other Languages

salsa	siesta
mattress	cargo
tycoon	vanilla
burrito	tsunami
bandana	iguana
tomato	plaza
poncho	caravan
dungarees	hammock
lasso	pajamas
patio	gallant

Fluency

Accuracy

Grammar

Contractions

Writing

Write to Narrate

Focus Trait:
Voice

Decoding

Stress in Three-Syllable Words

Vocabulary Strategies

Idioms

▼ TARGET VOCABULARY

antique	quests
plagued	noble
pierced	ignorance
thrust	faithful
transformed	exploits

Key Skills This Week

Target Skill:
Understanding Characters

Target Strategy:
Question

Vocabulary Strategies:
Idioms

Fluency:
Accuracy

Decoding:
Stress in Three-Syllable Words

Research Skill:
Paraphrasing vs. Plagiarism

Grammar:
Contractions

Spelling:
Words from Other Languages

Writing:
Write to Narrate:
Personal Narrative

✔ Assess/Monitor

☑ **Vocabulary**
p. T346

☑ **Comprehension**
p. T346

☑ **Decoding**
p. T347

☑ **Fluency**
p. T347

☑ **Language Arts**
p. T347

Whole Group

READING

Paired Selections

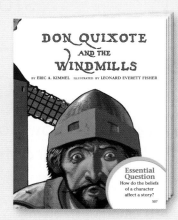

"Don Quixote and the Windmills"
HUMOROUS FICTION
Student Book, pp. 506–516

Accelerated Reader
Practice Quizzes for the Selection

"LitBeat: Live from La Mancha"
SOCIAL STUDIES PLAY
Student Book, pp. 518–521

Vocabulary

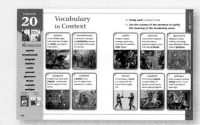

Student Book, pp. 502–503

Background & Comprehension

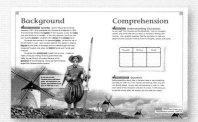

Student Book, pp. 504–505

LANGUAGE ARTS

Grammar
Student Book, pp. 522–523

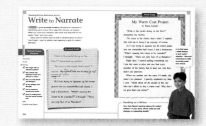

Writing
Student Book, pp. 524–525

Small Group

See pages T354–T355 for Suggested Small Group Plan.

TEACHER-LED

Leveled Readers

 Struggling Readers

▲ **On Level**

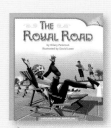

■ **Advanced**

◆ **English Language Learners**

Vocabulary Reader

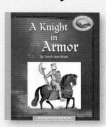

WHAT MY OTHER STUDENTS ARE DOING

Ready-Made Work Stations

Word Study

Think and Write

Comprehension and Fluency

Digital Center

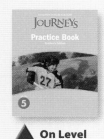

● **Struggling Readers**

■ **Advanced**

◆ **English Language Learners**

▲ **On Level**

Grab-and-Go!

Lesson 20 Blackline Master
- Target Vocabulary 20.1
- Selection Summary 20.2
- Graphic Organizer 20.3–20.6 ●▲■◆
- Critical Thinking 20.7–20.10 ●▲■◆
- Running Records 20.11–20.14 ●▲■◆
- Test Power 20.15
- Weekly Tests 20.1–20.9

Graphic Organizer Transparency 1

Additional Resources
- Genre: Fiction, p. 4
- Reading Log, p. 12
- Vocabulary Log, p. 13
- Listening Log, p. 14
- Proofreading Checklist, p. 15
- Proofreading Marks, p. 16
- Writing Conference Form, p. 17
- Writing Rubric, p. 18
- Instructional Routines, pp. 19–26
- Graphic Organizer 1: Column Chart, p. 27

JOURNEYS DIGITAL Powered by DESTINATION Reading

For Students
- Student eBook
- Comprehension Expedition CD-ROM
- Leveled Readers Online
- WriteSmart CD-ROM

For Teachers
- Online TE and Focus Wall
- Online Assessment System
- Teacher One-Stop
- Destination Reading Instruction

Intervention

STRATEGIC INTERVENTION: TIER II

Use these materials to provide additional targeted instruction for students who need Tier II strategic intervention.

Supports the Student Book selections

Interactive Work-text for Skills Support

Write-In Reader:

The Tale of the Unlucky Knight

- Engaging selection connects to main topic.
- Reinforces this week's target vocabulary and comprehension skill and strategy.
- Opportunities for student interaction on each page.

Assessment

Progress monitoring every two weeks.

For this week's Strategic Intervention lessons, see Teacher's Edition pages S42–S51.

INTENSIVE INTERVENTION: TIER III

- The materials in the Literacy Tool Kit help you provide a different approach for students who need Tier III intensive intervention.
- Interactive lessons provide focused instruction in key reading skills, targeted at students' specific needs.
- Lesson cards are convenient for small-group or individual instruction.
- Blackline masters provide additional practice.
- A leveled book accompanies each lesson to give students opportunities for additional reading and skill application.
- Assessments for each lesson help you evaluate the effectiveness of the intervention.

Lessons provide support for

- Phonics and Word Study Skills
- Vocabulary
- Comprehension Skills and Literary Genres
- Fluency

ELL English Language Learners

JOURNEYS DIGITAL — Powered by DESTINATIONReading®
- Leveled Readers Online
- Picture Card Bank Online

SCAFFOLDED SUPPORT

Use these materials to ensure the students acquire social and academic language proficiency.

Language Support Card

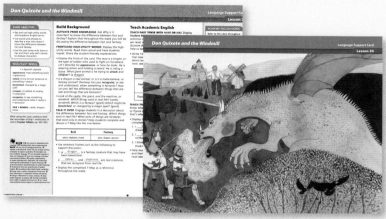

- Builds background for the main topic and promotes oral language.
- Develops high-utility vocabulary and academic language.

Leveled Reader

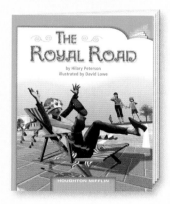

- Sheltered text connects to the main selection's topic, vocabulary, skill, and strategy.

Scaffolded Support

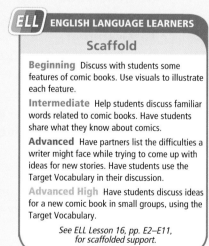

ELL ENGLISH LANGUAGE LEARNERS

Scaffold

Beginning Discuss with students some features of comic books. Use visuals to illustrate each feature.

Intermediate Help students discuss familiar words related to comic books. Have students share what they know about comics.

Advanced Have partners list the difficulties a writer might face while trying to come up with ideas for new stories. Have students use the Target Vocabulary in their discussion.

Advanced High Have students discuss ideas for a new comic book in small groups, using the Target Vocabulary.

See ELL Lesson 16, pp. E2–E11, for scaffolded support.

- Notes throughout the Teacher's Edition scaffold instruction to each language proficiency level.

Vocabulary in Context Cards 191–200

- Provide visual support and additional practice for Target Vocabulary words.

For this week's English Language Learners lessons, see Teacher's Edition, pages E42–E51.

Lesson 20
Weekly Plan

Whole Group

	Day 1	**Day 2**
Oral Language Listening Comprehension	**Teacher Read Aloud** "King Arthur: Fact or Legend?," T304–T305 ☑ Target Vocabulary, T305	**Turn and Talk**, T311
Vocabulary Comprehension Skills and Strategies **Reading** 	☑ **Comprehension** Preview the Target Skill, T305 ☑ **Introduce Vocabulary** Vocabulary in Context, T306–T307 **Develop Background** ☑ Target Vocabulary, T308–T309 	**Introduce Comprehension** ☑ **Understanding Characters,** T310–T311 Question, T310–T311 **Read "Don Quixote and the Windmills,"** T312–T322 Focus on Genre, T312 Stop and Think, T317, T319, T321
Cross-Curricular Connections Fluency Decoding	☑ **Fluency** Model Accuracy, T304	☑ **Fluency** Teach Accuracy, T330

Whole Group Language Arts

	Day 1	**Day 2**
Spelling Grammar Writing	☑ **Spelling** Words from Other Languages: Pretest, T336 ☑ **Grammar** Daily Proofreading Practice, T338 Teach Contractions with *not*; Apostrophe, T338 ☑ **Write to Narrate: Write a Personal Narrative** Draft, T342	☑ **Spelling** Words from Other Languages: Word Sort, T336 ☑ **Grammar** Daily Proofreading Practice, T339 Teach Contractions with Pronouns, T339 ☑ **Write to Narrate: Write a Personal Narrative** Draft, T343
Writing Prompt	*Explain how Cervantes's life influenced his decision to become a writer.*	*Describe how your classmates would react if you began to act like a knight.*

COMMON CORE
Correlations

Introduce Vocabulary RL.5.4, L.5.4a
Develop Background RL.5.4, L.5.4a
Fluency RF.5.4b
Spelling L.5.2e
Write to Narrate W.5.3a, W.5.3b, W.5.3d, W.5.4, W.5.5

Turn and Talk SL.5.1c
Introduce Comprehension RL.5.1
Read RL.5.1, RL.5.4, RL.5.10, L.5.3b
Fluency RF.5.4b
Spelling L.5.2e
Write to Narrate W.5.3a, W.5.3b, W.5.3d, W.5.4, W.5.5

Suggestions for Small Groups (See pp. T354–T355.)
Suggestions for Intervention (See pp. S42–S51.)
Suggestions for English Language Learners (See pp. E42–E51.)

JOURNEYS DIGITAL Powered by **DESTINATION**Reading®
Teacher One-Stop: Lesson Planning

Day 3

Turn and Talk, T323
Oral Language, T323

Read "Don Quixote and the Windmills," T312–T322
Develop Comprehension, T314, T316, T318, T320, T322
☑ **Target Vocabulary**
"Don Quixote and the Windmills," T314, T316, T318, T320, T322
Your Turn, T323
☑ **Deepen Comprehension**
Analyze Characters' Traits, T328–T329

Cross-Curricular Connection
Science, T315
☑ **Fluency** Practice Accuracy, T315
☑ **Decoding**
Stress in Three-Syllable Words, T331

☑ **Spelling**
Words from Other Languages: Word Origins, T337
☑ **Grammar**
Daily Proofreading Practice, T339
Teach Pronoun Contractions and Homophones, T339
☑ **Write to Narrate: Write a Personal Narrative**
Draft, T343

Explain why some qualities of knighthood should still be practiced today.

Oral Language SL.5.1a
Read RL.5.1, RL.5.4, RL.5.10, RF.5.4b, L.5.3b
Your Turn W.5.9a, SL.5.1a
Deepen Comprehension RL.5.1, SL.5.1a, SL.5.1c
Fluency RF.5.4b
Decoding RF.5.3a
Spelling L.5.2e
Write to Narrate W.5.3a, W.5.3b, W.5.3d, W.5.4, W.5.5

Day 4

Text to Self, T327

Read "LitBeat: Live from La Mancha," T324–T326
Connect to Social Studies, T324
Target Vocabulary Review, T325
Develop Comprehension, T326
Weekly Internet Challenge, T326–T327
Making Connections, T327
☑ **Vocabulary Strategies**
Idioms, T332–T333

☑ **Fluency**
Practice Accuracy, T325

☑ **Spelling**
Words from Other Languages: Connect to Writing, T337
☑ **Grammar**
Daily Proofreading Practice, T340
Review Contractions, T340
☑ **Write to Narrate: Write a Personal Narrative**
Revise, T344

Write a brief dialogue between Quixote's horse and Sancho's donkey.

Read RL.5.10
Making Connections RL.5.9, RI.5.9, W.5.3a, W.5.7, W.5.8, W.5.10
Vocabulary Strategies RL.5.4, L.5.3b, L.5.5b
Fluency RF.5.4b
Spelling L.5.2e
Write to Narrate W.5.3a, W.5.3b, W.5.3d, W.5.4, W.5.5, W.5.6

Day 5

Listening and Speaking, T335

Connect and Extend
Read to Connect, T334
Independent Reading, T334
Extend Through Research, T335

☑ **Fluency**
Progress Monitoring, T347

☑ **Spelling**
Words from Other Languages: Assess, T337
☑ **Grammar**
Daily Proofreading Practice, T340
Connect Grammar to Writing, T340–T341
☑ **Write to Narrate: Write a Personal Narrative**
Revise, Edit, and Publish, T344

Describe how a quest you undertook might affect the people in your life.

Listening and Speaking SL.5.4, SL.5.5
Connect and Extend W.5.7, W.5.8, SL.5.1a, SL.5.1c
Fluency RF.5.4b
Spelling L.5.2e
Write to Narrate W.5.3a, W.5.3b, W.5.3d, W.5.4, W.5.5, W.5.6

Your Skills for the Week

☑ **Vocabulary**
Target Vocabulary
Strategies: Idioms

☑ **Comprehension**
Understanding Characters
Question

☑ **Decoding**
Stress in Three-Syllable Words

☑ **Fluency**
Accuracy

☑ **Language Arts**
Spelling
Grammar
Writing

Extending the Common Core State Standards

Read RL.5.1, RL.5.3, RL.5.5, RL.5.10
Comprehension RL.5.1, RL.5.2, W.5.9a
Vocabulary L.5.5b
Listening and Speaking SL.5.6, L.5.6
Grammar L.5.1a
Writing W.5.3b, W.5.3c, W.5.4, W.5.5, W.5.10, L.5.6

Differentiated Support for This Week's Targets

 **TARGET SKILL**

Understanding Characters

TARGET STRATEGY

Question

TARGET VOCABULARY

antique	quests
plagued	noble
pierced	ignorance
thrust	faithful
transformed	exploits

Additional Tools

Vocabulary in Context Cards

Comprehension Tool: Graphic Organizer Transparency 1

? Essential Question

How do the beliefs of a character affect a story?

Vocabulary Reader

Build Target Vocabulary

Level U

- Introduce the Target Vocabulary in context and build comprehension using the Target Strategy.

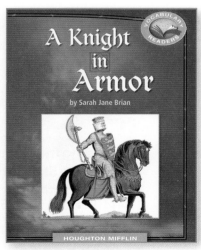

A Knight in Armor

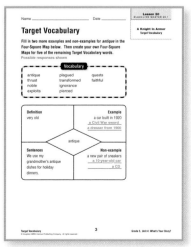

Blackline Master 20.1

Intervention

Scaffolded Support

- Provide extra support in applying the Target Vocabulary, Target Skill, and Target Strategy in context.

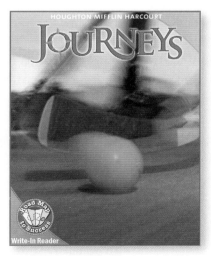

Write-In Reader

 For Vocabulary Reader Lesson Plans, see pp. T356–T357.

Leveled Readers

 Level Q

Struggling Readers

Objective: Use Understanding Characters and the Question strategy to read "Donald Quixote."

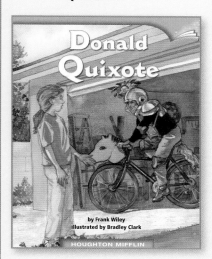

Blackline Master 20.3

 Level S

On Level

Objective: Use Understanding Characters and the Question strategy to read "El Camino Real."

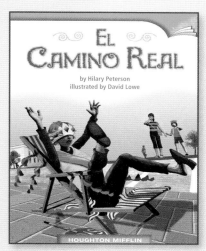

Blackline Master 20.4

 Level X

Advanced

Objective: Use Understanding Characters and the Question strategy to read "A Night in the Kingdom."

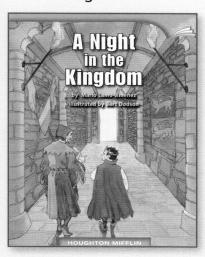

Blackline Master 20.5

Level S

English Language Learners

Objective: Use Understanding Characters and the Question strategy to read "The Royal Road."

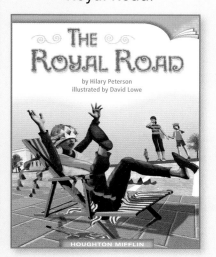

Blackline Master 20.6

 For Leveled Reader Lesson Plans, see pp. T360–T363.

Ready-Made Work Stations

Managing Independent Activities

Use the Ready-Made Work Stations to establish a consistent routine for students working independently. Each station contains three activities. Students who experience success with the *Get Started!* activity move on to the *Reach Higher!* and *Challenge Yourself!* activities, as time permits.

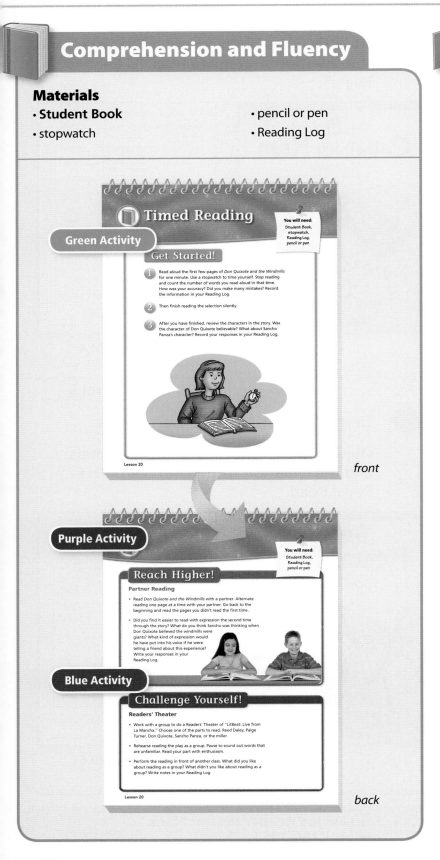

Comprehension and Fluency

Materials
- **Student Book**
- stopwatch
- pencil or pen
- Reading Log

Timed Reading

You will need:
Student Book,
stopwatch,
Reading Log,
pencil or pen

Green Activity

Get Started!

1. Read aloud the first few pages of *Don Quixote and the Windmills* for one minute. Use a stopwatch to time yourself. Stop reading and count the number of words you read aloud in that time. How was your accuracy? Did you make many mistakes? Record the information in your Reading Log.

2. Then finish reading the selection silently.

3. After you have finished, review the characters in the story. Was the character of Don Quixote believable? What about Sancho Panza's character? Record your responses in your Reading Log.

Lesson 20
front

Purple Activity

Reach Higher!

Partner Reading
- Read *Don Quixote and the Windmills* with a partner. Alternate reading one page at a time with your partner. Go back to the beginning and read the pages you didn't read the first time.
- Did you find it easier to read with expression the second time through the story? What do you think Sancho was thinking when Don Quixote believed the windmills were giants? What kind of expression would he have put into his voice if he were telling a friend about this experience? Write your responses in your Reading Log.

Blue Activity

Challenge Yourself!

Readers' Theater
- Work with a group to do a Readers' Theater of "LitBeat: Live from La Mancha." Choose one of the parts to read: Reed Daley, Paige Turner, Don Quixote, Sancho Panza, or the miller.
- Rehearse reading the play as a group. Pause to sound out words that are unfamiliar. Read your part with enthusiasm.
- Perform the reading in front of another class. What did you like about reading as a group? What didn't you like about reading as a group? Write notes in your Reading Log.

Lesson 20
back

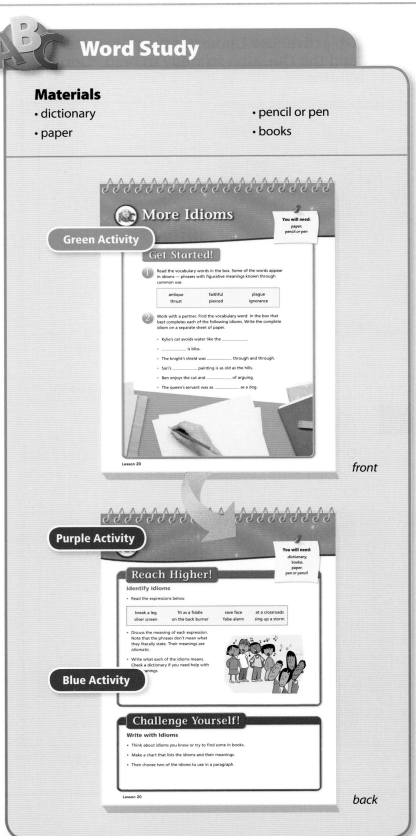

Word Study

Materials
- dictionary
- paper
- pencil or pen
- books

More Idioms

You will need:
paper,
pencil or pen

Green Activity

Get Started!

1. Read the vocabulary words in the box. Some of the words appear in idioms — phrases with figurative meanings known through common use.

| antique | faithful | plague |
| thrust | pierced | ignorance |

2. Work with a partner. Find the vocabulary word in the box that best completes each of the following idioms. Write the complete idiom on a separate sheet of paper.
- Kylie's cat avoids water like the _____.
- _____ is bliss.
- The knight's shield was _____ through and through.
- Sari's _____ painting is as old as the hills.
- Ben enjoys the cut and _____ of arguing.
- The queen's servant was as _____ as a dog.

Lesson 20
front

Purple Activity

Reach Higher!

Identify Idioms
- Read the expressions below.

| break a leg | fit as a fiddle | save face | at a crossroads |
| silver screen | on the back burner | false alarm | sing up a storm |

- Discuss the meaning of each expression. Note that the phrases don't mean what they literally state. Their meanings are *idiomatic*.
- Write what each of the idioms means. Check a dictionary if you need help with meanings.

Blue Activity

Challenge Yourself!

Write with Idioms
- Think about idioms you know or try to find some in books.
- Make a chart that lists the idioms and their meanings.
- Then choose two of the idioms to use in a paragraph.

Lesson 20
back

Think and Write

Materials
- **Student Book**
- library books, magazines
- paper and pencil or pen
- colored pencils or markers

Notes to a Knight

Green Activity

You will need:
Student Book,
paper,
pencil or pen

Get Started!

1. Review *Don Quixote and the Windmills* with a partner. Pretend you can send a letter back in time.

2. One partner will write a letter to Don Quixote and the other will write to Sancho Panza. Tell them what life is like in the 21st century. Ask them for interesting details about their daily lives, their adventures, and their battles.

3. Then trade letters with your partner. Each partner should respond to the letter as if he or she were Don Quixote or Sancho Panza.

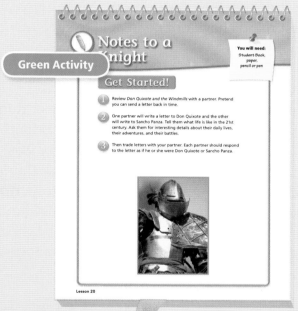

Lesson 20

front

Purple Activity

Reach Higher!

Knight Knowledge

You will need:
computer with
Internet access,
library books,
magazines,
colored pencils
or markers,
paper,
pencil or pen

- Work with a small group to write about medieval European knights. Have each member of the group choose a different topic about knights to research. Use books, magazines, or the Internet to do your research.

- Each person in the group writes a paragraph. Work as a group to combine your paragraphs into a short report. Work together to write an introductory paragraph and a conclusion for the report. Create a title page and include photos or art that you found.

- Share your finished report with the class or a small group. Allow time for students to ask questions about your report.

Blue Activity

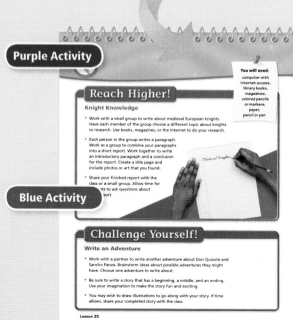

Challenge Yourself!

Write an Adventure

- Work with a partner to write another adventure about Don Quixote and Sancho Panza. Brainstorm ideas about possible adventures they might have. Choose one adventure to write about.

- Be sure to write a story that has a beginning, a middle, and an ending. Use your imagination to make the story fun and exciting.

- You may wish to draw illustrations to go along with your story. If time allows, share your completed story with the class.

Lesson 20

back

Independent Activities

Have children complete these activities at a computer center or a center with an audio CD player.

LAUNCH **>** ## Comprehension and Grammar Activities

Practice and apply this week's skills.

LAUNCH **>** ## Student eBook

Read and listen to this week's selections and skill lessons.

LAUNCH **>** ## WriteSmart CD-ROM

Review student versions of this week's writing models.

LAUNCH **>** ## Audiotext CD

Listen to books or selections on CD.

Single Log In

Teacher Read Aloud

Model Fluency

Accuracy Explain that good readers recognize many words automatically, but they use their decoding skills to sound out unfamiliar words.

- Display **Projectable 20.1**. Have students listen for correct pronunciation and usage of words as you read aloud.

- Reread the text, substituting several incorrect words. Explain how misreading words can confuse meaning.

- Reread the text together with students, practicing accuracy and listening for mistakes.

King Arthur: Fact or Legend?

They say he surfaced during Britain's darkest hour, when war and famine **plagued** the land. They say he rode a proud, white horse, uniting feuding armies to defeat the Saxons. They called his sword Excalibur; before it **pierced** the enemy, he'd pulled it from a stone. They named him Arthur, the Once and Future King, and told his tale across centuries.

King Arthur . . . Knights of the Round Table . . . Lancelot and Guinivere . . . Merlin the Magician. When we think of knights and castles, we recall these legendary characters. But is the legend of King Arthur really a legend? For centuries, historians have studied this very question. Even after years of research, the best minds have not been able to separate fact from fantasy.

We have all heard the story: Arthur emerged during a time of chaos. Most people were uneducated, with **ignorance** and fear fueling violent rivalries. Years of Roman rule had brought stability. When the Romans left, Britain was fair game to invaders. It didn't help that the country was divided among competing kingdoms. Then came Arthur. He **transformed** Britain by uniting everyone under one **noble** king and drove out the invaders. From Camelot, his shining castle on a hill, he presided over a golden time of peace and prosperity. He gathered **faithful** knights around a round

Projectable 20.1

Don Quixote and the Windmills | Fluency | Accuracy

Read Aloud: Model Oral Fluency

King Arthur: Fact or Legend?

They say he surfaced during Britain's darkest hour, when war and famine **plagued** the land. They say he rode a proud, white horse, uniting feuding armies to defeat the Saxons. They called his sword Excalibur; before it **pierced** the enemy, he'd pulled it from a stone. They named him Arthur, the Once and Future King, and told his tale across centuries.

King Arthur . . . Knights of the Round Table . . . Lancelot and Guinivere . . . Merlin the Magician. When we think of knights and castles, we recall these legendary characters. But is the legend of King Arthur really a legend? For centuries, historians have studied this very question. Even after years of research, the best minds have not been able to separate fact from fantasy.

A castle

table. These men **thrust** themselves into **quests** for good, with Arthur directing their **exploits**.

Historians know that most legends contain a kernel of truth. Centuries ago, most people were illiterate. People got their news from traveling storytellers. However, tellers added a little description here, a dose of adventure there, or an extra character to sweeten the plot. Many of the characters in Arthur's story actually lived. Was Arthur a true king? Or, as some suggest, was his character based on a heroic soldier?

Historians have pinpointed the era when an Arthur-like character may have lived— between the fifth and sixth centuries A.D., right after Roman rule. Using this fact, they determined that six hundred years passed before the first written account of Arthur appeared. Unfortunately, these **antique** pages—which contain elements of fantasy and myth—don't resolve the issue.

Here's what historians do agree on—the long lack of written evidence could mean one of three things: 1) An earlier account does exist, but it just hasn't been discovered yet; 2) the tale of Arthur is a true story that first existed only in oral form; 3) the legend of Arthur is pure myth.

Arthur enthusiasts continue to search for evidence. These are among the facts: One castle in the legend—Tintagel in Cornwall—is real. And the Camelot Research Committee is digging under a hill thought to be the site of Camelot. But, sifting fact from fantasy is a job for historians. Whether it is partly real or wholly imagined, we can feel free to enjoy King Arthur's tale for what it is: a great story.

Listening Comprehension
Preview the Target Skill

Read aloud the passage with accuracy. Then ask the following questions.

1 Ask Questions *Was King Arthur doing the right thing by uniting the kingdoms? Why or why not? Sample answer: Yes, he was making everyone safer from invasion by uniting them.*

2 Understanding Characters *What can you learn about King Arthur from the support the people gave him? King Arthur was a fair, just, wise, and strong leader.*

3 Understanding Characters *What kinds of traits might the Knights of the Round Table have had? They probably were brave people who believed in doing the right thing.*

4 Persuasion *Do the facts present enough evidence to make you think Camelot was real? Sample answer: No. If it were real, they would have found the remains of Camelot by now.*

 Target Vocabulary

- Reread "King Arthur: Fact or Legend?" aloud.
- As you read, pause briefly to explain each highlighted vocabulary word.
- Discuss the meaning of each word as it is used in the Read Aloud.

plagued constantly troubled or bothered

pierced poked a hole into; punctured

ignorance being unaware of important things; lack of knowledge

transformed totally changed

noble honest, brave, and unselfish

faithful someone or something you can always depend on; loyal

thrust thrown or pushed forcefully

quests journeys undertaken in order to find something

exploits unusual, brave, or funny experiences

antique an object made in an earlier time period

✔️ Introduce Vocabulary

SHARE OBJECTIVE

- Understand and use the Target Vocabulary words.

Teach

Display the **Vocabulary in Context Cards**, using the routine below. Direct students to **Student Book pp. 502–503**. See also **Instructional Routine 9**.

1 **Read and pronounce the word.** Read the word once alone, then together with students.

2 **Explain the word.** Read the explanation under *What Does It Mean?*

3 **Discuss vocabulary in context.** Together, read aloud the sentence on the front of the card. Help students explain and use the word in new sentences.

4 **Engage with the word.** Ask and discuss the *Think About It* question with students.

Apply

Give partners or small groups one or two **Vocabulary in Context Cards**.

- Help students start *Talk It Over* on the back of their card.
- Have students complete activities for all the cards during the week.

Lesson 20

✔️ **TARGET VOCABULARY**

quests

transformed

plagued

faithful

noble

pierced

ignorance

thrust

exploits

antique

Vocabulary Reader

Context Cards

502

Vocabulary in Context

1 quests
In the Middle Ages, lords sent their knights on quests, journeys to help others.

2 transformed
A ceremony changed, or transformed, squires into knights after years of training.

3 plagued
Knights may have been plagued, or bothered, by the weight of their armor.

4 faithful
A faithful horse was a knight's loyal companion in battle.

ELL ENGLISH LANGUAGE LEARNERS

Scaffold

Beginning Use actions to show the meanings of *pierced* and *transformed*. Then have students perform the action as you say each word.

Advanced Have partners ask and answer questions about each Vocabulary word. For example, *How would you handle an antique?*

Intermediate Have students complete sentence frames for each Vocabulary word. For example, *James Pearson was Renner's loyal and _____ friend; he was always ready to help her.* (faithful)

Advanced High Ask students questions to confirm their understanding. For example, *What do you think the phrase "ignorance is bliss" means?*

See ELL Lesson 20, pp. E42–E51, for scaffolded support.

- Study each **Context Card**.

- Use the context of the sentence to clarify the meaning of the Vocabulary word.

5 noble

Knights needed courage, generosity, and honor to perform noble deeds.

6 pierced

Tournament weapons were blunted to prevent knights' armor from being pierced.

7 ignorance

Medieval royalty, nobility, and clergy were educated. Others lived in ignorance.

8 thrust

In swordplay, a thrust is a lunge with the sword held straight out.

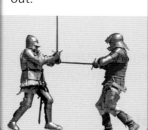

9 exploits

The fictional exploits, or great deeds, of heroes include stories about slaying dragons.

10 antique

Many museums display antique armor. It was made hundreds of years ago.

503

Monitor Vocabulary

Are students able to understand and use Target Vocabulary words?

IF...	THEN...
students have difficulty understanding and using most of the Target Vocabulary Words,	▶ use **Vocabulary in Context Cards** and differentiate the **Vocabulary Reader**, *A Knight in Armor*, for Struggling Readers, p. T356. *See also Intervention Lesson 20, pp. S42–S51.*
students can understand and use most of the Target Vocabulary words,	▶ use **Vocabulary in Context Cards** and differentiate the **Vocabulary Reader**, *A Knight in Armor*, for On-Level Readers, p. T356.
students can understand and use all of the Target Vocabulary words,	▶ use **Differentiate Vocabulary Reader**, *A Knight in Armor*, for Advanced Readers, p. T357.

 Vocabulary Reader, pp. T356–T357
Group English Language Learners according to language proficiency.

VOCABULARY IN CONTEXT CARDS 191–200

quests

In the Middle Ages, lords sent their knights on quests, journeys to help others.

quests

What Does It Mean?
Quests are journeys undertaken in order to find something.

Think About It.
What kinds of **quests** would you be willing to go on? What is something you would like to find?

Talk It Over.
Read each of the sentences below. Decide which sentences describe **quests**. Discuss your answers with a partner. Then create a new sentence that describes a **quest**, and write it on a separate sheet of paper.
- The prince went to find and slay the dragon.
- The boy went on a journey to find his lost dog.
- I went to the grocery store for cat food.
- You went to Antarctica to see live penguins.

front   back

Develop Background

 ENGLISH LANGUAGE LEARNERS

Scaffold

Beginning Help students understand the concept of *windmills* by drawing a picture on the board and writing the word. Point to the word *windmills* as students say it with you.

Intermediate Pre-teach words that may be found in "Don Quixote and the Windmills" using gestures, visuals, and simple sentences. Help students use the words in their own sentences.

Advanced Discuss with students some unfamiliar characteristics associated with the fantasy genre. Ask students to use the Target Vocabulary to describe an adventure they would like to go on someday.

Advanced High Tell students that Sancho Panza is Don Quixote's best friend. Have partners use the Target Vocabulary to discuss characteristics of an ideal best friend.

See ELL Lesson 20, pp. E42–E51, for scaffolded support.

 Target Vocabulary

1 Teach/Model

- Point out the picture of the windmills on **Student Book p. 504.** Tell students that "Don Quixote and the Windmills" is about a **noble** knight who thinks windmills are giants and goes to battle them.

- Use **Vocabulary in Context Cards** to review the student-friendly explanations of the Target Vocabulary words.

- Have students silently read **Student Book p. 504.** Then read the passage aloud.

2 Guided Practice

Ask students the first item below and discuss their responses. Continue in this way until students have answered a question about each Target Vocabulary word.

1. What are some typical summer vacation **exploits**?

2. Describe a **noble** act that you have witnessed.

3. Would you be surprised if a round eraser **pierced** a piece of paper? Why or why not?

4. How does an **antique** stove differ from a modern stove?

5. What personal **quests** might be part of your future?

6. What steps could you take if you were **plagued** by insects at a picnic?

7. How does a **faithful** friend act?

8. Name your favorite superheroes and how they change when they have **transformed**.

9. How would you feel if someone **thrust** a meal you didn't like toward you? Explain.

10. Why do people sometimes do things out of **ignorance**?

Background

✔ **TARGET VOCABULARY** **Cervantes** Spain's Miguel de Cervantes Saavedra (1547–1616) published *Don Quixote de la Mancha* in 1605. This famed tale follows the exploits of Don Quixote, a poor but noble man who thinks he is a knight. In the next selection, you'll see why Don Quixote pierced a windmill with a thrust of his antique lance.

Cervantes was unlucky in his personal quests. He lost the use of his left hand in a war. Later, pirates sold him into slavery in Algeria. Plagued by five years of bondage and four failed escape attempts, he gained freedom only when his faithful family and friends paid a ransom.

Cervantes then transformed himself into a writer. Unable to make a living by writing, he took government jobs. Sadly, he was thrown into prison because of his ignorance of record keeping. Some say that Cervantes began *Don Quixote* while in prison.

By the time he died, Cervantes was a well-known writer. His masterpiece, *Don Quixote*, was published in two parts, in 1605 and in 1615.

3 | Apply

- Have partners take turns reading a paragraph on **Student Book p. 504** to each other.

- Tell partners to pause at and explain each of the highlighted vocabulary words as they read.

Some **antique** stoves can still keep a room warm.

Introduce Comprehension

SHARE OBJECTIVES

- Identify characters' traits.
- Question characters' actions.

SKILL TRACE

Understanding Characters

Introduce	T310–T311
Differentiate	T358–T359
Reteach	T366
Review	T328–T329
Test	Weekly Test, Lesson 20

ELL ENGLISH LANGUAGE LEARNERS

Scaffold

Beginning Write the names of the characters in the passage on the board. Model for students how to make statements about the characters' qualities. Provide this sentence frame: *Pablo is someone who _____.*

Intermediate Work with students to use simple sentences to describe the characters in the passage.

Advanced Have students name and describe a character from a familiar story. Tell them to use the chart from Projectable 20.2.

Advanced High Have partners write sentences describing a character from a familiar story or play.

See ELL Lesson 20, pp. E42–E51, for scaffolded support.

✓ Understanding Characters; Question

1 Teach/Model

AL *Academic Language*

question to ask yourself questions about a selection before, during, and after you read

traits ways of speaking and acting that show what a character is like

---

- Tell students that **questioning** and understanding the **traits** of story characters can help them understand the story as a whole.

- Read and discuss with students **Student Book p. 505**. Have them use the Academic Language and other related terms.

- Display **Projectable 20.2**. Have students read "Pablo's Relaxing Day."

UNDERSTANDING CHARACTERS Point out that taking note of what the characters think, do, and say, and relating it to their own experiences will help readers understand the characters.

- Explain that you will use the Column Chart to record characters' thoughts, actions, and words to help understand their traits.

Think Aloud *I'll start by recording details about Pablo's thoughts. For example, he thinks it's a nice day for a nap.*

QUESTION Explain that asking questions about text details, such as characters' behaviors and actions, can help readers better understand the characters and the plot.

Think Aloud *Why does Pablo focus on eating lunch instead of fishing? If I did that, it would mean that I enjoy eating more than fishing. I can infer that this is the same reason for Pablo's behavior.*

Projectable 20.2

Don Quixote and the Windmills | Introduce Comprehension | Understanding Characters; Question

Understanding Characters; Question

Pablo's Relaxing Day

Pablo was happy to be relaxing by the stream on a glorious day. He planned to catch a large fish and have a nice fried fish dinner. The day was peaceful and quiet, perfect for a snooze. What made it even better was his lunch. He munched on his food happily, forgetting to bother setting up his fishing pole.

Suddenly a stranger rode up to him on a bony old horse. "You, peasant," shrieked the stranger, "how are you this day?" Pablo thought the man was odd and spoke in a very old-fashioned manner.

"You speak very strangely," Pablo said, his mouth full.

"I am a knight. This is how knights speak to peasants!" said the stranger, proudly.

Understanding Characters Use the Column Chart to record details you notice and make inferences about how Pablo feels about the stranger.

Characters' Thoughts	Characters' Actions	Characters' Words
Pablo wants to enjoy the peaceful day. He thinks it would be a nice day for a nap. He thinks the stranger speaks in an odd way.	Pablo wants a fish dinner, but forgets to set up his fishing pole. He begins to eat his lunch and is interrupted.	The stranger says, "You, peasant, how are you this day?" Pablo tells him, "You speak very strangely."

Question You can understand the characters in a story by asking questions about what they do and why they do it. Think of some questions based on the details in the Column Chart.

Comprehension

Understanding Characters

As you read "Don Quixote and the Windmills," look for thoughts, actions, and words that tell you about a character's feelings and motives. Use a graphic organizer like the one below to help you determine Don Quixote's motives from his thoughts, actions and words.

Thoughts	Actions	Words
•	•	•
•	•	•
•	•	•

Question

Asking questions about why a character does or says something can help you infer his or her motives and feelings when they are not directly stated. As you read, ask questions in order to make more sense of the characters and plot of a story. It will allow you to see the humor when the answers are not what you expect!

JOURNEYS DIGITAL **Powered by** DESTINATION Reading
Comprehension Activities: Lesson 20

505

Monitor Comprehension

Are students able to identify characters' traits?

IF...	THEN...
students have difficulty inferring characters' traits,	▶ **Differentiate Comprehension** for Struggling Readers, p. T358. *See also Intervention Lesson 20, pp. S42–S51.*
students can infer characters' traits,	▶ **Differentiate Comprehension** for On-Level Readers, p. T358.
students can question characters' actions to infer characters' traits,	▶ **Differentiate Comprehension** for Advanced Readers, p. T359.

 Differentiate Comprehension, pp. T358–T359. *Group English Language Learners according to language proficiency. See also ELL Lesson 20, pp. E42–E51 for scaffolded support.*

2 Guided Practice

Guide students to copy and complete their own Column Charts for "Pablo's Relaxing Day." Guide practice with the strategy using **Projectable S5**. Then review their charts with them.

3 Apply

Turn and Talk
Have partners ask each other questions about characters' actions in order to make inferences about the characters.

Then have small groups analyze and ask questions about characters in another story they have read. Have them use a Column Chart to organize their thoughts. Ask students to explain the role each character plays in the story's plot.

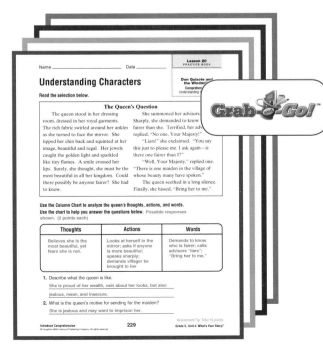

Reading Practice Book p. 229
See Grab-and-Go™ Resources for additional leveled practice.

Introduce the Main Selection

TARGET SKILL

UNDERSTANDING CHARACTERS

Explain that as they read, students will use **Graphic Organizer 1: Column Chart** to help them understand Don Quixote's and Sancho Panza's

- traits, feelings, actions, and motives.
- roles, functions, and relationships.

TARGET STRATEGY

QUESTION Students will use **Graphic Organizer 1** to ask questions about characters' thoughts, feelings and actions.

GENRE: Humorous Fiction

- Read the genre information on **Student Book p. 506** with students.
- Share and discuss the **Genre Blackline Master: Fiction.**
- Preview the selection and model identifying characteristics of the genre.

> **Think Aloud**
> *The title and illustrations make me think this story is about a knight. In the illustrations, he attacks a windmill. I think the story might be funny. It may be humorous fiction.*

- As you preview, ask students to find other features of humorous fiction.

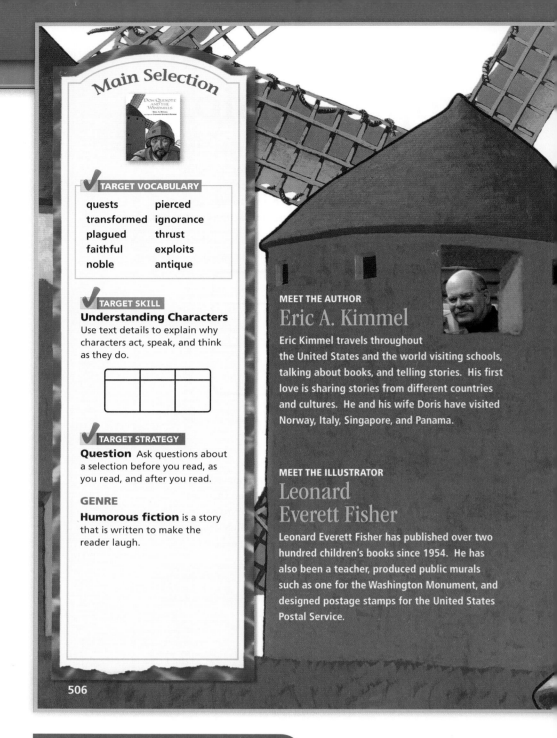

Main Selection

✓ TARGET VOCABULARY

quests	pierced
transformed	ignorance
plagued	thrust
faithful	exploits
noble	antique

✓ TARGET SKILL

Understanding Characters
Use text details to explain why characters act, speak, and think as they do.

✓ TARGET STRATEGY

Question Ask questions about a selection before you read, as you read, and after you read.

GENRE

Humorous fiction is a story that is written to make the reader laugh.

506

MEET THE AUTHOR
Eric A. Kimmel

Eric Kimmel travels throughout the United States and the world visiting schools, talking about books, and telling stories. His first love is sharing stories from different countries and cultures. He and his wife Doris have visited Norway, Italy, Singapore, and Panama.

MEET THE ILLUSTRATOR
Leonard Everett Fisher

Leonard Everett Fisher has published over two hundred children's books since 1954. He has also been a teacher, produced public murals such as one for the Washington Monument, and designed postage stamps for the United States Postal Service.

Reading the Selection

	Pre-Reading	Reading
Supported	**SELECTION SUMMARY** Use **Blackline Master 20.2** to give students an overview before they read. **AUDIOTEXT CD** Have students listen to the selection as they follow along in their books.	**AUTHOR'S MESSAGE** After reading the selection, discuss with students the author's message about beliefs, humor, and fantasy.
Independent	**PREVIEW** Have students look at the title and illustrations and discuss predictions and clues. Some students may read the story independently.	**TEXT EVIDENCE** Have student pause after pp. 509, 511, and 515. Ask them to write questio and note where the answers are found. After reading, have students discuss their responses

DON QUIXOTE AND THE WINDMILLS

BY ERIC A. KIMMEL   ILLUSTRATED BY LEONARD EVERETT FISHER

Essential Question

How do the beliefs of a character affect a story?

507

Essential Question

- Read aloud the **Essential Question** on **Student Book p. 507.** *How do the beliefs of a character affect a story?*
- Tell students to think about this question as they read "Don Quixote and the Windmills."

Set Purpose

- Explain that good readers set a purpose for reading, based on their preview of the selection and what they know about the genre, as well as what they want to learn by reading.
- Model setting a reading purpose.

Think Aloud *I am interested in stories about knights' adventures. I don't know if this story will be true to life or a fantasy because, based on the illustrations, this knight seems unusual. One purpose may be to find out more about how this tale differs from other stories about knights I have read.*

- Have students share their personal reading purposes and record them in their journals.

JOURNEYS DIGITAL Powered by DESTINATIONReading
Student eBook: Read and Listen

Develop Comprehension

Pause at the stopping points to ask students the following questions.

1 **Identify Author's Purpose**
Why does the author begin the selection by asking a series of questions? Sample answers: to catch the reader's attention; to introduce themes of the story

2 ✓ **TARGET VOCABULARY**
What do you think The **Exploits** of Esplandián *is about?* Sample answer: stories about the great deeds Esplandián accomplished

3 **Predict Characters' Actions**
Based on evidence in the text, what do you think Señor Quexada will do now that he believes that he is a knight? Sample answer: He will go on a quest and fight a monster.

508

ELL **ENGLISH LANGUAGE LEARNERS**

Scaffold

Beginning Use the illustrations to preview the selection with students. Have them repeat the names of people, animals, and objects.

Advanced Have students read p. 509, restate ideas about Señor Quexada, and ask clarifying questions.

Intermediate Read aloud p. 509. Explain these words using visuals or simplified language and discuss with students: *armor, ogres, damsels.*

Advanced High Have students brainstorm words related to knights and fantasy that they may encounter in the story.

See ELL Lesson 20, pp. E42–E51, for scaffolded support.

re you one who loves old stories? Does your heart beat faster when you hear tales of knights in armor? Of castles and dragons? Of ogres, giants, and damsels in distress? Beware! Those tales can drive you mad. It happened to a certain Spanish gentleman who lived four centuries ago in the province of La Mancha (lah MAHN chah). **1**

Señor Quexada (sehn YOHR keh HAH dah) was his name. He had a tall, lean figure and wore a woeful expression on his face, as if his heart held some secret sorrow.

Indeed, it did. Señor Quexada longed to live in days gone by, when gallant knights battled for the honor of ladies fair. Books of their adventures filled his library. *Amadis of Gaul, The Mirror of Chivalry,* and *The Exploits of Esplandián* were but a few of the volumes that tumbled from his shelves. **2**

Señor Quexada buried himself in these books. He read all day and far into the night, until his mind snapped. "Señor Quexada is no more," he announced to his astonished household. "I am the renowned knight and champion Don Quixote (kee HOH teh) de la Mancha." **3**

509

CROSS-CURRICULAR CONNECTION

Science

Explain to students that wind is one of Earth's renewable energy sources and that people have made use of it for thousands of years.

Tell students that the ancient Egyptians first used wind to sail boats. Later, the Chinese harnessed the power of wind to pump water. People in Persia (Iran) developed the earliest known windmills, which were used to grind grain into flour. The American colonists used windmills to pump water, grind grain, and cut wood at sawmills. In the early 1900s, Americans used windmills to generate electricity. Today, people are interested in windmills again, as an alternative energy source to replace oil and gas. Have students work in small groups to research other forms of energy. Have them write a brief summary of their findings.

✔ **TARGET STRATEGY**

Question

Model the Strategy

- Remind students that asking questions about characters' thoughts and actions can help them make more sense of the characters and the plot.

- Model how to ask questions about why a character acts as he does.

Think Aloud *Before I read, I see the drawing on p. 508. I ask myself,* Who is this man, and why is he so sad? *I discover that Señor Quexada is sad because he wants to live in a time that doesn't seem real. I then find that he reads so many books about knights' adventures that he thinks he is one. I ask myself,* How will this idea change this character?

- Tell students to ask questions about characters' thoughts and actions as they read to clarify any confusion they might have.

Practice Fluency

Accuracy Before you read aloud the fourth paragraph on **Student Book p. 509**, model previewing the text and using a dictionary to figure out words that students might not recognize automatically.

- Discuss with students why figuring out difficult words before reading helps improve accuracy.

- Have students choral-read the paragraph along with you.

See **p. T330** for a complete Fluency lesson on reading with accuracy.

Develop Comprehension

4 ✓ **TARGET VOCABULARY**

Why would a knight go on a **quest***?*
Sample answer: to help someone in need

5 Analyze Story Structure

Why is Sancho Panza's decision to go with Don Quixote important to the plot? Sample answer: Don Quixote and Sancho Panza become knight and squire; the story of their adventures begins with Sancho Panza's decision.

6 Character Traits

How does Señor Quexada change when he becomes Don Quixote? Sample answer: Before, he is sad and stays to himself; after, he is confident and bold.

7 Infer Character Motives

Why does Don Quixote behave like knights from stories?
Sample answers: The knights are his heroes; he wants to have adventures like they did.

I n the attic he found a rusty suit of armor, his grandfather's sword, a round leather shield, and an antique lance. His helmet was a foot soldier's steel cap that lacked a visor. Don Quixote made one out of paperboard and tied it on with ribbons. It would serve until he won himself a proper helmet on the field of battle.

A knight must have a noble steed. Don Quixote owned a nag as tall and bony as himself. He named the horse Rocinante (ROH sihn AHN teh), which means "Nag No More."

A knight must also have a squire, a faithful companion to share his quests. Don Quixote invited Sancho Panza (SAHN choh PAHN sah), a short, fat farmer from the neighborhood, to accompany him. "Come with me, Sancho," Don Quixote said. "Within a week I will conquer an island and make you king of it."

4

510

ELL **ENGLISH LANGUAGE LEARNERS**

Scaffold

Beginning Ask questions in a way that allows students to provide one-word responses. Help students shape responses into sentences and repeat the full sentences.

Intermediate Give a partial response for each question. Have students complete each one. Then have them repeat the complete response and confirm their understanding.

Advanced Have students respond to questions in complete sentences. Provide corrective feedback as needed.

Advanced High Have students use details from the story to support their answers to questions.

See ELL Lesson 20, pp. E42–E51, for scaffolded support.

"That will be no bad thing," Sancho replied. "If I were king of an island, my wife would be queen, and all my children princes and princesses." So Sancho agreed to come along. Although he was not as crackbrained as Don Quixote, he certainly saw no harm in seeing a bit of the world. **5**

Finally, a knight must have a fair lady to whom he has pledged his loyalty and his life. "A knight without a lady is like a tree without leaves or fruit, a body without a soul," Don Quixote explained to Sancho. After considering all the damsels in the district, he chose a pretty farm girl—Aldonza Lorenzo—from the village of Toboso.

Don Quixote rechristened his lady as he had rechristened his horse. He called her "Dulcinea," (dool see NEH ah) meaning "Sweetness." The very word breathed music and enchantment.

"Dulcinea of Toboso . . . Dulcinea . . . Dulcinea . . ." **6** The knight's heart overflowed with devotion as he **7** whispered the sacred name.

> **STOP AND THINK**
> **Question** Ask yourself what you have learned about knights in shining armor. How does Don Quixote compare to these knights?

511

STOP AND THINK

 **TARGET STRATEGY**

Question

- Remind students that asking questions before, during, and after they read helps them better understand the characters and plot.

- Have students complete the **Stop and Think** activity on **Student Book p. 511.**

- If students have difficulty asking and answering questions about the text, see **Comprehension Intervention** below for extra support.

- Display **Projectable 20.3a.** Tell students that a Column Chart can help them keep track of details that will help them understand characters.

- Have students use **Graphic Organizer 1** to begin their own Column Charts, adding details about the characters' thoughts, actions, and words.

COMPREHENSION INTERVENTION

 **TARGET STRATEGY**   Question

STRATEGY SUPPORT Remind students that asking questions about why a character does or says something can help them make sense of the character's feelings or behavior. Use this model:

I ask myself, What is a knight really like? I know Don Quixote has read many books about knights and their adventures. I'll pay attention to what he thinks, how he acts, and what he says. On p. 510, Don Quixote puts together an outfit from things in the attic. He finds a suit of armor, a sword, a shield, a helmet, and a lance. I think he does this because a knight wears these things. Have students add to their graphic organizers, and remind them to clarify their understanding by asking questions as they read.

Projectable 20.3a

Don Quixote and the Windmills | Comprehension Understanding Characters

Column Chart: Understanding Characters

Title or Topic _Don Quixote and the Windmills_

Characters' Thoughts	Characters' Actions	Characters' Words
Señor Quexada longed to live in the time of gallant knights. He imagines he is a great knight with a squire and a lady.	He gives himself a new name and finds a suit of armor. Don Quixote asks Sancho Panza to be his squire.	

Develop Comprehension

8 ✔ **TARGET VOCABULARY**

What is something that has **plagued** *you? Explain.* Answers will vary.

9 ## Character Traits

What does the dialogue between Don Quixote and Sancho Panza on p. 512 tell you about them? Sample answer: Don Quixote is determined to find adventure and has lost touch with reality; Sancho Panza is not interested in brave deeds and knows reality from fantasy.

10 ## Analyze Author's Purpose

How does the author use his description of the windmills to tell readers an important idea about his purpose? Sample answer: The author uses words that make the windmills seem human, giving the sense that they actually are like giants preparing to fight; the author's word choice adds humor and enjoyment because Don Quixote charges the windmills.

11 ## Understanding Characters

What does Don Quixote's speech before he charges the windmills tell you about him and his quest? Sample answer: Don Quixote exaggerates and is humorous without knowing it; his quest is a fantasy.

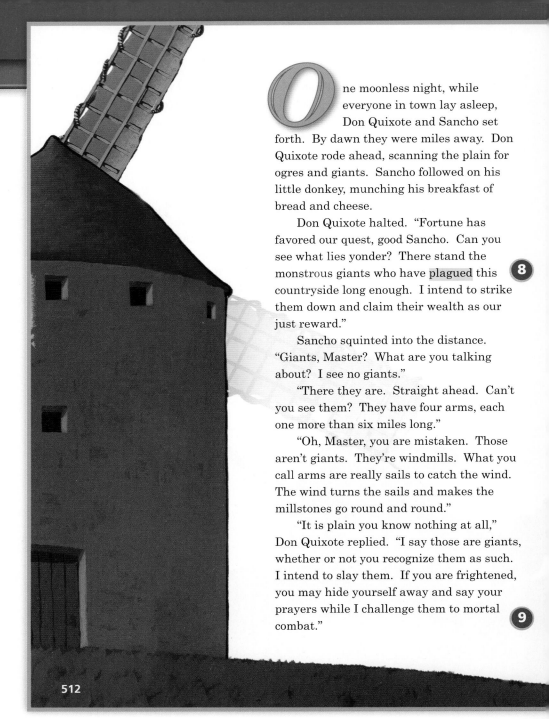

One moonless night, while everyone in town lay asleep, Don Quixote and Sancho set forth. By dawn they were miles away. Don Quixote rode ahead, scanning the plain for ogres and giants. Sancho followed on his little donkey, munching his breakfast of bread and cheese.

Don Quixote halted. "Fortune has favored our quest, good Sancho. Can you see what lies yonder? There stand the monstrous giants who have plagued this **8** countryside long enough. I intend to strike them down and claim their wealth as our just reward."

Sancho squinted into the distance. "Giants, Master? What are you talking about? I see no giants."

"There they are. Straight ahead. Can't you see them? They have four arms, each one more than six miles long."

"Oh, Master, you are mistaken. Those aren't giants. They're windmills. What you call arms are really sails to catch the wind. The wind turns the sails and makes the millstones go round and round."

"It is plain you know nothing at all," Don Quixote replied. "I say those are giants, whether or not you recognize them as such. I intend to slay them. If you are frightened, you may hide yourself away and say your prayers while I challenge them to mortal **9** combat."

512

Having said this, Don Quixote lowered his visor and put his spurs to Rocinante. He galloped across the plain to do battle with the windmills.

"Take to your heels, cowardly giants! Know that it is I, the noble Don Quixote, Knight of La Mancha, who am attacking you!"

"Master! They are only windmills!" Sancho called after him.

The wind picked up. The sails billowed. The great arms of the windmills began to turn.

Don Quixote laughed with scorn. "Do you think to frighten me? Though you have more arms than the giant Briareus, I will still make an end of you!" He lifted his eyes toward heaven. "Beautiful damsel, Dulcinea of Toboso, in your honor do I claim the victory. If I am to die, let it be with your sweet name upon my lips." **10**

Shouting defiance, he charged at the nearest windmill. **11**

> **STOP AND THINK**
> **Understanding Characters** What have you learned about Don Quixote so far that explains why he attacks the windmills?

513

STOP AND THINK

✓ **TARGET SKILL**

Understanding Characters

- Remind students that they can better understand characters and their motivations by paying attention to their thoughts, actions and words.

- Have students complete the **Stop and Think** activity on **Student Book p. 513**.

- If students have difficulty understanding characters, see **Comprehension Intervention** below for extra support.

- Have students continue their graphic organizers. Display **Projectable 20.3b** and work with students to add to the Column Chart.

COMPREHENSION INTERVENTION

✓ **TARGET SKILL** Understanding Characters

STRATEGY SUPPORT Remind students that they can use story details to understand more about characters. Paying attention to characters' thoughts, actions, and words can tell them about a character's feelings and motives. Model using Don Quixote's thoughts, actions, and words on **Student Book p. 513** to better understand why he attacks the windmills.

Think Aloud *Don Quixote lowers his visor and rides across the plains, charging the windmills that he is convinced are giants. He says things like, "Do you think to frighten me?...I will still make an end of you." I can see that he is involved in his fantasy about knights and adventure to the point that he isn't thinking realistically.*

Projectable 20.3b

Don Quixote and the Windmills | Comprehension | Understanding Characters

Column Chart: Understanding Characters

Title or Topic Don Quixote and the Windmills

Characters' Thoughts	Characters' Actions	Characters' Words
Señor Quexada longed to live in the time of gallant knights. He imagines he is a great knight with a squire and a lady.	He gives himself a new name and finds a suit of armor. Don Quixote asks Sancho Panza to be his squire. The two take off in search of adventure. Don Quixote charges at the windmills.	Don Quixote says, "There stand the monstrous giants who have plagued this countryside." Don Quixote says, "It is plain you know nothing at all."

Develop Comprehension

12 ✓ **TARGET VOCABULARY**

Why did Don Quixote's lance cause him another problem when he **pierced** *the sail with it? The lance stabbed through the cloth and then got caught in the ropes.*

13 **Infer Character Motives**

Based on what you know about Sancho Panza, why does he try to save Don Quixote? Sample answer: The author describes Sancho as a "faithful squire"; Sancho would not want his master to get hurt.

14 **Analyze Character Motives**

Does Sancho's reaction fit in with what you already know about him? Why or why not? Sample answer: Yes; he is Don Quixote's faithful servant, but his master did something foolhardy that risked their lives. Sancho seems amazed, exasperated, and maybe a little fearful.

His lance **pierced** the canvas sail and became tangled **12** in the ropes. Attempting to pull free, Don Quixote became caught as well. The windmill's rumbling arm dragged him out of the saddle, carrying him higher and higher.

Don Quixote drew his sword. "Release me, Giant, before you feel the sharp sting of my blade!" He slashed at the ropes. The windmill's arm swept past its zenith. It began hurtling toward the ground at an ever-increasing speed.

Sancho trotted up on his donkey. "Master, I will save you!" He grasped Don Quixote's ankle when the knight swept by. The **13** faithful squire found himself pulled off his donkey and carried aloft with his master.

514

ELL **ENGLISH LANGUAGE LEARNERS**

Scaffold

Beginning Use gestures and the illustrations on pp. 514–515 to explain the steps in Don Quixote's attack on the windmills.	**Advanced** Ask: *How would you describe Don Quixote on these pages?* Make a word web with words students say to describe him.
Intermediate Work with students to describe the steps in Don Quixote's attack on the windmills.	**Advanced High** Have students work in pairs to describe what Don Quixote is like. Ask partners to write sentences that describe him, based on his actions.

See ELL Lesson 20, pp. E42–E51, for scaffolded support.

"Do not fear, good Sancho. I feel the giant weakening. I will soon make an end of this villain." Don Quixote hacked at the ropes with renewed vigor.

Sancho saw the cords begin to fray. "Master! Spare the poor giant a few moments of life. At least until he brings us closer to the ground."

"Giant, in the name of my lady, Dulcinea of Toboso, I command you to yield or die."

Don Quixote made one last thrust. The ropes parted. The sail blew away. Don Quixote, with Sancho clinging to his ankle, plunged straight down. Together they would have perished, knight and squire, dashed to a hundred pieces, had the sail of the following arm not caught them and sent them rolling across the plain.

They tumbled to a stop at Rocinante's feet. Sancho felt himself all over for broken bones. "Ay, Master!" he groaned. "Why didn't you listen to me? I tried to warn you. Could you not see that they were only windmills? Whatever possessed you to attack them?" **(14)**

> **STOP AND THINK**
> **Author's Craft** The phrase "dashed to a hundred pieces" is an example of imagery. How does it help you understand the danger Don Quixote and Sancho are in?

515

STOP AND THINK
Author's Craft: Imagery

- Explain to students that **imagery** is a literary device that authors use to create clear pictures that help readers visualize how something looks, sounds, smells, tastes, or feels.

- Write the following sentence on the board: *The curtain of blizzard cut off my view of the road.* Point out that this is an example of imagery. The author's words help you see and feel the thickness of the snow.

- Have students complete the **Stop and Think** activity on **Student Book p. 515.**

? Essential Question

Discuss how Don Quixote's beliefs affect the story and cause certain events to occur.

Develop Comprehension

15 ✔ TARGET VOCABULARY

Give another example of something in this story that has **transformed**.
Sample answers: Don Quixote's appearance when he wears armor; Sancho's life as a farmer

16 ## Analyze Supporting Details

What evidence does the author provide to support the conclusion that Sancho Panza wants to continue as Don Quixote's squire?
Sample answers: Don Quixote resolves to meet his enemy, the ogre, again and overpower him, and Sancho replies that that would be good because they could not survive another battle like the last one; Sancho says that when Don Quixote describes the knight's life of fame and honor, Sancho believes the dream of his island might be within reach.

D on Quixote dusted off his battered armor. He tied the crushed visor back onto his helmet. "Be silent, Sancho. Your words reveal your ignorance. You know nothing about these matters. It is true that the giants now have the appearance of windmills. This is because they were bewitched by my enemy, the ogre, Frestón. At the last moment,

15 he transformed the giants into windmills to deprive me of the glorious victory that was rightfully mine. Never fear, Sancho. We will meet him again. All his power will not save him when he feels the edge of my mighty sword."

"I hope so," said Sancho as he pushed Don Quixote back onto Rocinante. "Another tumble like this and we will all go home in pieces."

Don Quixote took the reins in hand. "Never fear, faithful Sancho. The road to victory is often paved with misfortune. A true knight never complains. Follow me, and I promise we will dip our arms up to the elbow in what common people call 'adventures.' Our names and the stories of our matchless deeds will resound through the ages."

"Ay, Master! When I hear you say those words, I can almost believe they are true. Perhaps I really will have my island someday."

"Of course you will, Sancho. Why would you ever doubt it?"

Sancho mounted his donkey and went trotting after

16 Rocinante, vowing to follow Don Quixote wherever fortune's winds might carry him.

516

Your Turn

What Lies Yonder?

Make a Prediction Sancho Panza's thoughts, actions, and words reveal his motives for choosing to follow Don Quixote. Write a paragraph explaining how Sancho feels about Don Quixote and their quest. Then use this information to predict whether you think Sancho will join Don Quixote on his next adventure.
SHORT RESPONSE

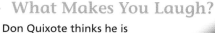

Mighty Monsters

Draw Don Quixote's Giant Don Quixote tells Sancho Panza that the ogre Frestón has given the giants "the appearance of windmills." Work with a small group to illustrate one of Don Quixote's "giants." Use details from the story to make your illustration of the giant come alive. When your picture is complete, add a caption explaining the action.
SMALL GROUP

What Makes You Laugh?

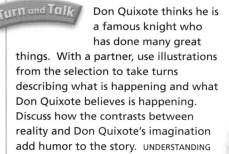
Turn and Talk Don Quixote thinks he is a famous knight who has done many great things. With a partner, use illustrations from the selection to take turns describing what is happening and what Don Quixote believes is happening. Discuss how the contrasts between reality and Don Quixote's imagination add humor to the story. UNDERSTANDING CHARACTERS

517

Retelling Rubric

4	**Excellent**	Students **clearly and thoroughly** retell Don Quixote's adventure.
3	**Good**	Students **accurately** retell most of Don Quixote's adventure.
2	**Fair**	Students **give a limited** retelling of Don Quixote's adventure.
1	**Unsatisfactory**	Students **cannot** retell Don Quixote's adventure.

Your Turn

Have students complete the activities on **page 517.**

What Lies Yonder? Have students use an idea-support map to plan their paragraph. Tell them to find evidence in the selection to support their description of Sancho Panza's feelings. Remind them that their prediction should be based on evidence from the selection.
(SHORT RESPONSE)

Mighty Monsters Have students review the selection to find details about what Don Quixote sees when he looks at the windmills. Remind them that what Don Quixote sees is different from what Sancho Panza sees. Tell students to base their illustration and caption on Don Quixote's idea of the "giant." Have groups share their illustrations with the class. (SMALL GROUP)

What Makes You Laugh? Have partners refer to the text to clarify their understanding of each illustration. Point out that the dialogue between Don Quixote and Sancho Panza often reveals what is actually happening as opposed to what Don Quixote thinks is happening. (COMPARE AND CONTRAST)

Oral Language

Have partners use the illustrations in the selection to review key events from the story. Then have students retell Don Quixote's adventure. Use the Retelling Rubric at the left to evaluate students' responses.

Connect to Social Studies

PREVIEW THE PLAY

- Tell students this selection is a play about the literary character, Don Quixote. Remind students that a play is a story that can be performed for an audience. Ask students to read the title and cast of characters on **Student Book p. 518**. Then have students read the play independently.

DISCUSS CHARACTERS

- Point out that the list of characters is usually found at the beginning of a play.

- A character's name is followed by the lines of dialogue, or words, that the character speaks.

- Tell students that the story of a play is told through the words and actions of the characters. What the characters say and how they say it helps readers better understand the story.

- Work with students to create a chart like the following about plays and the characters in them.

plays	stories that can be performed for an audience
characters	the people or animals in a story that show what they are like by what they say and do

Connect to Social Studies

✓ TARGET VOCABULARY

quests	transformed
plagued	faithful
noble	pierced
ignorance	thrust
exploits	antique

GENRE

A **play**, like this dramatic adaptation, tells a story through the words and actions of its characters.

TEXT FOCUS

Characters In a play, characters are often listed first. Each character is named before his or her lines of dialogue so readers know who is speaking.

518

LitBeat: Live from La Mancha

Retold by Rob Hale

Cast of Characters

Reed Daley, Anchor
Paige Turner, Reporter
Don Quixote
Sancho Panza
Miller

Reed Daley: This is LitBeat, bringing you breaking news from the world of literature. We go now to reporter Paige Turner, who is following a story outside of Toboso, Spain. Paige?

ELL ENGLISH LANGUAGE LEARNERS

Scaffold

Beginning Guide students to identify the title, cast of characters, and their lines of dialogue. Use the pictures to name characters.

Intermediate Have students answer simple questions about Paige Turner and Don Quixote. Discuss with students their responses and clarify understanding.

Advanced Discuss the different features of a news report. Work with students to brainstorm a list of words appropriate to newscasts.

Advanced High Have partners work together to make a list of words they might expect to see in a newscast.

See ELL Lesson 20, pp. E42–E51, for scaffolded support.

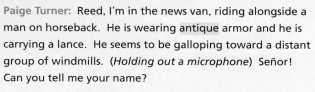

Paige Turner: Reed, I'm in the news van, riding alongside a man on horseback. He is wearing antique armor and he is carrying a lance. He seems to be galloping toward a distant group of windmills. (*Holding out a microphone*) Señor! Can you tell me your name?

Quixote: I am Don Quixote de La Mancha!

Paige: Can I ask you why you are charging toward those windmills? Do you have something against wind power?

Quixote: I will overlook your ignorance. Those are giants, madam, not windmills! They have plagued our land for too long. I will battle them, in the name of the lady I honor, the fair Dulcinea!

Paige: Okay, good luck with that. Here comes someone else—a man on a donkey. Your name, señor?

Panza: Sancho Panza. I am a humble farmer who will someday rule an island.

Paige: I see. Are you a friend of Don Quixote's, by any chance?

Panza: ¡Sí! My master's life is filled with daring exploits. He gets a bit confused sometimes, but I remain his faithful servant.

Paige: Very noble. Wait—(*To camera operator*) can you zoom in? Yes, Don Quixote is attacking one of the windmills! He has pierced a sail with his lance and now he seems to be caught in some rope. The windmill has pulled him right off his horse!

Panza: Master! I am coming!

519

Practice Fluency

Accuracy Have students listen as you read aloud the page of dialogue on **Student Book p. 519.**

- Remind students that good readers read each word correctly and accurately. To understand a play, the reader may need to slow down to be sure of who is speaking.

- Have students read Paige, Quixote, and Panza's lines on **p. 519.** Remind them to read each line carefully and accurately in order to understand the characters' words and actions.

JOURNEYS DIGITAL
Powered by DESTINATIONReading®
Student eBook: Read and Listen

TARGET VOCABULARY REVIEW

✓ **TARGET VOCABULARY**
Vocabulary in Context Cards – Character Vocabulary

Have students work in groups. Tell them to review the **Vocabulary in Context Cards.** Then ask them to take turns using each word in a sentence that gives information about one of the characters in *LitBeat: Live from La Mancha.* For example, the student who chooses the word *faithful,* could use it in the following sentence: *Sancho Panza was a faithful servant to Don Quixote.*

CONTEXT CARDS 191–200

front   back

Develop Comprehension

Reread the selection with students. Pause at stopping points to ask students the following questions.

1 Understanding Characters
What can you tell about Paige Turner's role from her first line of dialogue on p. 519? Sample answers: Paige Turner is covering a news story about Don Quixote and his adventure.

2 ✔ TARGET VOCABULARY *What does Don Quixote mean when he says, "I will overlook your ignorance"? Sample answer: He won't respond to the fact that Paige doesn't see the windmills as giants.*

3 Author's Purpose
The author uses phrases such as "Okay, good luck with that." What does this suggest about his purpose for writing? Sample answer: He is using conversational language to entertain.

Identify Characters

- Tell students that "LitBeat: Live from La Mancha" is a play that tells a story about a news reporter interviewing Don Quixote as he battles windmills. We learn about the play's characters through their dialogue and actions.

- Model the thinking.

Think Aloud *On p. 520, Panza groans as he speaks because he just fell from the windmill trying to help Don Quixote. I think that Panza would like a break from these silly adventures.*

Paige: Sancho Panza is trying to pull him back down, but—Oh, no, this is terrible! Both men are caught in the ropes. Those giant sails are pulling them up...up...like a Ferris wheel!

Quixote: Unhand me, villain! Take that! And that!

Paige: With each thrust of his sword, the ropes are giving way, Reed, but the men are too far up! They're going to fall!

Panza: Help!!!

Paige: Wait! Luckily another windmill sail has caught them and broken their fall! They have rolled onto the ground...(*She runs over.*) Señor Quixote, are you all right?

Quixote: A few bruises, nothing more. Look, Sancho! The giants have been transformed into windmills.

Panza: (*Groaning*) Please, master, let's not go on any more quests for a while.

Miller: (*Off in the distance*) Hey! Who is going to pay for my broken windmill?

Paige: This is Paige Turner for LitBeat. Back to you, Reed!

520

Weekly Internet Challenge

Using Information

- Review Internet Strategy, Step 5: Synthesize.
- Review with students the importance of gathering information from multiple reliable sites.
- Explain that good researchers learn to pull together the relevant information from a variety of sources.

INTERNET STRATEGY

1. **Plan a Search** by identifying what you are looking for and how to find it.

2. **Search and Predict** which sites will be worth exploring.

3. **Navigate** a site to see how to get around it and what it contains.

4. **Analyze and Evaluate** the quality and reliability of the information.

5. **Synthesize** the information from multiple sites.

Making Connections

Text to Self

Write a Story If you could be a hero for one day, what good deeds would you do? Write an imaginative story about the adventures you might have during your day as a hero. Include in your story a believable setting and an interesting plot. When you are finished, read your story to a small group.

Text to Text

Compare Literary Forms "LitBeat: Live from La Mancha" is a play based on the characters and events in the story "Don Quixote and the Windmills." Compare and contrast the ways in which these two selections tell about Don Quixote's adventure. How are the story and the play similar? How are they different?

Text to World

Research Windmills Today, many people are interested in wind as a source of renewable energy to produce electricity. Use print and electronic resources to research how windmills work. Then write a paragraph explaining your findings. Brainstorm and discuss with a small group other possible ways to use wind power as a renewable energy source. Take notes as you listen to others speak. Use your notes to write a short summary of your group's ideas.

521

"LitBeat: Live from La Mancha" Challenge

- Ask students to research ways in which different communities honor their heroes.

- Have students locate multiple sites related to their research question. Remind them to skim and scan each site quickly and make an evaluation about the site's reliability before spending time searching it for information.

- Have students gather information from several websites and write a summary pulling together information from the websites. Then have them present their summaries to the class.

Making Connections

Text to Self

Guide students to consider different ways to present their stories. Point out that stories may be written as plays, narratives, or even through journal entries. Students may wish to brainstorm interesting plot ideas to include in their stories.

Text to Text

To help students identify similarities and differences between the selections, have them create a Venn diagram. This will help them compare and contrast the ways in which the play and the story present Don Quixote's adventures.

Text to World

Remind students that writers always have a purpose, or reason, for writing. Ask students to consider a purpose for writing about windmills. Point out that when writers want to inform, they begin by gathering facts about their topic.

Deepen Comprehension

SHARE OBJECTIVES

- Analyze characters' roles and behavior.
- Analyze how characters' behavior impacts the plot.

SKILL TRACE

Understanding Characters

Introduce	T310–T311
Differentiate	T358–T359
Reteach	T366
▶ **Review**	**T328–T329**
Test	Weekly Tests, Lesson 20

ELL ENGLISH LANGUAGE LEARNERS

Scaffold

Beginning Discuss with students some of the important events on pp. 509–516. Work with students to identify characters in the text.

Intermediate Write example questions on the board: *Who are the characters? Where is the story set? What happens in the story? How do the characters affect the plot?* Discuss the questions with students and guide them to respond in complete sentences.

Advanced Have partners take turns asking and answering questions about characters in the selection. Have them use Graphic Organizer 1 to aid discussion.

Advanced High Have students analyze the influence of characters on the plot. Tell them to write a detailed paragraph that explains the effects that Don Quixote's and Sancho Panza's actions have on the story's events.

See ELL Lesson 20, pp. E42–E51, for scaffolded support

✓ Analyze Characters' Traits

1 | Teach/Model

AL *Academic Language*

archetype a character who matches a traditional character from other stories

---

- Explain that authors often use character types that have appeared in literature for many years. A story character who matches a traditional character from other stories is know as an **archetype**. A brave knight on a quest is one such archetype. Point out that Don Quixote mostly fits this archetype, but the times when he doesn't provide humor for the reader.

- Have students reread **Student Book p. 509**.

- Display **Projectable 20.4**. Discuss **Deepen Comprehension Question 1**.

- Remind students that a Column Chart helps to organize details about characters so that readers can fully understand them and the impact of their behavior on the plot.

- Model analyzing Señor Quexada to complete the Column Chart and answer the question.

Projectable 20.4

Don Quixote and the Windmills | Deepen Comprehension | Understanding Characters

Column Chart: Understanding Characters

Deepen Comprehension Question 1

What leads Señor Quexada to his important decision to pursue adventure? p. 509

Characters' Thoughts:	Characters' Actions	Characters' Words
He wants to live in the time of great knights; He is secretly sad and lonely.	Señor Quexada buries himself in books about the time of knights.	"Señor Quexada is no more. I am the renowned knight and champion Don Quixote de la Mancha."

Deepen Comprehension Question 2

What effect does Don Quixote's decision to live in a fantasy world have on the story? Use details from pp. 510–512 to support your answer.

Characters' Thoughts:	Characters' Actions	Characters' Words
Don Quixote pretends he has a squire and a lady.	He leaves his town and dreams up adventures.	"I say those are giants, whether or not you recognize them as such."

Deepen Comprehension Question 3

What qualities make Sancho Panzo a good sidekick for Don Quixote as he embarks on his adventures? pp. 511–516

Think Aloud *I know that Señor Quexada wants to live in the past and is lonely. To feel better, he buries himself in books about the time of knights. I'll write that in the middle column. When he declares, "Señor Quexada is no more. I am the renowned knight and champion Don Quixote de la Mancha," I know he has lost touch with reality and has decided to pursue adventures.*

Monitor Comprehension

Are students able to analyze characters' traits and behavior?

IF...	THEN...
students have difficulty analyzing characters' traits and behavior,	▶ use the Leveled Reader for **Struggling Readers** Donald Quixote, p. T360. See also Intervention Lesson 20, pp. S42–S51.
students can analyze characters' traits and behavior,	▶ use the Leveled Reader for **On-Level** Readers, El Camino Real, p. T361.
students can analyze characters' traits and behavior and how these impact the plot,	▶ use the Leveled Reader for **Advanced** Readers, A Night in the Kingdom, p. T362.

Leveled Readers, pp. T360–T363
Use the Leveled Reader for **English Language Learners**, The Royal Road, p. T363.

Group English Learners according to language proficiency level. See also ELL Lesson 20, E42–E51, for scaffolded support.

2 Guided Practice

- Reread pp. 510–512 of "Don Quixote and the Windmills" with students. Read and discuss **Deepen Comprehension Question 2** on **Projectable 20.4.** Use these prompts to guide students:

- *What does Don Quixote believe he needs to be a knight?* a squire and a lady

- *What does Don Quixote do once he has fully created his own character?* He leaves town and dreams up adventures.

- Complete the Column Chart for Question 2 with students.

GUIDED DISCUSSION Have students discuss ways in which Don Quixote's imagination affects the plot. Prompt students with questions like the one below:

- *How do Don Quixote's fantasies affect the story?* The story's conflicts arise because Don Quixote cannot tell the difference between his imagination and reality.

3 Apply

Turn and Talk Have partners make a Column Chart and complete **Deepen Comprehension Question 3** on **Projectable 20.4.** Have students share their responses with the class. *Sancho is a farmer who's willing to follow Don Quixote on his adventures. He's a follower rather than a leader, but is able to see the world as it actually is. As a result, he contrasts with Don Quixote, who isn't able to see the differences between what's real and what's imaginary.*

WRITE ABOUT READING Have students write another adventure for Don Quixote and Sancho Panza. Remind them to make the characters' behavior consistent with what is shown in the selection. Then have them explain to a partner how Don Quixote's and Sancho Panza's actions in their story affect the plot and conflict.

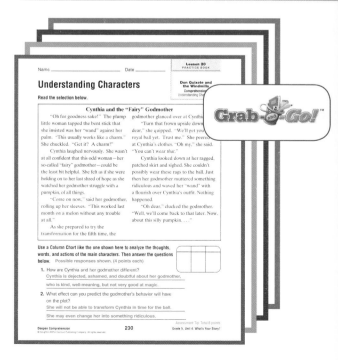

Practice Book p. 230
See Grab-and-Go™ Resources for additional leveled practice.

Fluency

Accuracy

1 Teach/Model

- Tell students that good readers recognize many words automatically when they read, and they work to figure out words they do not know.

- Have students look at the third paragraph on **Student Book p. 511.** Model scanning the paragraph for difficult words and finding pronunciations in a dictionary if necessary.

- Explain that previewing a selection and identifying difficult words before reading helps improve accuracy.

2 Guided Practice

- Together, read aloud **Student Book p. 511.**

- Work with students to identify difficult words and their correct pronunciations.

- If students are struggling with reading accurately, read the passage aloud to them, reviewing the difficult words. Finally, let them practice reading it to each other until they can read it smoothly and accurately.

- See also **Instructional Routine 5.**

3 Apply

- Tell students that with practice, they can improve their accuracy.

- Have students choral-read a paragraph of the selection while practicing automatic word recognition and accuracy. Listen as students read to monitor fluency.

- Allow students to read the paragraph three or four times.

Decoding

 ## Stress in Three-Syllable Words

1 Teach/Model

ANALYZE THREE-SYLLABLE WORDS Tell students that every syllable of a word must contain a vowel sound. Say the word *interrupt,* clapping for each syllable. Write *interrupt* on the board, divide the syllables with slashes, and point out the vowels in each syllable: in | ter | rupt

- Explain that in a word with more than one syllable, one syllable is pronounced with more stress, or emphasis, than others. Underline the final syllable *rupt.* Point out that we stress the final syllable in *interrupt* most heavily, and the middle syllable is unstressed.

- Review the concepts of stressed syllables and unstressed syllables. Stressed syllables are emphasized more, and vowel sounds can be clearly heard. Vowel sounds in unstressed syllables are less clear and may have the schwa sound.

- Write the words *civilized* and *underarmed* on the board. Model how to decode the first two words step by step: civ | il | ized, un | der | armed.

2 Practice/Apply

DECODE WORDS WITH THREE SYLLABLES Write the words from the chart below on the board.

Find stressed syllables...	by saying the word.	
in|ter|rupt unstressed | unstressed | stressed	civ | il | ized un | der | armed re | load | ed	*mis | giv | ings* *stam | ped | ing* *set | tle | ment*

- Have partners work in pairs to decode the remaining words. Ask students to say each word aloud and discuss which syllable is stressed and which syllables are unstressed.

- For additional practice, have students divide the words *burrito, bandana, tomato, dungarees, patio, tsunami* into three syllables.

- Use **Corrective Feedback** if students need additional help.

Corrective Feedback

If students have trouble decoding three-syllable words, use the model below.

Correct the error. Say the word aloud. *set | tle | ment*

Model the correct way to identify the stressed syllables. *Listen for the syllables as you say the word set / tle / ment. Listen for which syllable you stress a little more than the others. set / tle / ment*

Guide students to identify the stressed and unstressed syllables. *What are the syllables? (set/tle/ment) Which syllable is stressed? (the first) Which are unstressed? (the second and third)*

Check students' understanding. *What is the word? (settlement)*

Reinforce Have students repeat the process with the word *furious.*

Vocabulary Strategies

SHARE OBJECTIVE

• Understand and explain idioms, adages, and common sayings.

SKILL TRACE

Idioms	
Introduce	T114–T115, Unit 2
Differentiate	T364–T365
Reteach	T366
▶ Review	**T332–T333;** T122–T123, Unit 6
Test	Weekly Tests, Lesson 20

ELL ENGLISH LANGUAGE LEARNERS

Scaffold

Beginning Write *It's raining cats and dogs* on the board. Draw a house being pelted by raindrops. Explain that all languages have colorful phrases to describe things. These expressions have their own meanings apart from the meanings of the individual words.

Intermediate Explain that an adage is a well-known saying that often gives advice. Help students understand the adage *the early bird gets the worm.*

Advanced Ask students to explain what an idiom is and to work together to determine what the idiom and adage *don't burn any bridges* means.

Advanced High Have students find idioms in selections they have read recently and discuss with a partner what the idioms mean.

See ELL Lesson 20, pp. E42–E51, for scaffolded support.

✓ Idioms

1 Teach/Model

AL *Academic Language*

idiom an expression whose meaning cannot be learned from the usual meanings of the words

adage a traditional expression that has proven to be true over time

common saying a well-known expression, such as a proverb or slogan

• Explain that idioms are phrases or expressions whose meanings cannot be understood from the ordinary meanings of the individual words in the phrase.

• Tell students that other kinds of expressions, such as adages and proverbs, may also be idioms. Point out that these kinds of expressions often are examples of figurative language. Provide these adage and proverb examples and discuss their meanings with students: *Every rose has its thorns. Slow and steady wins the race.*

• Explain that idioms must be learned individually, as a chunk of language with a single meaning. Point out that even if they encounter an idiom that does not make sense, the general meaning of the phrase may be implied by the context of the sentence or selection. Tell students that context can help them determine the meanings of all kinds of expressions.

• Write these sentences on the board and read them aloud for students. *I'm not one to do anything without proper planning. I always look before I leap.*

• Model how to understand the meaning of the adage "look before you leap" by using context clues.

Think Aloud *The phrase "look before you leap" does not make sense to me. The sentence before it states "I am not one to do anything without proper planning." This means that a person plans and organizes rather than doing something hurriedly or without thought. Using context clues, I guess that the idiom "look before you leap" must not mean actually looking before you leap or jump. Instead, I think the idiom means planning and thinking carefully about your actions before doing them.*

2 Guided Practice

- Display the top half of **Projectable 20.5** and read "Nothing Ventured, Nothing Gained" aloud.

- Display the Column Map on the bottom half of **Projectable 20.5**.

- Help students identify the idioms in the passage. Circle or highlight the phrases.

- Have students use context clues to figure out the meanings of the idioms in the passage. Guide students as necessary, or use a dictionary or an idiomatic dictionary on the Internet.

- Guide students to determine the meanings of the idioms. Write each meaning in the Column Map. Discuss with students why certain idioms might have come to mean what they do.

Projectable 20.5

Don Quixote and the Windmills Vocabulary Strategies Idioms

Idioms

Nothing Ventured, Nothing Gained

Some folks like to make resolutions for the new year. Me? I prefer to stick with what I already know. For instance, I always plan ahead and make sure to look before I leap. I have friends who believe that ignorance is bliss, but that kind of unpreparedness really gets on my nerves. I always try to keep my cool and never, ever blow my top. Still, I've got big dreams to fulfill, and they're going to take a lot of hard work to accomplish. When someone tells me to relax and settle down, I get out my planner and show them my schedule for the next 10 years. Hey, I'm a busy girl with a lot to get done. After all, Rome wasn't built in a day!

Vocabulary
- blow
- bliss
- ventured
  - *aventurado*
- gained
- leap
- ignorance
  - *ignorancia*
- nerves
  - *nervios*

*Spanish cognates

Look before you leap	Ignorance is bliss	Gets on your nerves	Keep your cool	Blow your top	Rome wasn't built in a day
To think carefully about the possible consequences before doing something	If you don't know about something, you can't worry about it.	When someone or something irritates you	Remaining calm in a difficult or stressful situation	To become very angry	Big projects take a lot of time and effort to complete properly.

3 Apply

- Have partners use the Internet or other sources to find examples of idioms, adages, and common sayings. Tell them to work together to determine the meaning of each expression and to use it in a sentence. Tell students they may use a dictionary to help confirm their understanding. Then have two groups explain their idioms, adages, and common sayings to the other group.

Monitor Vocabulary Strategies

Are students able to identify and use idioms?

IF...	THEN...
students have difficulty identifying and using idioms,	▶ **Differentiate Vocabulary Strategies** for Struggling Readers, p. T364. *See also Intervention Lesson 20, pp. S42–S51.*
students can identify and use idioms most of the time,	▶ **Differentiate Vocabulary Strategies** for On-Level Readers, p. T364.
students can consistently identify and use idioms,	▶ **Differentiate Vocabulary Strategies** for Advanced Readers, p. T365.

SMALL GROUP Options

Differentiate Vocabulary Strategies: pp. T364–T365. *Group English Language Learners according to language proficiency.*

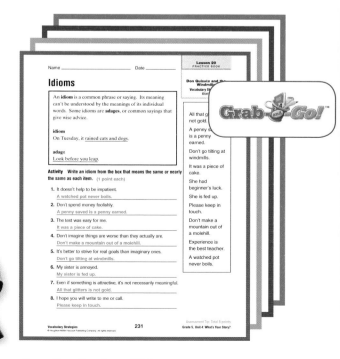

Idioms

An **idiom** is a common phrase or saying. Its meaning can't be understood by the meanings of its individual words. Some idioms are **adages**, or common sayings that give wise advice.

idiom
On Tuesday, it rained cats and dogs.

adage
Look before you leap.

Activity Write an idiom from the box that means the same or nearly the same as each item. (1 point each)

1. It doesn't help to be impatient.
   A watched pot never boils.
2. Don't spend money foolishly.
   A penny saved is a penny earned.
3. The test was easy for me.
   It was a piece of cake.
4. Don't imagine things are worse than they actually are.
   Don't make a mountain out of a molehill.
5. It's better to strive for real goals than from imaginary ones.
   Don't go tilting at windmills.
6. My sister is annoyed.
   My sister is fed up.
7. Even if something is attractive, it's not necessarily meaningful.
   All that glitters is not gold.
8. I hope you will write to me or call.
   Please keep in touch.

All that glitters is not gold. A penny saved is a penny earned. Don't go tilting at windmills. It was a piece of cake. She had beginner's luck. She is fed up. Please keep in touch. Don't make a mountain out of a molehill. Experience is the best teacher. A watched pot never boils.

231

Practice Book p. 231
See Grab-and-Go™ Resources for additional leveled practice.

Connect and Extend

- Make connections across texts.
- Read independently for a sustained period of time.
- Differentiate between paraphrasing and plagiarism.
- Discuss and apply tips for viewing symbols and images.

Don Quixote and the Windmills   **LitBeat: Live from La Mancha**

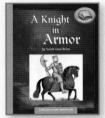

Vocabulary Reader

Struggling Readers   *On-Level Readers*

Advanced Readers   *English Language Learners*

Read to Connect

SHARE AND COMPARE TEXTS Have students compare and contrast this week's reading selections. Use the following prompts to guide discussion:

- Explain why it is important to understand the difference between fact and fantasy when you read about history.
- Explain how two or more texts from this week's literature might be helpful to someone who wants to write a realistic fiction piece based on history.

CONNECT TEXT TO WORLD Use these prompts to help deepen student thinking and discussion. Accept students' opinions, but encourage them to support their ideas with text details and other information from their reading.

- Why is it important to know the difference between fact and fantasy when you prepare a report for school?
- Which type of writing or reading do you enjoy more—informational or fantasy? Why?

Independent Reading

BOOK TALK Have partners discuss their independent reading for the week. Tell them to refer to their Reading Log or journal and summarize the main ideas. Have them paraphrase a favorite section, maintaining its meaning and order. Then have students discuss the following:

- how the cultural or historical context of each text supports their understanding
- the selections' theme
- the selections' story structure

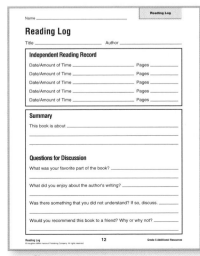

Reading Log

Extend Through Research

PARAPHRASING VS. PLAGIARISM Tell students that when they conduct research for a report and take notes from reference texts, it is important for them to paraphrase, or retell the information in their own words. Explain to students that using an author's exact words in their own writing is called *plagiarism*. It is taking credit for someone else's work, which is not acceptable.

- Show students an excerpt from a reference source. Choose a sentence from the text and write on the board examples of paraphrasing and plagiarism. Guide students to identify the examples correctly.

- Ask students to select a research topic that connects to what they learned this week and frame a research question.

- Have students locate two sources that contain information about their research topic. Then have them write a short composition in which they paraphrase information from the source to answer their research question. Have partners review each other's work to confirm they did not plagiarize. Discuss with students the importance of paraphrasing, not plagiarizing, words or ideas from a source when conducting research.

Listening and Speaking

VIEW SYMBOLS AND IMAGES Tell students that they will be viewing different kinds of symbols and images and discussing why they are important. Explain that a symbol can convey a large amount of information using no words at all. Tell students to think about the American flag. There are no words on the flag, yet it symbolizes many ideals. Explain that with a partner, they will choose a symbol or image that conveys information. Have them conduct research in appropriate reference sources to understand the symbol and its meanings. Then have them present the symbol to the class and explain what it represents and why it is important.

Allow students time to prepare their presentations. Tell them to focus on
  - speaking at an appropriate rate or speed;
  - making eye contact with the audience;
  - using an appropriate volume; and
  - adapting their language to their audience and purpose.

While students give their presentations, have audience members use the Listening Log to record what they have learned.

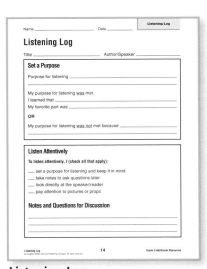

Listening Log

Spelling Words from Other Languages

- Spell words from other languages.

Spelling Words

Basic

salsa	dungarees	iguana
mattress	lasso	plaza
tycoon	patio	caravan
burrito	siesta	hammock
bandana	cargo	pajamas
tomato	vanilla	✪ gallant
poncho	tsunami	

Review

canyon, ✪ mirror, magazine, rodeo, monkey

Challenge

mosquito, cathedral, alligator, tambourine, sombrero

✪ Forms of these words appear in "Don Quixote and the Windmills."

ELL ENGLISH LANGUAGE LEARNERS

Preteach

Spanish Cognates

Write and discuss these Spanish cognates for Spanish-speaking students.

lasso • *lazo*

caravan • *caravana*

gallant • *galante*

Day 1

❶ TEACH THE PRINCIPLE

- Administer the **Pretest**. Use the Day 5 sentences.

- Explain that many of our words come from other languages. Point out that *tomato* is from the Spanish word *tomate* and *tycoon* is from the Japanese word *taikun*. Discuss pronunciation and syllabication using the chart below.

2 syllables	tycoon (tī/kün)
3 syllables	tomato (tə /mā/tō)

❷ PRACTICE/APPLY

Guide students to correctly pronounce the remaining Spelling Words.

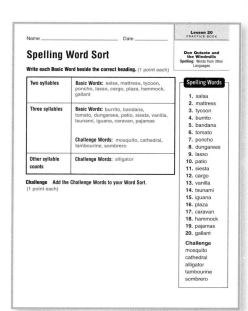

Practice Book p. 232

Day 2

❶ TEACH WORD SORT

- Set up two rows as shown. Model adding a Spelling Word to each row.

two syllables	sal/sa
three syllables	pa/ti/o

❷ PRACTICE/APPLY

- Have students add words from "Don Quixote and the Windmills."

Practice Book p. 233

Day 3

1 TEACH USING WORD ORIGINS

- **WRITE** *The company grew under the leadership of a tycoon.*

- Read aloud the sentence and underline *tycoon*. Remind students that its origin is Japanese. Have students use a dictionary to define *tycoon*.

- Explain that a word's origins can sometimes give readers a deeper understanding of that word.

- Work with students to use an online dictionary to look up the origin of *tycoon*. Point out that the idea of the Japanese Shogun, or military general, gives a better understanding of how a tycoon might run a business.

2 PRACTICE/APPLY

- Have partners choose five Spelling Words.

- Tell partners to use an online dictionary to look up the meaning and the origin of their chosen words. Have them discuss the relationships between each word's meaning and origin, and how the origin of the word can help readers better understand its meaning.

- Have partners use a dictionary or an etymology website to locate words derived from roots in languages such as German, French, and Spanish. Have them determine the word meaning and use each in a sentence.

Day 4

1 CONNECT TO WRITING

- Read and discuss the prompt below.

> ✏️ **Write to Narrate**
> Write a narrative paragraph about a person who is unique or special in some way.

2 PRACTICE/APPLY

- Guide students as they plan and write their narratives.

- Remind students to proofread their writing for errors in spelling. See p. T344.

Name _____ Date _____

Proofreading for Spelling

Find the misspelled words and circle them. Write them correctly on the lines below. (2 points each)

Dear Donnie,

We are having fun in Mexico, despite a tunami of chores before we left Laredo. I think the cargoe includes everything but a matress! Our carivan of three left early while it was still dark. I was still in my pajammas! While we drove along, I read *Don Quixote*. He is so gallent! He reminds me of you.

For lunch today, I ate a buritto with saulsa and vannilla flan in a little plazza. Yesterday, during my midday seista in a woven-rope hammack I watched a fat, lazy iguana on the hotel patio. I named him Sancho Panza. Today I am shopping for a ponchoe for you to wear as you ride among the giants.

Dulcy

1. tsunami
2. cargo
3. mattress
4. caravan
5. pajamas
6. gallant
7. burrito
8. salsa
9. vanilla
10. plaza
11. siesta
12. hammock
13. iguana
14. patio
15. poncho

Lesson 20
PRACTICE BOOK

Don Quixote and the Windmills
Spelling: Words from Other Languages

Spelling Words
1. salsa
2. mattress
3. tycoon
4. burrito
5. bandana
6. tomato
7. poncho
8. dungarees
9. lasso
10. patio
11. siesta
12. cargo
13. vanilla
14. tsunami
15. iguana
16. plaza
17. caravan
18. hammock
19. pajamas
20. gallant

Challenge
mosquito
cathedral
alligator
tambourine
sombrero

Practice Book p. 234

Day 5

ASSESS SPELLING

- Say each boldfaced word, read the sentence, and then repeat the word.

- Have students write the boldfaced word.

Basic

1. Nina served chips and **salsa**.
2. My old **mattress** is lumpy.
3. The **tycoon** owns many companies.
4. I had a **burrito** for lunch.
5. He wore a **bandana** on his head.
6. Please cut the **tomato** for the salad.
7. This **poncho** will keep you warm.
8. The laborer wore **dungarees**.
9. The cowgirl can **lasso** a cow.
10. We had dinner on the **patio**.
11. You cannot take a **siesta** in class.
12. What **cargo** does that ship carry?
13. Leon likes **vanilla** ice cream.
14. The **tsunami** destroyed the village.
15. Does an **iguana** make a good pet?
16. A crowd gathered in the **plaza**.
17. People travel by **caravan** in the desert.
18. Dad fell asleep on the **hammock**.
19. The child put on his **pajamas**.
20. The **gallant** knight killed the dragon.

Grammar ✓ Contractions

- Use apostrophes in contractions.
- Use contractions with pronouns.

ELL ENGLISH LANGUAGE LEARNERS

Scaffold

Beginning Tell students that negative contractions are made by joining a verb with the word *not*. Display the sentences below. Read them aloud and have students repeat. Explain to them that although one uses a contraction and one does not, the meanings are the same.

I do not have a pet. I don't have a pet.

Intermediate Have students change the words in parentheses to contractions to complete the sentence frames below.

Why _____ you going to school today? (are not) (aren't)

I _____ have any more food to share. (do not) (don't)

I _____ spent any more money. (have not) (haven't)

Advanced Write verbs on the board with *not*. Have students combine the words and spell out the contractions, including the apostrophe.

Advanced High Have students work in pairs. Have one partner say a contraction. Have the other partner explain how the contraction is formed. Then have them use the contractions in sentences.

*See ELL Lesson 20, pp. E42–E51,
for scaffolded support.*

JOURNEYS DIGITAL **Powered by** DESTINATIONReading®
Grammar Activiies: Lesson 20

Day 1 TEACH

DAILY PROOFREADING PRACTICE
Who became Don Quixotes wife. *Quixote's; ?*

❶ TEACH CONTRACTIONS WITH *NOT*; APOSTROPHE

PROJECTABLE **20.6**

- Display **Projectable 20.6**. Explain that contractions are two words joined together into a shorter word, and are typically used in conversation and informal writing. A common type of contraction is made by joining *not* with a verb, such as *are, can,* and *do*. An apostrophe takes the place of *o* in the word *not*.

- Write: *It'll be a great story if there isn't a sad ending.* Model identifying a contraction with *not*.

> **Think Aloud** *To identify a contraction with* not, *I look for words with* n, *an apostrophe, and* t. *I ask this Thinking Question: Which contraction is made with the word* not? *I see that the word* isn't *is made with the word* not, *so it must be the contraction.*

❷ PRACTICE/APPLY

- Complete **Projectable 20.6** with students.

- List on the board: *is, should, do, could, are, have.* Have students combine the words with *not* and call out the contractions. Then have them spell each one. *isn't, shouldn't, don't, couldn't, aren't, haven't*

- Tell students to avoid using another "no" word with a "not" contraction. Tell them that doing so creates a **double negative**. Discuss with students why the following sentence is incorrect. Then work with them to fix it. *He doesn't want no one's help. anyone's help*

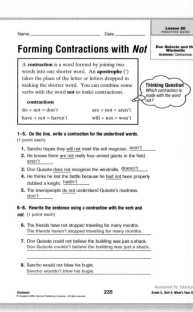

Practice Book p. 235

Day 2 TEACH

DAILY PROOFREADING PRACTICE

Sancho never could not have seen a giant. *delete "never"; couldn't*

① TEACH CONTRACTIONS WITH PRONOUNS

- Display **Projectable 20.7.** Point out to students that some contractions are made by combining a pronoun with a verb. An apostrophe is used to replace the missing letters. Discuss the examples provided.

- Model identifying contractions with pronouns in the example sentence: *They're telling us a story.*

Think Aloud *To identify a contraction that combines a pronoun with a verb, I look for words with a pronoun and an apostrophe. I ask this Thinking Question: Which word is made up of a pronoun and a verb? The word* they're *is made up of* they *and* are, *so it is the contraction.*

② PRACTICE/APPLY

- Complete items 1–8 on **Projectable 20.7** with students.

- List on the board: *he will, they will, you will, we are, they are, you are, she would, they would, you would.* Have students combine the pronouns and verbs to make contractions. Make sure they include the apostrophe correctly.

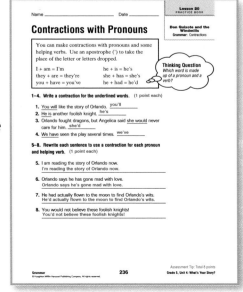

Practice Book p. 236

Day 3 TEACH

DAILY PROOFREADING PRACTICE

Theyre going to do battle with the windmills. *They're; windmills*

PROJECTABLE
20.8

① TEACH PRONOUN CONTRACTIONS AND HOMOPHONES

- Display **Projectable 20.8.** Point out to students that a variety of contractions can be made by combining two words and using an apostrophe to replace missing letters.

- Remind students that a contraction is a way to say the same thing using just one word rather than two. Model how using a contraction shortens a sentence: *We are not wearing our armor today. We aren't wearing our armor today.*

Think Aloud *To shorten a sentence, I ask this Thinking Question: Which words can be combined to make a contraction? The words* are *and* not *can be shortened to* aren't.

② PRACTICE/APPLY

- Complete items 1–7 on **Projectable 20.8** with students.

- Tell students that homophones are words that sound the same, but have different spellings and meanings. Write *you're* next to *your* on the board. Explain that *you're* means "you are," but *your* means "something that belongs to you." Have students think of sentences using both words. Continue with other word pairs, such as *its/it's; we'll/wheel.*

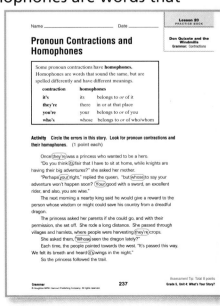

Practice Book p. 237

Day 4 REVIEW

DAILY PROOFREADING PRACTICE

Quixote weren't afraid and he winned the battle.
wasn't; won

1 REVIEW CONTRACTIONS

• Remind students that a negative contraction is made by joining a verb with the word *not*. The apostrophe takes the place of the missing letter *o*. Contractions can be made by combining a pronoun and a verb. Some contractions are homophones.

2 SPIRAL REVIEW

Easily Confused Verbs Tell students that the meanings of some verbs are easily confused with the meanings of others. One pair of verbs that are frequently confused are *can* and *may*. Write the following sentences on the board:

Can you reach the top of the ladder?

May I call you later?

• Explain that the verb *can* means "to be able," while *may* means "to be allowed." Have students practice using *can* and *may* by identifying the correct verb in the sentences below.

Bears (can, may) hibernate for months at a time. *(can)*

(Can, May) I visit you at work today? *(May)*

(Can, May) we go outside to play? *(May)*

Practice Book p. 238

Day 5 CONNECT TO WRITING

DAILY PROOFREADING PRACTICE

Sancho said, "Ill save your!" *I'll; you*

1 CONNECT TO WRITING

• Tell students that forming contractions correctly and checking to make sure to avoid double negatives is important to keep the writing clear and easy to read.

• Point out that an important part of proofreading is to make sure that the apostrophe in a contraction is placed correctly.

2 PRACTICE/APPLY

• Have students turn to **Student Book** p. 522. Review the rules for joining two words to make a contraction, combining a verb with the word *not* to make a negative, and making contractions with personal pronouns and verbs. Then have students complete the *Try This!* activity.

• Display the following paragraph. Have students find words that can be combined into a contraction.

Don Quixote did not have a helmet. He would not get a proper helmet until he won his first battle. His friend Sancho could not see any giants. He has helped Don Quixote a lot. *didn't, wouldn't, couldn't, He's*

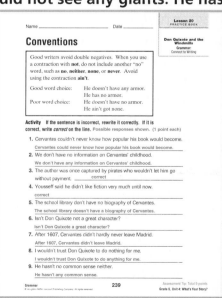

Practice Book p. 239

Grammar

What Is a Contraction? A **contraction** is a word formed by joining two words into one shorter word. An **apostrophe** (') takes the place of the letter or letters that are dropped in making the shorter word. You can combine some verbs with the **negative** word *not* to make contractions. You can also combine personal pronouns with verbs such as *is, are, have, had,* and *will* to make contractions.

Academic Language

contraction
apostrophe
negative

Examples of Contractions Made with Verbs Plus *Not*			
do not	don't	were not	weren't
does not	doesn't	will not	won't
is not	isn't	has not	hasn't

Examples of Contractions Made with Pronouns Plus Verbs			
I am	I'm	I have	I've
he is	he's	he has	he's
you are	you're	you have	you've
they are	they're	they have	they've
you will	you'll	you had	you'd

Try This! **Rewrite each sentence below on another sheet of paper. Replace each pair of boldfaced words with a contraction.**

1. You **are not** going to believe this tale.
2. **It is** about a knight on a quest.
3. **He is** determined to slay dragons.
4. **They are** nowhere to be found.
5. You **will not** guess what he attacks instead!

522

Conventions When using a contraction, make sure you put the apostrophe in the correct place. In a contraction with a pronoun and a verb, make sure the verb agrees in number with the pronoun. When using a contraction with *not,* avoid including another "no" word and creating a double negative. Finally, avoid using the contraction *ain't.*

Incorrect	Correct
He does'nt like giants.	He doesn't like giants.
They's watching the battle.	They're watching the battle.
He doesn't fear nobody.	He doesn't fear anybody.
Once again, he ain't the winner.	Once again, he isn't the winner.

Connect Grammar to Writing

As you edit your personal narrative, make sure you have used and written contractions correctly. Be sure to correct any contraction errors you find.

523

Try This!

1. *aren't*
2. *It's*
3. *He's*
4. *They're*
5. *won't*

CONNECT GRAMMAR TO WRITING

- Have students turn to **Student Book p. 523**. Read the Conventions paragraph with students.

- Read the sentences in the chart. Point out to students how each of the errors on the left side has been corrected on the right.

- Tell students that as they revise their personal narratives, they should check to make sure that their contractions are used correctly.

- Review the Common Errors at right with students.

COMMON ERRORS

Error: Were going to battle soon.

Correct: We're going to battle soon.

Error: I dont know if **its** good or bad.

Correct: I don't know if **it's** good or bad.

Error: I do not think I **have got no** helmet.

Correct: I don't think **I've** got a helmet.

Error: She **isnt** going to the party.

Correct: She **isn't** going to the party.

Days 1–3

Write to Narrate   Write a Personal Narrative

SHARE OBJECTIVES

- Draft a personal narrative.
- Write, revise, and edit drafts.
- Publish final drafts.

Academic Language

dialogue conversation between characters in a story

descriptive details ideas that provide more information about characters, events, and settings and that help to reveal the author's thoughts and feelings

voice how a writer's feelings are conveyed in his or her writing

ELL ENGLISH LANGUAGE LEARNERS

Scaffold

Beginning Provide sentence frames such as *My story made me feel _____.* Guide students in creating a narrative that includes thoughts and feelings. Work with them to complete the sentence frames.

Intermediate Ask students to describe something they did during the day today. Ask them to describe their thoughts and feelings about the event.

Advanced Have students choose a familiar story they know and write their own attention-grabbing beginning to the story.

Advanced High Before they begin writing their drafts, ask partners to discuss different beginnings they can use for their stories. Have them write two possible attention-grabbing beginnings.

JOURNEYS DIGITAL | **Powered by** DESTINATIONReading®
WriteSmart CD-ROM

Day 1 DRAFT

❶ TEACH DRAFTING

- Tell students that they will be writing drafts of the personal narratives that they planned last week. Discuss the following:

> What Is a Personal Narrative?
>
> - It is a story about someone's own experiences from his or her point of view.
> - It includes details about the author's thoughts and feelings.
> - It includes descriptive details about events and ideas in the story that show the reader how the author feels.

- Explain that a good personal narrative begins in a way that draws readers into the story, making them want to find out what happens next.

- Read aloud the first paragraph on **Student Book p. 524**. Discuss how the author introduces the story elements. Ask: *How does the author begin the narrative?* with a quotation *What do you think the story will be about? It will be about how the main character solves a problem of having no room in the closet.*

❷ PRACTICE/APPLY

- Have students use their completed events chart from Lesson 19 to begin drafting their personal narratives.

- Remind them that the beginning should grab the reader's attention and draw them into the story.

LESSON	FORM	TRAIT
16	Friendly Letter	Voice
17	Character Description	Word Choice
18	Personal Narrative Paragraph	Voice
19	Prewrite: Personal Narrative	Ideas
20	**Draft, Revise, Edit, Publish: Personal Narrative**	**Voice**

Language Arts

Writing

Day 2 DRAFT

① INTRODUCE THE FOCUS TRAIT: VOICE

- Remind students that the voice of a piece of writing can help the reader get a better sense of the story by helping them to relate to the characters and to understand how the author feels about those characters.

Connect to "Don Quixote and the Windmills"

Instead of this...	...the author wrote this.
Don Quixote thought the windmills in the distance were giants.	"There stand the monstrous giants who have plagued this countryside long enough." (p. 512)

- Read aloud the rest of **Student Book p. 512** and discuss how the dialogue of Don Quixote helps give the story a voice.

② PRACTICE/APPLY

- Have students continue to draft their personal narratives. Remind them to think about the voice of their narrative. Have them include their thoughts and feelings about the events in their narrative.

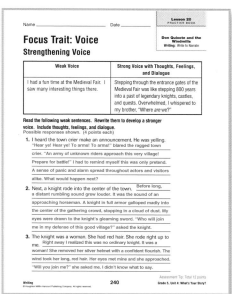

Practice Book, p. 240

Day 3 DRAFT

① TEACH OPENINGS

- Explain that good writers use a strong opening to hook the reader's attention and guide them to continue reading.

- Read aloud the passage opening on **Student Book p. 509.** Discuss what makes this a good opening.

Think Aloud *The opening talks directly to the reader and asks questions about the kinds of stories that are most exciting. It makes the reader wonder how such stories can affect someone who spends a lot of time thinking about them. It makes readers want to continue reading.*

- Point out that good openings help to get the reader interested in what the writer has to say.

② PRACTICE/APPLY

- Work with students to brainstorm a list of possible openings that might hook the reader and make them interested in reading more.

- Give students an opportunity to rewrite this sample opening so that it is more exciting to the reader:

  The school fair starts today at 3:00.

- Have students review their completed events chart to identify events that might help make an opening interesting.

- Explain to students that as they complete the first draft of their personal narratives, they should make sure they thought about a good opening for their story.

- Have students complete the first draft of their personal narratives.

Day 4 REVISE

1 INTRODUCE THE STUDENT MODEL

- Have students turn to **Student Book p. 524**. Read aloud the top of the page and the Writing Process Checklist for Revising.

- Read aloud the Revised Draft on **Student Book p. 524**. Discuss the revisions made by the student writer. Ask: *What kind of changes did Rama make to his draft? He made his opening more interesting and added more dialogue.*

- Reread **Student Book p. 524**. Have students identify descriptive details that help the reader understand the events of the story.

2 PRACTICE/APPLY

- Have students read the first drafts of their narratives and use the Writing Process Checklist to revise them.

- Remind them to make sure they have written the best opening that they can to hook the reader's attention.

- Point out that they should look for opportunities to include descriptive details about events and ideas in their narrative.

- Have student pairs evaluate each other's writing, focusing on openings and places in the narrative where more detail or description is needed.

Day 5 REVISE, EDIT, AND PUBLISH

1 TEACH/MODEL

- Have students turn to **Student Book p. 525**. Read Rama's Final Copy as a class and discuss the *Reading as a Writer* questions.

- Display **Projectable 20.9**. Read the Student Model aloud, and model how to proofread using proofreader marks. Then, work with students to revise the rest of the draft.

2 PRACTICE/APPLY

- Have students revise and edit their drafts and include changes based on peer and teacher feedback.

- **Proofreading** Have students proofread their revised first drafts. For support, have students use the **Proofreading Checklist Blackline Master**.

- **Publish** Tell students to create a final copy of their stories. Provide the following publishing options:

1. **Dramatic Reading** Writers can give dramatic readings of their stories.

2. **Booklet** Students can illustrate their stories and publish them in booklets.

3. **Classroom Literary Journal** Students can collect their stories in a classroom literary journal.

Projectable 20.9

Don Quixote and the Windmills Revising Write to Narrate

Revising Rama's Personal Narrative

Proofread Rama's draft. Use proofreading marks to correct any errors or make any improvements.

"What is this jacket doing on the floor?" demanded my mother.

"No room in the closet, that's what," I replied.
My mother told me to hang up my coat.

As I was trying to squeeze my fat winter jacket into our overstuffed hall closet, I had a brainstorm. "What's causing this closet to be crowded?" I thought. "There are only four of us Ramdevs".

When my mother saw the mess I'd made, she wasn't too pleased. I explained my idea. I said, "Think about all the people in this city who can't buy a coat. Why don't we give them our extras?"

Reading-Writing Workshop: Revise

Write to Narrate

☑ **Voice** A good **personal narrative** tells about an important or interesting event in your life in ways that only you can express. When you revise your narrative, add words and ideas that let the reader "hear" your own voice.

Rama used his events chart to draft a narrative about his Warm Coat Project. Later, he added a new opening to grab his readers' attention.

Writing Process Checklist

Prewrite

Draft

▶ Revise
- ☑ Did I begin with an attention-grabber?
- ☑ Did I include only important events and tell them in order?
- ☑ Did I use vivid details and dialogue?
- ☑ Do my feelings come through?
- ☑ Are my sentences smooth and varied?
- ☑ Does my ending show how the events worked out?

Edit

Publish and Share

524

Revised Draft

"What is this jacket doing on the floor?" demanded my mother.

"No room in the closet, that's what," I replied. ~~My mother~~ She told me to hang up ~~my~~ it anyway, of course. ~~coat.~~

As I was trying to squeeze my fat winter jacket into our overstuffed hall closet, I had a brainstorm. "What's causing this closet to be crowded?" I thought. "There are only four of us Ramdevs."

Final Copy

My Warm Coat Project
by Rama Ramdev

"What is this jacket doing on the floor?" demanded my mother.

"No room in the closet, that's what," I replied. She told me to hang it up anyway, of course.

As I was trying to squeeze my fat winter jacket into our overstuffed hall closet, I had a brainstorm. "What's causing this closet to be crowded?" I thought. "There are only four of us Ramdevs."

Right then, I started pulling everything out. I put the coats in piles and saw that every member of the family had at least one coat they didn't use anymore.

When my mother saw the mess I'd made, she wasn't too pleased. I quickly explained my idea. I said, "Think about all the people in this city who can't afford to buy a warm coat! Why don't we give them our extras?"

> In my final paper, I added dialogue to grab readers' attention. I also used contractions to make my writing sound more natural.

Reading as a Writer

How does Rama's opening capture his readers' interest? In your story, where could you add dialogue or interesting details?

525

Writing Traits Scoring Rubric

	Focus/Ideas	☑ **Organization**	**Voice**	☑ **Word Choice**	☑ **Sentence Fluency**	**Conventions**
4	Adheres to the topic, is interesting, has a sense of completeness. Ideas are well developed.	Ideas and details are clearly presented and well organized.	Connects with reader in a unique, personal way.	Includes vivid verbs, strong adjectives, specific nouns.	Includes a variety of complete sentences that flow smoothly, naturally.	Shows a strong command of grammar, spelling, capitalization, punctuation.
3	Mostly adheres to the topic, is somewhat interesting, has a sense of completeness. Ideas are adequately developed.	Ideas and details are mostly clear and generally organized.	Generally connects with reader in a way that is personal and sometimes unique.	Includes some vivid verbs, strong adjectives, specific nouns.	Includes some variety of mostly complete sentences. Some parts flow smoothly, naturally.	Shows a good command of grammar, spelling, capitalization, punctuation.
2	Does not always adhere to the topic, has some sense of completeness. Ideas are superficially developed.	Ideas and details are not always clear or organized. There is some wordiness or repetition.	Connects somewhat with reader. Sounds somewhat personal, but not unique.	Includes mostly simple nouns and verbs, and may have a few adjectives.	Includes mostly simple sentences, some of which are incomplete.	Some errors in grammar, spelling, capitalization, punctuation.
1	Does not adhere to the topic, has no sense of completeness. Ideas are vague.	Ideas and details are not organized. Wordiness or repetition hinders meaning.	Does not connect with reader. Does not sound personal or unique.	Includes only simple nouns and verbs, some inaccurate. Writing is not descriptive.	Sentences do not vary. Incomplete sentences hinder meaning.	Frequent errors in grammar, spelling, capitalization, punctuation.

See also ***Writing Rubric Blackline Master*** and Teacher's Edition pp. R18–R21.

Progress Monitoring

Assess

- Weekly Tests
- Fluency Tests
- Periodic Assessments

Respond to Assessment

☑ Vocabulary
Target Vocabulary
Strategies: Idioms

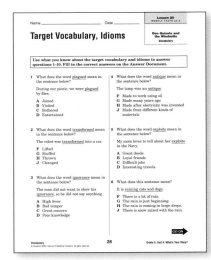

Weekly Tests 20.2–20.3

IF	a Student Scores...	THEN...
7–10 of 10	▶ Continue Core Instructional Program.
4–6 of 10	▶ **Reteaching Lesson,** page T366
1–3 of 10	▶ **Intervention** Lesson 20, pp. S42–S51

☑ Comprehension
Understanding Characters

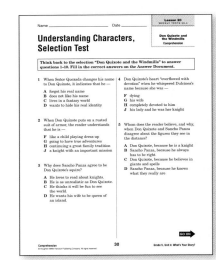

Weekly Tests 20.4–20.5

IF	a Student Scores...	THEN...
7–10 of 10	▶ Continue Core Instructional Program.
4–6 of 10	▶ **Reteaching Lesson,** page T366
1–3 of 10	▶ **Intervention** Lesson 20, pp. S42–S51

Powered by
DESTINATIONReading®
- Online Assessment System
- Weekly Tests

☑ Decoding
Stress in Three-Syllable Words

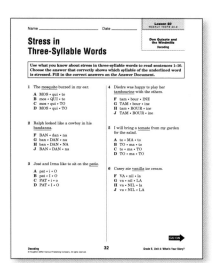

Weekly Tests 20.6–20.7

IF a Student Scores...	THEN...
7–10 of 10	▶ Continue Core Instructional Program.
4–6 of 10	▶ Reteaching Lesson, page T367
1–3 of 10	▶ Intervention Lesson 20, pp. S42–S51

☑ Language Arts
Grammar: Contractions

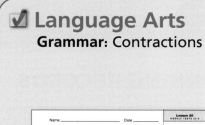 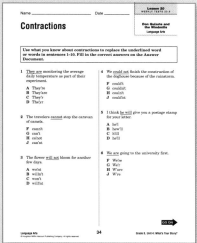

Weekly Tests 20.8–20.9

Writing Traits Rubrics
See *TE* pp. R18–R21.

IF a Student Scores...	THEN...
7–10 of 10	▶ Continue Core Instructional Program.
4–6 of 10	▶ Reteaching Lesson, page T367
1–3 of 10	▶ Intervention Lesson 20, pp. S42–S51

☑ Fluency

Fluency Assessment Plan
Assess one group per week.
Use this suggested plan below.

● Struggling Readers	Weeks 1, 3, 5
▲ On Level	Week 2
■ Advanced	Week 4

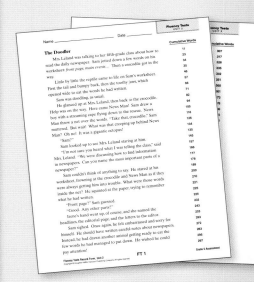

Fluency Record Form

Fluency Scoring Rubric
See *Grab-and-Go™ Resources Assessment* for help in measuring progress.

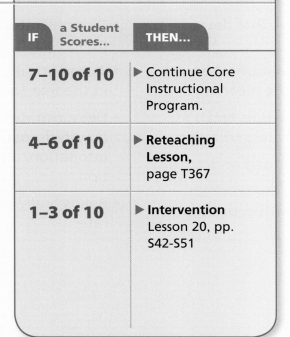
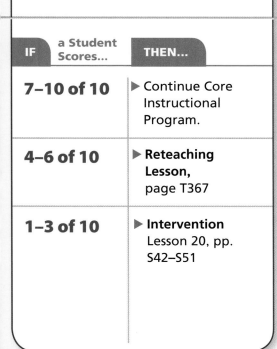

Progress Monitoring

 ## Small Group

RUNNING RECORDS

To assess individual progress, occasionally use small group time to take a reading record for each student. Use the results to plan instruction.

 Struggling Readers

 On Level

 Advanced

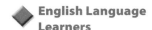 English Language Learners

For running records, see **Grab-and-Go™ Resources: Lesson 20,** pp. 13–16.

Behaviors and Understandings to Notice

- Self-corrects errors that detract from meaning.
- Self-corrects intonation when it does not reflect the meaning.
- Rereads to solve words and resumes normal rate of reading.
- Demonstrates phrased and fluent oral reading.
- Reads dialogue with expression.

- Demonstrates awareness of punctuation.
- Automatically solves most words in the text to read fluently.
- Demonstrates appropriate stress on words, pausing and phrasing, intonation, and use of punctuation.
- Reads orally at an appropriate rate.

Discuss Reading Strategies

Remind students that the strategies of successful readers can help them read passages on a test. Tell students that they should try using different strategies during practice tests and think about the strategies that best help them understand what they read. Display and discuss with students the following strategies:

• Read the title and preview the text.

• Look at the photographs and illustrations. Read the captions.

• Read the questions after the passage to help you focus as you read.

• Underline or make a note about anything that seems to be important.

• Ask yourself questions as you read: *How can I find the meaning of a new word that is used in both the nonfiction selection and the fiction story?*

Also remind students of the Target Strategies they have learned. Tell them to practice using the strategies with test passages as well.

- **Question**
- **Infer/Predict**
- **Analyze/Evaluate**
- **Monitor/Clarify**
- **Summarize**
- **Visualize**

SKILL TRACE

Test Power Focus	
Unit 1	Read Fiction
Unit 2	Read Nonfiction
Unit 3	Read Fiction
Unit 4	Compare Texts
Unit 5	Compare Texts

1 Teach/Model

Tell students that a test may ask them to read two selections back to back and then answer questions about how the pieces of writing are alike and how they are different.

- Tell students that paired reading selections on a test will have something in common. They may have similar main ideas, subjects, themes, plots, characters, or organization.

- Have students turn to **Student Book pp. 526–527**. Call on a volunteer to read aloud the direction line on Student Book p. 526.

Read the next two selections. Think about the author's purpose in each selection.

Skateboarding Through the Decades

Skateboarding has been around for more than fifty years. It all began in the 1950s. When the waves were flat and real surfing wasn't an option, surfers still wanted to have some fun. Maybe they could "surf the sidewalks"! Someone attached roller skate wheels to the bottom of a wooden board. Skateboarding was born.

In the early 1960s, companies manufactured huge numbers of skateboards. More than 50 million of them were sold in three years! There were skateboarding contests. A famous music group sang "Sidewalk Surfing" while riding a skateboard across the stage. Then, in the late 1960s, skateboarding's popularity crashed. It seemed that the fad was over.

Things picked up again in the 1970s. That's when urethane skateboard wheels were invented. Wheels made from this tough material gave a smooth and stable ride. Other improvements were made, too. Now skateboarders had better control. They could do new tricks, such as the "ollie." In this trick, skaters kick the tail of the board down while jumping, making the board pop into the air. During the 1970s, concrete skate parks sprang up—but closed when insurance rates skyrocketed.

During the 1980s, skaters took to the streets. Any place that offered a ramp, a wall, or a set of steps would do. People built wooden skate ramps in backyards and empty lots.

In 1995, ESPN's Extreme Games showed skateboarding events. Skateboarding stars appeared in commercials. Skateboarding clothing became a fashion style.

As the new century rolled around, so did the wheels of millions of skateboards. Cities built new skate parks. There were skateboarding camps. In 2004, a new holiday was created. Every year on June 21st, skateboarders around the globe take part in Go Skateboarding Day.

Extreme Sports Journal

526

ELL ENGLISH LANGUAGE LEARNERS

Scaffold

Beginning Help students preview the selections by discussing the topic and pronouncing unfamiliar words. Work with students to help them name the parts of the skateboard in the illustrations.

Intermediate To advance students' understanding of content-area vocabulary, have students use a dictionary to identify the meaning of each of these words: *invented, improvements, style.*

Advanced After previewing the selections, have partners write and discuss questions they have about skateboarding.

Advanced High Based on their preview of the selections, have students list and discuss vocabulary terms they think they might encounter in the selections.

The Best Place to Skateboard

Sam, Marco, and Jade stood in front of the sign, staring in disbelief. "Construction zone. Do not enter!" Sam read.

"Unbelievable!" said Jade. "That was the perfect place to skateboard. Where are we supposed to skateboard now?"

Glumly, Marco spun the urethane wheels on his board. "The nearest skate park is too far away," he said.

Sam looked thoughtful. "I have some work to do in the library," he said.

For the rest of the week, Sam went to the library every day after school. Marco and Jade hardly saw him.

Finally, Jade said to Sam, "You don't have to give up skateboarding just because we don't have a good place to practice! Why are you always at the library?" Sam just said that he was working on something. Marco and Jade didn't see him after school the next week, either.

On Saturday, Sam showed up at Marco's house. Marco and Jade were in the driveway on their skateboards. "Ask your parents if you can walk with me to the warehouse where my mom works," Sam said. "Bring your boards and your gear. I want to show you something."

The three friends walked to the warehouse. Sam led the way to an area behind the building.

"Look at those ramps!" said Jade.

"Where did you get the money to buy them?" asked Marco.

"I didn't buy them," answered Sam. "I built them. I researched the plans in the library. Then I got the wood from the warehouse. It was left over from a job. My mom's boss said I could use the wood to build the ramps. He even said that we could skate here on the weekends!"

"Way to go, Sam!" said Marco. "Now, let's practice some ollies!"

527

- Call on volunteers to read aloud the two passages on **Student Book pp. 526–527** aloud as the other students follow along. You may want to pause after the first selection to have students summarize the journal article. Pause periodically during reading to discuss similarities students have noticed between the selections.

- Then distribute **Blackline Master** 20.15. Work with students to help them answer the questions, using the passages in the **Student Book**.

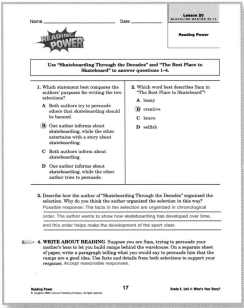

Blackline Master 20.15

Unit 4 Wrap-Up

The Big Idea

- Read the activity with students, and discuss the kinds of stories told by different characters in Unit 4 tell. Ask: *How do the characters make their stories interesting for readers?*

- Help students find a "way in" to writing their own story. Some may find it easiest to write a story about something that they have actually done or experienced. Others may find it helpful to draw a picture of the setting before they begin to write. Still others may come up with a story idea by freewriting.

- Have students use a graphic organizer, such as a story map or flow chart, to plan their writing.

Listening and Speaking

- So that they consider a variety of styles and approaches to illustration, encourage students to choose no more than one illustration from any selection.

- Tell students to consider not just *what* is pictured in each illustration, but also *how* scenes are illustrated and why they might be shown in this way. For example, such elements as color and line can reflect the mood of the selection. Similarly, illustrations that show characters with exaggerated features may reflect the humorous

Unit 4 Wrap-Up

The Big Idea

What's Your Story? In Unit 4, you read about several young writers and their creations. Write a short story that *you* would like to tell. Draw a picture that captures the setting of your story. Then write a caption that tells about the picture.

Listening and Speaking

Worth 1,000 Words Take another look at the illustrations in the selections you read in Unit 4. Choose the three you like best. Then tell a partner why you think they are the best, and explain how the illustrations add to the selection.

528

Weekly
Small Group Instruction

Day 1

Vocabulary Reader
- *A Knight in Armor*, T356

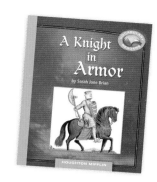

Day 2

Differentiate Comprehension
- Target Skill: Understanding Characters, T358
- Target Strategy: Question, T358

Day 3

Leveled Readers
- ● *Donald Quixote*, T360
- ▲ *El Camino Real*, T361
- ■ *A Night in the Kingdom*, T362
- ◆ *The Royal Road*, T363

Day 4

Differentiate Vocabulary Strategies
- Idioms, T364

Day 5

Options for Reteaching
- Vocabulary Strategies: Idioms , T366
- Comprehension Skill: Understanding Characters, T366
- Language Arts: Contractions/Write to Narrate, T367
- Decoding: Stress in Three-Syllable Words, T367

Ready-Made Work Stations

Independent Practice
- Comprehension and Fluency, T302
- Word Study, T302
- Think and Write, T303
- Digital Center, T303

Comprehension and Fluency   **Word Study**   **Think and Write**   **Digital Center**

Teacher-Led

	Day 1	Day 2	Day 3
Struggling Readers	**Vocabulary Reader** *A Knight in Armor*, Differentiated Instruction, p. T356	**Differentiate Comprehension** Understanding Characters; Question, p. T358	**Leveled Reader** *Donald Quixote*, p. T360
On Level	**Vocabulary Reader** *A Knight in Armor*, Differentiated Instruction, p. T356	**Differentiate Comprehension** Understanding Characters; Question, p. T358	**Leveled Reader** *El Camino Real*, p. T361
Advanced	**Vocabulary Reader** *A Knight in Armor*, Differentiated Instruction, p. T357	**Differentiate Comprehension** Understanding Characters; Question, p. T359	**Leveled Reader** *A Night in the Kingdom*, p. T362
English Language Learners	**Vocabulary Reader** *A Knight in Armor*, Differentiated Instruction, p. T357	**Differentiate Comprehension** Understanding Characters; Question, p. T359	**Leveled Reader** *The Royal Road*, p. T363

What are my other students doing?

	Day 1	Day 2	Day 3
Struggling Readers	• **Reread** *A Knight in Armor*	• **Vocabulary in Context Cards** 191–200 *Talk It Over* Activities • **Complete** Leveled Practice, SR20.1	• **Listen** to Audiotext CD of "Don Quixote and the Windmills"; Retell and discuss • **Complete** Leveled Practice, SR20.2
On Level	• **Reread** *A Knight in Armor*	• **Reread** "Don Quixote and the Windmills" with a partner • **Complete** Practice Book, p. 229	• **Reread** for Fluency: *El Camino Real* • **Complete** Practice Book, p. 230
Advanced	• **Context Cards** 191–200 *Talk It Over* Activities	• **Reread and Retell** "Don Quixote and the Windmills" • **Complete** Leveled Practice, A20.1	• **Reread** for Fluency: Leveled Reader *A Knight in the Kingdom* • **Complete** Leveled Practice A20.1
English Language Learners	• **Reread** *A Knight in Armor*	• **Listen** to Audiotext CD of "Don Quixote and the Windmills"; Retell and discuss • **Complete** Leveled Practice.	• **Vocabulary in Context Cards** 191–200 *Talk It Over* Activities • **Complete** Leveled Practice., ELL20.2

Ready-Made Work Stations

Assign these activities across the week to reinforce and extend learning.

Comprehension and Fluency
Timed Reading

Word Study
More Idioms

Day 4

Differentiate Vocabulary Strategies
Idioms, p. T364

Differentiate Vocabulary Strategies
Idioms, p. T364

Differentiate Vocabulary Strategies
Idioms, p. T365

Differentiate Vocabulary Strategies
Idioms, p. T365

Day 5

Options for Reteaching,
pp. T366–T367

Options for Reteaching,
pp. T366–T367

Options for Reteaching,
pp. T366–T367

Options for Reteaching,
pp. T366–T367

- **Partners: Reread** for Fluency
  Donald Quixote
- **Complete** Leveled
  Practice, SR20.3

- **Vocabulary in Context Cards**
  191–200 *Talk It Over* Activities
- **Complete** Practice Book, 231

- **Reread** for Fluency: "Don Quixote
  and the Windmills"
- **Complete** Leveled Practice, A20.1

- **Partners: Reread** for Fluency:
  The Royal Road
- **Complete** Leveled
  Practice, ELL20.3

- **Reread** for Fluency: "Don Quixote
  and the Windmills"
- **Complete** Work Station activities
- **Independent Reading**

- **Complete** Work Station activities
- **Independent Reading**

- **Complete** Work Station activities
- **Independent Reading**

- **Reread** *A Knight in Armor* or
  "Don Quixote and the Windmills"
- **Complete** Work Station activities
- **Independent Reading**

Think and Write
Notes to a Knight

JOURNEYS DIGITAL Powered by DESTINATION Reading

Digital Center

Weekly To-Do List

This Weekly To-Do List helps students
see their own progress and move on
to additional activities independently.

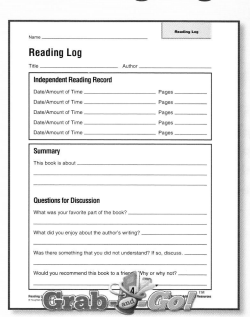

Reading Log

Vocabulary Reader

A Knight in Armor

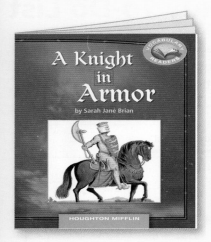

Summary

William Marshal (1144–1219) was one of the bravest knights that ever lived. This selection tells of the major battles and events in William's life.

TARGET VOCABULARY	
antique	quests
plagued	noble
pierced	ignorance
thrust	faithful
transformed	exploits

Struggling Readers

- Explain to students that about a thousand years ago during the Middle Ages, many boys dreamed of becoming knights. Have students tell what they know about knights of the Middle Ages. Explain that they will read about a real person, William Marshal, a great knight who served five kings.

- Guide students to preview the **Vocabulary Reader**. Read aloud the headings. Ask students to describe the images, using Target Vocabulary when possible.

- Have students alternate reading pages of the text aloud. Guide them to use context clues to determine the meanings of any unfamiliar words. As necessary, use the **Vocabulary in Context Cards** to review the meanings of vocabulary words.

- Assign the **Responding Page** and **Blackline Master 20.1**. Have partners work together to complete the pages.

On Level

- Have students tell what they know about knights of the Middle Ages. Explain that they will read about a real person, William Marshal, a great knight who served five kings. Point out that to be a knight required great strength and stamina. A suit of armor could weigh between 45-60 pounds. Guide students to preview the **Vocabulary Reader**.

- Remind students that context clues can help them determine the meaning of an unknown word. Tell students to use context clues to confirm their understanding of Target Vocabulary and to learn the meanings of new words.

- Have students alternate reading pages of the text aloud. Tell them to use context clues to determine the meanings of unknown words.

- Assign the **Responding Page** and **Blackline Master 20.1**. Have students discuss their responses with a partner.

Advanced

- Have students preview the **Vocabulary Reader** and make predictions about what they will read, using information from the preview and prior knowledge.

- Remind students to use context clues to help them determine the meanings of unknown words.

- Tell students to read the text with a partner. Ask them to stop and discuss the meanings of unknown words as necessary.

- Assign the **Responding Page** and **Blackline Master 20.1**. For the Write About It activity, remind students to use facts and details to support their ideas. Ask students to list the events that led to William Marshal's rise to power and influence in England.

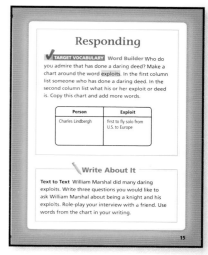

A Knight in Armor, p. 15

ELL English Language Learners

Group English Language Learners according to academic ability and language proficiency.

Beginning

Preview the selection with students, examining the illustrations. Whenever possible, use the Target Vocabulary words in the discussion. Read the Vocabulary Reader aloud with students, clarifying word meanings as needed.

Advanced

Have students work with a partner to write a synonym for each of the following Target Vocabulary words: *antique, exploits, faithful, pierced, plagued, quests, transformed.*

Intermediate

Provide sentence frames such as the following for students to practice the Target Vocabulary: *This sword is very old. It is an _____.* Then have students use the words in their own oral sentences.

Advanced High

Have students reread *A Knight in Armor*. Have them write a short summary of the story, telling the major events in the life of Marshal. Have them use as many vocabulary words from Lesson 20 as they can.

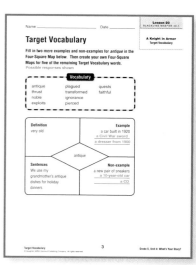

Blackline Master 20.1

Differentiate Comprehension

☑ Understanding Characters; Question

Struggling Readers

I DO IT

- Explain that readers can ask themselves questions to understand characters better.

- Read aloud p. 509 and model asking questions about the characters' words, thoughts, and actions.

Think Aloud *Señor Quexada spends all his time reading books about adventure. Why would he want to do that?*

WE DO IT

- Have students read p. 510 of "Don Quixote and the Windmills. "

- Have them identify who or what the passage is about.

- Guide students to formulate questions about characters' thoughts/feelings, actions, and words.

- Work with students to locate the answers to their questions in the text.

YOU DO IT

- Have students fill in Column Charts for the selection. Have them title the columns left to right: *What Character Thinks, What Character Does,* and *What Character Says.*

- Have them list questions about the characters in "Don Quixote and the Windmills."

- Have them look for answers in the text and complete their charts. Then have them share their charts with a partner.

On Level

I DO IT

- Read aloud p. 510 of "Don Quixote and the Windmills."

- Explain that questioning a character's relationships can help them understand the story.

- Model questioning how Don Quixote feels about and speaks/ acts towards Sancho in a Column Chart.

Thoughts	Actions	Words
Don Quixote thinks Sancho is loyal.	Don Quixote invites Sancho to accompany him.	He says he will give Sancho an island to rule.

WE DO IT

- Have students read p. 511 of "Don Quixote and the Windmills".

- Have a volunteer describe Sancho, and another describe Don Quixote.

- Work together to identify text details that support the students' descriptions.

YOU DO IT

- Have students complete the Column Chart for the two main characters. Have them head the columns left to right: *What Character Thinks, What Character Does,* and *What Character Says.*

- Have them work in pairs to compare and contrast the two characters using information in their Column Charts.

Advanced

I DO IT	WE DO IT	YOU DO IT
• Read aloud p. 516 of "Don Quixote and the Windmills." Explain that Don Quixote is an optimist.	• Discuss the character traits Sancho displays on p. 516.	• Have students use their Column Charts to write a paragraph comparing Sancho and Don Quixote.

Think Aloud *On this page, Don Quixote is an optimist who is looking forward to his next adventure despite his recent failure. He is ready to take on any problem.*

• List Sancho's characteristics on the board. Explain how these characteristics show him to be a realist, or a down-to-earth, sidekick.

• Have students discuss how the character traits of Don Quixote and Sancho affect their relationship. Ask why they may make a good "team."

• Invite students to model how they used the Question strategy to complete their Column Charts.

ELL English Language Learners

Group English Language Learners according to academic ability and language proficiency. Write the following sentence frames on the board: Don Quixote says____. Don Quixote feels____. Don Quixote does____. Ask students to help you fill in the blanks with examples of Don Quixote's words, thoughts, and actions. Then choose one of the following activities for additional support, as appropriate.

Beginning

Read aloud the first sentence frame. Fill in an example from the selection. Point to the example in the text as students follow. Have volunteers offer synonyms for *says*. *speaks, talks.* Repeat for *feels, does.*

Intermediate

With students, list examples of things Don Quixote says. Ask: *What does this tell you about the kind of person he is?* Repeat the exercise for examples of his thoughts and actions.

Advanced

Ask students to write a sentence explaining how Don Quixote thinks of himself. *Don Quixote thinks he is a brave knight.* Next, have students write a sentence describing how Don Quixote really is. *He is not a brave knight.*

Advanced High

Have students write about a few of Don Quixote's character traits. Remind them to include evidence from the selection. They should focus on examples of his words, feelings, and actions. Then have students share their sentences with a partner.

 **TARGET SKILL**

Understanding Characters

 **TARGET STRATEGY**

Question

 **TARGET VOCABULARY**

antique	quests
plagued	noble
pierced	ignorance
thrust	faithful
transformed	exploits

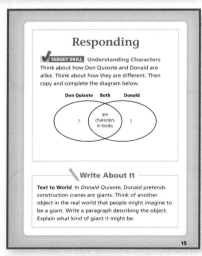

Donald Quixote, p. 15

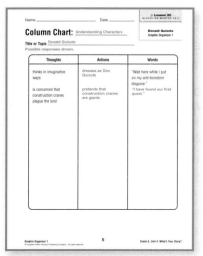

Blackline Master 20.3

Leveled Readers

Struggling Readers

 Donald Quixote

GENRE: HUMOROUS FICTION

Summary Sandra always looks forward to her Uncle Donald's visits. He's an art student and full of creative ideas. When Sandra shows him an adventure book about Don Quixote, who loved to act out adventures, she knows she's in for some adventures of her own.

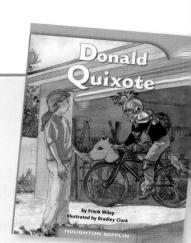

Introducing the Text

- *Don Quixote* was written by the Spanish author Miguel de Cervantes Saavedra in 1605. It is considered a great work of fiction.

- Remind students that using a Column Chart can help them understand the characters by recording their thoughts, words, and actions.

Supporting the Reading

- As you listen to students read, pause to discuss these questions.

UNDERSTANDING CHARACTERS p. 3 *Why did Uncle Donald paint a mural on the fence at Sandra's house? He's an artist and has a unique way of seeing things. He thought the street needed more color.*

QUESTION p. 7 *How does Uncle Donald create an adventure? He dresses in a suit of armor from things he finds in the garage and calls himself Donald Quixote.*

Discussing and Revisiting the Text

CRITICAL THINKING After discussing *Donald Quixote*, have students read the instructions on **Responding p. 15**. Use these points as they revisit the text.

- Have partners identify character traits for Don Quixote and Uncle Donald. Have them write these traits under the name of each character on **Blackline Master 20.3**.

- Ask students to compare and contrast the characters.

- Distribute **Blackline Master 20.7** to develop students' critical thinking skills.

FLUENCY: ACCURACY Model reading with accuracy. Then have partners echo read p. 7 and help them with any difficult vocabulary or ideas. Have partners listen to one another and correct for accuracy.

On Level

▲ *El Camino Real*

GENRE: HUMOROUS FICTION

Summary Teresa and Clara Montez enjoy using their imaginations to pretend that their street, El Camino Real, is a royal road. Unfortunately, some funny disasters occur as they live out this fantasy.

Introducing the Text

- Explain that the English translation of the Spanish street, "El Camino Real," is the "Royal Road."

- Remind students that using a Column Chart can help them understand the characters by recording their thoughts, words, and actions.

Supporting the Reading

- As you listen to students read, pause to discuss these questions.

UNDERSTANDING CHARACTERS pp. 3–5 *How are Teresa and her grandfather alike? They both have active imaginations and like to tell stories.*

QUESTION p. 18 *After the disasters, why would Alfonso, Marva, and Rosa come to the girls' door? They must have understood that the girls were just using their imaginations and didn't mean any harm.*

Discussing and Revisiting the Text

CRITICAL THINKING After discussing *El Camino Real*, have students read the instructions on **Responding p. 19**. Use these points to revisit the text.

- Have partners identify character traits for both Teresa and Clara. Have them write them under the name of each character on **Blackline Master 20.4**. Ask students to compare and contrast the characters.

- Distribute **Blackline Master 20.8** to develop students' critical thinking skills.

FLUENCY: ACCURACY Have partners read p. 3 aloud, making sure that what they read makes sense to them. If they make a mistake, they should stop and correct it.

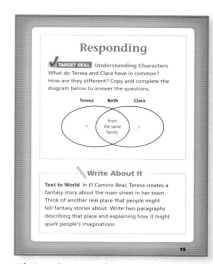

El Camino Real, p. 19

Blackline Master 20.4

SMALL GROUP Options

Targets for Lesson 20

✓ **TARGET SKILL**

Understanding Characters

✓ **TARGET STRATEGY**

Question

✓ **TARGET VOCABULARY**

antique	quests
plagued	noble
pierced	ignorance
thrust	faithful
transformed	exploits

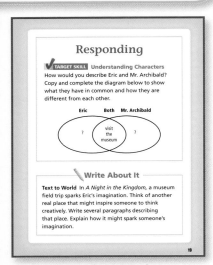

A Knight in the Kingdom p. 19

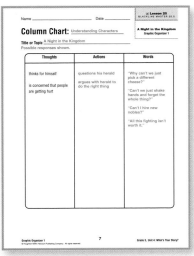

Blackline Master 20.5

Leveled Readers

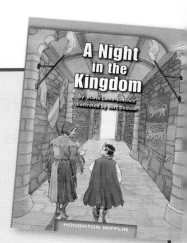

Advanced

 A Night in the Kingdom

GENRE: HUMOROUS FICTION

Summary Eric finds the Museum of Medieval History incredibly boring. When his sister lends him the book, *When Knights Were Bold*, he dreams that he is a king during Medieval times. Suddenly he is living an adventure complete with knights and jousting tournaments.

Introducing the Text

- Explain that *When Knights Were Bold* is a real children's story written by Eva March Tappan.

- Remind students that using a Column Chart can help them understand the characters' relationships and motives.

Supporting the Reading

- As you listen to students read, pause to discuss these questions

UNDERSTANDING CHARACTERS p. 2 *What was Eric's attitude toward the class field trip to the Museum of Medieval History? He was happy to get out of class, but he thought it would be boring.*

QUESTION pp. 15–16 *What did Eric learn about the cheese joust when he finally met with the king of Archibald? They were both told what to say to each other. Neither of the kings wanted to be at odds with the other.*

Discussing and Revisiting the Text

CRITICAL THINKING Discuss *A Night in the Kingdom* and have students read the instructions on **Responding p. 19**. Use these points as they revisit the text.

- Have students identify character traits for Eric and Mr. Archibald and list them on **Blackline Master 20.5**.

- Have them compare and contrast the two characters.

- Distribute **Blackline Master 20.9** to develop students' critical thinking skills.

FLUENCY: ACCURACY Have partners read aloud p. 4. Remind students to stop to correct any mistakes.

JOURNEYS DIGITAL **Powered by** DESTINATIONReading®
Leveled Readers Online

 English Language Learners

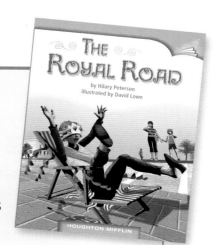

◆ *The Royal Road*

GENRE: HUMOROUS FICTION

Summary Teresa and Clara Montez pretend that their street, El Camino Real, is a royal road. Their grandfather reminds the girls to use their imaginations wisely. The sisters forget this advice as they begin to believe in their fantasy.

Introducing the Text

• Explain that in English, the Spanish road name "El Camino Real" means "Royal Road."

• Remind students that using a Column Chart can help them understand the characters by recording their words, thoughts/feelings, and actions.

Supporting the Reading

• As you listen to students read, pause to discuss these questions.

UNDERSTANDING CHARACTERS p. 6 *Clara looks a bit worried when her sister tells her that The Great Bear constellation eats little girls. What does this tell you about Clara? She listens to what her sister says.*

QUESTION p. 8 *Why is Teresa sent to the principal's office? She is daydreaming during class and gives a silly answer when her teacher asks her the capital of Minnesota.*

Discussing and Revisiting the Text

CRITICAL THINKING After discussing *The Royal Road*, have students read the instructions on **Responding p. 19**. Use these points as they revisit the text.

• Have students work with partners to identify character traits for Teresa and Clara. Then have them identify two or more character traits and list them in the boxes on **Blackline Master 20.6**. Ask them to tell how Teresa and Clara are alike and different.

• Distribute **Blackline Master 20.10** to develop students' critical thinking skills.

FLUENCY: ACCURACY Have pairs take turns reading aloud p. 2, slowing down when necessary in order to maintain accuracy.

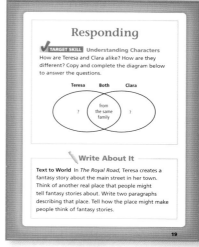

The Royal Road, p. 19

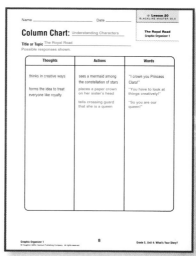

Blackline Master 20.6

Differentiate Vocabulary Strategies ☑ Idioms

Struggling Readers

I DO IT

- Remind students that we use many idioms in English.

- Tell students that an idiom is an expression or a group of words that, when used together, have a different meaning than the individual words.

- Explain that it can take time to learn common idioms. Using context when reading or listening can help determine the meaning of idioms.

WE DO IT

- Write the following on the board: *John ate a piece of cake.*

- Discuss the meaning of the underlined phrase. *a kind of baked sweet*

- Then say: *Climbing that hill was a piece of cake.* Ask students what the words mean now. *Easy to do.* Point out that used this way, the phrase is an idiom. The phrase means something different than the sum of the individual words.

YOU DO IT

- Have students copy the idiom into their notebooks.

- Have them write the literal meaning of the words and then write what the idiom means.

- Have students write 2 sentences, one with the literal meaning of *a piece of cake,* and one with *a piece of cake* used as an idiom.

On Level

I DO IT

- Tell students that idioms are a group of words that mean one thing as individual words, but, when put together, mean something completely different.

- Remind students that idioms are everyday sayings. We often use idioms to stress a point or to make language more interesting or colorful.

- Explain that readers must learn common idioms so they can understand an author's intended meaning. Context can help them determine the meanings of idioms.

WE DO IT

- Write the following phrase on the board: *paid an arm and a leg.*

- Have a student read the phrase aloud. Discuss with students the literal meaning of the words.

- Then say: *Joe paid an arm and a leg for his new backpack.* Ask students what the words mean now. *The backpack was very expensive.*

- Point out that if Joe *really* paid by giving up his arm and his leg, it would be an extraordinary price to pay!

YOU DO IT

- Write the following phrases on the board: *beats me, call it a day, bent out of shape.*

- Have students write the literal meaning of the words and then write what the idiom means.

- Have students write three sentences using the idioms.

- For fun, students may draw cartoons that illustrate the literal meaning of the phrases.

Advanced

I DO IT

- Remind students that idioms are expressions or groups of words that mean one thing as individual words, but when put together mean something completely different.

- Remind students that we often use idioms to stress a point or to make language more interesting or colorful.

- Explain that idioms are not meant to be taken *literally*, or exactly word-for-word.

WE DO IT

- Write the following on the board:

  I'm really broke this week.

  That song makes me feel blue.

  Relax. Just go with the flow.

- Have students read the sentences and underline the idiom. Use a dictionary to confirm the meanings. Work with students to explain the meaning of each.

YOU DO IT

- Have students work in groups to write a short skit using as many idioms as possible in the dialogue. Get them started with this list: *do an about face, grab a bite, lend me a hand, change your mind, cut it out, drag your feet.*

- Have groups perform their skits for each other. Students not performing should keep a list, writing down as many of the idioms they hear in the skits as they can.

ELL English Language Learners

Group English Language Learners according to academic ability and language proficiency. Write *quests, transformed, plagued, faithful, noble, pierced, ignorance, thrusts, exploits,* and *antique.* Have students repeat after you as you pronounce each word.

Beginning

Display the following sentence: *Señor Quexada buried himself in his books.* Discuss the word *bury* and its usual meaning. Then explain the meaning as it is used in the sentence. Ask: *Does Señor Quexada read a lot?* yes

Intermediate

Display the following sentence: *Señor Quexada's mind snapped.* Explain what an idiom is, and have students find the idiom in the sentence. Guide students to tell what the sentence means. *He went crazy.*

Advanced

Have students find at least one idiom in "Don Quixote and the Windmills." Have them read the sentences containing the idiom(s) and tell what they mean. Write the meanings on the board.

Advanced High

Have students identify parts of the selection that may be substituted with idioms they know. Have them rewrite the sentence(s) adding the idiom(s) but maintaining the original meaning.

✓ Options for Reteaching

Vocabulary Strategy

✓ Idioms

I DO IT

- Remind students that idioms are everyday expressions or sayings.
- Write the following sentence on the board: *That really made me blow my top.*

WE DO IT

- Underline the words *blow my top*. Explain to students that this is an idiom.
- Explain to students that an idiom is a group of words that have a meaning that is different from the literal meaning of the words, or from the meanings of the individual words.
- Model for students how to determine what *blow my top* means.

  Think Aloud *The top of me is my head. I know it doesn't really mean that my head exploded. To blow up can mean to get angry, so this must mean that something made me want to blow up, or get angry, almost as if there was an explosion in my head.*

YOU DO IT

- Have each student write a sentence using the idiom *blow my top* or *keep my cool*. Have them illustrate what the sentence would mean if understood literally.
- Have volunteers share their illustrations, and then explain what the idiom actually means.

Comprehension Skill

✓ Understanding Characters

I DO IT

- Remind students that the relationships between characters in a story tell a lot about who the characters are. They can also affect the plot, or story line.
- Point out that Don Quixote imagines he is the *archetype*—that is, a near perfect example—of a knight. Sancho, his squire, is an ordinary man.

WE DO IT

- Have students read **Student Book p. 516** aloud.
- Model how to analyze the relationship between the traditional knight, Don Quixote, and his squire, Sancho.

  Think Aloud *I notice that Don Quixote has a very romantic idea of what it means to be a true knight. He talks of his "glorious victory" and his "mighty sword." Sancho calls Don Quixote "Master" and Don Quixote gives him orders. This tells me Don Quixote's relationship with Sancho is that of a hero and a sidekick. It is the kind of relationship a traditional knight would want.*

- Help volunteers identify more dialogue that reveals Sancho and Don Quixote's relationship.

YOU DO IT

- Distribute **Graphic Organizer 1**.
- Have students label the left column of their T-Maps "Don Quixote," the middle column "Sancho," and the right column "Relationship".
- Have them work in pairs to scan the story for dialogue from each character that reveals their relationship.
- Review the completed graphic organizers.

Language Arts

 # Contractions

I DO IT

- Remind students that a contraction is a combination of two words into one. An apostrophe takes the place of missing letters.
- List the following contractions on the board: *can't, I'll, it's*. Point out what words these contractions stand for.

Think Aloud *I know that* can't *is made from the two words* can *and* not. *The apostrophe takes the place of the letters* n *and* o.

- Continue with *I'll* and *it's*.

WE DO IT

- Guide students to identify the contractions and the words they are made from in the following sentences. *I'm from Dallas, Texas. I don't like when I lose my glasses. It's good to eat vegetables.* Have students identify the contractions and tell you the two words they stand for.
- Have partners work together to write sentences using contractions. Have them identify what two words the contraction stands for, and point out the apostrophe in each.

YOU DO IT

- Have pairs of students write three sentences using contractions. Have them write the two words each contraction stands for after their sentences.
- Invite volunteers to explain to the class how they formed each contraction.

Decoding

 # Stress in Three-Syllable Words

I DO IT

- Recall that each syllable in a word has a vowel sound.
- In multi-syllable words, one syllable is usually stressed, or said with more force than the others.
- Write *tomato*. Model how to decode tomato.

Think Aloud *I will say the word aloud three times, stressing a different syllable each time. To/MA/to sounds correct.*

WE DO IT

- Write *bandana* and *siesta* on the board.
- Help students decode each word and put the stress on the correct syllable.
- Discuss how to use a dictionary to find the correct way to pronounce an unfamiliar word.

YOU DO IT

- Write *ignorance, government, selection, personal,* and *quietly* on the board.
- Have partners decode the words.
- Have them identify the stressed syllables, using a dictionary if needed.
- Use the **Corrective Feedback** on p. T331 if students need additional help.

Teacher Notes

STRATEGIC INTERVENTION

Lesson

16 **"Making Movies"** (Write-In Reader pages 154–160)

Target Vocabulary: episodes, incredibly, launch, mental, thumbed
Author's Purpose
Monitor/Clarify

Lesson

17 **"In the Year 2525"** (Write-In Reader pages 164–170)

Target Vocabulary: admitted, destination, impressed, produced, suspense
Story Structure
Infer/Predict

Lesson

18 **"Making a Magazine"** (Write-In Reader pages 174–180)

Target Vocabulary: background, career, formula, insights, required
Fact and Opinion
Analyze/Evaluate

Lesson

19 **"Sojourner Truth: Speaker for Equal Rights"** (Write-In Reader pages 184–190)

Target Vocabulary: dependent, effective, exception, issue, urge
Persuasion
Summarize

Lesson

20 **"The Tale of the Unlucky Knight"** (Write-In Reader pages 194–200)

Target Vocabulary: pierced, plagued, quests, thrust, transformed
Understanding Characters
Question

SHARE OBJECTIVES

- Use descriptive adjectives.
- Ask students to think of clubs or organizations that are common in schools.
- Read to build meaning for Target Vocabulary words.

MATERIALS

Write-In Reader pages 152–153

ACADEMIC LANGUAGE

adjective

Oral Grammar

Descriptive Adjectives

- Explain that adjectives such as *interesting*, *beautiful*, and *exciting* do not give enough information. When we write or talk, we should try to describe something so well that the readers or listeners can picture it.

- Play "I spy." In the first clue, use an adjective such as *interesting* or *beautiful* that does not give specific information. In the next clues, use adjectives that give specific descriptive information. For example:

  I spy an interesting object.

  It has wavy red lines on it.

  It has deep blue flowers on it.

  It has intricate embroidery on the edge.

  What is it? (Jill's skirt)

Talk About It

Help focus students' attention on making a movie. Ask, *What does it take to make a movie?*

Discuss the question, emphasizing these points:

- First the story, or script, must be written.

- The story must be organized into scenes or episodes.

- Pictures, or storyboards, are drawn to plan how the scenes will look.

- The film crew discusses the film.

- Decisions about whether or not to proceed with the project are made.

Target Vocabulary

Write-In Reader pages 152–153

• Read and discuss each paragraph. Then discuss the meaning of each Target Vocabulary word. Suggest that students underline words or phrases that provide clues to meaning. Also point out the following:

In this story, the meaning used for *launch* is "to officially start," as in, *The company will launch its new website on Thursday.* The word can also mean "a large motorboat," as in, *The launch was used to transport passengers from the cruise ship to the shore. Launch* can also mean "to send a vessel into the air or space," as in, *NASA might launch a rocket to Mars within the next twenty years.*

• Allow students time to formulate their responses. Then ask students to choose an answer they would like to read aloud.

Possible responses:

   1. interested members; equipment

   2. a short time

   3. sketch it or describe it aloud

   4. extremely; fabulously

   5. Students might have an episode for each year of their lives.

Quick Check Target Vocabulary

Ask each student to use one of the Target Vocabulary words in a sentence.

✔ **TARGET VOCABULARY**

Episodes are separate parts of a series of events.

Something that happens **incredibly** occurs in a way that is amazing or hard to believe.

To **launch** something means to officially start it.

Something that is **mental** happens in the mind.

A person who **thumbed** pages turned and looked through them quickly.

EXTRA PRACTICE

Build Fluency Have students read **Write-In Reader** pages 152–153 with a partner or a family member.

SHARE OBJECTIVES

- Read words with vowel pair syllables.
- Determine the author's purpose.
- Read to apply skills and strategies.

MATERIALS

Write-In Reader pages 154–157

ACADEMIC LANGUAGE

author's purpose

Multisyllable Words

Focus: Vowel Pair Syllables

Write these words on the board or on a pad.

1	railroad	maintain	cookout
2	snowplow	moonbeam	raincoat
3	outreach	downstream	rowboat

Row 1: Ask, *What is one way to divide these words?* (Many are compound words, so they can be divided between the words, as in *railroad*. We can use vowel-consonant-consonant-vowel letter patterns to divide words such as *maintain*.) Then circle the vowel pairs in each word (highlighted in list). Remind students of the sound that each vowel pair stands for.

Row 2: Have volunteers divide the words, then circle the vowel pair syllables in each word. Choral read the words with students.

Row 3: Listen to each student read the words. Make corrections as needed. Record your findings.

RETEACH

Author's Purpose

- Hold up a classroom nonfiction book. Read the title and some of the chapter titles. Then ask, *Why do you think the author wrote this book?*

- Remind students that the author's purpose is the reason he/she writes a book. Point out that an author can have more than one purpose. Say, *I think the author wrote this book to inform. The book also has lots of diagrams, illustrations, and photos that describe. Have you read a book that informed and described?*

- Explain that knowing the author's purpose can help a reader determine at what speed to read. Ask, *Would you read a nonfiction book quickly or slowly? Why?*

- Make a list of author's purposes: to inform, to express, to describe, to persuade, or to entertain.

Quick Check | Comprehension

Ask students to name another book that had two purposes.

READ

"Making Movies"

Write-In Reader pages 154–157

- Preview the selection with students using the **Think Aloud** to set a purpose for reading. Record their ideas.

Think Aloud *The title is* Making Movies. *That's one thing I can read to find out about. Some of the pictures seem to show different scenes. I'm also going to read to find out what the movie is about. What other clues help you to set a purpose for reading?*

Together, review the steps to the Monitor/Clarify Strategy, **Write-In Reader** page 304. As needed, guide students in applying the strategy as they read.

READ

Have students take turns reading the selection with partners. Discuss, confirm, and revise student predictions based upon text details.

REREAD

Call on individuals to read aloud while others follow along. Stop to discuss each question. Point out *downstream*, an example of a word with a vowel pair syllable. Allow time for students to write their responses before proceeding. Sample answers are provided.

Page 154: Why do you think the author shows every person in the club speaking? You can give more than one reason. (The author wants to introduce the characters in the story. The author wants to show that teamwork is an important part of being in a club.)

Help unpack meaning, if needed, by asking, *How many members are in the video club?* (five) *How many people do you think it takes to make a movie?* (many people: directors, actors, producers, extras)

Unpack Meaning: For questions on pages 155–157, you may want to use the notes in the right-hand column.

Page 155: In what ways are episodes in a TV series connected? (Each episode builds on the previous events in the series. Episodes also involve the same characters.)

Turn and Talk **Page 156:** What do you think of when you make a mental picture of a river? (Students' mental pictures may involve long and thin bodies of moving water.)

Page 157: Why does the author have Sally and Julio tell the story instead of Jin? (The author shows that Jin has written a good story that is easily followed and understood by the reader.)

UNPACK MEANING

Use prompts such as these if students have difficulty with a **Stop•Think•Write** question:

Page 155 *What does the word* episodes *mean?* (separate parts of a series of events) *Why do viewers continue to watch a TV series week after week?* (They enjoy certain characters, or they may be excited to see what will happen next.)

Page 156 *What is the shape of many rivers?* (long and thin) *How would you describe the water in a river?* (moving)

Page 157 *See page 156. How does Julio react when he skims Jin's story?* (He says the story is fantastic.) *How do Julio and Sally tell the others about the story?* (They give the main idea of the story, highlighting a major event.)

EXTRA PRACTICE

Build Fluency Have students read **Write-In Reader** pages 154–157 with a partner or a family member.

SHARE OBJECTIVES

- Use descriptive adjectives.
- Read aloud fluently to improve rate.
- Read to apply skills and strategies.

MATERIALS

Write-In Reader pages 158–160

ACADEMIC LANGUAGE

descriptive adjective   rate

Warm Up

Oral Grammar

Descriptive Adjectives

- Make a statement about an object or person in the room. Have students provide descriptive adjectives. Elicit a variety of adjectives.

Teacher prompts	Students respond
Samantha is great.	kind, caring, helpful, sweet, athletic, smart, intelligent, musical, generous, friendly, considerate, warm-hearted
Rob's shirt looks nice.	colorful, tailored, loose, tight, wild, distinctive, silky, rough, smooth
Those clouds are Interesting.	billowy, white, black, fluffy, grey, large, small, enormous, ominous, dark, rain-filled

RETEACH

Fluency: Rate

Write-In Reader page 158

Explain that you are going to read from page 158 in two different ways, and you want students to evaluate your reading.

- First, read the first paragraph on the page extremely slowly. Pause unnaturally between words and to indicate punctuation marks. Then read the paragraph a second time. This time, read very quickly. Run words together and avoid pausing as indicated by punctuation.

- Ask, *What did you think of my first reading? Explain. Was my second reading better? Explain.* Be sure students recognize how hard it is to grasp meaning when someone reads too quickly or too slowly.

- Now read the text at an appropriate pace. Ask, *What did you think of this reading? Why?*

- Have students choose paragraphs from pages 154–157 and practice reading them aloud at an appropriate rate.

READ

"Making Movies"

Write-In Reader pages 158–160

Review the first part of the story with students. Ask, *What have we learned so far?* Then preview today's reading. If necessary, have students predict how the story may end.

READ

Ask students to read to confirm their predictions. Have students take turns reading the selection with partners. Discuss, confirm, and revise predictions based upon text details. Ask if there was anything about the way the story ended that surprised them.

REREAD

Call on individuals to read aloud while others follow along. Stop to discuss each question. Allow time for students to write their responses before proceeding. Sample answers are provided.

Page 158: Why do you think the author tells about Talia's eyes and mouth? (The author is showing how the story's exciting plot makes her feel.)

Help unpack meaning, if needed, by asking, *How might a person's face appear when they are watching something scary?* (Their eyes might be wide open. Their mouths might be wide open. They may cover their eyes with their hands.)

Unpack Meaning: For questions on pages 159–160, you may want to use the notes in the right-hand column.

Page 159: What do you think of the video club's plans? What are they forgetting? (Their plans sound impractical for a school project. They will need access to a trained bear and a river to make the movie.)

Turn and Talk **Page 160:** What does Wanda mean when she says the Video Club has to go "back to the drawing board"? (They will have to come up with a more practical movie idea.) Have partners discuss this question and then share with the group.

Quick Check Retelling

Have students retell the end of the story. Support the retelling by asking: *How does Sally picture the scene with the bear? Why does Wanda remind the other members that they live in the city?*

UNPACK MEANING

Use prompts such as these if students have difficulty with a **Stop•Think•Write** question:

Page 159 *Look at page 158. Why is Wanda quiet?* (She knows the others aren't thinking realistically about Roy's story.) *In Hollywood, how do movie directors get animals to do what they want?* (They get help from experienced animal trainers.)

Page 160 *What does Wanda say about the idea?* (It is great but has a few problems.) *What does she suggest he do with the story idea?* (save it for Hollywood) *It's obvious that the club won't make the film. What can you assume that "back to the drawing board" means?* (They will have to start over again; come up with another idea.)

EXTRA PRACTICE

Build Fluency Have students reread **Write-In Reader** pages 158–160 with a partner or a family member.

SHARE OBJECTIVES

- Read words with vowel pair syllables.
- Identify adjectives.
- Answer questions using evidence from the text.

MATERIALS

Write-In Reader pages 154–161

ACADEMIC LANGUAGE

adjective

Warm Up

Multisyllable Words

Focus: Vowel Pair Syllables

Write these words on the board or on a pad.

1	break / down	Broad / way	drive / way
2	free / way	green / house	try / out
3	blood / hound	show / boat	steam / boat

Row 1: Divide the words, explaining, *A compound word can be divided between the two words that make up the compound.* Then circle the vowel pair syllables in each word (highlighted in list). Explain that we use the phonics rules we know to read and blend the syllables to read the words.

Row 2: Have volunteers divide the words after the first vowel pair syllable and circle both vowel pair syllables. Then read and blend both syllables.

Row 3. Listen to each student read the words. Make corrections as needed. Record your findings.

RETEACH

Adjectives

- Review that adjectives describe nouns and can tell *what kind* or *how many.* Have students name adjectives that might be used to describe a famous movie.

- Have students turn to page 160 and read the first paragraph aloud. Say, *How many adjectives can you find in the first paragraph?* (great, few, wild, stray, public)

- Write: *We want to see a hollywood movie.* Have students identify the adjective. (Hollywood) Point out that the adjective is formed from the place name, so it should begin with a capital letter.

Turn and Talk Have students read page 159 to find other examples of adjectives.

Quick Check Grammar

Have students find four other examples of adjectives in the story. Ask students to write each adjective and noun it describes.

Look Back and Respond

Write-In Reader pages 154–161

Help students complete the Look Back and Respond page. Model how to use the hint in question 1 to find evidence that can be used to support answers.

- Explain that evidence is proof, clues, or information.

- Remind students that they can circle or underline the specific words in the selection that they used as evidence for their answers.

1. How would you describe Julio and Sally? (They are enthusiastic and good at visualizing the story as a movie.)

Help unpack meaning, if needed, by asking, *What does Julio do after he reads Jin's story?* (He makes a mental picture.) *What do Julio and Sally do as they read through Jin's story?* (They excitedly summarize the story's events for the other club members.)

Turn and Talk Have students work independently on questions 2, 3, and 4. When students have completed the page, have partners discuss their responses and then share them with the group. Sample responses are provided. Accept reasonable responses.

Unpack Meaning: For questions 2–4, you may want to use the notes in the right-hand column to guide the discussion about student responses.

2. How does the author show that this video club is not very experienced in planning or making movies? (They get very excited about making a movie before thinking about the practicality of their plans.)

3. What clue does the author give early in the story that Wanda is the most practical of all the club members? (She reminds the others that they need a good story before they can make any decisions about the movie.)

4. What does Wanda mean when she tells Rob to save his story for Hollywood? (She means that Rob's story is better suited for much more experienced moviemakers.)

UNPACK MEANING

Use prompts such as these if students have difficulty with a question:

2. *What clues in the story tell you that the video club members are inexperienced?* (It takes Jin only a weekend to write a script. They would have to film near a river and have a trained bear in order to make the movie.)

3. *What evidence can you find on page 155 to help you respond?* (Wanda warns the club members that they should think about the story before they think about episodes.)

4. *What do the club members realize at the end of the story?* (They need to find a simpler story to film.) *Who works in Hollywood?* (professionals in the movie industry: producers, directors, actors, etc.)

EXTRA PRACTICE

Retell Have students retell "Making Movies" to a partner or a family member.

MATERIALS

Context Cards: *assuming, developed, episodes, feature, incredibly, launch, mental, record, thumbed, villains*

Write-In Reader pages 154–160

Leveled Reader: *Dog Walker, Inc.*

ACADEMIC LANGUAGE

story structure   infer

predict

✔ TARGET VOCABULARY

Assuming is supposing or accepting that something is true.

When something is **developed**, it comes into being or becomes more complete.

To **feature** something means to give it special importance.

A **record** is the most remarkable, or best, achievement in a category.

Villains in a story are characters who oppose the heroes.

Warm Up

Multisyllable Words
Cumulative Review

- Write these sentences on the board or on a pad.

  1. The raging river carries him downstream.
  2. They hold tryouts for their short film.
  3. They could save Mike if they had a rowboat.

- Tell students to be on the lookout for clues they can use to divide and read long words. Have students circle all of the words with vowel pair syllables.

- Assign students to work with a partner to practice reading the sentences. Then listen to each student read one sentence. Make corrections as needed. Record your findings.

REVIEW

Target Vocabulary
Context Cards

- Display the **Context Cards** for *episodes, incredibly, launch, mental,* and *thumbed*. Review the meanings of these words. Then have students use the words in oral sentences about different clubs or organizations on a school campus.

- Add the **Context Cards** for *assuming, developed, feature, record,* and *villains*. Give one card to each student. Have students imagine they are writing a screenplay for a famous Hollywood film producer. Have students use their words in original sentences that describe the characters, plot, and setting of the screenplay. Have students share their sentences with the class.

✏ WRITE ABOUT IT

- Ask students to write a letter to a well-known actor. In the letter, they should ask the actor to visit their school to give a lecture on filmmaking. Tell students to use the word *assuming* in their letters.

PRETEACH

Story Structure
Infer/Predict

Write-In Reader pages 154–160

- Introduce skill and strategy. Say, *In the next lesson, we are going to focus on the structure of a story. We'll also work on ways to make inferences and predictions about what you are reading.*

- Explain, *Well-written stories often include an introduction, a plot, rising action, a climax, and a resolution. These elements build the story structure.*

- Ask, *What does the author tell us in the beginning of the story?* (The author introduces the characters, setting, and plot of the story: members of a school video club planning to make their own movie.)

- Have students help you make a list on the board of information the author gives the reader in each section of the story.

  Page 156: Rising Action – The author develops the plot by having John and Sally summarize Rob's exciting story.

  Page 159: Climax – After hearing Rob's story, the members enthusiastically agree that it would make a great movie.

  Page 160: Resolution – Wanda reminds the others that they live in the city and that Rob's story isn't very practical for their video club.

- Turn to and review the Infer/Predict Strategy found on page 304 in the **Write-In Reader**. Tell students that when reading a selection, they should make inferences about what they are reading and make predictions about what will come next. Have students think about the story and use what they read and what they already know to make a prediction about the club's next idea.

APPLY READING SKILLS

Introduce *Dog Walker, Inc.* Choral read the first few pages with students. Depending on their abilities, have students continue reading with partners or as a group.

● **Leveled Reader**

Quick Check Fluency

Listen to individual students as they read the **Write-In Reader** selection. Make specific notes about words that presented difficulty to them.

INFER/PREDICT STRATEGY

When you make an **inference**, you use clues in the text and what you already know to figure out what the author does not tell you.

Look for clues like these to help you make an inference:

- what characters say
- characters' actions
- plot events
- description of the setting
- main ideas and details
- characteristics of the genre
- your prior knowledge and experiences

A **prediction** is a type of inference. When you make a prediction, you use clues to guess what will happen next.

EXTRA PRACTICE

Independent Reading Have students read from a book of their choice and describe what they read in their reading logs.

SHARE OBJECTIVES

- Identify adverbs that show frequency and intensity.
- Discuss science fiction stories.
- Read to build meaning for Target Vocabulary words.

MATERIALS

Write-In Reader pages 162–163

ACADEMIC LANGUAGE
adverb   frequency

Oral Grammar

Adverbs of Frequency/Intensity

- Write these adverbs of frequency on the board.

| usually | sometimes | seldom | scarcely | never |

- Explain that some adverbs describe frequency or how often something happens.

- Tell students that you will say a sentence. Students will say a sentence using an adverb of frequency. Students may use adverbs not listed on the board.

Teacher prompts	Students respond
Mike plays baseball.	Mike **always** plays baseball.
The noisy grey bird flies into the pine tree.	The noisy grey bird **rarely** flies into the pine tree.
Susan watches TV shows about science.	Susan **sometimes** watches TV shows about science.

Talk About It

Tell students that a "virtual vacation" is a "make-believe journey" that people take using computers, pictures of faraway places, and sound effects. Help focus students' attention on what it might be like to take a virtual vacation. Ask, *What is so great about taking a virtual vacation?*

Discuss the question, emphasizing these points:

- You can "travel" millions of miles without taking a step.

- You can travel back in time.

- You can travel forward in time.

- You don't have to pack anything to bring along with you.

- You don't have to drive there.

- You can see interesting and unusual things.

- You can visit dangerous places like volcanoes, but still be completely safe.

Target Vocabulary

Write-In Reader pages 162–163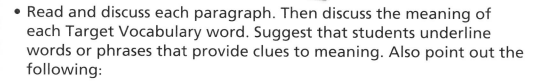

- Read and discuss each paragraph. Then discuss the meaning of each Target Vocabulary word. Suggest that students underline words or phrases that provide clues to meaning. Also point out the following:

  Contrast the meaning of *admitted* as it's used in the first paragraph with another meaning for the word, "to enter or to allow to enter," as in, *We were not admitted to the concert because we forgot our tickets.*

  Produced can also mean "made a public presentation of," as in, *The community theater group produced a new musical.* But *produced* can also mean "caused to exist," as in, *Last year, the car company produced a new, electric car.*

- You may want to have partners or students in small groups read aloud the paragraphs with the correct answers in place.

  Responses:

  1. admitted

  2. impressed

  3. suspense

  4. destination

  5. produced

Quick Check Target Vocabulary

Ask each student to use one of the Target Vocabulary words in a sentence.

✔ **TARGET VOCABULARY**

If you **admitted** something, you said that it is true.

A **destination** is a place where someone is going.

A person who **impressed** you had a strong, favorable effect on you.

If you **produced** something, you made it.

Suspense is anxious uncertainty about what will happen.

EXTRA PRACTICE

Build Fluency Have students read **Write-In Reader** pages 162–163 with a partner or a family member.

SHARE OBJECTIVES

- Read multisyllable words with vowel pair syllables.
- Identify story structure, including characters, setting, and plot.
- Read to apply skills and strategies.

MATERIALS

Write-In Reader pages 164–166

ACADEMIC LANGUAGE

conflict	resolution
infer	predict

Multisyllable Words

Focus: Vowel Pair Syllables

Write these words on the board or on a pad.

1	be / neath	can / teen	dug / out
2	prevail	window	decay
3	Sunday	repeat	yellow

Row 1: Identify the VCCV and VCV letter patterns, and use them to divide these words as shown.

Circle the vowel pair syllables in each word (highlighted in red). Point out that two words, *beneath* and *dugout,* have VCV letter patterns. The first syllable in *beneath* is open and the vowel is long. The first syllable in *dugout* is closed, so the vowel is short.

Row 2: Have students divide words between consonants, circle the vowel pair syllable, then choral read the words.

Row 3: Listen to each student read the words. Make corrections as needed. Record your findings.

RETEACH

Story Structure

- Name a movie that you saw recently, and briefly summarize the plot. Ask, *What was the conflict in the movie?* Remind students that a plot is usually based on a conflict. **Conflict** involves a struggle between two opposing forces and creates interest and suspense. Often, the character has a goal that motivates him or her to solve the problem.

- Review that a reader learns more about the characters through the plot. **Resolution** is the successful solution to the problem that forms the plot.

- Draw a flow chart on the board with these headings: *Problem, Attempts to Solve Problem, Resolution.* Use a recent book that students have read, and have them help you fill in the chart.

Quick Check | **Comprehension**

Have students explain a real life situation when they tried to solve a problem.

READ

"In the Year 2525"

Write-In Reader pages 164–166

- Preview the selection with students using the **Think Aloud** to predict what the story is about. Record their ideas.

Think Aloud *The title* In the Year 2525 *tells me that the story takes place in the future. On page 165, I see that one of the characters is visiting a place called "Volcano Vacationland." I think this story is about a trip in the future to a very unusual place. What other clues help you predict what the story will be about?*

- Together, review the steps to the Infer/Predict Strategy, **Write-In Reader** page 304. As needed, guide students in applying the strategy as they read.

READ

Ask students to read to confirm their predictions. Have students take turns reading the selection with partners. Discuss, confirm, and revise student predictions based on text details.

REREAD

Call on individuals to read aloud while others follow along. Stop to discuss each question. Point out words with vowel pair syllables such as *explained* and *heated*. Allow time for students to write their responses before proceeding. Sample answers are provided.

Page 164: As the story begins, what is the Ortiz family doing? (visiting the office of Virtual Vacations to talk to a travel agent)

Help unpack meaning, if needed, by asking, *What is one of the first things people do when they decide to go on vacation?* (They think about where they want to go.) *Once people have decided where to go, what do they do next?* (They find out more about the destination.)

Unpack Meaning: For questions on pages 165–166, you may want to use the notes in the right-hand column.

Turn and Talk **Page 165:** What is one <u>destination</u> you usually have each day? Can you think of two or three others? (Responses will vary, but might include school, a friend's or relative's house, a store.) Have partners discuss their answers and then share with the group.

Page 166: In the story, images are produced by computers. What is a synonym for <u>produced</u>? (made, created, established)

UNPACK MEANING

Use prompts such as these if students have difficulty with a **Stop•Think•Write** question:

Page 165 *What does* destination *mean?* (a place where someone goes) *What kinds of places could be considered destinations?* (buildings, parks, cities, tourist attractions)

Page 166 *What does* produced *mean?* (made or created) *If a computer produces an image, what does it do?* (The computer creates an image.)

EXTRA PRACTICE

Build Fluency Have students read **Write-In Reader** pages 164–166 with a partner or a family member.

SHARE OBJECTIVES

- Identify adverbs that show frequency and intensity.
- Read aloud fluently to improve intonation.
- Read to apply skills and strategies.

MATERIALS

Write-In Reader pages 167–170

ACADEMIC LANGUAGE

adverb	intensity	pitch
intonation	stress	

Warm Up

Oral Grammar

Adverbs of Frequency/Intensity

- Write these adverbs of intensity on the board.

too	very	completely	extremely	fairly

- Explain that some adverbs describe the intensity of an action, adjective, or another adverb. Tell students that you will say a sentence in which an adverb describes an adjective. Identify the noun, then ask students to identify the adjective and the adverb of intensity.

Teacher prompts	Students respond	
	Adjective	**Adverb**
The very pretty dog played with the ball. The noun is dog.	pretty	very
An extremely cold wind blew across the snow. The noun is wind.	cold	extremely

RETEACH

Fluency: Intonation

Write-In Reader page 167

Tell students you are going to read page 167 and you want them to evaluate your reading.

- Read the page in a monotone voice, giving equal stress to each word. For example, you might read the first paragraph, as a run-on sentence in a flat, robotic voice.

- Ask, *What did you think of my reading? Why?* Discuss that intonation is the rising and falling of your voice as you read, as well as the stress or emphasis of certain words and phrases. Explain that adjusting your voice as you read helps to emphasize important ideas and feelings in a story.

- Have students follow along as you reread the paragraph with the appropriate intonation. Then discuss how using intonation helped make it easier to understand the passage. Have students practice reading aloud sentences from the page, focusing on intonation as they read.

READ

"In the Year 2525"

Write-In Reader pages 167–170

Review the first part of the story with students. Ask, *What have we learned so far?* Then preview today's reading. Have students look for clues to help them predict how this story will end.

READ

Ask students to read to confirm their predictions. Have students take turns reading the selection with partners. Discuss, confirm, and revise predictions based upon text details. Ask if there was anything about the way the story ended that surprised them.

REREAD

Call on individuals to read aloud while others follow along. Stop to discuss each question. Allow time for students to write their responses before proceeding. Sample answers are provided.

Page 167: What happens first to the Ortizes in the Virtual Vacation Room? (They see a strange creature with two heads.)

Help unpack meaning, if needed, by asking, *What does* virtual *mean?* (It means it isn't real, but it looks real.) *What isn't real in the Virtual Vacation Room?* (the two-headed creature)

Unpack Meaning: For questions on pages 168–170, you may want to use the notes in the right-hand column.

Page 168: How would you describe Jill? (Responses will vary, but students might suggest that she is not a careful person.)

Page 169: Why do you think the Ortizes huddled together in suspense? (They were worried about where Jill might mistakenly send them next and they wanted to stay together.)

Turn and Talk **Page 170:** Where does the end of the story take place? (The Ortizes are at Volcano Vacationland.) Have partners discuss this question and then share with the group.

Quick Check **Retelling**

Have students retell the humorous events from this story. Support their retelling by asking, *Where did Jill accidentally send the Ortizes? What did they see in each place? What did they see when they finally reached Volcano Vacationland?*

UNPACK MEANING

Use prompts such as these if students have difficulty with a **Stop•Think•Write** question:

Page 168 *What does Jill do first when she tries to send the Ortizes on vacation?* (She pushes the wrong button and sends them to the planet Frufee.) *Does Jill's next attempt get the Ortizes to the right place?* (No, she pushes another button sending them into a battle in 1781.)

Page 169 *What does* suspense *mean?* (anxious uncertainty about what will happen) *What kinds of situations can cause suspense?* (Responses will vary, but may include going to new places, scary movies or books, waiting to hear good or bad news.)

Page 170 *Do the Ortizes finally get to the destination they wanted?* (Yes, they end up at Volcano Vacationland.) *Why do the Ortizes forget where they are?* (The experiences in the Virtual Vacation Room seem very real.)

EXTRA PRACTICE

Build Fluency Have students read **Write-In Reader** pages 167–170 with a partner or a family member.

SHARE OBJECTIVES

- Read multisyllable words with vowel pair syllables.
- Use adverbs.
- Answer questions using evidence from the text.

MATERIALS

Write-In Reader pages 164–171

ACADEMIC LANGUAGE
adverb

Multisyllable Words

Focus: Vowel Pair Syllables

Write these words on the board or on a pad.

1	subway	checkpoint	reveal
2	tattoo	textbook	prevail
3	retreat	obtain	elbow

Row 1: Identify the VCCV and VCV letter patterns that can be used to divide these words. Also, demonstrate dividing between compound words. Demonstrate, as shown below.

s u b / w a y	check / point	r e / v e a l
V C C V	(compound)	V C V

Then circle and identify the vowel pair syllables (highlighted in list). Then read and blend the syllables. Repeat the word.

Row 2: Have volunteers divide words using strategies they have learned. Then choral read the words.

Row 3: Listen to each student read the words. Make corrections as needed. Record your findings.

RETEACH

Adverbs

- Review that adverbs describe verbs by telling how, when, or where something is done. Adverbs can describe other adverbs by telling to what extent. Many adverbs end in -*ly*.

- Write the sentence shown below on the board. Ask volunteers to suggest words to fill in the blanks.

  The beautiful boat sailed along the water _____ and _____. (adverb, adverb)

Turn and Talk Have students review the story to find examples of adverbs used in sentences. Invite students to write their sentences on the board.

Possible Answers: She carefully pushed the button. We're finally at Volcano Vacationland.

Quick Check **Grammar**

Have students use adverbs that show frequency and intensity.

Look Back and Respond

Write-In Reader pages 164–171

Help students complete the Look Back and Respond page. Model how to use the hint in question 1 to find evidence that can be used to support answers.

• Explain that evidence is proof, clues, or information.

• Remind students that they can circle or underline the specific words in the selection that they used as evidence for their answers.

1. What settings are there in the story? (Virtual Vacations office, a bedroom on the planet Frufee, Virtual Vacation Room, American Revolution battlefield, Volcano Vacationland)

Help unpack meaning, if needed, by asking, *What is the "setting" of a story?* (The setting is where the story takes place.) *What kinds of places can be used as settings for stories?* (Responses will vary, but may include houses, schools, buildings, parks, cities, planets, and outer space.)

Turn and Talk Have students work independently on questions 2, 3, and 4. When students have completed the page, have partners discuss their responses and then share them with the group. Sample responses are provided. Accept reasonable responses.

Unpack Meaning: For questions 2–4, you may want to use the notes in the right-hand column to guide the discussion about student responses.

2. What happens to the Ortizes the first two times they try to go on their vacation? (The first time they are in the Virtual Vacation Room looking at a sleeping two-headed creature. The second time they are on a battlefield in 1781.)

3. How are the Ortizes finally able to visit Volcano Vacationland? (Jill must have finally pushed the right button.)

4. If you could go on a Virtual Vacation, where would you go? Why? (Responses will vary greatly.)

UNPACK MEANING

Use prompts such as these if students have difficulty with a question:

2. *What did Jill have to do to send the Ortizes on a virtual vacation?* (She had to push a button on a computer.) *Are the Ortizes happy about the first two places they visit? Why or why not?* (They are not happy because neither place is where they wanted to go.)

3. *What happened the first two times that the Ortizes tried to go on their virtual vacation?* (Jill pressed the wrong button.) *What happened the third time?* (Jill pushed the correct button.)

4. *Do you think virtual vacations will be possible someday?* (Responses will vary, but students may say they think technology will be developed to make these kinds of vacations possible.)

EXTRA PRACTICE

Retell Have students retell In the "Year 2525" to a partner or a family member.

Day 5

SHARE OBJECTIVES

- Read multisyllable words with vowel pair syllables.
- Demonstrate understanding of Target Vocabulary words.
- Preview Fact and Opinion and the Analyze/Evaluate Strategy.

MATERIALS

Context Cards: *admitted, collected, compliment, concentrate, destination, impressed, original, produced, rumor, suspense*

Write-In Reader pages 133–139

Leveled Reader: *Robot Rescue*

ACADEMIC LANGUAGE

fact	opinion
analyze	evaluate

 TARGET VOCABULARY

Someone who is **collected** is calm and sensible.

A **compliment** is a positive, admiring, or respectful comment about someone.

To **concentrate** is to focus one's attention on something.

Something that is **original** is the first of its kind.

A **rumor** is a statement that is believed to be true even though there are no facts to prove it.

Multisyllable Words

Cumulative Review

- Write these sentences on the board or on a pad.
  1. Jill repeats the computer program.
  2. They retreat to the safety of their home.
  3. Will there be textbooks in the future?
- Tell students to be on the lookout for clues they can use to divide and read long words. Have students circle the multi-syllable words with vowel pair syllables.
- Assign students to work with a partner to practice reading the sentences. Then listen to each student read one sentence. Record your findings.

REVIEW

Target Vocabulary

Context Cards

- Display the **Context Cards** for *admitted, destination, impressed, produced,* and *suspense.* Review the meanings of these words. Then have students write the words in sentences about virtual vacations. Ask students to share their sentences.
- Show the **Context Cards** for *collected, compliment, concentrate, original,* and *rumor.* Assign one card to each student. Have students make up riddles for their words. Have the rest of the group identify the vocabulary word that solves the riddle.

WRITE ABOUT IT

- Ask students to write a one- or two-paragraph description of a virtual vacation destination site for a travel brochure. Students' destinations can be real or make-believe. Tell students to use the word *destination* in their article.

PRETEACH

Fact and Opinion
Analyze/Evaluate

Write-In Reader pages 133–139

- Introduce skill and strategy. Say, *In the next lesson, we are going to focus on fact and opinion. We'll also work on analyzing and evaluating a text.*

- Explain, *Writers use both facts and opinions to tell their stories or teach the reader about a subject. A fact is a statement that can be proven true or false. An opinion is a statement that expresses a thought, feeling, or idea.*

- Explain, *Sometimes, writers include signal words that help readers recognize that they are reading an opinion. These words include* first, best, greatest, see, most, I think, I feel, *and* I believe.

- Say, *Let's look back at* Nero Hawley's Dream. *Turn to page 137 and read the first paragraph.*

- Ask, *Which sentences are statements of fact? Which sentences are opinions? Explain.* (Sentences 1, 2, and 4 are facts that can be checked; sentences 3 is an opinion.)

- Turn to and review the Analyze/Evaluate Strategy, found on page 303 in the **Write-In Reader**. Tell students that when they analyze a story, they pay close attention to important details that help them understand events, settings, or characters. Analyzing details helps them evaluate, or form an opinion about what they have read. Have students practice the skill by forming an opinion of *Nero Hawley's Dream*.

APPLY READING SKILLS

Introduce *Robot Rescue*. Choral read the first few pages with students. Depending on their abilities, have students continue reading with partners or as a group.

Quick Check | Fluency

Listen to individual students as they read the **Write-In Reader** selection. Make specific notes about words that presented difficulty to them.

● Leveled Reader

ANALYZE/EVALUATE STRATEGY

When you **analyze** and **evaluate** a text, you study the text to form an opinion about it.

1. Analyze a text by looking at the ideas and by thinking about what the author wants readers to know and feel.

   Think about the text:
   - characteristics of the genre
   - setting, characters, and plot
   - facts and ideas
   - graphic features
   - organization of ideas

   Think about the author:
   - purpose and message
   - words and phrases
   - opinions

2. Evaluate a text by forming opinions about what you read.

   Think about you:
   - How much did you enjoy the text?
   - How do you feel about the characters?
   - How do feel about the author's message?
   - Do you agree with the author's opinions?
   - Did the author achieve his or her purpose?

EXTRA PRACTICE

Independent Reading Have students read from a book of their choice and describe what they read in their reading logs.

Warm Up

Oral Grammar

Prepositional Phrases

- Write these prepositions on the board:

in	to	for	on	of
by	up	from	toward	into

- Explain that a prepositional phrase usually contains the preposition, sometimes followed by an article or adjective, followed by a noun or pronoun.

- Tell students that you will start a sentence. Students will add a prepositional phrase to describe the verb in the sentence. Call on several students to suggest a variety of prepositional phrases.

Teacher prompts	Students respond
I ran . . .	I ran over the bridge. I ran up the hill.
I sat . . .	I sat on the chair. I sat by the window.
The dogs chased the cat . . .	The dogs chased the cat up the tree. The dogs chased the cat through the tunnel.

Talk About It

Help focus students' attention on writers and publications. Ask, *What goes into making a magazine?*

Discuss the question, emphasizing these points:

- People decide how the magazine should look.
- They discuss possible story ideas.
- They conduct research to learn more about a topic.
- They conduct interviews.
- They check their facts.
- People look for or take photos to support the story.
- The story is designed.
- Mistakes are corrected.
- The magazine is printed.

Target Vocabulary

Write-In Reader pages 172–173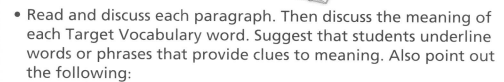

- Read and discuss each paragraph. Then discuss the meaning of each Target Vocabulary word. Suggest that students underline words or phrases that provide clues to meaning. Also point out the following:

    Contrast the meaning of *background* in this instance, "a person's past experience, training, and education," with another meaning for the word, "the part of a picture or pattern that appears off in the distance or behind the main subject," as in *In the background, we saw tall snow-covered mountains.*

    A *formula* is "a set of rules or steps to produce a desired result." The word can also refer to specially produced milk for newborns, as in *For the first six months, my little brother drank only baby formula.*

- Allow students time to respond. Then ask students to choose an answer they would like to read aloud.

Possible responses:

1. clear, expressive writing abilities; editing skills; imagination

2. I would like a career in the military because I would like to serve my country.

3. Being around animals all day would give a person plenty of opportunity to observe the animals' behavior.

4. delicious food, good music, interesting guests

5. experience, education, training

Quick Check | **Target Vocabulary**

Ask each student to use one of the Target Vocabulary words in a sentence.

✔ **TARGET VOCABULARY**

Background is a person's past experience, training, and education.

A **career** is a job that becomes a person's life's work.

A **formula** is a set of rules or steps to produce a desired result.

Insights are ideas about the true nature of a situation.

When something is necessary or called for, it is **required**.

EXTRA PRACTICE

Build Fluency Have students read **Write-In Reader** pages 172–173 with a partner or a family member.

SHARE OBJECTIVES

- Read multisyllable words.
- Distinguish between fact and opinion in a text.
- Read to apply skills and strategies.

MATERIALS

Write-In Reader pages 174–177

ACADEMIC LANGUAGE

fact   opinion   analyze   evaluate

Multisyllable Words

Focus: Vowel Pair Syllables

Write these words on the board or on a pad.

1	unbounded	dismounted	mistreated
2	ingrown	recounted	disjoin
3	subgroup	unfairly	repaying

Row 1: Say, *To make words easier to read, we can divide after a prefix and before an ending.* Divide the words, then circle the vowel pair syllable (in red). Review the sound represented by each vowel pair.

Row 2: Ask volunteers to divide words, then circle the vowel pair syllables. Choral read the words.

Row 3: Listen to each student read the words. Make corrections as needed. Record your findings.

RETEACH

Fact and Opinion

- Read a paragraph from a movie or television review in a newspaper or magazine. Reread a sentence that gives a fact and ask, *Is this information a fact or an opinion? Why?*

- Point out that a fact is a statement that can be proven to be true or false. Facts can be checked in a reference source or with an expert in the field. Ask, *How could you check the fact that I just read?*

- Remind students that an opinion expresses a thought or belief. Read a sentence from the review that gives an opinion. Ask, *Are there signal words that let you know that this is an opinion? What are these words?*

- Discuss the author's purpose in writing a review. Ask, *What does this author want you to do or not do? Does he/she want you to see this movie/TV show? What reasons do authors have for using facts and opinions in a review?*

Quick Check **Comprehension**

Ask students to share a fact and an opinion from a story they recently read or a movie they recently saw.

READ

"Making a Magazine"
Write-In Reader pages 174–177

- Preview the selection with students using the **Think Aloud**. Record their ideas.

> Think Aloud *In the text, I see headings such as,* Learning from an Expert, Planning Stories, Conducting an Interview, *and* Putting It All Together. *I think this selection will be about publishing a magazine. What other clues help you predict what the story is about?*

- Together, review the steps to the Analyze/Evaluate Strategy, **Write-In Reader** page 303. As needed, guide students in applying the strategy as they read.

READ
Ask students to read to confirm their predictions. Have students take turns reading the selection with partners. Discuss, confirm, and revise student predictions based upon text details.

REREAD
Call on individuals to read aloud while others follow along. Stop to discuss each question. Sample answers are provided.

Page 174: What is <u>required</u> to make a sandwich? (bread, mayonnaise or mustard, meat, lettuce, tomato, etc.)

Help unpack meaning, if needed, by asking, *What does the word* required *mean?* (necessary or called for) *Can you make a sandwich without bread?* (no) *Without a filling?* (no)

Unpack Meaning: For questions on pages 175–177, you may want to use the notes in the right-hand column.

Page 175: When Mr. Gomez calls Annie the best magazine writer in the nation, is he stating a fact or an opinion? Explain. (An opinion; someone else might not think that Annie is the best.)

Turn and Talk Page 176: What is Annie's <u>formula</u>? How does it help students choose what to write about? (Annie's formula is to interview interesting people who are local. Her method guided students as they began searching for their own story ideas.) Have partners discuss their answers and then share with the group.

Page 177: Which statements on this page are opinions? Explain. (My team had come up with a great idea; nobody is interested in chickens; that's a great idea. None can be proven true.)

UNPACK MEANING

Use prompts such as these if students have difficulty with a **Stop•Think•Write** question:

Page 175 *What is a fact?* (something that can be proven true or false) *Can it be proven that Annie is the best writer in the nation?* (No; even if one source or expert in the field thinks she is the best, another may disagree.)

Page 176 *What does the word* formula *mean?* (a set of rules or steps to produce a desired result) *Underline the words in the text that tell about Annie's formula.* (We'd interview interesting people in our own neighborhood.)

Page 177 *What is an opinion?* (a particular person's feelings or beliefs) *Can an opinion be proven true or false?* (no)

EXTRA PRACTICE

Build Fluency Have students read **Write-In Reader** pages 174–177 with a partner or a family member.

SHARE OBJECTIVES

- Identify prepositions and prepositional phrases.
- Read aloud fluently, focusing on phrasing and punctuation.
- Read to apply skills and strategies.

MATERIALS

Write-In Reader pages 174, 178–180

ACADEMIC LANGUAGE

phrasing   punctuation

Oral Grammar

Prepositional Phrases

Tell students that you will read a sentence. Students will give the thumbs-up signal when they hear the preposition. Then they will say the entire prepositional phrase. (Prepositions are boldface.) If there is time, have students suggest different prepositional phrases for the sentences.

1. *Our magazine is **about** farm animals.*
2. ***During** the storm, we ran home.*
3. *Shana knew a family who lived **near** the park.*
4. *Jill walked **through** the tunnel yesterday.*
5. *Glenn drove **along** the long bumpy road.*
6. *The dogs ate lots **of** food.*

RETEACH

Fluency: Phrasing

Write-In Reader page 174

Explain that you are going to read from page 174 in two different ways, and you want students to evaluate your reading.

- First, read the last paragraph on the page without paying attention to punctuation. Run sentences together. Do not adjust the tone of your voice to indicate question marks. Do not pause after commas or stop after periods. Then reread the paragraph, modeling how to chunk groups of words into meaningful phrases and pause appropriately after punctuation marks.

- Ask, *Which reading was better? Explain.* Be sure students recognize that phrasing and adjusting your speed to indicate punctuation marks makes a reading more enjoyable and easier to understand.

- Have students practice reading aloud the same paragraph, paying close attention to phrasing and punctuation. As an alternative, students can choose another paragraph from pages 174–177 to practice their reading fluency.

READ

"Making a Magazine"

Write-In Reader pages 178–180

Review the first part of the story with students. Ask, *What have we learned about making a magazine so far?* Then preview today's reading. Have students look for clues to help them predict what the rest of the selection will be about.

READ

Ask students to read to confirm their predictions. Have students take turns reading the selection with partners. Discuss, confirm, and revise predictions based upon text details.

REREAD

Call on individuals to read aloud while others follow along. Stop to discuss each question. Allow time for students to write their responses before proceeding. Sample answers are provided.

Page 178: Why did Laura start the community garden? (She had moved to the United States from her farm in Italy and missed growing things.)

Help unpack meaning, if needed, by asking, *What did the students find out about how Laura learned to grow things?* (Laura grew up on a farm in Italy.) *What did she miss about the farm after moving to the United States?* (She missed growing things.)

Unpack Meaning: For questions on pages 179–180, you may want to use the notes in the right-hand column.

Page 179: Why did the writers show their photographs to another team? (They wanted a second opinion on which photographs to use.)

Turn and Talk **Page 180:** Why do the students print out just one copy of their magazine at first? (They want to check it for errors before printing more copies.) Have partners discuss this question and then share their answers with the group.

Quick Check **Retelling**

Have students retell the end of the selection. Support the retelling by asking, *What did the students do after they finished writing their stories? Who did they print copies of the magazine for?*

SHARE OBJECTIVES

- Read words with vowel pair syllables.
- Identify prepositions and prepositional phrases.
- Answer questions using evidence from the text.

MATERIALS

Write-In Reader pages 174–181

ACADEMIC LANGUAGE

preposition   prepositional phrase

Warm Up

Multisyllable Words

Focus: Vowel Pair Syllables

Write these words on the board or on a pad.

1	uncrowded	misread	disdainful
2	misleading	redrawing	rereading
3	releasing	detaining	unknown

Row 1: Say, *To make words easier to read, we can divide after a prefix and before an ending.* Divide the words, then circle the vowel pair syllable (in red). Review the sound represented by each vowel pair.

Row 2: Ask volunteers to divide words, then circle the vowel pair syllables. Choral read the words.

Row 3: Listen to each student read the words. Make corrections as needed. Record your findings.

RETEACH

Prepositions

- Review that a preposition connects a noun to other words in a sentence. Prepositions can introduce objects or give information about time and place. Review that a phrase containing a preposition and its object is called a prepositional phrase.

- Have students read the second paragraph on page 178 aloud. Ask, *Can you find examples of prepositional phrases in this paragraph?* Write students' answers in a chart.

Preposition	+	Object	=	Prepositional Phrases
about		background		about her background
on		a farm		on a farm
in		Italy		in Italy
to		the United States		to the United States

Turn and Talk Have students find prepositional phrases in the second and third paragraphs on page 179.

Answers: <u>in</u> the library; <u>on</u> the Internet; <u>about</u> community gardens; <u>to</u> our story; <u>of</u> photographs; <u>to</u> another team

Quick Check | Grammar

Have students write a sentence using a preposition.

Look Back and Respond

Write-In Reader page 174–181

Help students complete the Look Back and Respond page. Model how to use the hint in question 1 to find evidence that can be used to support answers.

- Explain that evidence is proof, clues, or information.

- Remind students that they can circle or underline the specific words in the selection that they used as evidence for their answers.

1. What great idea do the students have for their magazine? (to write about activities that usually take place in the country)

Help unpack meaning, if needed, by asking, *Where do the students live?* (in the city) *What comes to mind when you think of city living?* (tall buildings, cars and traffic, sidewalks, fast pace)

Turn and Talk Have students work independently on questions 2, 3, and 4. When students have completed the page, have partners discuss their responses and then share them with the group. Sample responses are provided. Accept reasonable responses.

Unpack Meaning: For questions 2–4, you may want to use the notes in the right-hand column to guide the discussion about student responses.

2. What insights about community gardens might Laura give that wouldn't be found in books? (why someone might start a community garden; why gardens are great for the community)

3. Why does the team do more research after they have interviewed Laura? (to learn more facts about community gardens to add to their story)

4. On page 180, the narrator says, "There were mistakes!" Is the statement a fact or an opinion? Explain. (Fact; the narrator can prove that there were mistakes in the magazine.)

UNPACK MEANING

Use prompts such as these if students have difficulty with a question:

2. *What sort of information would you expect to find in a book about community gardens?* (facts about how to start one, what sorts of tools are needed, etc.) *Are Laura's reasons for starting her garden something that would be in a book?* (no)

3. *Do you think Laura knows everything there is to know about community gardens?* (probably not) *What do you look for when you do research?* (facts about a subject)

4. *What sorts of mistakes might there be on a magazine page?* (spelling, punctuation, and grammatical errors) *How could you prove that a spelling or grammatical error is a mistake?* (check a dictionary or grammar book)

EXTRA PRACTICE

Retell Have students retell "Making a Magazine" to a partner or a family member.

SHARE OBJECTIVES

- Read words with vowel pair syllables.
- Demonstrate understanding of Target Vocabulary words.
- Preview Persuasion and the Summarize/Paraphrase Strategy.

MATERIALS

Context Cards: *background, career, destruction, edition, formula, household, insights, publication, required, uneventful*

Write-In Reader pages 124–130

Leveled Reader: *Maria Tallchief: American Ballerina*

ACADEMIC LANGUAGE

persuasion   summarize   paraphrase

✓ TARGET VOCABULARY

Destruction is vast damage and ruin.

An **edition** is a printing, or version, of a publication.

The people who live together in a residence make up a **household**.

A **publication** is printed material offered for public sale or distribution.

Something **uneventful** had nothing important or significant taking place.

Warm Up

Multisyllable Words
Cumulative Review

- Write these sentences on the board or on a pad.

  1. The writer recounted the story in great detail.

  2. He revealed more about his background.

  3. Some parts of the story are unknown.

- Tell students to be on the lookout for clues they can use to divide and read long words. Have students circle multisyllable words with vowel pair syllables.

- Assign students to work with a partner to practice reading the sentences. Then listen to each student read one sentence. Make corrections as needed. Record your findings.

REVIEW

Target Vocabulary
Context Cards

- Display the **Context Cards** for *background, career, formula, insights,* and *required.* Review the meanings of these words. Then have students use the words in oral sentences about different types of writers and their work.

- Add the **Context Cards** for *destruction, edition, household, publication,* and *uneventful.* Give one card to each student. Have students imagine they are journalists and are researching a news story. Tell them to choose a topic for their news stories and use their words in original sentences that give facts about the topic. Have students share their sentences with the class.

WRITE ABOUT IT

- Ask students to write about a career they find interesting, using the word *career* in their descriptions.

PRETEACH

Persuasion
Summarize

Write-In Reader pages 124–130

- Have students review *Women of the American Revolution*. Then introduce the skill and strategy. Say, *In the next lesson, we are going to focus on the use of persuasion in a text. We'll also work on ways to summarize or paraphrase what you are reading.*

- Explain, *Authors have many different purposes for writing. One purpose may be to convince readers to think a certain way or agree with a particular idea. This is called persuasion.*

- Ask, *What idea does the author introduce in the first paragraph of page 124?* (that while men did most of the fighting in the American Revolution, women played an important role, too) *How does the author try to persuade the reader that women played an important role in the war?* (by naming some of the contributions they made and by telling the stories of individual women)

- Have students turn to page 129. Say, *The author says that Abigail Adams was a "hero." Is this a fact or an opinion?* (opinion) *How does the author try to persuade us to agree with this opinion?* (by providing examples of how Abigail stood up for women and advised her husband on important decisions)

- Review the Summarize Strategy on page 302 in the **Write-In Reader**. Tell students that they can summarize what they have read to help them better remember the most important points. Have students tell key points from *Women of the American Revolution*. List their ideas on the board. Then work with students to summarize the selection.

APPLY READING SKILLS

Introduce *Maria Tallchief: American Ballerina*. Choral read the first few pages with students. Depending on their abilities, have students continue reading with partners or as a group.

● **Leveled Reader**

Quick Check **Fluency**

Listen to individual students as they read the **Write-In Reader** selection. Make specific notes about words that presented difficulty to them.

SUMMARIZE STRATEGY

When you **summarize**, you briefly explain the most important ideas in a text in your own words. Organize a summary in a way that makes sense, and do not change the meaning of the text. A summary can be as short as one or two sentences.

In narrative texts, explain

- who the main character is and where the story takes place.
- the problem that the main character faces.
- the most important events.
- how the problem is resolved.

In informational texts, explain

- the main idea.
- the most important details that support the main idea.

When you **paraphrase**, you restate the author's words in another way. A paraphrase can be about the same length as the original text.

You can paraphrase by

- using synonyms to replace words the author used.
- changing the order of words in a sentence in a way that makes sense.
- combining sentences that have related ideas.

EXTRA PRACTICE

Independent Reading Have students read from a book of their choice and describe what they read in their reading logs.

Day 1

SHARE OBJECTIVES

- Use possessive nouns.
- Discuss the importance of individual rights.
- Read to build meaning for Target Vocabulary words.

MATERIALS

Write-In Reader pages 182–183
Context Cards: *dependent, effective, exception, issue, urge*

ACADEMIC LANGUAGE
possessive noun

Oral Grammar

Possessive Nouns

- Students will benefit by practicing the use of possessive nouns before they begin practicing possessive pronoun replacement. The format below strengthens the inclusion of the /s/ (representing *apostrophe -s*) in phrases such as *the girl's music.*

- Model, using the first prompt and response. Signal students to respond to your prompt in the following sentences.

Teacher prompts	Students respond
That music is the girl's. It is…	the girl's music.
This leash is his dog's. It is…	his dog's leash.
The horse is the farmer's. It is…	the farmer's horse.
This map is Dad's. It is…	Dad's map.
That house is my aunt and uncle's. It is…	my aunt and uncle's house.
This team belongs to our school. It is…	our school's team.

Talk About It

Help focus students' attention on the importance of equal rights. Ask, *What are some important rights that all Americans have?*

Discuss the question, focusing on the following:

- Speech: All Americans are entitled to voice their opinions, regardless of who they are and where they live.

- Vote: All American citizens of voting age are guaranteed the right to take part in government by voting.

- Housing: By law, all Americans are free to live in any community despite their race, religion, or ethnic background.

- Religion: All Americans have the right to practice their own religion without restrictions.

Target Vocabulary

Write-In Reader pages 182–183

- Read and discuss each section. Use **Context Cards** to review the meanings of the Target Vocabulary words. Then discuss the meaning of each Target Vocabulary word. Suggest that students underline words or phrases that provide clues to meaning. Also point out the following:

  Issue has several meanings. In this instance, *issue* is "a topic that is being focused on, discussed, or argued." The word can also be used as a verb—(1) "to supply or distribute" as in "to issue a revision of a book"; (2) "to make a public statement" as in "The mayor will issue an apology."

  When used as an adjective—as in this lesson—*dependent* describes a person who relies on others. *Dependent* can also be used when talking about animals and things such as "My cat is dependent on us for food" or "Earth is dependent on the Sun for heat and light." When used as a noun, a *dependent* is the person (or thing) that is reliant on someone (or something). For example, a child is a *dependent* of his or her parents.

- Have volunteers read aloud the numbered sentences with the correct vocabulary word in place.

Responses:

1. issue
2. urge
3. dependent
4. exception
5. effective

Quick Check | Target Vocabulary

Ask each student to use one of the Target Vocabulary words in a sentence.

✔ **TARGET VOCABULARY**

Someone who is **dependent** relies on others.

Something **effective** is successful and achieves desired results.

An **exception** does not fit into a general rule.

An **issue** is a subject or problem that people think and talk about.

To **urge** is to recommend or argue for strongly.

EXTRA PRACTICE

Build Fluency Have students read **Write-In Reader** pages 182–183 with a partner or a family member.

Warm Up

Multisyllable Words

Focus: Vowel Pair Syllables

Write these words on the board or on a pad.

1	underground	overbook	overgrown
2	overboard	undercoat	overloaded
3	intergroup	disbelief	undersea

Row 1: Say, *To make words easier to read, we can divide after a prefix and before an ending.* Then circle the vowel pair syllable (highlighted in list). Review the sound represented by each vowel pair. Read each word.

Row 2: Ask volunteers to divide words, then circle the vowel pair syllables and read them. Choral read the words.

Row 3: Listen to each student read the words. Make corrections as needed. Record your findings.

RETEACH

Persuasion

- Have students suggest a community project such as building a public pool or clearing a nature trail.

- Have students state their goal (position) such as to convince the local government to act on their suggestion.

- Have students provide support (facts and reasons) that could be used to persuade officials to create the trail. List their ideas on the board. For example, a trail would give families a place to spend time together; provide a place to learn about nature.

- Tell students that sometimes authors write to persuade readers to think or act in a certain way. These authors will provide details and use certain language to achieve their goal.

- Emphasize that identifying persuasive text helps readers understand how an author feels about a subject and how he or she may be trying to influence others.

Quick Check Comprehension

Have students share facts and reasons they would use to convince a parent to allow them to have a sleepover party.

READ

"Sojourner Truth: Speaker for Equal Rights"

Write-In Reader pages 184–187

- Preview the selection with students using the **Think Aloud** to predict the topic. Guide students to make predictions.

Think Aloud *The section heads include words like* rights *and* slavery. *I think this story is about slavery and human rights. What other clues help you predict the topic of the story?*

- Together, review the Summarize Strategy, **Write-In Reader** page 302. As needed, guide students in applying it.

READ

Ask students to read to confirm their predictions. Have students take turns reading the selection with partners. Discuss, confirm, and revise student predictions based upon text details.

REREAD

Call on individuals to read aloud while others follow along. Point out words with vowel pair syllables, including *owner, speaker,* and *beliefs.* Stop to discuss each question. Sample answers are provided.

Page 184: Why were equal rights so important to Isabella Baumfree? (Baumfree was born a slave.)

Help unpack meaning, if needed, by asking, *Was Baumfree born a free person?* (no) *What was her childhood like?* (She was sold many times.) *How was Baumfree treated by her masters?* (badly)

Unpack Meaning: For questions on pages 185–187, you may want to use the notes in the right-hand column.

Page 185: It took Baumfree a year to win her case and get her son back. Why do you think the author includes this information? (to persuade the reader to think that Baumfree was strong and determined)

Turn and Talk **Page 186:** What does the author say to convince readers that Baumfree was an <u>effective</u> speaker? (People listened closely. Her words gave them courage and hope.) Have partners discuss the question and then share with the group.

Page 187: Sojourner Truth and Frederick Douglass both escaped slavery. How do you think this helped them as abolitionist speakers? (Since they both experienced slavery, their words against it would have great meaning.)

UNPACK MEANING

Use prompts such as these if students have difficulty with a **Stop•Think•Write** question:

Page 185 *The author wants us to know that Baumfree fought for a year to get her son back. How do you think Baumfree felt during that year?* (She probably felt tired and frustrated.) *Why do you think she kept up the fight?* (She wanted her son back.) *What does Baumfree's year-long struggle tell us about her?* (that she was a strong and determined woman)

Page 186 *Which sentences in the text give information about Baumfree as a speaker?* (She gave speeches. She shared her beliefs in the speeches. She was an effective speaker. People listened closely. Her words gave them courage and hope.) *Which of these sentences tell you about her ability as a speaker?* (People listened closely. Her words gave them courage.)

Page 187 *What did abolitionist speakers give speeches about?* (They spoke out against the cruelness of slavery.) *What did Sojourner Truth and Frederick Douglass learn about slavery in their own lives?* (They learned that slavery was cruel and unjust.)

EXTRA PRACTICE

Build Fluency Have students read **Write-In Reader** pages 184–187 with a partner or a family member.

SHARE OBJECTIVES

- Use possessive pronouns.
- Read aloud to improve fluency by stressing words for emphasis.
- Read to apply skills and strategies.

MATERIALS

Write-In Reader pages 188–190

ACADEMIC LANGUAGE

possessive pronoun   persuade

stress

Oral Grammar

Possessive Pronouns

- Write on the board or on a pad: *Those shoes belong to Victoria.* Explain, *We can say this another way.* Write: *They are Victoria's shoes.*

- Remind students that pronouns can take the place of nouns. The pronouns *my, your, his, her, its, our,* and *their* show ownership. Ask, *Can you use a pronoun to say almost the same thing?* Write: *They are her shoes.*

- Give a sentence and prompt. Have students respond.

Sample prompts	Students respond
This notebook is my mom's. It is…	her notebook.
This leash is the dog's. It is…	its leash.
That is my aunt and uncle's house. It is…	their house.
This team belongs to all of us. It is…	our team.

RETEACH

Fluency: Stress

Write-In Reader page 188

Remind students that good readers stress, or emphasize, certain words. Tell students that you are going to read from page 188 in two different ways, and you want them to evaluate your reading.

- First, read the last paragraph in a monotone voice. Then reread the paragraph modeling how to stress words for emphasis. For example, stress the following words: *look, plowed, planted, gathered, work as much, eat as much,* and *man.*

- Ask, *Which reading gave you a better idea of what Sojourner Truth was feeling? Why?* Emphasize that stressing key words and phrases can change the meaning of a reading as well as make it more interesting to listen to. Have small groups practice reading aloud the same paragraph, applying what they learned about stress.

READ

"Sojourner Truth: Speaker for Equal Rights"

Write-In Reader pages 188–190

Review the first part of the story with students. Ask, *What have we learned about Sojourner Truth so far?* Then preview today's reading. Have students predict what else they might learn.

READ

Ask students to read to confirm their predictions. Have students take turns reading the selection with partners. Discuss, confirm, and revise predictions based upon text details. Ask if there was anything about the way the story ended that surprised them.

REREAD

Call on individuals to read aloud while others follow along. Stop to discuss each question. Sample answers are provided.

Page 188: Why did Sojourner Truth <u>urge</u> women to gain their rights? (Possible answer: She knew that women could do anything that men could do, so they deserved the same rights.)

Help unpack meaning, if needed, by asking, *What does* urge *mean?* (to push people to do or feel something) *What rights did men have that women did not?* (the right to vote; the right to hold most jobs) *Did Sojourner Truth think women were as strong as men?* (yes)

Unpack Meaning: For questions on pages 189–190, you may want to use the notes in the right-hand column.

Page 189: What things show that Sojourner Truth was brave? (She helped African Americans adjust to life after slavery at a time when some people may not have been supportive or welcoming.)

Turn and Talk **Page 190:** How do these facts help you know Sojourner Truth better? (Possible answer: They show what a remarkable and unusual life she had from her youth through her adulthood.) Have partners discuss this question and then share with the group.

Quick Check Retelling

Have students retell the end of the story. Support the retelling by asking, *What did Sojourner Truth do to help women gain their rights? How did she continue to help others after slavery was ended? What did you learn about her?*

UNPACK MEANING

Use prompts such as these if students have difficulty with a **Stop•Think•Write** question:

Page 189 *How were enslaved African Americans treated?* (They were treated unfairly and with cruelty.) *Do you think everyone began treating African Americans more kindly when slavery ended? Why or why not?* (Probably not; people's opinions and behavior usually don't change overnight.) *What kind of person would be willing to challenge people who still treated blacks unfairly?* (a brave and determined person)

Page 190 *What did you learn about Sojourner Truth's childhood?* (Dutch was her first language; by the age of 13, she had been sold three times.) *What did you learn about her adult life?* (She journeyed through 22 states, speaking out against slavery; because she was six feet tall, she wasn't afraid of angry crowds; she met Abraham Lincoln.)

EXTRA PRACTICE

Build Fluency Have students read **Write-In Reader** pages 188–190 with a partner or a family member.

SHARE OBJECTIVES

- Read words with vowel pair syllables.
- Identify possessive pronouns, indefinite pronouns, and interrogative pronouns.
- Answer questions using evidence from the text.

MATERIALS

Write-In Reader pages 184–191

ACADEMIC LANGUAGE

indefinite pronoun
interrogative pronoun
possessive pronoun

Multisyllable Words

Focus: Vowel Pair Syllables

Write these words on the board or on a pad.

1	overcoach	underway	semiweekly
2	underfeeding	overpayment	overcrowded
3	overlook	undercook	overstay

Row 1: Say, *To make words easier to read, we can divide after a prefix and before an ending.* Divide the words, then circle the vowel pair syllables (highlighted in chart). Review the sound represented by each vowel pair.

Row 2: Ask volunteers to divide words, then circle the vowel pair syllables. Choral read the words.

Row 3: Listen to each student read the words. Make corrections as needed. Record your findings.

RETEACH

Possessive Pronouns

Review that possessive pronouns show ownership and stand for another noun. They include *my, your, his, her, its, our,* and *their.* Note that possessive pronouns do not include an apostrophe as in the possessive form of a common noun.

- Read the first sentence on page 182 aloud. Ask, *What is the possessive pronoun?* (their) *What noun does it stand for?* (enslaved people)

Turn and Talk Have students read all of page 185 and list the possessive pronouns and the nouns they stand for used in sentences describing Sojourner's experience.

Answers: her (Isabella); his (the owner); her (Isabella); her (Isabella); their (a kind couple); her (Isabella)

Quick Check Grammar

Have students write a sentence for each of the following possessive pronouns: *my, his,* and *our.*

Look Back and Respond

Write-In Reader pages 184–191

Help students complete the Look Back and Respond page. Model how to use the hint in question 1 to find evidence that can be used to support answers.

- Explain that evidence is proof, clues, or information.

- Remind students that they can circle or underline the specific words in the selection that they used as evidence for their answers.

1. What issues were important to Sojourner Truth? (ending slavery and giving women the right to vote)

Help unpack meaning, if needed, by asking, *What details about Sojourner Truth's life and beliefs can you find on page 184?* (She fought for equal rights for all people. She was born a slave.) *How did these things affect her life?* (She wanted to end slavery.) *What details about Sojourner Truth's life can you find on page 188?* (She felt she was as strong as a man and should have the same rights that men did.) *How did these things affect her life?* (She fought to get women the right to vote.)

Turn and Talk Have students work independently on questions 2–4. When students have completed the page, have partners discuss their responses and then share them with the group. Sample responses are provided. Accept reasonable responses.

Unpack Meaning: For questions 2–4, you may want to use the notes in the right-hand column to guide the discussion about student responses.

2. What details about Sojourner Truth did the author provide to persuade readers to admire her? (Possible answers: She fought in court for a year to get her son back; her hard life made her want to help others; her speech at the Women's Rights Convention in 1851.)

3. What words would you use to describe Sojourner Truth? (Possible answer: Sojourner Truth was a strong and determined woman who fought hard for what she believed in.)

4. In what ways do people like Sojourner Truth help make our world better? (Possible answer: They overcome great challenges and use what they learned in the process to teach others.)

Use prompts such as these if students have difficulty with a question:

2. *What evidence can you find on page 185 to help you write your answer?* (Truth fought for a year to get her son back.) *What did this tell you about her?* (Not only was Sojourner Truth a good mother, she also was a fighter who would not give up!) *What other clues in the story helped you to answer the question?*

3. *What part of your answer to questions 1 and 2 can help you answer this question?* (Question 1 was about the issues that were important to Sojourner Truth—women's rights and ending slavery. Question 2 was about clues in the text that showed what a good person Truth was.) *How can you use this information to respond to the question?* (Question 1: Truth's interest in ending slavery and giving women equal rights tells me that she was a wise woman who believed in fairness for all. Question 2: Truth's hard life made her want to help others—this piece of information tells me that Truth was very unselfish; instead of being bitter about her own life, she worked to protect others from having to go through the same things she did.)

4. *What words did you come up with in question 3 to describe Sojourner Truth?* (strong and determined) *How do strong and determined people help to make our world better?* (They fight with great determination to bring fairness and equality to all people under all circumstances.)

EXTRA PRACTICE

Retell Have students retell "Sojourner Truth: Speaker for Equal Rights" to a partner or a family member.

SHARE OBJECTIVES

- Identify words with vowel pair syllables.
- Demonstrate understanding of Target Vocabulary words.
- Preview Understanding Characters and Questioning.

MATERIALS

Context Cards: *dependent, deteriorating, effective, exception, granted, issue, minimum, ordinance, urge, violations*

Write-In Reader pages 104–110

Leveled Reader: *The Big Interview*

ACADEMIC LANGUAGE

character   question

✔ TARGET VOCABULARY

When something is **deteriorating**, it is becoming worse.

Something **granted** is given in an official way.

A **minimum** is the very least.

An **ordinance** is a law or rule made by authorities.

Violations are acts that break the rules.

Warm Up

Multisyllable Words

Cumulative Review

- Write these sentences on the board or on a pad.

    1. They spoke to the crowds on a semiweekly basis.

    2. The hall was overcrowded the Sunday she spoke.

    3. The Underground Railroad helped slaves get their freedom.

- Tell students to be on the lookout for clues they can use to divide and read long words. Have students circle the vowel pair syllables in the multisyllable words that appear here.

- Assign students to work with a partner to practice reading the sentences. Then listen to each student read one sentence. Make corrections as needed. Record your findings.

REVIEW

Target Vocabulary

Context Cards

- Display the **Context Cards** for *dependent, effective, exception, issue,* and *urge*. Review the meanings of these words. Then have students use the words in oral sentences about women's struggle for equal rights.

- Add the **Context Cards** for *deteriorating, granted, minimum, ordinance,* and *violations*. Give one card to each student. Have them make up a riddle for their word. Have the rest of the group guess the answer.

✏ **WRITE ABOUT IT**

- Ask students to think of an issue that is important to them, such as a problem facing their school, their community, or their state. Explain that they will write a letter to a government leader to convince that person to address the issue. In their letters, students should describe their concern and give at least two reasons why it needs to be dealt with. Students should use the word *issue* in their letters.

PRETEACH

Understanding Characters Question

Write-In Reader pages 104–110

- Introduce skill and strategy. Say, *In the next lesson, we are going to focus on understanding characters. We'll also work on asking questions as you read.*

- Explain, *In fiction, characters are the people (or sometimes animals) in the story. Writers tell different things about their characters including what they look like, how they sound, what they like to do, and how they feel.*

- Explain, *Sometimes an author tells the readers everything they need to know about a character. Other times, readers use text clues to figure out characters' viewpoints, how they feel, or why they are acting in a certain way.*

- Ask, *What clues in the text helped you to know that Jack Bunker in* The Story of Bunker's Cove *wanted America to be free from Great Britain?* (In addition to other clues, on page 107 the author states, "He [Jack Bunker] didn't want the British to be able to use it [the *Falmouth Packet*] to fight the Patriots.)

- Turn to and review the Question Strategy found on page 305 in the **Write-In Reader.** Tell students that when they use this strategy, they will ask questions *before, during,* and *after* a reading. Have students share questions they had about Sojourner Truth. Then have them identify which questions were and were not answered in the selection.

APPLY READING SKILLS

Introduce *The Big Interview.* Choral read the first few pages with students. Depending on their abilities, have students continue reading with partners or as a group.

Quick Check | Fluency

Listen to individual students as they read the **Write-In Reader** selection. Make specific notes about words that presented difficulty to them.

QUESTION STRATEGY

One way to check and improve your understanding of a text is to **ask yourself questions** before, during, and after reading. Use questions like these:

- What does the author mean here?
- What is the main idea?
- What does this word mean?
- Who or what is this about?
- Why did this happen?
- How does this work?
- What is the author's purpose?
- What caused this character to act this way?
- Which ideas connect to the topic or theme?
- Which ideas are important to understand and remember?

Look for the answers to your own questions to make sure you understand the text.

Question Words

Words such as *who, what, when, where, why, how,* and *which* will help you form questions.

Leveled Reader

EXTRA PRACTICE

Independent Reading Have students read from a book of their choice and describe what they read in their reading logs.

SHARE OBJECTIVES

- Use pronoun contractions correctly.
- Discuss castles, including how they were built, how they were used, and who lived inside them.
- Read to build meaning for Target Vocabulary words.

MATERIALS

Write-In Reader pages 192–193

ACADEMIC LANGUAGE

pronoun   contractions

Warm Up

Oral Grammar

Pronoun Contractions

- List on the board or on a pad.

Pronoun and Verb	Contraction
I am	I'm
you are	you're
it is	it's
we would	we'd
they have	they've

- Explain that pronoun contractions give us a quick way to say something. Then say each sentence.

Teacher says, then asks, *Contraction?*	Students respond
I am going to the beach.	I'm going to the beach.
We are studying the American Revolution.	We're studying the American Revolution.
You have been working hard.	You've been working hard.
They are not ignoring their work.	They're not ignoring their work.
She is a hard worker.	She's a hard worker.

Talk About It

Help focus students' attention on the story. Ask, *What do you know about tales?*

Discuss the question, emphasizing these points:

- Tales sometimes include make-believe characters such as dragons.
- Tales are fiction.
- Tales often take place in castles and kingdoms of long ago.
- The characters in tales are sometimes kings, queens, and knights.
- The characters learn an important lesson about themselves or life.

Target Vocabulary

Write-In Reader pages 192–193

• Read and discuss the passage. Then discuss the meaning of each Target Vocabulary word. Suggest that students underline words or phrases that provide clues to meaning. Also point out the following:

Contrast the meaning of *thrust* as it's used in the story, "to push in forcefully," with another meaning for the word, "to force someone to accept or deal with something," as in *The candidate's victory thrust her into the spotlight.*

As used in the story, *pierced* means "to have a hole poked into something." Pierced can also mean "to have a sudden intense effect on someone," as in *My heart was pierced with sadness when my dog ran away. Pierced* can also mean "to sound or shine suddenly," as in *The quick flicker of a match pierced the darkness.*

Quests are journeys undertaken to achieve something. The singular form of the word, *quest,* is a synonym for the words *mission, purpose,* and *goal.*

• Ask students to choose an answer they would like to read aloud.

Responses:

1. pierced

2. plagued

3. quests

4. thrust

5. Possible response: With the drawbridge up, attackers had to swim across the moat to reach the castle. Arrows, rocks, or tar could be dropped on them from above.

6. Possible responses: skin and cloth.

Quick Check Target Vocabulary

Ask each student to use one of the Target Vocabulary words in a sentence.

✔ **TARGET VOCABULARY**

If something is **pierced**, a hole has been poked in it.

If someone is **plagued**, he or she is constantly bothered by something.

Quests are journeys undertaken in order to find something.

To **thrust** is to push in forcefully.

If something is **transformed**, it is totally changed.

EXTRA PRACTICE

Build Fluency Have students read **Write-In Reader** pages 192–193 with a partner or a family member.

SHARE OBJECTIVES

- Read words with vowel pair syllables.
- Understand characters in a story.
- Read to apply skills and strategies.

MATERIALS

Write-In Reader pages 194–197

ACADEMIC LANGUAGE

character   trait   question

Multisyllable Words

Cumulative review

- Write these sentences on the board or on a pad.

    1. The knight prevails over the dragon.

    2. It is unlikely that all castles had moats.

    3. The prince's story sounded misleading.

- Tell students to be on the lookout for clues they can use to divide and read long words. Have students circle multisyllable words with vowel pair syllables.

- Assign students to work with a partner to practice reading the sentences. Then listen to each student read one sentence. Record your findings.

RETEACH

Understanding Characters

- Display a book that your students have recently read. Have students name one of the main characters. Ask, *What do you know about this character? What details from the story support your thinking?*

- Remind students that **behavior** is the way a character acts. **Traits** are ways of speaking and acting that show what a character is like.

- Guide students to analyze the character that they named. Draw a T-Map on the board. On the left side, record students' ideas about the behavior and traits of the character. Then discuss each idea with students, using the information to draw conclusions about the character's thoughts, feelings, and motivations. Record students' ideas on the right side of the T-Map. Encourage students to think about dialogue in the story, the character's relationships, and the character's actions.

Quick Check | Comprehension

Ask students to analyze a different character in the same book. Use a T-Map to record students' ideas.

READ

"The Tale of the Unlucky Knight"

Write-In Reader pages 194–197

- Preview the selection with students using the **Think Aloud** to predict what the characters might be like. Record their ideas.

> Think Aloud   *I know from the title that the story is about an unlucky knight. I also see a king and queen. I'll read to find out if they help him. What other clues help describe the characters?*

- Together, review the Question Strategy on **Write-In Reader** page 305. Guide students in applying.

READ

Ask students to read to confirm their ideas about the characters. Have students take turns reading the selection with partners. Discuss, confirm, and revise student descriptions based upon text details.

REREAD

Call on individuals to read aloud while others follow along. Stop to discuss each question. Sample answers are provided.

Page 194: How would you describe Sir Edward? (Sir Edward has good manners.) What does he do or say to make you think this? (He kneels before the throne.)

Help unpack meaning, if needed, by asking, *What did the king and queen do that was unusual?* (They invited Sir Edward in, although they did not know him.) *How did the queen describe Sir Edward's face?* (as a friendly face)

Unpack Meaning: For questions on pages 195–197, you may want to use the notes in the right-hand column.

Page 195: What is the reason for Sir Edward's <u>quests</u>? (He's in search of some way to prove his bravery.)

Page 196: How would you describe the queen? (The queen is kind.) What does she do to make you think this? (She offers Sir Edward food and encouragement.)

Turn and Talk   **Page 197:** Why do you think the king offers Sir Edward his lance? (to give Sir Edward something that will make him think his luck can change) Have partners discuss their answers and then share with the group.

UNPACK MEANING

Use prompts such as these if students have difficulty with a **Stop•Think•Write** question:

Page 195 *What is a* quest*?* (a journey in search of something) *What quests do the king and queen ask Sir Edward if he has performed?* (fighting a dragon and saving a lady in danger)

Page 196 *How does the queen feel?* (She feels sorry for Sir Edward.) *Why does the queen change the subject from Sir Edward's bad luck to food?* (She wants to make him feel better.)

Page 197 *Why does the king tell Sir Edward he has used the lance many times?* (to make Sir Edward think the lance is dependable) *What does the king want Sir Edward to think when he says the lance "has never failed me"?* (The lance will not fail Sir Edward either.)

EXTRA PRACTICE

Build Fluency Have students read **Write-In Reader** pages 194–197 with a partner or a family member.

SHARE OBJECTIVES

- Use contractions with *not*.
- Read aloud fluently to improve accuracy.
- Read to apply skills and strategies.

MATERIALS

Write-In Reader pages 198–200

ACADEMIC LANGUAGE

contraction   negative statement   accuracy

Warm Up

Oral Grammar

Contractions with *not*

- On the board or on a pad, list contractions with *not*.

> can't, don't, won't, doesn't, hasn't, haven't, aren't, didn't

- Tell students that you are going to make a statement, and you want them to turn it into a negative statement using one of the contractions with *not*. Explain that double negatives are not used in English (unlike many other languages). Therefore, if a contraction with *not* is used, another negative should not be used (including *never, neither, no, nobody, nothing, none,* or *nowhere*).

Teacher prompts	Students respond
I hear something.	I **can't** hear anything. I **didn't** hear anything.
Jamal eats everything.	Jamal **doesn't** eat anything. Jamal **won't** eat anything. Jamal **can't** eat anything.
Sam likes everyone.	Sam **doesn't** like anyone. Sam **doesn't** like anybody.

RETEACH

Fluency: Accuracy

Write-In Reader page 198

Tell students to follow along as you read the first two paragraphs on page 198. As you read, pronounce the word *tear* as a "a tear in a cloth," rather than as a "tear from an eye." Also, pronounce the word *through* as *throw* and the word *hope* as *hoop*.

- Ask, *What did you think of my reading? Explain.* Be sure students recognize that your reading was inaccurate because you mispronounced several words. Emphasize that inaccurate word recognition can confuse listeners as well as change the meaning of a story or passage.

- Have students listen as you read the passage correctly. Discuss how the passage's meaning changed. Then have students practice reading aloud the rest of the page, concentrating on accuracy as they read.

READ

"The Tale of the Unlucky Knight"

Write-In Reader pages 198–200

Review the first part of the story with students. Ask, *What have we learned about the characters in this story so far?* Then preview today's reading.

READ

Ask students to read to confirm their ideas. Have students take turns reading the selection with partners. Discuss, confirm, and revise predictions based upon text details. Ask if there was anything about the way the story ended that surprised them.

REREAD

Call on individuals to read aloud while others follow along. Stop to discuss each question. Sample answers are provided.

Page 198: How do the king and queen feel as they wait for Sir Edward's return? (They're anxious and worried.) How can you tell? (They both shed tears and have trouble sleeping.)

Help unpack meaning, if needed, by asking, *Why does the queen hope the knight's luck has changed?* (She knows Sir Edward needs all the help he can get in facing a dragon.) *Why does the king not answer the queen when she asks, "Do you think he has fought the dragon?"* (The king knows that Sir Edward's chances are not good against a dangerous dragon.)

Unpack Meaning: For questions on pages 199–200, you may want to use the notes in the right-hand column.

Page 199: What does Sir Edward mean when he says that the king's lance <u>pierced</u> the dragon's tough skin? (The lance put a hole in the dragon's skin.)

Turn and Talk **Page 200:** How does Sir Edward feel about King Al and Queen Bess at the end of the story? (He is grateful to them.) Have partners discuss their answers and then share with the group.

Quick Check | Retelling

Have students retell the end of the story. Support the retelling by asking: *What happened after the king gave Sir Edward the lance? What did Sir Edward think about the lance? How was Sir Edward finally transformed?*

UNPACK MEANING

Use prompts such as these if students have difficulty with a **Stop•Think•Write** question:

Page 199 *How could a lance pierce tough skin?* (It must have been very sharp.) *Why did the dragon run away screaming?* (He must have been hurt.)

Page 200 *Has someone ever helped you get past some problem in your life?* (Responses will vary.) *How did you feel toward the person or persons who helped you?* (Responses will vary.)

EXTRA PRACTICE

Build Fluency Have students reread **Write-In Reader** pages 198–200 with a partner or family member.

SHARE OBJECTIVES

- Read words with vowel pair syllables.
- Identify contractions and the words they replace.
- Answer questions using evidence from the text.

MATERIALS

Write-In Reader pages 194–201

ACADEMIC LANGUAGE

contractions

Warm Up

Multisyllable Words

Cumulative Review

- Write these sentences on the board or on a pad.
    1. He was disdainful of the other knights.
    2. She dismounted her horse.
    3. Releasing the dragon would be unwise.

- Tell students to be on the lookout for clues they can use to divide and read long words. Have students circle multisyllable words with vowel pair syllables.

- Assign students to work with a partner to practice reading the sentences. Then listen to each student read one sentence. Record your findings.

RETEACH

Contractions

- Remind students that a contraction is two words put together shortened. To write a contraction, we leave out one or more letters and use an apostrophe in their place. As needed, review how to form contractions with not and pronouns.(Examples: *can't, didn't, you're, they've, I'm, that's*)

- Have students reread page 195. Say, *The word* let's *must be a contraction that stands for* let us. *I can check by using the words* let us *in place of the contraction in the sentence.* Read the first sentence, replacing let's with let us. *Say, Yes, the sentence still makes sense and has the same meaning.*

- Have students identify the contraction and the words it replaces in Paragraph 2 *(don't; do not)*.

- Ask students to reread the first paragraph on page 198. Point out that the words *king's* and *knight's* are possessive nouns, not contractions.

Turn and Talk Have partners find and list other contractions in the story and identify the words they replace.

Sample Answers: page 196–*let's us*; pages 197, 199–*I'm, I am*; page 200–*it's, it is*

Quick Check Grammar

Write several contractions on the board or a pad. Have students identify the words the contractions have replaced.

Look Back and Respond

Write-In Reader pages 194–201

Help students complete the Look Back and Respond page. Model how to use the hint in question 1 to find evidence that can be used to support answers.

• Explain that evidence is proof, clues, or information.

• Remind students that they can circle or underline the specific words in the selection that they used as evidence for their answers.

1. What do King Al's actions and what he says to Sir Edward show about the king? (He is wise and caring.)

Help unpack meaning, if needed, by asking, *Why does King Al tell Sir Edward there is a dragon roaming nearby?* (He knows Sir Edward must face his fear of being unlucky.) *Why does King Al have trouble sleeping while Sir Edward is off fighting the dragon?* (He is worried about Edward.)

Turn and Talk Have students work independently on questions 2–4. When students have completed the page, have partners discuss their responses and then share them with the group. Sample responses are provided.

Unpack Meaning: For questions 2–4, you may want to use the notes in the right-hand column to guide the discussion about student responses.

2. How are King Al and Queen Bess alike? (They are both sensitive, caring people.) How are they different? (Queen Bess shows her love for Sir Edward by offering him food and encouragement. King Al shows a tough kind of love for Sir Edward by pushing him to face the dragon and his fear of being unlucky.)

3. What effect does King Al's lie have on Sir Edward? (He thinks the lance has been lucky for King Al, so Sir Edward feels empowered as he rides out to face the dragon.)

4. How do you think Sir Edward's life will be different from now on? (Responses will vary, but may include that Sir Edward will have greater self-confidence.)

UNPACK MEANING

Use prompts such as these if students have difficulty with a question:

2. *On page 195, what do the king and queen do for Sir Edward?* (They listen carefully to his story.) *Why does the king say, "Nonsense!" on page 197?* (He offers a different kind of encouragement to Sir Edward.)

3. *Why does Sir Edward think he is unlucky?* (He hasn't been successful in his past quests.) *What do you think luck is?* (Responses will vary, but may include belief in oneself.)

4. *How has a negative experience affected you?* (Responses will vary.) *What can help you overcome a negative experience?* (Responses will vary.)

EXTRA PRACTICE

Retell Have students retell "The Tale of the Unlucky Knight" to a partner or a family member.

SHARE OBJECTIVES

- Read words with vowel pair syllables.
- Demonstrate understanding of Target Vocabulary words.
- Preview Sequence of Events and the Visualize Strategy.

MATERIALS

Context Cards: *antique, exploits, faithful, ignorance, noble, pierced, plagued, quests, thrust, transformed*

Write-In Reader pages 194–200

Leveled Reader: *Donald Quixote*

ACADEMIC LANGUAGE

sequence   visualize

 **TARGET VOCABULARY**

An **antique** object is one that was made many years ago.

Exploits are brave or daring actions.

Someone **faithful** is someone you can always depend on; he or she is loyal.

Ignorance is a lack of knowledge or awareness of important things.

A **noble** person is honest, brave, and unselfish.

Warm Up

Multisyllable Words

Cumulative Review

- Write these sentences on the board or on a pad.

  1. He was rereading the story to his mother.

  2. She liked to retreat into fantasy stories.

  3. The ending is sometimes left unknown.

- Tell students to be on the lookout for clues they can use to divide and read long words. Have students circle multisyllable words with vowel pair syllables.

- Assign students to work with a partner to practice reading the sentences. Then listen to each student read one sentence. Record your findings.

REVIEW

Target Vocabulary

Context Cards

- Display the **Context Cards** for *pierced, plagued, quests, thrust,* and *transformed*. Review the meanings of these words. Then have students use the words in oral sentences about the adventures of a knight long ago.

- Show the **Context Cards** for *antique, exploits, faithful, ignorance,* and *noble*. Have students take turns giving a synonym or an antonym for one of the words. Have the rest of the class identify the correct vocabulary word.

✏️ **WRITE ABOUT IT**

Ask students to write a humorous story about Sir Edward's next quest. Have them describe the event, using the word *exploits* in their descriptions.

PRETEACH

Sequence of Events
Visualize

Write-In Reader pages 194–200

- Introduce skill and strategy. Say, *In the next lesson, we are going to focus on the sequence of events in a story. We'll also work on ways to visualize in order to understand the story's characters and events.*

- Explain, *A writer's story has an organized story line, or plot. This story line or plot is made of a series, or sequence of events. Usually—but not always—writers tell the events in the order in which they take place.*

- Ask, *What happens first in* The Tale of the Unlucky Knight? (A knight arrives at the castle of King Al and Queen Bess. The king and queen invite him in, and the unlucky knight introduces himself.)

- Ask, *What happens on each page of the story?* Use page numbers to draw a timeline on the board. Invite students to identify events on each page of the story.

- Turn to and review the Visualize Strategy, found on page 305 in the **Write-In Reader**. Discuss the strategy as a class, emphasizing that visualizing the characters, settings, and events in a story can make the story easier to understand and more enjoyable. Have students identify the descriptive words and phrases that they used to form mental pictures of the action.

APPLY READING SKILLS

Introduce *Donald Quixote*. Choral-read the first few pages with students. Depending on their abilities, have students continue reading with partners or as a group.

Leveled Reader

Quick Check | Fluency

Listen to individual students as they read the **Write-In Reader** selection. Make specific notes about words that present difficulty to them.

VISUALIZE STRATEGY

When you **visualize**, you use details in a text to help you create mental pictures. Use the author's words plus your own knowledge and experiences. Visualizing can help you understand and remember what you are reading.

In narrative texts, visualize

- how characters look and act.
- settings and plot events.
- how one event leads to the next event.

In informational texts, visualize

- what an object, a real person, or place looks like.
- how something works or how it is built.
- steps to complete a task.
- how one event leads to another event.
- how things are alike and different.

Be ready to change your mental pictures as you read new details.

EXTRA PRACTICE

Independent Reading Have students read from a book of their choice and describe what they read in their reading logs.

Teacher Notes

ELL ENGLISH LANGUAGE LEARNERS

Lesson

16 "Lunch Money"

Build Background: How can pictures tell a story?

Comprehension: Author's Purpose; Monitor/Clarify

Target Vocabulary: assuming, developed, episodes, feature, incredibly, launch, mental, record, thumbed, villains

High-Utility Words: fold, illustration, pages, price, sell

Lesson

17 "LAFFF" from "Best Shorts"

Build Background: What inspires authors to write?

Comprehension: Story Structure; Infer/Predict

Target Vocabulary: admitted, collected, compliment, concentrate, destination, impressed, original, produced, rumor, suspense

High-Utility Words: backward, contest, forward, future, genius, travel

Lesson

18 "The Dog Newspaper" from "Five Pages a Day"

Build Background: What makes a good story?

Comprehension: Fact and Opinion; Analyze/Evaluate

Target Vocabulary: background, career, destruction, edition, formula, household, insights, publication, required, uneventful

High-Utility Words: boring, exciting, interesting, interview, report

Lesson

19 "Darnell Rock Reporting"

Build Background: In what ways can you speak up for what you believe?

Comprehension: Persuasion; Summarize

Target Vocabulary: dependent, deteriorating, effective, exception, granted, issue, minimum, ordinance, urge, violations

High-Utility Words: decide, meeting, opinion, speech, support

Lesson

20 "Don Quixote and the Windmill"

Build Background: Why is it important to know the difference between fact and fantasy?

Comprehension: Understanding Characters; Question

Target Vocabulary: antique, exploits, faithful, ignorance, noble, pierced, plagued, quests, thrust, transformed

High-Utility Words: appearance, attack, bewitched, conquer, recognize

SHARE OBJECTIVES

- Participate in discussion about making comic books.
- Say, read, and use Target Vocabulary and high-utility words.
- Identify author's purpose and complete a T-Map.

MATERIALS

Language Support Card 16

Context Cards

Dialogue ELL16.1 (Making Comic Books, Making Money)

Student Book (pp. 406–416)

Main Selection Summary ELL16.2

Graphic Organizer Transparency 12

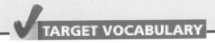

✓ TARGET VOCABULARY

• = *Spanish cognate*

assuming	
developed	
episodes	• *episodios*
feature	
incredibly	• *increíblemente*
launch	
mental	• *mental*
record	• *récord*
thumbed	
villains	• *villanos*

ACADEMIC LANGUAGE

author's purpose   • *propósito del autor*

Listening, Speaking, and Viewing

USE LANGUAGE SUPPORT CARD
Present **Language Support Card 16**. Use the activities on the back of the card to introduce concepts and vocabulary from "Lunch Money" and to practice **Academic English**.

Develop Target Vocabulary

USE CONTEXT CARDS Show the **Context Cards** for *mental* and *developed*. Present the cards using Steps 1–3 of the Introduce Vocabulary routine on **Teacher's Edition** p. T14.

- Help students use *mental* and *developed* to discuss how pictures help to tell a story.

USE ORAL LANGUAGE DIALOGUE Distribute **Dialogue ELL16.1**. Read the title aloud, and have students repeat. Have students look at the title, images, and other information on the page. Have them predict what they think the dialogue will be about.

BLM ELL16.1

- As you read the dialogue aloud, display the **Context Cards** for *episodes, mental,* and *developed*. After you read the dialogue, have students read it chorally with you.

- Draw a Column Chart with the heads *Word, Meaning,* and *Examples*. Write *episodes* in column 1, and provide an example of how the word can be used in context.

- Help students generate and list a meaning for *episodes* in the middle column. List examples of episodes in the last column.

- Read or have a student read each row aloud. Use the remaining Target Vocabulary words to complete the chart as a class.

- Allow students to include language from **Dialogue ELL16.1**. Encourage them to use high-utility words. Record student responses on the chart and display it as a reference.

▬▬▶ **WRITE-PAIR-SHARE** Display sentence frames such as the following and have partners use them to write complete sentences.

1. Greg wrote the first ____episodes____, or parts, about his character Creon.

2. Greg helped readers create ____mental____ pictures with his final episode about Eeon's adventures.

Scaffold Comprehension

PREVIEW "LUNCH MONEY" Explain that, before reading, students will skim "Lunch Money" in order to predict what the selection is about. Help students scan heads and captions, and other text features on **Student Book** pp. 406–416. Have them predict one thing they may learn by reading the text.

USE MAIN SELECTION SUMMARY Distribute **Summary ELL16.2**. Read the summary aloud, then have students chorally reread with you.

BLM ELL16.2

RETEACH

Author's Purpose

TEACH/MODEL Read aloud **Summary ELL16.2**. Write **author's purpose**. Say the words aloud and have students repeat. *A purpose is a reason for doing something. An author's purpose is the author's reason for writing something.*

• Remind students that an author's purpose in a story is to communicate ideas to the reader about the characters and plot.

GUIDED PRACTICE Have students read **Summary ELL16.2**.

• Display **Graphic Organizer Transparency 12**. Explain that a T-Map can help identify the author's purpose by recording details. Label the chart with these headings: *Detail* and *Author's Purpose*.

• Write the following details from the summary under the *Detail* heading: *Greg sold a record of seventeen comics. Greg planned many episodes that would feature his characters. Greg made up some villains to fight his characters.*

• *Why did the author include these details in the story? How do they help you understand the story or the author's purpose?* Help students explain what the author's purpose was for including each detail, for example, *The author wants readers to know that Greg's comics were a success.*

Do students…

• correctly pronounce and use vocabulary words in discussion?

• identify an author's purpose?

REVIEW TOGETHER

• Have partners use **Context Cards** to review the Target Vocabulary words and their meanings. Have them complete the activities on the backs of the cards.

• Have partners choose a detail from their own lives and tell why they would include it in a story about themselves.

Graphic Organizer

Name _____ Date _____

Graphic Organizer 12

T-Map: _____

Title or Topic _____

Detail	Author's Purpose
Greg sold a record of seventeen comics.	Readers know that Greg's comics were a success.
Greg planned many episodes that would feature his characters.	Readers know that Greg is a serious writer.
Greg made up some villains to fight his characters.	Readers know that Greg is creative.

Graphic Organizer 12

✏️ Scaffolded Practice and Application

Beginning In the left column of the T-Map, have students write *to draw, to fold, to sell, to write.* Help students include phrases such as these or other infinitives in their reponses.

Intermediate In the left column, have students write *Greg developed a plan; Greg learned drawing skills.* On the right, write reasons for why the author included each detail.

Advanced Under the heading *Detail* list details from the summary, for example *Creon, Leon, Eeon.* In the right column, have students give the author's reason for including the detail.

Advanced High Under the heading *Detail* list details that provide clues to Greg's character, such as: *loves drawing.* Have students infer the author's reason for including this: *shows Greg is an artist.*

- Use Target Vocabulary words to preview and discuss "Lunch Money."
- Listen to and recite a dialogue about making comic books.
- Identify word parts and inflectional endings.
- Monitor and clarify details from "Lunch Money."

MATERIALS

Student Book (pp. 406–416)

Audiotext CD

Dialogue ELL16.1 (Making Comic Books, Making Money)

Context Cards

Main Selection Summary ELL16.2

Language Support Card 16

ACADEMIC LANGUAGE

• = *Spanish cognate*

realistic fiction   • *ficción realística*

inflectional ending

monitor

clarify   • *clarificar*

Scaffold Comprehension

DISCUSS "LUNCH MONEY" Use the following picture-text prompts to discuss "Lunch Money." Remind students that "Lunch Money" is **realistic fiction**. Realistic fiction is a present-day story with events that could take place in real life.

PAGE 407: Have students read the title aloud and look at the first illustration. Identify the boy as Greg. *What does Greg use his comic books to do?* (His comic books use pictures to tell stories.)

PAGE 410: *What book is Greg reading?* (a drawing book) *Why is he reading this book?* (He wants to learn to draw.)

PAGES 412–413: *What process is described here?* (the process of making a comic book) *Does the process look difficult to you?* (Answers will vary.)

AUDIOTEXT CD Make the **Audiotext CD** for "Lunch Money" available. Have students follow in the **Student Book** as they listen.

Practice Target Vocabulary

USE ORAL LANGUAGE DIALOGUE Distribute **Dialogue ELL16.1**. Have a student read the title aloud.

BLM
ELL16.1

- Read the dialogue aloud or have proficient readers model reading aloud.

- Have students identify Target Vocabulary and high-utility words in the dialogue and read the words aloud with you.

- Have them restate each Target Vocabulary word and use it in an original sentence. Then have them complete the activity on the page.

PRACTICE FLUENCY: INTONATION Read **Dialogue ELL16.1** aloud, varying intonation at the phrase or sentence level. Have students follow along on their pages as they listen. Then have them echo the reader, reminding them to focus on their own intonation.

Word Parts and Inflectional Endings

INTRODUCE *An **inflectional ending** is a change in a word or root that is based on how the word is used. Inflectional endings for* walk, *for example, are* -s, -ing, *and* -ed: *Sam walks home. Sam is walking home. Yesterday, Sam walked home. Some suffixes, such as* -ed, *are also inflectional endings.*

PRACTICE Have students use **Context Cards**, the dialogue, the summary, or "Lunch Money" to look for and name words with word parts and inflectional endings. (*developed, assuming*)

Monitor/Clarify

TEACH/MODEL Remind students that to **monitor** means to follow something closely. *When you **monitor** your understanding, you think about what you read as you read it. You also try to **clarify**, or make clear, anything you don't understand.* Use a Think Aloud to model monitoring and clarifying "Lunch Money."

> Think Aloud   *In this story the author talks about ways kids can make money. Why did the author include this detail in the story? I can probably find the answer by reading on and looking for more information about this detail.*

GUIDED PRACTICE Have students read aloud selected paragraphs from "Lunch Money." Help them clarify information from the paragraph.

- Review **Teach Academic English** on **Language Support Card 16**. Remind students to use infinitives and the phrase *in order to* to tell why an author includes a given detail in a selection.

Do students…
- demonstrate fluency as they recite the dialogue using proper intonation?
- identify word parts and inflectional endings?
- monitor and clarify details from "Lunch Money"?

- Have partners take turns reading **Dialogue ELL16.1** aloud. Encourage them to read the roles of the dialogue, focusing on intonation.
- Have partners work together to identify the word ending in each case: *record:* no ending; *recorder:* -er, *records:* -s, *recording:* -ing, *recorded:* -ed.
- As a class, write two or three key details from "Lunch Money." Ask students to clarify or restate the details in their own words.

✏️ Scaffolded Practice and Application

Beginning Have students copy sentences from "Lunch Money" that include phrases such as: *to walk and play with their dog.* Have students circle the phrases and tell what they mean.	**Intermediate** Have students copy two or three phrases from "Lunch Money." Work with students to provide *why* questions that correspond to each phrase.	**Advanced** Have students find key details in "Lunch Money." Have students explain why the author included each detail in the story.	**Advanced High** Have students find key details in "Lunch Money." Have students write sentences explaining how each detail reveals something important about a character or event.

SHARE OBJECTIVES

- Use Target Vocabulary words to discuss "Lunch Money."
- Read and discuss a summary of "Lunch Money."
- Identify word origins.
- Examine author's purpose.

MATERIALS

Student Book (pp. 406–416)
Main Selection Summary ELL16.2
Audiotext CD
Dictionaries
Language Support Card 16
Context Cards

ACADEMIC LANGUAGE

• = *Spanish cognate*

author's purpose   • *propósito del autor*

Scaffold Comprehension

REVIEW "LUNCH MONEY" Use the Think Aloud and the following prompts to lead students on a guided review of "Lunch Money." Remind students that reviewing and retelling what they read will help them understand and remember it.

Think Aloud **PAGE 409:** *Greg's comic books are called* Chunky Comics. *I think his comic books are called that because they are short and sturdy.*

PAGE 412: *What does this page tell you about Greg?* (It tells you that Greg can draw.) *What does it tell you about the comic book?* (It tells you that the comic book requires a lot of work.)

PAGES 412–413: *Why does the author include information about making a comic book?* (to show what goes into making a comic book)

PAGE 416: *What does this tell you about how Greg feels about his work?* (He seems proud.)

CHECK COMPREHENSION If students need additional support with the main selection, direct them to **Summary ELL16.2**. Read the summary aloud, and have them listen and follow along on their pages.

BLM ELL16.2

Have students take turns reading sections of the summary aloud. Have them answer the following comprehension questions:

1. What kind of business does Greg have?

2. What does Greg know how to do?

3. What did he use to print the pages?

Have students work in pairs to circle high-utility words and highlight Target Vocabulary words found in **Summary ELL16.2**. Have them take turns reading each sentence containing a vocabulary word and paraphrasing the meaning of that sentence.

AUDIOTEXT CD Make the **Audiotext CD** for "Lunch Money" available. Have students follow in the **Student Book** as they listen.

Do students…
- use Target Vocabulary words appropriately to discuss "Lunch Money"?
- correctly answer questions about the summary?
- identify word origins?
- examine the author's purpose?

PRETEACH
Word Origins

INTRODUCE *Foreign words are words that come from other languages. A word origin explains where a word comes from.*

- Write *villain*. Define a *villain* as a person who causes problems. Point out that *villain* has Latin and French origins.

THINK-PAIR-SHARE Have students look up *library, orange, salad*, and *tomato* in a dictionary. Partners should identify the origin of each word: *library* (Latin), *orange* (Sanskrit, India), *salad* (French, Spanish), and *tomato* (Aztec, Mexico). Have students use the words to orally complete the following sentences:

1. I went to the ___library___ to find a recipe for a salad.

2. The recipe included a ripe ___orange___ and a red tomato.

RETEACH
Author's Purpose

TEACH/MODEL Explain that an **author's purpose** is the author's reason for writing something. *The words, facts, and details that an author chooses give clues to the author's purpose.*

GUIDED PRACTICE Read aloud the paragraph on the first page of "Lunch Money" that begins: "He got to pick the name because he was the author of all the Chunky Comics stories." *What information does the author give in this paragraph?* (He describes all the things Greg does to make Chunky Comics.) *Why do you think the author chose to include these details?* (He wants readers to know that Greg really wants to succeed.)

- Review **Teach Academic English** on **Language Support Card 16**.

- Remind students that *to* with infinitives and *in order to* with infinitives can be used to examine the author's purpose.

- Provide additional practice with **Context Cards**.
- Have partners take turns reading aloud **Summary ELL16.2**.
- Have partners match the following words (written in random order): *chocolate, lemon, alarm*, and *algebra*, with their foreign origin words, also in random order: *tchocoatl (chocolate*, Mexico*), limung (lemon*, China*), alarm (alle' arme*, Italian*)*, and *algebra (al jabr*, Arabic*)*.
- As a class discuss the following question: *Why do you think the author wrote about someone like Greg?* Suggest the following responses: Greg can do many things. The author may want to write about someone who does everything on his own.

✏️ Scaffolded Practice and Application

| **Beginning** Have students name important details in the story that will help determine the author's purpose. Suggest details such as: *Greg, comic books, characters, villains*, and *copy machine*. | **Intermediate** Have students use short phrases and sentences to name important details that might help the ideas of the author become clearer for readers. | **Advanced** Have students list a basic goal of the story's characters and the author's purpose in using it. Then have students use the phrases to explain the author's purpose. | **Advanced High** Have students write several sentences to describe the basic goals of the story's characters and the author's purpose in using them. |

Day 4

SHARE OBJECTIVES

- Use Target Vocabulary words to discuss "Zap! Pow! A History of Comics."
- Identify adjectives in sentences.

MATERIALS

Student Book (pp. 416, 418–420)
Leveled Reader
Context Cards

ACADEMIC LANGUAGE

• = *Spanish cognate*

informational text	• *texto informativo*
adjective	• *adjetivo*

Scaffold Content-Area Reading

DISCUSS "ZAP! POW! A HISTORY OF COMICS" Use the following picture-text prompts to lead students on a review of "Zap! Pow! A History of Comics." Remind them that "Zap! Pow! A History of Comics" is **informational text**. Remind them that informational text gives facts and examples about a topic.

PAGE 418: Point to the timeline. *What does this timeline show?* (the history of comics) *What happened in 1933?* (The first comic books appeared.)

PAGE 419: Have a student read aloud the first paragraph. *What was the first comic? (Yellow Kid) Where did it appear?* (in a Sunday paper) *What did early comic artists draw to show characters speaking?* (speech balloons)

PAGE 420: Have a student read aloud the first paragraph. *How did people get the first comic books?* (They came with products.) Have a student read aloud the second paragraph. *What character started the golden age of comic books?* (Superman)

- Have a student read aloud the third paragraph. *When did the golden age of comic books end?* (1954) *Which classic comic books are still popular today? (Batman* and *Superman)*

Leveled Reader

READ *THE LOST COMIC BOOK* To read more about how pictures can tell a story, direct students to the **Leveled Reader**. Have partners or small groups take turns rereading the selection aloud to one another.

◆ English Language Learners

BUDDY READING Pair an adult or more proficient reader with a slightly less proficient reader. Have buddies take turns reading to each other. Below are tips for more proficient readers when their buddies read with them:

1. Help with pronunciation when you know words that your buddy doesn't know.

2. Skip difficult words. Try to read the rest of the sentence.

3. Ask questions to help your buddy understand the story:

   • What is happening in this picture?

   • Who are the people in the story?

   • What is the problem in the story?

Adjectives

TEACH/MODEL Write *adjective.* Point to the picture showing a *Chunky Comic* on **Student Book** p. 416. Write *Chunky Comics are small.*

- Explain that the word *small* is an adjective. *Adjectives are words that describe nouns, or name words. Some adjectives tell what kind. Other adjectives tell how many. The* small *bird. The* hard *floor. The* old *car. The* green *shirt. Greg sold* seventeen *units.*

GUIDED PRACTICE Write *The comic books were short. The books were also sturdy. You can combine sentences by using* and *to join adjectives when those adjectives follow a form of the verb* be. Write *The comic books were short and sturdy.*

- Have a student underline the adjectives in the new sentence.

- Have students suggest and combine other sentences containing adjectives. Have them then suggest adjectives to replace those in the combined sentence.

> **Transfer Skills**
> **Adjective Order**
> Point out that in English, the adjective usually comes before the noun. In Spanish, Vietnamese, Hmong, and Haitian Creole, adjectives usually follow the noun. Provide practice with phrases and sentences containing adjectives that follow the noun, for example, *The dog is small. The shirt is yellow.*

Do students…
- use Target Vocabulary words appropriately to talk about "Zap! Pow! A History of Comics" and *The Lost Comic Book*?
- identify adjectives?

- Provide additional practice with **Context Cards.**
- Have partners read sections of "Zap! Pow! A History of Comics" and *The Lost Comic Book* to each other.
- Review the definition of *adjective* as a group.

Scaffolded Practice and Application

Beginning Write the following words: *smooth, pencil, quiet, warm, chair, bad.* Have students identify the adjectives and copy them.

Intermediate Write *Greg draws a small comic.* Have partners copy the sentence and circle the adjective. Ask students to read the sentence aloud.

Advanced Write these sentences: *These great comics sell. He chewed the warm bread.* Have partners write similar sentences containing adjectives. Have students define *adjective* orally.

Advanced High Have students write their own sentences that contain adjectives. Students should circle adjectives and point to each noun they modify. Then, have students define *adjective* in their own words.

SHARE OBJECTIVES

- Discuss and compare different types of comic books.
- Make a chart to compare and contrast the different types of comic books.
- Use vocabulary words to write about comic books.

MATERIALS

Student Book (pp. 406–416, 418–420, 424–425)
Leveled Reader
Grab-and-Go ™ Resources (p. 18)

ACADEMIC LANGUAGE

• = *Spanish cognate*

narrate   • *narrar*
friendly letter

Compare Texts

MAKE COMPARISONS Use the model below to help students complete a chart comparing different types of comic books. Have students refer to their **Leveled Reader** and **Student Book** pp. 406–416 and 418–420.

Comic	Main Characters	When and Where Sold	Special Powers
Yellow Kid	Yellow Kid	1896 in newspapers	none
Chunky Comics	Creon, Leon, Eeon	last summer, school cafeteria	time travel
Superman	Superman	1938 to present, in stores	super strength, can fly
Incognito	Incognito	about twenty years ago, in stores	can change form

- Have students orally form sentences based on the information in the chart. Provide sentence frames such as the following:

1. The *Yellow Kid* started in _____1896_____ and was sold in __the Sunday newspaper__.

2. *Chunky Comics* started __last summer__ and is sold in __the school cafeteria__.

3. *Superman* started in ____1938____ and is sold in ____stores____.

4. *Incognito* started __about twenty years ago__ and was sold in ____stores____.

DISCUSS COMPARISONS To help students compare and contrast different types of comic books, ask questions such as *How are the comic books and their characters the same? How are they different?* Have students rank the comics with respect to super powers, publication date, and format. Provide sentence frames such as:

5. The oldest comic is __Yellow Kid__. __Superman__ came next, followed by __Incognito__ and __Chunky Comics__.

6. Superman can fly and has super ____strength____. __Incognito__ can change his form. Yellow Kid has no __special powers__.

7. __Yellow Kid__ was published in a newspaper, but __Incognito__ and __Superman__ were sold in stores.

Write to Narrate

TEACH/MODEL Review the features of a **friendly letter**. Review what it means to **narrate**. *When you narrate, you tell about something that happened. When you write a letter, you should write about something you experienced. It should include details that express how you feel about what happened. It should sound almost like a conversation you have with your best friend.*

- Read and discuss the Writing Traits Checklist on **Student Book** p. 424.

- Read and discuss the Writing Model on **Student Book** pp. 424–425. Point out examples of showing feelings by developing voice.

GUIDED PRACTICE Explain that the class will work together to write a friendly letter. Explain that the group will write a letter to someone who has participated in a class event, for example a parent, teacher, or local official.

- Write the following questions: *Who are we writing to? What event do we want to tell about, or narrate?* Brainstorm ideas with students and begin listing events to include in the shared letter. As you write, help students list details that illustrate the events in your letter. Record and summarize student responses in sentence form.

> **Extend Language**
> **Letter-Writing Words**
> name, address, date, title, greeting, format, heading, body, closure

- As the writing proceeds, remind students that a letter should also include details that express their feelings about the event. *How did you feel about the event? Which details were important to your feelings?*

- When the letter is finished, have a student read it aloud.

CHECK PROGRESS

Do students…

- participate in discussion about the different types of comic books?
- correctly identify similarities and differences between each selection about comic books and how they tell a story?
- express their feelings in their writing?

REVIEW TOGETHER

- Have students work in pairs or small groups to read and review the rows and columns of the different types of comic books comparison chart.
- Have partners help each other check for and include vocabulary words in their writing.
- Have students review the **Writing Rubric** on p. 18 of the **Grab-and-Go™ Resources**.

✏️ Scaffolded Practice and Application

| **Beginning** Provide the frame: *I want to write a letter to _____.* Have students draw pictures to illustrate what their letter is about. | **Intermediate** Provide the frame: *I want to write a letter to _____, about _____.* Have students list four key details they would include in their letter. | **Advanced** Have partners work together to create a letter to a friend. Have students read their letters to the class. | **Advanced High** Have students write brief letters to friends that narrate an event. Letters may or may not include illustrations. |

SHARE OBJECTIVES

- Participate in discussion about time travel.
- Say, read, and use Target Vocabulary and high-utility words.
- Practice story structure and complete a Story Map.

MATERIALS

Language Support Card 17
Context Cards
Chant ELL17.1 (Time Travel)
Student Book (pp. 430–444)
Main Selection Summary ELL17.2
Graphic Organizer Transparency 11

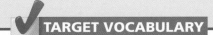
✔ TARGET VOCABULARY

	• = *Spanish cognate*
admitted	• *admitió*
collected	
compliment	
concentrate	• *concentrarse*
destination	• *destino*
impressed	• *impresionado*
original	• *original*
produced	• *producir*
rumor	• *rumor*
suspense	• *suspenso*

ACADEMIC LANGUAGE

story structure	• *estructura de la historial*
character	
conflict	• *conflicto*
resolution	

Listening, Speaking, and Viewing

USE LANGUAGE SUPPORT CARD
Present **Language Support Card 17**. Use the activities on the back of the card to introduce concepts and vocabulary from "LAFFF" and to practice **Academic English**.

Develop Target Vocabulary

USE CONTEXT CARDS Show the **Context Cards** for *impressed* and *suspense*. Present the cards using Steps 1–3 of the Introduce Vocabulary routine on **Teacher's Edition** p. T86.

- Help students use *impressed* and *suspense* to discuss what inspires authors to write.

- Encourage students to use high-utility words in their responses.

USE ORAL LANGUAGE CHANT Distribute **Chant ELL17.1**. Read the title aloud, and have students repeat. Have students look at the title, images, and other information on the page. Then have them predict what they think the chant will be about.

BLM ELL17.1

- As you read the chant aloud, display the **Context Cards** for *original, impressed, destination*, and *suspense*. After you read the chant, have groups read it chorally for the class.

- Have students draw a picture of something they imagine they would see if they traveled to the future. Have them describe their picture to a partner, using one or more vocabulary words if possible.

- Have partners present each other's drawings to the class, describing the picture and answering questions.

- Allow students to include language from **Chant ELL17.1**. Encourage them to use high-utility words. Have students vote on their favorite picture or original idea.

WRITE-PAIR-SHARE Display sentence frames such as the following and have partners use them to write complete sentences.

1. If I traveled to the future, I would probably be impressed by ___Answers will vary___.

2. Michael heard a ___rumor___ that a time machine would be produced by scientists.

Scaffold Comprehension

PREVIEW "LAFFF" Explain that, before reading, students will skim "LAFFF" in order to predict what the selection is about. Help students scan the illustrations, highlighted words, and other text features on **Student Book** pp. 430–444. Have them predict one thing they may learn by reading the text.

USE MAIN SELECTION SUMMARY Distribute **Summary ELL17.2.** Read the summary aloud, then have students read each line aloud, going around the room so that all students participate.

BLM
ELL17.2

RETEACH

Story Structure

TEACH/MODEL Read aloud the first paragraph in **Summary ELL17.2.** Write *story structure*. Say the words aloud and have students repeat.

- Explain that a story's structure is the way it is organized. *A story often begins by introducing* **characters.** *Then the characters face a* **conflict.** *That conflict causes them to take action. Their actions are events in the story. Finally, something happens that solves the conflict and the story ends. This is the* **resolution.**

GUIDED PRACTICE Have students read the first paragraph in **Summary ELL17.2** and circle the names of characters.

- Display **Graphic Organizer Transparency 11.** Explain that a Story Map can help students understand a story's structure.

- *Who are the main characters of the story?* Write the answer in the *Characters* section of the Story Map. (Peter, Angela)

- Help students use the summary to complete the Story Map.

- Display a completed Story Map as a reference throughout the week. Have students continue to fill out their maps as they read and discuss the main selection.

Graphic Organizer

Name _____ Date _____

Graphic Organizer 11

Story Map: _____

Title _____

Setting	Characters
	Peter, Angela

Plot

Problem (Conflict)
Angela feels bad about stealing the story.

Events
Peter made a time machine. Angela went to the future. Angela won the writing contest.

Solution (Resolution)
Peter helps Angela realize she did not steal the story; it was her own.

Graphic Organizer 11
© Houghton Mifflin Harcourt Publishing Company. All rights reserved.

✏️ **Scaffolded Practice and Application**

Beginning Help students write the names of the characters in the correct section of their Story Maps. Have students read each character's name.	**Intermediate** Have students brainstorm and list events in their Story Map. Then have them write a sentence that tells about the conflict.	**Advanced** Have students write sentences about the events, conflict, and resolution to complete their Story Maps. Have them share their ideas with a partner.	**Advanced High** Have students use their completed Story Maps to write sentences about the story's structure. Have them read their paragraphs to the class.

Scaffold Comprehension

DISCUSS "LAFFF" Use the following picture-text prompts to discuss "LAFFF." Remind students that "LAFFF" is **science fiction**. A science fiction story is a fantasy that is usually based on scientific ideas and often set in the future.

PAGE 431: Have students read the title aloud. *Is LAFFF a word? What do you think it could mean?* (No; the letters stand for something and sound like *laugh*.)

PAGE 435: *What does Peter produce for Angela to show her that he traveled into the future?* (a rose from his mother's garden) *Why is the rose proof that his time machine works?* (The story is set in December, and the rose only blooms in June.)

PAGE 442: Read aloud the third paragraph. *Why is Angela in suspense while she waits to hear who won the story-writing contest?* (She wants to find out if she won, and she is waiting to see if anyone accuses her of stealing the story.) *What is happening in the picture?* (Angela is being named the winner of the contest.)

AUDIOTEXT CD Make the **Audiotext CD** for "LAFFF" available. Have students follow in the **Student Book** as they listen.

Practice Target Vocabulary

USE ORAL LANGUAGE CHANT Distribute **Chant ELL17.1**. Have a student read the title aloud.

BLM ELL17.1

- Read the chant aloud or have a proficient reader model reading aloud.

- Have students identify Target Vocabulary and high-utility words in the chant and read the words aloud with you.

- Have them restate each Target Vocabulary word and then try to restate the line from the chant by replacing the word with a synonym or phrase that means nearly the same thing. Then have them complete the activity on the page.

PRACTICE FLUENCY: RATE Read or have a fluent reader read **Chant ELL17.1** aloud, reading at a rate that is appropriate for the difficulty of the text. Have students follow along on their pages as they listen. Then have partners read the chant to each other, focusing on adjusting their reading rate so that they can read accurately and with reasonable comprehension.

CHECK PROGRESS

Do students…
- demonstrate fluency as they recite the chant while focusing on reading rate?
- correctly identify common word parts?
- make inferences and predictions about "LAFFF"?

REVIEW TOGETHER

- Have partners take turns reading **Chant ELL17.1** aloud. Encourage them to vary their reading rate according to the difficulty of the text.
- Have partners work together to identify words with various word parts from the weekly selections. Have them write each word and identify each word part.
- Have partners reread pages from "LAFFF" and make inferences and predictions before they continue reading.

PRETEACH

Recognizing Common Word Parts

INTRODUCE *Words are made up of parts that are put together, like building blocks. Each **word part** changes the meaning of a word.*

- Write *estimated*. *The word* estimated *means judged, or given a value. It contains the suffix* -ed. *If we add the prefix* under- *to* estimated, *we get the new word* underestimated, *which means "assigned a lower value than is correct." Estimated, a neutral word, becomes* underestimated, *a negative word.*

PRACTICE Have students use **Context Cards**, the chant, the summary, or "LAFFF" to look for and name words that are made with various word parts. *(immigrated, scientist, impressed)*

RETEACH

Infer/Predict

TEACH/MODEL Write *infer* and ***predict*** and explain the terms. Remind students that when you predict, you make informed guesses about what will happen next in a story. *To infer means to figure out something that is not clearly said or written in a story.* Use a Think Aloud to model inferring and predicting information from "LAFFF."

Think Aloud *On page 437, it says that Angela really wanted to win the contest. I can infer that she wants to make her parents proud. I predict she'll find a way to win the contest.*

GUIDED PRACTICE As a class, read paragraphs from "LAFFF" and make inferences and predictions based on the information you have read.

- Review **Teach Academic English** on **Language Support Card 17**.
- Remind students to use *might* when making predictions.

✏️ Scaffolded Practice and Application

Beginning Have students answer inference and prediction questions about the selection in one- or two-word answers.	**Intermediate** Have partners write an inference and a prediction about the selection using sentence frames such as *I think that ____* and *I predict that ____.*	**Advanced** Have partners write inferences and predictions about the selection, using *might*. Have students read their sentences to each other and discuss whether they agree.	**Advanced High** Have students write a paragraph that gives their inferences and predictions about the selection, using *might*. Have them read their paragraph to the class.

- Use Target Vocabulary words to discuss "LAFFF."
- Read and discuss a summary of "LAFFF."
- Use a dictionary to find the meanings and parts of speech of words.
- Infer and predict conflicts.

MATERIALS

Student Book (pp. 430–444)
Main Selection Summary ELL17.2
Audiotext CD
Dictionaries
Language Support Card 17
Context Cards

ACADEMIC LANGUAGE

• = *Spanish cognate*

dictionary entry
parts of speech
infer   • *inferir*
predict   • *predecir*
conflict   • *conflicto*

Scaffold Comprehension

REVIEW "LAFFF" Use a Think Aloud and the following prompts to lead students on a guided review of "LAFFF." Remind students that reviewing and retelling what they read can help them understand the material better in order to make inferences and predictions.

> Think Aloud

PAGE 431: *This picture shows a girl in a strange machine. It looks like light or energy is being produced by the machine. Something very strange must be happening!*

PAGE 432: *What is Peter doing in this picture?* (thinking) *What do people think of Peter?* (He is a genius; he is strange.)

PAGE 433: *What rumor were people spreading about Peter?* (that he was building a machine)

PAGES 434–435: *What does Angela think about the time machine at first?* (that it is a joke)

PAGE 441: *What is Angela doing here? Why?* (reading the winning story from the writing contest; She wants to copy the story so she can win first place.)

CHECK COMPREHENSION If students need additional support with the main selection, direct them to **Summary ELL17.2**. Read the summary aloud, and have them listen and follow along on their pages.

BLM ELL17.2

Have students take turns reading sections of the summary aloud. Have them answer the following comprehension questions:

1. Why couldn't Angela copy the whole story from the future?

2. Why did Angela feel bad about using Peter's machine?

3. What made Angela feel better?

Have students work in pairs to circle high-utility words and highlight Target Vocabulary words found in **Summary ELL17.2**. Have them take turns reading each sentence containing a vocabulary word and then using the word in an original sentence.

AUDIOTEXT CD Make the **Audiotext CD** for "LAFFF" available. Have students follow in the **Student Book** as they listen.

Using Reference Sources

INTRODUCE Write *dictionary entry* and *parts of speech*. *An entry in a dictionary is a word followed by its meaning. Parts of speech are different types of words such as verbs, nouns, pronouns, adjectives, and adverbs.*

- Write *rumor (n.)*. *In a dictionary entry for* rumor, *the n. shows the part of speech: noun.*

THINK-PAIR-SHARE Write *original, collected,* and *admitted*. Have partners look up each word and its part of speech in a dictionary. Discuss the meanings as a class. Have students use the words to orally complete the following sentences:

1. Nobody ___admitted___ who broke the window.

2. Although Maria was nervous about speaking to the judges, she seemed very ___collected___.

3. Have you seen Misha's ___original___ artwork on display in the hall?

Story Structure

TEACH/MODEL Write and pronounce *predict, infer,* and *conflict.* Have students repeat. Explain that we infer information that isn't directly stated in a text by using clues and what we already know. *We can use clues and what we know to infer what the conflict, or problem, of the story is. Then we can predict what might happen next.*

GUIDED PRACTICE *In "LAFFF," Angela peeks into the garage. We can infer that she wasn't supposed to do that. What conflict can we predict?* (Peter might get angry because Angela was spying on him.)

- Review **Teach Academic English** on **Language Support Card 17**.

- Remind students that they can infer and predict using *might*.

CHECK PROGRESS

Do students…

- use Target Vocabulary words appropriately to discuss "LAFFF"?
- correctly answer questions about the summary?
- use a dictionary to find the meanings and parts of speech of words?
- infer and predict conflicts in "LAFFF"?

REVIEW TOGETHER

- Provide additional practice with **Context Cards**.
- Have partners take turns reading aloud **Summary ELL17.2**.
- Have partners look up unfamiliar words from the selection using a dictionary and use each word in a sentence.
- Have students name one conflict from the main selection and tell what information helped them infer this conflict.

✏️ **Scaffolded Practice and Application**

Beginning Help students use *might* to answer true or false prediction questions about the selection. For example, *Peter might win the writing contest, true or false?*	**Intermediate** Have partners write an inference and a prediction about the selection using sentence frames such as *Angela might feel _____.* and *Peter might _____.*	**Advanced** Have partners write several inferences and predictions about conflicts in the selection. Have students discuss why they think each idea could be a conflict.	**Advanced High** Have students write a paragraph that gives inferences and predictions about conflicts in the selection. Have them read their paragraphs to the class.

Scaffold Content-Area Reading

DISCUSS "FROM DREAMS TO REALITY" Use the following picture-text prompts to lead students on a review of "From Dreams to Reality". Remind them that "From Dreams to Reality" is **informational text**. Remind them that informational text gives facts and examples about a topic.

PAGE 446: Point to the illustration. *Where is this picture of a space capsule from?* (a Jules Verne novel) Have students read the caption. *What is the space capsule's destination?* (the Moon)

- Have students read the first paragraph. *Why are people impressed by sci-fi authors?* (They sometimes predict the future in their stories.)

PAGE 447: Have students describe what is happening in the picture. (The *Saturn V* is going to the Moon.)

- Point out the title of Verne's story on the page, and have students read aloud the second paragraph. *What details did Verne write that are similar to the first real trips to the Moon?* (Each rocket had three persons, left from Florida, and was similar in size.)

PAGE 448: *Look at the picture of automobile plant robots. How are they different from the picture of the original factory robots in RUR?* (The original robots looked like people, but the auto plant robots do not.)

Leveled Reader

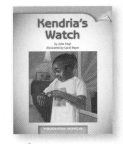

READ "KENDRIA'S WATCH" To read more about inventions, direct students to the **Leveled Reader**. Have partners or small groups take turns rereading the selection aloud to one another.

PAIRED READING Pair students of approximately the same level of reading proficiency. Display these tips for partners to use when reading together:

◆ **English Language Learners**

1. Sit side by side and look at the book together.

2. Take turns holding the book.

3. Look at the pictures and try to predict what will happen next.

4. When you finish, ask your buddy about his or her favorite character or part of the selection.

RETEACH

Adverbs

TEACH/MODEL Write *adverb*. Remind students that an adverb modifies a verb, often by telling how, when, or where the action happened. Then remind students that they should try not to use many short sentences in a row in their writing. *Often short sentences about the same topic can be combined into longer sentences. Adverbs can help us do this.*

- Have students look at the picture on **Student Book** page 435. Write *The rose disappeared suddenly. Peter admitted that his machine had problems. How could we combine these sentences?* Have students give suggestions, then write *When the rose disappeared suddenly, Peter admitted that his machine had problems.* Point out that *when* is also an adverb that helps us combine sentences.

GUIDED PRACTICE Write *Jonas sat down. He sighed loudly.* Have students identify the adverb *loudly.* *You can combine these two sentences by using the adverbs* when *and* loudly. Write *When Jonas sat down, he sighed loudly.*

- Write *The bell was big. It rang loudly. You can combine these two sentences by changing the order of some of the words and eliminating others.* Write *The big bell rang loudly.*

Transfer Skills
Adverbs and Adjectives

In Hmong and Haitian Creole, the adjective form is used after the verb. This may lead students to use adjectives instead of adverbs in English, as in *Talk slow.* Remind students that adjectives describe nouns and adverbs describe verbs. Provide additional practice in the formation and placement of adverbs, for example, *talk quietly, walk quickly.*

CHECK PROGRESS

Do students…
- use Target Vocabulary words appropriately to talk about "From Dreams to Reality" and *Kendria's Watch?*
- identify and use adverbs correctly?

REVIEW TOGETHER

- Provide additional practice with **Context Cards**.
- Have partners read sections of "From Dreams to Reality" and *Kendria's Watch?* to each other.
- Review as a group the ways that adverbs are used. Have students name adverbs and use them in sentences.

✏️ Scaffolded Practice and Application

Beginning Write *I ran today. I ran quickly.* Have partners write down the sentences and then work together to combine them into one sentence.	**Intermediate** Write *The scientist speaks about the invention. She is nervous.* Have students combine the sentences by changing the adjective to an adverb.	**Advanced** Have students write several sentences that combine ideas using adverbs. Have partners exchange sentences and check each other's work for correctness.	**Advanced High** Have students write a paragraph that includes several sentences that are combined using adverbs. Have students try to combine three ideas in one sentence within their paragraph.

Compare Texts

MAKE COMPARISONS Use the model below to help students complete a chart comparing inventions and the future. Have students refer to their **Leveled Reader** and **Student Book** pp. 430–444 and 446–448.

Invention	Real or Fictional?	Inventor	Function
Time machine	Fictional	Peter Lu	takes people on short trips to the future
Saturn V rocket	Real	NASA	transported astronauts to the Moon in 1969
Space capsule in *From the Earth to the Moon*	Fictional	Jules Verne	transported astronauts to the Moon
Watch	Fictional	Aunt Laqueta	makes the wearer invisible

- Have students orally form sentences based on the information in the chart. Provide sentence frames such as the following:

1. Peter's ___time machine___ could travel to the ___future___ .

2. The ___*Saturn V* rocket___ was invented by NASA.

3. One fictional invention is ___a time machine___ .

DISCUSS COMPARISONS To help students compare and contrast inventions and the future, ask questions such as *What do these fictional and real inventions have in common? Is it possible to really make any of these fictional inventions? Is it possible to travel to the future?* Provide sentence frames such as:

4. Both ___the *Saturn V* rocket___ and ___Verne's space capsule___ were invented to transport people to the Moon.

5. Neither Peter's ___time machine___ nor Aunt Laqueta's ___watch___ were real inventions.

6. The ___time machine___ was made to travel to the future, but the ___space capsule___ and ___the *Saturn V* rocket___ were made to travel to the Moon.

RETEACH

Write to Narrate

TEACH/MODEL Review the features of a **descriptive paragraph**.
*When you **narrate**, you tell a story. A descriptive piece of writing tells what something is like. Often, it describes a **character**, or a person in the story.*

- Read and discuss the Writing Traits Checklist on **Student Book** p. 452.

- Read and discuss the Writing Model on **Student Book** pp. 452–453. Point out examples of word choice.

GUIDED PRACTICE Explain that the class will work together to write a descriptive paragraph about a character.

> **Extend Language**
> **Descriptive Words**
> imaginative, cheerful, talkative, athletic, curious, hard-working, studious, adventurous, popular

- Have students give suggestions about which person to write about, such as a character from a well-known story or one that the group creates on its own. Write the name of the person.

- Brainstorm the characteristics of the person and list them. Discuss things that the person would say and do.

- Have students suggest sentences to describe the person, including dialogue. For example, write *Julie is the funniest person I know. She often says you should laugh more.* Help students revise the sentences to add natural speech and combine short sentences using adverbs: *Julie, the funniest person we know, often says, "If you can't laugh, you aren't living."*

- Read the paragraph aloud chorally. Have students suggest ways to include the paragraph in a longer piece of narrative writing.

CHECK PROGRESS

Do students…
- participate in discussion about inventions and the future?
- correctly identify similarities and differences between inventions and the future?
- use exact words, vivid details, and dialogue in their writing?

REVIEW TOGETHER

- Have students work in pairs or small groups to read and review the rows and columns of the inventions and the future comparison chart.
- Have partners help each other check for and include vocabulary words in their writing.
- Have students review the **Writing Rubric** on p. 18 of the **Grab-and-Go™ Resources**.

Scaffolded Practice and Application

Beginning Write the frame *I think _____ is _____*. Write adjectives such as *funny, smart*, and *popular* in the second blank. Help students complete the sentence frame and read it chorally.	**Intermediate** Have students complete the sentence frame *I think _____ is _____, because _____*. Have partners read each other's sentences and offer suggestions that add detail to the reason.	**Advanced** Have students write sentences describing a person they know. Have partners exchange papers and help each other add dialogue to several of the sentences.	**Advanced High** Have students write a paragraph describing a person they know, including dialogue and complex sentences in their writing. Have them read their paragraphs to the class.

Listening, Speaking, and Viewing

USE LANGUAGE SUPPORT CARD
Present **Language Support Card 18**. Use the activities on the back of the card to introduce concepts and vocabulary from "The Dog Newspaper" and to practice **Academic English**.

Develop Target Vocabulary

USE CONTEXT CARDS Show the **Context Cards** for *insights* and *background*. Present the cards using Steps 1–3 of the Introduce Vocabulary routine on **Teacher's Edition** p. T162.

- Help students use *insights* and *background* to discuss what makes a true story interesting.

- Encourage students to use high-utility words in their responses.

USE ORAL LANGUAGE CHANT Distribute **Chant ELL18.1**. Read the title aloud, and have students repeat. Have students look at the title, images, and other information on the page. Then have them predict what they think the chant will be about.

BLM
ELL18.1

- As you read the chant aloud, display the **Context Cards** for *required, uneventful, publication*, and *insights*. After you read the chant, have partners read it together.

- Show students the Web from the **Language Support Card**. *We wrote ideas about good stories. Now let's write ideas about bad stories.*

- Draw another Web with the words *Bad Stories* in the center circle. Ask students what words describe a true story that isn't interesting.

- Allow students to include language from **Chant ELL18.1**. Encourage them to use vocabulary words and high-utility words. List responses in the Web.

▬▬▶ WRITE-PAIR-SHARE Display sentence frames such as the following and have partners use them to write complete sentences.

1. An interesting true story often has helpful ___insights___.

2. An uninteresting true story may be ___uneventful___.

Scaffold Comprehension

PREVIEW "THE DOG NEWSPAPER" Explain that, before reading, students will skim "The Dog Newspaper" in order to predict what the selection is about. Help students scan the illustrations and other text features on **Student Book** pp. 458–466. Have them predict one thing they may learn by reading the text.

USE MAIN SELECTION SUMMARY Distribute **Summary ELL18.2**. Read the summary aloud, then have partners take turns reading it.

BLM
ELL18.2

RETEACH

Fact and Opinion

TEACH/MODEL Read aloud the first paragraph of **Summary ELL18.2**. *This paragraph includes both* **facts** *and* **opinions***. To find the facts, we'll ask: Can this be proven? To find the opinions, we'll look for value words that signal what someone thinks or feels.*

GUIDED PRACTICE Have students read the first two paragraphs of **Summary ELL18.2**. After each sentence, ask, *Is this something that could be proven, or is it something a person feels or believes?*

- Display **Transparency 12**. Explain that a T-Map can help students **analyze,** or look closely at, facts and opinions.

- Write *Facts* above the left column and *Opinions* above the right. Read each sentence, and ask, *In which column does this sentence belong?* List the sentences in the appropriate columns. Ask: *How many facts did we find? How many opinions did we find? Do any of the facts support the opinions?* (There are three opinions: Peg thought the neighbors' stories were boring; B.J. had a very interesting background; it was a terrible war.)

- Display a completed T-Map as a reference throughout the week.

CHECK PROGRESS

Do students…
- correctly pronounce and use vocabulary words in discussion?
- identify facts and opinions?

REVIEW TOGETHER

- Have partners use **Context Cards** to review the Target Vocabulary words and their meanings. Have them complete the activities on the backs of the cards.
- Have partners read the opinions on their T-Maps. *How many of the opinions include the words I think that or I feel that? How many of them include value words that show how someone feels?*

Graphic Organizer

Name _____ Date _____
Graphic Organizer 12

T-Map: _____
Title or Topic _____

Facts	Opinions
Started a newspaper at age ten	Peg thought that the neighbors' stories were boring.
Interviewed neighbors	
	B.J. had a very interesting background.
Wrote about her own dog, B.J.	
	It was a terrible war.
Born in Germany during World War II	
B.J. rescued by American soldiers	

Graphic Organizer 12
© Houghton Mifflin Harcourt Publishing Company. All rights reserved.

Scaffolded Practice and Application

Beginning Have partners answer this question: *Which facts in paragraph 2 support the opinion that "B.J. had a very interesting background"?*	**Intermediate** Have partners complete the T-Map together. Have them identify the value words that identify each opinion.	**Advanced** Have students complete the T-Map independently. Have them identify the words that identify each opinion.	**Advanced High** Have students analyze other paragraphs in the summary. Ask them to circle each opinion that is supported by facts.

Day 2

SHARE OBJECTIVES

- Use Target Vocabulary words to discuss "The Dog Newspaper."
- Listen to and recite a chant about what makes a true story interesting.
- Recognize suffixes.
- Analyze and evaluate facts and opinions in "The Dog Newspaper. "

MATERIALS

Student Book (pp. 458–466)
Audiotext CD
Chant ELL18.1 (Spread the News!)
Context Cards
Main Selection Summary ELL18.2
Language Support Card 18

ACADEMIC LANGUAGE

• = Spanish cognate

autobiography	• autobiografía
suffix	• sufijo
base word	• palabra base
analyze	• analizar
evaluate	• evaluar

Scaffold Comprehension

DISCUSS "THE DOG NEWSPAPER" Use the following picture-text prompts to discuss "The Dog Newspaper." Remind students that "The Dog Newspaper" is an **autobiography**. An autobiography tells about events in a person's own life, written by that person.

PAGE 459: Have students read the title aloud. *What kind of news might be in a publication called* The Dog Newspaper? (Possible responses: stories about new dogs, dogs that had puppies, dogs that won awards or did something brave)

PAGE 461: *Look at the picture of the soldiers. How does this picture connect to B.J.'s background?* (The soldiers rescued B.J. from the destruction of World War II.)

PAGE 462: *How did B.J. come to live in Peg's household?* (Uncle Bill won the drawing to see who would keep the dog; he lived in Peg's house.)

AUDIOTEXT CD Make the **Audiotext CD** for "The Dog Newspaper" available. Have students follow in the **Student Book** as they listen.

Practice Target Vocabulary

USE ORAL LANGUAGE CHANT Distribute **Chant ELL18.1**. Have a student read the title aloud.

BLM ELL18.1

- Read the chant aloud or have a proficient reader model reading aloud.

- Have students identify Target Vocabulary and high-utility words in the chant and read the words aloud with you.

- Have them restate each Target Vocabulary word and tell how it connects to writing good news stories. Then have them complete the activity on the page.

PRACTICE FLUENCY: INTONATION Read each line of **Chant ELL18.1** aloud, and then call on a student to reread it aloud with proper intonation. Have readers focus on the pitch in their voices as they read.

Do students…
- demonstrate fluency as they read the chant, using proper intonation?
- identify suffixes?
- analyze and evaluate opinions in "The Dog Newspaper"?

REVIEW TOGETHER

- Have partners take turns reading **Chant ELL18.1** aloud. Encourage them to choose one stanza in the chant to reread with proper intonation to a partner.
- Have partners identify the base word and the suffix in each of these words: *required, requirement, insightful, publisher, publishing*
- Have partners read two pages of the selection together. Ask them to analyze and evaluate any opinions that the author states on those pages.

Recognizing Suffixes

INTRODUCE Write *event* and *eventful*. Tell students that *event* is a **base word**, a word to which other word parts can be added.

- *An event is something that happens. What letters did I add to* event *to form* eventful? *The letters* -ful *are a* **suffix**, *a word part that can be added at the end of a base word.* Eventful *means "full of events, busy, or exciting."*

- Write the words *excite, exciting*, and *excitement*. Have students identify the suffixes in *exciting* and *excitement*.

PRACTICE Have students use **Context Cards**, the chant, the summary, or "The Dog Newspaper" to look for and name words that contain suffixes. (*writing, reporter*)

RETEACH

Analyze/Evaluate

TEACH/MODEL Remind students that when we **analyze** a text, we study its details carefully. *When we* **evaluate** *a text, we judge how well the author uses details to support his or her ideas.* Use a Think Aloud to model analyzing and evaluating "The Dog Newspaper."

Think Aloud *When I read about Peg's interviews with her neighbors, I analyzed the details of the stories the neighbors told about their dogs. Then I evaluated Peg's opinion that the stories were boring. I agreed with her opinion.*

GUIDED PRACTICE Have students read the second paragraph on page 463 of "The Dog Newspaper." Ask them to analyze and evaluate this opinion: "Even though my lead story required little research, this sixty cents was not easy money."

- Review **Teach Academic English** on **Language Support Card 18**. Remind students to use *I feel* and *I think that* when evaluating an opinion.

✏️ Scaffolded Practice and Application

| **Beginning** Help students identify and evaluate facts that showed that Peg worked hard. | **Intermediate** Have partners complete this sentence frame: *I think that Peg's opinion is/is not right because _____.* | **Advanced** Have students complete a T-Map of Peg's opinion and supporting facts. Then have them write a sentence in which they evaluate her opinion. | **Advanced High** Have students write a paragraph in which they evaluate Peg's opinion. Have them include a topic sentence and paraphrase details from the text. |

Scaffold Comprehension

REVIEW "THE DOG NEWSPAPER" Use a Think Aloud and the following prompts to lead students on a guided review of "The Dog Newspaper." Remind students that reviewing and retelling what they read will help them evaluate an author's opinions.

Think Aloud **PAGE 460:** *Look at the picture of Peg interviewing her neighbor. I can tell that the neighbor is enjoying talking to her and that Peg is taking careful notes. I think Peg has the personality and skills required for a career as a reporter.*

PAGE 464: *On this page, I see some of the headlines for Peg's newspaper stories. Find some of these headlines, in quotation marks. Do they sound exciting or boring?* ("Skippy Gets a Bath," boring)

PAGE 465: *Look at the mess Peg found after the destruction of B.J.'s gingerbread house. Why do you think she decided to write about this for the next edition of her publication?* (She thought it was an exciting event in B.J.'s usually uneventful life.)

CHECK COMPREHENSION If students need additional support with the main selection, direct them to **Summary ELL18.2**. Read the summary aloud, and have them listen and follow along on their pages.

BLM
ELL18.2

Have students take turns reading sections of the summary aloud. Have them answer the following comprehension questions:

1. Peg began her writing career at age ten. What publication did she start?

2. Describe the interesting background of Peg's dog B.J.

3. Why did the neighbors stop buying *The Dog Newspaper*?

Have students work in pairs to circle high-utility words and highlight Target Vocabulary words found in **Summary ELL18.2**. Have them use the words in sentences about what kinds of true stories they like to read.

AUDIOTEXT CD Make the **Audiotext CD** for "The Dog Newspaper" available. Have students follow in the **Student Book** as they listen.

CHECK PROGRESS

Do students…

- use Target Vocabulary words appropriately to discuss "The Dog Newspaper"?
- correctly answer questions about the summary?
- use analogies to compare synonyms and antonyms?
- evaluate the author's message by analyzing facts and opinions?

PRETEACH

Analogies

INTRODUCE Write *analogy, synonym*, and *antonym*. *An analogy compares one pair of words to another pair of words. Sometimes, each pair of words are synonyms, or words with the same meaning. Sometimes each pair of words are antonyms, or words with the opposite meaning.*

- Write *required : needed :: enjoyed :* _____liked_____. Model how to read the analogy: Required *is to* needed *as* enjoyed *is to* _____liked_____. *Do* required *and* needed *have the same meaning or the opposite meaning?* (same) *What word means the same as* enjoyed? *(liked, loved)*

- Write *eventful : uneventful :: big :* _____small_____ *Do the first two words mean the same or the opposite?* (opposite) *What is the opposite of* big? *(small, little)*

THINK-PAIR-SHARE Have partners orally complete the following analogies:

1. destruction : ruin :: house : _____home_____

2. exciting : boring :: good : _____bad_____

3. formula : rule :: story : _____tale_____

RETEACH

Fact and Opinion

TEACH/MODEL Write and pronounce *analyze, fact,* and *opinion*. Have students repeat. Explain that when we carefully study the facts and opinions in a text, we can **evaluate**, or judge, the author's message.

GUIDED PRACTICE Read aloud the third paragraph on the last page of "The Dog Newspaper." *These opinions are the author's message. Let's list some facts in the text that support these opinions.*

- Review **Teach Academic English** on **Language Support Card 18**.

- Remind students that they can use value words to express and evaluate opinions.

REVIEW TOGETHER

- Provide additional practice with **Context Cards**.
- Have partners take turns reading aloud **Summary ELL18.2**.
- Have partners write their own analogies, using synonyms and antonyms. Then have them share their analogies with the class.
- Write this message: *You can learn a lot by writing stories about your own neighborhood. What facts in the selection support this message? Do you agree or disagree with this message? Why?*

✏️ **Scaffolded Practice and Application**

| **Beginning** Use these sentence frames: *For her first story, Peg wrote about _____. In her second issue, she wrote about _____.* | **Intermediate** Have partners answer the following questions: *What did Peg write about in her first issue? How many people bought it?* | **Advanced** Have students compare and contrast the first three issues of Peg's newspaper to find facts that support the author's message. | **Advanced High** Have students write a paragraph that evaluates the author's message. Have them give facts and opinions that support their opinions. |

Scaffold Content-Area Reading

DISCUSS "POETRY ABOUT POETRY" Use the following picture-text prompts to lead students on a review of "Poetry About Poetry." Remind them that "Poetry About Poetry" includes works of **poetry**. Remind them that poetry uses the sound and rhythm of words in a variety of forms to suggest images and express feelings.

PAGE 468: Point out that "To Write Poetry" includes an English text and a Spanish text. Read the English text, and then invite a Spanish speaker to read the Spanish text.

- *Which of the five senses does the poet mention?* (touch, smell, taste) *Why is it important for poets to use their senses?* (so they can create vivid images that readers can picture in their minds)

PAGE 469: *This poem is based on the poet's childhood background. What do we learn about her household and her career?* (She and her sister were close; she started her writing career when she was a child.)

- *A genius is a person with very special talents. What does the sister mean when she says, "We have a genius in the house"?* (She thinks her sister's poem is very good.)

PAGE 470: *Listen while I read this poem. It describes how poetry can "turn on a light in someone's mind." How does the poem's shape match its message?* (The words are written in the shape of a light bulb.)

Leveled Reader

READ *THE LIFE OF B.B. KING* To read more about what makes a good story, direct students to the **Leveled Reader**. Have partners or small groups take turns rereading the selection aloud to one another.

English Language Learners

PAIRED READING Share the following tips with partners of different proficiency levels:

1. Sit side by side and partner-read each sentence.

2. Take turns reading after you have read a few sentences each.

3. Remember to read at a rate that helps you understand the text.

Prepositions and Prepositional Phrases

TEACH/MODEL Write *The cat walked under the table. The cat walked on the table.* Circle *under* and *on*. *These words are* **prepositions.** *In these sentences, the prepositions* under *and* on *show a connection between the table, what the cat did, and where the cat was.*

- *A noun or pronoun always follows a preposition. This noun is called the* **object of the preposition.** *What is the object of each preposition?* (table)

- *Together, the preposition, its object, and all the words in between are called a* **prepositional phrase.** *Underline* under the table *and* on the table. *These are prepositional phrases.*

GUIDED PRACTICE Have students find the prepositional phrases in the following sentences:

1. The dog jumped over the fence. (over the fence)

2. Peg walked around her neighborhood. (around her neighborhood)

3. Peg wrote ideas in her notebook. (in her notebook)

Transfer Skills

Prepositions

Cantonese does not have an exact equivalent of English prepositions, so Cantonese-speaking students may be unfamiliar with them. Common Spanish prepositions include *bajo* (under), *con* (with), *en* (in, on), *entre* (between), *sin* (without), and *sobre* (on, over). Provide additional practice with prepositions and prepositional phrases, for example, *on the wall, off the floor.*

CHECK PROGRESS

Do students…

- use Target Vocabulary words appropriately to talk about "Poetry About Poetry" and *The Life of B.B. King?*

- identify and use prepositions and prepositional phrases?

REVIEW TOGETHER

- Provide additional practice with **Context Cards.**

- Have partners read sections of "Poetry About Poetry" and *The Life of B.B. King* to each other.

- Have groups of students write riddles about objects in your room, using prepositional phrases. For example: *I am on the teacher's desk. I am next to her book. You can use me to write on paper. What am I?* (pen) Have them share the riddles with the class to see if students can guess the answers.

🖍 Scaffolded Practice and Application

Beginning Have students draw pictures to show prepositional phrases: *on the table, under the table, above the table, around the table, beside the table.* Then have them write a sentence to describe each picture.

Intermediate Have students complete sentence frames with prepositions to describe things in the room: *The clock is _____ the wall. The chair is _____ the desk. Hector sits _____ Maya.*

Advanced Have students write sentences about the room, using prepositional phrases. Provide prepositions: *above, across, behind, in front of, around, between, by, under, with, next to.*

Advanced High Have students identify prepositional phrases in the summary. Have them circle the preposition and underline its object. Then have them write original sentences, using the same prepositions.

- Discuss and compare the careers of three creative people.
- Make a chart to compare and contrast careers of three creative people.
- Use vocabulary words to write about the careers of three creative people.

MATERIALS

Student Book (pp. 458–466, 468–470, 474–475)
Leveled Reader
Grab-and-Go™ Resources (p. 18)

ACADEMIC LANGUAGE

• = *Spanish cognate*

personal narrative	• *narativa personal*
voice	• *voz*
brainstorm	
main idea	
lead sentence	
details	• *detalles*
conclusion	• *conclusión*

Compare Texts

MAKE COMPARISONS Use the model below to help students complete a chart comparing the careers of three creative people. Have students refer to their **Leveled Reader** and **Student Book** pp. 458–466 and 468–470.

Creative Person	Peg Kehret	Nikki Grimes	B.B. King
Kind of Career	writer of fiction and nonfiction	poet	blues singer and guitarist
When He/She Began Practicing	when she was ten	as a child	as a child
Expresses Insights About	her background and experience/ dogs/unique stories	her background and experience	feelings, blues, people, guitars

- Have students orally form sentences based on the information in the chart. Provide sentence frames such as the following:

1. Peg Kehret began her writing career when she was <u>ten years old</u>.

2. B.B. King has a successful career as a <u>blues singer and guitarist</u>.

3. Nikki Grimes writes <u>poems</u> and expresses insights about <u>her background and experiences</u>.

4. In his music, B.B. King expresses insights about <u>feelings</u>.

DISCUSS COMPARISONS To help students compare and contrast the careers of three creative people, ask questions such as, *How are these people alike? How are they different?* Provide sentence frames such as:

5. All three people began practicing their talent when they were <u>children</u>.

6. Peg Kehret and Nikki Grimes are writers, but B.B. King is <u>a singer and guitarist</u>.

7. Both Peg Kehret and Nikki Grimes express insights about <u>their own backgrounds and experiences</u>.

8. Of the three creative people, <u>B.B. King</u> is probably the most famous.

Write to Narrate

TEACH/MODEL Review the features of a **personal narrative**.
*A personal narrative is a true story about your own life. It should tell about interesting events. It should also be told in your **voice**, or words that show your thoughts and feelings.*

- Read and discuss the Writing Traits Checklist on **Student Book** p. 474 and the Writing Model on **Student Book** pp. 474–475. Point out examples of words and phrases that express the writer's voice, or thoughts and feelings.

GUIDED PRACTICE Explain that the class will work together to begin writing a personal narrative.

- *Let's think about what we need to do to write a personal narrative about something interesting that happened in our class this year. First, we would **brainstorm,** or think of as many ideas as we can.* List students' ideas.

- *Let's suppose we are going to write about our favorite visitor to the class. First, we would express our **main idea** in a lead sentence that shows our voice, or the way we really talk.* Write *We had a great time the day that _____ came to our class.*

> ### Extend Language
> **Words About Thoughts and Feelings**
> like, dislike, best, worst, happy, sad, bored, excited

- *What are some **details** we could add to show how much fun we had?* List students' suggestions in their own words. Point out words that convey thoughts and feelings.

- *Now we need a **conclusion** that sums up why the day was so special. What should we write?*

- Suggest that students use the details you have written to write a letter of appreciation to the person who visited your class.

Do students…
- participate in discussion about the careers of three creative people?
- correctly identify similarities and differences between the careers of three creative people?
- use words and phrases that express thoughts and feelings in their writing?

- Have students work in pairs or small groups to read and review the rows and columns of the careers of three creative people comparison chart.
- Have partners help each other check for and include vocabulary words in their writing.
- Have students review the **Writing Rubric** on p. 18 of the **Grab-and-Go™ Resources**.

✏️ Scaffolded Practice and Application

Beginning Have students copy each sentence as you write it. Have them name other details to add about the visitor.	**Intermediate** Have partners use some of the sentences above to write a personal narrative paragraph. Have them paraphrase some of the sentences to show their own voice and to add additional details.	**Advanced** Have students write a personal narrative on a topic of their choice. Have partners read each other's narratives and suggest places they could revise to express their personality and feelings.	**Advanced High** Have students write a personal narrative on a topic of their choice. Have them use the Writing Traits Checklist to revise their narrative independently. Remind them to use words that express their voice.

SHARE OBJECTIVES

- Participate in discussion about presenting a speech.
- Say, read, and use Target Vocabulary and high-utility words.
- Practice persuasion and complete an Idea-Support Map.

MATERIALS

Language Support Card 19
Context Cards
Dialogue ELL19.1 (Persuading the Council)
Student Book (pp. 480–492)
Main Selection Summary ELL19.2
Graphic Organizer Transparency 7

✔ TARGET VOCABULARY

• = Spanish cognate

dependent	• depender
deteriorating	• deteriorar
effective	
exception	• excepción
granted	
issue	
minimum	• mínimo
ordinance	
urge	
violations	• violaciones

ACADEMIC LANGUAGE

persuasion • persuasión

Listening, Speaking, and Viewing

USE LANGUAGE SUPPORT CARD
Present **Language Support Card 19**. Use the activities on the back of the card to introduce concepts and vocabulary from "Darnell Rock Reporting" and to practice **Academic English**.

Develop Target Vocabulary

USE CONTEXT CARDS Show the **Context Cards** for *issue* and *effective*. Present the cards using Steps 1–3 of the Introduce Vocabulary routine on **Teacher's Edition** p. T232.

- Help students use *issue* and *effective* to discuss ways people can speak up for what they believe in.

USE ORAL LANGUAGE DIALOGUE Distribute **Dialogue ELL19.1**. Read the title aloud, and have students repeat. Have students look at the title, images, and other information on the page. Then have them predict what they think the dialogue will be about.

BLM ELL19.1

- As you read the dialogue aloud, display the **Context Cards** for *exception, minimum,* and *urge*. After you read the dialogue, help students paraphrase each line.

- Have students work in small groups. Have one student play the role of Brianna presenting her opinion. Have the rest of the group play the City Council, by listening and responding with questions.

- Have the students playing City Council members debate and vote on whether the buildings where Brianna lives should be repaired.

- Hold a vote by a show of hands. Then, have students list which repairs must be made.

- Allow students to include language from **Dialogue ELL19.1**. Encourage them to use high-utility words.

▶ **WRITE-PAIR-SHARE** Display sentence frames such as the following and have partners use them to write complete sentences.

1. Brianna tries to ____urge____ the City Council to do something about the deteriorating condition of the buildings.

2. Brianna feels the ____issue____ is that the building should be clean and safe.

Scaffold Comprehension

PREVIEW "DARNELL ROCK REPORTING" Explain that students will skim "Darnell Rock Reporting" in order to predict what the selection is about. Help students scan the introduction, summary, illustrations, and other text features on **Student Book** pp. 480–492. Have them predict one thing they may learn by reading the text.

USE MAIN SELECTION SUMMARY Distribute **Summary ELL19.2**. Read the summary aloud, then have students chorally reread it.

BLM
ELL19.2

RETEACH
Persuasion

TEACH/MODEL Read aloud the last two paragraphs in **Summary ELL19.2**. Explain that to use **persuasion** is to try to convince a person that an idea is right. *Writers use persuasion to convince readers to agree with them.*

- Point out that techniques of making writing persuasive include giving examples, evidence, and reasons that support ideas. *A writer's ideas are more convincing when they are supported by examples and evidence.*

GUIDED PRACTICE Have students read the second paragraph in **Summary ELL19.2** and underline the reasons Darnell lists for his idea.

- Display **Graphic Organizer Transparency 7**. Explain that an Idea-Support Map can help students identify reasons and supporting details people use to make ideas persuasive.

- *Who did Darnell want to help with the garden?* (homeless people) Record the response, and have students copy it.

- *What reasons did Darnell give to support the idea that the garden should be used to help the homeless?* (The garden would help the homeless. They could grow food there.)

- Display a completed Idea-Support Map as a reference throughout the week.

Graphic Organizer

Name _____ Date _____   Graphic Organizer 7

Idea-Support Map: _____
Title or Topic Darnell wanted to help homeless people.

Homeless people could grow food in the garden.

The garden would help the homeless.

Graphic Organizer 7
© Houghton Mifflin Harcourt Publishing Company. All rights reserved.

✏️ Scaffolded Practice and Application

Beginning Provide sentence pairs about Darnell's idea. In each pair, include one neutral and one persuasive sentence. Help students identify the persuasive sentences.	**Intermediate** Provide sentence starters about Darnell's idea. Ask students to complete them with information that makes the ideas persuasive.	**Advanced** Provide sentences that explain Darnell's idea. Help students rewrite or add to the sentences to make them persuasive.	**Advanced High** Ask students to explain Darnell's idea using reasons that might have been more persuasive to the City Council.

- Use Target Vocabulary words to discuss "Darnell Rock Reporting."
- Listen to and recite a dialogue about a speech to the City Council.
- Identify common suffixes.
- Summarize "Darnell Rock Reporting."

MATERIALS

Student Book (pp. 480–492)
Audiotext CD
Dialogue ELL19.1 (Persuading the Council)
Context Cards
Main Selection Summary ELL19.2
Language Support Card 19

ACADEMIC LANGUAGE

• = *Spanish cognate*

realistic fiction	• *ficción realista*
suffix	• *sufijo*
summarize	
summary	

Scaffold Comprehension

DISCUSS "DARNELL ROCK REPORTING" Use the following picture-text prompts to discuss "Darnell Rock Reporting." Remind students that "Darnell Rock Reporting" is **realistic fiction**. Realistic fiction is a present-day story with events that could happen in real life.

PAGE 481: Have students read the title aloud. *This is Darnell Rock. What does* reporting *mean?* (writing or telling news)

PAGE 482: Read aloud the introduction. *What does Darnell want to do with a basketball court near the school?* (turn it into a garden to feed the homeless) *What does the City Council want to do with it?* (turn it into a parking lot for teachers)

PAGES 486–487: Point to the girl in the illustration. *Linda does not agree with Darnell.* Read aloud the last two paragraphs on page 487. *What does Linda say during her speech?* (Schools are for teaching students, not helping the homeless.)

PAGE 492: Read aloud the last four paragraphs. *What does Darnell accomplish in his speech?* (He persuaded a listener to donate land for a garden. Also, he was asked to write another newspaper article.)

AUDIOTEXT CD Make the **Audiotext CD** for "Darnell Rock Reporting" available. Have students follow in the **Student Book** as they listen.

Practice Target Vocabulary

USE ORAL LANGUAGE DIALOGUE Distribute **Dialogue ELL19.1**. Have a student read the title aloud.

BLM
ELL19.1

- Read the dialogue aloud or have proficient readers model reading aloud.

- Have students identify Target Vocabulary and high-utility words in the dialogue and read the words aloud with you.

- Have them restate each Target Vocabulary word and quiz each other on the definitions of the words. Then have them complete the activity on the page.

PRACTICE FLUENCY: PHRASING: PUNCTUATION Have students listen as the narrator phrases sentences based on punctuation in **Dialogue ELL19.1**. Have students repeat the phrasing accurately.

Common Suffixes

INTRODUCE Write **suffix**. *A suffix is a group of letters that is attached to the end of a word and changes the word's meaning.*

- Write and pronounce the word *effective*. Underline *effect*, and circle *-ive*. *What does* effect *mean?* Confirm that an effect is a change that comes about because of a cause.

- *The suffix* -ive *means "causing." So* effective *means "causing an effect."* Explain that an effective speech is a speech that changes the minds of listeners.

PRACTICE Have students use **Context Cards**, the dialogue, the summary, or "Darnell Rock Reporting" to look for and name words that have suffixes. *(violations, exception, dependent)*

Summarize

TEACH/MODEL Remind students that when we **summarize**, we tell the most important parts of a selection. Use a Think Aloud to model summarizing "Darnell Rock Reporting."

> **Think Aloud** *Darnell had an article in the local newspaper for his idea to use the basketball court to help the homeless. He presented his idea to the City Council. These are two very important details to include in a summary of the events in "Darnell Rock Reporting."*

GUIDED PRACTICE Place students into groups. List events from "Darnell Rock Reporting," and ask groups to decide which details to include in a **summary** of the story.

- Review **Teach Academic English** on **Language Support Card 19**. Remind students to use complex sentences with noun phrases plus *is that* as they explain.

CHECK PROGRESS

Do students…
- demonstrate fluency as they use punctuation to guide phrasing?
- identify words with suffixes and their meanings?
- summarize "Darnell Rock Reporting"?

REVIEW TOGETHER

- Have partners take turns reading **Dialogue ELL19.1** aloud. Encourage them to reread the dialogue using punctuation as a guide for proper phrasing.
- Write words with suffixes in one column and definitions in a second column. Have students match the words to their definitions.
- Have partners reread "Darnell Rock Reporting" and summarize it in pairs.

✏️ Scaffolded Practice and Application

Beginning Help students copy the events you wrote. Have them circle and read aloud the words and phrases they think are most important.	**Intermediate** Help partners identify and list important details from "Darnell Rock Reporting" in the order in which they take place.	**Advanced** Have students brainstorm important details and events from "Darnell Rock Reporting" and use them to write two or three sentences about the story.	**Advanced High** Have students write important details from "Darnell Rock Reporting" and use them to write a summary paragraph about the story events.

Scaffold Comprehension

REVIEW "DARNELL ROCK REPORTING" Use a Think Aloud and the following prompts to lead students on a guided review of "Darnell Rock Reporting." Remind students that reviewing and retelling what they read helps them recall the opinions of characters.

Think Aloud **PAGE 482:** *This is a newspaper article by Darnell. He urged the City Council to turn a basketball court into a garden. I wonder if they agreed with his opinion.*

PAGE 483: *This is a newspaper article by Linda Gold. She doesn't support Darnell's opinion. What does Linda urge City Council members to do?* (to turn the basketball court into a parking lot for teachers)

PAGE 489: Read aloud the paragraph. *How did Darnell's opinion change?* (He wanted to help the students as well as the homeless people.) *Why was the new argument more persuasive?* (His new argument showed how the garden would benefit the students in the school, not only the homeless.)

PAGES 491–492: Read aloud the last sentence on page 491. *Did Darnell persuade City Council members?* (no) Read aloud page 492. *What support did Darnell receive?* (A man donated land for a garden, and the city newspaper asked Darnell to write an article.)

CHECK COMPREHENSION If students need additional support with the main selection, direct them to **Summary ELL19.2**. Read the summary aloud, and have them listen and follow along on their pages.

BLM
ELL19.2

Have students take turns reading sections of the summary aloud. Have them answer the following comprehension questions:

1. What was wrong with the basketball court?

2. Who went with Darnell to support him?

3. How did the City Council vote on the issue?

Have students work in pairs to circle high-utility words and highlight Target Vocabulary words found in **Summary ELL19.2**. Have students call out a definition, while partners identify the word it explains.

AUDIOTEXT CD Make the **Audiotext CD** for "Darnell Rock Reporting" available. Have students follow in the **Student Book** as they listen.

Greek and Latin Suffixes

INTRODUCE Remind students that a **suffix** is a group of letters added to the end of a word. *Greek and Latin suffixes give us clues about word meanings.*

- Write and pronounce the word *doable*. *The suffix -able is Latin. It means "can." So* doable *means "can be done." Someone in the story believed Darnell's idea was doable. How do we know this?* (A person donated land to make the idea a reality.)

THINK-PAIR-SHARE Write *affordable, reasonable*, and *considerable*. Circle the *-able* in each word and confirm each meaning. Then have students orally complete the following sentences:

1. Darnell felt the garden would be an ___affordable___ way for homeless people to help themselves.

2. The speech had ___considerable___ influence. One man even volunteered to give away land for the garden.

3. It was ___reasonable___ of Linda to prefer a parking lot.

Persuasion

Teach/Model Explain that when we **evaluate** a **persuasive** message, we study its reasons and the support for those reasons.

GUIDED PRACTICE Write the following ideas: *Homeless people can learn from working in a garden. Students can use a garden to do community service.* Help students generate ideas in support of each proposal. *Which is more persuasive? Why and to whom?* (A school community is probably more likely to support a proposal in favor of students.)

- Review **Teach Academic English** on **Language Support Card 19**. Remind students to use noun phrases such as *my opinion* when trying to persuade.

CHECK PROGRESS

Do students…

- use Target Vocabulary words appropriately to discuss "Darnell Rock Reporting"?
- correctly answer questions about the summary?
- use Greek and Latin suffixes to understand word meanings?
- evaluate persuasive messages?

REVIEW TOGETHER

- Provide additional practice with **Context Cards**.
- Have partners take turns reading aloud **Summary ELL19.2**.
- Write the words with the suffix *-able*. Have students use the suffix to guess the word meanings and confirm them in a dictionary.
- List a few reasons that support Linda's idea of making the basketball court into a parking lot. Ask students to study the reasons and identify those that are the most persuasive.

> ✏️ **Scaffolded Practice and Application**

| **Beginning** Have students copy the two ideas. Ask which idea is more persuasive. Have students answer with one or two words. | **Intermediate** Have partners identify the persuasive message behind each idea. Have them write two to three sentences restating each message. | **Advanced** Have partners write sentences evaluating the persuasive message behind each idea, then explain their evaluation by citing reasons and support. | **Advanced High** Have students write a paragraph that evaluates the persuasive message behind each idea presented by Linda and Darnell in "Darnell Rock Reporting." |

SHARE OBJECTIVES

- Use Target Vocabulary words to discuss "De Zavala: A Voice for Texas."
- Identify more kinds of pronouns.

MATERIALS

Student Book (pp. 494–496)
Leveled Reader
Context Cards

ACADEMIC LANGUAGE

• = *Spanish cognate*

persuasive text	• *texto persuasivo*
pronoun	• *pronombre*
possessive pronoun	• *pronombre posesivo*

Scaffold Content-Area Reading

DISCUSS "DE ZAVALA: A VOICE FOR TEXAS" Use the following picture-text prompts to lead students on a review of "De Zavala: A Voice for Texas." Remind them that "De Zavala: A Voice for Texas" is **persuasive text**. Remind them that persuasive text seeks to make readers think or act in a certain way.

PAGE 494: Read aloud the first three sentences. *Texans had to decide whether to follow ordinances from a cruel dictator or follow a new leader.*

- Read the title aloud. *Do you think De Zavala supported Texans or the cruel dictator?* (Texans)

PAGE 495: Read aloud the first and last sentences. *In his speech, what did De Zavala want to persuade listeners to think?* (that Texas should be independent)

PAGE 496: Read aloud the first paragraph. *Why did De Zavala mention that the freedom of Texans was deteriorating?* (to persuade listeners to think that Texas should be independent)

- Read aloud the last paragraph. *How do readers know that De Zavala convinced people to follow him?* (He became the first vice-president of the Republic of Texas.)

- *What happened shortly after this?* (Texas joined the United States as the twenty-eighth state.)

Leveled Reader

READ *THE OLD TREE* To read more about how people speak up for their beliefs, direct students to the **Leveled Reader**.

1. Provide sentence strips for each student pair.

2. Direct pairs to write or dictate one or two sentences summarizing a different page of *The Old Tree*.

English Language Learners

3. Post sentence strips in order, and fill in any missing story events.

4. Make other modifications to form a summary. This may include omitting unimportant details or shortening sentence length.

5. Read the summary chorally.

More Kinds of Pronouns

TEACH/MODEL Remind students that a **pronoun** is a word that replaces a noun. *Some pronouns show ownership.*

- Write *Darnell's article persuaded readers. His speech persuaded listeners.*

- Underline *Darnell's*. Explain that *Darnell's* is a possessive noun.

- Point to *his*. Explain that *his* is a **possessive pronoun**.

GUIDED PRACTICE Explain that a possessive pronoun tells who or what a noun belongs to.

- List other possessive pronouns: *my, your, his/her/its, our,* and *their*. Explain that each shows ownership. *Using possessive pronouns helps us avoid repeating nouns.*

- Write *Darnell and Linda gave speeches. Darnell's and Linda's opinions were different.* Underline *Darnell's* and *Linda's*.

Transfer Skills
Possessive Pronouns
Explain that possessive pronouns are used differently in some languages. For example, in Spanish, the possessive pronoun *su* is used to replace both masculine and feminine nouns. In Russian, the possessive of a noun depends on the gender of the noun it describes, rather than the noun the pronoun replaces. Provide additional practice forming statements using possessive pronouns, for example, *His book is on the desk. Her soccer game was canceled.*

- Point out that the second sentence is awkwardly written. *Let's use a possessive pronoun to make the sentence sound more natural.*

- Point to the list of possessive pronouns. *Which possessive pronoun can we use to replace the possessive nouns Darnell's and Linda's?* (*their*)

Do students…
- use Target Vocabulary words appropriately to talk about "De Zavala: A Voice for Texas" and *The Old Tree*?
- identify and form possessive pronouns?

- Provide additional practice with **Context Cards**.
- Have partners read sections of "De Zavala: A Voice for Texas" and *The Old Tree* to each other.
- As a group, review possessive pronouns and the nouns they replace.

Scaffolded Practice and Application

Beginning	Intermediate	Advanced	Advanced High
List nouns in one column and possessive pronouns in another column. Have students draw lines to connect each noun with the possessive pronoun that would replace it.	Provide frames about "Darnell Rock Reporting" with possessive nouns. Have students replace the nouns using possessive pronouns.	Provide sentence pairs about "Darnell Rock Reporting" with possessive nouns that repeat. Have students replace the nouns with possessive pronouns where appropriate.	Ask students to write a paragraph about "Darnell Rock Reporting." Ask them to use both possessive nouns and pronouns.

Compare Texts

MAKE COMPARISONS Use the model below to help students complete a chart comparing situations in which people speak up for what they believe. Have students refer to their **Leveled Reader** and **Student Book** pp. 480–492 and 494–496.

Person	Issue	Opinion	Support
Darnell Rock	how to use the old basketball court	Darnell wants to make a garden for students and homeless people.	He says the garden will help students think about their lives.
De Zavala	whether Texas should be independent	De Zavala wants Texas to be independent.	He says the rich leaders don't consider average Texans in decisions.
Elena	whether to save a tree or build an auditorium	Elena wants to save the tree.	She says the tree is like a 150-year-old monument.

- Have students orally form sentences based on the information in the chart. Provide sentence frames such as the following:

1. The issue De Zavala speaks about is ___the independence of Texas___.

2. As support for her opinion, Elena says that ___the tree is like a 150-year-old monument___.

3. Darnell Rock wanted to ___build a garden___ because he felt it would help students and homeless people.

DISCUSS COMPARISONS To help students compare and contrast situations in which people speak up for what they believe, ask questions such as, *How were the issues Elena, Darnell, and DeZavala faced similar? How were they different?* Provide sentence frames such as:

4. Both Darnell and Elena had an opinion about ___how to use a deteriorating area at school___.

5. DeZavala's opinion was similar to Darnell's because ___he wanted to help people___.

6. Darnell and Elena differed in that ___Darnell wanted to help people, but Elena wanted to protect the environment___.

Write to Narrate

TEACH/MODEL Review the features of a **personal narrative**. Explain that a personal narrative is a story that happened to the writer. *A personal narrative should include events, and details that are organized in logical order.* Point out that writers should choose an interesting topic and consider the audience as they explain events.

- Read and discuss the Writing Process Checklist on **Student Book** p. 500.

- Read and discuss the Writing Model on **Student Book** pp. 500–501. Point out examples of prewriting.

GUIDED PRACTICE Explain that the class will work together to write an events chart for a personal narrative.

- Guide students in a prewriting activity of brainstorming topics. List topics as students suggest them. *Who are we writing the narrative for?* (other students) *How will this affect the tone?* (It should be informal.)

- Have the group identify a topic for the personal narrative. (Example: *This morning something unusual happened to me.*)

> **Extend Language**
> **Verbs to Express Opinion**
> think, believe, feel, suspect, imagine, suppose, assume

- *What are some details or events that could follow and explain this topic?* List answers from students. (*I got ready and left for school on time. No one was at school when I arrived. Then I realized that my clock was an hour fast.*)

- Ask students to help you arrange the events in logical order.

- Read the completed events chart chorally. Have students suggest additional details if they feel any are missing.

CHECK PROGRESS

Do students…
- participate in discussion about situations in which people speak up for what they believe?
- correctly identify similarities and differences between situations in which people speak up for what they believe?
- generate events and details for a personal narrative?

REVIEW TOGETHER

- Have students work in pairs or small groups to read and review the rows and columns of the situations in which people speak up for what they believe comparison chart.
- Have partners help each other check for and include vocabulary words in their writing.

✏️ Scaffolded Practice and Application

| **Beginning** Have students write about events that happened using one or two sentences. Have students number the events if possible. | **Intermediate** Have students list events that happened using complete sentences. Have them number the events in the order in which they happened. | **Advanced** Have students write sentences about events that happened, including supporting details. Have them use time-order transition words to show the order in which the events happened. | **Advanced High** Have students write sentences using time-order transitions to tell about events that happened. Then have them include details that describe the events. |

- Participate in discussion about a man who doesn't know the difference between fact and fantasy.
- Say, read, and use Target Vocabulary and high-utility words.
- Practice analyzing characters and complete a T-Map.

MATERIALS

Language Support Card 20
Context Cards
Dialogue ELL20.1 (Noble Hero or Silly Fool?)
Student Book (pp. 506–516)
Main Selection Summary ELL20.2
Graphic Organizer Transparency 12

✓ TARGET VOCABULARY

	• = *Spanish cognate*
antique	• *antigua*
exploits	
faithful	
ignorance	• *ignorancia*
noble	• *nobles*
pierced	
plagued	• *plagados*
quests	
thrust	
transformed	• *transformó*

ACADEMIC LANGUAGE

character	
inference	• *inferencia*

Listening, Speaking, and Viewing

USE LANGUAGE SUPPORT CARD
Present **Language Support Card 20**. Use the activities on the back of the card to introduce concepts and vocabulary from "Don Quixote and the Windmills" and to practice **Academic English**.

Develop Target Vocabulary

USE CONTEXT CARDS Show the **Context Cards** for *ignorance* and *exploits*. Present the cards using Steps 1–3 of the Introduce Vocabulary routine on **Teacher's Edition** p. T306.

- Help students use *ignorance* and *exploits* to discuss why it is important to know the difference between fact and fantasy.

USE ORAL LANGUAGE DIALOGUE Distribute **Dialogue ELL20.1**. Read the title aloud, and have students repeat. Have students look at the title, images, and other information on the page. Then have them predict what they think the dialogue will be about.

BLM ELL20.1

- As you read the dialogue aloud, display the **Context Cards** for *quests, noble, exploits,* and *transformed*. After you read, tell students that Don Quixote dreamed of living long ago, when knights were heroes in the same way that fictional superheroes are today.

- Display the T-Map you started with the **Language Support Card**. Ask: *In fact, what real thing did Don Quixote attack?* Write *windmill* in the *Real* column.

- *Don Quixote did not know the difference between fact and fantasy. In his fantasy, what did he think he was attacking?* Write *giant* in the *Fantasy* column.

▶ **WRITE-PAIR-SHARE** Display sentence frames such as the following and have partners use them to write complete sentences.

1. Don Quixote thought a giant could be transformed into a ____windmill____.

2. This belief showed his ___ignorance___ of the difference between fact and fantasy.

Scaffold Comprehension

PREVIEW "DON QUIXOTE AND THE WINDMILLS" Explain that students will skim "Don Quixote and the Windmills" in order to predict what the selection is about. Help students scan the illustrations and other text features on **Student Book** pp. 506–516. Have them predict one thing they may learn by reading the text.

USE MAIN SELECTION SUMMARY Distribute **Summary ELL20.2**. Read the summary aloud, then have partners take turns reading it.

BLM
ELL20.2

RETEACH

Understanding Characters

TEACH/MODEL Read aloud the first two paragraphs of **Summary ELL20.2**. *To understand story* **characters,** *we have to notice what they say and do. Then we ask ourselves why they act the way they do. We make* **inferences** *to figure out why characters say and do things.*

GUIDED PRACTICE Have students read the first two paragraphs of **Summary ELL20.2**. *Don Quixote was an old man who made a lot of changes in his life. Let's make inferences, or guesses, to figure out why.*

- **Display Graphic Organizer Transparency 12.** Explain that a T-Map can help students note what a character says and does and figure out why a character says and does these things. Write *What Character Did* above the left column and *Inference About Character* above the right column.

- *What did Señor Quexada do in the second paragraph?* (changed his name, found a lance, made Sancho his squire, pretended a farm girl was a noble lady) *Why do you think he did these things?* (He wanted to be a knight; he wanted to have adventures.)

- Display a completed T-Map as a reference throughout the week.

Do students…
- correctly pronounce and use vocabulary words in discussion?
- understand characters?

- Have partners use **Context Cards** to review the Target Vocabulary words and their meanings. Have them complete the activities on the backs of the cards.
- Have partners read the last three paragraphs of the summary. Then have them complete these sentence frames about Sancho: *I have figured out that Sancho was _____. That's why he _____.*

Graphic Organizer

| Name | Date | Graphic Organizer 12 |

T-Map: _____

Title or Topic _____

What Character Did	Inference About Character
changed his name; found an old lance; imagined his horse was a steed; made Sancho his faithful squire; pretended a farm girl was a noble lady	Señor Quexada wanted to be a knight. He wanted to have adventures like the ones in his books.

Graphic Organizer 12
© Houghton Mifflin Harcourt Publishing Company. All rights reserved.

✏️ **Scaffolded Practice and Application**

| **Beginning** Guide partners to complete these sentence frames: *I have figured out that Señor Quexada was an old man who _____. That's why he _____.* | **Intermediate** Have partners complete these sentence frames: *I have figured out that Señor Quexada was _____. That's why he _____.* | **Advanced** Have students write two sentences describing what they have figured out about Señor Quexada, and telling what he does and why he does those things. | **Advanced High** Have students write a paragraph describing what they have figured out about Señor Quexada, and telling what he does and why he does those things. |

Scaffold Comprehension

DISCUSS "DON QUIXOTE AND THE WINDMILL" Use the following picture-text prompts to discuss "Don Quixote and the Windmill." Remind students that "Don Quixote and the Windmill" is a work of **humorous fiction**. Humorous fiction is written to make the reader laugh.

PAGE 506: Have students read the title aloud. Point to the windmill. *Why would Don Quixote attack a windmill?* (He didn't know the difference between fact and fantasy. To him, the windmill had the appearance of a giant.)

PAGES 508–509: *Look at the giant, the knight, the dragon, and the noble lady. Why does the picture show them falling out of Don Quixote's book?* (To him, these fantasy images have become real. He thinks they exist.)

PAGES 510–511: Point to Don Quixote's armor, his horse, his antique lance, his faithful squire, and his noble lady. *Are they like the people and things you would read about in a story about knights? Why not?* (No: His helmet is made of paper; his lance is old; his horse is bony; his squire and lady are farmers.)

AUDIOTEXT CD Make the **Audiotext CD** for "Don Quixote and the Windmill" available. Have students follow in the **Student Book** as they listen.

Practice Target Vocabulary

USE ORAL LANGUAGE DIALOGUE Distribute **Dialogue ELL20.1**. Have a student read the title aloud.

BLM
ELL20.1

- Read the dialogue aloud or have proficient readers model reading aloud.

- Have students identify Target Vocabulary and high-utility words in the dialogue and read the words aloud with you.

- Have them restate each Target Vocabulary word and use it in a sentence about knights or fantasy. Then have them complete the activity on the page.

PRACTICE FLUENCY: STRESS Read aloud **Dialogue ELL20.1** with appropriate stress. Review several sentences with students. Read them with correct stress and then without stress so that they can hear the difference. Then have pairs read the dialogue aloud, using appropriate stress.

Stress in Three-Syllable Words

INTRODUCE Write, *ignorance, appearance,* and *understand.* Say the words aloud and have students repeat.

- Tell students that *ignorance, appearance,* and *understand* all have three **syllables,** or word parts. Explain that a different syllable is **stressed** in each word. Remind them that a stressed syllable is said a little louder and a little longer than an **unstressed** one.

- Clap out the rhythm of each word, and have students identify the stressed syllable in each. (*ignorance*: first; *appearance*: second; *understand*: third)

PRACTICE Have students use **Context Cards**, the dialogue, the summary, or "Don Quixote and the Windmills" to look for and name words that have three syllables. (*exciting, victory, recognize*)

RETEACH

Question

TEACH/MODEL Write *question* and *infer,* and explain the terms. Remind students that they can ask questions about a character's actions and relate them to their own lives. Use a Think Aloud to model asking questions about "Don Quixote and the Windmills."

> **Think Aloud** *Why did Sancho agree to go with Don Quixote? I wouldn't do that unless I believed my friend or wanted an adventure. I can infer that's why Sancho agreed.*

GUIDED PRACTICE Have students ask questions about the characters' actions on pages 514–515 of "Don Quixote and the Windmills." Then have them infer why the characters acted the way they did.

- Review **Teach Academic English** on **Language Support Card 20**. Help students use the present perfect tense in complex sentences to ask and answer questions about the selection.

CHECK PROGRESS

Do students…

- demonstrate fluency as they recite the dialogue with appropriate stress?
- identify the stressed syllable in three-syllable words?
- ask questions and make inferences about "Don Quixote and the Windmills"?

REVIEW TOGETHER

- Have partners take turns reading **Dialogue ELL20.1** aloud. Encourage them to switch roles for the dialogue and use appropriate stress for each role.
- Have students make a Column Chart with one of these three-syllable words at the top of each column: *ignorance, appearance, understand.* Then have them sort this list of words into the correct columns by stressed syllable: *Quixote, gentleman, underneath, adventures, attacking, interfere, loyalty.*
- Have partners read the last page of "Don Quixote and the Windmills" together. Have them question what the characters say and do to figure out their motivations. Then guide them to infer why the characters behaved as they did.

✏️ Scaffolded Practice and Application

| **Beginning** Give sentence frames: *Sancho wanted to save Don Quixote. That's why he _____. Don Quixote thought he was fighting a giant. That's why he _____.* Work with students to complete them. | **Intermediate** Ask: *Why did Sancho grab Don Quixote's ankle? Why did Don Quixote cut at the ropes? Why did Sancho ask him to stop?* Have students make inferences to answer the questions. | **Advanced** Have students imagine themselves in the characters' situation to figure out why the characters behaved as they do. Have them ask questions and make inferences together. | **Advanced High** Have students work independently to ask questions and make inferences about a character's behavior. |

Scaffold Comprehension

REVIEW "DON QUIXOTE AND THE WINDMILLS" Use a Think Aloud and the following prompts to lead students on a guided review of "Don Quixote and the Windmills." Remind students that reviewing and retelling what they read will help them understand a story's characters and plot.

Think Aloud **PAGE 508:** *Look at Señor Quexada's face. He looks so sad. He is plagued by his fantasies of an exciting life. That's why he transformed himself into Don Quixote.*

PAGES 512–513: *Who is the knight charging ahead on his faithful horse?* (Don Quixote) *What is he going to attack with his antique lance?* (a windmill)

PAGES 514–515: *After Don Quixote's lance pierced the sail of the windmill, what happened next?* (The sail pulled him up into the air.)

PAGE 516: *Listen while I read the first two paragraphs. Don Quixote says that Sancho reveals his ignorance. How does Don Quixote reveal his own ignorance?* (He thinks the fantasy creatures from his books are real.)

CHECK COMPREHENSION If students need additional support with the main selection, direct them to **Summary ELL20.2**. Read the summary aloud, and have them listen and follow along on their pages.

BLM
ELL20.2

Have students take turns reading sections of the summary aloud. Have them answer the following comprehension questions:

1. Why did Señor Quexada change his name and leave home with his faithful friend Sancho?

2. Why did Don Quixote attack the windmill?

3. After the attack, Sancho said the giants were really windmills. What did Don Quixote say?

Have students work in pairs to circle high-utility words and highlight Target Vocabulary words found in **Summary ELL20.2**. Have them use the words to make up their own story about a knight and his faithful squire.

AUDIOTEXT CD Make the **Audiotext CD** for "Don Quixote and the Windmills" available. Have students follow in the **Student Book** as they listen.

Idioms

INTRODUCE Write *figurative language, idiom,* and *adage*. *Figurative language uses words to create a picture in your mind. Idioms are a form of figurative language. An idiom is an expression whose meaning cannot be figured out from its individual words.*

- Write: *Some parents have eyes in the back of their heads. What do you think this idiom means?* (Many parents know what their kids are doing even if they can't see them.)

- *At the end of the story, Don Quixote uses an adage, or a traditional saying about life.* Write: *The road to victory is often paved with misfortune. What do you think he means?* (You don't always succeed the first time you try to do something.)

THINK-PAIR-SHARE Help partners orally figure out these idioms

1. Don't count your chickens before they hatch. (You don't always know how things will turn out.)

2. Don't bite off more than you can chew. (Don't try to do more than you are able to do.)

RETEACH
Understanding Characters

Teach/Model Explain that a character's **traits** are aspects of his or her personality. *Many stories and movies have two characters who work together: a leader and a follower. What are some traits a leader would have?* (strong ideas, persuasive arguments) *Who has the character traits to be the leader in this story?* (Don Quixote) *Who is the follower?* (Sancho)

GUIDED PRACTICE *Let's list other stories or movies we know that have a leader and follower.* (Sample answer: Batman and Robin)

- Review **Teach Academic English** on **Language Support Card 20**. Remind students that they can use a T-Map to make inferences about characters' traits.

✏️ **Scaffolded Practice and Application**

| **Beginning** Give students sentence frames to compare character types: *Sancho is Don Quixote's follower, but he also helps _____.* | **Intermediate** Ask questions to help students compare recurring character types: *How are Don Quixote and Batman alike? How are they different?* | **Advanced** Have students write a paragraph that compares Don Quixote and Sancho to another pair of leader/follower characters from a favorite story or movie. | **Advanced High** Have students write a paragraph with this topic sentence: *Stories about a leader and his loyal follower are always popular.* Have them give examples. |

CHECK PROGRESS

Do students…
- use Target Vocabulary words appropriately to discuss "Don Quixote and the Windmills"?
- correctly answer questions about the summary?
- identify idioms and adages?
- analyze characters' traits?

REVIEW TOGETHER

- Provide additional practice with **Context Cards**.
- Have partners take turns reading aloud **Summary ELL20.2**.
- Have partners discuss and interpret these idioms: *The early bird gets the worm. A stitch in time saves nine. Birds of a feather flock together.*
- Have students draw pictures and make posters depicting their favorite leader/follower characters from stories or movies. Under the picture, have students write each character's name, and the character's traits.

Scaffold Content-Area Reading

DISCUSS "LITBEAT: LIVE FROM LA MANCHA" Use the following picture-text prompts to lead students on a review of "LitBeat: Live from La Mancha." Remind them that "LitBeat: Live from La Mancha" is a **play**. Remind them that a play tells a story through the words and actions of its characters.

PAGE 519: *Don Quixote is wearing his* antique *armor while a TV reporter describes his exploits. Why is this humorous?* (It combines a character from long ago with one from the present day.)

- *What does Paige say after Don Quixote explains the reason for his attack on the windmills?* (She says, "Okay, good luck with that.") *Why did the author include this remark?* (It's modern slang and shows a sarcastic attitude toward Don Quixote's quest. The author wants to make us laugh.)

PAGE 520: *Who complains after Don Quixote breaks the windmill?* (the Miller, the man who owns it) *Why did the author include this remark?* (to make us laugh)

- *How is this selection like* "Don Quixote and the Windmills"? *How is it different?* (Same: two of the characters, most of the plot, same theme about fact and fantasy, both humorous; Different: play, not story, some modern characters, some modern, sarcastic dialogue)

Leveled Reader

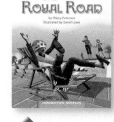

READ *THE ROYAL ROAD* To read more about telling the difference between fact and fantasy, direct students to the **Leveled Reader**. Have partners or small groups take turns rereading the selection aloud to one another.

◆ **English Language Learners**

PAIRED READING Share these tips with readers of approximately the same proficiency level:

1. Sit side by side and look at the book together.

2. Take turns holding the book.

3. Look at the pictures and try to predict what will happen next.

4. When you finish, ask your buddy about his or her favorite character or part of the story.

Contractions

TEACH/MODEL Write these sentences from *The Royal Road*: *"Don't feel silly,"* Grandfather said. *"It's good to get lost in a story."*

- Underline *don't* and *it's*. *These words are* **contractions**, *or shortened ways of saying something.* Don't *is a short way of saying* do not. It's *is a short way of saying* it is. *What letter did I drop from* do not *to write* don't? **(the o in not)** *I used an* **apostrophe** *to show that there is a letter missing. What letter did I drop from* it is? **(the i in is)**

GUIDED PRACTICE Write *He is attacking a windmill. He does not know what it really is.* Underline *He is. How can I make these two words into a contraction?* **(Drop the i in is and add an apostrophe.)** Write *He's.*

- Underline *does not. How can I make these two words into a contraction?* **(Drop the o in not and add an apostrophe.)** Write *doesn't.*

- Help students form contractions from the following phrases: *did not, she is, you are, is not, are not, we are.*

Transfer Skills
Contractions

Spanish uses contractions when the masculine definite article *el* follows the prepositions *a* (*to*) and *de* (*from*). For example, Spanish speakers write *al hombre* (*to the man*) instead of *a el hombre*. They write *del hombre* (*from the man*) instead of *de el hombre*. Notice, however, that Spanish contractions do not include an apostrophe. Provide additional practice forming contractions, for example, *He isn't in the room.*

Do students…

- use Target Vocabulary words appropriately to talk about "LitBeat: Live from La Mancha" and *The Royal Road*?
- use contractions correctly?

- Provide additional practice with **Context Cards**.
- Have partners read sections of LitBeat: Live from La Mancha and *The Royal Road* to each other.
- Have groups read two pages of *The Royal Road* together. Have them identify contractions and tell what each contraction means.

✏️ Scaffolded Practice and Application

Beginning Have students copy the contractions. Have them rewrite these sentences with contractions: *She is my friend. You are late. I did not do it. We are coming. They are not here.*	**Intermediate** Have students copy the contractions. Then have partners write an original sentence using each contraction.	**Advanced** Have partners talk about what they like to do with their friends. Then have them write sentences from their dialogue, using contractions.	**Advanced High** Have students write a scene for a play. Tell them to include contractions in the dialogue.

- Discuss and compare selections about the difference between fact and fantasy.
- Make a chart to compare and contrast selections about the difference between fact and fantasy.
- Use vocabulary words to write about selections that show the difference between fact and fantasy.

MATERIALS

Student Book (pp. 506–516, 518–520, 524–525)
Leveled Reader
Grab-and-Go™ Resources (p. 18)

ACADEMIC LANGUAGE

• = *Spanish cognate*

personal narrative   • *narrativa personal*
voice   • *voz*

Compare Texts

MAKE COMPARISONS Use the model below to help students complete a chart comparing selections about the difference between fact and fantasy. Have students refer to their **Leveled Reader** and **Student Book** pp. 506–516 and 518–520.

Selection	"Don Quixote and the Windmills"	"LitBeat: Live from La Mancha"	*The Royal Road*
Genre	humorous fiction	play	humorous fiction
Setting: Place and Time	Spain: long ago	Spain: modern times	U.S.: modern times
Characters	Don Quixote, Sancho	Don Quixote, Sancho, TV reporter, Miller	Teresa Montez, her family and friends
Theme	It's important to know what is fact and what is fantasy.	It's important to know what is fact and what is fantasy.	It's important to know what is fact and what is fantasy.

- Have students orally form sentences based on the information in the chart. Provide sentence frames such as the following:

1. <u>LitBeat: Live from La Mancha</u> is a play.

2. <u>The Royal Road</u> is set in the United States in modern times.

3. Teresa Montez is the main character in <u>The Royal Road</u> .

4. The theme of "Don Quixote and the Windmills" is that <u>it's important to know what is fact and what is fantasy</u>

DISCUSS COMPARISONS To help students compare and contrast selections about fact and fantasy, ask questions such as, *How are the three selections similar? How are they different?* Provide sentence frames such as:

5. All three selections have the same <u>theme</u> .

6. "Don Quixote and the Windmills" and *The Royal Road* are works of <u>humorous fiction</u>, but "LitBeat: Live from La Mancha" is a <u>play</u> .

7. "LitBeat: Live from La Mancha" and *The Royal Road* are both set in modern times, but <u>Don Quixote and the Windmills</u> is set long ago in the past.

8. Both "Don Quixote and the Windmills" and <u>LitBeat: Live from La Mancha</u> include the characters of Don Quixote and Sancho.

Write to Narrate

TEACH/MODEL Review the features of a **personal narrative**.

A personal narrative is a true story about your life. It tells interesting events. A personal narrative should be in your own **voice**, *or in words that show your personal thoughts and feelings. It should also have a good ending that shows how the events worked out.*

- Read and discuss the Writing Process Checklist on **Student Book** p. 524 and the Writing Model on **Student Book** pp. 524–525. Point out examples of voice.

GUIDED PRACTICE Explain that the class will work together to complete the personal narrative that was started last week.

- Recall the list of topics that the class generated last week. Invite a student to name the chosen topic. The review the completed events chart. Remind students that the events need to be in a logical order.

- Use the events chart to draft complete sentences. and remind them that the tone should grab the reader's attention and sound like the voice of a fifth grader.

- Use students' suggestions to write a beginning that adequately uses voice to capture the reader's interest.

- Have individuals suggest important events and vivid details. Include them in supporting paragraphs.

- Have a pair of students read the completed personal narrative aloud. Discuss the narrative, and have students suggest changes to the order of the sentences.

CHECK PROGRESS

Do students…
- participate in discussion about selections that show the difference between fact and fantasy?
- correctly identify similarities and differences between selections about fact and fantasy?
- use voice in their writing?

REVIEW TOGETHER

- Have students work in pairs or small groups to read and review the information about each selection in the fact and fantasy comparison chart.
- Have partners help each other check for and include vocabulary words in their writing.
- Have students review the **Writing Rubric** on p. 18 of the **Grab-and-Go™ Resources**.

▶ Scaffolded Practice and Application

Beginning Have students copy the narrative. Have them name other thoughts and feelings that they might use in the narrative.	**Intermediate** Have partners revise the opening sentences of the personal narrative by writing in their own voice. Have them role-play the situation first.	**Advanced** Have students write and revise a personal narrative on a topic of their choice. Have partners read each other's narratives and suggest ways to improve the beginning so that it captures a reader's interest.	**Advanced High** Have students write a personal narrative on a topic of their choice. Have them use the Writing Process Checklist to revise their narrative independently. Remind them to use words that express their voice.

Teacher Notes

Resources

Contents

Use Newspapers

1 | Teach/Model

Summarize the purpose and features of a newspaper. Have students refer to different newspaper sections during the discussion.

- Usually published daily or weekly, newspapers report on recent events, including local, national, and world news. Well-written articles cover the *who, what, when, where, how,* and *why* of events. Point out that many newspapers make their content available on the Internet.

- In addition to news, newspapers offer editorials and entertainment and human-interest articles.

- Newspapers also review books, films, and live performances. Reviews usually start with an overview of the content and background information about the author or group. Then the reviewer analyzes and evaluates the quality of the work or the performances.

2 | Practice/Apply

- Have groups of students analyze sections of a local newspaper and tell who would be interested in the information and why. Then have them access an online newspaper and compare and contrast online and print formats.

- Have the groups locate a book, movie, or live performance review in an online or print newspaper and label the type of content it contains.

Persuasive Techniques

1 | Teach/Model

Review with students that **persuasive techniques** are used to influence how people think or act. Discuss with students the following persuasive techniques:

- An **overgeneralization** is a broad statement which is not based on facts or evidence. It does not hold true for more than one or two isolated groups or ideas. For example: "Smart athletes drink Power Gulp."

- A **testimonial** persuades people through the support of a celebrity or expert: "Pop star Gina G. wears Sneaky Sneaks!"

- The **bandwagon** technique tries to persuade people to do something on the basis that "everyone else" is doing it.

- Faulty cause and effect connects the use of a product with a positive result: "Eat *Pow! Flakes* and you'll kick the winning goal."

Stress that students should be critical readers and thinkers by analyzing the claims and assertions made by people attempting to persuade with these strategies.

2 | Practice/Apply

- Have partners reread **Student Book pp. 87–88,** "Vote for Me!" and analyze the two election posters for examples of persuasive techniques.

- Have partners search magazines and newspapers to find examples of persuasive techniques to share with the class.

Note Text Structure

SHARE OBJECTIVE

Analyze different types of text structure.

MATERIALS

Student Book

1 Teach/Model

Explain to students that authors organize information and ideas in a logical manner to show how ideas are related. Point out to students that looking for these text structures can help them better understand information that the author wants them to know. Authors leave clues for the reader that reveal the text structure. Discuss the following types of text structure.

- **Cause and effect**: Authors include primary causes and effects, and these are main topics of reading selections. Main ideas will be supported by details that elaborate and clarify.

- **Compare and contrast**: To understand two or more ideas, it useful to know how they are the same and different. Words such as *like* and *compared to* are clues that the author is comparing and contrasting.

- **Order of importance**: Authors list the most important facts and ideas as main topics and less important facts as details or subtopics.

- **Proposition and support**: Propositions or opinion statements may be main topics, with reasons provided to support them.

2 Practice/Apply

- Have students use their **Student Books** to identify selections that include examples of these different types of text structures. Have student pairs analyze one example to determine how it helps readers understand the information in the text. Then have them write a short summary paragraph explaining their analysis.

Media Effect

SHARE OBJECTIVE

Discuss and analyze the effect of the public media on daily life.

MATERIALS

newspapers; magazines; radio; computers with Internet access

1 Teach/Model

Discuss with students the different forms of public media that they experience and interact with on a daily basis. Have them note their purpose and importance. Review the following forms of media and their content with students.

- **Newspapers**: news, weather, sports, comics, entertainment, editorials, obituaries, feature articles, listings (e.g., employment), announcements, advertisments

- **Magazines**: in-depth articles on a variety of general or special-interest topics, advertisments

- **TV**: information such as news, weather, political commentary, and documentaries; entertainment including talk shows and reality shows; advertising

- **Radio**: music, talk shows, news, sports, events

- **Internet**: websites of people and institutions, information, advertisements, entertainment, blogs, videos, e-mail

Discuss with students the need to constantly evaluate the information and the purpose of that information in the media.

2 Practice/Apply

- Have partners select one of the types of media, find examples of that type, and then analyze its purpose, content, and appeal.

- Have partners develop and deliver a brief presentation about the form of media they selected. The presentations should include a discussion of the advantages and disadvantages of the medium, and how it impacts lives.

Study Skills

How to Outline

SHARE OBJECTIVE

Prepare outlines using structural patterns in informational texts.

MATERIALS

Student Book

1 Teach/Model

Remind students that **outlining** helps organize or recap information briefly but clearly. Remind them that authors carefully organize their writing to help readers better comprehend the text.

- Tell students that the text structures authors use can also be used to structure an outline. These include sequence of events; causes and effects; comparisons and contrasts (likes/differences); order of importance; propositions and supporting facts; and categorization related to the topic.

- Display an outline for students as you explain the process for creating one.

- Tell students that when writing an outline, the first step is to decide which organizing structure to use. The next step is to determine the content of the main categories, followed by the subcategories, and to arrange them in logical order. Last, key details are added. Each of the steps may be labeled with numbers and/or letters depending on how formal the outline needs to be.

2 Practice/Apply

- Have partners choose 2 to 3 pages of informational text from the **Student Book** to outline.

- Have pairs exchange their outlines with another pair. Have each pair explain which organizing structure they chose and why. Pairs should then critique each other's outlines for both content and structure.

Rhetorical Devices

SHARE OBJECTIVE

Identify and analyze rhetorical devices used for intent and effect.

MATERIALS

Student Book

1 Teach/Model

Explain that speakers use many different techniques to hold their listeners' attention and emphasize important ideas. Discuss examples of these **rhetorical devices**:

- **Cadence** is the rhythmic rise and fall of words, giving a musical flow to speech.

- **Repeating words or phrases** stresses important details ("I have a dream"). Another type of repeating pattern is the repetition of initial sounds ("a gruesome grin"), called **alliteration**.

- **Onomatopoeia** is the use of words that imitate the sound they describe (*pow, zoom,* and *roar*).

- **Hyperbole** uses exaggeration to make a point ("I am starving").

- **Personification** gives human qualities to objects, animals, or ideas ("the words leapt from his lips").

2 Practice/Apply

- Have partners think of two additional examples of each type of rhetorical device. Then have them look through the **Student Book** or other books they have already read for two additional examples of each.

- Have partners share with the class both the examples they thought of and the examples they found. Compile a master list on the board.

Preparing an Oral Presentation

SHARE OBJECTIVE

Organize thoughts before speaking.

MATERIALS

note cards

1 Teach/Model

Explain that before giving an **oral presentation**, students must gather and organize their information and plan what they will say. Discuss these steps for preparing an oral presentation.

- Choose a topic. As needed, research the topic and gather information for the presentation.

- Organize research information and personal ideas and opinions that will be part of the presentation. Decide what ideas are most important to include in the presentation.

- Write notes telling important ideas about the topic on note cards or paper. Organize the note cards or ideas in an order that makes sense.

- Practice speaking aloud, using the notes to help remember what to say.

2 Practice/Apply

- Have students prepare a brief oral presentation about an important event in their lives.

- Have students decide on their topics and list their thoughts about the event, using a graphic organizer, such as a web, to organize and prioritize the information.

- Next, students should write the most important ideas about their topics on note cards or paper in a logical order.

- Have students exchange their notes with a partner. Have partners evaluate the effectiveness of the strategy used to organize the presentation.

Delivering an Oral Presentation

SHARE OBJECTIVE

Give a speech about a favorite activity.

MATERIALS

notes on index cards

1 Teach/Model

Remind students that prior to giving an **oral presentation**, the speaker must organize the content of the speech. Once the notes are written and the speech has been practiced, the speaker is ready to present it. Remind students to remember the following points when giving a speech:

- Stay on the topic that was chosen.

- Present the information in an organized manner.

- Speak loudly enough for the audience to hear all of the words. Speak clearly and with expression.

- Be sure to look at the audience, even when using note cards. Use the audience's reaction to gauge whether communications are effective.

2 Practice/Apply

Have students prepare an oral presentation on an important event in their lives. Follow the guidelines of the previous Study Skill lesson as needed to help students prepare for their presentations.

- Create a schedule so that students know when to get ready.

- Allow time for students to practice their presentations.

- Have students present to small groups.

- Provide time for group members to give each other constructive feedback after their oral presentations.

Word Histories

1 Teach/Model

Explain that the history of a word is called its **etymology**. Many dictionaries give complete or partial etymologies for entry words, providing interesting insights into how words and their meanings develop and change over time.

Use this example to discuss an etymology:

can•dle [ME candel < OE < Lat. candela < *candēre*, to shine]

- An etymology traces a word's history from its most recent English stage (given first) to its earliest known stage (given last).

- The < symbol means "derived from."

- The abbreviations name the languages from which a word was "borrowed." In this example, the languages include ME (Middle English), OE (Old English), and Lat. (Latin).

- Symbols and abbreviations in etymologies are listed in the Guide to the Dictionary, which is often found at the beginning of the book.

- Many times the meaning of a word's earliest known stage or its affixes and roots is given.

2 Practice/Apply

- Ask students to research the etymologies of any five Target Vocabulary words from Unit 4. Then have them write a sentence with each word.

- Have students share the etymology of one word with the class.

Multimedia Presentation

1 Teach/Model

Explain that a **multimedia presentation** combines text, images, and sound to communicate with, inform, and entertain an audience. Computer software is often used for multimedia presentations.

Review how to plan a multimedia presentation: research the topic; organize ideas and details; decide which images/sounds will best illustrate ideas and details; plan graphics such as diagrams or graphs; identify free, noncopyrighted images, audio clips, movies, or songs to use; create a script based on main ideas and details, and images and graphics being used. Discuss the following steps to complete a multimedia presentation:

- Finalize the content and put it into a logical order.

- Choose where to use images and graphics to illustrate the content.

- Decide where sound might be used to illustrate or enhance information.

- Decide on whether there are other appropriate ways to enhance the content, such as humor, anecdotes, and stories.

- Practice speaking in a strong, expressive voice.

2 Practice/Apply

- Have small groups assemble a multimedia presentation on a topic related to the Unit 4 Big Idea or Essential Questions.

- Give students time to practice their presentations.

- Have groups present to the class.

SHARE OBJECTIVE

Plan an Internet search and use search engines for appropriate websites.

MATERIALS

computers with Internet access

Internet Strategies

1 Teach/Model

Review Internet basics and safety. Then use the following points to discuss and review planning a search and using search engines.

- **Web browser** software provides Internet access. **Search engines** identify websites with specific information.

- Internet searches require deciding on the topic and planning how best to find it. Students should identify **key words** or terms that focus on specific areas of the topic. Key words provide more usable data by narrowing the search.

- Remind students that search engine entries or **"hits"** include descriptions, or excerpts from the site, the URL (web address) and an electronic link. Extensions such as *.gov, .org,* or *.edu* help identify sources of reliable information. Discuss why other sites might be less appropriate or useful.

2 Practice/Apply

- Have partners choose a topic related to the Unit 4 Big Idea or Essential Questions and identify key words to use for an Internet search. Have them conduct their search, revising their key words as needed. Ask students to predict which of the resulting websites will be useful.

- Have students go to the sites and select three with the most useful information. Have them share these sources with the class. Compile a class list of sources for future research projects.

Word Lists

Unit 1 — School Spirit!

	TARGET VOCABULARY			Spelling Words			Academic Language
Lesson 1	disturbing	struggled	collapsed	breath	numb	comic	story structure
	interrupted	staggered	numb	wobble	hymn	bundle	summarize
	squashing	wobbled	shifted	blister	shovel	solid	conflict
	specialty			crush	gravity	weather	resolution
				direct	frantic	energy	rising action
				promise	swift	stingy	simple subject
				grasp	feather		simple predicate
							fragment
Lesson 2	function	flawed	axis	awake	display	sheepish	graphic features
	delicate	acute	simulate	feast	braces	release	text features
	adjusted	version	tethered	stray	thief	remain	question
				greet	ashamed	sway	caption
				praise	sleeve	training	imperative and
				disease	waist	niece	exclamatory
				repeat	beneath		sentences
							setting
Lesson 3	debate	gradually	stalled	sign	compose	odor	compare
	inflated	hesitated	beckoned	groan	dough	spider	contrast
	shaken	scanned	prodded	reply	height	control	infer
	decorated			thrown	excite	silent	compound sentence
				strike	apply	brighten	complete subject
				mighty	slight	approach	complete predicate
				stroll	define		dialogue
							point of view
Lesson 4	unison	identical	intimidated	glue	loose	route	sequence of events
	uniform	element	recite	flute	lose	cartoon	monitor
	mastered	routine	qualifying	youth	view	avenue	clarify
	competition			accuse	confuse	include	chronological order
				bruise	cruise	assume	initials
				stew	jewel	souvenir	acronym
				choose	execute		abbreviations
							exact details
Lesson 5	officially	embarrassed	supposedly	ounce	haunt	August	theme
	preliminary	typically	sweeping	sprawl	scowl	auction	visualize
	opponents	gorgeous	obvious	launch	naughty	royal	collective nouns
	brutal			loyal	destroy	coward	singular noun
				avoid	saucer	awkward	plural noun
				basketball	pounce	encounter	voice
				moist	poison		point of view

Unit 2 — Wild Encounters

	TARGET VOCABULARY			Spelling Words			Academic Language
Lesson 6	basking	fatal	ordeal	glory	pardon	beware	cause
	analyzing	treating	marine	aware	warn	absorb	effect
	juvenile	calling	intensive	carton	vary	armor	infer
	stunned			adore	barely	stairway	antonyms
				aboard	torch	perform	main verb
				dairy	barge	former	helping verb
				ordeal	soar		linking verb
							transition words
Lesson 7	frantic	wheeled	strained	earth	worthwhile	thirsty	motive, motivation
	lunging	bounding	romp	peer	nerve	reverse	traits
	stride	shouldered	picturing	twirl	pier	worship	visualize
	checking			burnt	squirm	career	behavior
				smear	weary	research	analyze
				further	alert	volunteer	compound direct object
				appear	murmur		figurative language
Lesson 8	endangered	conserving	attracted	steel	lessen	berry	author's viewpoint
	unique	restore	regulate	steal	who's	bury	persuade
	adapted	guardians	responsibility	aloud	whose	hanger	assumption
	vegetation			allowed	manor	hangar	evaluate
				ring	manner	overdo	conjunctions
				wring	pedal	overdue	goal
				lesson	peddle		opinion
							reason
Lesson 9	critical	bundle	commotion	wildlife	light bulb	overboard	conclusion
	secured	clammy	demolished	uproar	well-known	post office	predict
	realization	squalling	elite	home run	throughout	outspoken	generalization
	annoyance			headache	life preserver	up-to-date	root
				top-secret	barefoot	awestruck	complex sentence
				teammate	part-time	newscast	subordinating conjunction
				wheelchair	warehouse		topic sentence
Lesson 10	unobserved	ferocious	vary	cellar	passenger	calendar	main idea
	available	resemble	contentment	flavor	major	quarter	supporting detail
	detecting	particular	keen	cougar	popular	lunar	synonym
	mature			chapter	tractor	proper	antonym
				mayor	thunder	elevator	analogy
				anger	pillar	bitter	quotations
				senator	border		opinion

Word Lists

Unit 3 — Revolution!

Lesson	TARGET VOCABULARY			Spelling Words			Academic Language
Lesson 11	cramped distracted viewpoint shattered	surveyed pressing representatives	embark bracing conduct	bargain journey pattern arrive object suppose shoulder	permit sorrow tunnel subject custom suggest perhaps	lawyer timber common publish burden scissors	cause effect thesaurus subject pronoun object pronoun antecedent concluding sentence
Lesson 12	benefit repeal advantages temporary	contrary prohibit previously	midst objected rebellious	human exact award behave credit basic vivid	evil modern nation robot panic select cousin	item police prefer menu novel deserve	fact opinion reasons context synonym future tense position evidence
Lesson 13	legendary formal gushed strategy	retreat foes shimmering	magnificent revolution plunged	conflict orphan instant complex simply burglar laundry	laughter employ anchor merchant improve arctic mischief	childhood purchase dolphin partner complain tremble	conclusion generalization thesaurus antonym regular verb irregular verb goal persuade
Lesson 14	persuade apprentice contributions influential	aspects authorities bondage	provisions dexterity tentative	actual cruel influence diet museum casual ruin	pioneer trial visual realize create riot genuine	area annual audio dial theater patriot	sequence of events summarize chronological order word root active voice passive voice persuade logical order
Lesson 15	mimic mocking efficient personally	lacked rural tedious	organize summons peal	formal whistle label puzzle legal angle normal	needle angel pupil struggle level local bicycle	channel global stumble quarrel article fossil	compare contrast prefix irregular verb helping verb opinion paraphrasing

Unit 4 — What's Your Story?

	TARGET VOCABULARY			Spelling Words			Academic Language
Lesson 16	record mental launch assuming	episodes developed feature	incredibly villains thumbed	scrubbed listening stunned knitting carpeting wandered gathering	beginning skimmed chatting shrugged bothering whipped quizzed	suffering scanned ordered totaled answered upsetting	author's purpose monitor clarify author's viewpoint word origin adjective decriptive adjective
Lesson 17	impressed admitted produced destination	original concentrate collected	rumor suspense compliment	tiring borrowed freezing delivered whispered losing decided	amazing performing resulting related attending damaged remarked	practicing supported united expected amusing repeated	plot resolution story structure adverb frequency intensity vivid detail dialogue
Lesson 18	career publication household edition	required formula background	insights uneventful destruction	duties earlier loveliest denied ferries sunnier terrified	abilities dirtier scariest trophies cozier enemies iciest	greediest drowsier victories horrified memories strategies	evaluate opinion fact analogies antonyms synonyms prepositional phrases
Lesson 19	issue deteriorating dependent exception	granted effective urge	violations ordinance minimum	lately settlement watchful countless steadily closeness calmly	government agreement cloudiness delightful noisily tardiness forgetful	forgiveness harmless enjoyment appointment effortless plentiful	author's goal persuade summarize assumption bias suffix indefinite pronouns personal narrative
Lesson 20	antique plagued pierced thrust	transformed quests noble	ignorance faithful exploits	salsa mattress tycoon burrito bandanna tomato poncho	dungarees lasso patio siesta cargo vanilla tsunami	iguana plaza caravan hammock pajamas gallant	question traits behavior idiom adage contraction apostrophe negative

Word Lists

Unit 5 — Under Western Skies

Lesson	TARGET VOCABULARY			Spelling Words			Academic Language
Lesson 21	undoubtedly salvation shuffled stunted	evident pace seep	vain mirages factor	nature certain future villain mountain mixture pleasure	captain departure surgeon texture curtain creature treasure	gesture fountain furniture measure feature adventure	chronological order sequence of events visualize analyze synonym irregular verb procedure transitions

Lesson 22	reasoned
	margins
	envy
	upright
		bared
		spared
		nerve
			banish
			astonished
			deserted
				storage
				olive
				service
				relative
				cabbage
				courage
				native
					passage
					voyage
					knowledge
					image
					creative
					average
					justice
						detective
						postage
						cowardice
						adjective
						village
						language
							theme
							infer
							predict
							past perfect tense
							present perfect
							  tense
							future perfect
							  tense

Lesson 23	extending dominated residents flourished	acquainted prospered hostile	acknowledged sprawling decline	entry limit talent disturb entire wisdom dozen	impress respond fortress neglect patrol kitchen forbid	pirate spinach adopt frighten surround challenge	main idea details summarize paraphrase word families base word word root transition words

Lesson 24	rustling
	balked
	lectured
	disadvantage
		quaking
		beacon
		mishap
			surged
			torment
			fared
				mislead
				dismiss
				insincere
				unable
				indirect
				mistreat
				disaster
					dishonest
					insecure
					unknown
					incomplete
					unequal
					unstable
					misspell
						disagree
						informal
						discover
						unwise
						mislaid
						disgrace
							cause
							effect
							comparative
							  adjectives and
							  adverbs
							superlative
							  adjectives and
							  adverbs

Lesson 25	expedition barrier despite fulfilled	range techniques resumed	edible tributaries trek	elect election tense tension react reaction confess	confession decorate decoration contribute contribution express expression	imitate imitation connect connection admire admiration	author's viewpoint author's purpose analogy underline italics research source

Journey to Discovery

	Review Vocabulary			Spelling Words			Academic Language
Lesson 26	disturbing	gradually	routine	produce	commotion	prospect	visuals
	struggled	scanned	gorgeous	company	contest	confirm	caption
	function	identical	sweeping	protect	prefix	preflight	diagram
	flawed			preview	progress	provide	chart
				contain	computer	propose	graph
				combat	confide	promotion	mpa
				prejudge	convince		multiple-meaning words
Lesson 27	stunned	adapted	realization	vacant	urgent	frequent	analyze
	analyzing	conserving	available	insistent	pessimist	laughable	behavior
	ordeal	critical	resemble	reversible	comfortable	radiant	traits
	checking			honorable	absorbent	collectible	theme
				contestant	optimism	novelist	sufix
				patriotism	finalist	journalism	abbreviations
				observant	terrible		imagery
Lesson 28	viewpoint	legendary	aspects	telephone	paragraph	saxophone	fact
	surveyed	retreat	rural	autograph	symphony	telescope	opinion
	advantages	persuade	organize	microscope	telegraph	calligraphy	distinguish
	previously			photograph	megaphone	xylophone	question
				televise	microwave	homophone	idiom
				biology	photocopy	homograph	adage
				microphone	biography		common saying
Lesson 29	record	required	effective	inspect	porter	disrupt	conclusion
	incredibly	insights	plagued	export	report	portable	generalization
	destination	dependent	noble	erupt	spectacle	transport	infer
	suspense			predict	deport	spectator	predict
				respect	interrupt	verdict	Greek root
				bankrupt	dictator	dictionary	Latin root
				dictate	import		appositve
Lesson 30	undoubtedly	underestimated	balked	ballet	barrette	garage	topic
	pace	extending	techniques	echo	depot	khaki	main idea
	reasoned	residents	barrier	bouquet	courtesy	crochet	supporting detail
	nerve			cassette	petite	chorus	summarize
				coupon	denim	essay	word origin
				safari	brunette	alphabet	genre
				portrait	buffet		multigenre college

Using Rubrics

*A **rubric** is a tool a teacher can use to score a student's work.*

*A **rubric** lists the criteria for evaluating the work, and it describes different levels of success in meeting those criteria.*

__Rubrics__ are useful assessment tools for teachers, but they can be just as useful for students. In fact, rubrics can be powerful teaching tools.

RUBRIC

Rubrics for Retelling and Summarizing

- There is a separate rubric for narrative and for nonfiction. Before students begin their retellings or summaries, ask them which rubric should be used. Then point out the criteria and discuss each one.

- Have students focus on the criteria for excellence listed on the rubric so that they have specific goals to aim for.

RUBRIC

Rubric for Presentations

- Before students make a presentation, discuss the criteria listed on the rubric. Have students focus on the criteria for excellence listed on the rubric so that they can aim for specific goals.

- Discuss the criteria for listening with students who will be in the audience. Point out the criteria for excellence listed on the rubric so that they can target specific goals.

RUBRIC

Rubrics for Writing

- When you introduce students to a new kind of writing through a writing model, discuss the criteria listed on the rubric, and ask students to decide how well the model meets each criterion.

- Before students attempt a new kind of writing, have them focus on the criteria for excellence listed on the rubric so that they have specific goals to aim for.

- During both the drafting and revising stages, remind students to check their writing against the rubric to keep their focus and to determine if there are any aspects of their writing they can improve.

- Students can use the rubrics to score their own writing. They can keep the marked rubric in their portfolios with the corresponding piece of writing. The marked rubrics will help students see their progress through the school year. In conferences with students and family members, you can refer to the rubrics to point out both strengths and weaknesses in students' writing.

- See *Grab-and-Go™ Resources* for weekly writing rubrics.

Scoring RUBRIC for Retelling Narratives

Score of ④

The student:

- names and describes the main and supporting characters and tells how they change or learn.
- tells about the setting.
- retells the plot in detail.
- describes the problems and resolutions in the story.
- uses phrases, language, vocabulary, sentence structure, or literary devices from the story.
- accurately describes the theme or meaning of the story.
- provides extensions of the story, such as making connections to other texts, relating relevant experiences, and/or making generalizations.
- requires little or no prompting.

Score of ③

The student:

- names and describes the main characters.
- tells about the setting.
- retells most of the plot accurately.
- describes some of the problems and resolutions in the story.
- uses some phrases, language, vocabulary, or literary devices from the story.
- relates some aspects of the theme or meaning of the story.
- provides some extensions of the story, such as making connections to other texts or relating relevant experiences.
- may require some prompting.

Score of ②

The student:

- tells some details about the story elements, including characters, setting, and plot, with some omissions or errors.
- uses little language and vocabulary from the story.
- shows minimal understanding of the theme or meaning of the story.
- provides minimal extensions of the story.
- requires some prompting to retell the story.

Score of ①

The student:

- tells few, if any, details about the story elements, with errors.
- has little or no awareness of the theme of the story.
- provides no extensions of the story.
- is unable to retell the story without prompting.

Scoring RUBRIC for Summarizing Nonfiction

Score of 4

The student:

- provides a summarizing statement.
- relates the main idea and important supporting details.
- creates a focused, coherent, logical, and organized structure; stays on topic; and relates important points to the text.
- understands relationships in the text such as cause-and-effect, chronological order, or classifying, grouping, comparing, or contrasting information.
- discriminates between reality and fantasy, fact and fiction.
- uses phrases, language, vocabulary, or sentence structure from the text.
- clearly tells the conclusion or point of the text with details.
- identifies the author's purpose for recreating the text.
- provides extensions of the text, such as making connections to other texts, relating relevant experiences, and/or making generalizations.
- requires little or no prompting.

Score of 3

The student:

- tells the topic of the text.
- relates the main idea and relevant details.
- creates a coherent structure and stays on topic.
- mostly understands relationships in the text, such as cause-and-effect, chronological order, or classifying, grouping, or comparing information.
- discriminates between reality and fantasy.
- uses some phrases, language, or vocabulary from the text.
- tells the conclusion or point of the text.
- identifies the author's purpose.
- provides some extensions of the story, such as making connections to other texts or relating relevant experiences.
- may require some prompting.

Score of 2

The student:

- minimally relates the topic of the text.
- shows minimal understanding of the main idea, and omits many important details.
- provides some structure; might stray from topic.
- understands few, if any, relationships in the text, such as chronological order, classifying, or grouping.
- uses little or no language and vocabulary from the text.
- does not fully understand the conclusion or point of the text.
- shows some awareness of the author's purpose.
- provides few, if any, extensions of the text.
- requires some prompting.

Score of 1

The student:

- shows little or no understanding of the topic of the text.
- shows little or no understanding of the main idea, and omits important details.
- provides a poorly organized or unclear structure.
- does not understand relationships in the text.
- does not understand the conclusion of the text.
- provides no extensions of the text.
- is unable to summarize the text without prompting.

Scoring RUBRIC for Presentations

	SPEAKING	VISUALS	MARKERS	WORD PROCESSING	HANDWRITING
Score of 4	The speaker uses very effective pace, volume, intonation, and expression.	The writer uses visuals such as illustrations, charts, graphs, maps, and tables very well. The text and visuals clearly relate to each other.	The title, subheads, page numbers, and bullets are used very well. They make it easy for the reader to find information in the text. These markers clearly show organized information.	Fonts and sizes are used very well, which helps the reader enjoy reading the text.	The slant of the letters is the same throughout the whole paper. The letters are clearly formed and the spacing between words is equal, which makes the text very easy to read.
Score of 3	The speaker uses effective pace, volume, intonation, and expression.	The writer uses visuals fairly well.	The title, subheads, page numbers, and bullets are used fairly well. They usually help the reader find information.	Fonts and sizes are used fairly well, but could be improved upon.	The slant of the letters is usually the same. The letters are clearly formed most of the time. The spacing between words is usually equal.
Score of 2	The speaker uses somewhat effective pace, volume, intonation, and expression.	The writer uses visuals with the text, but the reader may not understand how they are related.	The writer uses some markers such as a title, page numbers, or bullets. However, the use of markers could be improved upon to help the reader get more meaning from the text.	Fonts and sizes are used well in some places, but make the paper look cluttered in others.	The handwriting is readable. There are some differences in letter shape and form, slant, and spacing that make some words easier to read than others.
Score of 1	The speaker's techniques are unclear or distracting to the listener.	The visuals do not make sense with the text.	There are no markers such as title, page numbers, bullets, or subheads.	The writer has used too many different fonts and sizes. It is very distracting to the reader.	The letters are not formed correctly. The slant spacing is not the same throughout the paper, or there is no regular space between words. The paper is very difficult to read.

Scoring Rubrics

Scoring RUBRIC for Narrative Writing

	FOCUS/IDEAS	ORGANIZATION	VOICE	WORD CHOICE	SENTENCE FLUENCY	CONVENTIONS
Score of 4	The narrative fits the purpose for writing and the intended audience very well. The ideas are very interesting.	A beginning introduces characters, setting, and problem. A middle tells events in order. An ending gives the solution.	Characters and events are presented in rich detail, in a very clear and authentic way.	There are many exact, vivid, and sensory words and some dialogue.	All of the sentences are smooth and varied.	There are no grammar, spelling, capitalization, or punctuation errors.
Score of 3	The narrative fits the purpose for writing and the intended audience well. The ideas are interesting.	A beginning introduces characters and problem. Events in the middle are not always in order. An ending gives the solution.	Characters and events are presented in some detail, in a mostly clear and authentic way.	There are some exact, vivid, and sensory words and some dialogue.	Most of the sentences are smooth and varied.	There are a few grammar, spelling, capitalization, or punctuation errors.
Score of 2	The purpose for writing and the intended audience are not very clear. The ideas are not very interesting.	There is no clear beginning, middle, or ending. There is a problem, but not a good solution. Events are not in order.	Characters and events are presented with few details and not enough authenticity.	There are few descriptive words and no dialogue.	Few of the sentences are smooth, and there is little sentence variety.	There are some grammar, spelling, capitalization, and punctuation errors.
Score of 1	The purpose for writing and the intended audience are not clear. The ideas are uninteresting.	There is no beginning, middle, or ending. There is no problem. Events are hard to follow.	Characters and events are presented with little detail and authenticity.	There are no descriptive words and no dialogue.	None of the sentences are smooth, and there is no sentence variety.	There are many grammar, spelling, capitalization, and punctuation errors.

Scoring RUBRIC for Expository Writing

	Score of 4	Score of 3	Score of 2	Score of 1
FOCUS/IDEAS	Writing adheres to a clearly stated topic. All of the main ideas are supported by facts.	Writing mostly adheres to the topic. Most of the main ideas are supported by facts.	Writing does not always adhere to the topic. Some of the main ideas are supported by facts.	Writing does not adhere to the topic. There are few main ideas and supporting facts.
ORGANIZATION	Facts and examples are always presented in a clear and logical order.	Facts and examples are mostly presented in a clear and logical order.	Facts and examples are sometimes presented in a clear and logical order.	Facts and examples are rarely presented in a clear and logical order.
VOICE	The writing shows a strong and confident connection to the topic.	The writing mostly shows a confident connection to the topic.	The writing sometimes shows a confident connection to the topic.	The writing shows a weak connection to the topic.
WORD CHOICE	All of the facts are clear and exact, and all words readers might not know are defined.	Most of the facts are clear and exact, and many words readers might not know are defined.	Some of the facts are clear and exact, and some words readers might not know are defined.	Few of the facts are clear and exact, and none of the words readers might not know are defined.
SENTENCE FLUENCY	There is excellent sentence variety, and all the verb tenses are the same.	There is adequate sentence variety, and most of the verb tenses are the same.	There is some sentence variety, and some of the verb tenses are the same.	There is little sentence variety, and the verb tenses are confusing and often different.
CONVENTIONS	There are no grammar, spelling, capitalization, or punctuation errors.	There are a few grammar, spelling, capitalization, or punctuation errors.	There are some grammar, spelling, capitalization, and punctuation errors.	There are many grammar, spelling, capitalization, and punctuation errors.

Scoring Rubrics

Scoring RUBRIC for Persuasive Writing

	FOCUS/IDEAS	ORGANIZATION	VOICE	WORD CHOICE	SENTENCE FLUENCY	CONVENTIONS
Score of 4	The position is very clear and well supported by three or more good reasons. There is a strong call to action.	There are plenty of facts and details arranged in a logical order.	Feelings about the topic are very clear and strongly expressed.	There are many exact words and phrases.	There is excellent variety in sentence types and lengths.	There are no grammar, spelling, capitalization, or punctuation errors.
Score of 3	The position is clear and supported by two good reasons. There is a call to action.	There are adequate facts and details, mostly arranged in a logical order.	Feelings about the topic are mostly clear and adequately expressed.	There are some exact words and phrases.	There is adequate variety in sentence types and lengths.	There are a few grammar, spelling, capitalization, or punctuation errors.
Score of 2	The position is not clearly stated and is inadequately supported. There is a vague call to action.	There are few facts and details and no logical order.	Feelings about the topic are somewhat clear and weakly expressed.	There are a few exact words and phrases.	There is some variety in sentence types and lengths.	There are some grammar, spelling, capitalization, and punctuation errors.
Score of 1	The position is unclear, and there are no supporting reasons. There is no call to action.	There are no facts or details.	Feelings about the topic are not clear, and there is no personal expression.	There are no exact words and phrases.	There is little variety in sentence types and lengths.	There are many grammar, spelling, capitalization, and punctuation errors.

Scoring RUBRIC for Multipurpose Writing

	FOCUS/IDEAS	ORGANIZATION	VOICE	WORD CHOICE	SENTENCE FLUENCY	CONVENTIONS
Score of 4	Adheres to the topic, is interesting, has a sense of completeness. Ideas are well developed.	Ideas and details are clearly presented and well organized.	Connects with reader in a unique, personal way.	Includes vivid verbs, strong adjectives, specific nouns.	Includes a variety of complete sentences that flow smoothly, naturally.	Shows a strong command of grammar, spelling, capitalization, punctuation.
Score of 3	Mostly adheres to the topic, is somewhat interesting, has a sense of completeness. Ideas are adequately developed.	Ideas and details are mostly clear and generally organized.	Generally connects with reader in a way that is personal and sometimes unique.	Includes some vivid verbs, strong adjectives, specific nouns.	Includes some variety of mostly complete sentences. Some parts flow smoothly, naturally.	Shows a good command of grammar, spelling, capitalization, punctuation.
Score of 2	Does not always adhere to the topic, is somewhat interesting, has some sense of completeness. Ideas are superficially developed.	Ideas and details are not always clear or organized. There is some wordiness or repetition.	Connects somewhat with reader. Sounds somewhat personal, but not unique.	Includes mostly simple nouns and verbs, and may have a few adjectives.	Includes mostly simple sentences, some of which are incomplete.	Some errors in grammar, spelling, capitalization, punctuation.
Score of 1	Does not adhere to the topic, has no sense of completeness. Ideas are vague.	Ideas and details are not organized. Wordiness or repetition hinders meaning.	Does not connect with reader. Does not sound personal or unique.	Includes only simple nouns and verbs, some inaccurate. Writing is not descriptive.	Sentences do not vary. Incomplete sentences hinder meaning.	Frequent errors in grammar, spelling, capitalization, punctuation.

Handwriting

Individual students have various levels of handwriting skills, but they all have the desire to communicate effectively. To write correctly, they must be familiar with concepts of

- size (tall, short)
- open and closed
- capital and lowercase letters
- manuscript vs. cursive letters
- letter and word spacing
- punctuation

To assess students' handwriting skills, review samples of their written work. Note whether they use correct letter formation and appropriate size and spacing. Note whether students follow the conventions of print such as correct capitalization and punctuation. Encourage students to edit and proofread their work and to use editing marks. When writing messages, notes, and letters, or when publishing their writing, students should leave adequate margins and indent new paragraphs to help make their work more readable for their audience.

Stroke and Letter Formation

Most manuscript letters are formed with a continuous stroke, so students do not often pick up their pencils when writing a single letter. When students begin to use cursive handwriting, they will have to lift their pencils from the paper less frequently and will be able to write more fluently. Models for manuscript and D'Nealian handwriting are provided on pages R24–R27.

Position for Writing

Establishing the correct posture, pen or pencil grip, and paper position for writing will help prevent handwriting problems.

Posture Students should sit with both feet on the floor and with hips to the back of the chair. They can lean forward slightly but should not slouch. The writing surface should be smooth and flat and at a height that allows the upper arms to be perpendicular to the surface and the elbows to be under the shoulders.

Writing Instrument An adult-sized number-two lead pencil is a satisfactory writing tool for most students. As students become proficient in the use of cursive handwriting, have them use pens for writing final drafts. Use your judgment in determining what type of instrument is most suitable.

Paper Position and Pencil Grip The paper is slanted along the line of the student's writing arm, and the student uses his or her nonwriting hand to hold the paper in place. The student holds the pencil or pen slightly above the paint line—about one inch from the lead tip.

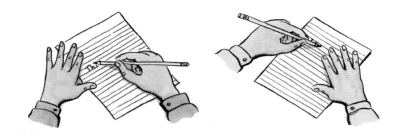

Developing Handwriting

The best instruction builds on what students already know and can do. Given the wide range in students' handwriting abilities, a variety of approaches may be needed.

Writing for Different Purposes   For students who need more practice keeping their handwriting legible, one of the most important understandings is that legible writing is important for clear communication. Provide as many opportunities for classroom writing as possible. For example, students can

- **Make a class directory listing the names of their classmates.**
- **Draw and label graphic organizers, pictures, and maps.**
- **Contribute entries weekly to their vocabulary journals.**
- **Write and post messages about class assignments or group activities.**
- **Record observations during activities.**

Meaningful Print Experiences   Students should participate in meaningful print experiences. They can:

- **Write signs, labels for centers, and other messages.**
- **Label graphic organizers and drawings.**
- **Contribute in group writing activities.**
- **Write independently in notebooks.**

You may also want to have students practice handwriting skills in their first language.

Writing Fluently   To ensure continued rapid advancement of students who come to fifth grade writing fluently, provide

- **A wide range of writing assignments.**
- **Opportunities for independent writing on self-selected and assigned topics.**

A B C D E F G H

I J K L M N O P

Q R S T U V W

X Y Z

a b c d e f g h

i j k l m n o p

q r s t u v w

x y z

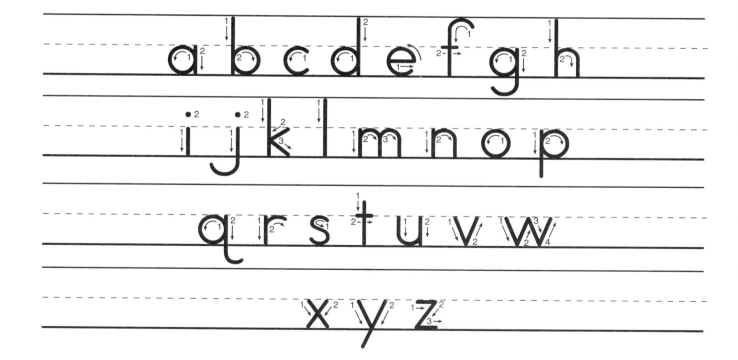

A B C D E F G H

I J K L M N O P

Q R S T U V W

X Y Z

a b c d e f g h

i j k l m n o p

q r s t u v w

x y z

ABCDEFGH
IJKLMNOP
QRSTUVW
XYZ

abcdefgh
ijklmnop
qrstuvw
xyz

Glossary

This glossary contains meanings and pronunciations for some of the words in this book. The Full Pronunciation Key shows how to pronounce each consonant and vowel in a special spelling. At the bottom of the glossary pages is a shortened form of the full key.

Full Pronunciation Key

Consonant Sounds

b	**bib**, ca**bb**age	kw	**ch**oir, **qu**ick	t	**t**igh**t**, stopp**ed**
ch	**ch**ur**ch**, sti**tch**	l	**l**id, need**l**e, ta**ll**	th	**b**a**th**, **th**in
d	**d**ee**d**, maile**d**, pu**ddl**e	m	a**m**, **m**an, du**mb**	th	ba**th**e, **th**is
f	**f**ast, **f**i**f**e, o**ff**, **ph**rase, rou**gh**	n	**n**o, sudd**en**	v	ca**v**e, **v**al**v**e, **v**ine
g	**g**a**g**, **g**et, fin**g**er	ng	thi**ng**, i**nk**	w	**w**ith, **w**olf
h	**h**at, **wh**o	p	**p**o**p**, ha**pp**y	y	**y**es, **y**olk, on**i**on
hw	**wh**ich, **wh**ere	r	**r**oar, **rh**yme	z	ro**s**e, **s**i**z**e, **x**ylophone, **z**ebra
j	**j**udge, **g**em	s	mi**ss**, **s**auce, **s**cene, **s**ee	zh	gara**g**e, plea**s**ure, vi**s**ion
k	**c**at, **k**ick, s**ch**ool	sh	di**sh**, **sh**ip, **s**ugar, ti**ss**ue		

Vowel Sounds

ă	p**a**t, l**au**gh	ŏ	h**o**rrible, p**o**t	ŭ	c**u**t, fl**oo**d, r**ou**gh, s**o**me
ā	**a**pe, **ai**d, p**ay**	ō	g**o**, r**ow**, t**oe**, th**ou**gh	û	c**i**rcle, f**u**r, h**ear**d, t**er**m, t**ur**n, **ur**ge, w**or**d
â	**ai**r, c**a**re, w**ear**	ô	**a**ll, c**au**ght, f**o**r, p**aw**		
ä	f**a**ther, k**o**ala, y**ar**d	oi	b**oy**, n**oi**se, **oi**l	yōō	c**u**re
ĕ	p**e**t, pl**ea**sure, **a**ny	ou	c**ow**, **ou**t	yōō	**a**b**u**se, **u**se
ē	b**e**, b**ee**, **ea**sy, p**ia**no	ōō	f**u**ll, b**oo**k, w**o**lf	ə	**a**go, sil**e**nt, penc**i**l, lem**o**n, circ**u**s
ĭ	**i**f, p**i**t, b**u**sy	ōō	b**oo**t, r**u**de, fr**ui**t, fl**ew**		
ī	r**i**de, b**y**, p**ie**, h**igh**				
î	d**ear**, d**eer**, f**ie**rce, m**e**re				

Stress Marks

Primary Stress ´: bi·ol·o·gy [bī **ŏl**´ ə jē]
Secondary Stress ´: bi·o·log·i·cal [bī´ ə **lŏj**´ ĭ kəl]

G1

A

aspect
Aspect comes from the Latin prefix ad- ("at") and the Latin word root specere, which means "to look." A spectator, which comes from the same word root, is a watcher. A prospect, which is something that is looked forward to, comes from the prefix pro-, "in front of" or "before," and specere.

attract
Attract comes from the Latin prefix ad- ("toward") and the Latin word root trahere, "to pull or to draw." The English word tractor, a vehicle that pulls another vehicle or object, also comes from trahere. Contract, an agreement between two or more parties, comes from the Latin prefix com- ("together") and trahere. Retract, which means "to take back," comes from the Latin prefix re- ("again") and trahere.

ac·knowl·edge (ăk nŏl´ ĭj) *v.* To recognize: *They were acknowledged as experts in science.*

ac·quaint·ed (ə kwānt´ id) *adj.* Familiar or informed: *People acquainted through mutual friends develop meaningful relationships.*

a·cute (ə kyōōt´) *adj.* Keen; perceptive: *The cat has an acute sense of hearing.*

a·dapt·ed (ə dăp´ tid) *adj.* Fitted or suitable, especially for a specific purpose: *A dog's claws are adapted for digging.*

ad·just (ə jŭst´) *v.* To change, set, or regulate in order to improve or make regular: *I adjusted the seatbelts in the car to fit the child.*

ad·mit (ăd mĭt´) *v.* To acknowledge or confess to be true or real: *He admitted that I was right.*

ad·van·tage (ăd văn´ tĭj) *n.* A beneficial factor or feature: *Museums and libraries are some of the advantages of city life.*

an·a·lyze (ăn´ ə līz) *v.* To break up into parts to learn what the parts are: *After analyzing the test results, doctors know how to help patients.*

an·noy·ance (ə noi´ əns) *n.*
1. Something causing trouble or irritation; a nuisance: *His tummy ache was a minor annoyance.*
2. Irritation or displeasure: *He swatted at the mosquito in annoyance.*

an·tique (ăn tēk´) *adj.* Belonging to, made in, or typical of an earlier period: *The castle was full of antique furniture.*

ap·pren·tice (ə prĕn´ tĭs) *n.* A person who works for another without pay in return for instruction in a craft or trade: *The blacksmith's apprentice was trained to make horseshoes.*

as·pect (ăs´ pĕkt) *n.* A way in which something can be viewed by the mind; an element or facet: *The doctor reviewed all aspects of the patient's history.*

as·sum·ing (ə sōō mĭng) *conj.* If; supposing: *Assuming our guests arrive on time, we'll have dinner at 6:00.*

as·ton·ish (ə stŏn´ ĭsh) *v.* To surprise greatly; amaze: *It astonished me that we finished our project on time.*

at·tract (ə trăkt´) *v.* To cause to draw near; direct to oneself or itself by some quality or action: *Crowds were attracted to the beautiful beach.*

au·thor·i·ty (ə thôr´ ĭ tē) *n.* A person or an organization having power to enforce laws, command obedience, determine, or judge: *City authorities closed the street for repairs.*

a·vail·a·ble (ə vā´ lə bəl) *adj.* Capable of being obtained: *Tickets are available at the box office.*

ax·is (ăk´ sĭs) *n.* A straight line around which an object rotates or can be imagined to rotate: *The axis of the earth passes through both of its poles.*

B

back·ground (băk´ ground´) *n.* A person's experience, training, and education: *Math knowledge is a perfect background for jobs in science.*

balk (bôk) *v.* To stop short and refuse to go on: *My pony balked at the gate and would not jump.*

ban·ish (băn´ ĭsh) *v.* To drive out or away; expel: *Banish such thoughts from your mind.*

bare (bâr) *v.* To open up to view; uncover: *The bear opened its mouth and bared its teeth at the wolf.*

bar·ri·er (băr´ ē ər) *n.* Something that blocks movement or passage: *Cows crossing the road are a barrier to traffic.*

bask (băsk) *v.* To rest in and enjoy a pleasant warmth: *The snake has been basking in the spring sunshine for an hour.*

bea·con (bē´ kən) *n.* A light or fire used as a warning or guide: *The flashing beacon on the lighthouse warned the ship that it was nearing the coast.*

beck·on (bĕk´ ən) *v.* To signal (a person), as by nodding or waving: *The principal beckoned us to her office.*

ben·e·fit (bĕn´ ə fĭt) *n.* Something that is of help; an advantage: *The field trip was of great benefit to the students.*

bon·dage (bŏn´ dĭj) *n.* The condition of being held as a slave or serf; slavery or servitude: *The slaves were held in bondage.*

bound (bound) *v.* To leap, jump, or spring: *The deer was bounding into the woods.*

brace (brās) *v.* To give support to; make firm; strengthen: *The camper is bracing a tent with poles.*

bru·tal (brōōt´ l) *adj.* Cruel; ruthless: *The enemy launched a brutal attack.*

bun·dle (bŭn´ dl) *v.* To dress (a person) warmly: *She made sure to bundle up before heading out in the snow.*

beacon

ă rat / ā pay / â care / ä father / ĕ pet / ē be / ĭ pit / ī pie / î fierce / ŏ pot / ō go / ô paw, for / oi oil / ōō book

G2

C

call·ing (kô′ ling) *n.* Job, occupation, profession, or career: *She always felt that nursing was her calling.*

ca·reer (kə rîr′) *n.* A profession or occupation: *She is considering a career in medicine.*

check (chĕk) *v.* To stop or hold back: *The defenders were in charge of checking the opposing offense during the soccer match.*

clam·my (klăm′ ē) *adj.* Unpleasantly damp, sticky, and usually cold: *My feet feel clammy in wet boots.*

col·lapse (kə lăps′) *v.* To fall down or inward suddenly; cave in: *Part of the roof collapsed after the fire.*

col·lect·ed (kə lĕk′ tĭd) *adj.* In full control of oneself; composed; calm: *He did his best to stay cool and collected when making his speech.*

com·mo·tion (kə mō′ shən) *n.* A disturbance or tumult: *The argument created a commotion in the hall.*

com·pe·ti·tion (kŏm pĭ tĭsh′ ən) *n.* A test of skill or ability; a contest: *The soccer match was a competition between two talented teams.*

com·pli·ment (kŏm′ plə mənt) *n.* An expression of praise, admiration, or congratulation: *She gave me a compliment.*

con·cen·trate (kŏn′ sən trāt′) *v.* To keep or direct one's thoughts, attention, or efforts: *It's hard to concentrate on my homework when the television is on.*

con·duct (kŏn′ dŭkt) *n.* The act of directing; management: *The coach was responsible for the team's conduct.*

con·serve (kən sûrv′) *v.* To protect from loss or harm; preserve: *Conserving energy is important.*

con·tent·ment (kən tĕnt′ mənt) *n.* The condition of being content; satisfaction: *Cats purr with contentment when they are satisfied.*

con·trar·y (kŏn′ trĕr ē) *adj.* Stubbornly opposed to others; willful: *Little children often become contrary when they need a nap.*

con·tri·bu·tion (kŏn′ trĭ byōō′ shən) *n.* Something that is given: *We made contributions of food to the poor.*

cramped (krămpt) *adj.* Confined and limited in space: *A family of four lived in a cramped little apartment.*

crit·i·cal (krĭt′ ĭ kəl) *adj.* Extremely important or decisive: *The surgeon performed a critical surgery.*

D

de·bate (dĭ bāt′) *n.* A discussion or consideration of the arguments for and against something: *The class held a debate to discuss the fairness of the school dress code.*

de·cline (dĭ klīn′) *n.* The process or result of going down in number or quality: *Some people think the neighborhood is in decline.*

dec·o·rate (dĕk′ ə rāt′) *v.* To furnish with something attractive, beautiful, or striking; adorn: *The students decorated the auditorium with flowers for graduation.*

del·i·cate (dĕl′ ĭ kĭt) *adj.* Easily broken or damaged; fragile: *Don't drop a delicate china cup.*

de·mol·ish (dĭ mŏl′ ĭsh) *v.* To tear down completely; level: *They demolished the old building.*

de·pend·ent (dĭ pĕn′ dənt) *adj.* Relying on or needing the help of another for support: *Plants are dependent upon sunlight.*

de·sert·ed (dĕ zûrt′ ĭd) *adj.* Left alone; abandoned: *The girl felt deserted when her friends walked away from her.*

de·spite (dĭ spīt′) *prep.* In spite of: *Lewis and Clark traveled to the Pacific despite the unknown dangers.*

des·ti·na·tion (dĕs′ tə nā′ shən) *n.* The place to which a person or thing is going or is sent: *The destination of that package is written on the label.*

de·struc·tion (dĭ strŭk′ shən) *n.* The condition of having been destroyed: *The tornado caused great destruction.*

de·tect (dĭ tĕkt′) *v.* To discover or determine the existence, presence, or fact of: *Detecting the smell of smoke could save your life.*

de·te·ri·o·rate (dĭ tîr′ ē ə rāt′) *v.* To make or become inferior in quality, character, or value; worsen: *The moisture is deteriorating the cover of the old book.*

de·vel·op (dĭ vĕl′ əp) *v.* To bring into being: *The author developed the book's plot gradually.*

dex·ter·i·ty (dĕks tĕr′ ĭ tē) *n.* Skill or grace in using the hands, body, or mind: *A silversmith with dexterity can make beautiful pots.*

competition

destruction
Destruction comes from the Latin prefix *de-* ("off" or "down") and the Latin root *struere*, which means "to construct." Related words are *structure*, "something that is constructed," and *instruct*, "to teach," which come from the same Latin word root.

à rat / ā **pay** / â care / ä **father** / ĕ **pet** / ē be / ĭ **pit** / ī **pie** / î **fierce** / ŏ **pot** / ō go /
ô **paw, for** / oi **oil** / ōō **book**

G4

ōō **boot** / ou **out** / ŭ **cut** / û **fur** / hw **which** / th **thin** / *th* **this** / zh vision / ə **ago,**
silent, pencil, lemon, circus

G5

---

dis·ad·van·tage (dĭs′ ăd văn′ tĭj) *n.* A circumstance or condition that makes it harder to do something or to be successful: *A disadvantage of river transportation is its slowness.*

dis·tract (dĭs trăkt′) *v.* To draw (the attention, for example) away from something: *The noise distracted the students in the library.*

dis·turb (dĭs tûrb′) *v.* To intrude upon; bother: *The visitors were disturbing the musician's practice.*

dom·i·nate (dŏm′ ə nāt′) *v.* To have controlling power or occupy a commanding position over: *The mayor dominated the town hall meeting.*

E

ed·i·ble (ĕd′ ə bəl) *adj.* Safe to eat: *James was surprised to learn that some flowers are edible.*

e·di·tion (ĭ dĭsh′ ən) *n.* The entire number of copies of a book or newspaper printed at one time and having the same content: *Today's edition of the paper is sold out.*

en·vy (ĕn′ vē) *n.* A feeling of discontent at the advantages or successes enjoyed by another, together with a strong desire to have them for oneself: *I was filled with envy when I saw their new car.*

ef·fec·tive (ĭ fĕk′ tĭv) *adj.* Having an intended or expected effect: *The vaccine is effective against the flu.*

ef·fi·cient (ĭ fĭsh′ ənt) *adj.* Acting or producing effectively with a minimum of waste, expense, or unnecessary effort: *High gas mileage makes this car an efficient vehicle.*

el·e·ment (ĕl′ ə mənt) *n.* A part of a whole, especially a fundamental or essential part: *The novel is a detective story with one element of a science fiction story.*

e·lite (ĭ lēt′) or (ā lēt′) *adj.* Relating to a small and privileged group: *The athletes were the elite stars of the sports world.*

em·bar·rass (ĕm băr′ əs) *v.* To cause to feel self-conscious or ill at ease; disconcert: *Not knowing the answer to the question embarrassed me.*

em·bark (ĕm bärk′) *v.* To set out on an adventure; begin: *The sailors embark on an ocean voyage.*

en·dan·gered (ĕn dān′ jərd) *adj.* Nearly extinct: *The endangered animals were put in a preserve.*

ep·i·sode (ĕp′ ĭ sōd) *n.* An incident that forms a distinct part of a story: *The story was divided into six episodes for television.*

ev·i·dent (ĕv′ ĭ dənt) *adj.* Easy to see or notice; obvious: *From the dark clouds, it was evident that it would soon rain.*

ex·cep·tion (ĭk sĕp′ shən) *n.* The act of leaving out or the condition of being left out: *All of our guests have arrived, with the exception of two.*

ex·pe·di·tion (ĕk′ spĭ dĭsh′ ən) *n.* A group making a journey for a specific purpose: *The expedition cheered when they reached the top of Mt. Everest.*

ex·ploit (ĕk′ sploit′) *n.* An act or deed, especially a brilliant or heroic one: *The exploits of Robin Hood helping the poor are legendary.*

ex·tend (ĭk stĕnd′) *v.* To stretch out; reach: *We saw a clothesline extending from the tree to the house.*

F

fac·tor (făk′ tər) *n.* Something that brings about a result: *A willingness to work hard is an important factor in achieving successes.*

faith·ful (fāth′ fəl) *adj.* Loyal and dutiful; trustworthy: *My dog is a faithful friend.*

fare (fâr) *v.* To get along; progress: *How are you faring with your project?*

fa·tal (fāt′ l) *adj.* Causing death: *Disease can prove fatal to humpback whales.*

fea·ture (fē′ chər) *v.* To give special attention to; offer prominently: *The exhibit will feature Native American pottery.*

fe·ro·cious (fə rō′ shəs) *adj.* Extremely savage; fierce: *The tiger's ferocious roar frightened the deer.*

flaw (flô) *v.* To make defective: *The report was flawed with several errors.*

flour·ish (flûr′ ĭsh) *v.* To do well; prosper: *Their business flourished and they became rich.*

foe (fō) *n.* An enemy, opponent, or adversary: *Foes of the new city dump met to fight the plan.*

for·mal (fôr′ məl) *adj.* Structured according to forms or conventions: *The board of directors met in a formal meeting.*

for·mu·la (fôr′ myə lə) *n.* A method of doing something; procedure: *The teacher gave us the formula for writing a good research paper.*

fran·tic (frăn′ tĭk) *adj.* Very excited with fear or anxiety; desperate; frenzied: *She was frantic with worry.*

flaw
Flaw comes from the Norse word *flaga*, which originally meant "stone slab, flake." The word was first used to refer to a defect of character in 1586, and a defect in material things in 1604, probably referring to a fragment, or piece, broken off of a slab of stone.

ferocious

à rat / ā **pay** / â care / ä **father** / ĕ **pet** / ē be / ĭ **pit** / ī **pie** / î **fierce** / ŏ **pot** / ō go /
ô **paw, for** / oi **oil** / ōō **book**

G6

ōō **boot** / ou **out** / ŭ **cut** / û **fur** / hw **which** / th **thin** / *th* **this** / zh vision / ə **ago,**
silent, pencil, lemon, circus

G7

Glossary

household
Household is made up of *house*, meaning "a building made for people to live in," and *hold*, meaning "possession."

identical
Identical comes from a Latin word meaning "identity," the physical characteristics and personality characteristics that make up who a person is. Other English words relating to someone's identity come from the same Latin word root: *identity*, of course, *identify*, and *identification*.

inflate

ful·fill (fŏŏl fĭl′) *v.* To carry out: *Sharon fulfilled her responsibility when she finished cleaning her room.*

func·tion (fŭngk′ shən) *v.* To perform one's normal or proper activity: *The lungs function to take in oxygen.*

G

gor·geous (gôr′ jəs) *adj.* Dazzlingly beautiful or magnificent: *The snowcapped mountains were gorgeous in the sunset.*

grad·u·al·ly (grăj′ ŏŏ əl lē) *adv.* Occurring in small stages or degrees, or by even, continuous change: *The water level in the lake changed gradually.*

grant (grănt) *v.* To give or allow (something asked for): *The teacher granted us permission to leave early.*

guar·di·an (gär′ dē ən) *n.* A person or thing that guards, protects, or watches over: *Courts act as guardians of the law.*

gush (gŭsh) *v.* To flow forth suddenly in great volume: *Water gushed from the broken pipe.*

H

hes·i·tate (hĕz′ ĭ tāt) *v.* To be slow to act, speak, or decide: *We hesitated about whether to go over the rickety bridge.*

hos·tile (hŏs′ təl) *adj.* Not friendly: *Don't give me such a hostile look.*

house·hold (hous′ hōld′) *n.* The members of a family and others living together in a single unit: *Every household has its own rules.*

I

i·den·ti·cal (ī dĕn′ tĭ kəl) *adj.* Exactly equal and alike: *We're riding identical bicycles.*

ig·no·rance (ĭg′ nər əns) *n.* The condition of being unaware; lack of knowledge: *Ignorance of the law is no excuse for breaking it.*

im·press (ĭm prĕs′) *v.* To have a strong, often favorable effect on the mind or feelings of: *The worker impressed his manager and was promoted.*

in·cred·i·bly (ĭn krĕd′ ə blē) *adv.* Hard to believe; unbelievable: *The winner of the race ran incredibly fast.*

in·flate (ĭn flāt′) *v.* To cause to expand with air or gas: *She inflated the tires on her bicycle.*

in·flu·en·tial (ĭn′ flŏŏ ĕn′ shəl) *adj.* Having or exercising influence: *Our city has an influential newspaper.*

in·sight (ĭn′ sīt) *n.* The perception of the true nature of something: *The movie critic's review had brilliant insights about the meaning of the movie.*

in·ten·sive (ĭn tĕn′ sĭv) *adj.* Complete and carried out with care: *After the accident, Mary needed intensive care for a few days.*

in·ter·rupt (ĭn tər ŭpt′) *v.* To do something that hinders or stops the action or conversation of; break in on: *I was about to finish my joke when my brother interrupted me.*

in·tim·i·date (ĭn tĭm′ ĭ dāt) *v.* To fill with fear; frighten, or discourage: *The rough water intimidated us in our light canoe.*

is·sue (ĭsh′ ŏŏ) *n.* A subject being discussed or disputed; a question under debate: *The senator spoke about the issue of reforming campaign laws.*

J

ju·ve·nile (jŏŏ′ və nīl′) *adj.* Young: *The juvenile humpback played with the other young whales.*

K

keen (kēn) *adj.* Acute; sensitive: *The keen eyes of the owl help him to see at night.*

L

lack (lăk′) *v.* To be without: *The neighborhood lacked streetlights.*

launch (lônch) or (länch) *n.* The act of starting or setting into action: *The company was ready for the launch of its new research program.*

lec·ture (lĕk′ chər) *v.* To give an explanation or a scolding: *My father lectured me about going out after dark.*

leg·en·dar·y (lĕj′ ən dĕr′ ē) *adj.* Very well-known; famous: *Paul Revere's ride is legendary.*

lunge (lŭnj) *v.* To make a sudden forward movement: *She was lunging for the ball.*

M

mag·nif·i·cent (măg nĭf′ ĭ sənt) *adj.* Outstanding of its kind; excellent: *Jackie Robinson was a magnificent athlete.*

mar·gin (mär′ jĭn) *n.* An edge or border: *Weeds grew around the margins of the pond.*

ma·rine (mə rēn′) *adj.* Living in or connected to the sea: *Whales are marine mammals.*

mas·ter (măs′ tər) *v.* To become the master of; bring under control: *He mastered a foreign language.*

å rat / å pay / å care / ä father / ĕ pet / ē be / ĭ pĭt / ī pie / î fierce / ŏ pot / ō go / ô paw, for / oi oil / ŏŏ book

ŏŏ boot / ou out / ŭ cut / û fur / hw which / th thin / th this / zh vision / ə ago, silent, pencil, lemon, circus

numb
Numb comes from the Old English word *niman*, which literally means "to take." When you are numb, you cannot feel or move normally; feeling has been taken from you.

ma·ture (mə tyŏŏr′) or (mə tŏŏr′) or (mə chŏŏr′) *v.* To grow older: *Most puppies mature into full-grown dogs in a year or two. adj.* Having reached full growth or development: *A mature redwood can be hundreds of feet tall.*

men·tal (mĕn′ tl) *adj.* Occurring in or done in the mind: *Good writing creates a mental image in the reader's mind.*

midst (mĭdst) or (mĭtst) *n.* The middle position or part; the center: *They planted a tree in the midst of the garden.*

mim·ic (mĭm′ ĭk) *adj.* Acting as an imitation: *A snowman is a mimic person. v.* To resemble closely; simulate: *Children often mimic the mannerisms of their parents.*

min·i·mum (mĭn′ ə məm) *n.* The smallest amount or degree possible: *We need a minimum of an hour to make dinner.*

mi·rage (mĭ räzh′) *n.* An optical illusion in which something that is not really there appears to be seen in the distance: *In the desert we saw mirages that looked like lakes.*

mis·hap (mĭs′ hăp′) *n.* An unfortunate accident: *The trip ended without a mishap.*

mock (mŏk) *v.* To treat with scorn or contempt; deride: *I felt bad for Tom while his brother was mocking him.*

N

nerve (nûrv) *n.* Courage or daring: *It took all my nerve to talk to the new student in our class.*

no·ble (nō′ bəl) *adj.* Having or showing qualities of high moral character, as courage, generosity, or honor: *The knight performed a noble deed.*

numb (nŭm) *adj.* Deprived of the power to feel or move normally: *The boy's toes were numb with cold.*

O

ob·ject (əb jĕkt′) *v.* To be opposed; express disapproval: *We objected to the loud noises downstairs.*

ob·vi·ous (ŏb′ vē əs) *adj.* Easily perceived or understood; evident: *Large football players have an obvious advantage.*

of·fi·cial·ly (ə fĭsh′ əl lē) *adv.* By or in a way relating to an office or post of authority: *The winner was officially declared.*

op·er·a·tor (ŏp′ ə rā′ tər) *n.* A person who operates a machine or device: *The backhoe operator dug a ditch.*

op·po·nent (ə pō′ nənt) *n.* A person or group that opposes another in a battle, contest, controversy, or debate: *The two runners were opponents in the race.*

or·deal (ôr dēl′) *n.* An experience so difficult that it tests the ability to keep trying: *The wind was so strong that walking was an ordeal.*

or·di·nance (ôr′ dn əns) *n.* A statute or regulation, especially one enacted by a city government: *The ordinance requires that every dog be on a leash.*

or·gan·ize (ôr′ gən īz′) *v.* To put together or arrange in an orderly, systematic way: *She was told to organize her messy room.*

o·rig·i·nal (ə rĭj′ ĭ nəl) *adj.* Existing before all others; first: *Virginia is one of the original thirteen Colonies.*

P

pace (pās) *n.* Speed of motion or progress: *I love the fast pace of city life.*

par·tic·u·lar (pər tĭk′ yə lər) *adj.* Separate and different from others of the same group or category: *The painter wanted the walls a particular shade of blue.*

peal (pēl) *n.* A loud burst of noise: *A peal of thunder frightened the baby.*

per·son·al·ly (pûr′ sən əl lē) *adv.* In person or by oneself; without the help of another: *I thanked her personally.*

per·suade (pər swād′) *v.* To cause (someone) to do or believe something by arguing, pleading, or reasoning; convince: *He tried to persuade them to come with us.*

pic·ture (pĭk′ chər) *v.* To form a mental image of; visualize; imagine: *He pictured himself winning the bike race.*

pierce (pĭrs) *v.* To pass into or through (something) with or as with a sharp instrument: *The arrows pierced the target.*

plague (plāg) *v.* To annoy; pester; harass: *The manager was plagued with complaints from angry customers.*

pierce

plunge (plŭnj) *v.* To thrust, throw, or place forcefully or suddenly into something: *The farmer plunged the pitchfork into the hay.*

pre·lim·i·nar·y (prĭ lĭm′ ə nĕr′ ē) *adj.* Prior to or preparing for the main matter, action, or business; introductory: *The architect showed preliminary sketches for a building.*

press·ing (prĕs′ ĭng) *adj.* Demanding immediate attention; urgent: *Hunger is one of the world's most pressing problems.*

å rat / å pay / å care / ä father / ĕ pet / ē be / ĭ pĭt / ī pie / î fierce / ŏ pot / ō go / ô paw, for / oi oil / ŏŏ book

ŏŏ boot / ou out / ŭ cut / û fur / hw which / th thin / th this / zh vision / ə ago, silent, pencil, lemon, circus

provisions

pre·vi·ous·ly (prē´ vē əs lē) *adv.* Before something else in time or order: *Previously, the girls lived in New Orleans.*

prod (prŏd) *v.* To stir to action; urge: *She continually prodded him to do his homework.*

pro·duce (prə dōōs´) *v.* To create by mental or physical effort: *It takes time to produce a painting.*

pro·hib·it (prō hĭb´ ĭt) *v.* To forbid by law or authority: *The pool rules prohibit diving in the shallow end.*

pros·per (prŏs´ pər) *v.* To be fortunate or successful; thrive: *The man prospered after graduating from college.*

pro·vi·sions (prə vĭzh´ ənz) *n.* Stocks of foods and other necessary supplies: *Soldiers at war are given provisions.*

pub·li·ca·tion (pŭb lĭ kā´ shən) *n.* An issue of printed or electronic matter, such as a magazine, offered for sale or distribution: *The school's monthly publication is very informative.*

Q

quake (kwāk) *v.* To shiver or tremble, as from fear or cold: *I was so frightened that my legs were quaking.*

qual·i·fy (kwŏl´ ə fī´) *v.* To make eligible or qualified, as for a position or task: *She received all high grades, qualifying her for the Honor Society.*

quest (kwĕst) *n.* A search, especially for something held valuable or precious: *Space exploration represents the latest quest for knowledge of the universe.*

R

range (rānj) *n.* An extended group or series, especially a row or chain of mountains: *The Rocky Mountain range is in the western United States.*

re·al·i·za·tion (rē əl ĭ zā´ shan) *n.* The act of realizing or the condition of being realized: *The realization that he lost his wallet panicked him.*

rea·son (rē´ zən) *v.* To use the ability to think clearly and sensibly: *I reasoned that I should stay inside because it was raining outside.*

re·bel·lious (rĭ bĕl´ yəs) *adj.* Prone to or participating in a rebellion: *The rebellious farmer fought in the Revolutionary War.*

re·cite (rĭ sīt´) *v.* To repeat or say aloud (something prepared or memorized), especially before an audience: *The players recite the Pledge of Allegiance before each game.*

ă rat / ā pay / â care / ä father / ĕ pet / ē be / ĭ pit / ī pie / î fierce / ŏ pot / ō go / ô paw, for / oi oil / ŏŏ book

G12

rec·ord (rĕk´ ərd) *n.* The highest or lowest measurement known, as in sports events or weather readings: *Death Valley holds the record for least rainfall in a year in the United States.*

reg·u·late (rĕg´ yə lāt) *v.* To control or direct according to a rule or a law: *Rangers regulate park activities.*

re·peal (rĭ pēl´) *v.* To withdraw or cancel officially; revoke: *The Senate voted to repeal the law.*

rep·re·sen·ta·tive (rep´ rĭ zĕn´ ta tĭv) *n.* A person who acts for one or more others: *Rob and Peter were elected as class representatives.*

re·quire (rĭ kwīr´) *v.* To be in need of; need: *Practice is required for a person to become better at a sport.*

re·sem·ble (rĭ zĕm´ bəl) *v.* To have similarity or likeness to; be like: *Some house cats resemble cougars.*

res·i·dent (rĕz´ ĭ dənt) *n.* A person who lives in a particular place: *Residents of the building had to leave because the power was out.*

re·spon·si·bil·i·ty (rĭ spŏn´ sə bĭl´ ĭ tē) *n.* Something that one is responsible for; a duty or obligation: *The two cats are my responsibility.*

re·store (rĭ stôr´) *v.* To bring back to an original condition: *The carpenter wanted to restore the old building.*

re·sume (rĭ zōōm´) *v.* To continue: *Classes resumed after school vacation.*

re·treat (rĭ trēt´) *v.* The act or process of withdrawing, especially from something dangerous or unpleasant: *Patriots forced the Hessians to retreat from battle.*

rev·o·lu·tion (rev´ ə lōō´ shan) *n.* The overthrow of one government and its replacement with another: *The goal of the American Patriots during their revolution was to overthrow British rule.*

romp (rŏmp) *n.* Lively or spirited play: *The girls took their dogs for a romp in the park.*

rou·tine (rōō tēn´) *n.* A series of activities performed or meant to be performed regularly; a standard or usual procedure: *They were delayed by the guards' routine of checking their passports.*

ru·mor (rōō´ mər) *n.* A story or report, usually spread by word of mouth, that has not been established as true: *I heard a rumor that Peter is moving to China.*

rur·al (rŏōr´ əl) *adj.* Of, relating to, or characteristic of the country: *Farms are found in rural areas.*

rural

rus·tle (rŭs´ əl) *v.* To make a soft fluttering sound: *A rustling in the woods scared me away.*

S

sal·va·tion (săl vā´ shan) *n.* Someone or something that saves or rescues: *The spring was the salvation of the thirsty traveler.*

scan (skăn) *v.* To examine (something) closely: *She scanned the report card.*

se·cure (sĭ kyōōr´) *v.* To cause to remain firmly in position or place; fasten: *We secured the ship's hatches.*

seep (sēp) *v.* To pass slowly through small openings; ooze: *Cold air could seep in through the cracks.*

shake (shāk) *v.* To make uneasy; disturb; agitate: *She was shaken by the bad news.*

shat·ter (shăt´ ər) *v.* To break into pieces by force; smash: *The shattered glass was unfixable.*

shift (shĭft) *v.* To move or transfer from one place or position to another: *She shifted the heavy basket in her arms.*

shim·mer (shĭm´ ər) *v.* To shine with a subdued, flickering light: *The shimmering candle could be seen in the darkness.*

shattered

shoul·der (shōl´ dər) *v.* To place on the shoulder or shoulders for carrying: *The dad shouldered the boy so he could see over the crowd.*

shuf·fle (shŭf´ əl) *v.* To walk slowly, while dragging the feet: *I shuffled my feet because I was so tired.*

sim·u·late (sĭm´ ya lāt´) *v.* To have or take on the appearance, form, or sound of; imitate: *We saw a device that simulates space flight.*

spare (spâr) *v.* To show mercy or consideration to: *I spared your feelings by not telling you about the problems.*

spe·cial·ty (spĕsh´ əl tē) *n.* A special pursuit, occupation, talent, or skill: *His specialty is portrait painting.*

sprawl·ing (sprôl´ ĭng) *adj.* Spreading out in different directions: *I looked over the sprawling meadow.*

squal·ling (skwôl´ ĭng) *n.* Loud crying: *The mother stopped her baby's squalling by singing him to sleep. adj.* Crying loudly: *They found the squalling kitten under a bush.*

squash (skwŏsh) *v.* To beat or flatten into a pulp; crush: *He was squashing the peach on the pavement.*

ă rat / ā pay / â care / ä father / ĕ pet / ē be / ĭ pit / ī pie / î fierce / ŏ pot / ō go / ô paw, for / oi oil / ŏŏ book

G14

stag·ger (stăg´ ər) *v.* To move or stand unsteadily, as if carrying a great weight; totter: *Carrying the large boxes, she staggered clumsily.*

stall (stôl) *v.* To slow down or stop the process of; bring to a standstill: *The traffic stalled because of the accident ahead.*

strain (strān) *v.* To work as hard as possible; strive hard: *The boy strained to lift the heavy bag.*

strat·e·gy (străt´ ə jē) *n.* The planning and directing of a series of actions that will be useful in gaining a goal: *General George Washington came up with a strategy for the battle.*

stride (strīd) *n.* A single, long step: *The giraffe took long strides.*

strug·gle (strŭg´ əl) *v.* To make strenuous efforts; strive: *She struggled to stay awake.*

stun (stŭn) *v.* To make someone or something unable to sense what is going on: *The loud noise of the boat engine stunned the fish.*

stunt·ed (stŭn´ tĭd) *adj.* Slowed or stopped abnormally in growth or development: *The stunted tree did not grow because there was no water.*

sum·mon (sŭm´ ən) *v.* To call forth; muster: *The smell of turkey summons memories of past Thanksgiving dinners.*

sup·pos·ed·ly (sə pō´ zĭd lē) *adv.* Seemingly: *Until she lied, she was supposedly my friend.*

surge (sûrj) *v.* To move with gathering force, as rolling waves do: *The crowd surged forward.*

sur·vey (sər vā´) or (sûr´ vā´) *v.* To look over the parts or features of; view broadly: *We surveyed the neighborhood from a hilltop.*

sus·pense (sə spĕns´) *n.* The state or quality of being undecided or uncertain: *The movie left us in suspense.*

sweep·ing (swēp´ ĭng) *adj.* Moving in, or as if in, a long curve: *The castaways waved to the rescue plane with sweeping gestures.*

T

tech·nique (tĕk nēk´) *n.* A procedure or method for carrying out a specific task: *Jason learned techniques for carving wooden toys.*

te·di·ous (tē´ dē əs) *adj.* Tiresome because of slowness, dullness, or length; boring: *He didn't like math, so he thought the lecture was tedious.*

suspense
The word *suspense* comes from the Latin prefix *sub-*, meaning "from below," and the Latin word root *pendere*, "to hang." A *suspension bridge* is a bridge on which the roadway hangs from cables. The related word *depend*, which means "to rely on" or "be determined by," comes from the Latin prefix *de-*, "down from," and *pendere*.

tem·po·rar·y (tĕm′ pə rĕr′ ē) *adj.* Lasting, used, serving, or enjoyed for a limited time; not permanent: *The man was given a **temporary** license until he could get a permanent one.*

ten·ta·tive (tĕn′ tə tĭv) *adj.* Not fully worked out, concluded, or agreed on: *The publisher created a **tentative** production schedule.*

teth·er (tĕth′ ər) *v.* To fasten or restrict: *As a safety measure, the astronaut was **tethered** to the spaceship.*

thrust (thrŭst) *n.* A forceful shove or push: *The knight killed the dragon with a **thrust** of the sword.*

thumb (thŭm) *v.* To scan written matter by turning the pages with the thumb: *She **thumbed** through the magazine.*

tor·ment (tôr′ mĕnt′) *n.* Great physical or mental pain: *I was in a state of **torment** listening to the teacher explain the homework assignment.*

uni-
The basic meaning of the prefix *uni-* is "one." It comes from the Latin prefix *uni-*, which in turn comes from the Latin word root *unus*, "one." The word *unicorn*, a mythological one-horned horse, comes from *uni-* and the Latin word root *cornu*, "horn." *Uniform, unique, unison,* and *unicycle* all have "one" in their definitions.

trans·form (trăns fôrm′) *v.* To change the nature, function, or condition of; convert: *The caterpillar **transformed** into a butterfly.*

treat (trēt) *v.* To give medical care to a person or animal or for an illness: *Some doctors make a specialty of **treating** birds only.*

trek (trĕk) *n.* A long, hard journey, especially on foot: *Settlers made the **trek** to the West.*

trib·u·tar·y (trĭb′ yə tĕr′ ē) *n.* A river or stream that flows into a larger river or stream: *People enjoy boating on **tributaries** of the Mississippi River.*

typ·i·cal·ly (tĭp′ ĭ kəl lē) *adv.* In a way that is usual for a kind, group, or category: ***Typically**, school begins early in the morning.*

U

un·doubt·ed·ly (ŭn **dou**′ tĭd lē) *adv.* Beyond question; undisputedly: *He was **undoubtedly** glad he made it to the meeting on time.*

un·e·vent·ful (ŭn′ ĭ **vĕnt**′ fəl) *adj.* Having no significant events: *The trip was **uneventful**.*

u·ni·form (yōō′ nə fôrm′) *adj.* Being the same as another or others: *He built the porch out of planks of **uniform** length.*

u·nique (yōō **nēk**′) *adj.* Being the only one of its kind: *The puppy had a **unique** mark on his back.*

u·ni·son (yōō′ nĭ sən) or (yōō′ nĭ zən) *n.* At the same time; at once: *The rowers must work in **unison** to win.*

un·ob·served (ŭn′ əb **zûrvd**′) *adj.* Not seen or noticed: *We crept up the walkway **unobserved**.*

ă rat / ā pay / â care / ä father / ĕ pet / ē be / ĭ pit / ī pie / î fierce / ŏ pot / ō go / ô paw, for / oi oil / ŏŏ book

up·right (ŭp′ rīt′) *adv.* Straight up: *I taught my dog to sit **upright** and beg for a biscuit.*

urge (ûrj) *v.* To entreat earnestly and repeatedly; exhort: *The coach continues to **urge** us to stay in shape over summer vacation.*

V

vain (vān) *adj.* Having no success: *Firefighters made a **vain** attempt to save the burning building.*

var·y (vâr′ ē) *v.* To be different or diverse: *His diet will **vary** from day to day.*

veg·e·ta·tion (vĕj′ ĭ **tā**′ shən) *n.* The plants in an area or region; plant life: *There is little **vegetation** at the North Pole.*

ver·sion (vûr′ zhən) *n.* A type: *This new car is a reworked **version** of an older model.*

view·point (vyōō′ point′) *n.* A position from which something is observed or considered; a point of view: *From the **viewpoint** of the British, their navy was the best.*

vil·lain (vĭl′ ən) *n.* A wicked or very bad person; a scoundrel: *The evil brothers were the **villains** of the movie.*

vi·o·la·tion (vī ə **lā**′ shən) *n.* The act or an instance of breaking or ignoring or the condition of (a law or rule) being broken or ignored: *She was fined for traffic **violations**.*

W

wheel (hwēl) *v.* To turn or whirl around in place: *She **wheeled** to see what had made the loud sound behind her.*

wob·ble (wŏb′ əl) *v.* To move unsteadily from side to side: *The old table **wobbled**.*

villain
The meaning of *villain* has changed over the centuries. The word comes from the Latin word root *villa*, which means "country house." It originally meant a peasant or serf who lived in the country. It gradually changed to mean a person with coarse feelings or a foolish person, and then a wicked person.

vegetation

ōō boot / ou out / ŭ cut / û fur / hw which / th thin / th this / zh vision / ə ago, silent, pencil, lemon, circus

Acknowledgments

The Birchbark House written and illustrated by Louise Erdrich. Copyright © 1999 by Louise Erdrich. Reprinted by permission of Hyperion Books. All rights reserved.
Can't You Make Them Behave, King George? by Jean Fritz, illustrated by Tomie dePaola. Text copyright © 1977 by Jean Fritz. Illustrations copyright © 1977 by Tomie dePaola. Reprinted by permission of Coward-McCann, a division of Penguin's Young Readers Group, a member of Penguin Group (USA). Inc., and Gina Maccoby Literary Agency.
Cougars by Patricia Corrigan, illustrated by John F. McGee. Copyright © 2001 by Northword Press. Reprinted by permission of T & N Children's Publishing.
Dangerous Crossing by Stephen Krensky, illustrated by Greg Harlin. Text copyright © 2005 by Stephen Krensky. Illustrations copyright © 2005 by Greg Harlin. All rights reserved including the right of reproduction in whole or in any form. Reprinted by permission of Dutton Children's Books, a member of Penguin's Young Readers Group, a division of Penguin Group (USA) Inc., and The Gersh Agency.
Darnell Rock Reporting by Walter Dean Myers. Copyright © 1994 by Walter Dean Myers. Reprinted by permission of Random House Children's Books, a division of Random House, Inc.
"Deanie McLeanie" by Walter Dean Myers. Copyright © 1994 by Walter Dean Myers. Reprinted by permission of Miriam Altshuler Literary Agency.
"Disturbed, the cat" from *The Penguin Book of Japanese Verse* (1967). Translated by Geoffrey Bownas and Anthony Thwaite. Reprinted by permission of Geoffrey Bownas.
"The Dog Newspaper" from *Five Pages a Day: A Writer's Journey* by Peg Kehret. Text copyright © 2005 by Peg Kehret. Reprinted by permission of Albert Whitman & Company and Curtis Brown, Ltd.
Don Quixote and the Windmills, a retelling by Eric A. Kimmel from *The Ingenious Don Quixote De La Mancha* by Miguel de Cervantes Saavedra, pictures by Leonard Everett Fisher. Retelling copyright © 2004 by Shearwater Books. Pictures copyright © 2004 by Leonard Everett Fisher. Reprinted by permission of Farrar, Straus & Giroux, LLC.
El Diario de Elisa by Doris Luisa Oronoz. Text copyright © by Doris Luisa Oronoz. Reprinted by permission of the author.
Everglades Forever: Restoring America's Great Wetlands by Trish Marx, photographs by Cindy Karp. Text copyright © 2004 by Trish Marx. Photographs copyright © 2004 by Cindy Karp. Reprinted by permission of Lee & Low Books, Inc., NY, NY 10016.
"Genius" from *A Dime a Dozen* by Nikki Grimes. Copyright © 1998 by Nikki Grimes. Reprinted by permission of Dial Books for Young Readers, a division of Penguin Young Readers Group, a member of Penguin Group (USA) Inc. All rights reserved.
"Good Sportsmanship" from *All in Sport* by Richard Armour. Copyright © 1972 by Richard Armour. Reprinted by permission of Geoffrey Armour.
Interrupted Journey: Saving Endangered Sea Turtles by Kathryn Lasky, photographs by Christopher G. Knight. Text copyright © 2001 by Kathryn Lasky. Photographs copyright © 2001 by Christopher G. Knight. Reprinted by permission of Candlewick Press, Inc.
"James Forten" from *Now Is Your Time! The African-American Struggle for Freedom* by Walter Dean Myers. Copyright © 1991 by Walter Dean Myers. Reprinted by permission of HarperCollins Publishers.
"Karate Kid" by Jane Yolen from *Opening Day: Sports Poems*, published by Harcourt Brace & Co. Copyright © 1996 by Jane Yolen. Reprinted by permission of Curtis Brown, Ltd.
"LAFFF" by Lensey Namioka from *Within Reach: Ten Stories* edited by Donald P. Gallo. Copyright © 1983 by Lensey Namioka. Reprinted by permission of Lensey Namioka. All rights reserved by the author.
Lewis and Clark by R. Conrad Stein. Copyright © 1997 by Children's Press®, a division of Grolier Publishing Co., Inc. All rights reserved. Reprinted by permission of Scholastic Library Publishing.
Lunch Money by Andrew Clements. Text copyright © 2005 by Andrew Clements. Reprinted by permission of Simon & Schuster's Books for Young Readers, a division of Simon & Schuster's Children's Publishing Division, and Writer's House, LLC, acting as agent for the author.
"A Package for Mrs. Jewls" from *Wayside School is Falling Down* by Louis Sachar, illustrated by Adam McCauley. Text copyright © 1989 by Louis Sachar. Illustrations copyright © 2003 by Adam McCauley. Reprinted by permission of HarperCollins Publishers.
Off and Running by Gary Soto. Text copyright © 1996 by Gary Soto. Reprinted by permission of the author and BookStop Literary Agency. All rights reserved. Jacket cover reprinted by permission of Random House Children's Books, a division of Random House, Inc.
Old Yeller by Fred Gipson. Copyright © 1956 by Fred Gipson. Reprinted by permission of HarperCollins Publishers and McIntosh & Otis, Inc.
Rachel's Journal written and illustrated by Marissa Moss. Copyright © 1998 by Marissa Moss. All rights reserved. Reprinted by permission of Houghton Mifflin Harcourt Publishing Company and the Barbara S. Kouts Agency.
"Rockett Girls" from *Double Dutch: A Celebration of Jump Rope, Rhyme and Sisterhood* by Veronica Chambers. Copyright © 2002 by Veronica Chambers. Reprinted by permission of Hyperion Books for Children and the Sandra Dijkstra Literary Agency. All rights reserved.
"A Seeing Poem" from *Seeing Things* by Robert Froman, published by Thomas Y. Crowell, 1974. Copyright © 1974 by Robert Froman. Reprinted by permission of Katherine Froman.
Storm Warriors by Elisa Carbone. Copyright © 2001 by Elisa Carbone. Cover illustration copyright © 2001 by Don Demers. Reprinted by permission of Alfred A. Knopf, an imprint of Random House Children's Books, a division of Random House, Inc.

They Called Her Molly Pitcher by Anne Rockwell, illustrated by Cynthia von Buhler. Text copyright © 2002 by Anne Rockwell. Illustrations copyright © 2002 by Cynthia von Buhler. Reprinted by permission of Alfred A. Knopf, a division of Random House Children's Books, a division of Random House, Inc.
"Tiger" from *All the Small Poems and Fourteen More* by Valerie Worth. Copyright © 1987, 1994 by Valerie Worth. Reprinted by permission of Farrar, Straus and Giroux, LLC.
"A Tomcat Is" by J. Patrick Lewis from *Cat Poems*, published by Holiday House. Copyright © 1987 by J. Patrick Lewis. Reprinted by permission of Curtis Brown, Ltd.
"To Write Poetry/ Para escribir peosia" from *Iguanas in the Snow and Other Winter Poems/Iguanas en la nieve y otras poemas de invierno* by Francisco X. Alarcón. Copyright © 2001 by Francisco X. Alarcón. Reprinted by permission of Children's Book Press, San Francisco, CA, www.childrensbookpress.org
"Tucket's Travels" from *Tucket's Gold* by Gary Paulsen. Copyright © 1999 by Gary Paulsen. Reprinted by permission of Flannery Literary.
Ultimate Field Trip 5: Blasting Off to Space Academy by Susan E. Goodman, photographs by Michael J. Doolittle. Text copyright © 2001 by Susan E. Goodman. Photographs copyright © 2001 by Michael J. Dootlittle. Reprinted by permission of Atheneum Books for Young Readers, an imprint of Simon & Schuster Children's Publishing Division.
We Were There, Too! by Phillip Hoose. Text copyright © 2001 by Phillip Hoose. All rights reserved. Maps by Debra Ziss. Reprinted by permission of Farrar, Straus and Giroux, LLC.

Credits

Photo Credits

Placement Key: (t) top; (b) bottom; (l) left; (r) right; (c) center; (bg) background; (fg) foreground; (i) inset.
TOC 4 (b) ©Michael J. Doolittle; **TOC 6** (b) ©Michael H. Francis; **TOC 8** ©Don Farrall/Photodisc/Getty Images; **17A** ©Fancy Photography/Veer; **17B** (spread) ©Fancy Photography/Veer; (inset) ©Siede Preis; **18** (tl) ©Jim West/Alamy; (tr) ©Blend Images/Alamy; (bl) ©Patrick Giardino/Getty Images; (br) ©Inspirestock/Jupiter Images; **19** (tl) ©Charles Gupton/CORBIS; (tc) ©Tom Morrison/Getty Images; (tr) ©Blend Images/Alamy; (bl) ©Ableimages/Getty Images; (bc) ©Rick Gayle/Corbis; (br) ©Digital Vision Ltd./SuperStock; **20-21** ©Masterfile; **20** (inset) ©Masterfile; **22** (b) ©Courtesy of Bruce MacPherson; (t) ©HANDOUT/Newscom; **37** (t) ©Ron Levine/Getty Images; **39** C Squared Studios/Photodisc; **42** (tl) ©Digital Vision/Getty Images; (tr) © NASA/epa/CORBIS; (bl) ©NASA/Handout/epa/Corbis; (br) ©NASA/Roger Ressmeyer/CORBIS; **43** (tl) ©Mike Dunning/DK IMAGES; (tc) ©Roger Ressmeyer/CORBIS; (tr) ©NASA/Roger Ressmeyer/CORBIS; (bl) ©CHARLES W LUZIER/Reuters/Corbis; (bc) © Bloomimage/Corbis; (br) ©Corbis; **44-45** (bkgd) ©Corbis; **46** (t) ©Courtesty of Susan E. Goodman; **46-47** ©Michael J. Doolittle; **48-59** (t) ©Taxi/Getty Images; **48** (l) ©Michael J. Doolittle; **49** ©Michael J. Doolittle; **50** ©Michael J. Doolittle; **51** ©Michael J. Doolittle; **52** (b) ©Michael J. Doolittle; **53** ©Michael J. Doolittle; **54-55** ©Michael J. Doolittle; **55** (r) ©Michael J. Doolittle; (c) ©Michael J. Doolittle; **56** ©Michael J. Doolittle; **57** (b) ©Michael J. Doolittle; **58-59** ©Jeff Greenberg/PhotoEdit; **58** (inset) ©Nasa; **59** (tr) Photo Royalty Free; (br) Getty Images/PhotoDisc; **60** (inset) ©NASA; **61** (br) ©NASA Marshall Space Flight Center; **62-63** (bkgd) ©NASA/Getty Images; (starry sky) ©Ian McKinnell/Photographer's Choice/Getty Images; **63** (t) ©PhotoLink/APEX; **65** ©Plain Pictures/Jupiter Images; **68** (tl) ©Tony Freeman/PhotoEdit; (tr) ©Image Source Black/Alamy; (bl) ©Corbis; (br) ©Age Fotostock/SuperStock; (graph) ©Beard & Howell/Getty Images; **69** (tl) ©Amy Meyers/Shutter Stock; (tc) ©Paul Conklin/PhotoEdit; (tr) ©Spencer Grant/PhotoEdit; (bl) ©Mary Kate Denny/PhotoEdit; (bc) ©Adam Taylor/Getty Images; (br) ©LWA-Dann Tardif/CORBIS; **70** ©Michael Newman/PhotoEdit; **70-71** (bkgd) ©J. Schwanke/Alamy; **72** (b) ©Courtesy of Eric Velasquez; **86** (yellow button) ©1995 PhotoDisc; **88** (bkgd) ©Age fotostock/SuperStock; **91** ©David Young-Wolff/PhotoEdit; **94** (tl) ©BananaStock/SuperStock; (tr) ©Marc Vaughn/Masterfile; (bl) ©PNC/Getty Images; (br) ©Tom Rosenthat/SuperStock; **95** (tl) ©WireImageStock/Masterfile; (tc) ©David Sanger Photography/Alamy; (tr) ©Rudi Von Briel/PhotoEdit; (bl) ©Tim Pannell/Corbis; (bc) ©David Madison/Getty Images; (br) ©LWA-Dann Tardif/CORBIS; **96-97** ©John Fletcher/www.usajumprope.org; **98-99** ©John Fletcher/www.usajumprope.org; **98** ©Courtesy Hyperion Books for Children; **100** (t) ©Lawrence Manning/Corbis; **100-101** ©Debbie Egan-Chin; **102-103** ©Debbie Egan Chin; **103** (t) ©Debbie Egan-Chin; **104-105** (t) ©Bob Jacobson/Corbis; **104** ©Debbie Egan-Chin; **105** ©Debbie Egan-Chin; **106-107** ©Ron Tarver; 108 ©Ron Tarver; **109** (tr) PhotoDisc - royalty free; **109** (br) Stockbyte/Getty Images Royalty-Free; **110-111** (bkgd) ©George Shelley/CORBIS; 110 (inset) ©Tom Carter/PhotoEdit; **112-113** ©Warren Morgan/CORBIS; (tr) ©D. Hurst/Alamy; (br) ©www.imagesource.com; **115** ©Michael Newman/Photoedit; **118** (tl) ©ImageState/Alamy; (tr) ©Mike Powell/Allsport Concepts/Getty Images; (bl) ©Galina Barskaya/Shutter Stock; (br) ©Arco Images/Alamy; **119** (tl) ©Jamal A. Wilson/Stringer/AFP/Getty Images; (tc) ©Alistair Berg/Taxi/Getty Images; (tr) ©Nick Garbutt/npl/Minden Pictures; (bl) ©Andrew Fox/Alamy; (br) ©Peter Beck/Corbis; (bc) ©Digital Vision/Alamy; **120-121** ©Tom Carter/PhotoEdit; **122** (b) ©Courtesy of Jim Tsinganos; (t) ©Courtesy of Terry Trueman; **133** (tr) Brand X Pictures/GettyImages; (tr) Stockbyte Photo; (br) Corbis; **134-135** (t) © www.photo-hartmann.de; **136** (inset) © www.photo-hartmann.de; **137** (b) ©George S. de Blonsky/Alamy; **139** ©Susanna Price/Dorling Kindersley/Getty Images; **144** (b) ©Jeff Greenberg/Alamy; **145A** ©Richard Cummins/Lonely Planet Images; **145B** (spread) ©Judy Bellah/Lonely Planet Images; (inset) ©Richard Cummins/Lonely Planet Images; (title) ©Siri Stafford/Getty Images; **146** (tl) ©Roger Bamber/Alamy; (tr) ©Gerry Ellis/Getty Images; (bl) ©David Frazier/Corbis; (br) ©Raymond Gehman/CORBIS; **147** (tl) ©Kari K. Greer/911 Pictures; (tc) ©Mike Mcmillan/Spotfire Images; (tr) © Bruce

Turbeville; (bl) ©Andrea Pistolesi/Getty Images; (bc) ©Lucy Nicholson/Reuters/Corbis; (br) ©Michael Sales/ The Image Bank/Getty Images; **148-149** (bkgd) ©Mike Mcmillan/Spotfire Images; **148** (l) ©Kevin R. Morris/ CORBIS; (r) ©Mike Mcmillan/Spotfire Images; **150-151** (bkgd) ©Shoot/zefa/Corbis; **150** ©Courtesy Harcourt Children's Books; **151** (inset) ©Raymond Gehman/ CORBIS; **152** ©USDA Forest Service; **153** ©Raymond Gehman/CORBIS; **154** (t) ©Day 2 -- Taking shelter - Karen Tapia-Anderson/Los Angeles Times; **154-155** (b) ©Lonely Planet Images/Getty Images; **155** ©USDA Forest Service; **156** ©National Interagency Fire Center; **158-159** ©Kim Kulish/Corbis; **160-161** (b) ©Lonely Planet Images/ Getty Images; **160** (b) © California Department of Forestry and Fire Protection; **161** (t) © California Department of Forestry and Fire Protection; **162** (t) © California Department of Forestry and Fire Protection; **162-163** © California Department of Forestry and Fire Protection; **163** (br) Corbis; (tl) Corbis; (tr) Brand X Pictures; **167** (tr) ©Sandy Huffaker/Stringer/Getty Images; **172** (tl) ©The Granger Collection, New York; (bl) ©The Granger Collection, New York; (br) ©The Granger Collection, New York; (tr) ©The Granger Collection, New York; **173** (tl) ©Catherine Karnow/CORBIS; (tr) ©Steve Kaufman/CORBIS; (bl) ©Adam Woolfitt/CORBIS; (bc) ©The Granger Collection, New York; (br) ©Juniors Bildarchiv/Alamy; (tc) ©Layne Kennedy/Corbis; **174-175** (bkgd) ©The Granger Collection, New York; **176** (b) ©Courtesy of Mark Elliot ; (t) ©Thomas D. McAvoy/ Stringer/Time & Life Pictures/Getty Images; **187** (br) Digital Stock; **191** (tr) ©L. Zacharie/Alamy; **193** ©Marmaduke St. John/Alamy; **196** (tl) ©Daryl Benson/ Masterfile; (tr) ©David Frazier/PhotoEdit; (bl) ©Mary H. Swift/Alamy; (br) ©Peter Arnold, Inc./Alamy; **197** (tl) © Paul Glendell/Alamy; (tc) ©David Frazier/PhotoEdit; (tr) ©Michael DeFreitas Wildlife/Alamy; (bl) ©Photodisc/ SuperStock; (bc) ©Wolfgang Kaehler/CORBIS; (br) ©Jeff Greenberg/PhotoEdit; **198** (inset) ©Teake Zuidema/The Image Works; **198-199** (bkgd) ©Buddy Mays/Corbis; **200-201** ©2004 Cindy Karp/Lee & Low Books Inc.; **200** ©Courtesy of Trish Marx and Cindy Karp; **202** ©2004 Cindy Karp/Lee & Low Books Inc.; **203** (b) ©2004 Cindy Karp/Lee & Low Books Inc.; **204** (t) ©2004 Cindy Karp/ Lee & Low Books Inc.; **204-205** (b) ©2004 Cindy Karp/ Lee & Low Books Inc.; **206-207** ©2004 Cindy Karp/Lee & Low Books Inc.; **208** (l) ©2004 Cindy Karp/Lee & Low Books Inc.; **208-209** ©2004 Cindy Karp/Lee & Low Books Inc.; **210-211** ©2004 Cindy Karp/Lee & Low Books Inc.; **212-213** ©2004 Cindy Karp/Lee & Low Books Inc.; **213** (tl) Corel Stock Photo Library - royalty free; (br) Robin Hill/Digital Vision/Getty Images; **214-215** (bkgd) ©Mark A. Johnson/Corbis; **215** (inset) ©Craig Aurness/Corbis; **216-217** (bkgd) ©Scenics of America/PhotoLink; **216** (inset) ©Jeff Vanuga/Corbis; **217** (t) ©Renaud Visage/ Getty Images; **219** ©Theo Allofs/CORBIS; **222** (tl) ©Reuters/CORBIS; (tr) ©Joe Raedle/Staff/Getty Images; (bl) ©John Kershaw/Alamy; (br) ©Barbara Davidson/ Dallas Morning News/Corbis; **223** (tl) ©Jeff Curtes/ Corbis; (tc) ©Tony Freeman/PhotoEdit; (tr) ©Jean-Bernard Vernier/CORBIS SYGMA; (bl) ©Mark & Audrey Gibson; (bc) ©Michael Ventura/PhotoEdit; (br) ©RubberBall/SuperStock; **224-225** (bkgd) ©David A.

Harvey/Getty Images; **226** (b) ©Courtesy of James Ransome; (t) ©Courtesy Random House; **237** (br) Getty; **238-239** (bkgd) ©USCG Image Library; **240-241** (bkgd) ©USCG Image Library; **240** (inset) ©Courtesy of Sarah Manning Pope, Mount Olive NC/Chicamacomico Historical Association; **241** (t) ©Joe Skipper/CORBIS; **243** ©Mitchell Funk/Photographer's Choice/Getty Images; **246** (tl) ©Juniors Bildarchiv/Alamy; (tr) ©Mark C Ross/Getty Images; (bl) ©Richard Hamilton Smith/CORBIS; (br) ©CORBIS/Jupiter Images; **247** (tl) ©E. A. Janes/Photo Researchers, Inc.; (tc) ©Daniel J. Cox/CORBIS; (tr) ©Chad Johnston/Masterfile; (bl) ©Pete Oxford/Minden Pictures; (bc) ©Advance Images/Alamy; (br) ©Ian O'Leary/Stone/Getty Images; **248-249** (bkgd) Fr©ank Burek/Corbis; **250-251** ©W. Perry Conway/Aerie Nature Series, Inc; **252-253** ©Michael H. Francis; **254-255** (t) ©Michael H. Francis; **256** ©Tom & Pat Leeson; **257** ©Michael H. Francis; **258** (t) ©Erwin and Peggy Bauer/ Wildstock; **259** (b) ©W. Perry Conway/Aerie Nature Series, Inc; **260-261** ©DLILLC/Corbis; **261** (tl) Corel Stock Photo Library - royalty free; (br) Getty; **265** (b) ©DK Limited/CORBIS; **267** © Philip Schermeister/ National Geographic/Getty Images; **272** (b) ©Plush Studios/Getty Images; (t) ©Richard Cummins/Lonely Planet Images; **273A** ©Colonial Williamsburg; (title) ©Tom Grill/Getty Images; **273B** (bkgd) ©Colonial Williamsburg; (inset) ©Dorling Kindersley; **274** (tl) ©North Wind/North Wind Picture Archives; (tr) ©The Granger Collection, New York; (bl) ©Look and Learn/The Bridgeman Art Library; (br) ©Science Museum, London, UK/BridgemanArt Library; **275** (tl) ©National Geographic/Getty Images; (tc) ©North Wind/North Wind Picture Archives; (tr) ©Paul A. Souders/Corbis; (bl) ©The Granger Collection, New York; (bc) ©The Granger Collection, New York; (br) ©BATES LITTLEHALES/ National Geographic Image Collection; **276-277** (bkgd) ©Archivo Iconografico, S.A./CORBIS; **276** (l) ©Bridgeman Art Library; (r) ©The Corcoran Gallery of Art/CORBIS; **279** (frame) ©Image Farm; (b) ©Courtesy of Greg Harlin; (t) ©Courtesy of Stephen Krensky; **291** (tl) Corbis; (br) Steve Allen/Brand X/Corbis; **292-293** (bkgd) ©Mark Lewis/Getty Images; **293** (inset) ©Chris Hondros/ Getty Images; **294** ©Michael Ainsworth/Dallas Morning News/Corbis; **295** (t) ©Bridgeman Art Library; **297** ©Danny Lehman/Corbis; **300** (tr) ©The Granger Collection, New York; (bl) ©North Wind/North Wind Picture Archives; (br) A View of the House of Commons, engraved by B. Cole (fl.1748-75) (engraving), English School, (18th century) /Stapleton Collection, UK, /The Bridgeman Art Library; **301** (tl) ©The Granger Collection, New York; (tc) ©The Granger Collection, New York; (tr) ©The Granger Collection, New York; (bl) ©The Granger Collection, New York; (bc) ©Kevin Fleming/CORBIS; (br) ©Joseph Sohm; Visions of America/CORBIS; **302-303** (bkgd) ©SuperStock; **304** ©Courtesy of Penguin Young Readers Group; **315** (tl) C Squared Studios/PhotoDisc/ Getty Images; (br) Comstock; **319** (b) ©Paul Barton/ CORBIS; **321** (b ©The Granger Collection, New York; **324** (tl) ©The Granger Collection, New York; (tr) ©The Granger Collection, New York; (bl) ©Bettmann/CORBIS; (br) ©The Granger Collection, New York; **325** (tl) ©Bettmann/CORBIS; (tc) ©The Granger Collection, New

G20

York; (tr) ©The Granger Collection, New York; (bl) ©Bettmann/CORBIS; (bc) ©The Granger Collection, New York; (br) ©North Wind Picture Archives/Alamy; **326-327** (bkgd) ©The Granger Collection, New York; ©Courtesy Houghton Mifflin Trade and Reference Division; **339** (tr) Getty; **345** ©The Granger Collection, New York; **348** (tl) ©North Wind/North Wind Picture Archives ; (tr) ©The Colonial Williamsburg Foundation; (bl) © Kelly-Mooney Photography/Corbis; (br) ©Bettmann/CORBIS; **349** (tl) ©The Granger Collection, New York; (tc) ©Colonial Williamsburg Foundation; (tr) ©T. David Reed; (bl) ©North Wind/North Wind Picture Archives; (bc) ©Colonial Williamsburg Foundation; (br) ©The Granger Collection, New York ; **350-351** (bkgd) ©Dave G. Houser/Corbis; **350** (l) ©North Wind/North Wind Picture Archives; (r) ©Stock Montage/Contributor/ Hulton Archive/Getty Images; **352** (b) ©courtesy of Steve Noble; (t) ©Hugh Grannum/DETROIT FREE PRESS/ Newscom; **358** ©The Granger Collection, New York; **360** ©North Wind/North Wind Picture Archives; **362** ©Leon Gardiner Collection/Historical Society of Pennsylvania; **363** (tr) Corel Stock Photo Library - royalty free; **364-365** ©Hmco/Coppola Studios Inc.; **366** (t) ©Ross Warner/ Alamy; **369** ©The Granger Collection, New York; **372** (tl) ©The Granger Collection, New York; (tr) ©Colonial Williamsburg Foundation; (bl) ©North Wind/North Wind Picture Archives; (br) ©The Corcoran Gallery of Art/ Corbis; **373** (tc) ©The Granger Collection, New York; (tr) ©Colonial Williamsburg Foundation; (bl) ©The Colonial Williamsburg Foundation; (bl) ©Colonial Williamsburg Foundation; (br) ©Leif Skoogfors/Corbis; (tl) ©Colonial Williamsburg Foundation; **374-375** (bkgd) ©Hmco/ Coppola Studios Inc.; **374** (inset) ©Kevin Fleming/ CORBIS; **376-377** (bkgd) ©Alan Crostwaite/Acclaim Images; **376** (inset) ©Courtesy Phillip Hoose; **377** (bc) ©K. William Kautz; **378-388** border ©Saniphoto/ Shutterstock; **378** ©Museum of Fine Arts, Boston; **379** (r) ©The Granger Collection, New York; (r) © Burke/Triolo Productions/Brand X/Corbis; **380** ©JupiterImages/Brand X/Alamy; **381** ©The Granger Collection, New York; **382** ©Don Farrall/Photodisc/Getty Images; **383** ©Burke/ Triolo Productions/Brand X/Corbis; **384** ©Michael Freeman/Corbis; **385** ©The Granger Collection, New York; ©Burke/Triolo Productions/Brand X/Corbis; **386** (l) ©Colonial Williamsburg Foundation; **387** ©darlenebordwell.com; **388** ©United States Postal Service; **389** ©Alan Crostwaite/Acclaim Images; ©Jodie Coston/ Acclaim Images; (br) Getty Images/Digital Vision; **400** (b) ©Coinery/Alamy; (t) ©Dorling Kindersley; **401** (insert) ©Ariel Skelley/CORBIS; **402** (tl) ©Spencer Grant/ PhotoEdit; (tr) ©Lindsey Parnaby/epa/Corbis; (bl) ©Jeff Greenber/PhotoEdit; (br) ©Masterfile; **403** (tl) ©Seth Wenig/Reuters/Corbis; (tc) ©Lenora Gim/Getty Images; (bl) ©Paul Harris/Dorling Kindersley; (br) ©Everett Collection; **406** (b) ©Courtesy of Adam Gustavson; **418** (t) ©1934 by King Features Syndicate/Library of Congress; **419** (b) ©Hulton Archive/Handout/Getty Images; **423** ©Masterfile; **426** (tl) ©Bob Daemmrich/PhotoEdit; (tr) ©Stephen Bonk/ShutterStock; (bl) ©Stockbyte/ SuperStock; (br) ©Paul Gilham/Getty Images; **427** (tl) ©Jon Arnold Images/SuperStock; (tc) ©Clive Brunskill/ Getty Images; (tr) ©Chris Whitehead/Digital Vision/Getty

Images; (bl) ©Mathew Gavanaugh/Stringer/Getty Images; (bc) ©Timothy A. Clary/Staff/AFP/Getty Images; (br) ©David Young-Wolff/Getty Images; **428** (inset) ©Hulton Archive/Getty Images; **428-429** (bkgd) ©Stocktrek Images/ Getty Images; **430** (b) ©Courtesy of Hiromitsu Yokota; (t) ©Courtesy Lensey Namioka. Photo by Don Perkins of Liberty Studios; **445** (br) Creatas Royalty Free Stock Resources Brand X Pictures/Creatas Royalty Free Stock Resources; (tr) Getty; **446-447** (bkgd) ©NASA; **446** (inset) ©The Granger Collection, New York; **448-449** (bkgd) ©Masterfile; **448** (inset) ©BBC/Corbis; **451** ©POPPERFOTO/Alamy; **454** (tl) ©Bob Daemmrich/ PhotoEdit; (tr) ©Steve Hamblin/Alamy; (bl) ©Danita Delimont/Alamy; (br) ©Patrik Giardino/Corbis; **455** (tl) ©Dennis MacDonald/Alamy; (tc) ©Shaun Botterill/Getty Images Sport/Getty Images; (tr) ©Digital Vision/Getty Images; (bl) ©Nasa/Johnson Space Center; (bc) ©John Neubauer/PhotoEdit; (br) ©Steve Nudson/Alamy; **456-457** James Hardy/PhotoAlto Agency RF Collections/Getty Images; (bkgd) ©81A Productions/Corbis; **458** (b) ©Courtesy of Tim Jessel; (t) ©Courtesy of Peg Kehert; **467** (br) Artville / Getty Images; **469** (br) ©Penguin Young Readers Group; (c) ©Hmco; **470** (b) ©ImageSource/AGE Fotostock; **471** (t) ©JUPITERIMAGES/Brand X/Alamy; **473** ©Larry Williams/Corbis; **475** ©Peter Griffith/ Masterfile; **476** (tl) ©Masterfile; (tr) ©Mary Date Denny/ PhotoEdit; (bl) ©Jim West/Alamy; (br) ©Larry Lee/Larry Lee Photography/Corbis; **477** (tl) ©Blend Images/Alamy; (tc) ©Tim Wright/CORBIS; (tr) ©Myrleen Ferguson Cate/PhotoEdit; (bl) ©David Young-Wolff/ PhotoEdit; (bc) ©Kayte M. Deioma/PhotoEdit; (br) ©Rhoda Sidney/ PhotoEdit; **478-479** (bkgd) ©Chris Brown/Alamy; **480** (b) ©Courtesy of Jerome Lagarrigue; **481** (t) ©Nancy Kaszerman/Zuma Press/Newscom; **497** (t) ©JupiterImages/Comstock Images/Alamy; **499** ©Paul Doyle/Alamy; **502** (tl) ©The Granger Collection, New York; (tr) ©The Granger Collection New York; (bl) ©Tatiana Morozova/Shutter Stock; (br) ©Bridgeman Art Library/Getty Images; **503** (tl) Punchstock; (tc) ©Rick Rickman/NewSport/Corbis; (tr) ©The Granger Collection, New York; (bl) ©Demid/Shutter Stock; (bc) ©The Bridgeman Art Library; (br) ©Steve Hamblin/ Alamy; **504-505** (bkgd) ©Guenter Rossenbach/zefa/ Corbis; **504** (inset) ©1Apix/Alamy; **507** (t) ©Courtesy of Eric Kimmel; **517** (tr) Corbis; (br) Corbis; **518** (inset) ©The Granger Collection, New York; 519 (inset) ©The Granger Collection, New York; **520** (inset) ©The Granger Collection, New York; **523** ©Ablestock/Alamy; **528** (b) ©Jim West/PhotoEdit; **529A** ©Cliff Leight/Aurora; **529B** (bkgd) ©Panoramic Images/Getty Images; (inset) ©Photodisc/Nature wildlife Environment; **530** (tl) ©The Granger Collection, New York; (tr) ©H. Armstrong Roberts/ClassicStock/The Image Works; (bl) ©Nick Vedros & Assoc./Getty Images; (br) ©LMR Group/Alamy; **531** (tl) ©North Wind Picture Archives/Alamy; (tc) ©North Wind/North Wind Picture Archives; (tr) ©Vera Bogaerts/Shuuterstock; (bl) ©North Wind/North Wind Picture Archives; (bc) ©Bettmann/CORBIS; (br) ©Scott T. Smith/CORBIS; **532-533** (bkgd) ©Phil Schermeister/ CORBIS; **534** (b) ©Courtesy of Bill Farnsworth; (t) ©AL GRILLO/AP Images; **549** (br) PhotoDisc; (br) PhotoDisc - royalty free; (tr) Comstock; **550-551** (bkgd) ©Rusty Dodson/Shutter Stock ; **552-553** (bkgd) ©Ed Darack/

G21

Getty Images; **552** (inset) ©David Northcott/CORBIS; **553** (t) ©1995 PhotoDisc; **555** ©Tim Fitzharris/Masterfile ; **558** (tl) © Richard T. Nowitz/Corbis; (tr) ©Rodolfo Arpia/Alamy; (bl) ©Joel Sartore/Getty Images; (br) ©Jim and Jamie Dutcher/Getty Images ; **559** (tl) ©Louie Psihoyos/Getty Images; (tc) ©franco pizzochero/AGE fotostock; (tr) ©age fotostock/SuperStock; (bl) ©Doug Dreyer/Getty Images; (bc) ©Bill Bachman/Alamy; (br) ©age fotostock/SuperStock; **560-561** (bkgd) ©James P. Rowan Photography; **560** (inset) ©Illinois State Museum collections; **562** (b) ©Courtesy of S.D. Nelson; (t) ©Eric Miller/Associated Press; **586-587** ©Barry Moser ; **587-597** (border treatment) ©Craig Aurness/CORBIS; **588-589** ©Fine Arts Museums of San Francisco, Gift of Eleanor Martin; **573** (tl) PhotoDisc - royalty free; **574-575** (bkgd) © North Wind Picture Archives; **574** (br) ©Monroe P. Killy/Minnesota Historical Society; **575** (tr) ©Kenneth M. Wright Studos/Minnesota Historical Society; **576-577** (bkgd) ©Frances Densmore/Minnesota Historical Society; **577** (t) ©Michael Wildsmith/Getty Images; **579** ©Masterfile; **582** (tl) ©Time & Life Pictures/Getty Images; (tr) ©Richard Heinzen/SuperStock; (bl) ©William A. Allard/Getty Images; (br) ©Douglas Faulkner/CORBIS; **583** (tl) ©Bob Daemmrich/PhotoEdit; (tc) ©American Stock/Contributor Collection/Getty Images; (tr) ©Hind Sight Media/Alamy; (bl) ©Jeff R. Clow/Shutter Stock; (bc) ©Michael Rutherford /SuperStock; (br) ©WireImageStock/Masterfile; **584-585** (bkgd) ©age fotostock/SuperStock; **586** ©Evans Chan; **588** (inset) ©Yale University Library; **590-591** ©Oakland Museum/ The Art Archive; **592** (inset) ©Yale University Library; **594** (b) Library of Congress; **594-595** ©Gilcrease Museum, Tulsa, Oklahoma; **596** (t) ©Rio Grande Historical Collections, New Mexico State University; (b) Library of Congress; **597** (tl) Corbis; (tr) Corbis; (br) Digital Stock/ Corbis Corporation; **598-599** ©MasterFile; **599** (inset) ©Courtesy of John Stauffer; **600-601** (bkgd) ©Nancy Greifenhagen/Alamy; **601** (t) ©John and Lisa Merrill/ CORBIS; **602** ©John Kelly/Digital Vision/Getty Images; **606** (tl) ©Yellow Dog Productions/Getty Images; (tr) ©Thomas & Pat Leeson /Photo Researchers, Inc.; (bl) ©Layne Kennedy/CORBIS; (br) ©Kevin Foy/Alamy; (tc) ©Time & Life Pictures/Getty Images; **607** (tl) ©Jaume Gual/AGE fotostock; (tr) ©Kelvin Murray/Getty Images; (bl) ©Livia Corona/Getty Images; (bc) ©Veronique Krieger/DK Stock; (br) ©MasterFile; **608-609** (bkgd) ©Navaswan/Getty Images; **608** ©Bronte Parsonage Museum, Haworth, Yorkshire, U.K./Bridgeman Art Library; **610** (b) ©Courtesy of Megan Halsey; (t) ©Elias Stahl; **621** (br) Corbis - royalty free; **622-623** (bc) ©Art Resource, NY; **622** (bl) ©Snark/Art Resource, NY; **623** (br) ©The Reliable Contraband (engraving) (b/w photo) by Edwin Forbes (1839-95)/Bridgeman Art Library; **624-625** (bkgd) ©Underwood & Underwood/CORBIS; **624** (tr)

©The Granger Collection, New York; (l) ©Western History/Geneology Dept./Denver Public Library; **625** (t) ©James L. Amos/CORBIS; 630 (tl) ©ImageSource/Age Fotostock; (tr) ©Aurora/Getty Images; (bl) ©CORBIS; (br) ©Stapleton Collection/Corbis; **631** (tl) © Matt Stroshane/ Stringer/Getty Images; (tc) ©Ian Murphy/Getty Images; (tr) ©The Granger Collection, New York; (bl) Jim Bridger (1804-81) (b/w photo), American Photographer, (19th century)/© Private Collection, Peter Newark American Pictures /The Bridgeman Art Library; (bc) ©Stephen Alvaraez/National Geographic Image Collection; (br) ©Marcel Meys/Archives Larousse, Paris/Bridgeman Art Library, NY; **632** (tr) ©Peter Newark American Pictures/ The Bridgeman Art Library; **632-633** ©David David Gallery/SuperStock; **634-635** (bkgd) ©Darrell Gulin/ CORBIS; **635** (cl) ©Richard Cummins /SuperStock; (cr) ©Richard Cummins /SuperStock; (stamp) ©Richard Cummins/SuperStock; (inset) ©Courtesy of Elizabeth Cody Kimmel; **636** ©Smithsonian Museum of American History; **637** (bkgd) ©The Granger Collection, New York; **638** ©Greg Vaughn/Alamy; **639** (parchment) ©Dorling Kindersley/Getty Images; ©Gelen Rowell/Peter Arnold, Inc.; **640** (inset) ©David Frazier/The Image Works; **640-641** (bkgd) ©Gavin Hellier/agefotostock; **642-643** ©Connie Ricca/CORBIS; **644-645** ©DEA/G. SIOEN/ Getty Images; **645** (br) Getty; **651** ©Connie Ricca/ CORBIS; **656** (b) ©Masterfile; (t) ©Photodisc/Nature wildlife Environment; **665** © Jeremy Woodhouse/ PhotoDisc/Getty Images; **666** © SuperStock; **669** © PhotoDisc/Getty Images; **670** © PhotoDisc/Getty Images; **673** © PhotoDisc/Getty Images; **674** © PhotoDisc/Getty Images; **675** (t) © PhotoDisc/Getty Images; (b) © PhotoDisc/Getty Images; **678** © PhotoDisc/Getty Images

G22

Illustration

Cover Mike Wimmer; **4** David Klug; **6** James Ransome; **8** James Forten; **10** Tim Jessell; **12** S.D. Nelson; **22–33** Bruce MacPherson; **34–37** David Klug; **37** Ken Bowser; **38–39** David Klug; **41** Sally Vitsky; **44** Bob Kayganich; **63–65** David Klug; **67** Ken Bowser; **72–81, 84–85** Eric Velasquez; **89** Ken Bowser; **90–91** David Klug; **93** Jan Bryan-Hunt; **100, 104, 106–109** Jim Kelly; **114–115** David Klug; **120** Jim Kelly; **122–133** ©Jim Tsinganos; **136** Argosy Publishing; **137** Ken Bowser; **138** David Klug; **141** Ken Bowser; **143–144** Sally Vitsky; **164–167** Jago Silver; **168–169** David Klug; **171** Chris Lensch; **174** Susan Johnston Carlson; **176–187** ©Mark Elliot; **188–191** Hannah Bureau; **191** (inset) Ken Bowser; **192–193** David Klug; **202** Ortelius Design, Inc; **217** Ken Bowser; **218–219** David Klug; **221** Chris Lenseh; **224** Ortelius Design, Inc; **226–237** ©James Ransome; **241** Ken Bowser; **242–243** David Klug; **245** Sally Vitsky; **248** Ortelius Design, Inc; **262–265** Barbar Hranilovich; **265** Ken Bowser; **266–267** David Klug; **269** Jan Bryan-Hunt; **270–273** Sally Vitsky; **295** Ken Bowser; **296** David Klug; **299** Sally Vitsky; **316–319** Robert Barret; **320** David Klug; **323** Jan Bryan-Hunt; **326** Wood Ronsaville Harlin, Inc; **340–343** Marc Scott; **343** (b) Ken Bowser; **344** David Klug; **352–359, 363** Steven Noble; **367** (t) Ken Bowser; **367** (b) David Klug; **368** David Klug; **386** (r) Joe LeMonnier; **390–393** ©Bleu Turrell; **393** (t) David Klug; **393** (b) Ken Bowser; **394** David Klug; **397** Sally Vitsky; **400** Ken Bowser; **402–403** Promotion Studios; **404–405** Miracle Studios; **406–417** Adam Gustavson; **418–421** Miracle Studios; **421** (b) Ken Bowser; **422–432** David Klug; **425** Sally Vitsky; **430–445** ©Hiromitsu Yokota; **449** (t) Dave Klug; **449** (b) Ken Bowser; **450–451** David Klug; **453** Chris Lensch; **456** Argosy Publishing; **458–467** ©Tim Jessell; **471** Ken Bowser; **472–473** David Klug; **475** Sally Vitsky; **480–493** ©Jerome Lagarrigue; **494–497** Ron Himler; **495** Pam Thomson; **497** Ken Bowser; **498–499** David Klug; **514** Michael Jarozsko; **518–521** Igor Oleynikov; **522–523** David Klug; **525** Jan Bryan-Hunt; **525** Jan Bryan-Hunt; **526–527** Sally Vitsky; **534–549** Dave Klug; **553** Ken Bowser; **554** David Klug; **557** Sally Vitsky; **562–573** ©S.D. Nelson; **577** Ken Bowser; **578** David Klug; **581** Jan Bryan-Hunt; **584** Ortelius Design, Inc; **586–587** ©Barry Moser; **593** Karen Minot; **601** Ken Bowser; **602–603** David Klug; **605** Jan Bryan-Hunt; **612–621** Megan Halsey; **625** Ken Bowser; **626** David Klug; **632, 637** Susan Johnston Carlson; **646–649** Bill Farnsworth; **649** (t) Susan Johnston Carlson; **649** (b) Ken Bowser; **650–651** David Klug; **654–656** Sally Vitsky.

All other photos Houghton Mifflin Harcourt Photo Libraries and Photographers.

G23

Research Bibliography

Adams, M.J. (2000). *Beginning to Read: Thinking and Learning About Print*. Cambridge: MIT Press.

Armbruster, B., Anderson, T.H., & Ostertag, J. (1987). Does text structure/summarization instruction facilitate learning from expository text? *Reading Research Quarterly*, 22 (3), 331–346.

Armbruster, B., Lehr, F., & Osborn, J. (2001). *Put Reading First: The Research Building Blocks for Teaching Children to Read* (pp. 21–31). Washington, D.C.: National Institute for Literacy.

Askew, B.J. & Fountas, I.C. (1998). Building an early reading process: Active from the start! *The Reading Teacher,* 52 (2), 126–134.

Baker, S.K., Chard, D.J., Ketterlin-Geller, L.R., Apichatabutra, C., & Doabler, C. (in press). The basis of evidence for Self-Regulated Strategy Development for students with or at risk for learning disabilities. *Exceptional Children*.

Ball, E., & Blachman, B. (1991). Does phoneme awareness training in kindergarten make a difference in early word recognition and developmental spelling? *Reading Research Quarterly*, 26 (1), 49–66.

Baumann, J.F. & Bergeron, B.S. (1993). Story map instruction using children's literature: Effects on first graders' comprehension of central narrative elements. *Journal of Reading Behavior*, 25 (4), 407–437.

Baumann, J.F. & Kame'enui, E.J. (Eds.). (2004). *Vocabulary Instruction: Research to Practice.* New York: Guilford Press.

Baumann, J.F., Seifert-Kessell, N., & Jones, L.A. (1992). Effect of think-aloud instruction on elementary students' comprehension monitoring abilities. *Journal of Reading Behavior*, 24 (2), 143–172.

Bear, D.R. & Templeton, S. (1998). Explorations in developmental spelling: Foundations for learning and teaching phonics, spelling, and vocabulary. *The Reading Teacher,* 52 (3), 222–242.

Beck, I.L. (2006). *Making Sense of Phonics: The Hows and Whys*. New York: Guilford Press.

Beck, I.L. & McKeown, M. (2006). *Improving Comprehension with Questioning the Author: A Fresh and Expanded View of a Powerful Approach (Theory and Practice).* New York, NY: Scholastic.

Beck, I.L., McKeown, M., Hamilton, R., & Kucan, L. (1998). Getting at the meaning. *American Educator*, Summer, 66–71.

Beck, I.L., McKeown, M., Hamilton, R., & Kucan, L. (1997). *Questioning the Author: An Approach for Enhancing Student Engagement with Text*. Newark, DE: International Reading Association.

Beck, I.L., & McKeown, M.G., (2001). Text talk: Capturing the benefits of read-aloud experiences for young children. *The Reading Teacher*, 55 (1), 10–20.

Beck, I.L., McKeown, M.G. & Kucan, L. (2002). *Bringing Words to Life: Robust Vocabulary Instruction*. New York: Guilford Press.

Beck, I.L., Perfetti, C.A., & McKeown, M.G. (1982). Effects of long-term vocabulary instruction on lexical access and reading comprehension. *Journal of Educational Psychology*, 74 (4), 506–521.

Bereiter, C. & Bird, M. (1985). Use of thinking aloud in identification and teaching of reading comprehension strategies. *Cognition and Instruction*, 2, 131–156.

Biemiller, A. (2005). Size and sequence in vocabulary development: Implications for choosing words for primary grade vocabulary. In E.H. Hiebert & M.L. Kamil (Eds.), *Teaching and Learning Vocabulary* (pp. 223–242). Mahwah, NJ: Lawrence Erlbaum.

Biemiller, A. (2001) Teaching vocabulary: Early, direct, and sequential. *American Educator*. Spring.

Biemiller, A. (2001). Vocabulary development and instruction: A prerequisite for school learning. In D. Dickinson & S. Neuman (Eds.), *Handbook of Early Literacy Research*, (Vol. 2), New York: Guilford Press.

Biemiller, A. & Slonim, N. (2001). Estimating root word vocabulary growth in normative and advantaged populations: Evidence for a common sequence of vocabulary acquisition. *Journal of Educational Psychology*, 93 (3), 498–520.

Blachman, B. (2000). Phonological awareness. In M. Kamil, P. Mosenthal, P.D. Pearson, & R. Barr (Eds.), *Handbook of Reading Research*, (Vol. 3). Mahwah, NJ: Lawrence Erlbaum.

Blachman, B., Ball, E.W., Black, R.S., & Tangel, D.M. (1994). Kindergarten teachers develop phoneme awareness in low-income, inner-city classrooms: Does it make a difference? *Reading and Writing: An Interdisciplinary Journal*, 6 (1), 1–18.

Brown, I.S. & Felton, R.H. (1990). Effects of instruction on beginning reading skills in children at risk for reading disability. *Reading and Writing: An Interdisciplinary Journal*, 2 (3), 223–241.

Carlo, M. (2004). Closing the gap: Addressing the vocabulary needs of English-language learners in bilingual and mainstream classrooms. *Reading Research Quarterly*, 39 (2), 188–215.

Chall, J. (1996). *Learning to Read: The Great Debate (revised, with a new foreword)*. New York: McGraw-Hill.

Chard, D.J., Ketterlin-Geller, L.R., Baker, S.K., Doabler, C., & Apichatabutra, C. (2009). Repeated reading interventions for students with learning disabilities: Status of the evidence. *Exceptional Children,* 75 (3), 263–281.

Chard, D.J., Stoolmiller, M., Harn, B., Vaughn, S., Wanzek, J., Linan-Thompson, S., & Kame'enui, E.J. (2008). Predicting reading success in a multi-level school-wide reading model: A retrospective analysis. *Journal of Learning Disabilities,* 41 (2), 174–188.

Charity, A.H., Scarborough, H.E., & Griffin, D.M. (2004). Familiarity with school English in African American children and its relation to early reading achievement. *Child Development*, 75 (5), 1340–1356.

Chiappe, P. & Siegel, L.S. (2006). A longitudinal study of reading development of Canadian children from diverse linguistic backgrounds. *Elementary School Journal,* 107 (2), 135–152.

Coyne, M.D., Kame'enui, E.J., & Simmons, D.C. (2004). Improving beginning reading instruction and intervention for students with LD: Reconciling "all" with "each." *Journal of Learning Disabilities*, 37 (3), 231–239.

Coyne, M.D., Kame'enui, E.J., Simmons, D.C., & Harn, B.A. (2004). Beginning reading intervention as inoculation or insulin: First-grade reading performance of strong responders to kindergarten intervention. *Journal of Learning Disabilities*, 37 (2), 90–104.

Coyne, M.D., Zipoli Jr., R.P., Chard, D.J., Faggella-Luby, M., Ruby, M., Santoro, L.E., & Baker, S. (2009). Direct instruction of comprehension: Instructional examples from intervention research on listening and reading comprehension. *Reading & Writing Quarterly*, 25 (2), 221–245.

Coyne, M.D., Zipoli Jr., R.P., & Ruby, M. (2006). Beginning reading instruction for students at risk for reading disabilities: What, how, and when. *Intervention in School and Clinic*, 41 (3), 161–168.

Craig, H.K. & Washington, J.A. (2006). *Malik Goes to School: Examining the Language Skills of African American Students From Preschool-5th Grade*. Mahwah, NJ: Lawrence Erlbaum Associates.

Craig, H.K. & Washington, J.A. (2001). Recent research on the language and literacy skills of African American students in early years . In D. Dickinson & S. Neuman (Eds.), *Handbook of Early Literacy Research,* (Vol. 2), New York: Guilford Press.

Dixon, R.C., Isaacson, S., & Stein, M. (2002). Effective strategies for teaching writing. In E.J. Kame'enui, D.W. Carnine, R.C. Dixon, D.C. Simmons, & M.D. Coyne (Eds.), *Effective Teaching Strategies That Accommodate Diverse Learners* (2nd ed., pp. 93–119). Upper Saddle River, NJ: Merrill Prentice Hall.

Dowhower, S.L. (1987). Effects of repeated reading on second-grade transitional readers' fluency and comprehension. *Reading Research Quarterly*, 22 (4), 389–406.

Duke, N.K. (2000). 3.6 minutes a day: The scarcity of informational text in first grade. *Reading Research Quarterly*, 35 (2), 202–224.

Duke, N.K. & Pearson, P.D. (2002). Effective practices for developing reading comprehension. In A.E. Farstrup & S.J. Samuels (Eds.), *What Research Has to Say About Reading Instruction* (3rd ed., pp. 205–242). Newark, DE: International Reading Association.

Durán, E., Shefelbine, J., Carnine, L., Maldonado-Colón, E., & Gunn, B. (2003). *Systematic Instruction in Reading for Spanish-Speaking Students*. Springfield, IL: Charles C. Thomas.

Edwards Santoro, L., Chard, D.J., Howard, L., & Baker, S.K. (2008). Making the VERY most of classroom read alouds: How to promote comprehension and vocabulary in K-2 classrooms. *The Reading Teacher,* 61 (5), 396–408.

Ehri, L.C. (1998). Grapheme-phoneme knowledge is essential for learning to read words in English. In J. Metsala & L. Ehri (Eds.), *Word Recognition in Beginning Literacy* (pp. 3–40). Hillsdale, NJ: Lawrence Erlbaum Associates.

Ehri, L. & Nunes, S.R. (2002). The role of phonemic awareness in learning to read. In A.E. Farstrup & S.J. Samuels (Eds.), *What Research Has to Say About Reading Instruction* (3rd ed., pp. 110–139). Newark, DE: International Reading Association.

Ehri, L. & Wilce, L. (1987). Does learning to spell help beginners learn to read words? *Reading Research Quarterly*, 22 (1), 48–65.

Farr, R. (1990). Reading. *Educational Leadership,* 47 (5), 82–83.

Farr, R., Lewis, M., Faszholz, J., Pinsky, E., Towle, S., Lipschutz, J. & Faulds, B.P. (1990). Writing in response to reading. *Educational Leadership*, 47 (6), 66–69.

Fletcher, J.M. & Lyon, G.R. (1998) Reading: A research-based approach. In Evers, W.M. (Ed.), *What's Gone Wrong in America's Classroom?* Palo Alto, CA: Hoover Institution Press, Stanford University.

Foorman, B. (Ed.). (2003). *Preventing and Remediating Reading Difficulties*. Baltimore, MD: York Press.

Foorman, B.R., Francis, D.J., Fletcher, J., Schatschneider, C., & Mehta, P. (1998). The role of instruction in learning to read: Preventing reading failure in at-risk children. *Journal of Educational Psychology*, 90 (1), 37–55.

Francis D.J., Rivera, M., Lesaux, N., Kieffer, M., & Rivera, H. (2006). Practical Guidelines for the Education of English Language Learners: Research-based recommendations for instruction and academic interventions (Book 1). Texas Institute for Measurement, Evaluation, and Statistics. University of Houston for the Center on Instruction.

Francis D.J., Rivera, M., Lesaux, N., Kieffer, M., & Rivera, H. (2006). Practical Guidelines for the Education of English Language Learners: Research-based recommendations for serving adolescent newcomers (Book 2). Texas Institute for Measurement, Evaluation, and Statistics. University of Houston for the Center on Instruction.

Fuchs, L., Fuchs, D., & Hosp, M. (2001). Oral reading fluency as an indicator of reading competence: A theoretical, empirical, and historical analysis. *Scientific Studies of Reading*, 5 (3), 239–256.

Fukkink, R.G. & de Glopper, K. (1998). Effects of instruction in deriving word meaning from context: A meta-analysis. *Review of Educational Research*, 68 (4), 450–469.

Gambrell, L.B., Morrow, L.M., & Pennington, C. (2002). Early childhood and elementary literature-based instruction: Current perspectives… *Reading Online,* 5 (6), 26–39.

Gersten, R. (2005). Behind the scenes of an intervention research study. *Learning Disabilities Research & Practice,* 20 (4), 200–212.

Gersten, R. & Baker, S. (2000). What we know about effective instructional practices for English learners. *Exceptional Children*, 66 (4), 454–470.

Gersten, R., Baker, S.K., Haager, D., & Graves, A.W. (2005). Exploring the role of teacher quality in predicting reading outcomes for first-grade English learners: An observational study. *Remedial and Special Education,* 26 (4), 197–206.

Gersten, R. & Geva, E. (2003). Teaching reading to early language learners. *Educational Leadership,* 60 (7), 44–49.

Gersten, R. & Jiménez, R. (2002). Modulating instruction for English-language learners. In E.J. Kame'enui, D.W. Carnine, R.C. Dixon, D.C. Simmons, & M.D. Coyne (Eds.), *Effective Teaching Strategies That Accommodate Diverse Learners*. Upper Saddle River, NJ: Merrill Prentice Hall.

Gipe, J.P. & Arnold, R.D. (1979). Teaching vocabulary through familiar associations and contexts. *Journal of Reading Behavior*, 11 (3), 281–285.

Griffith, P.L., Klesius, J.P., & Kromrey, J.D. (1992). The effect of phonemic awareness on the literacy development of first grade children in a traditional or a whole language classroom. *Journal of Research in Childhood Education*, 6 (2), 85–92.

Guthrie, J. & Wigfield, A. (2000). Engagement and motivation in reading. In M. Kamil, P. Mosenthal, P. Pearson, & R. Barr, (Eds.), *Handbook of Reading Research, Vol. III*, 403–422.

Guthrie, J.T., Wigfield, A., Barbosa, P., Perencevich, K.C., Taboada, A., Davis, M.H., et al. (2004). Increasing reading comprehension and engagement through concept-oriented reading instruction. *Journal of Educational Psychology*, 96 (3), 403–423.

Hall, S.L. & Moats, L.C. (1999). *Straight Talk About Reading*. Chicago, IL: Contemporary Books.

Harm, M.W., McCandliss, B.D. & Seidenberg, M.S. (2003). Modeling the successes and failures of interventions for disabled readers. *Scientific Studies of Reading*, 7 (2), 155–182.

Harn, B.A., Stoolmiller, M., & Chard, D. (2008). Identifying the dimensions of alphabetic principle on the reading development of first graders: The role of automaticity and unitization. *Journal of Learning disabilities*, 41 (2), 143–157.

Hasbrouck, J. & Tindal, G.A. (2006). Oral reading fluency norms: A valuable assessment tool for reading teachers. *The Reading Teacher*, 59 (7), 636–644.

Research Bibliography

Hiebert, E.H. & Kamil, M.L. (Eds.). (2005). *Teaching and Learning Vocabulary: Bringing Research to Practice*. Mahwah, NJ: Lawrence Erlbaum Associates.

Hudson, R., (2006). Using Repeated Reading and Readers Theater to Increase Fluency. Reading First National Conference. Website: http://www3.ksde.org/sfp/rdgfirst/natl_rdgfirst_conf_2006/hudson_using_repeated_reading_to_increase_fluency.pdf.

Hudson, R., Lane, H., & Pullen, P. (2005). Reading fluency assessment and instruction: What, why, and how? *The Reading Teacher*, 58 (8), 702–714.

Juel, C. (1988). Learning to read and write: A longitudinal study of fifty-four children from first through fourth grades. *Journal of Educational Psychology*, 80 (4), 437–447.

Juel, C., & Minden-Cupp, C. (2000). Learning to read words: Linguistic units and instructional strategies. *Reading Research Quarterly*, 35 (4), 458–492.

Kamil, M.L., Mosenthal, P.B., Pearson, P.D., & Barr, R. (2000). *Handbook of Reading Research*. Vol. III. Mahway, NJ: Lawrence Erlbaum Associates.

Lehr, F. & Osborn, J. (2005). A Focus on Comprehension. Pacific Resources for Education and Learning (PREL) Monograph. U.S. Department of Education. Website: www.prel.org/programs/rel/rel.asp.

Lehr, F., Osborn, J., & Hiebert, E.H. (2004). A Focus on Vocabulary. Pacific Resources for Education and Learning (PREL) Monograph. U.S. Department of Education. Website: www.prel.org/programs/rel/rel.asp.

Lesaux, N.K. & Siegel, L.S. (2003). The development of reading in children who speak English as a second language. *Developmental Psychology*, 39 (6), 1005–1019.

Lipson, M.Y., Mosenthal, J.H., Mekkelsen, J., & Russ, B. (2004). Building knowledge and fashioning success one school at a time. *The Reading Teacher*, 57 (6), 534–542.

Lipson, M.Y. & Wixson, K.K. (2008). New IRA commission will address RTI issues. *Reading Today*, 26 (1), 1, 5.

Lonigan, C.J., Burgess, S.R., & Anthony, J.L. (2000). Development of emergent literacy and early reading skills in preschool children: Evidence from a latent-variable longitudinal study. *Developmental Psychology*, 36 (5), 596–613.

Lundberg, I., Frost, J., & Petersen O. (1988). Effects of an extensive program for stimulating phonological awareness in preschool children. *Reading Research Quarterly*, 23 (3), 263–284.

McCardle, P. & Chhabra, V. (Eds.). (2004). *The Voice of Evidence in Reading Research*. Baltimore: Brooks.

McIntosh, A.S., Graves, A., & Gersten, R. (2007). The effects of response to intervention on literacy development in multiple-language settings. *Learning Disability Quarterly*, 30 (3), 197–212.

McIntosh, K., Chard, D.J., Boland, J.B., & Horner, R.H. (2006). Demonstration of combined efforts in school-wide academic and behavioral systems and incidence of reading and behavior challenges in early elementary grades. *Journal of Positive Behavior Interventions*, 8 (3), 146–154.

McIntosh, K., Horner, R.H., Chard, D.J., Boland, J.B., Good, R.H. (2006). The use of reading and behavior screening measures to predict non-response to school-wide positive behavior support: A longitudinal analysis. *School Psychology Review*, 35 (2), 275–291.

McIntosh, K., Horner, R.H., Chard, D.J., Dickey, C.R., & Braun, D.H. (2008). Reading skills and function of problem behavior in typical school settings. *The Journal of Special Education*, 42 (3), 131–147.

McKenna, M.C. & Stahl, S.A. (2003). *Assessment for Reading Instruction*, New York: Guilford Press.

McKeown, M.G. & Beck, I.L. (2001). Encouraging young children's language interactions with stories. In D. Dickinson & S. Neuman (Eds.), *Handbook of Early Literacy Research* (Vol. 2). New York: Guilford Press.

McKeown, M.G., Beck, I.L., Omanson, R.C., & Pople, M.T. (1985). Some effects of the nature and frequency of vocabulary instruction on the knowledge and use of words. *Reading Research Quarterly*, 20 (5), 522–535.

Merino, B. & Scarcella, R. (2005). Teaching science to English learners. *University of California Linguistic Minority Research Institute Newsletter*, 14 (4).

Moats, L. (2004). Efficacy of a structured, systematic language curriculum for adolescent poor readers. *Reading & Writing Quarterly*, 20 (2), 145–159.

Moats, L. (2001). When older students can't read. *Educational Leadership*, 58 (6), 36–46.

Moats, L.C. (2000). *Speech to Print: Language Essentials for Teachers*. Baltimore, MD: Paul H. Brooks Publishing Co., Inc.

Moats, L.C. (1998). Teaching decoding. *American Educator,* 22 (1 & 2), 42–49, 95–96.

Moats, L.C. (1999). *Teaching Reading Is Rocket Science*. Washington, DC: American Federation of Teachers.

Morrow, L.M. (2004). Developmentally appropriate practice in early literacy instruction. *The Reading Teacher,* 58 (1), 88–89.

Morrow, L.M., Kuhn, M.R., & Schwanenflugel, P.J. (2006/2007). The family fluency program. *The Reading Teacher*, 60 (4), 322–333.

Morrow, L.M. & Tracey, D.H. (1997). Strategies used for phonics instruction in early childhood classrooms. *The Reading Teacher*, 50 (8), 644–651.

Morrow, L.M., Tracey, D.H., Woo, D.G., & Pressley, M. (1999). Characteristics of exemplary first-grade literacy instruction. *The Reading Teacher,* 52 (5), 462–476.

Mosenthal, J.H., Lipson, M.Y., Torncello, S., Russ, B., & Mekkelsen, J. (2004). Contexts and practices of six schools successful in obtaining reading achievement. *Elementary School Journal*, 104 (5), 343–367. ABSTRACT ONLY.

Nagy, W.E. & Scott, J.A. (2000). Vocabulary processes. In M.L. Kamil, P.B. Mosenthal, P.D. Pearson, & R. Barr (Eds.), *Handbook of Reading Research*, (Vol. 3, 269–284). Mahwah, NJ: Erlbaum.

National Center to Improve Tools of Educators. Website: NCITE: http://idea.uoregon.edu/~ ncite/.

National Commission on Writing. (2004). *Writing: A Ticket to Work...or a Ticket Out*. New York: The College Board.

National Reading Panel (2000). Teaching children to read: An evidence-based assessment of the scientific research literature on reading and its implications for reading instruction. NIH Publication No. 00-4754. Washington, DC: National Institute of Child Health and Human Development.

Neuman, S.B., & Dickinson, D.K., (Eds.). (2002). *Handbook of Early Literacy Research*. New York: Guilford Press.

O'Connor, R., Jenkins, J.R., & Slocum, T.A. (1995). Transfer among phonological tasks in kindergarten: Essential instructional content. *Journal of Educational Psychology*, 87 (2), 202–217.

O'Shea, L.J., Sindelar, P.T., & O'Shea, D.J. (1985). The effects of repeated readings and attentional cues on reading fluency and comprehension. *Journal of Reading Behavior*, 17 (2), 129–142.

Orkwis, R. & McLane, K. (1998, Fall). *A Curriculum Every Student Can Use: Design Principles for Student Access*. ERIC/OSEP Special Project, ERIC Clearinghouse on Disabilities and Gifted Education, Council for Exceptional Children.

Osborn, J. & Lehr, F. (2003). *A Focus on Fluency: Research-Based Practices in Early Reading Series.* Honolulu, HI: Pacific Resources for Education and Learning.

Paris, S.G., Cross, D.R., & Lipson, M.Y. (1984). Informed strategies for learning: A program to improve children's reading awareness and comprehension. *Journal of Educational Psychology*, 76 (6), 1239–1252.

The Partnership for Reading. (2003). *Put Reading First: The Research Building Blocks for Teaching Children to Read*. (2nd ed.). MD: National Institute for Literacy.

Payne, B.D., & Manning, B.H. (1992). Basal reader instruction: Effects of comprehension monitoring training on reading comprehension, strategy use and attitude. *Reading Research and Instruction*, 32 (1), 29–38.

Phillips, B.M. & Torgesen, J.K. (2001). Phonemic awareness and reading: Beyond growth of initial reading accuracy. In D. Dickinson & S. Neuman (Eds.), *Handbook of Early Literacy Research* (Vol. 2). New York: Guilford Press.

Pikulski, J.J., (1998). Business we should finish. *Reading Today*, 15 (5), 30.

Pikulski, J.J., & Chard, D.J. (2005). Fluency: Bridge between decoding and reading comprehension. *The Reading Teacher,* 58 (6), 510–519.

Pressley, M. (1998). *Reading Instruction That Works: The Case for Balanced Teaching*. New York: The Guilford Press.

Rasinski, T. (2003). *The Fluent Reader: Oral Reading Strategies for Building Word Recognition, Fluency and Comprehension*. New York: Scholastic.

Rasinski, T.V., Padak, N., Linek, W., & Sturtevant, E. (1994). Effects of fluency development on urban second-grade readers. *Journal of Educational Research*, 87 (3), 158–165.

Rayner, K., Foorman, B.R., Perfetti, C.A., Pesetsky, D., & Seidenberg, M.S. (2001). How psychological science informs the teaching of reading. *Psychological Science in the Public Interest*, 2 (2), 31–74.

Rayner, K., Foorman, B.R., Perfetti, C.A., Pesetsky, D., & Seidenberg, M.S. (2002) How should reading be taught? *Scientific American*, pp. 85–91.

Report from the National Reading Panel. (2000). *Teaching Children to Read: An Evidence-Based Assessment of the Scientific Research Literature on Reading and its Implications for Reading Instruction.* Bethesda, MD: National Institute of Child Health and Human Development. Website: http://www.nationalreadingpanel.org/Publications/summary.htm.

Rinehart, S.D., Stahl, S.A., & Erickson, L.G. (1986). Some effects of summarization training on reading and studying. *Reading Research Quarterly*, 21 (4), 422–438.

Robbins, C. & Ehri, L.C. (1994). Reading storybooks to kindergartners helps them learn new vocabulary words. *Journal of Educational Psychology*, 86 (1), 54–64.

Rosenshine, B., & Meister, C. (1994). Reciprocal teaching: A review of research. *Review of Educational Research*, 64 (4), 479–530.

Rosenshine, B., Meister, C., & Chapman, S. (1996). Teaching students to generate questions: A review of the intervention studies. *Review of Educational Research*, 66 (2), 181–221.

Samuels, S., Schermer, N., & Reinking, D. (1992). Reading fluency: Techniques for making decoding automatic. In S.J. Samuels, J. Samuels, & A.E. Farstrup (Eds.), *What Research Has to Say About Reading Instruction* (pp. 124–143). Newark, DE: International Reading Association.

Samuels, S.J. & Farstrup, A.E. (2006). *What Research Has to Say About Fluency Instruction*. Newark, DE: International Reading Association.

Scarcella, R. (2003) Academic English: A conceptual framework. *The University of California Linguistic Minority Research Institute, Technical Report* 2003-1.

Scarcella, R. English learners and writing: Responding to linguistic diversity. On-line pdf. http://wps.ablongman.com/wps/media/objects/133/136243/english.pdf.

Scarcella, R. (1990). *Teaching Language Minority Students in the Multicultural Classroom*. Englewood Cliffs, NJ: Prentice Hall Regents.

Scharer, P.L., Pinnell, G.S., Lyons, C., & Fountas, I. (2005). Becoming an engaged reader. *Educational Leadership,* 63 (2), 24–29.

Schleppegrell, M. (2004). *Teaching Academic Writing to English Learners,* 13 (2). Grant Report: University of California Linguistic Minority Research Institute.

Sénéchal, M. (1997). The differential effect of storybook reading on preschoolers' acquisition of expressive and receptive vocabulary. *Journal of Child Language*, 24 (1), 123–138.

Shanahan, T. (2005). FAQs about Fluency. http://www.springfield.k12.il.us/resources/languagearts/readingwriting/readfluency.html.

Shany, M.T. & Biemiller, A. (1995). Assisted reading practice: Effects on performance for poor readers in grades 3 and 4. *Reading Research Quarterly*, 30 (3), 382–395.

Shaywitz, S. (2003). *Overcoming Dyslexia*. New York: Alfred A Knopf.

Simmons, D.C., Kame'enui, E.J, Coyne, M.D. & Chard, D.J. (2002). Effective strategies for teaching beginning reading. In E.J. Kame'enui, D.W. Carnine, R.C. Dixon, D.C. Simmons, & M.D. Coyne (Eds.), *Effective Teaching Strategies That Accommodate Diverse Learners*. Upper Saddle River, NJ: Merrill Prentice Hall.

Sindelar, P.T., Monda, L.E., & O'Shea, L.J. (1990). Effects of repeated readings on instructional- and mastery-level readers. *Journal of Educational Research*, 83 (4), 220–226.

Snow, C., Burns, M., & Griffin, P. (Eds.). (1998). *Preventing Reading Difficulties in Young Children*. Washington, D.C.: National Academy Press.

Stahl, S.A. & Fairbanks, M.M. (1986). The effects of vocabulary instruction: A model-based meta-analysis. *Review of Educational Research*, 56 (1), 72–110.

Stanovich, K.E. (1986). Matthew effects in reading: Some consequences of individual differences in acquisition of literacy. *Reading Research Quarterly*, 21 (4), 360–407.

Research Bibliography

Stanovich, K.E. & Stanovich, P.J. (2003). Using research and reason in education: How teachers can use scientifically based research to make curricular & instructional decisions. Jessup, MD: National Institute for Literacy. Retrieved January, 26, 2006, from http://www.nifl.gov/partnershipforreading/publications/pdf/Stanovich_color.pdf.

Strickland, D.S. (2002). The importance of effective early intervention. In A.E. Farstrup & S.J. Samuels (Eds.), *What Research Has to Say about Reading Instruction* (3rd ed., pp. 69–86). Newark, DE: International Reading Association.

Strickland, D.S. & Morrow, L.M. (2000). *Beginning Reading and Writing*. Newark, DE: International Reading Association.

Strickland, D.S., Snow, C., Griffin, P., Burns, S.M. & McNamara, P. (2002). *Preparing Our Teachers: Opportunities for Better Reading Instruction*. Washington, D.C.: Joseph Henry Press.

Tabors, P.O. & Snow, C.E. (2002). Young bilingual children and early literacy development. In S. Neuman & D.K. Dickinson (Eds.), *Handbook of Early Literacy Research* (pp. 159–178). New York: Guilford Press.

Templeton, S. (1986). Synthesis of research on the learning and teaching of spelling. *Educational Leadership,* 43 (6), 73–78.

Templeton, S., Cain, C.T., & Miller, J.O. (1981). Reconceptualizing readability: The relationship between surface and underlying structure analyses in predicting the difficulty of basal reader stories. *Journal of Educational Research,* 74 (6), 382–387.

Torgesen, J., Morgan, S., & Davis, C. (1992). Effects of two types of phonological awareness training on word learning in kindergarten children. *Journal of Educational Psychology,* 84 (3), 364–370.

Torgesen, J., Wagner, R., Rashotte, C., Rose, E., Lindamood, P., Conway, T., & Garvan, C. (1999). Preventing reading failure in young children with phonological processing disabilities: Group and individual responses to instruction. *Journal of Educational Psychology*, 91 (4), 579–593.

Torgesen, J.K. & Hudson, R. (2006). Reading fluency: Critical issues for struggling readers. In S.J. Samuels & A. Farstrup (Eds.), *What Research Has to Say About Fluency Instruction*. Newark, DE: International Reading Association.

Torgesen, J.K., & Mathes, P. (2000). *A Basic Guide to Understanding, Assessing, and Teaching Phonological Awareness*. Austin, TX: PRO-ED.

Torgesen, J.K., Rashotte, C.A., & Alexander, A. (2001). Principles of fluency instruction in reading: Relationships with established empirical outcomes. In M. Wolf (Ed.), *Dyslexia, Fluency, and the Brain*. Parkton, MD: York Press.

Valencia, S.W., Au, K.H., Scheu, J.A., & Kawakami, A.J. (1990). Assessment of students' ownership of literacy. *The Reading Teacher,* 44 (2), 154–156.

Valencia, S.W. & Buly, M.R. (2004). Behind test scores: What struggling readers *really* need. *The Reading Teacher,* 57 (6), 520–531.

Valencia, S.W. & Sulzby, E. (1991). Assessment of emergent literacy: Storybook reading. *The Reading Teacher,* 44 (7), 498–500.

Vaughn, S. & Linan-Thompson, S. (2004). *Research-Based Methods of Reading Instruction: Grades K-3*. Alexandria, VA: ASCD.

Vaughn, S., Linan-Thompson, S., Pollard-Durodola, S.D., Mathes, P.G. & Hagan, E.C. (2001). Effective interventions for English language learners (Spanish-English) at risk for reading difficulties. In D. Dickinson & S. Neuman (Eds.), *Handbook of Early Literacy Research* (Vol. 2, pp. 185–197). New York: Guilford Press.

Vaughn, S., Moody, S.W., & Shuman, J.S. (1998). Broken promises: Reading instruction in the resource room. *Exceptional Children*, 64 (2), 211–225.

Vellutino, F.R., & Scanlon, D.M. (1987). Phonological coding, phonological awareness, and reading ability: Evidence from a longitudinal and experimental study. *Merrill-Palmer Quarterly*, 33 (3), 321–363.

Vogt, M. (2004/2005). Fitful nights. *Reading Today*, 22 (3), 6.

Vogt, M. & Nagano, P. (2003). Turn it on with light bulb reading!: Sound-switching strategies for struggling readers. *The Reading Teacher*, 57 (3), 214–221.

Washington, J.A. (2001). Early literacy skills in African-American children: Research considerations. *Learning Disabilities Research and Practice,* 16 (4), 213–221.

White, T.G., Graves, M.F., & Slater, W.H. (1990). Growth of reading vocabulary in diverse elementary schools: Decoding and word meaning. *Journal of Educational Psychology*, 82 (2), 281–290.

Wixson, K.K. (1986). Vocabulary instruction and children's comprehension of basal stories. *Reading Research Quarterly*, 21 (3), 317–329.

Index

Listening and Speaking

Listening Comprehension. *See* Comprehension, Listening.

Literary Forms. *See* Genre.

Literary Response. *See* Writing, Prompts.

Literature. *See* Leveled Readers; Student Book; Teacher Read Alouds; Vocabulary Reader.

Magazine

Main Idea and Details. *See* Comprehension,
Target Skills.

Main Selections. *See* Student Book, Literature
Selections.

Making Connections. *See* Student Book, Making
Connections.

Mass Media. *See* Media.

Meeting Individual Needs. *See* Differentiated
Instruction.

Media
Extend Through Research: Media Literacy
   Analyze Formality/Informality of Digital
     Media, **5-1:** T335; **5-2:** T335
   Explain Different Ways to Present Messages,
     5-1: T43, T117; **5-2:** T45
   Identify the Media's Point of View,
     5-1: T263; **5-2:** T263
   Survey Different Media Techniques,
     5-1: T191; **5-2:** T117, T191
Study Skills
   Computer Basics, **5-1:** R4
   Internet Strategies, **5-1:** R7; **5-2:** R7;
     5-3: R7; **5-4:** R7; **5-5:** R7
   Media Effect, **5-4:** R3
   Multimedia Presentation, **5-4:** R6

Word Processing Skills: Keyboarding, **5-1:** R4

Model, Analyze. *See* Writing, Process.

Modeling. *See* Fluency, Think Aloud.

Monitor Comprehension. *See* Comprehension.

Monitor/Clarify. *See* Comprehension, Target
Strategies.

Multiple-Meaning Words. *See* Vocabulary,
Strategies.

Myth. *See* Genre.

Narrative Nonfiction. *See* Genre.

Narrative Writing. *See* Writing, Forms.

Negatives. *See* Grammar.

Nonfiction. *See* Genre; Writing, Forms;
Writing, Mode.

Nouns. *See* Grammar.

Ongoing Assessment. *See* Assessment, Periodic
Assessment.

On-Level Readers. *See* Differentiated Instruction;
Leveled Readers.

Online TE and Planning Resources. *See*
Technology Resources.

Open and Closed Syllables. *See* Decoding.

Options for Reteaching. *See* Differentiated
Instruction.

Oral Language. *See* Listening, Speaking,
Viewing; Your Turn.

Organization. *See* Writing, Traits.

Paragraphs. *See* Writing, Forms.

Parent Involvement. *See* Grab-and-Go™,
School-Home Connection.

Periodic Assessment. *See* Assessment.

Periodic Progress-Monitoring. *See*
Assessment, Progress Monitoring.

Periods. *See* Grammar, Punctuation.

Personal Narratives. *See* Writing, Forms.

Persuasion. *See* Comprehension, Target Skills.

Persuasive Speech. *See* Genre.

Persuasive Text. *See* Genre.

Phonics. *See* Decoding.

Photo Cards. *See* Student Book, Vocabulary
in Context.

Phrasing. *See* Fluency.

Planning. *See* Focus Wall; Small Group Plan;
Suggested Weekly Plan; Unit Planning and Pacing;
Week at a Glance; Technology Resources.

Plays. *See* Genre; Student Book, Literature
Selections.

Plot. *See* Comprehension, Target Skills, Story
Structure.

Plural Nouns. *See* Grammar, Nouns.

Poetry. *See* Genre; Student Book, Literature
Selections; Writing, Forms.

Poetry Place. *See* Magazine.

Possessive Pronouns. *See* Grammar, Pronouns,
Possessive.

Predictions, Make. *See* Comprehension, Target
Strategies, Infer/Predict.

Prefixes. *See* Decoding; Vocabulary, Strategies.

Prepositions and Prepositional Phrases.
See Grammar.

Prewriting. *See* Writing, Process; Writing,
Traits, Ideas.

Prior Knowledge. *See* Develop Background;
Differentiated Instruction, English Language
Learners.

Progress Monitoring. *See* Assessment.

Pronouns. *See* Grammar.

Proofreading. *See* Writing, Process.

Proper Mechanics. *See* Grammar.

Proper Nouns. *See* Grammar, Nouns.

Prosody. *See* Fluency.

Publishing. *See* Writing, Process.

Punctuation. *See* Fluency, Phrasing; Grammar.

Purpose Setting, 5-1: T21, T93, T167, T241,
T313; **5-2:** T21, T95, T167, T241, T313; **5-3:** T21,
T95, T167, T239, T311; **5-4:** T21, T93, T169, T239,
T313, **5-5:** T21, T97, T169, T241, T313; **5-6:** T17,
T61, T107, T153, T197

Purposes for Listening, 5-1: T13, T85, T159,
T191, T233, T305; **5-2:** T13, T87, T159, T191,
T233, T305; **5-3:** T13, T87, T117, T159, T231,
T261, T303; **5-4:** T13, T85, T161, T231, T305;
5-5: T13, T89, T161, T233, T305; **5-6:** T9, T55,
T101, T145, T189

Purposes for Reading. *See* Reading, Purpose
Setting.

T

U

All photos from the HMH Photo Library or shot by Houghton Mifflin Harcourt Photographers.

Teacher Notes

Teacher Notes

Teacher Notes

Teacher Notes

Teacher Notes

Teacher Notes

Teacher Notes